The
Times
of
My Life

The
Times
of
My Life

and My Life with 𝕿𝖍𝖊 𝕿𝖎𝖒𝖊𝖘

Max Frankel

RANDOM HOUSE • NEW YORK

Library of Congress Cataloging-in-Publication Data
Frankel, Max.
    The times of my life: and my life with The Times / Max Frankel.
        p.   cm.
    Includes index.
    ISBN 0-679-44824-1
    1. Frankel, Max, 1930– . 2. Journalists—United States—20th
century—Biography. 3. New York Times. 4. Jews, German—United
States—Biography. 5. Jews—Germany—History—1933–1945. I. Title.
PN4874.F615T56   1999
070'.952—dc21
    [B]   98-16831

Random House website address: www.atrandom.com
Printed in the United States of America on acid-free paper
9876543

DESIGN BY MERCEDES EVERETT

For **MomPop**

With Joyce, David, Margot, and Jon

Contents

REPORTER: COLD WAR WEST
1961–1972

EDITOR
1972–1994

ABOUT *The Times of My Life*

EVERY TIME I MARVELED AT THE CHAIN OF ABSURD circumstance that plucked us from a town in Nazi Saxony mere moments before the Holocaust and eventually delivered us to the ark America, Mom would scoff, speak a word for God or Fate, and tell me to get on with life. She took pride, of course, in her "world-trotting journalist" and "editor of the Greatest Paper on Earth," but she had no patience for his sense of vainglorious melodrama. "*Every*body who got out has got a story to tell," she would say dismissively, never realizing how much she stirred my desire to recount ours.

"Tyrannies We Have Known" was the title I imagined for volume 1, to cover our international adventures: one family's survival of both Hitler and Stalin and my lifelong fascination with the disease of totalitarianism. "Secrets I Have Known and Blown" seemed suitable for volume 2, to recount my newspaper experiences and recall the scoops, leaks, and hemorrhages of Cold War journalism. To complete the tale, I dreamt of risking a philosophical treatise for volume 3, honoring the plaintive request to Mom from Berlin's commissioner of police in 1940 with the title "Will You Tell Them We're Not All Bad?"—a suitable epitaph for twentieth-century civilization.

My pretentious trilogy will not be written. As Mom tried to teach me, *every* life is a journey, a narrative in search of meaning. Nonetheless I dredged her memory over the years, and Pop's, and finally my own, for the simple reason that our predicaments conspired to make me a professional witness to the times of my life. A paid teller of stories, I judged my own as worth adding to the many I had already spun.

It is the story of a fugitive, beginning with a desperate pursuit of permits and passports to get our family past the borders of hate and barriers of indifference that defined our times. It describes a search for identity as well as safety, a yearning to belong but also to keep on running, to make a career of my rovings, my outsiderhood.

I escaped into America, and beyond it. The idea of America became my proud passport. A passion to conform made me a patriot. The discovery of words turned me into a skeptic. And the journalist's press pass sent me vaulting across borders to gain a spectacular perspective on our era. Like the astronauts floating in outer space, I've had a rare glimpse of the earth in my times, and it gave me an irrepressible urge to record the journey.

—MAN BEER BILL FACES
—EAT, THEN AMENDMENT;
—OSED BY BOTH PARTIES

ROOSEVELT SEEKS
LAW TO REGULATE
NEW SECURITIES

PRESIDENT SPEEDS
$900,000,000 CUTS
IN HIS FIRST MONTH

HITLERITES ORDER BOYCOTT
AGAINST JEWS IN BUSINESS,
PROFESSIONS AND SCHOOLS

NAZI MOBS RUN WILD
IN HEART OF VIENNA

REFUGEE

1930–1940

—SEVELT PUSHES
—000,000,000 PLAN
—CUT FARM DEBTS

BIG GAIN BY BANKS
THROUGHOUT NATION
RESERVE REPORTS

HARRIMAN INQUIRY
BY PECORA ORDERED

NEW YORK UNLIKELY
TO GET BEER APRIL 7
DUE TO ALBANY ROW

Jarges Dodd State of Hope
In Message After 2 Months

ROOSEVELT PUSHES
$2,000,000,000 PLAN
TO CUT FARM DEBTS

BIG GAIN BY BANKS
THROUGHOUT NATION
RESERVE REPORTS

HITLER CABINET GETS POWER
TO RULE AS A DICTATORSHIP;
REICHSTAG QUITS SINE DIE

Text of Dictatorship Act

—AUSTRIA AFTER HITLER ULTIMATUM
—TROOPS INVITED TO MAINTAIN ORDE—
—NQUART CHANCELLOR; POWERS PRO—

The Austrian Situation

GERMAN ARMY ATTA—
CITIES BOMBED, POR—
DANZIG IS ACCEPT—

Hitler Acts Against Poland

The New York Times front page reproduction.

1 · WHERE TO?

I WAS NOT YET THREE YEARS OLD WHEN ADOLF HITLER came to power in 1933, and I could have become a good little Nazi in his army. I loved the parades; I wept when other kids marched beneath our window without me. But I was ineligible for the Aryan race, the Master Race that Hitler wanted to purify of Jewish blood and other pollutants so that it could rule the world for "a thousand years."

Besides blood, what most defined a person in Hitler's Germany was a passport. But at my age I was ineligible for that as well and had to be inscribed in Mom's. Mutti, I called her, and she and everyone else called me Biba. Like many little boys in Germany, I was nicknamed Bubi but promptly mispronounced it to create the unique identity of Biba. We lived in Weissenfels, a well-scrubbed town in Saxony, near Leipzig, which manufactured shoes, staffed the Leuna chemical works, and served as a minor railroad hub for central Germany. My parents' passports were Polish, not German, although neither spoke Polish and had not lived in Poland since early childhood. Actually, they never lived in "Poland" at all; when Papa and Mutti were born, in 1902 and 1904, Poland had undergone one of its periodic dismemberments. Their native villages, proverbial *shtetlach* named Busk and Sokal, were dots on the map in a region called Galicia of what was then the Austro-Hungarian Empire. The region became Polish again after World War I, in 1919; it became Soviet at the start of World War II, in 1939, then German, then Soviet, and finally Ukrainian at the end of the Cold War, in 1991. The Jews of Galicia could have amassed a colorful array of passports if only they had survived these permutations.

The Fränkels of Busk and the Katzes of Sokal migrated separately before World War I to the city of Gera in German Thuringia and took apartments in adjoining streets. They came in search of economic opportunity, which they found by buying and selling rags and cheap clothes, but they never lost the stigma of being *Ostjuden*, Eastern Jews. Even without the ethnic instruction of the Nazis, the German Jews looked down upon the scruffier ones from the East and not infrequently wondered aloud why they didn't go back where they came from. The *Ostjuden* looked too Jewish and talked too Jewish; they were embarrassing obstacles to the German Jews' "assimilation," which was an exercise more in hiding than in merging. The bent and bearded caricatures of *Ostjuden* that German Jews carried in their heads looked very much like the pictures the Nazis drew to portray all Jews everywhere.

Still, Papa and Mutti lived easily with these distinctions. They thought of themselves as born in Austria-Hungary and only perversely branded Polish; they felt like Jews and lived like Germans. The quest for their own business took them from Gera to Weissenfels shortly after I was born. The chemical workers promised to be good customers of my grandfather, a peddler, and his son, who dreamed of opening their own dry goods store. There were no major tensions between the 120 Jews and 40,000 Germans of Weissenfels. The Jews were prominent among the merchants, lawyers, and physicians; many of them had assimilated clear into mixed marriages. The fathers of our town's German Jews had fought for Kaiser Wilhelm II in World War I, and they would have fought for Germany again if allowed. We were the only Jews in town who did not possess German citizenship, and our political views were a smidgen less Germanic than those of the rest, but we were respected members of the Jewish congregation and accepted members of the larger society.

Mom often testified that until the Nazis came along anti-Semitism was something her parents talked about only in tales of the old country. In Weissenfels, she said, the most common distinction between Jew and

Gentile arose in discussions of servants: people thought a German girl trained in a Jewish household was less desirable—she was "too spoiled."

Fränkel became a well-known name in Weissenfels on New Year's Day in 1933, when it appeared in large letters above the entrance of a store at one corner of the town's main marketplace. The store carried stockings and handkerchiefs, suits, dresses, and some shoes, and on special order it could provide tables, beds, and sofas, even an occasional icebox or piano. Opa Isaak Fränkel, my grandfather, and his energetic son, Jakob, acquired their goods in Leipzig or Berlin, added a modest profit, and delivered wherever you wished. And if the buttons on your suit had to be moved or a dress needed shortening, Jakob's wife, Mary, was at hand a few hours each day with pins in her mouth to make the garment fit. The appeal of the Fränkels lay not only in their cheerful one-stop service but in their apparently trusting nature: they let even 1,000-mark items out of the store with only a small down payment, and, after months of weekly collections, when you were close to settling the debt, they would urge you to take home some other goods with "nothing down." As in his prior peddling enterprise, Pop kept bundles of neat account cards for the installment buyers and used a secret code to brand each one as a good risk, doubtful, or bad. The business was full of promise had Germany not gone berserk.

It was only twenty days after the store's grand opening that Adolf Hitler became Germany's chancellor. The *Führer* was a well-advertised phenomenon. He and his brown-shirted hoodlums had demonstrated their skill at government by blaming economic distress on the Jews and by bashing skulls, even in little Weissenfels, of people like Herr Franz, my nursemaid's husband, because he called himself a socialist. The Jews and socialists of Weissenfels, and also a great many other people, were uneasy about the *Führer's* accession. But many expected the Nazis to fail and disappear in short order; they had promised much too much, it was said. Others were more impressed that this charismatic foreigner, an Austrian, so well understood Germany's humiliation in war and desperation after economic collapse. Like him or not, most Germans said, Hitler came to power lawfully, a very important fact in such a fastidious society.

Germany's failure to distinguish between the lawful and the just allowed the Nazis to run wild. But brutal despotism was not a uniquely German phenomenon in midcentury Europe. Utopian fascism, like communism, exalted the power of the state and defined the word *totalitarian* as benign. In any case, the law by which the Nazis governed was not human law or natural law, only national law, and wherever a choice appeared between national ambition and some higher moral force, the Nazis were more forthright than most regimes about their priorities: revenge, recovery, and room to breathe—*Lebensraum*. Thus were millions of Germans brought to believe that their Germanity took priority over their humanity.

In our town, folks began to waver about this choice on Saturday, April 1, 1933, the day on which the Nazis ordered a nationwide boycott of every Jewish business. Two brown-shirted storm troopers patrolled the front of our store with signs instructing people not to buy from Jews; presumably, they also carried blackjacks to enforce the request. No one came that day. But on the following Monday, my third birthday, the troopers were gone and a good number of our faithful patrons returned, some through the front door and a fair number, including Gestapo detectives, through a back door. They were elaborately apologetic about the boycott and asked forgiveness for their cowardice. *You know how it is*, they kept saying, and they guiltily purchased an extra sheet or dress. In a sense, we Jews were fortunate to have been spared their humiliating dilemma.

Still, maybe half our customers gradually disappeared, and the least honest among them even stopped paying their debts. Jewish lawyers soon lost the right to press our claims in court. Hitler's 1,000-mark bonus for newlyweds could no longer be redeemed in Jewish stores. Some of our non-Jewish competitors atoned for their greedy pursuit of our customers by paying Pop "commissions" for "referrals." The Jewish owners of large department stores in Leipzig and Berlin were thrown into panic; they advertised frantically that they no longer employed Jewish salesclerks so that customers could be assured of dealing only with pure Aryans. Some of their suddenly unemployed clerks arrived in Weissenfels, where our Jewish community tried to absorb them. But no amount of improvisation could long shield us from the rain of Nazi decrees.

Over the next two years, Jews were barred from most professions and even from most public places. The Jewish salesmen who supplied our store were forbidden to enter hotels and restaurants and could barely function. We could no longer sit in the coffeehouse or go to the movies or swim at the Saale River beach. Mom's dressmaker no longer found time for her orders, and her beautician no longer granted appointments. By the end of 1935, even the minimally Jewish German Jews, who had successfully camouflaged themselves and whom we Easterners derisively called *yekkes* (probably because they wore *Jacken*—jackets) had been stripped of their German citizenship. Such Germans became Jews again, even if they were only half Jews, quarter Jews, or one-eighth Jews. Those who had struggled hardest to acquire the coloration of their surroundings were among the most conspicuous now that their environment was transformed. They no longer fit in anywhere.

By necessity, the Jews of Weissenfels drew themselves into a tighter community. They founded Zionist clubs and prepared their youngsters for flight to Palestine. The Jewish Agency, looking to claim that holy land by outnumbering the Arabs, recruited settlers under the age of thirty-five and also "capitalists" of any age if they paid their way with 1,000 smuggled English pounds (about $5,000) each. Older folks thought of leaving, too, but the fear of change, the dread of a new language, the separation from relatives, and the loss of familiar comforts held them back. They would tolerate segregation and discrimination for a time and vied in the invention of new hopes: they might be legally exchanged to some other country (Madagascar was prominently mentioned); surely the 1936 Olympics in Berlin would require the Nazis to display a new spirit of tolerance; maybe Hitler would overreach and fall from power, or the civilized world, whatever that was, would finally intervene and throw him out. Much as safety often produces dread of disaster, fear created endless hallucinations of rescue. The more miserable our condition, the more certain we became that it would not, could not, get worse. No one even imagined death camps.

In those still early Nazi years, only two Weissenfels Jews were actually arrested: young Hoffman, the playboy son of a cattle dealer, and young Tasselkraut, a salesman's son, both in their early twenties. Hoffman, people thought, went to a dance with a non-Jewish girl and probably infuriated some Nazi suitor. Tasselkraut's offense has been forgotten, though the charge against both was something about reading forbidden newspapers. Their sentence was a year in Buchenwald, the nearest concentration camp. Both were released after two months on condition that they leave the country. Hoffman went to Palestine, Tasselkraut to Britain. It's assumed that their parents paid handsome ransoms; indeed, extortion may have been the impetus for their arrests. The non-Jews who still confided in the Fränkels were suspicious of the legal proceedings, but they could not bring themselves to concede that the boys were altogether innocent. Maybe they were Communists, people said, with a delusionary logic that I would encounter again in many places.

I remember Pop and his closest friend, Hermann Birnbach, whispering over chess about how Hoffman had been warned not to discuss his experiences in Buchenwald. Their whispering was a sure sign that they were again debating the pros and cons of leaving Germany. The isolation and persecution of Jews were clearly intended to drive us out. Since no one expected to be killed, and since so much income had already been lost, there seemed to be time to plan an orderly exit. The chess players whispered about smugglers who took money, jewels, and even people across borders for exorbitant fees, and they speculated about assorted havens. By collecting the coupons of the hundreds of packs of cigarettes that Papa and Birnbach smoked on these evenings, I acquired an illustrated album about the 1936 Berlin Olympics and learned the flags of all the countries that were so urgently under review: Argentina, Brazil, Chile, Australia, Poland, Britain, Italy, and, again and again, the United States, more often called by the paradisial name of America.

From the age of memory, I was learning to cope with the world's bizarre delineations of nations and each one's rules and rituals of exit, entry, and citizenship. Maps, visas, permits, and passports were among my toys and lesson plans. I was being trained for refugeedom, primed to be dropped into a Palestinian desert or a Latin American jungle. And I learned not only to distinguish between lawful and illegal transactions across borders but also when and where and with whom one could safely discuss such things. In short, I was well rehearsed for the melodrama of our flight from Hitler, even though our family botched it in performance.

———————

I had learned to read pretty well before entering Herr Weber's first-grade class. I also wrote well, except for the damned inkblots for which you had your knuckles rapped with a ruler. (Tearing a page out of the penmanship book was a capital offense.) But I bore a greater grievance against Weber. Twice each week, before the *Hitlerjugend* hour, he would gently order me, the school's only Jew, to leave for home. I hated that isolation, as I hated being the only kid in school without a brownshirt uniform and the only one living behind windows that didn't fly a flag on holidays. I flew into a screaming, stomping rage one night when I spotted Herr Weber and my classmates bearing fiery torches and bloodred swastika banners past our house behind a loud, magnificent marching band. Weber regularly consulted my parents to ask how else he could shield me from the name-calling and pummeling at school and also how he might soothe my wounded pride. He was such a kind man, Mom kept telling me as she explained that we Jews just had to put up with distinctions, like not having a Christmas tree.

Since I ate Christmas herring and boiled potatoes and stollen at the home of Frau Franz, our housekeeper, and enjoyed eight days of Chanukah celebrations at home, I felt no religious deprivation. It was the exclusions at school that hurt and that compelled me to find anchor in a mostly adult world. I had only one playmate, Dieter, the barber's son, who lived downstairs and with whom I drove soccer balls the length of our apartment's corridor. I played cards with Opa and chess with Papa and solitary games with myself; I worked easy crossword puzzles, scratching the answers with pins when forbidden to "write" on the Sabbath. I walked alone to school and to synagogue, breaking into a trot whenever I passed through the tunnel beneath the railroad tracks so that I could imagine myself winning a long-distance race; I used the tunnel's echo to produce the sound of a cheering throng. Since I was not a fast runner, the race was an obvious metaphor by which a lonely kid devised his own paths of triumph.

The evidence that their six-year-old needed a more wholesome object of loyalty than Nazi parades intensified the family's impatience with life in Germany. Hitler's first territorial excursion into the Rheinland had not met any of the predicted resistance from France or Britain. The cosmopolitan merriment surrounding the Olympics in Berlin had brought no relief to Jews in the provinces. Opa Isaak and Mutti's parents in nearby Gera urged us to flee, confident that they themselves could survive in obscure retirement. First Papa and finally Mutti agreed. But they would not flee in panic, running like some other Jews over borders by night. They built a new structure of hope on the assumption that they could still escape with dignity.

Where to?

Pop was hefty and athletic but, approaching thirty-five, too old to qualify as a "youth settler" in Palestine; besides, the only thing he could reliably settle was a bad debt. He had been a peddler and storekeeper all his life. Wit and calculation were his only professional skills. Inside his chunky frame there coexisted a restless vigor and a scrupulous wile, an impulse to command and a desire to conform. Pop habitually threw himself into a battle of wits against overpowering authority, yet he submitted deferentially to the lowliest of its agents. These were qualities that might have made him an intellectual, and they certainly combined to help him outlive two tyrannies. But he was not a farmer or frontiersman.

Mom, in any case, did not want to sit in some Arab village plucking chickens, as she put it. She had been what we call a sheltered girl, an only child, plump, pretty, and spoiled, trained to observe events more than to act in them, and to imitate her mother's habit of distilling epigrammatic wisdom from her observations. A half century later she could have been a journalist. Endurance was her strong suit; confrontation pained her. She almost always retreated from combat and appeased combatants, unafraid to be considered meek, which she was not. She vowed to endure the Nazis long enough, she said, to plan an "orderly" flight. Refugees in search of a haven are about as rational as young people seeking a mate.

We were "Poles," and we assumed we could go to Poland. But Jews in Poland, while by no means hounded as efficiently as in Germany, were being widely blamed for that country's stagnant economy and unstable government. Our relatives there wrote that they would welcome a Hitler for a time, that subsisting on welfare in the German manner was probably preferable to a normal Polish existence. Our rejection of Poland felt good, too, because it preserved the illusion that we had a choice of destinations.

Our Polish passports would have permitted migration to Italy, at least to await something better, but we didn't know that; it was one of the few intricacies of migratory law that escaped us. (After World War I, as Austria-Hungary was being dismembered into Poland, Czechoslovakia, Hungary, et cetera, my grandparents could have chosen Austrian citizenship and then qualified easily for the "Austrian quota" of the United States, but they hadn't known about *that* or imagined that it would ever matter.) Belgium, Holland, and France rejected all immigrant applications, though they did not turn back the refugees who crept across their borders by night. Some people argued that life in a Belgian, Dutch, or French jail was clearly preferable to freedom in Nazi Germany, but Papa thought the odds that he, Mutti, and I could safely smuggle ourselves through those well-patrolled frontiers were slim. Britain admitted only domestic servants with a firm promise of a position or industrialists with plainly desirable talents and capital. Mom and Pop felt they could not qualify as a maid-and-butler team to some Anglican lord.

Australia seemed so far away its merits were difficult to discern. Canada required the posting of a bond—that we would not become public charges—from Canadian relatives that we did not have. There was no real objection to several Latin American countries that offered asylum, but neither was there any particular attraction. If people we knew were headed for Cuba or Brazil, we might have joined them. But no one was.

The best place, clearly, was the United States, specifically New York—so clearly that it felt like the only right place. The three most famous symbols of America for every European—Franklin Roosevelt, Fiorello La Guardia, and Columbia University—were New York institutions. Millions of Jews lived in New York and, it was said, were unafraid to speak Yiddish, not just in the streets but even on the radio! How that news delighted us. Papa had visions of muddling through with his Yiddish while he established himself in the same Jewish retail circles in which he felt so comfortable in Leipzig and Berlin. Ever the prudent realist, he also purchased a set of language books called *One Thousand Words of English*, whose cover bore an illustration of one man asking another, "Pardon me, can you tell me the way to the Stock Exchange?"

We would go to America.

———

The rituals by which America, the nation of refugees, screened other refugees were, politely put, complicated. The procedures seemed to us to be built on the premise that to help others in distress was to confer a privilege upon the undeserving. And indeed, the rules were designed to hold down the influx of ethnic undesirables and to favor the national and racial tribes living in the United States, not in 1936 but back in 1920.

The total number of immigrants admitted by the United States each year was fixed by Congress, and that number was apportioned among different nationality groups in the same proportion as the ancestral lineages of the country's 1920 population. The annual supply of visas, therefore, was distributed not in response to demand or need but by nationality quotas—so many for Britons, so many for Greeks, and oh so few for Poles. If in any year there happened to be too few British applicants but a surplus of Greeks, that was too bad; the quotas were not transferable. Nor could the applicants change their qualifications by changing citizenship; in the eyes of the United States, as in Hitler's, my parents were Poles because they were born in what had since become Poland. I was "Polish" by inheritance but German by birth; had I been twenty-one and held my own passport or had the United States wanted to admit a parentless child, I would have qualified for the much larger German quota. The system was logical, if not sensible or generous.

The United States also required a sponsor for each immigrant family, an American citizen who promised to keep the newcomers off the relief rolls. The sponsor had to demonstrate a capacity to honor this promise and a close enough kinship to make it credible. Until adolescence, I never knew that the word *affidavit* meant something more than the sworn statement of such a sponsor, although we informally referred to the required affidavits as the Papers.

Mutti had two cousins in New York who seemed to be the only possible sponsors. One was Felix Pfeffer, a brooding and remote man who had deserted from the Austro-Hungarian army before World War I and wandered to America, where he became rich. He owned textile mills and apartment houses and contributed large sums to Zionist causes. He kept aloof from most of the family, but he had successfully sponsored dozens of people for immigration to America, many of them virtual strangers.

The other available cousin was his distant relative Pauline Pfeffer, whose married name we didn't even know. She was the daughter of a well-known Yiddish journalist who had edited a big New York paper and, we reasoned, must have married well. Indeed she had, we discovered; although the Depression had not been kind to her husband, Victor Schwebel, he was the sort of man who would run to the ends of the Earth to help a person in distress.

We did not really need the promise of much financial aid. Pop had moved some money out of Germany to Poland and to America, of which about $3,000 remained at the end of the smugglers' discount trail in a New York bank. But we could hardly risk disclosing this illegal stash in correspondence with our relatives or applications to the American embassy.

The Papers came on Friday, March 11, 1938. I remember the date because it was also the day that, for the first time in my brief experience as a geographer, an entire nation disappeared. Cousin Felix's listed income was impressive, and Cousin Victor's promises added weight to the dossier. Friends came to share a festive Sabbath dinner, and our high spirits almost caused us to forget to turn on the shortwave radio. There had been rumors about momentous events in Austria, and Pop wanted to get the true version; so he sealed the windows, drew the drapes, moved chairs close to the console, and faintly tuned in the forbidden transmission of Radio Vienna. He did so just in time to hear a man deliver a weeping farewell address. "*Gott schütze Österreich!*"—God Protect Austria!, Chancellor Schuschnigg was saying. And then they played "Deutschland über Alles," the Haydn quartet and German anthem that Pop hastily explained was a piece of music belonging to all people and happened to be Austria's anthem, too. Pop switched the dial to a German station, which played a military march and announced the "liberation" of Austria, leaving me to wonder whether the Austrian flag now had to be torn out of my Olympics album.

The pace of arrests in Germany quickened, and almost any scoundrel could get a Jew arrested by claiming that she had been overcharged in the store (which she should not have been patronizing) or had overheard us telling an anti-Nazi joke. So the family's only thought now was to get out. Our daily expectation was a letter from the United States consulate in Berlin promising a visa to the promised land.

When the letter came, it said the Papers were no good. Cousin Victor's income wasn't large enough to support us, and Cousin Felix's large claims were insufficiently buttressed to be believed. The consul would be happy to receive additional evidence. Incidentally, the letter added, the Polish quota was now oversubscribed and closed for several years—but our application had come just in time to make it onto the end of the waiting list.

Whatever mistake had been made in composing our relatives' affidavits, we were sure, could be swiftly corrected. We besieged New York with telegraphed requests for further evidence of our cousins' wealth, for tax returns, more papers, more promises, more of everything. But we still had no doubt of the outcome. Papa refused to jeopardize our chances by offering bribes to the allegedly susceptible flunkies at the American consulate. He also passed up visas to Latin America, now openly for sale.

No one expected what became new months of delay. Cousin Felix responded not with his tax returns but with warnings that life was tough in America and were we sure we really wanted to come? Next he wrote that he heard the Polish quota was closed and that more evidence from him would not help. We could only speculate about his hesitations; maybe people he had sponsored were becoming a burden; maybe some legal problems prevented disclosure of his tax returns. Not until Willy Gottfried, an old friend who had received an American visa with much less impressive financial backing, reached New York could we safely reveal our secret New York bank account and urge urgency upon our possibly burdened relatives.

To enhance our chances, Mom and I rushed to a "vacation" in Poland to learn the names of still more remote cousins in America. This was truly a voyage back to where we had come from: the village of Sokal, whose muddy lanes resembled the storied streets of Sholom Aleichem and the paintings of Marc Chagall. Like characters in one such story, we encountered an uncle who'd never forgotten or forgiven his quarrel with Opa and therefore refused to divulge the New York addresses that we craved. But we eventually came by the names and, returning home, fired off another round of pleading letters. It was only a half century later that I learned the true source of our difficulty. State Department archives revealed that even world-famous applicants were being turned away in response to Washington's orders "to require additional evidence and to resort to various administrative devices which would postpone and postpone and postpone the granting of visas."

Willy Gottfried's arrival in New York and Cousin Victor's energetic response to our predicament finally produced a breakthrough. They formed a Committee to Get the Fränkels Out and drew up new Papers galore, and their augmented dossier reached the American consulate in Berlin on November 1, 1938—just a few hours after we were arrested and kicked out of Germany.

2 · NO-MAN'S-LAND

SOMEONE, AS KAFKA PUT IT, MUST HAVE BEEN TELLING lies about Papa. Without having done anything wrong, he was arrested one afternoon, a Thursday afternoon, October 27, 1938. He was alone at the store when two policemen—ordinary "Schuppos," not Gestapos—came and ordered him to head-quarters, up near the castle overlooking the town. The Schuppos did not know why. Yes, of course, he could send someone to tell his wife.

Mom rushed to the store to await my return from Hebrew school and kissed Pop good-bye. Had someone reported a tax evasion? Did that wretch of a woman pronounce his goods over-priced? Was he headed for Buchenwald? or Dachau? There was no relief from the awful ignorance until he heard them locking Regina Wechsler, a friend, into the next cell. Whatever it was, at least it was plural, not personal.

Three hours later the Schuppos reappeared at the store. They were gentler now and very sorry, but Mom and I were also under arrest. They didn't know why, but they thought we would be joining Herr Fränkel.

The Weissenfels chief of police was even more apologetic. Nothing personal, he announced; in fact, why hadn't Frau Fränkel and little Max disappeared in the few hours of grace he had contrived to leave us? Now he would have to check our names on the list sent down from Halle. The list requisitioned every Jew of "Polish origin" for deportation to Poland, he explained. He hoped we understood that he would be held responsible for every Jew in hand.

So it would be Poland after all, Mom mused while considering what use to make of this news. Pop had to be reassured; if I got to see him, she told me carefully, I was to tell him that we, too, were now at the police station and that we were going to Poland.

Then she thought of all the money in the store safe; 7,000 marks could be useful on a long journey. And all the clothes at the apartment, already packed for America. And now, from the next room, she heard the voice of Herr Kranz, dear, drunken Kranz, the Gestapo big shot who only weeks before had anxiously pleaded that his name be removed from the Fränkels' file of customers and who, it was said, never rejected a little income on the side.

Would Herr Kranz let her return to the store to lock it up properly while little Max stayed with his father? Yes, of course, replied the equally quick-witted Kranz; why, he himself would be her escort.

Mindful of the urgent news that Mom had entrusted to me, I was led into Pop's jail cell to begin my career as a reporter.

We are going to Poland, I blurted out.

Oh? asked Pop, *Who is we?*

Mutti and I. I don't know about you.

Mutti was more successful with her part in the intrigue. She returned to the store with her high-ranking escort and persuaded him to break the seal already soldered to the safe. She reached for the pile of high-denomination bills, handed Kranz 300 marks, and stuffed 6,700 into her pocketbook.

Here, she said, *let's split it.*

Now, she continued, could she make a final inspection of our apartment and pick out some warm clothes for the journey? Of course, said Kranz, ordering his uniformed entourage to keep a discreet distance from our house on the Friedrichstrasse to spare Frau Fränkel any embarrassment. He was such a gentleman; he alone would accompany Mom inside. She scooped up two suitcasefuls of mothballed woolens from the America pile and let Kranz wallow in a supply of cigars and schnapps.

Not until Mom rejoined us in the family cell with her haul and her tale did Pop obtain a coherent account of our predicament. And he passed the news to our town's other "Poles" in the neighboring cells—the Wechslers, with baby, and the three Sternreichs. Eastward was not the direction of flight we had hoped for, and police vans were not the transport of choice, but Mom kept stressing that we were at last leaving Germany, a counsel that induced a perverse sense of security in all of us.

All three families, including the Wechsler baby carriage, were driven to Halle, the regional center to which other "Polish" Jews were being ferried that night from Eisenach, Erfurt, Dürnberg, and other cities. Only slowly did we learn of the frightening efficiency displayed that night in every German city, town, and hamlet. In an ominous rehearsal for later assignments, the Gestapo and SS had rounded up 15,000 Jews of Polish descent in a single day. Hitler was claiming the "Germanic" territories of Silesia from Poland, and he was giving Poland "her Jews" in exchange.

Actually, our irrational status as "Poles" had become even more tenuous. The Polish government had recently decreed that Polish passports would be valid only if they bore a certain purple rubber stamp, which was, conveniently, unavailable to most Jews, particularly those living outside of Poland. And it was these disowned Poles who lacked the purple stamp that Hitler was now offering up for barter.

A few of the 15,000 slipped through his net because, like Opa Isaak, they were traveling on roundup day. And a good number, like Mom's parents in Gera, were deported in relative comfort, aboard passenger trains. As these trains hit the border, a diplomatic storm erupted. To defend itself against the unwanted Jews, the Polish government hastily rounded up some of its "Germans," including many Jews, and threatened to push them westward in retribution. Out of this grotesque reciprocity there finally came a feeble "compromise": the Nazis would take back some of the Jew-bearing trains if Poland would admit others.

These negotiations were still being organized when we were registered in Halle and warned that we could take only 10 marks out of the country. At Pop's insistence, Mom surrendered her cache of 6,700 marks but received a carefully composed, duly stamped receipt. How they loved to show a solicitous side to their victims. The policeman who stood guard over the railroad car that was taking us toward the border jumped off at most stops to buy milk for the children and cigarettes for the adults. One of the four Gestapo agents commanding the train told jokes in a better Yiddish than that spoken by any of his charges.

Our last stop in Germany has no name in any of our memories. We couldn't even see the town's lights through the rain. Some local Jews served up coffee, sandwiches, and terror: the trains were not getting through to Poland, they said; we were to be marched to the border under armed guard. When twenty local policemen reported for escort duty, the Gestapo chief airily dismissed them. *I need men with iron nerves*, he announced. We waited hours more until a platoon of black-shirted SS troopers marched up at midnight.

They prodded our group of about 200 along a dirt road that had turned into a muddy brook until we faced the SS leader beneath an umbrella of trees. The rain beat so hard against the police van that served as his platform we barely heard his words. But their gist was clear: as of 1:03 A.M., October 29, 1938, we were officially expelled from Germany; directly ahead lay a strip of no-man's-land and beyond that Poland, where we belonged; whoever set foot on German soil again would be shipped to a concentration camp. Heil Hitler!

They are going to shoot us in the back! a woman screamed.

Mutti, they are going to shoot! I yelled.

I promise you, Mom insisted, *no one will shoot. Now give me your hand and let's go. It's just a few minutes to Poland.*

It felt like a rutted potato field, but it might have been just another rain-drenched road. No one talked, but some other children were crying, especially the Wechsler baby, whose bucking carriage Regina, Mutti's friend, refused to abandon because the pillows concealed a precious cargo of gold. We slushed ahead for an hour, but we probably traveled only a few hundred yards.

Suddenly, silhouetted against the dark sky, there stood the square mortarboard caps and pointed rifles of four Polish soldiers. They were stomping wildly in the mud to restrain the growling dogs that each held on a taut leash. We stopped in fear. They stared in wonderment. Finally even the dogs grew still, and we discovered that only two men in our crowd of 200 "Poles" could speak any Polish. They requested at least provisional shelter because the Germans had threatened arrest for anyone caught on German soil. At least while awaiting instructions, would the border guards take us to those flickering lights in the distance? The children, especially, needed shelter from the rain.

Follow us, the soldiers commanded. Now that we thought ourselves in friendly hands, the weight of the suitcases became more bearable, and even the preciously laden Wechsler carriage rolled more easily. The road curved so much that we decided it would still be a long time before we reached the lights. The group allowed itself some nervous laughter and chatter until the mood was shattered again by a clearly German voice: *Halt!*

We were back in Germany. Up ahead, instead of the four Polish guards, stood three or four or twenty Germans, barking a babel of orders to retreat. Behind us, the Polish guards were disappearing down the road. We ran like a herd, our Polish speakers in the lead, begging for an explanation. One of the Poles just turned, raised his weapon, and fired a shot into the air.

Mutti, you promised, I yelled, but Mom and Pop shoved me to the ground. We all dived into the mud—soft and safe no-man's-mud. The Germans lined up behind us, the Poles up ahead, all of them ranged in the rain along the lines that ruled their minds: national frontiers.

But there was no more shooting and no more shouting, so we gradually raised our heads and settled on the wet ground to await our fate. People coughed and sneezed and had little else to say. An unarmed emissary from the German group offered to shelter women with children in a frontier shack until the rain let up, but the men vetoed that idea. These confusing signals of brutality and courtesy overwhelmed the senses; we were truly in no-man's-world.

This was my fifth border crossing. I had traveled, more comfortably by train, to and from Czechoslovakia the year before and to and from Poland just a few months earlier, experiences that left me deeply scarred. When we were returning from Carlsbad, German customs agents confiscated the Czech chinaware I had won at bingo because Mom refused to pay an exorbitant tariff. Leaving Poland, I had to watch strange hands crawling through the underwear in my suitcase. At least this time, I decided, there would be no customs inspection.

I awoke at dawn in Mom's arms beneath a tree at the apex of a triangular meadow. Pop was blowing cigarette smoke into the fog through a pneumonial cough. Along the hypotenuse of our triangle ran a road between two *Schlagbäume*—felled trees—the red-and-white-striped border poles that marked every European border. An SS man walked to the edge of our plot from the German side; come what may, he said, we would have to get into Poland. Nor did anyone want to turn back. Without any special command, our crowd gathered up its parcels and suitcases and lumbered to the road and leaned against the Polish border pole. A half-dozen soldiers stood guard there with their ferocious dogs leashed and muzzled but not well controlled. We pressed against the pole to overhear the debate between our two Polish speakers and the soldiers. Many heads were shaking negatively, and the pole stayed down.

Some SS guards, leering, gathered behind us and linked arms. *Go, go,* they yelled, laughing, and when they grew tired of that they took to flirting with the prettier girls inside our corral. The Polish guards stood their ground impassively, except when one of the dogs gained too much leash and tore the overcoat off a man in the front row. At intervals, a Polish farmer drove up in a horse-drawn wagon, and the guards of both nations would clear a path so he could serve milk to the children. I suppose we might have retreated back to the triangle, but the apt symbolism of our predicament, between the poles, seemed to hold us in place.

We rocked back and forth on that strip of road for six or seven hours until noon, when two Polish army officers arrived and ordered their *Schlagbaum* raised and the Jews admitted. By international agreement, they announced, we would be welcomed in Poland, not as refugees but as tourists, without prejudice to our ultimate fate. All those who wished— *sic!*—could pass through a customs inspection at the shack ahead and have their passports duly stamped. Welcome to Poland!

We crossed the line without elation, and Pop's thoughts advanced immediately to the next step, getting out again, to America. He was speculating about possibilities and simultaneously instructing his son in the essentials of flight: size up every predicament and spot the exits. Fugitives aspire not to control their environment, only to map it and escape when possible.

The customs people worked quickly enough until they got to Mutti and the two suitcases filled with clothes for America. They were brand-new clothes, with the price tags still affixed, the Polish agents pointed out—and they were now content to speak in German. We could pay a duty at least ten times greater than the 10 marks we'd been allowed to carry or surrender the goods.

For the first time in all my observations of parental encounters with authority, Mutti lost her composure. She would rather send the clothes back to Germany than surrender them here, she shouted.

Well, Madam, Germany is that way.

And before any of us grasped what was happening, Mutti went that way, a suitcase in each hand, and disappeared into the German frontier shack. A moment later she reappeared, waving excitedly to summon me and Pop back to Germany.

Those damned Poles, the German customs man intoned. *What do they want you to do, freeze in this weather? We won't send those things back. You go into that room and put them all on.*

So we stripped off our wet clothes and donned as many shorts, shirts, sweaters, and jackets as our overcoats could encompass. We asked the German official to dispose of the soiled garments, bade him well, and, with our now empty and duty-free suitcases, waddled back into Poland.

3 · ENEMY ALIEN

BORDERS, OF COURSE, ARE ONLY THE MOST CONSPICUOUS barriers among peoples. I already understood that uniforms, language, music, and religion were also barricades to be fought over as fiercely as boundaries. Now that we had crossed a conventional frontier, we were going to confront many more unmarked barriers. In every fresh environment, we faced a choice between two paths to safety: hiding inside the herd of refugees or escaping into a new conformity. We chose a little of each.

Our next vehicle of flight was a horse-drawn cart that dumped its human cargo at the first Polish village, outside a huge barn. Pop, whose generosity toward his fellowman never precluded suspicion of him, expected that we would be imprisoned here indefinitely, and so he took to tinkering with his gold watch, the only likely ransom, looking for a target. Our crowd of 200 deportees was no longer a group; we shared information and speculation and straw to lie upon, but each family now charted its own path out of the hay.

Our plan led toward Kraków, the medieval city of Polish kings, the city to which Pop had long ago smuggled some of his money and where we could live with the most delicious relative a boy of eight could imagine: Uncle Isaak Pfeffer, the chocolate maker.

As Mom habitually reminded me, it's when you've got bad luck that you really need good luck. We soon felt lucky indeed to have qualified for Hitler's first mass deportation. For on the night of November 9–10, barely a week after we entered Poland, he ordered the massive Kristallnacht pogrom, sending his storm troopers to smash most synagogues and stores owned by Jews, to seize Jews' property, and to arrest most of the Jewish males who did not cheat the Nazis with suicide. We learned later that our landlord in Weissenfels had shrewdly protected our apartment on the pretext of defending his building and that the policemen who had sealed our store defended it as now "public property." But most of the Jewish men in Weissenfels were hauled off to concentration camps, and only the few who could emigrate immediately were released in the succeeding months. Tales of wild beatings and weird tortures in the camps filtered to Poland, though Mom and Pop had trouble believing them. They could credit any slur against Poles, whom they didn't really know, but they tended to hold out for evidence against Germans, whom they knew to be kind as well as cruel.

Within days of our arrival in Poland, I was bundled off to school, provided with language tutors on the side, and tethered to a "normal" routine. Mom's latest epigram was that the only way to survive an undesirable condition was to treat it as permanent; think it temporary and you're likely to be trapped forever. So we pretended to adjust to a life we longed to escape.

Ominously, the exits remained blocked. Months passed without further word from the American consulate in Berlin. Presuming our visas to be at hand, we didn't dare disclose our change of address lest that provoke a new round of complications. Instead, Pop put his faith in the German post office; he directed the Weissenfels branch to route our mail to friends who could be counted on to forward it to Kraków. But since none had arrived by the spring of 1939, it was decided to risk Mom's return to Germany to learn what had gone wrong.

That became possible, despite the horrors of Kristallnacht, when the Germans once again moderated their evil decrees with a burst of bureaucratic rectitude. They had conducted a bizarre negotiation with the Poles over the fate of the assets of the deported Jews, and now, instead of delivering those assets to Poland, they offered to readmit to Germany a single member of every deported family for a month's "orderly liquidation" of property. And since a lingering chivalry seemed to make it safer for Jewish women than men in Germany, it was mostly women who took advantage of this amnesty and dared to go back "to save something."

Frau Franz, my nursemaid, greeted Mom with flowers at the Weissenfels train station in early June. And the town's police chief, plainly embarrassed about our expulsion, offered "all possible assistance." At the provincial center of Magdeburg, Mom claimed the 6,700 marks that had been receipted so meticulously during the night of our expulsion; she was paid in denominations of her choice.

Aren't you afraid we'll get to Poland before you get to America? the Nazi paymaster mocked.

If you do, I'll serve you coffee, Mom replied, to his delight.

Fatefully, she was getting the hang of these joustings.

The money she received, however, was not allowed out of Germany, so Mom went on a shopping spree and packed a huge lift van for shipment to New York. Under the tolerant gaze of Weissenfels inspectors, she crated our furniture and clothing, the dairy dishes and meat dishes and Passover dishes and gilt coffee service, the Czech crystal and lace and German cutlery and silver, and also some hastily bought English luggage, shirts and suits, French silk dresses and Persian rugs, plus a considerable portion of the Fränkel store's inventory of linens, stockings, and handkerchiefs. Herr Kranz and his Gestapo cronies toasted the sealing of this huge wooden container with our whiskey and gratefully carted off the souvenirs that Mom bestowed upon them.

With three weeks remaining on her reentry permit, she devoted every remaining hour to a siege of the American consulate in Berlin, the elegant granite building around the corner from the Brandenburg Gate, just off Unter den Linden, not far from Hitler's future bunker and Ulbricht's future Wall. The anteroom was a tense, unhappy place, aptly depicted in Gian Carlo Menotti's opera *The Consul.* The visa supplicants sat hour after hour, never daring to read a book or newspaper lest they miss an official's telling glance or chance remark or the encouraging albeit envied smile of another applicant's triumph. They were silent worshipers reaching out separately and alone to the unseen Supreme Judge, behind the door marked CONSUL GENERAL.

On Mom's very first day she reached a vice-consul, who shuffled a few dossiers and announced, *Your affidavits are no good.*

Why not?

Insufficient promise of support from one relative and insufficient sup-

port of the promise of another. The wealth of some of the sponsoring relatives who would keep us off the welfare rolls was pronounced inadequate
and the assurances of others were held not credible. Moreover, the sponsors seemed too distantly related to be reliable guarantors of anything.
Next, please.

But we are a healthy family, Mom pleaded, *ready to earn an honest living.*

*No matter, Madame, the law requires a credible guarantee that you won't be
a burden on the state, and yours is not credible.*

Is there nothing else to be done?

Probably not.

Should we apply to another country and wait for American visas there?

That's up to Madame.

––––––––––

Final as all this sounded, Mom had nothing better to do than return to the
consulate's antechamber, day after day after day. Perhaps she would hear
something more encouraging, maybe she'd run into someone with "connections." Each morning she sheathed her sinking spirit in stunning
clothes, so that she might appear a worthy bet instead of an unworthy beggar. She was conforming to yet another new environment.

One noontime, with only one week of her allotted month in Germany
remaining, she saw a tall man, tanned and tailored, crossing the anteroom
with a striking blond woman on his arm. He must be influential, she decided, and leapt into his path to ask for five minutes of his time. In a terrible German, which she took as confirmation of his high diplomatic rank,
the man asked why. Well, there was trouble with her visa and she had only
a few days left in Berlin and she was sorry to burden him but she didn't
know where else to turn.

For an awkwardly long minute, the man studied her, down to the
shoes, then said, *Certainly, Madame.* He had a luncheon date but would
speak with her if she returned at three o'clock. But the consulate was
closed on Wednesday afternoons, Mom injected, losing some of her composure. The man smiled at her anxiety. He would alert the doorman, he
said, to admit the "elegant lady."

The Fränkel folder lay on the consul general's desk when the doorman signaled Mom's return.

How many dependents are there now? he asked.

*Still only one child—Max. Who would have more under these circum-
stances?*

What is the family doing now?

Living in Kraków, Mom said hesitantly. She was afraid of this previously unrevealed fact, but also afraid to lie. Omitting the melodrama, she described our deportation.

And what do you do in Poland? the consul inquired.

Well, one lie might help, Mom decided. *We cash the checks that our rich relatives send from the United States,* she said.

Really?

Yes. How else could we live? she added, calling attention to her newly purchased clothes.

Very well, Frau Fränkel, you will hear from us.

Mom walked out of the empty consulate with the buoyant gait she had observed in other successful hurdlers. She sensed at once what we formally learned three weeks later, that we had at last won the grand prize, three visas to America.

We were to appear in person to receive them at the consulate in Berlin, on September 12, 1939.

———————

Not even Kafka could have imagined the next obstacle on Mom's course. As she was returning to Kraków through the border town of Zbonscin, the Poles seized her passport without explanation. And when she refused to travel on without it, she was thrown into a camp where 7,000 refugees had been penned for six months. Quickly losing the attachment to her passport, she agreed to leave empty-handed, and rejoined us in Kraków, where she learned that Pop's passport, too, had been "rescinded." We now had the prospect of visas at last, but no passports into which they could be stamped.

We were not Poles, the Poles had decided, so we did not deserve Polish passports of any kind. Very well, we said, we do not want to be Poles, but we need passports to depart. In a burst of ingenuity, the Polish government invented a new and appropriately absurd document: the stateless passport—or, literally, "Identity Card of a Stranger." Our bleached status was symbolized by its color, almost pure white, a novel passport color that proved to be our salvation but for the moment seemed only a ludicrous concoction.

The next and, we dared hope, final bump in the road to America was permission to answer the consulate's summons to Berlin, precisely on September 12. Any Jew's return to Germany was by now a mad and suicidal venture. Jewish men were imprisoned or living in terror, and even some women and children had been taken to the camps. We were prepared to risk a quick few days in mid-September, but how could we be sure that the Nazis' consul in Kraków would grant the necessary transit permit on or just before September 12? And if we failed to appear in Berlin that day, would we lose the visas altogether?

The Polish-German agreement that had allowed Mom to return to Germany in June also permitted transit through Germany by all Jews migrating to other countries. Hitler was cleansing Germany, not yet all the Earth, of Jews. But the offer expired on July 31, meaning we would have to linger in Germany for six long weeks, which Pop refused to consider. He would risk no more than seventy-two hours on the Nazis' turf and so would come to Berlin only at the last moment. If the Germans denied him transit, he could always have himself smuggled across the border—so long as he was not encumbered by family. So Mom and I ventured legally back to Germany on the last possible day, July 31, and sought safety in the familiar surroundings of Weissenfels. We took along Pop's new stateless passport in the hope that we could get him a transit visa for the crucial days in September.

But Weissenfels, alas, no longer felt safe. In the few weeks since Mom had packed the lift van, the familiar police and Gestapo agents had decided they could no longer risk dealings with us. Most of the Jewish men were gone, and their families had fled to the anonymity of big cities. We, too, decided to bed down in a furnished room in Leipzig, getting police permission on the pretext that we needed access to kosher food. With the last of the Fränkel assets, Mom had bought passage for three to New York on a German steamship, leaving Hamburg on September 14. The German-America Line told her not to worry about Pop; it would get him permission to pass through Berlin. Mom had also sought a pass for Pop to join us in Leipzig, and the police there arranged for her to seek it from the appropriate authorities in Berlin. It was on our way to that appointment, on September 1, that all our plans, and all Europe, collapsed.

Standing in line to buy rail tickets to Berlin, we suddenly heard Hitler's voice raging from every pillar at the Leipzig station. Germany was on the march, he screamed, avenging an "attack" by Poland.

Germany's invasion of yet another country struck me as unspectacular news, but this time I heard the word *Krieg*—meaning war. Mom explained that the Polish army would resist and get help from England and France. But she quickly sensed that war compounded our jeopardy. Now we were not only hunted Jews but also enemy aliens. And the *Blitzkrieg* raged across terrain separating us from Pop.

From behind us, we heard a comment that Mom memorized and repeated often. *I knew when I saw the synagogues burn,* an elderly German mumbled, *I knew then that we would someday pay for it.*

––––––––––

Mom's only thought was to get out of Germany fast. In her search for a destination, Germany's new enemies—Poland, Britain, and France—were obviously disqualified. But most of the nonbelligerents and neutrals wouldn't have us. Mom shuttled from one consulate to another in Leipzig with her evidence of an imminent visa to America and of paid passage across the Atlantic, concentrating on the Swedes, who had assumed Poland's diplomatic functions, and the Danes, Dutch, and Belgians. All turned us away. Only the Hungarians seemed touched by her desire to "rejoin a husband" in Poland. They granted a three-day transit permit through Budapest, but as luck would have it the German army was pre-empting all eastbound trains. Civilians were directed to a train leaving from Berlin the next day, Saturday, September 9, giving Mom a chance to visit the American consulate one more time.

The consulate was closed on Saturdays, but for 10 marks the doorman agreed to see who might be working. A pleasant woman about Mom's age appeared and was moved to tears by the response she had to deliver. *I couldn't give you an earlier appointment than the twelfth,* she said, *but in any case, you have a new problem. If your husband does not appear with you on the twelfth, you won't get your visa. We don't divorce couples. I feel so sorry for you.*

Losing the visas only hours before we were to receive them seemed a fate even worse than remaining in Germany. Recklessly, Mom decided that we would stay in Berlin and let the precious Hungarian permit lapse. She sent Pop's passport off to Kraków through Danish diplomatic channels to let him pursue his own course, and she fired off a telegram to New York: WE ARE IN BERLIN, BUT SEPARATED BY WAR. NEED PAPER IMMEDIATELY SAYING I CAN COME ALONE, WITH MAX. It was the last message she could toss into the ocean, for the very next morning the Gestapo decreed that Jews could no longer send telegrams without special permission.

The Jewish Community Center, or what was left of its welfare branch, found us a furnished room far from the center of Berlin. Fearing internment as enemy aliens, we still had not registered with the police, and being unregistered, we were afraid during the nightly air-raid alerts to enter a public shelter. A house far from the center seemed safer, although the occasional British and Polish planes overhead dropped more leaflets than bombs and inflicted only feeble damage.

By Monday morning, our American sponsors had grasped our predicament and telegraphed agreement to receive us without Pop. But we still had to wait one more day for the consulate's formal hearing. And it was not until we had passed the medical exams and completed other formalities on the twelfth that we learned of the final agony. The consul had just received a new German regulation: he could issue visas only to persons holding valid "exit permits" from the Berlin police. He understood those permits would be difficult to obtain, especially for Jews, but he promised to reserve our visas for up to four months before assigning our quota numbers to other applicants.

So our ship sailed without us. Berlin lay in darkness each night, and we lay in fear. There was no hoping for a legal exit unless we first registered our presence with the police, in the "Jewish Enemy Alien" line. On Rosh Hashana, the Jewish New Year, all the remaining Jewish men were arrested. On Yom Kippur, the Day of Atonement, storm troopers knocked on our door and confiscated all radios. No physicians were permitted to treat a Jew. Being ineligible for ration cards, we could buy only bread and, occasionally, pork sausage, which, to spare my sensibilities, Mom passed off to me as kosher. We lacked winter clothes, but Mom obtained a fluffy snowsuit from the welfare organization so that I could attend the makeshift Jewish school across town. When I wore the suit to synagogue one Friday evening, they threw me out as improperly dressed. We no longer belonged even where we belonged.

Mom ran each day to the Jewish Community Service and to every conceivable German official, smuggler, and crook to learn how to get an exit permit. At police headquarters they would not admit that they lacked the authority to grant it, hiding their impotence in taunts. *What do you expect? The Poles are killing our boys, and you, a Polish Jew, want to go traveling around the world?*

German soldiers returning from Kraków were more helpful. They brought two postcards from Mom's parents. One urged that we return to Poland if we could; the second implored us by all means to stay away. Pop, they indicated, had fled eastward from the advancing German army.

The second postcard frightened Mom, and her curiosity overwhelmed her judgment. It led her, during Christmas week, to wangle a military pass for an overnight trip by troop train to Kraków. With what she always remembered as stupid abandon, she left me in darkened Berlin with her friend Regina Wechsler.

Mom learned in Kraków that her father, Opa Mathes Katz, had died of a heart attack, one of the last European Jews to die as people are meant to die. But the rest of Kraków's Jews could hardly be described as living. They stumbled around the city with large yellow Stars of David on their clothing to mark them for humiliation by both the defeated Poles and the conquering Nazis. Kraków's Jewish Community Center was a pitiful remnant of the energetic welfare agency we had frequented just months earlier; no one even heard of such a thing as an exit permit out of occupied Poland. For what she knew would be the last time, Mom hugged her mother good-bye and turned her mind to saving her child.

———————

The sign on the door at Berlin's police headquarters said, ENTRANCE STRICTLY FORBIDDEN. Mom had passed it often. This time she peeked inside.

Can't you read? the commissioner bellowed.

Yes, I'm sorry, but I'm desperate, Mom replied. She described her predicament and asked for an exit permit.

Red-faced, the commissioner rose, looked outside his office, and shut the door. *Sit down,* he commanded. *If you tell anyone about our meeting and what I am about to say, you will never get out of the country alive, do you understand?*

Mom nodded.

Don't you know that police permits and exit visas are not issued by the police? We only rubber-stamp the papers.

Then who decides?

The Gestapo, of course.

Where do I go?

To Gestapo headquarters. To Dr. Joachim Schüller.

Thank you, thank you.

Mom had turned to leave when she was asked, *Where did you say you want to go?*

To America.

If you get there, will you tell them we're not all bad?

———————

At Berlin's Jewish Community Center they would not even reveal the location of Gestapo headquarters. *You are not allowed on that street and you won't come out alive,* the woman said, *and no one will come to get you out.*

But there was no restraining Mom in this fourth and last month of our gestating visa. She got the address somehow and, wearing her best suit of clothes, set forth, stationing her friend Regina around the corner to take charge of me in case she failed to reappear.

Only uniformed Nazi officials were scurrying in and out of the formidable building, flashing special identity cards to an SS trooper at the door. Mom presented her passport, that white, stateless creation with the embossed Polish eagle on the cover. Though it listed her nationality as Jewish, it did not conspicuously brand her, like German documents for Jews, with the mandatory middle name of Sarah. It bore the Polish variant of her name: Maria Fraenkel.

I've come to see Dr. Joachim Schüller, Mom said.

The blackshirt studied the strange white document, surely the first such he had ever seen. *Are you Swiss?* he wondered, not unintelligently naming the only other country that issued white passports with some French words inside.

Mom gave no answer, and so the trooper reported a Swiss lady at the door.

The manicured Dr. Schüller smiled. *I thought you said you were Swiss?*

Your guard said that, not I, Mom answered, with a hint of contempt for the security arrangements.

Yes, Schüller allowed, *it is getting more and more difficult to get intelligent help behind the front. Even the Aryan race has its idiots.*

Still, the idiots redeemed themselves fast enough. The doctor pressed a button, spoke peremptorily into a telephone, and in less than a minute the Fränkel family dossier, much fatter than the one at the American consulate, lay before him. It told him everything he could possibly want to know about us, including the reason for Mom's visit, but he seemed to enjoy prodding the weak.

How come your name is now Maria? Are you converted?

No, I am a Jew. My name is Marie. The Poles wrote it Maria.

Where do you want to go?

To America.

Really?

No, not really. But no one here seems to want us.

Why don't you go to your Americans for help?

They aren't my Americans. I have lived in Germany most of my life, and I do not want to leave. You give us no choice.

Why didn't you stay in Poland?

I have no connection with Poland. My father was Austrian and fought for Austria in World War I. No one wants us anymore.

It was all going reasonably well until the doctor hit an obvious question that Mom had failed to anticipate.

Where is your husband?

In Lwów.

Oh? What is he doing all the way over there?

Mom groped for an alibi that would not admit Pop's fear of the Nazis.

He was to have joined us here for the trip to America, she began. *Our ship—a* German *ship—sailed from Hamburg on September fourteenth. I had reservations for three—here, I can show you.*

And then she hit upon an alibi: *He went to Lwów to say good-bye to his mother, and then the war broke out.*

Precisely. We're at war with Poland, and you, a Pole, want privileges from us?

I told you, I have nothing to do with Poland. I am "stateless." Here, I can prove it to you another way. There is a transit visa through Hungary in that passport. It would have gotten me out of Germany right after the war started, to Poland. But I hate them so, I didn't go.

Dr. Schüller smiled again and reached for pad and pen. *When do you want to leave?*

As soon as I can. I would have to make arrangements.

Go and make them.

You mean we will get the exit visas? Is it sure?

The doctor stopped smiling. *If I say something, it is sure.*

One week later, it was.

Only one door out of Germany remained open for Jews—a remote border station between Oldenburg and the Dutch city of Groningen. We were the only passengers on the two-car train that covered the last twelve miles, and we seemed to be the custom guards' first customers in quite a while. Instead of elation at last we felt greater anxiety than at any time in the past six months; what else could possibly go wrong? Yet Mom was determined to get her gold watch, diamond ring, wedding band, and pearl earrings out of Germany. The guards searched her pocketbook first, and, as they led her away to be undressed, she dropped the jewelry inside the bag and casually handed it to me. I was expected to know enough about borders to walk off nonchalantly with that handbag; in fact, I cradled it while offering to help another inspector in his struggle to open our luggage.

After customs came a last German passport check, by two blackshirts.

You are going to America?

Yes, I said.

Will you have more oranges to eat there?

Yes.

Do you realize that the ocean is full of our mines? Can you swim?

Yes, I lied.

Have you ever passed a border before?

Oh, yes.

Have you ever been through anything like this?

Nothing so thorough, Mom interjected, hiding her sarcasm.

The SS men were pleased and wished us a pleasant trip.

Strolling the cobblestones of Groningen, I expressed my exuberance by pronouncing them the cleanest streets I had ever seen. Mom said Holland was a neat and tidy country. We toasted Holland with coffee, the first good coffee in months. I asked whether we could afford a second cup, which we could because our American relatives were to have cabled fifty dollars to Rotterdam, where we were to board the SS *Volendam*.

Rotterdam in my memory is lights, a brilliant and blazing contrast to blacked-out Berlin. We lived for two days with a Mr. Monderer, a Jew of considerable wealth who was now charitably dispensing some of it to refugees. It happened that Pop—from whom we had heard nothing in months—was one of his patrons, because Monderer was linked to the chain of smugglers who passed our money along to New York. We laughed about the coincidence, even if it turned on the missing member of our family. We'd have laughed at almost anything that day.

As the SS man said, there were mines in the English Channel, and British pilots needed two days to guide our ship past smaller vessels that were listing badly or broken in two. Once out in the Atlantic, I navigated every corridor and befriended passengers in every class of service. I learned to draw the *Volendam* from every perspective and collected grapefruit halves at every meal to carve them into ashtrays. They were the first grapefruits I had ever seen.

We reached New York on February 22 after an otherwise uneventful crossing, except that Mom lost one of her pearl earrings aboard ship. About two months later, a few days before Holland was overrun by the Nazis, the earring arrived in the mail with a note from the *Volendam*'s captain. It had been found on the second crossing after ours, he wrote, and he hoped we were well. When we asked where to find him, we learned that he had been killed in an attack at sea.

Cousins Vic and Felix and all the unknown relatives greeted us at the Holland-America Line's pier in Hoboken, across the river from New York. I asked to be alerted when Vic's car crossed the state border, but we sped so fast through the Holland Tunnel that I barely caught sight of the frieze in which dirty tiles spelled out the words NEW JERSEY and NEW YORK on either side of a vertical line. No barrier, no customs, not even a policeman's salute.

I still give silent tribute to that neglected marker every time I pass through the tunnel. Its utter lack of significance is for me a sure sign, and source, of America's greatness.

PATRIOT

1940–1948

4 · THE FOURTH REICH

NO MATTER HOW COMFORTING THE REFUGE, IT IS vexing to be a refugee. Speech, dress, and manners that were elegant in the old country are suddenly gauche in the new. Hands offered for shaking are left dangling in midair. Naked knees jutting from short pants shout "alien" to every passerby. No one explains, through weeks of embarrassment, that *language* doesn't rhyme with *sandwich*. America offers safety, but not an end of striving.

And despite the extraordinary intimacy achieved on our journey, Mom and I now strove on separate paths. She needed the security of a refugee ghetto. I needed the immunity of assimilation.

In a sense, I became a chronic fugitive, forever looking to escape the mundane, to find new soil and stimulation. But becoming American also meant becoming a chronic conformist, acquiring new camouflage for a new environment. No more kneesocks and overcoats, Mutti; I want corduroy knickers and a mackinaw jacket! Schoolbooks are bound with a belt, Mutti, not packed inside a briefcase! Lunch belongs in a brown bag, not a metal box! The month-old American, aged ten, patronized his Mutti with his vast knowledge of the New World, and she, thirty-five, lovingly accepted this inversion. Mutti became Mom, and I even tried not answering when she addressed me in German. She proposed a compromise: she would speak German only inside our home and I could reply in English. Arrogantly, I assumed she was serving her own convenience; only to her grandchildren did she explain how she wanted to preserve a chance for her husband and her son to communicate in a common language.

She was right to worry, and not just linguistically. For seven years we had only a few faint hints that Pop was alive in the Soviet Union. Mom searched for him relentlessly; she sent weekly letters and monthly packages of marketable food and clothing into a Russian void. One year the Red Cross conveyed an address for Pop in remote Siberia. One other time we received a postcard in his hand. In our absorbing new habitat, my sense of Pop was fast eroding. Mom's devotion to him became more real than my memory of him.

And my arrogance grew faster than my shoe size. I began to imagine that my rescue from Europe's shipwreck was somehow earned, even ordained. Though surrounded by embittered refugees, I abhorred their hurt and rejected their life of grievance. Insensitive to the pain around me, I considered my survival in America a reward and a validation of hope. I was still running my solitary race, as in the Weissenfels tunnel, and I could still hear the encouraging roar of a faceless crowd.

Mom disdained vainglorious fantasy. She constantly remarked on the dumb luck of our escape. We were lucky to have been expelled from Germany just two weeks before the Kristallnacht terror. We were luckier still to have returned to Germany a month before Hitler invaded Poland and herded Opa Fränkel and Oma Katz and Uncle Israel, the chocolate maker, and Jerzy, my Polish tutor, into the ghetto. She never imagined that even the ghetto was not the end of the horror.

We were lucky to land one of the last American visas issued to Jews in Berlin and to have passed through Holland only weeks before it was overrun by the Nazis. And, luck upon luck, we began our lives as Americans just as Americans regained their post-Depression optimism, prepared to get rich in war and outgrow their own anti-Semitism.

Mom ascribed her brilliant improvisations to desperation. Everyone who escaped has a remarkable story, she'd say. You just have to be lucky. And ready. Being ready was the dominant theme of her child rearing; even luck was useless for the unprepared. Always be ready. Finish your homework tonight, you might oversleep in the morning. Lay out the clothes you'll wear, your ride may come early. Stop wasting time on that broken zipper; find another way. Decades later, colleagues who never knew Mom nonetheless detected her promptings in their editor's habitual refusal to butt against obstacles. They remarked on my tendency, whatever the barrier ahead, to quickly map an alternate route, or even a new destination. I bore the faith of a fugitive that there must be a way out.

Still, to ride the waves is not to control them. While mastering some circumstances, Mom never let me forget our vulnerability in others. In fact, I invented an entire cosmology to explain the powers that governed people's fate. Before I ever heard of atoms, electrons, quarks, or matryoshka dolls, I became convinced that a whole world of tiny creatures lived inside every dense object, like the leg of my chair. Whenever I pushed my chair away from a table, I experienced a flush of divine might, for I would picture millions of tiny creatures scrambling inside the chair for safety, their world convulsed by an earthquake whose cause they could never know. But I felt simultaneously inferior, at the mercy of other creatures, because I imagined *our* world to be encased inside the chair of some monstrous giant. Our rain was probably his sneeze. Our earthquakes occurred when he pushed too brusquely from his breakfast table.

My cosmos was infinite. The little ones inside my chair surely had *their* chairs, containing yet other worlds of still tinier beings. And the giant inside whose chair I existed must himself be living inside the chair of a still larger being. Like all mythologies, mine served to explain otherwise unfathomable events. It even provided a key to human nature: if each of us is simultaneously godlike and antlike, omnipotent and feeble, then we all have reason to feel as I have always felt, simultaneously domineering and humble, compelling and complying.

My mythology aptly suited America, which inspires the ambition to command even as it rewards efforts to conform. As I could have taught Einstein, invoking my theory of chairs: Where you sit is where you stand.

Within a week of our arrival in New York, I had to sit for more than an hour a day in the most uncomfortable possible chairs. They were foot-high stools that placed me in the midst of a chorus of six-year-olds chanting "dog" and "cat" and "cow" as their teacher held up flash cards bearing those words. Sullenly, I was cramming English sounds and spellings into synapses that only a year before had been painted full of Polish.

Since he could not interview me in English to determine my grade level, the principal of P.S. 197 in Flatbush had chosen a long-division problem from the fourth-grade text and watched me solve it by a method that he found amusing but effective. He ruled that I could join other ten-year-olds in Grade 4B but that for two periods a day I had to practice English vocabulary and spelling in Class 1A. If only today's teachers in multilingual programs could have observed the pedagogic power of my daily humiliation. Never again did I pursue learning with the zeal induced by my desire to graduate from that circle of six-year-old midgets.

Like most of the world's Jews, of course, I had the advantage of a multilingual childhood. I read and wrote German in two alphabets, Roman and Gothic, and was taught to read and write Hebrew for synagogue without even understanding much of it. I understood Yiddish, that admixture of German, Slavic, and Hebrew that Mom and Pop invoked with their parents or friends whenever they wanted to be instantly intimate, and I still retained a fair amount of Polish. So to my encounter with English I brought a musical ear and an agile tongue; I was actually a vastly better language mimic than student. Within three months, I spoke a much better New York American than I realized, and I improved it daily by drilling the traces of German out of my pronunciation. *This*, not *zis; world*, not *verld; ring*, not *rink*. By the summer of 1940, my outermost German skin had been shed. I was a well-spoken though largely illiterate American, a discrepancy that would, in time, produce a career-shaping pedagogical crisis.

To be sure, my first encounter with English reduced me to tears. Our valiant cousins, Vic and Pauline Schwebel, drove us from the boat to their Brooklyn home, preparing to care for us indefinitely as they had promised to a thickheaded U.S. government. Pauline spoke Yiddish, the language in which her father became a famous New York newspaper editor. But Vic could only smile his instant affection. My first memory of their sons, Jack and Steve, finds them wrestling on the floor over some entry in a ledger containing mystifying numbers, which, I later learned, recorded the feats of every Brooklyn Dodger. But Jack and Steve, aged fifteen and eleven, became enthusiastic custodians of their second cousin in short pants and propelled him through several disastrous ventures in hospitality. On that first February weekend, they promoted a family outing to a plush movie palace on Kings Highway, thinking that pictures of the city would not only impress their visitor but also facilitate his understanding of the plot of *Little Old New York*. But I was not impressed, understood nothing, and dissolved in tears. So to make amends, they proposed the restaurant next door, which featured a spicy vegetable glop and chow mein noodles. One forkful of this alien food changed their cousin's mood from mere depression to hysteria.

Obviously persistent, the Schwebel boys also escorted me to the playground at Madison High, where I was fitted with a large left-hand glove and urged to catch and throw a grapefruit-size ball. With a whole team of instructors, I slowly qualified as a second baseman and gradually learned, along with *dog, cat,* and *cow,* to say *bat, ball,* and *base, home, up,* and *out.* By April, I was promoted back up and out of the first-grade misery. And the Schwebels' persistence propelled them to remarkable careers; Jack became a multimillionaire in fiberglass, Steve the president of the International Court of Justice.

Up and out was also Mom's objective, except that for her it meant back into a community of refugees. She wanted to be among friends in Washington Heights, where once proudly assimilated Jews had drawn together to share the anxieties of acclimation and their despair about the news, or lack of news, from relatives in Europe. The Heights, a huge outcropping of Manhattan schist commanding the confluence of the Hudson and Harlem Rivers, was by turns a heavily fortified American and English stronghold during the Revolution. Even when New York City expanded northward, large estates survived in the Heights into the twentieth century, most notably the one John James Audubon bought with the earnings of his famous bird portraits. When the Broadway subway tunneled into the region in 1906, developers followed and imposed Manhattan's street grid on the high hills and rocks. They built from south to north in strips parallel to Broadway, and so the lava of humanity streaming up from downtown settled, before and after World War I, into long, narrow ethnic corridors.

The better-off Irish workers from the Lower East Side were the first to ride the trains to the tenements thrown up east of Broadway. Black elites, many from the Caribbean, moved into the more elegant apartment houses overlooking Coogan's Bluff and the Giants' Polo Grounds beside the Harlem River. East European Jews flocked to the area between Broadway and the Hudson, attracted by six-story buildings with elevator service and spacious, well-heated apartments. The finest of these buildings looked out on the river and the spectacular Palisades cliffs of New Jersey or onto tree-lined Fort Washington Avenue, where they could claim names like Chambold Court and Chateau d'Armes.

In the 1930s, the riverside parkland was further enriched by vistas of that splendorous new span, the George Washington Bridge. But many of the apartments were vacated and devalued in the Great Depression. They became affordable quarters for refugees who were accustomed to middle-class comforts yet needed now to rent out rooms to other families. By 1940, about 20,000 German Jews had moved in among the East Europeans, who were "the Yankees" in this Frankfurt am Hudson. The Yankees bemoaned the neighborhood's decline; they didn't really mean it when they cursed the immigrants back to where they came from, but they did wish they'd stop prattling in German. The newcomers drew class boundaries among themselves as well. The first arrivals, who had left Germany in orderly fashion with most of their belongings, settled up north, on Manhattan's highest hills and near the area's finest shops along West 181st Street. Down a notch, between the bridge, at 178th Street, and Columbia's Presbyterian Medical Center at 168th, lived a mixture of less affluent German and Eastern Jews. They shared a street-level oasis, Wright Park, and Upper Manhattan's most sumptuous movie house, the air-conditioned Moorish palace profanely named Loew's 175th. It was destined to survive, just as incongruously, when the Heights turned Dominican, as the Reverend Ike's United Church ("Come In, Or Smile As You Pass").

The Frankels—we needed no *umlaut a* in English to be pronounced correctly—moved to the southern, poorest third of the Jewish ridge. Our Loew's, the Rio, and also the Audubon and Costello movie theaters, offered only "air-cooled" relief in summer and second- or third-run romances. But if you flexed your knees at the box office and passed for under twelve, you paid just ten cents (plus a penny tax after Pearl Harbor) for two full-length films, a newsreel, a cartoon, and each Saturday's installment of *The Mark of Zorro*. The Costello soon became an Orthodox shul and ultimately a shuttered relic. The quaintly tiled Audubon lay in ruins after Malcolm X was gunned down in its ballroom, but Columbia's Medical Center agreed to make his rostrum a shrine at the end of the century in a deal to build research labs behind the facade. The Rio became a *grocería* for the Puerto Rican and Dominican immigrants who climbed the Heights after us.

Mom's closest friends from Gera, the Gottfrieds, lived on 162d Street, and she found a four-bedroom apartment close by, at 645 West 160th. It came with a "concession"—three months' free rent for the signing of a two-year lease—and offered the area's typical amenities: iron fire escapes for storing pails and mops and stringing laundry lines; a refrigerator with trays that automatically made ice cubes; "built-in" closets, some with lights; central heating and hot running water; an intercom buzzer to admit visitors to the faux marble lobby; a swift Otis elevator; and a pay phone and washing machine in the basement.

Barely six weeks off the boat, Mom couldn't read the lease she was signing, but she knew what she was doing. Our smuggled nest egg of $3,000, which Willy Gottfried had faithfully banked, had earned some interest and loomed as an immigrant's fortune. She would pay the monthly rent of $53 by subletting three of our rooms, kitchen privileges included. Standing by to move in were the Oppenheimers, a devout family of three supported by the father's painting and paperhanging; Mrs. Lederer, who was always heading "downtown" in veiled hats and leather gloves to take coffee and *schlag* at Rumpelmayer's with, she claimed, Hollywood-bound film moguls she knew from Vienna; and Erna Reisler, an excitable young woman from Gera whose main virtue in my eyes was a brother who delivered cases of seltzer in bulbous squirt bottles.

Alas, when our lift van was pried open, our furniture stood in pools of water that had been poured over the giant crate to protect it from a fire on a New York pier. We had fire insurance, of course, but our belongings, unfortunately, had not burned. And who could have foreseen needing flood insurance? We discarded the mildewed carpets and mattresses and rosewood furnishings that were stripped of their veneers. The upright piano was ruined, though it took a few months before I agreed to abandon it. We salvaged the upper half of a massive credenza, odd chairs whose seats could be recovered, dishes and cutlery, some clothing, and a glass-keyed typewriter on which neighbors now helped to compose our appeals for compensation. (The *z* on that Erika portable was located, German style, where American machines place the *y*, leaving me with a strange accent in typing long after I had shaken off all oral traces.) Mom eventually settled for an insurance payment of $300, less than she spent at the Salvation Army for the furnishings we needed to retain our tenants. For the first time, she also invaded the precious bank account to tide us over until she found work.

Her first job, paying seven dollars a week, was sewing buttons in Brooklyn onto Simon Ackerman suits—my brand, eventually, because Mom vouchsafed the workmanship and knew the pants to be spacious in the seat. Despite advancement there, she moved to an even more distant shop that promised to teach her the tricks of attaching buttons and button loops to Persian lamb coats. That paid eight dollars a week, but the owner often pleaded poverty and merely wrote out worthless IOUs. He did, however, provide instruction, not only in buttoning but also in lining fur coats with silk and inserting pockets or shortening the hems as changing fashions required. Within a year, Mom had a career as a finisher at Steinfink Furs, a second-story establishment at Broadway and Ninety-first Street. It brought her a dollar an hour at the start and her own workroom with an Emerson radio that delivered the depressing news of the war and the uplifting drama of a succession of soaps. Her English vocabulary soared even as her fingers turned black and callused.

Mom worried about leaving me "in the street," even though our streets pulsed with adolescent life. Most afternoons, curb ball and stickball contests filled every block; they were suspended only when a police car actually responded to complaints that a window had been broken. In particularly tense innings, automobile drivers could be persuaded by posted younger brothers to await the third out before steering their cars through the playing field.

Street life became a much greater challenge than schoolwork. Whatever my deficiencies in reading and writing in the fifth and sixth grades, I must have compensated with feats of arithmetic and with the elaborate maps and drawings that always decorated my history and geography reports. I was clearly Mrs. Ritter's favorite in 6A and 6B and, at her recommendation, won the coveted citizenship medal bestowed at final assembly by the Daughters of the American Revolution. Mom proudly displayed that decoration when she visited federal offices in Washington to enlist their help in locating Pop. The medal was less an achievement than a badge of belonging, the end of statelessness. And with the medal came the ultimate reward for good grades: a captainship in the "patrol," a platoon of crossing guards that wore the insignia of the American Automobile Association and white canvas shoulder belts that conferred authority to stop cars and pedestrians, to come late to class, and to leave early, ahead of the crowd. I valued the autonomy even more than the power and celebrity.

Autonomy beckoned after school, as well. Curb ball lost some of its charm, especially because the infield patter often lapsed into German slang and profanity. I recoiled from playmates who flaunted their *Brüderschaft* and the German accents that they were too old, by a year or two, to shed. Instead of joining the Maccabee social and soccer club, I drifted into the community of the Wall.

A winding stoop of stone atop a grassy knoll on Riverside Drive, the Wall was the upper deck of our Hudson voyage. Spring, summer, and fall, clusters of friends and neighbors would stroll from their apartment warrens toward the river, there to occupy virtually reserved places at the Wall. Some brought deck chairs; most just sat atop the stone, so committed to conversation that they were indifferent to the sun's brilliant plunge behind the New Jersey cliffs and to the tiaras of lights worn by both the great bridge up north and the giant Ferris wheel in the Palisades Amusement Park to the south. The Wall offered a rich diet of debate, gossip, and flirtation, which I would sample each night while steering a steady course toward affiliation with the "American" kids nestled a few yards north of 161st Street.

Their attraction was magnetic. Herbie Tanzer, two years older, always knew someone planning a weekend drive to Rye Playland. He also gave girls a charming blush with off-color jokes. Lenny Frank was a sober guide to the pairings and infidelities of neighborhood couples. Joe Holtzer, a lanky star at sinking basketballs in bushel baskets hung from fire escapes, symbolized the compatibility of athletic prowess and intellectual ambition by gaining admission to Townsend Harris High for high achievers. And gawky Ann Lichtenstein welcomed a chubby and shy newcomer by consenting to "go steady" and recruiting me to the circle of girls who turned their living rooms into studios that trained clumsy males in the fox-trot, rumba, and lindy hop. As only Mom noticed, I never roosted among the refugees at the Wall and never even once went to the movies with an immigrant girl.

Sabbath worship opened yet another chance to shed the refugee skin. As in Germany, the immigrant Jews observed religious rituals largely in the style of their former Christian neighbors—liberally if they lived among Lutherans, Orthodox if among Catholics. In our corner of the Heights, most refugee families flocked to the Orthodox services of Rabbi Lieber, a fellow immigrant sustained financially by an assembly line of war-inspired weddings for which his wife could cook and cater. I, however, made myself important as an usher at the reformist Hebrew Tabernacle. I fell under the spell of the sonorous sermons upstairs of Rabbi Opher— "What an actor!" Mom kept remarking with unusual scorn—and the loving Hebrew instruction of Mr. Mendelsohn downstairs. Even after my religious ardor waned and I learned to recognize Opher's hypocrisies, my career at the Tabernacle flourished. Cantor Ehrenburg nursed my cracking soprano into a cantorial tenor during bar mitzvah preparations and often let me sing his part at services with the full operatic backing of organ and choir, to great acclaim from the "Yankee" congregation. That led to leading roles in the musical comedies being produced in the basement and an introduction to the meetings there of Boy Scout Troop 750, a milestone on my patriotic trajectory.

Four months before I was old enough to take the Scout oath, while I was still rehearsing to tie a dozen Tenderfoot knots and to ignite a nest of woolly hemp with flint and steel, the Japanese attacked Pearl Harbor. And Hitler, for reasons no one has ever explained to me, declared war on the United States. The German Jews on the Heights were thrilled to see America drawn into the war at last and shifting the balance of power against the still rampaging Nazi armies. Those of military age were proud to join the army, especially if, like Henry Kissinger, they were assigned to intelligence units training for the inevitable occupation of the Master Race.

I, too, wanted a uniform. And Mom, delighted that I had found yet another off-street activity, blew a precious fifty dollars for my Boy Scout khakis, kerchief, and beaver hat. To justify the investment, I volunteered for every form of uniformed duty. We hauled in newspapers, scrap metals, and tin cans to be recycled. We studied enemy airplane silhouettes and stood as spotters on neighborhood roofs. We solicited blood donations and distributed warnings against loose talk about military sailing dates. If we had not left Pop and other hostages in Europe, the war as I first experienced it might have been purposeful fun. Compared with the deprivations Mom and I had suffered with our Jewish food coupons in Berlin, America's rationing of sugar and a few other staples was a most minor annoyance.

Incredible as it will always seem, until late in the war we did not know and did not want to believe the darkest intimations about the massacre of Europe's Jews. The ghastly truth was kept from us not only by the Nazis but also by admired leaders like Franklin Roosevelt, who had verified the slaughter but chosen to feel helpless to intervene. Even some of America's foremost Jews were reluctant to demand the rescue of their European brethren; they did not want to ask a Christian and widely anti-Semitic nation to delay the war effort and run military risks to save Jewish lives. That our patriotism might conflict with our humanity was not an idea I could handle in early adolescence. Not until the stench of Auschwitz reached the world's nostrils toward the end of the war did Jewish communities clamor for special notice, focusing our remorse on demands for a Jewish state and haven in Palestine.

Had I been editor of *The New York Times* in 1942, would I have pursued the reports of genocide and featured them on Page One? As a Jew, no matter how compelling my credentials, I would not have been editor of *The Times* in 1942, or for twenty years thereafter. Arthur Hays Sulzberger, the Jew of German descent who had married into control of the paper, feared "special pleading," as did most other assimilated American Jews of prominence. He did not want it said that he ran a "Jewish" newspaper or that he bent his influence toward Jewish causes. In mid-1942, when *The Times* was much more than now the arbiter of important news, it devoted a mere two inches deep inside the paper to an account of what was described as "the greatest mass slaughter in history"—the report of Poland's Jewish labor Bund that the Nazis had decided "to annihilate all the Jews in Europe" and had so far slaughtered 700,000. If true, why not Page One?

If doubtful, why print anything? *The Boston Globe* and other papers had given the report much more prominence the day before. But the fate of Polish, Baltic, and Ukrainian Jews trapped in the maw of the Nazi war machine was not going to engage the interest of this self-conscious, apologetically Jewish enterprise. Even the unavoidable news about a 1942 rally of 30,000 people protesting the Nazis' genocide in Madison Square Garden, a few blocks from *The Times*, was described antiseptically on its front page as a "mass demonstration against Hitler atrocities."

Not until 1943 did *The Times*'s editorials acknowledge the urgency of special efforts to rescue Jews from annihilation. And that change of tone occurred only after a plainly non-Jewish member of the editorial board, Anne O'Hare McCormick, wrote of another rally that "the shame of the world filled the Garden Monday night." If there was shame, it evoked no action. And the Roosevelt White House labored to avoid any expression of special concern for Europe's Jews. When Anthony Eden, Britain's foreign minister, called on the president, he warned explicitly that any offer of asylum to Jews could well provoke Hitler into allowing a "mass movement" of them to the West. The danger of pleading for the Jews was that it might succeed! Not Roosevelt or Secretary of State Cordell Hull or Under Secretary Sumner Welles or Harry Hopkins, the note taker, objected to the brutality of that judgment.

Eden, of course, was worried about alienating the Arabs and losing their oil and Britain's colonies in the Middle East. We Jews understood that much. We were none too comfortable about being allied to a Britain that dared to block boatloads of desperate Jewish refugees from reaching the coast of Palestine. You didn't have to be a Zionist training to settle in the Holy Land to subscribe to the view that for Jews to feel safe again anywhere they would need a land of their own somewhere, a place to be the majority, to speak their own language, to write their own laws and recruit their own police. They needed a beacon of nationhood and a passport of their own. We nourished that dream long before we learned how few European Jews would survive to realize it.

Even we refugees from Germany were predisposed to disbelieve the reports of genocide. Did the Nazis persecute Jews? Yes, of course, we knew that. Did they kill Jews along with Poles and Russians as they marched on Moscow? Undoubtedly. Did they ship Jews to labor camps? Why, sure, they needed slaves to manufacture guns and to clear the rubble from their bombed cities.

But gas chambers? Ovens? Lampshades made from Jewish skins? People like Opa and Oma buried alive in ditches they'd been forced to dig?

Unbelievable.

Unimaginable.

The Germans had fallen under the spell of a Chaplinesque tyrant who besotted them with dreams of conquest and vengeance for the humiliations of their youth. But Germans were not barbarians. That is what people in the Fourth Reich said about the Third. We were reckless and stupid in our optimism. And Hitler's most monstrous legacy is that such noble disbelief, such faith in culture and in reason, will forevermore be naive.

5 · Breaking Out

IT WAS ONLY A FEW MONTHS AFTER I HAD BEEN HAULED aboard the ark America that I first heard the command to get back where I came from. The incident is important only for its consequences—imagined consequences at that. She was a fat Jewish matron who sat precariously perched atop a stool in my favorite candy store—a New York forties candy store that was mostly soda fountain, cigarette dispenser, newspaper stand, and teenage hangout. The woman's handbag, shopping net, and elbows lay sprawled across the counter space of three stools. And of course the two remaining seats at the rear, near the phone booth, were reserved for the horse and numbers players. So when I arrived to order an egg cream, I slid as gently as a perspiring ten-year-old could onto the stool at the fat woman's left. Inevitably, our elbows touched, and without losing cadence she interrupted her speech about the congenital kleptomania of the goyim to direct her hate at me. "Why don't you go back where you came from?" she screeched.

You often heard that taunt in our little corner of New York. It was a crude synonym for Dirty Refugee, Stinking Nigger, or

Nazi Hoodlum. I was told to go back where I came from when I fumbled the ball on the baseball field and also when I performed with annoying speed in arithmetic class. And we newcomers mustered only two forms of rebuttal. When, for example, a summer night quarrel over seats on the Wall caused a second-generation American to call a first-generation American a Lousy Refugee and told him to go back where he came from, the latecomer, no matter how feeble his English, had usually learned to reply, "So, *you* were here with the Indians?" Or when a strong Yiddish accent vied with a strong German accent for a spot in line at the butcher's and ordered the rival back whence she came, the victim would mutter, even in retreat, "I suppose *you* came over on the *Mayflower*?"

The odd thing about that taunt to return where I came from is that it took root in my ambition in wholly unexpected ways. I'm quite sure that I decided in those youthful traumatic moments that I would indeed go back someday, not to live but to gloat, not to reclaim Europeanhood but to flaunt my Americanism. Or so it seems, for the memory of that Fat One keeps recurring even now. It is evidence that where we yearn to go is forever conditioned by where we have been.

My ultimate response was to dream, like the kids in William Steig's cartoons, of glory: I pursued visions of escape from Fat Ones and from Washington Heights, of living beyond the zone of refugees, of acquiring the accent, dress, opinions, and aspirations of impeccable Americans, of becoming an opera star and intoning stirring tenor renditions of "God Bless America" on the stage of the Metropolitan or at Yankee Stadium, or of becoming a political star and delivering moving testimonials to the plight of refugees on the floor of the United States Senate, or of making trench-coated journeys across Europe, brandishing my press card and American passport before a whole continent of displaced persons, back indeed where I came from, the master avenger subduing the Master Race, the most envied American of them all.

How quickly those pipe dreams took form! I gave up on opera and politics at an early age, but I had knickers instead of short pants as soon I could pronounce *corduroy* and long pants before mother could afford them. I conquered the pronunciations of *bottle* (not *boddle*!) and *waver* (not *wafer*!). I memorized three stanzas of "America," down to alabaster cities, whatever they were. I "went steady" and had a business of my own, M. FRANKEL, SIGNS & POSTERS, ENGLISH ONLY. I earned the "citizenship" merit badge one week after becoming a Boy Scout Tenderfoot. I hated the dirty Japs (though never quite all Germans) and took endless tests in engineering, mathematics, and fine arts until I won admission to a public high school safely outside the borders of our German-Jewish ghetto.

Even in congenial New York, with its Jewish policemen and Jewish radio and Jewish signs in stores and Jewish stars in films, being Jewish was not an entirely painless condition. Though I aspired to melt in the American pot and routinely befriended non-Jewish classmates, white and black, I had only to cross Broadway to experience the inadequacy of my liberal ideology. Crossing Broadway meant facing danger, shaped by ethnic rage. Crossing Broadway was a journey to the other America, where truth and power were defined by tribal affiliation.

On our side there were Jewish bakeries and a kosher delicatessen, an all-night grocery and a seven-day drugstore, the immigrant jeweler and the umbrella store whose sale signs and window tags were often ordered from the Frankel Sign Co. Our ice-cream parlor offered booths and egg creams, but at much higher prices than those of the "candy" stores whose sodas were subsidized by a heavy traffic in cigarettes and newspapers—the *News* and the *Mirror,* the *Sun,* the *Journal-American,* the *World-Telegram,* *The New York Times,* the *Herald Tribune,* *PM,* *The Daily Worker,* *The Daily Forwarts,* *Die Freiheit,* *Die Staats-Zeitung,* and, most important to the refugees, the weekly *Aufbau,* which advertised for relatives around the world and conferred pride and distinction upon the scattered remnants of German Jewry.

Down the middle of Broadway ran islands of trees and grass, tended as only Park Avenue's are today, their shaded benches claimed by weary shoppers and by the elderly who preferred to avoid the hills leading to the Wall on Riverside Drive.

On the far side of Broadway, two taverns, a shellfish market, and a photo studio featuring freckled faces signaled an abrupt demographic shift. Although Jews and Puerto Ricans could be found among that side's customers, they were tourists in an alien land. The blocks running up toward Amsterdam Avenue belonged mainly to the Irish, the Pilgrims of Washington Heights. And their turf was fiercely guarded, or so it seemed, by belligerently Catholic adolescents. Stacks of books that I had borrowed from the public library used to gather dust for weeks under my bed, each overdue and accumulating fines of a penny a day, because I dreaded the trip to the library through Irish terrain. Once, maybe even twice, when postcards that I intercepted were demanding huge sums of Mom for "lost" volumes, I began lifting nickels and dimes from her pocketbook to purchase safety with larceny. With a dollar or so, I could pay the fines and also hire a mercenary to make the risky journey on my behalf. I'm sure Mom would have approved of my prudence, if not my theft, had I dared to confess.

The Irish kids called us Christ killers, and they carried ingenious weapons to avenge their Lord. Every Halloween they would invade our turf, swinging cotton stockings filled with pebbles and powdered chalk; each white or pink spot on our clothing signified a painful hit. When passage through their turf was unavoidable—to take the short path home from the Eighth Avenue subway line—I felt relieved if I absorbed just a few bare-knuckled blows. What really stung, for days, was a fist grasping the metal handle of an ash can, even if you ran fast and took the blow to the arm instead of the head. And then came zip guns: homemade wooden revolvers that fired metal bottle caps or sharp-edged bullets of linoleum with the force of a thick rubber band stretched along the top of the barrel. We captured a few fancy models and manufactured copies for ourselves, but the real risk of taking out someone's eye led us repeatedly into arms control negotiations, with occasional success.

An armistice with the Irish assured safe passage through their blocks just as I entered the seventh grade at Edward W. Stitt Junior High at the edge of the Negro neighborhood. But neither diplomacy nor authority could rescue me from a disastrous encounter with a knife-wielding gang of blacks near that school. In my very first days there, I became their daily prey.

A smug, smirking character had accosted me in a stairwell, asking to borrow a nickel and a fountain pen. When I obliged, he shoved me aside and ran off with the loot. Humiliated, I told Mom I had lost the pen and gratefully accepted money for another. But when a few days later the same bully took that one, too, I had to endure a stern lecture about carelessness. So I took to hiding the pen in my shoe, along with the money for milk. But when in my next stairwell confrontation even a search failed to yield money or pen, I was forced to surrender my leather gloves, gloves from Germany that had survived even the flood on the pier. Unwilling to face Mom with that news, I reported the theft to our teacher, who of course retrieved the gloves, reprimanded the culprit, and secured for "this here white-boy snitcher" a thorough after-school thrashing.

Two pummelings by a gang of toughs were all that I would endure. For three days, I pleaded stomach cramps, while Mom, fearing some grave malady in her normally eager student, took precious time from work to pursue the mystery. *This is not like you. You and I should have no secrets from one another. What's gone wrong? Is the work too hard? Can you see from the back of the room? Are the teachers no good?*

Tearful silence was all she got, even when she took to reciting the sum of her lost wages. I was not just afraid to return to school, I was ashamed of having mishandled the whole calamitous chain of events, of my cowardice and my racist nightmares. I had lied about losing the first two pens. I had tattled to the authorities, a treason in every culture. Worst of all, I was indiscriminately reading hostility into every black face loitering near school—I, who had so boldly proclaimed a brotherhood in scouting with Americans of every color; I, who had worshiped Joe Louis for decking Hitler's favorite, Max Schmeling; I, who had memorized Paul Robeson's rendering of "Ballad for Americans" ("In '76 the sky was red, thunder rumbling overhead . . .").

I understood that by benefiting from America's wealth and values, I had also inherited its debts and sins. But like most Jews, I expected exemption from the hostility that blacks felt toward whites; we shared so many vulnerabilities and dreams of justice. I never expected that Jews' devotion to civil and individual rights would one day collide with black demands for group reparations and that the alliance with blacks that we Jews coveted would eventually be bestowed on Muslims instead. Even as I preached equality, I experienced fear, a paradox that would last a lifetime.

Mom extracted the truth about the Stitt affair only after she conferred with my teacher and promised that I would not have to return there. The teacher said she was helpless to protect me outside of school. The principal said scornfully that instead of learning Hebrew after school I should have been learning how to defend myself. In desperation, Mom turned to Mrs. Ritter back at P.S. 169, who advised conspiring with friends to violate the law: give little Max a new address and register him up at Junior High 115. And that is what we did. Hiding our crime and real address from prying classmates was stressful, but not nearly so much as trudging alone for a mile in each direction in every kind of weather. I began to plot yet another escape.

I resolved that I would not attend George Washington High. It had an excellent reputation but was rooted in the neighborhood and required me to trudge to junior high for three full years. Instead, I bucked for the "rapid" class that would let me leave P.S. 115 after only three semesters if I qualified for one of New York's "special" public high schools. I was good at math, and so I shocked Mom one day by applying for the test to Brooklyn Tech.

You're going to be an engineer?

Yes, or an architect. Why not?

Don't be foolish. What do you know about being an architect?

I'll show you I can draw, and not only maps.

But it's more than an hour each way! You'll be exhausted, and for what? They don't teach mathematics at George Washington? If it's good enough there for Lenny and Herbie, why not for you?

Fate intervened yet again on a visit to Cousin Felix Pfeffer, our main sponsor for admission to America, the owner of a textile mill, apartment houses, and a spacious home in Flushing, Queens. Doris and Barbara, his daughters, traveled the length of the city to the High School of Music & Art to get what their mother considered "the finest education anywhere." When I showed interest, Mom did too, if only to finesse Brooklyn Tech. Music & Art was just two subway stops from ours, actually closer to the south than George Washington to the north.

But it's too late to learn the piano, Mom lamented. *You have to be a musician or an artist.*

I told you, I can draw.

With the encouragement of a flattered art teacher at 115, I drew feverishly to fill the required portfolio. For the mandatory portrait, I traced a *Life* magazine cover photo of Gen. Douglas MacArthur smoking his corncob, then copied my tracery freehand and destroyed the telltale carbons. For the requested landscape, I drew the long curve of the Wall counterpoised against the graceful span of the George Washington Bridge; I did it from memory, actually improving on the composition that a less embarrassed artist would have found outdoors. And for the still life, I scattered apples, pears, and pillows all over our apartment, wearing out my soap eraser and cursing the limited range of the colors in my box of Crayolas.

On the day of the live test, there was no time for such laborious creativity. It was my first visit to that lovely Castle on the Hill at 135th Street and Convent Avenue, past the Gothic towers of City College. Intimidating oil portraits and glorious tempera landscapes hung in the halls of M & A, and girls in long tweed skirts walked those halls swinging their cased clarinets or oboes, violins or violas, I didn't know the difference. Scariest of all were the giant easels and tall stools on which we were to sketch a live model in pencil in just thirty minutes and render a white plaster bust surrounded by colorful drapes, bowls, and fruits in pastel crayons in just one hour. Only years later, while helping to administer such a test, did I learn what simple aptitudes were wanted from us. The portrait of the student model did not have to capture her looks or even her shape with any accuracy; the trick was to demonstrate a sense of space by fully fitting the figure onto a paper that was larger by far than any I had ever worked on. And the still life was meant to test our innate sense of color, to see whether we had the discretion and the nerve to limit ourselves to a few purposeful hues.

With a few unconscious scribblings, I qualified for admission to this extraordinary institution, a luminous palace of culture conceived in the darkest days of the Depression and staffed, like so many of New York's public schools, by teachers who in fairer times would have pursued grander ambitions than the nurture of adolescent delusions. How deluded we were! I was going to be an artist, yes, selling paintings. Mom wondered politely whether I might not also think about drawing posters or designing magazine covers. Somebody or other in the next block was making a nice living decorating store windows. *Come, we'll take the bus downtown and I'll show you very artistic windows. In any case, you have time to decide. Keep an open mind. Other things will excite you.*

Words to live by. Barely three months later I was plotting a summer in North Carolina, in a place where I would be invited to sacrifice my career in art to the still higher calling of opera.

They'll pay me fifty dollars for eight weeks, Mom.

Where?

In a children's camp in North Carolina.

Where is that?

North Carolina, Mom. The Great Smoky Mountains. Cool and safe. The Pfeffer girls have been there. Herbie Tanzer is going too.

Carolina? That's near Florida, no? Can't you find something closer?

Mom knew better than to sail into the wind of my ambition. Better to put a gentle hand on the tiller.

Do you remember your first summer away from home? she asked. I was six and enrolled in a Jewish camp far, far away, on the Baltic, near Rostock. Mom recalled taking me to the train station in Leipzig to join a group of children I had never met. She told me not to worry if I felt a little homesick, that was only natural. At the barrier where passengers were divorced from visitors, she suppressed her tears, she remembered, and kissed me farewell. But her eyes flooded as she watched me trundle down the long platform.

I'll never forget it as long as I live, Mom said. *You never looked back!*

6 · ARTFUL DODGER

INEVER LOOKED BACK BECAUSE I NEVER DOUBTED THAT Mom would always be there, promising a better tomorrow on the worst of days and pretending that no pain or separation was ever permanent.

Her great equanimity made a blur even of the end of the war in Europe. The prospect of Pop's reappearance must have stirred both hope and anxiety in her heart, but I find no traces of them in the files of my mind. Perhaps the Nazis' final surrender was anticlimactic, long anticipated in the news. Perhaps it lies buried beneath two more vivid images. In one, I am leaping out of bed as a voice on the radio—a correspondent named Hicks, I could swear—shouts graphic descriptions of the armada spread before him in the English Channel clear across to the beaches of Normandy. Mom and I had sailed that channel four years earlier, past jackknifed vessels crippled by German mines and along the coastline that was now aflame with the promise of victory. In the other memory, I see myself irresistibly in the newsreel pictures of emaciated youths in striped uniforms, their hollow eyes staring through a fence into the lenses of their liberators. I am sure that I would be standing among them, not lying among the skeletons piled high in stinking trucks and ditches. But I also imagine myself guilty of having purchased survival with humiliating appeasements of Nazi guards and shameful betrayals of fellow inmates.

Everyone felt some kind of guilt. The world had to choose: ignorance or indifference? Many Germans probably had an easier choice than anyone; they made themselves ignorant of evils they were powerless to resist. On average, their conscience never reached indifference. Who knew what when? Most Germans obviously saw Jews disappearing from their midst. But did they talk about them being gassed? Did Californians talk about the disappearance of Japanese Americans? Did they inquire into their fate? Does persecution normally portend annihilation? Are we all complicit in the annihilation of America's Indians and the enslavement of blacks?

I embarrassed Mom in these debates, not because she disagreed with my speculations about the complexity of guilt but because so many of her friends considered my moral relativism to be a monstrous insult to the memory of our Six Million. American Jews who had never even met any Germans simply condemned them all. To confirm my Americanism, I genuinely tried indiscriminate hating, but it was not in my nature, which is to say it was not in Mom's nature. She believed that all people were created equally capable of good and evil and that God had randomly sprinkled virtue and sin among all His children. After experiencing the kindness of even a single German, she was true to her promise to the Berlin police commissioner. *If you get there, will you tell them we're not all bad?* Of Mom's many gifts to me, the most precious is this shield against blinding hatred.

Toward the end of the war, the guilt question also acquired a practical side. Henry Morgenthau, the secretary of the Treasury and most prominent Jew in President Roosevelt's circle—the only cabinet member who had fervently wanted to rescue more Jews from Europe—proposed that vanquished Germany be plowed under her own rubble, turned into an agrarian society, and forever denied the industrial capacity to wage another war. The government's much less admirable "realists," however, recalled how the subjugation of Germany after World War I had produced the conditions that brought Hitler to power. I sided passionately with these realists. I was sure that the United Nations would be as feeble a watchdog as the League of Nations had been against the military aggressions of Italy, Japan, and Germany. Democracy would take hold among our enemies only if planted in a bed of prosperity. Hungry people would sooner or later defy any legal system that denied them bread. And without legality there is only anarchy, never liberty.

My hope that America would end the war wisely relied heavily on Roosevelt. His death and not the Nazis' anticlimactic surrender made that spring memorable. It froze forever my generation's extravagant memory—and expectation—of the presidency. FDR's warm and confident presence left no doubt about the outcome. The war that so many millions fought became his victory. The prosperity that the war created became his recovery. Jews and Negroes were particularly enthralled by Roosevelt's ministry, not so much for what he did for them as for the enemies he made. He did little to save the Jews of Europe or to advance the rights of American blacks, but the people who hated Jews and Negroes also hated Roosevelt, Hitler above all. Roosevelt's serene and inspirational leadership haunted not just Harry Truman but all succeeding presidents. They were only as good as their imitations of him.

The moment of his death lingers in the romantic, right half of my memory; all of Music & Art was summoned to an assembly and heard the senior orchestra perform the mournful movement of Beethoven's Seventh. But the rest of that climactic year is a mere jumble of left-brain abbreviations: V-E Day; A-bombs; V-J Day; UN. For in my first summer of peace, I was separated from all prior experience, bridling horses, threshing rye, and pitching hay in the Great Smoky Mountains, far from home and Mom.

───────────

"Write often," Mom commanded as she studied my maps and read anxious accounts of the polio epidemics all around. So I sent her a stream of postcards, depicting Mount Pisgah from every side, the Cherokee Indian reservation we had visited and the dams of the Tennessee Valley Authority we had crossed. Amazing, I wrote: to build Fontana Dam, Roosevelt had to appease the locals by doubling the number of toilets and drinking fountains and separating them into "White" and "Colored" facilities. On federal property! Most of my cards, however, said only "Hi"—what else was there to say on every other day? Poor Mom imagined me lying paralyzed by polio in some hospital ward, incapable of writing more. The cards inspired what must have been her first phone call across the Mason-Dixon Line.

High Valley camp housed about a hundred youngsters and offered a unique mix of the customary sports—riding, swimming, singing, necking—and three hours of daily farm labor. The counselors were school-teachers and camp alumni, but a few local lads and Herbie Tanzer and I were recruited to add heft to the labor battalions, hauling in the hay, stacking the rye, grooming the horses, and canning the peaches and black-berries that the entire camp picked. The more exotic the chores and di-alects of our Anglo-Saxon farmhands, the more I cherished this journey through yet another America. But Herbie Tanzer preferred relaxation to labor and was soon sent packing. Also dismissed was the clumsy counselor to the Midgets, creating a vacancy that triggered my promotion from la-borer to boss of the six- to eight-year-olds' cabin. For telling bedtime sto-ries and responding to anxious parental inquiries, I earned a cornucopia of new privileges: all the Luckies I could smoke after lights out, all the coffee I could drink, and all the sexy gossip I could comprehend from the faculty lives of the counselors who were teachers in Tuscaloosa. I had stumbled into what became a four-year career as a High Valley counselor. I learned to double-clutch a truckload of kids down a steep mountain road; to promenade a lady to a fiddler's merry call; to forge a dozen postcards for moms whose kids would otherwise lose dessert; to spoon with pretty campers while dining with the management. And I met Sol.

Sol Cohen, a former concertmaster of the Hollywood Bowl Sym-phony, had retired to North Carolina to teach music and manage the camp's summer entertainment. Perpetually bent at the sacroiliac, he could nonetheless leap from the piano stool, pluck his violin for a few bars of Buttercup, then pound the keys again from a crouched position and, be-tween chords, bare-handedly conduct the *H.M.S. Pinafore* finale. Indefati-gable and infinitely tolerant of children of every age, Sol supplied candy *before* dinner, even lunch, and he let lazy campers hide in his cabin during work period—if, that is, they'd sit still for a symphony.

Once Sol heard me sing I became a four-year project. I drifted to his piano as I had drifted toward Kaffee kapellas in Germany, ever closer like a bee to nectar. Music aroused me, and it consoled me long before I was exposed to the bizarre syntax and vocabulary in which it is written. In suc-cessive years, Sol cast me as his lead in *Pinafore*, *The Mikado*, and *Naughty Marietta*. He showed me off at Methodist vespers in Waynesville and ran me through all the songs in his trunkload of sheet music, transposing them higher and higher until my voice cracked. He'd written about me to Julius, his brother, a voice teacher, who had asked that he test the purity of my A, and even B-flat. Finally Julius appeared, and the Cohen brothers swore that I could make it to the Metropolitan Opera. They arranged for lessons in New York with the personal coach of Jennie Tourel, the Met soprano, who evoked a steady high B once he had me breathing correctly, and he was sure I would eventually produce a reliable C. But now I would need piano lessons and theory lessons and Italian lessons, then French. Aghast at the price of such a commitment in time and money, and needing four tedious lessons to master the phrasing of just one page of an Italian air, I quit opera forever.

Mom, who'd been frightened by the whole enterprise, was equally alarmed by my ruthless abandonment of it. I may be another Richard Tucker, I told her. But if not, or if something goes wrong with my throat, I'll spend my life singing at weddings and bar mitzvahs.

Opera's loss was the art world's gain, for I now gave myself fully to Miss Ridgaway's arduous watercolor instruction. Prim, pince-nezed Helen Ridgaway was my homeroom teacher for the entire four years at Music & Art. And through her reserve, she let me discern a spinster's affection that I was eager to reward with achievement. She had us painting "warm" apples, then "cool" apples, "heavy" apples and "light" apples, "smooth" apples and "rough" apples. Was painting going to be as tedious as vocalizing? *You must sketch at least an hour a day*, Miss Ridgaway warned. *You have to learn to see, not just to look.*

Leah Rosen, in the second year, was even more demanding. An austere Greenwich Village sculptor who each day wore a different silver pendant of her own invention, she made us stand through her entire ninety-minute exercise in design. She said it was the only way to muster the energy needed to transform a flat sheet of paper into an imaginary, three-dimensional box—the object of almost all painting. For one whole month we worked with only large and small cutout squares, moving them around the imaginary box to create the illusion of depth between them. When we finally added color, Miss Rosen allowed only reds and greens, and the shapes of each color had to dance a pleasing, separate pattern as well as work harmoniously together. Little did we realize that we were retracing the intellectual journeys of the leading artists of the twentieth century—notably Braque and Picasso, Kandinsky and Mondrian, Moore and Davis—and applying a theory of relativity. As Miss Rosen pointed out, a green among greens appears to be a different color than the same green among reds. Just as Einstein taught us to see phenomena from different perspectives, Picasso taught us to depict a vase from different angles. What you perceived, they agreed, depended on where you sat, and multi-dimensional perceptions taken together produced an altogether new sight, and insight.

That did not wholly explain why the color of a thing should depend on the color of its surroundings. But then I remembered how in Carolina my normally accent-free English acquired a southern lilt and drawl. A greenhorn among rednecks was no longer quite so green.

The students at Music & Art were as remarkable as the teachers. They came disproportionately from Jewish homes that exposed youngsters to art or paid for music lessons and from black families that encouraged singing at church. Though we were tested only for artistic or musical aptitude, we turned out to be well above average intelligence, attracting and inspiring the best of the teachers that the Depression had trapped in the public school system. Our politics were bohemian, and mostly sung in ballads. We ranged from liberal to progressive, from grudging support of Harry Truman to enthusiasm for Henry Wallace.

In my main venture into elective politics, I was sacrificed on the altar of progressivism. Though a popular orator at school assemblies—*How dare they censor Schnitzler's "Golden Cockatoo"! Reinstate Mr. Manheim!*—I was soundly defeated by an electorate eager to be the first in New York to choose a black youth as president of an integrated student body. I taught myself affirmative reaction. My disappointment was further eased by the resuscitative skills of my campaign manager, Ronnie Myers—eventually New York Councilwoman Ronnie Eldridge. She anticipated a national trend by steering her defeated candidate into a profitable commercial career; she arranged to have me chosen president of the student co-op, which sold canvases and paints, bow waxes and oboe reeds, and paid our customers rebates at the end of the year.

We were a community beyond our own understanding. In our school society, talent trumped both rank and age. A fellow freshman, Si Heifetz, played first-row violin in the senior orchestra. Elliot Zuckerman's fluid cityscapes hung in the halls beside the oils of third-year veterans. Zohra Lampert and Julie Bovasso acted leading roles in every year's dramas. Art students built sets for operas and illustrated journals of poetry. Choirs from every grade performed solemn memorials at assemblies and led us all in the school song—by Brahms, of course. And what swing bands we fielded at after-school dances!

Just twenty-five blocks from home, two stops on the IRT, and a queasy walk up San Juan Hill, I had found a castle of joy. Self-esteem was acquired there not through one's own pretensions but from the talents of classmates and the worldly successes of graduates. Many years passed before I fully understood the extent of my own development in high school. I learned to recognize America as something more than a destination for explorers and refugees. In Mr. Graham's Socratic "civics" lectures, America became a grid of blackboard lines and boxes, illustrating a diffusion of power among competing institutions and peoples—power that he thought was properly mistrusted, checked, and balanced. Under Miss Lewin's gently mocking management of debates in the student government, America became a clash of ideas and personalities, a contest between what was right and who was charming. And in Mr. Gold's gritty discourse on the Constitution, America became the big bang of history, an explosion of ideals and interests in Philadelphia that produced an ever-expanding universe of rights and obligations, inspiring individuals, states, and finally whole nations to learn to surrender some sovereignty to a higher, federal authority and its promise of safety and prosperity.

Mr. Gold had us reenact the Constitutional Convention so that we could each discover in the characters we played the tugs of greed, ambition, and personality that shape all political ideals. We did not just read about compromise, we experienced it. I acted the part of Alexander Hamilton, an immigrant New Yorker of mixed or unknown parentage who had ingratiated himself with General Washington, peddling federalist visions and handsome profits to New York's merchant class—the Kissinger of his day. I learned to admire Hamilton's political wisdom as distinct from his personal ambitions, and discovered more credible portraits of him in Madison's convention journal than in the hostile histories produced by an academic claque of Jeffersonians.

My poorest subject was English, and my nemesis was Elsie Herrmann. Elsie Frieda Herrmann. Tall and angular, she was whispered to have yearned to dance ballet. Somehow she mutated into a teacher of English. She had crisp, clear speech and a bold, loud handwriting. Her *NO!* could forever banish a misspelling, and her *Well Done!* made a composition immortal. She seized my scruff in fifth term and never let go.

I had arrived in her class a liar and a cheat. Plodding through *Ivanhoe* and *Silas Marner* in the prior year had exhausted my tolerance for English fiction. To find a half-dozen puzzling words on every page had sapped my linguistic confidence. To look them up or lazily guess wrong about their meaning rendered the narratives incomprehensible. And to sit in fear of being called on in class turned the nightly torture into morning terror. To survive Miss Herrmann's daily quiz about the assigned pages of *A Tale of Two Cities*, I would prepare secret crib sheets about the characters and, for added security, position my chair for easy inspection of a classmate's test paper, offering to reciprocate the courtesy in Math or German.

Near the end of the semester came the fateful summons. Miss Herrmann extracted a confession that I was not doing the nightly reading and had fallen hopelessly behind in comprehending Dickens's great classic. On the strength of my passable compositions, I might still qualify for a grade of 80, she said, but that was an alarming prospect for a student whose other grades averaged 95 or more. She had a theory: only by learning to write might I still learn to read. And the place to concentrate on writing was her sixth-term journalism course, whose select students produced *Overtone*, the glossy school paper. To qualify me for admission, she would have to inflate my grade beyond my just deserts and, if she were wrong about my potential, I would come to the fateful Regents exam a year later with an even greater literary handicap. But since I wasn't reading well in any case, why not try it her way and come to Journalism?

Miss Herrmann's grade fraud proved to be an exciting investment. In another era, it would be called affirmative action. She habitually sent three or four of us in pursuit of the same news or interview and had our reports discussed by the entire class. Eventually, after considerable rewriting, one of these articles was published in the monthly paper and prominently signed by the winning author. Miss Herrmann left no doubt that journalism was a competitive sport ending in bylined gratification.

She also prescribed a nightly workout. Mine required analyzing the feature stories in her favorite paper, the *World-Telegram and Sun*, and a "Profile" or "Talk of the Town" vignette in *The New Yorker* to detect the writer's "angle"—meaning angle of vision, perspective, theme, or just plain gimmick. A topic is not an angle, she instructed; a subject is not an idea. You don't just write about an English teacher; you write about the success of an English teacher's pedagogy. Miss Herrmann's most exacting pedagogic device was to demand a cover sheet on all our writings, inscribed with the geometric symbol for angle, a drawn ∠, beneath which we had to proclaim our theme. Usually, she'd order it rewritten: "Needs a better ∠!" But if clearly promised and delivered—"The ∠: Visiting artists draw inspiration from the Fulton Fish Market at dawn"—an angle could evoke her exuberant response: "I'll take it, hook, line, and sinker!"

Reading for Miss Herrmann was suddenly fun and functional. *The New Yorker*'s hyperfactual reportage, allusive cartoons, and stinging ripostes to the errors in other publications gave us not just an enlarged vocabulary but an entirely new language of observation. We all wrote Ogden Nash verses and Philip Hamburger profiles. David Wise, our editor in chief, borrowed S. J. Perelman's pen to mock the school authorities, and my "Globalism" columns owed everything to E. B. White's "Talk of the Town" editorials. As defined by Miss Herrmann and performed by *The New Yorker*, journalism provided a congenial, comic stance even toward the most serious subjects.

I know precisely when it happened: when art yielded permanently to journalism. I stood struggling with an oil scene of tree trunks in Mr. Bloomstein's class while Elliot Zuckerman just poured his palette onto canvas at the next easel, brushing a vibrant cityscape in a single afternoon. I was constructing a painting with an architect's calculation; Elliot was creating a mood with an artist's vision. Ever aspiring to be the best, I fled. Off I ran to the *Overtone* office, to a medium that I felt I could command. And every afternoon thereafter, I would sneak through the forest of easels when Mr. Bloomstein wasn't looking to spend an hour dummying *Overtone* layouts, editing "Gallery Ganderings," gathering news for "Palette Patter" and "Intermission Chatter." It turned out, of course, that I was fleeing more than failure. I was trading the life of a performer for the life of an observer. I was abandoning involvement and choosing detachment and becoming a perpetual refugee.

At the end of sixth term, seven of us were promoted from reporter to editor and rewarded with another semester in Miss Herrmann's custody. With more pride than even I dared to show, she announced that I would be her editor in chief. Only I knew how much satisfaction she derived from her pedagogical gamble and how profound her influence had been on me. Propelled by her force and faith, I entered the privileged guild of ink-stained busybodies.

Journalism? Mom wondered. That didn't sound very portable, not readily usable in another country if it ever came to that. Better to have something in reserve, something you can do with your hands. *If you want to be in newspapers, why not first learn printing?*

7 · Sojourn in Siberia

WHILE MOM SAVED US BY CONFRONTING NAZIS, POP saved himself by eluding them. When Hitler and Stalin, by prearrangement, each seized half of Poland in September 1939, the danger to Pop in Kraków became palpable. Jews were disappearing in broad daylight, carted off by truck to dig trenches for German troops and graves for themselves. Pop's new "stateless" passport, which Mom had mailed through diplomatic channels, was destroyed when the Nazis burned down the Kraków post office. All that remained of his official persona was a worthless photostat of that already useless original.

In the registry of the Kraków Jewish Community, however, the Gestapo found a treasure chest of listings; a well-registered refugee like Pop was among the first to be hunted. With thousands of Jews and socialists—two species that Hitler always had trouble telling apart—Pop rode a train eastward and had himself smuggled into the Soviet zone and to Lwów, the capital of the Galicia region, where he was born thirty-seven years before. Seven years under the heel of the Nazis had been quite enough.

He did not know that night, of course, that he was destined to spend a symmetrical seven years under the heel of the Bolsheviks.

Lwów, a sleepy Slavic relic of Austria's Hapsburg house, was suddenly swollen with refugees and convulsed by the natives' scramble for security. Poles, Ukrainians, Belorussians, and Jews had to decide whether the new Soviet masters were friends or foes, whether they had been saved from Hitler or captured by Stalin. In Lwów's coffeehouses, patrons traded passports and identities and purchased favor from the Soviet *nachalniki*, who were free at last to indulge their bourgeois fantasies. When the Russians closed down private businesses as decadent relics of another era, many Poles tried to save their own possessions by turning in Jews as the preeminent "capitalists." The Soviets gratefully accepted their confiscatory assistance, but they were not primarily interested in planting Marxism or spreading revolution. They wanted half of Poland as a buffer to secure their hold on the Ukraine and the recently seized territories of Latvia, Estonia, and Lithuania in the north and Bessarabia in the south.

Pop found shelter with distant relatives, but when he learned of our passage to New York he tried urgently to get to Romania, the last open corridor out of Eastern Europe. With his tattered reproduction of a worthless passport and the precious promise of a visa to America, he reenacted Mom's desperate quest for an exit permit. A Yiddish-speaking Soviet official assured him it would soon be granted—kept assuring him right up to the moment of Pop's arrest. Though Pop's closest friend from Germany, Hermann Birnbach, ran a thriving business smuggling people from Lwów to Romania, he coldly ignored Pop's importunings. It is a fair gauge of that time that a friend who had never before envied Jakob Fränkel his family or financial success was now consumed with envy of his American visa.

One of the few legible entries in the photostat of Pop's stateless passport identified him as a *kupiec*—a merchant. And it was Kupiec Frenkel whom the NKVD, the Soviet secret police, arrested in March 1940 in what was proclaimed to be a campaign to spread the blessings of Soviet citizenship. Once again, Pop's offense was not personal. The citizenship drive was intended to make the Soviet annexation of Polish territory unalterable, which is precisely why tens of thousands resisted. When Nikita Khrushchev, then head of the Ukraine's Communist party, recalled touring the region in his memoir, he declared himself "shocked" at how many Jews stood on long lines, seeking to return to Nazi-held cities just to avoid the pressure to become Soviet citizens.

Those whose refusal could be attributed to "bourgeois hostility" were rounded up for trial as "class enemies" and marked for deportation to the east. Pop, being a merchant, was automatically found guilty. Having purged and murdered millions of their own people, the Soviets needed to replace the dead souls in their mines and forests, to revive the country's economy, and to prepare for its defense. As captured documents later revealed, the NKVD men had to fill monthly quotas of arrests just as Siberian milkmaids were given quotas to fill their pails. And the NKVD, ever faithful to bureaucratic imperatives, preferred hauling off "confessed" criminals. So they interrogated their prey until they broke their spirits, sparing only the bodies for the labor ahead.

Pop's deportation was a disguised blessing; it took him out of the eventual path of the German army. It was also more bearable than a German prisoner transport. The Russians taught their passengers how to drill a hole in the floorboards to form a toilet; how to heat water on the kerosene stove in the corner; how to flavor the daily pound of bread with two spoonfuls of sugar. When his train reached its destination, the 700 passengers were formed into work battalions and housed in a compound guarded from huge wooden watchtowers. They were somewhere in Gorki Region, 250 miles east of Moscow, appropriately enough near Dzerzhinsk, the city named for the first (and Polish) chief of the Soviet secret police. They were in a labor camp, which the Russians, like the Germans, called a *lager*.

Socialists, capitalists, communists, peasants, kulaks, criminals, Jews, Latvians, Estonians, Romanians, Ukrainians, Russians: workers of the world united, in two-story barracks from which they marched each dawn to the kitchen for bread, potatoes, and hot water, then for an hour to the forest to chop trees, trim branches, and load logs onto lumber rails until dark. As Comrade Stalin had written in the 1936 Soviet Constitution, he who does not work does not eat. By extension, whoever worked less, ate less. After just a few weeks, each morning found two or three of the prisoners collapsing by the side of the road. No one knew precisely how many died and how many were restored to a questionable existence. The healthy ones, their bellies swollen and their faces wizened, chopped on to earn their rations and, with whatever energy remained in the evening, rewound the rotted strips of leather that were the remnants of their shoes for the next day's march.

One day in late 1940, the day on which the Russian sun suddenly vanishes and winter descends unannounced to challenge the tolerance of an entire continent, Pop calculated that he had lost forty pounds and could last only two or three more months. Instead of waiting for that fateful day, he feigned exhaustion beside the forest trail, banking on that frail line of decency that distinguished Bolshevik cruelty from Nazi barbarity. The Russians did not burn their human refuse; frugally, where a body could still be salvaged, they nursed the wounds they had inflicted.

A horse-drawn wagon carried Pop to a hospital two hours away, a collection point for the reparable shells of prisoners from dozens of camps in the steppe. The hospital, too, was surrounded by watchtowers and overseen by NKVD guards, but its managers were prisoners under the direction of Boris Abramovich, an Odessa physician serving a twenty-year sentence for something or other. He imposed a ruthless cleanliness; everyone wore white tunics, and every patient, no matter how ill and no matter what the temperature outside, was dragged each day to the communal *banya* for a thorough scrubbing.

In a leap of ethnic faith, the instinct by which Yiddish-speaking Jews the world over exchanged extraordinary favor, Pop revealed his ruse to Boris Abramovich. And the doctor returned his trust by employing Yakov Isakovich Frenkel in a most delicate assignment: collecting the valuables that arriving prisoners kept hidden so that they could be sold to the NKVD for more generous rations for the entire hospital population. And instead of returning Pop to hard labor after six weeks, as required, the doctor arranged for his permanent employ at the hospital. He would be a sanitaire, or male nurse, for ten rubles a month—and a jewel procurer for nothing.

Pop remained a prisoner, of course, and in Russian eyes a Pole, even though he spoke only German and Yiddish. He learned in April 1941, a full year after his arrest, that he had finally been sentenced to a term of five years for the crime of "capitalism." He cried at the thought of incarceration until 1946, but Boris Abramovich, the twenty-year termer, roared with laughter. *The luckiest capitalist in Russia* is how he introduced Pop to new inmates.

Luckier still, for Pop as for the world, was Hitler's decision in June to invade the Soviet Union. On the petition of the Polish government in exile to a Soviet government that was now its ally, 150,000 surviving Poles in Russia were released from the labor camps. They were suddenly free to settle anywhere except in major cities, and with most Russian men off fighting the Germans, they had a wide choice of employment. With his privately distilled vodka, Boris Abramovich presided over a celebration of Yakov Isakovich's "freedom," offering a final toast with two bits of Russian wisdom: go East, young man, as far as possible from the advancing Nazis, and get to a farm, where no one ever starves.

Pop found a collective farm, the Sanitsinoye Kolkhoz, in Ishim, near

Sverdlovsk, as far east as one can go without leaving Europe. He was one of twenty strangers who arrived in time to help with the harvest, and the farmers took special care to convert this *kupiec* into a *kolkhoznik*, a collective farmer. Pop lived with a succession of peasants who generously shared their food, always gave him the bench-bed nearest the stove, and refused his frequent offers to pay with his wedding band, his only remaining treasure. In the fall, Pop was asked to let a young boy show him how to look after a dozen cows, how to lead them to pasture, sit or sleep under a tree till dusk, whistle for their return, and watch the cows march home again. That was to be his hibernal career had he shown the slightest competence. But at 10:00 P.M. on his first day, Pop was suddenly hauled before a village assembly and accused of stealing a cow. Had he sold it for profit? Did he trade it to another village? Could he retrieve it? The trial lasted until midnight, when the missing cow straggled home and Pop at once applied for safer work.

He was sent to a shoe factory in Ishim to hammer nails into soles on a primitive assembly line and to the city's warehouse to help carry bundles. As the doctor had warned, food in town was in short supply, and since he lacked connections to the black market, Pop went hungry and again landed in a hospital. Another spring gave him another new life, and now he found room and board with a Jewish woman who needed a man to do her chores. Her husband had been dragged off during the 1937 purges; she and her twelve-year-old son trafficked in ration coupons. With Pop's wedding ring, she acquired a week's supply of bread and enough money to bribe an official to send his telegram to America. But Pop lost this desirable connection in the spring of 1943, when he was wrongly charged with the young boy's routine thefts of bread.

Russia's war effort was approaching a climax, and the entire population was mobilized for a more efficient use of civilian labor. Duly registered, Pop was assigned to a brigade of thirty men to erect telegraph poles between Ishim and Tyumen, a Siberian city about 200 miles to the east. That winter, back in Ishim, he was given a sedentary post office job, which meant a chance to try to send mail to New York. After only a month, however, envious authorities had him fired as a "security risk." Twice in Ishim, Pop received mail from us, each letter containing a postal order for fifty dollars. But that bought only four pounds of meat on the black market. The paper itself, used to roll cigarettes and start fires, was more valuable than any denomination printed thereon. When he saw his first Sunday *New York Times*, Pop estimated that in wartime Siberia it would have fed him for a year.

Mobilization assignments took him back to the shoe factory, then to a meat-canning combine, and, in January 1944, to the Glavnofaneroprom in Tyumen, a veneer factory that made matches, finished furniture, and compressed wood for the airplane industry. Even in deepest Siberia, Pop could not escape the swirl of class and ethnic tensions that had landed him there. It was not good enough, the authorities insisted, that he swept the factory floor with zeal and hammered nails with care and observed all the rules of barracks life. What *kind* of Pole was he? Was he a reactionary supporter of the Polish exiles in London? Or a progressive follower of the Polish Communists harbored in Russia? Pop hadn't heard much about the brewing conflict over Poland's future, and he couldn't have cared less. But he understood his predicament and refused to choose. Loyalty to London risked a return to the lumber *lager;* joining up with the Communists required accepting a "temporary" Soviet citizenship. He said he wanted to end up in America, not Poland.

Why, Comrade Frenkel?

My wife and child are there.

We have plenty of women and fatherless children here—now. Ho, ho!

Indeed, a widow, her daughter, and her daughter's child were Pop's roommates in Tyumen. She considered him a lucky find because she had lost her husband in the purges and the daughter's husband was a soldier at the front. Once again Pop enjoyed the planks of honor beside the stove; he figured prominently in the woman's nightly thanksgiving prayer before her icon because he always brought waste wood from the factory to feed the fire. When possible, Pop also stole some protein-rich casein cheese extracts before they were dumped into vats to make plastics.

Normally, he ate at the factory's cafeteria, submitting to a complex rationing scheme that correlated slices of bread with hours of achievement, including bonuses for overtime and overfulfilled quotas. Fair-minded and good with numbers, Pop was eventually chosen to manage this system, and when 150 German prisoners of war were assigned to the factory, they were placed in his charge. Now Tovarich Frenkel was called Meister Fränkel, and he labored two shifts a day to instruct the prisoners and to guard the few hammers and screwdrivers that had been kept off the black market. He was not so successful at protecting the legs of chairs and tables awaiting assembly; Pop himself took home a few legs each week for firewood until a Moscow inspector placed the whole factory on probation for mishandling state property.

Everyone stole. Legs, hammers, paper bags, bread. Pop and his German charges once worked around the clock for a week to complete a veneered buffet for the Sverdlovsk regional party chief, yet soon thereafter

Pop spotted the buffet in the home of the foreman. For the promise of a few sticks of wood, the armed guards at the factory gate would let anything pass. When Germany surrendered, Russia stole what she could outside her borders, even whole factories, in compensation for her losses. Pop's German charges were kept prisoner five years after the war, even longer if they knew anything about rocketry.

Among the things Stalin stole after the war was the slice of Poland he had tried to take in 1939. Poland was re-created and moved westward, compensated for the lost eastern land with a slice of Germany duly cleansed of Germans. But even this Poland was not entrusted to patriotic Poles; Stalin sent Russified Poles to Warsaw with the Red Army, and, within a year, these Communists seized control of the country from the democrats who had spent the war in London. Since Stalin thought Roosevelt and Churchill had ceded him control of Poland at the Yalta Conference in early 1945, he kept his promise to release all the Poles who survived his labor camps. Pop and all the rest were gathered up in the spring of 1946 for the train trip "home."

It was a chaotic journey. The train would stop for hours, or days, at sidings or in small towns, and its passengers would rush off to scavenge for food or drink. Some were lost along the way. Pop jumped off the train in Moscow and raced to the American embassy, where he had his first taste ever of governmental warmth. As the spouse of an American citizen, he was advised to race right back to the railroad station, that a train in the hand was better than a Soviet exit permit in the bush. Luckily the train was still waiting in Moscow and his visa to America was waiting in Warsaw. He needed a few more months to get himself to Sweden and to bribe his way to the head of the line of passengers awaiting a berth to New York. Pop arrived in America on Columbus Day 1946. To everyone's surprise, he had only warm words for Stalin and all Russia. After all, he insisted, they had saved his life.

8 · HOME AND HARLEM

AT THE PIER, PEOPLE KEPT SHOVING AND STRAINING TO see over our heads, and the tactics of self-defense became a distraction from my anxiety. I thrust out a hip and an elbow to hold one woman at bay when I could have easily granted her another foot of space. It was hardly the spirit in which to begin Pop's education in democracy.

Mom and I came alone. A forty-two-year-old woman on the arm of her sixteen-year-old son, she was proud and beautiful, no matter how weary. But I, with only a nine-year-old's memory of the father I had come to greet, was a frightened child. So pride and fear had it out as we watched the husky, surprisingly gray figure scamper along the wide, endless pier toward our barrier. His legs churned with such small, quick steps it seemed as if his suitcases were a team of horses drawing him on. His eyes, pumping tears onto a beaming face, wandered without much purpose, as if to feign a lack of interest in the melodrama of which we were all a little ashamed—until those eyes found us in the crowd. Then he lunged forward and wept.

Mom wanted this to be the end of adventure, the end of barriers and boundaries, new languages, homes, and jobs. She had raised a son and reunited a family and conquered a country and outlived Hitler and outfoxed Stalin, and when she thought about things that way, which was not often, it all seemed perfectly logical and inevitable, not remarkable, but tiring. She always weighed her *tsouris*, her troubles, on a universal scale and had long since decided that ours belonged on the fortunate side. That meant she could pity as well as despise her tormentors. Germans in her mind were not only the sadists who had butchered her mother and uncles and cousins but also the frightened customers who had risked entering our store in Weissenfels by the back door. They were the border guards conspiring to help her save shirts and sweaters from forfeit to Polish customs and bemused Gestapo chieftains feeling like Christians as they let a Jewish mother and child escape their persecution. The Russians, in her imagination, were miserable peasants, unskilled in barbarity but also untutored in civility, robbing people of husbands in the prime of life with little awareness of their sin. If the Germans were to blame for Hitler, she would ask, weren't the Russian people to blame for Stalin?

Americans were still foreigners to Mom. She spoke of them appreciatively but objectively, in the third person. They had given her citizenship and a passport, bountiful status and free range, the kind of support she had from her mother and had given her child. And Americans had saved her child not only from physical harm but also from statelessness, which counted for almost as much. It was from her son that Mom learned most about Americans, but she had her own firm convictions about them. Although they pushed you horribly in the subway, cheated you at the butcher's, and let their children behave like wild Indians, and although they were innocent of most of the pain in the world, Americans produced diverting movies and handy kitchen gadgets, gave work to anyone unafraid of exertion, let a Jew be a Jew, and felt an obligation to help a woman to reunite with her husband. All that Americans demanded in return was that you not look too poor or wretched, that you not play the beggar or refugee or otherwise remind them of their debt to the world and the war that had enriched them. This nation of businessmen had no stomach for philosophical accounts. When she had gone to Washington to arrange for Pop's immigration papers, the commissioners were solemnly solicitous and most impressed by the medal the DAR had pinned on her son in elementary school. They never bothered with the customary questions about how Pop would avoid becoming a public charge. They heard her story and looked her over and felt good for not asking. People who make them feel proud to be Americans are the people Americans like the best, and they liked Mom a lot.

Neither to me nor to anyone else did Mom ever comment or even hint about how it felt to go to bed alone for seven years, to sew linings into other women's fur coats, or to leave her only child to find his own amusements in the streets each afternoon. She chased away every envy. She felt proud that she had learned to work with her hands so late in life, even if it permanently stained them Persian lamb black. All people should know how to do something with their hands, she decided. If you want to write for newspapers, you ought to know how to operate and oil the Linotype machines. Just look at Dr. Weiss washing dishes in the Catskills and Cantor Rauh raising chickens in New Jersey and the novelist Willie Katz canning meatballs in Brooklyn. Illness was the only insurmountable calamity. Success was a trap, especially if encountered too soon in life. Dreams are best fulfilled slowly; people need something to look forward to. Money is best if gradually acquired; too much money burns holes in your pockets and warps your judgment. Fighting never solves anything.

There was a bond between us that we feared Pop would resent. Deep down, I felt not so much deprived by Pop's long absence as empowered by it. I had enjoyed the undivided love of a wise and resourceful woman but also limitless freedom to chart my own path into American culture. How would Pop fit into this arrangement and avoid being an alien in his own home? Mom and I drew up a last secret protocol: there would be no secrets from Pop, no hesitation in proclaiming him sovereign over our family, and no ganging up against him, even if he proclaimed black to be white or white to be black. And then we went to the pier.

Democracy, I insisted, *means free choice by the people. There are no free elections in Russia, just as there were no free elections in Germany, so the Communists are as bad as the Nazis.*

No, not as bad, Pop replied, quietly but vigorously. *They didn't kill the Jews in Russia. They are anti-Semites, but they didn't kill Jews for being Jews.*

Why must everything always be judged in terms of Jews?

Ha. Because we are Jews!

But Jewish is only a religion, like Catholic or Protestant. I'm an American, and you are going to be an American.

You are an American. I am not.

Everyone can be an American here. Naturalized citizens have almost the same rights as native-born citizens, and the same protections in court. I can't be president, but I can be elected to the Senate. That's democracy! Either people are free or they are not free. You don't have to be so eternally grateful to the Russians that you don't say a bad word about them.

Russians are kind and generous. They gave me the place of honor wherever I went, always near the stove. They love their country. They are religious. They suffer in silence. They endure. Hitler could not have been defeated without them. I would have been killed without them.

But they almost killed you!

Not me because I'm me, just a lot of people, to survive.

And that makes them different? That makes a Soviet lager *better than a Nazi* lager? *If you kill people you kill people! We have laws here and courts to enforce them that protect people's rights. Have you ever heard of habeas corpus? Over there, all that matters is what one man says.*

It's not that simple.

I can't talk to you! I screamed. *What's white you call black and what's black you call white. This is a free country and Russia is not a free country and Germany was not a free country.*

Someday you will learn the difference.

I'm not a child anymore.

No, but you don't understand everything, yet.

I certainly understand the difference between a free country and a dictatorship.

Maybe.

Not maybe! Yes! You come over here and don't know anything about this country, have never seen an election here, have never seen people argue on street corners and say whatever they like about the government, and you sit there like a know-it-all defending those Russian murderers!

I am not defending them. Seventy-five percent of the people would agree with me.

Ninety percent would call you a fool.

Enough! Mom said. *Enough!*

We always fought about politics, but of course we were really fighting each other. Cruelly, I would emphasize that I felt a higher loyalty to America than to Pop. He would insist that he had a wisdom greater than any found in my textbooks. Within a year, we'd prove that the issues we debated were actually irrelevant to our contest. That's when Pop started to denounce Stalin as a maniac while I conceded that Harry Truman was not always right, that in persecuting the Hollywood writers America was behaving like Russia. Pop would counter that a society had to protect itself and that I was underestimating the Communist menace.

As the spouse of a citizen, Pop became a citizen in just two years. Now

I could tell him how to vote and he would reject my counsel even though he followed it once inside the booth. We recognized each other in each other, proving that we were father and son and learning to love each other as we were.

———

As for the meaning of America, Pop didn't need my lectures. He announced his plans the morning after he arrived. Mother had worked long enough, he said, and would quit sewing at the end of the year. If she wanted to help out for a few weeks at the height of each fur season, he would not object. But he alone would now provide for the family. He would look for work that very day.

Don't be silly, Mom replied. *Relax and rest. Learn English and think carefully about what you could do. Don't work for someone else. We're not going to starve, and another year or two of sewing won't kill me.*

Was she insane? Pop yelled. *Another year or two? Who ever heard of anything like that? Nine out of ten people would agree that she was talking nonsense. It only proved that she was overworked.* She had better quit at once. Was he a cripple or something? Other men had learned to support their families in America. He was, thank God, healthy and didn't need to rest. *Und mein Eng-lish ist good!*

Yes, his English was good, Mom consoled. *Only please stop shouting.*

No one is shouting, Pop shouted. *But this has to be settled, right now.*

Very well, anything he wanted she would accept. *But please: find a business you know something about.*

Now, that is reasonable, Pop concluded.

Within a month of his arrival in late 1946, Pop owned a business and his Germanic English acquired a southern accent. Through an ad in *Aufbau* and with the savings Mom had added to their smuggled nest egg, Pop purchased a business that bore a striking resemblance to the one he and his father had created in Weissenfels twenty years earlier. It was a peddler's route through Harlem—bearing dresses and underwear and stockings to working-class homes and extending them credit to be collected at the rate of a dollar or two a week. But the enterprise had been depleted. Pop acquired about a hundred delinquent accounts, a half-dozen battered suitcases, an assortment of housecoats, aprons, towels, and other goods that had failed to sell, and a 1936 Chevrolet, which functioned tolerably on level ground. Pop did not know how to drive, of course, so he also acquired a chauffeur, another refugee, who lacked the talent to steal away good customers once Pop decided which they were.

Over my objections, the old nightgowns and socks and brassieres were stored in floor-to-ceiling metal shelving in my room. Each morning, long before I rose for school, Pop played solitaire with his account cards on the kitchen table, mapping a promising route for the day. Everyone asked why he wasn't afraid to carry money so conspicuously around Harlem.

What is there to be afraid of? he wanted to know.

Well, the questioner was not prejudiced, but you know, Harlem is a dangerous place.

Not to Pop, who was still color-blind. He did not feel the nauseous fear that gripped his democratic son whenever I was recruited to help collect on a few accounts. All that Pop knew about Negroes was that they were dark-skinned working people, just as loyal as his best customers in Germany, he'd insist. They offered him cool drinks on hot days, shared family confidences, and pointed him toward new customers. So before the women of Harlem went to work in the morning and long after they came home in the evening, Pop would chug through the littered streets in his chauffeur-driven Chevy—dubbed Heinrich—dispensing lollipops and balloons to the crowds of kids who celebrated his arrival. Now forty-five years old, he charged up and down six-story walk-ups with his heavy suitcases. He collected debts—or tales of woe about lost jobs and missing husbands. If there was an extra dollar left in the cookie jar next week, Ol' Mistah Franklin would be sure to get it. And if the purchase of a black lace negligee was to be consummated, Ol' Mistah Jacob had to keep it secret! The lazy deadbeats were weeded from Pop's roster, and the hardworking, honest folks were given smartly printed account books: JACOB FRANKEL, SUITS, DRESSES, SUNDRIES. Even those already in hock for a secondhand Cadillac and TV set were encouraged to buy just a little something they hadn't planned on if they could afford to pay a dollar each week—and to recommend some cousins or daughters if they couldn't. Within just six months, the route supported both Pop and the chauffeur, and within a year Pop had learned to drive himself.

Years later, after he had collapsed from exhaustion, the customers he had shrewdly chosen went right on paying their debts to his wife and son and sending their good wishes with floral greeting cards. And years later, after Pop had been beaten up and robbed on a dimly lit stair and, as in Germany, had moved his whole operation into a small store on Amsterdam Avenue, the same customers still came, by bus if necessary, to pay off their accounts and to incur new debts. He ran the store until the mid-1960s, surviving a labor union's extortion racket and two holdups—by "out-of-the-neighborhood" hoods, he always emphasized. A blow to the head in yet another robbery finally finished the store, but to Pop's amazement the mail continued to bring in dollar bills to pay down 80 percent of the outstanding debt. Pop retired with profound respect for his customers, the people who restored his authority as a provider, husband, and father and left him with a satisfying sense of opportunity in America.

SKEPTIC

1948–1955

"All the News That's Fit to Print"

The New York Times.

LATE CITY EDITION

TRUMAN ASKS $17 BILLION TO RESTORE EUROPE; MARSHALL SAYS PEACE MUST AWAIT RECOVERY; CONGRESS VOTES STOP-GAP AID, LATER ADJOURNS

Meyers, Lamarre Indicted; General Is Cited on 6 Counts

$540,000,000 IS SET

SECRETARY IS BLUNT

PRESIDENT IS GRAVE

Final Grant Is Far Under Administration Wish —China Is Included

Pact on Germany Linked to Struggle With East on European Aid Plan

SHARP ROW IN SENATE

FREEDOM HELD BASIC

Bridges Opposes Plants for Soviet—Pacts Are Cited by Vandenberg

He Resists Reparations on Thesis 'We Put In, Russians Take Out'

SPECULATION BILL SIGNED BY TRUMAN

FIELDING REPORTS RELIEF CASE DROP

Program High on Agenda For Session Opening Jan. 6

PRIVATE FUND FLOW TO EUROPE DESIRED

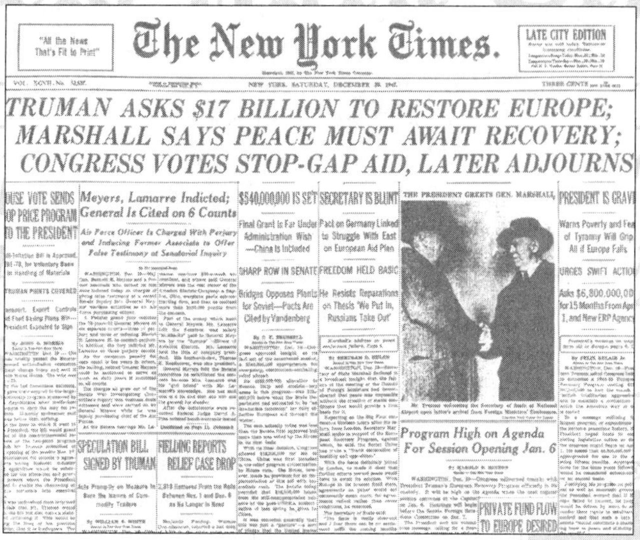

9 · Global Village

ARE YOU A PACIFIST?
No.
An anarchist?
No.
A fascist?
No.
A communist?
No.
Would you take up arms to defend your country?
Yes.
Have you ever been convicted of a crime?
No.
What is the Bill of Rights?
The first ten amendments to the Constitution.
What is the First Amendment about?
Freedom of speech, freedom of the press, freedom of worship.
Congratulations. You have fulfilled all the requirements for naturalization as a citizen of the United States of America. In

testimony whereof the seal of the Court is hereunto affixed this 1st day of March in the year of our Lord nineteen hundred and 48, and of our Independence the one hundred and 72nd. Please recite after me:

I pledge allegiance . . . *but could a native be a fascist?* . . . to the Flag . . . *or a communist?* . . . of the United States of America . . . *if I became a pacifist tomorrow* . . . and to the Republic for which it stands . . . *would I have sworn falsely today?* . . . one Nation . . . *and be deported?* . . . indivisible . . . *but I think I would fight for America* . . . with liberty . . . *so I didn't lie* . . . and justice . . . *I would even kill* . . . for all.

Please safeguard this certificate; it may not be copied or reproduced in any manner.

———

Luckily, the judge never asked whether I was a federalist. Having finished high school in January, I took that oath while waiting to enter college in the fall and in the interim pursued an incendiary—some would have said subversive—career. I celebrated my admission to citizenship with fellow mimeographers and envelope stuffers in the basement of an East Side town house from which we distributed the propaganda and solicitations of the United World Federalists. We were agitating through chapters in every state for a World Government, to save humanity from atomic war. Just as the American colonies found safety and prosperity by uniting in a more perfect federal union, we thought the nations of the world had to federate to finally put an end to international anarchy. I spent my days insisting that the "United Nations" were not at all united because each nation retained the sovereign right to make war on every other. And I spent my evenings down in Greenwich Village with K, of the membership division upstairs, helping her shop for straw-hat ribbons, Chianti, and Dylan Thomas poetry and suffering her news of an encounter with a most eligible scholar of science who perfectly complemented her flair for literature and drama. K, which is how she signed her name, was a blithe spirit of twenty-three who had selected the worldly innocent in the basement, barely eighteen, for a crash course in Village values and female friendship.

Unlike K, I was never a guest at the Village gatherings at which Fifth Avenue matrons and Bedford Street artists debated Adler's expositions of Freudian doctrine. Loitering in a crowd of sidewalk chatterers on Grove Street was the closest I came to the important art and brilliant verse that I enviously imagined them to be toasting and producing on every Village street. Bars and coffeehouses that came alive after midnight were reason enough for me to envision myself a future Village resident, harvesting unwrapped Italian loaves from an Albanian baker, unpackaged French cheeses from a Greek grocer, and unground Colombian beans from, of all things, a Chinese chandler. Decades later, these pungent products would have spread to every suburban mall, but in the white-bread America of 1948, they made a walk down Christopher Street feel like a stroll on the Left Bank, conjuring dreams of uninhibited maidens dispensing wit and whimsy in candlelit garrets. I was sure that I would occupy such a garret one day, furnished in primary colors against stark white walls hung with huge cubist canvases. The Village was Music & Art, plus sex, a beckoning Mecca. Forever my fantasy.

It was in the basement of an elegant Upper East Side brownstone that we labored by day for a world federation to govern the village that the world had become. Heeding Mom's injunctions about manual labor, I had gone so far as to teach myself touch typing. So when the United World Federalists advertised for an Addressograph operator, I presented myself, accurately, as a skilled member of the faith and, falsely, as needing a few years' income before entering college. The machinery in question, which I had never seen, stamped addresses onto metal plates, which in turn printed envelopes or labels for our propaganda and solicitations. We possessed not only the addresses of thousands of dues-paying members but also drawerfuls of plates bearing the names of legislators and congressmen, mayors and governors, and, most preciously, celebrities and philanthropists. I color-coded these steely files and made myself indispensable to the powers upstairs, where memberships were processed and where strategies were devised under the direction of our rangy leader, Cord Meyer, Jr., who, I can only assume, was not then what he was later revealed to have become, the spymaster of the Central Intelligence Agency.

Most of America, however, was already obsessed with treason that winter, and we were all required to choose sides between God-fearing Americanism and godless communism. Our vulnerability to Soviet bombs and espionage, the putsch that brought Communists to power in Czechoslovakia, and the advance of Communist guerrillas in China seemed a reprise of the fascist conquests of Germany, Italy, and Japan in the 1930s. The Red tide stranded the remaining romantic American Marxists in the camp of the enemy. A more moderate leftish "progressivism" was offered by FDR's jilted vice president, Henry Wallace, and it attracted the guitar-strumming boys and tweed-skirted girls of my high school crowd. But I smelled Stalinists in the Wallace camp and soon recoiled to the safer ranks of Truman Democrats. Sadly, Truman betrayed my ideal of America when he felt compelled to compete with Republican Red hunting and extracted "loyalty" oaths from all federal servants—as if spies would shrink from taking oaths. He also ordered his attorney general to publish a list of political, professional, social, and cultural organizations whose alleged sympathy for communism or fascism made all their members suspect and unfit for positions of trust, like teaching children or acting in soap operas. Not to be so easily outdone, the Republicans countered with congressional inquisitions into "un-American" activities, crediting the testimony of former Communists who now gained fame and fortune by confessing that they had trafficked in American secrets and Soviet lies. It was from those apostates that the country was asked to learn loyalty.

One of the evangelical turncoats was Whittaker Chambers, an editor at *Time* magazine, who persuaded a media-wise, Red-baiting young congressman, Richard Nixon, that one of his sources for diplomatic secrets had been Alger Hiss, a former high official of the State Department and scion of the liberal East Coast establishment. For me and virtually every other political citizen, choosing between Chambers and Hiss became an urgent and revealing decision, a truly defining moment.

I studied the case but disdained them both. Hiss looked into his accuser's mouth to discern the ill-formed dentures that he had once known in a man named George Crosley, but he denied the treasonous relationship that Chambers described. Hiss persisted with his denials even after Chambers produced a microfilmed sampler of stolen State Department documents from their hiding place inside a pumpkin on his Maryland farm. The Pumpkin Papers led to Hiss's indictment for perjury in 1948 and two sensational trials in Foley Square, which I followed assiduously and attended occasionally. Four of the first trial's jurors and all the people I most admired—liberals, artists, and intellectuals—let Lloyd Paul Stryker, the Clarence Darrow of his day, persuade them that there had been an FBI frame-up of Hiss to discredit the Democrats. Yet while I despised the smug certitudes of Chambers, I concluded from the evidence that Hiss had indeed lied. And I took my lonely stand as further proof of my suitability for the practice of disinterested journalism. Most people to my left and right seemed to regard political opinion as a fashion, worn as a badge of social or economic class. It was difficult to hold my ground against a majority of friends and colleagues, but journalism offered protection, a place to stand legitimately, even proudly, apart from the crowd.

———

I was drawn to other unfashionable conclusions. Under the influence of E. B. White's brilliant editorials in *The New Yorker* ("when a man hangs from a tree it doesn't spell justice unless he helped write the law that hanged him"), I favored hanging the top Nazis without trial, without the pretense that they violated a nonexistent law. And applying Augie Gold's instruction in the coup by which our Founding Fathers produced a federal constitution, I predicted the inability of the United Nations to keep the peace. Even while swearing allegiance to my wonderful America, I blamed nationalism for the century's two World Wars and for the barbarism of both Hitler and Stalin, and I had come to this East Side brownstone to help create a higher authority than the nation-state.

The most popular book on our basement shelves, a one-dollar reprint of Emery Reves's *The Anatomy of Peace*, defined our cause with propositions that still seem irrefutable. Wars, he wrote, have never been deterred for long by treaty, weaponry, or common sense. They ceased to occur among families, tribes, villages, cities, provinces, and states only as each warring unit gave up the "sovereign right" to injure another and created a canopy of law, a higher form of government. Federalism was as American as apple pie, a more powerful invention even than the assembly line. That is why our other best-seller was Carl Van Doren's history of the making and ratifying of the American Constitution, which he titled *The Great Rehearsal*—for world government. Van Doren encouraged us to believe that the nation-states of our century were repeating the error of the first American government, that the League of [Sovereign] Nations after World War I and yet again the United [Sovereign] Nations after World War II were as feeble as the Articles of Confederation that failed to unite the American colonies. Without a higher authority, Reves wrote, all great powers must behave like gangsters and all small nations like prostitutes.

Thus equipped in six months with a political philosophy, instilled with bohemian appetites, and thoroughly practiced in touch typing, I quit my job with the Federalists and went off to college.

10 · LEARNING MEANING

I THINK I KNEW THAT CARL VAN DOREN, THE WORLD FED-
eralist among historians, had a brother, a poet named Mark,
who taught at Columbia University. And I knew that Columbia
passed out awards each year to competing high school newspapers. But otherwise, I knew Columbia only as the fourth station down from home on the Broadway subway. I'd never heard
of Joseph Wood Krutch, Lionel Trilling, Jacques Barzun, Irwin
Edman, Dumas Malone, David Truman, Moses Hadas, Charles
Frankel, C. Wright Mills, and all the other celebrated scholars
who became my mentors when oh so ignorantly I decided to
enroll in Columbia College and chanced upon what was probably the country's finest undergraduate curriculum. Like General of the Army Dwight D. Eisenhower, who arrived at the
same time to be the university's president, I picked Columbia
for essentially unworthy reasons. And like Ike, I exploited the
place shamelessly.

Bright New York youngsters from poor families were supposed to go to CCNY, the City College of New York, which

Jews called "our Harvard," and with reason. City College fielded a gifted faculty and offered a first-class education at taxpayer expense. It opened access to the finest graduate schools—more so than other colleges when you consider that Ivy League bastions still used informal quotas to hold down their number of New York Jews. But CCNY served only city kids, and the still striving refugee inside me mistook that for provincialism. I yearned to cross yet another frontier and invested extraordinary energy in the journey. Unlike CCNY, the private colleges demanded that I take the College Board entrance exam, an alarming prospect.

My desultory reading habits were finally taking their toll: I could not recognize half the words on the sample vocabulary test the College Board sent me. I could not begin to match word pairings like "hammer:nail" with "despot:peon." Self-help manuals, like *Thirty Days to a More Powerful Vocabulary*, did not relieve the crisis. And the College Board boasted that cramming was useless; it was testing a "lifetime of learning."

My vocabulary may have been shallow, but my skepticism ran deep. I resolved to cram and somehow prove them wrong. I discovered that the library at Columbia's Teachers College housed a file of all College Board exams ever devised. In just half a dozen visits, I copied out every unfamiliar word and word pairing, filling two shoe boxes with index cards that bore the strange words on one side, their definitions on the other. For months, I traveled everywhere with some of those cards until I had memorized, although in no true sense acquired, this new vocabulary. When I came upon the boxes a decade later, I was startled to find how many of those once intimidating words appeared routinely in *The New York Times*, and in my own writings. But at the time, the cards were cork to a drowning swimmer. When I finally took the board test, I recognized three fourths of the words, enough to qualify for all three of the private colleges to which I had applied.

At the top of the list was the University of Chicago, whose curriculum struck me as suitably bohemian and whose campus was attractively far from home. Chicago taught the Great Books without even requiring that you attend class. It was led by Robert M. Hutchins, the university's president before he was thirty, who banished football and not only favored world government but composed and published its constitution. Then, too, Chicago would let me hover near Sandy, a high school flame who had incomprehensibly committed herself to a rival suitor. Mom's prayers against Chicago were answered only when it denied me financial aid. I would have to stay inside the borders of New York after all and take advantage of the state's scholarship, worth a significant $350 a year. That was almost enough to cover tuition at NYU and more than half the cost of Columbia.

Pop argued fervently for Columbia. It was famous even in Europe, he insisted, so its degree would always be worth more. His endorsement would have surely soured me on Columbia if I hadn't heard the siren songs of David Wise, my predecessor as editor of *Overtone* at Music & Art. Dave had followed his father to Columbia and told rhapsodic tales about writing for *The Columbia Daily Spectator*—the *Monday-to-Friday Spectator!* As a daily, he emphasized, *Spec* was hungry for new recruits; NYU and City offered only weeklies, he scoffed. Besides, at Columbia you met "downtown journalists" who came to cover campus events and to teach at the Graduate School of Journalism. Dave had already sold two features to International News Service!

That's how I chose Columbia; I followed the ink. I reported for duty at the *Spectator* a full week before the start of classes, an order of priority that remained immutable for four fateful years.

In just one week, Columbia bleached out all my frustrated ambitions for elective office. Though shy, chubby, and unimposing, I'd been emboldened by Mom's faith to believe that I could be a popular as well as articulate leader. But the absurdity of it dawned at the first meeting of the freshman class, when we were invited to nominate ourselves for the posts of class president and secretary-treasurer. The winners would cast votes on the Student Board, arrange assorted "smokers" with professors and dances with Barnard girls, and, of course, get a leg up on admission to good medical and law schools. A dozen classmates ran eagerly toward the stage, and I, too, felt the undertow of high school campaigns yanking at me. In an epiphanous moment, still vivid a half century later, I stopped in midmotion for a rush of calculation: stick with journalism and you'll be writing about these clowns; give up frivolous self-promotion and deal instead with "real" issues. With a memorable thud, I sat back down, never to feel the candidate urge again.

My immersion in campus journalism seemed to have the university's highest sanction. In Ike's first speech to our class, he promised a new gym and a better football field and stressed the importance of "nonacademic" pursuits. "The day that goes by that you don't have fun, that you don't enjoy life," Eisenhower said, with a syntax prophetic of his political career, "is to my mind not only unnecessary but un-Christian." Indeed, we non-Christians were drawn in great numbers to the fourth floor of John Jay Hall and the adjacent offices of the *Spectator,* the chess club, the debate team, the *Review,* the *Jester,* and the Varsity Players. Religious or not, we devoutly believed in extracurricular fun and turned those rooms into bustling fraternity houses, and more: a place where individual growth also produced communal value.

Sniffing out the trustees' secret plot to raise tuition and spreading the news turned out to be more gratifying even than deciphering a Shakespeare sonnet. Embarrassing the dean about the girls-in-the-room rule—*Could the order to keep doors open by at least "the thickness of a book" be satisfied with a slim volume of poetry?*—was far more amusing than defining the comic nature of Don Quixote. I could not resist the lures of journalism: the license to pry into all corners of campus life, the chance to champion remedies for discovered wrongs, the easy access to persons of every rank, and the reliable armor to shield an otherwise debilitating shyness.

Columbia, with a wisdom since abandoned, did not then require undergraduates to "major" in any one subject, so we prejournalism dilettantes majored aggressively in *Spec.* We hung around its shabby offices, eager to take any reporting assignment or to run photographs to the engravers, to dummy page layouts or to change typewriter ribbons. Although I slept at home and was due in my first freshman class at 8:00 A.M., I cheerfully volunteered for frequent duty at Cocce Press down in Greenwich Village, where we cobbled stories into their pages until dawn, then hastily skimmed a Saint Augustine essay on the subway ride home. I soon suspected that I lacked the necessary devotion for a career in scholarship.

Even so, the seductions of Columbia's core curriculum were not easily resisted. Two freshman courses in particular imposed massive nightly readings and opened our minds to an intoxicating flood of ideas. Each met four times a week in intimate settings of about fifteen students. Humanities Lit burdened us with a big book a week, from Aristophanes to Zola. And with so few targets in the room, there was no ducking the provocations of senior professors: *How would you compare Yahweh's character in Genesis with that of the gods of Sophocles, Mister Frankel?*

Still more demanding was "CC"—Introduction to Contemporary Civilization in the West. It dragged us through a parade of Western ideas with excerpts from the writings of scores of philosophers like Aquinas, Machiavelli, Hobbes, Kant, Mill, and Adam Smith. Despite the density of these texts, they magically transformed our adolescent sense of history. The ancient Greeks ceased to be just authors of myths and fairy tales and became impressive tutors in the meanings of tyranny and democracy. Europe's past ceased to be a tiresome succession of monarchs and emerged

instead as a cascade of speculations about the nature of man and the ideologies that might tame him. These readings let us connect the debates of
sages like Plato and Marx, Aquinas and Kant. We were encouraged to join
in this chain of conversation across the ages and taught the fundamental
laws of disputation. My clarifying moment came in an encounter with
Prof. Charles Frankel (no relation), in an instruction that has focused all
my reading ever since. Explaining why he, a liberal, and C. Wright Mills,
a Marxist, were willing to wrestle so publicly and passionately in our
weekly philosophy seminar, he said: *"You never know what anyone is for until
you know what he is arguing against."*

That whole categories of humanity, especially women, were left out of
our readings and discussions did not then strike us as remarkable. In our
sense of the natural order of things, the girls across Broadway at Barnard
College, with obvious exceptions, were preparing for mate- and motherhood; they were the engines of biology, not of philosophy. Little did we
realize that those very women would become a driving force in our generation's history.

———————

Though *Spec* remained my major, Ideas were at least my college minor.
And together these interests shaped both my political stance and my personality. I became a secular liberal, plainly more devoted to political analysis than to action.

I made the satisfying discovery of Moses, who commanded the worship of law instead of the golden calf, and of Jesus, who proclaimed the
equality of mankind in God's love. And I came to understand that since
people are not in fact equal in talent and strength, their equal rights to life,
liberty, and opportunity had to be defined and secured by law. It took four
years to get from that first sentence to the second, but it was an exhilarating journey.

The ultimate riddle of these formative years was how the worshipers
of Moses and Jesus could have abandoned their prophetic teachings and
succumbed to a pathetic, murderous tribalism. I finally found the answer
in my year-long study of a single book, *The Open Society and Its Enemies,*
Karl R. Popper's investigation during World War II of the roots of totalitarianism. My guide, once again, was Prof. Charles Frankel, who held out
Popper as our century's most relevant prophet of liberalism. He was even
more than that for me because he finally resolved my youthful struggle to
link the tyrannies that had shaped our family's fortune.

The doctrines that produced both Hitler and Stalin, Popper observed, could be traced through Hegel and Marx all the way back to Plato, to a family of ideas that proclaimed utopian truths and certitudes whose imposition by force required the construction of "closed" societies. The utopian tyrannies insisted that history had "Meaning" and that it imposed an inexorable logic on events. The Nazis proposed to reach a Platonic Golden Age by purifying a racial tribe, Popper taught, while the Communists idealized a single tribe or class of proletarians. But their doctrines were equally wicked:

> The more we try to return to the heroic age of tribalism, the more surely do we arrive at the Inquisition, at the Secret Police and at a romanticized gangsterism. Beginning with the suppression of reason and truth, we must end with the most brutal and violent destruction of all that is human. *There is no return to a harmonious state of nature. If we turn back, then we must go the whole way—we must return to the beasts.*

I found that to be the only plausible explanation of the Holocaust. Popper persuaded me that the claim that history has a single Meaning leads inevitably to the rule of brutes and the closed society. The only defense was to recognize that "History" had no purpose or meaning, no utopian past or future, and that social justice had to be found in the present, through a process of "piecemeal social engineering"—constant experiment, debate, and corrections of course. Only in an "open society" could reason prevail and violence be curbed, because experiment required universal skepticism and the freedom to dissent.

Thus did Professors Popper and Frankel ratify my commitment to journalism. For once you conclude that freedom requires society to live by reason—by experiment, analysis, correction, and piecemeal engineering—then language and discourse become more than instruments of self-expression. As Popper put it:

> Rationalism is therefore bound up with the idea that the other fellow has a right to be heard, and to defend his arguments. . . . Also the idea of impartiality leads to that of responsibility; we have not only to listen to arguments, but we have a duty to respond, to answer, where our actions affect others. Ultimately, in this way, rationalism is linked up with the recognition of the necessity of social institu-

tions to protect freedom of criticism, freedom of thought and thus the freedom of men. And it establishes something like a moral obligation towards the support of these institutions.

So working for *Spec* became not only fun but a duty. Journalism became not just gratifying but a moral imperative.*

---

* If history had "meaning," Charles Frankel would have been allowed to live out a brilliantly rational life. But the war in Vietnam cut short his career in Washington administering the government's international education programs, and when he returned to Columbia, the student rebellion sent him fleeing to the presidency of the National Humanities Center in North Carolina. He kept his beloved country home near New York, where one day in early 1979, Frankel, his wife, Helen, and two houseguests were murdered in their beds by random robbers. No meaning indeed.

11 · UPTOWN, DOWNTOWN

AS I BEGAN MY SOPHOMORE YEAR, DAVE WISE WAS blazing a new trail to journalistic glory. The chum who had lured me to Columbia and the *Spectator* had succeeded Richard Dougherty as campus stringer for the *Herald Tribune*. Besides attending class and reporting for *Spec*, Dave now traveled downtown most days to write for the *Trib* about tiresome education conferences at Teachers College, about new habits being pulled out of rats in Columbia's psychiatry labs, and about Eisenhower homilies to alumni concerning God and country. And Dave brought back to campus the irreverent celebrations of such news from veteran *Trib* reporters, stoking our ambition to labor among them.

Dave plotted his life the way he eventually plotted his spy novels and pathbreaking exposés of the CIA—elaborately and furtively. In his most conspiratorial manner, he summoned me to lunch one day to report that crusty Nancy Edwards, a graduate student then covering campus news for *The New York Times*, had received a humiliating but nonetheless tempting offer from that paper: to write up wedding notices in its Society Department. Nan, who had developed a bark worthy of Hildy Johnson in *The Front Page*, pined like all of us to cover cops and politicians, but staff was staff, and so she was likely to settle for brides and births. If she did, Dave said, she would let Dave choose between staying at the *Trib* and succeeding her at *The Times*. Whatever his choice, they had agreed to try to pass the remaining job to me.

Dave had already cast me as the more Timesian by temperament, a judgment that I stuffily took to be a compliment. More practically, we both believed that young men rose faster on the livelier—and stingier—*Tribune*. We both aspired to cover politics, progressing from general assignments to stalking the mayor, the governor, and finally the president in the White House. We reckoned that, with luck, reaching those heights would take maybe six years at the *Trib* but ten, or even fifteen, at *The Times*. So Dave decided to stay at the *Trib* and encouraged Nan to nominate me for *The Times*.

Bob Garst, *The Times*'s city editor, was politely incredulous. A courtly Virginian, he blushed and patiently explained his demurral. The campus correspondency had occasionally gone to a college senior, he recalled, but a mature graduate student, like Nan, was best. If she knew no one better than a sophomore, he could surely interest one of his students at Columbia's Graduate School of Journalism; several even had professional experience with smaller papers.

Garst spoke with such courteous deliberation that Nan had time to invent a final argument. Well, yes, she said, there are undoubtedly good reporters at the J-School, but they're busy all day chasing assignments around town. Frankel, by contrast, spent all day and many nights at the *Spectator*, and in this Eisenhower era, with so much news at Columbia, *The Times* would be getting not one pair of legs but fifty!

A rarity among editors, Garst enjoyed contradiction. Even in society news, he welcomed imagination and spunk. He smiled appreciatively at Nan. *Well, all right, send him down. We'll take a look.*

Buttoned into in my most Timesian jacket, I followed Nan into the marble lobby on West Forty-third Street and into the vast third-floor newsroom that stretched a full city block from Garst's chair at the City Desk. I expected him to explore my knowledge of Columbia, but Garst chose to test my maturity. How would I ever find the time to work for both *Spec* and *The Times* while going to school? I said Dave Wise had proved it was possible; in any case, I would never let an amateur interest interfere with a professional obligation. Since I hoped one day to join the staff of *The Times*, I would not dare to cheat on my responsibilities.

That was that. It was my first regular job, and my last.

The pay was twenty dollars a week, nearly twice the cost of tuition. Unlike most newspaper stringers—so called because they were part-timers paid by the measurement of a string, or ruler, at the rate of a dollar or two per inch—I would be earning only about fifty cents an inch, or a penny a word. But the steady income meant that I could be trusted not to press for the printing of worthless news and not to pad every item just to enlarge my income. Overnight, I had become a news professional, empowered to discard the chaff churned out by the university's public relations office. Overnight, I had become a sophomore of renown, familiar to campus authorities as the lad who could spread their boasts and promotions around the world. And overnight I had become a wage earner, freed from parental cash subsidies. I could afford dinner at Toffenetti's in Times Square while awaiting *The Times*'s first edition with my cherished prose— and the early *Trib*, to make sure that I hadn't been scooped by Dave. I could even afford an occasional steak at Bleeck's, at the *Trib*'s back door, where the biggest bylines in New York gathered to trade stories too bawdy to print, all delightful, some even true. It was a heady transformation. And occasionally, my beat produced some very delicious news.

Ike's Beer and Hot Dogs speech was that kind of news. It was also a memorable demonstration of how journalism, like science, progresses by hypothesis, by shrewd conjecture that anticipates events and evidence.

Around the *Spectator*, our most persistent hypothesis was that Dwight D. Eisenhower had been brought to Columbia by a cabal of influential trustees to be "demilitarized" for an eventual run at the White House. Democrats and Republicans alike had clamored to run him in 1948, but he'd put them off, refusing even to hint at his political philosophy and surprising everyone by taking the Columbia presidency instead. He had no prior connection to the university and obviously lacked any interest in scholarship or scholars. And his speeches were insipid models of the platitudinous: "As a fellow freshman at Columbia, let me just say this: I have learned on the field of battle what I think you can learn more easily in these pleasant surroundings. Our need is for moral rectitude and a spiritual rededication to the principles upon which this great nation was built."

Whenever Dave and I heard Ike pronounce on the country's "need," we would immediately mutter "moral rectitude and spiritual rededication" and strain to suppress our snide front-row laughter. Maybe Ike enjoyed begging for donations from alumni or courting publicity for Columbia. But we suspected that the ringleaders on the board of trustees, including Arthur Hays Sulzberger, the publisher of *The Times*, hoped to use Columbia as a platform to launch Ike's career as a Republican. They needed him to rescue the party from Midwest isolationists and from the irresponsibility bred by the party's twenty years in opposition.

The evidence for our hypothesis was skimpy but intriguing. As only a few of us had noticed, a *Spectator* photograph of the trustees' black-tie welcome for Eisenhower in 1948 had shown a single alien figure standing at the edge of the group; it was Henry Cabot Lodge, a Republican who lacked any connection to Columbia but who became an early advocate of "drafting" Ike for the White House and then served as his campaign spokesman. Meanwhile, at Eisenhower's elbow in his Columbia office, sat retired Col. Kevin McCann, for many years the general's most trusted confidant, speechwriter, and political counselor. Stephen Ambrose, Ike's admiring biographer, doesn't think much of our theory, noting that most of Columbia's trustees supported Thomas Dewey in 1948 and expected him to win and serve eight years. But Columbia's first offer to Ike was made in 1946, and the deal was sealed in mid-1947, when Sen. Robert Taft, the Ohio isolationist, looked to be in firm command of the GOP.

And a most remarkable offer it was, clearly foreshadowing Eisenhower's casual approach to the White House. Ambrose reports that Ike was promised no "involvement" in academics, no "responsibility" for fund-raising, no "excessive" entertaining, and no "burdensome" administration. Even so, Ike confided to a friend five months into the job that he'd made a mistake, never realizing what a "big operation" Columbia was.

Eisenhower was relieved of his misery by a wily President Truman, who did his best to keep Ike in uniform, maybe because he needed him but maybe also to restrain him politically. Truman summoned the general to Washington for half the 1948–49 academic year and early in 1951 sent him back to Europe as supreme commander of the Allied armies. From the start, these absences made a mockery of Eisenhower's academic pretensions, and we *Spectator* reporters could not get even an off-the-record commitment from him that he planned eventually to return to the university. Like most Columbia teachers and students, we were openly contemptuous of Ike's campus caper.

Ever the cool professionals, Dave and I were less interested in mocking Ike than in teasing out evidence of the political plans that we were sure existed. That is why the rumors of a few overlooked sentences in one of Ike's off-campus speeches, to the Saint Andrews Society at the Waldorf-Astoria, struck us, and us alone, as pregnant with significance. Buried in a text that an amused Colonel McCann eagerly provided, we found unmistakable evidence that Ike was ready to be labeled a Republican, a fervent opponent of the New Deal and Fair Deal social policies. He had defined a liberal as "a man in Washington who wants to play Almighty with your money," and he'd chided liberals, meaning Democrats, for encouraging folks to want "champagne and caviar when they should have beer and hot dogs."

How colorfully our hypothesis had found supporting evidence! Ike's campaign had begun, we concluded. But no one downtown had noticed. So we gave our little scoop to *Spec*, never expecting it to gain a second life when the seniors in charge of the student paper wrote an editorial assaulting the general as no one had assaulted him since the Battle of the Bulge:

> General Eisenhower, who doubles as president of this University, delivered himself of several remarkable statements last Wednesday evening. . . . If the speech was a trial balloon, we think public reaction will soon flatten it. . . . Being content with beer and hot dogs has never been part of the American tradition we know. The one we know assures any citizen that he may some day eat champagne and caviar, and in the White House at that. We don't know, of course, but we are willing to bet that beer and hot dogs weren't on the menu at the Waldorf-Astoria last Wednesday night either.

The Times and the *Trib*, having missed the story on the first bounce, were delighted to let their campus stringers resurrect it now. Though I was new to the job, my article about *Spec*'s editorial—"Student Daily Chides Eisenhower as Belittling 'Personal Security' "—ran prominently, and the news reverberated through press and radio. So great was the excitement that *The Times* a week later took three more of my paragraphs on the subject, reporting that eight frankfurters and rolls had mysteriously appeared in the cupped right hand of the campus statue of Alexander Hamilton. And a week after that, *The Times* admitted yet another short dispatch, this one about the campus Christmas party at which Ike tried to disarm his now loud critics. He said he couldn't give a sermon because the chaplain was present; he couldn't address "scholarly things" because scholars were present; and, to much applause, "certainly I'm not going to talk about politics. . . . I never have."

Neither Ike's eight years in the White House nor my forty-five at *The Times* would wipe away the memory of the Beer and Hot Dogs excitement. That was my first successful deduction of a truth about power and my first thrill of shouting news through the megaphone that is *The New*

York Times. For the first time, I applied Prof. Charles Frankel's philosophical counsel—*"You cannot know what a man is for until you know what he's against"*—to journalism. And for the first time I understood that a reporter is no mere stenographer, that facts and quotes are not necessarily truthful until they have context.

In time, I realized that many newspapers too often assaulted readers with facts and quotes without exploring what they meant. *Who, what, when,* and *where,* but rarely *why.* There was too little *why,* even in *The Times.* "Good and Gray" was its nickname because it delivered page after page of disembodied fact and text, lately relieved only by the articles of a few stars, like Mike Berger and James Reston. In his illuminating prose from Washington, Reston dared to suggest that statesmen had motives for what they said, did, and failed to do and that the hidden pressures they felt were both more interesting and more complex than their public words. Reston's insightful articles were so unusual his editors didn't dare present them as part of their "objective" news. But they were so obviously fair, accurate, and well informed, they demanded to be published. So *The Times* invented a distinct typography for Reston's dispatches and labeled them "News Analysis," as had been done only a few times for Arthur Krock.

The conventional and more sterile style of newspaper writing had itself been innovative once, a reaction against the fevered fulminations of partisan editor-owners like Horace Greeley, James Gordon Bennett, William Randolph Hearst, and Joseph Pulitzer. Rejecting their crusades, *The Times* of Adolph Ochs presented itself as impartial and comprehensive. And as foreign wars and revolutions forced Americans to take notice of world events, a terse and simple writing style became doubly advantageous. Correspondents flashed the important facts at the top of their articles in case cable or radio communication was interrupted. And they were encouraged to write sparsely to hold down word-by-word cable costs. Moreover, in World War II, most American papers took their foreign news from wire services, whose haste and hunger for broad appeal drained the life from their prose. For many editors, also at *The Times,* "wire service" news set a false standard of "objectivity." But those of us knocking at newspaper doors in the 1950s aspired to be not just stenographic reporters but "correspondents" like Reston.

———————

In my college years, our most analytical and meaningful journalism was practiced uptown, at *Spec.* And what a media-mad crew we were. Dave Wise became the editor in chief of *Spec* and, as we had figured, was hired after graduation by the *Trib;* he reached the White House via City Hall and Albany as planned, in six years. When I succeeded him at *Spec,* my deputies included two future presidents of network news, Richard C. Wald and Lawrence K. Grossman; a third, Roone Arledge, labored down the hall editing our yearbook.

We used both the news and editorial columns of *Spec* to decipher the double-talk by which our college deans for too long tolerated the exclusion of blacks and Jews from fraternities. We decoded and denounced a university decree celebrating academic freedom but slyly barring Communists from appearing on campus. We questioned the fairness of deferring brainy students from the Korean draft. Uptown, we practiced being Reston, examining the complexities of community life. Downtown, we were dull apprentices, learning to polish mostly pallid, parochial news of little consequence:

EISENHOWER OPENS TERM AT COLUMBIA.
Again Calls for U.S. Faith in Democratic Aims

COLUMBIA SETS UP ISRAELI STUDY UNIT

10 "BORING CLASSICS" VOTED BY READERS.
Bunyan Wins First Place

Occasionally, of course, I would bag some news of major consequence, but in the stream of trivia, it attracted little notice:

George F. Kennan, counselor of the State Department, charged here last night that the "witch-huntings" of Communists in this country had dimmed considerably our understanding of the Russian people—a people, he said, that is "saturated" with liberal and moral concepts that "must some day" assert themselves and lead to the collapse of the present Soviet regime.

Only slowly did I understand why even the worldly *New York Times* carried so much provincial campus news. Its large local staff was really needed only at odd moments, when planes crashed into the Empire State Building or New York's electricity suddenly gave out. Between crises, the locals were sent to cover insipid business lunches, charity dinners, and professional conventions, and their reports were supplemented by yet more trivia from dozens of suburban part-timers and campus stringers like me. After designing a truly cosmopolitan Page One each night and giving foreign dispatches pride of place in the front of the paper, the editors of *The Times*, like those of every other American newspaper, ranked the importance of events by their proximity to the center of town. And the center of *The Times*'s town, after it moved there in 1903, was aptly called Times Square.

Local news sold papers, and local ads paid for news. That was newspapering. The most desirable local news named names, those of people who bought the paper or should be buying it. The New York papers played on a wider stage than most; their local stories sometimes extended all the way to the old country of their immigrant readers. And the papers' proximity to Wall Street and the world's busiest harbor impressed upon them the expanding range of the city's commerce. Business and trade were also local news. *So please, Mr. Frankel, let's be accurate about middle initials! A name in* The Times *is a name committed to history!*

Besides serving history, I had to worry about verbosity. Whenever I entered *The Times*'s vast newsroom, I would look to see whether the familiar green eyeshade was presiding over the City Desk that afternoon. It belonged to Don Marshall, the snarling night City editor, whose presence instantly decreed an extra hour of labor. Early in my *Times* career, Marshall had summoned me to his side to challenge an eight-line article in which I allowed a professor receiving a research grant to speak glowingly about his laboratory achievements.

"What is this bullshit?" Marshall bellowed, never looking up but running a fierce black pencil through half my prose. It felt like a public hanging because, like every summons in that cavernous office, his had been by loudspeaker—*"Mister Frankel, to the City Desk, please"*—and the entire staff could observe my long march back with a rejected typescript in hand.

A second such humiliation had to be avoided at all costs. Laboriously pruning my copy, especially when Marshall was on duty, became the best defense. But for safety's sake, I devised another. I began to seek a work space nearer the front, so that I could be summoned with a crook of a finger, without that dread loudspeaker. Among the desks arrayed like tombstones in two dozen rows, seven or eight abreast, stood a few whose owners did not bother to lock the flip-top typewriters, and so I gradually crept forward until, at Pete (Richard H.) Parke's invitation, I laid claim to an unused desk beside his, in the very first row. This was sacred turf, the first stand of the orchestra. And my other neighbor was the concertmaster himself, the soft-spoken star of the local staff, Mike (Meyer) Berger.

From that front-row perch, I could follow my copy being passed safely from hand to hand until a copy editor had penciled in a headline, impaled a dupe on his spike, and sent the original toward the pneumatic tubes that shuttled articles to the typesetters one flight up. Then I could linger among the many reporters who had finished for the night until Frank Adams, the deputy City editor, ambled over to confer a few premature "good nights" to clear the room so that he and the customary trio of political reporters, James Haggerty, Leo Egan, and Warren Moscow, could settle down for their regular game of bridge. Just to loiter among these reporters, some of whom had seen Mussolini hanging by his feet and Patton's Third Army surging through Weissenfels and who were now volunteering for combat in Korea and exploration in Antarctica, was to pine for a part in their magnificent enterprise—whether or not it included the right to write like Reston.

Pretty soon I discovered that I was rubbing my palms while composing at the typewriter, imitating Pete Parke, and sneaking off with a carbon of Abe Raskin's labor yarns to see what tiny changes the copy desk would dare to make in such pristine copy. Most lovingly I studied Mike Berger's notes, from which he produced the most chilling accounts of multiple murder and the most charming pictures of St. Patrick's Day parades.

Mike's clipboard was the only useful journalism text I ever had. It was astoundingly sparse: just names, addresses, sums of money, bits of spoken quotes, and whatever descriptive phrases occurred while he planned his story—a *prancing steed* in the park, a *Sabbath stillness* in the harbor. That's all he ever wrote down, and when I overheard him taking phoned reports from a crime scene, I began to understand why. Mike drew pictures in his head: *The guy went up one flight and turned left—or did you say right? Was the door wide open or just ajar? No, no, wait just a moment, please. Is there a light in the hall? Could you make out the wallpaper?—Okay, peeling, with pink flowers. And no one heard him in the corridor?—Must be a carpet of some kind, right?*

Ever since, whether reporting a Manhattan murder or a Moscow summit, I made sure to check the carpets and the wallpaper. For Mike's sake, I kept my eyes on the story and out of my notebook. Instead of grasping at dialogue, I tried to picture the plot. And I always separated my few jottings on paper with a circled *X*, the way Mike Berger did, expecting, no doubt, that by working like Mike, I might write like Mike.

Even in my last year at college, however, there was nothing distinctive about my writing except its volume. I was writing a lot, in three different venues, each demanding a different voice.

Over the summer, *The Times* had hired me as a full-time reporter, to serve mostly as a lobster-shift replacement in police "shacks." That meant sitting from 8:00 P.M. to 3:30 A.M. among friendly competitors who shared a rented apartment across the street from police headquarters in Manhattan and other boroughs and also across from the East and West Side command precincts. We would count fire bells, alert for four- or five-alarmers and lesser conflagrations in tony neighborhoods. And we'd listen to the chatter on police radios for crimes worth pursuing. The permanent shack dwellers enjoyed tutoring new kids from *The Times;* they would drive me, their own pistols at the ready, to the seedier parts of town to watch a tenement fire, an auto chase, or a crime-in-progress collar. We talked cop talk with cops and racist talk to racists; all our papers felt then that a "black-on-black" crime had little or no "news value." Only once or twice a week did I get a reportable incident; *The Times* favored jewel thefts—or anything worse—at fancy addresses or crimes that provided a certain anecdotal cuteness: MAN IN VICTIM'S SUIT SEIZED AS MURDERER or 2 JITTERY ROBBERS GET $10,000 IN LOOT—VICTIM CALMS THEM DOWN.

Back in school that fall, I had to muffle this vernacular voice to produce learned essays with titles like "On Equality" or "Mill's Epistemology." My classes were mostly once-a-week seminars in classical readings. I learned best in small discussion groups and welcomed the freedom to write the required papers at my convenience, in predawn somnolence. Now that I was editor of the *Spectator,* Mom and Pop were able to rationalize my moving out, even to a campus just forty-five blocks from home. I shared an apartment with *Spec*'s managing editors, Larry Grossman and Charlie Jacobs, whose courses overlapped with mine and permitted collaborations that our economics text called "efficiencies of scale."

I rarely had trouble tracking a material argument by John Locke or a mystical passage in Franz Kafka, but the simple syntax of newswriting downtown interfered with my production of suitably intricate, footnoted essays uptown. Perversely, my instructors seemed to find my colloquial approach to scholarly themes refreshing and gave me grades that were rarely warranted by the intellectual weight of my ideas.

If these extremes of uptown and downtown expression ever merged, it was in the editorials that our gang wrote for *Spec.* We disdained the pomposity of some of our predecessors, but the war in Korea also cured us of excessive frivolity. The now worldwide struggle against communism was claiming the lives of our generation and some of our freedoms, and we could hear the future's challenge: Where were *you* when it mattered?

Why, indeed, were we sitting out the war in college? We wrestled with that one until we figured how to eat our cake and have it too: We urged students to take the IQ tests for deferment from the draft so long as they were available, like tax loopholes. But we opposed the policy that sent mostly poor and undereducated men to fight our battles.

———————

Opportunists we were. But pop historians notwithstanding, we were not a "silent generation." We wrote mostly about campus affairs, but we yielded nothing in fervor. When the college refused to shut down fraternities whose national leaders insisted on racial and religious discrimination, we named the offending chapters and implored freshmen to boycott them. When the university tried censoring campus speakers by disqualifying "radical" organizations, we exposed the hypocrisy and urged alumni contributors to resist a threat to academic freedom. We chided Ike for refusing to forswear politics and not promising to return to Columbia when his European duties ended. We invented a comparison shopper, Charlie Marketwise, who found student loans at Chase National for 3.83 percent without collateral while the university was soaking students at 4.00 percent. We published the names, including our own, of seniors chosen for membership in "secret" service societies, praising their work but shattering their hurtful aura of mystery. And we preached liberty in the cheeky but civil spirit of Columbia's liberal values:

We were pleased to see the other day that the charming ladies of Sapulpa, Oklahoma, have decided to revive the felicitous custom of burning books. The ladies were quite surprised that their disposal of "books about sex and socialism" (there is some sort of connection, you know) raised such a fuss in outlying districts. . . . The appropriate fuel in ancient Rome was Christians, but this is no longer the style. One no longer burns individuals—one burns ideas. This is much more sanitary, humane, and final. Individuals have been known to die of their own accord, but the tenacity with which ideas cling to life in books is startling.

When the time came to surrender our *Spectator* pulpit, we ended with a closing thought that finally connected the three worlds of my Columbia experience:

It is to our great surprise that we find in the last 130 issues of *The Spectator* a theme . . . that to print the news and record ideas is a positive good . . . that there is nothing to be gained by secrecy, collusion and suppression of thought and deed, but that much is lost by such practices. In a year characterized by increased popular acceptance of the path of least resistance—the path of repression, conformity and shortsightedness—we have tried to convince our community that it must retain its liberal vitality.

12 · PRIVATE IN THE PENTAGON

LUCKILY FOR THE ARMY, FOR THE EISENHOWER PRESI-
dency, and for the cause of free inquiry in America, my draft
board lived up to its official name as a *Selective* Service. By deferring my military career for one more year after college, it let me
play a part in the downfall of Joe McCarthy, learn to leak atomic
secrets, and achieve a lock on a job at *The New York Times*.

Getting hired full-time by *The Times* after graduation
turned out to be the easy part. It was delayed when some Columbia trustees complained to their colleague Arthur Hays
Sulzberger that his newspaper's coverage of a strike of university cooks and kitchen workers had been slanted to favor the
union cause. Rare among publishers, Sulzberger avoided rash
judgment of his campus stringer and deferred to the opinion of
his editors. When I anxiously inquired about my job application
in June 1952, Bob Garst, the City editor, opened a folder containing all of my strike coverage, each article alarmingly under-
lined in red. My stories had been examined with dermatological
care, but Garst smiled, pronounced them fair after all, and declared himself free to hand me a press card.

My aim, however, was not just to get hired but to work at *The Times* for at least one year before army service so that the paper would be legally obligated to take me back. To make that happen, I developed an elaborate three-step scheme. I first petitioned the draft board for a further delay, to let me exploit my "academic momentum" and earn a master's degree in political science. I don't recall how I argued that such a degree would benefit the Republic, but I offered to compromise with the national interest by promising to finish the two-year master's program in a single academic year—"a mere nine months." Step 2 was to find a schedule of Columbia courses, five in each semester, that satisfied the degree requirements and whose lectures all occurred on two contiguous days of the week. Step 3, as I joined *The Times*, was to volunteer most magnanimously to work on weekends so that I could take my days off on Tuesdays and Wednesdays and spend them in class. Clever, but a fearful commitment to a year of virtually nonstop labor.

Tuesdays and Wednesdays found me at Columbia, nodding through the history and philosophy lectures of Jacques Barzun, Dumas Malone, and Franz Neumann and plotting an unusual master's thesis with David Truman—a portrait of "Robert B. Blaikie and His Irregular Regular Democratic Club." I learned to operate mechanical calculators in Columbia's statistical lab and prepared elaborate charts of voting patterns in the Irish, Jewish, and Puerto Rican districts around Columbia, all demonstrating the decline of the old clubhouse culture and influence. Instead of delivering votes, a new kind of district leader was winning judgeships and other patronage by periodically *opposing* his own party's ticket. He was mostly endorsing the voters' preferences rather than shaping them, even if that required supporting independent or Republican candidates like Dwight Eisenhower. "Leaders" were becoming followers, even in this one-party bastion of the Deep North. Now that voters got their welfare benefits directly from governments and took their impressions of candidates directly from television, they showed scant loyalty to the Democratic party. I had stumbled into an early manifestation of a tide that would shape American politics throughout my career.

Thursdays to Mondays, I put aside my academic texts and worked at overcoming my image as "the Columbia kid" at *The Times*. In a year of police reporting, late-night Rewrite duty, and legging events for more senior writers, I wanted to leave an impression that would last through the two years of my army absence. Adapting to the tribal culture of *The Times*, however, also required extensive political analysis.

One memorable day, for example, Pete Parke and I were sent to New

Haven to meet Adlai Stevenson's campaign train. As instructed, we watched for the moment the train crossed the border from Connecticut to Westchester County, for that was when it passed from National Desk turf into City Desk territory. As City staffers, we now assumed coverage of the Democratic candidate, displacing the formidable William Lawrence, our national political correspondent, and followed Stevenson to a rousing street rally on Harlem's 125th Street. Contrary to all my theorizing, some frontiers had their uses; there were benefits to be found even in such ludicrous assertions of sovereignty.

I soon learned that major news events regularly inspired such competitions among staff members. Foreign correspondents defended their turf as ferociously as border guards, challenging the incursions of other *Times* writers even if they brought special knowledge or experience to the coverage. Washington kept out New Yorkers, and New York claimed every inch of regional terrain. Only on night Rewrite, with deadlines descending, did we display genuinely selfless teamwork. The half-dozen Rewrite men reported for work at dinnertime, then sat around exchanging gossip, reading novels, or studying for history tests until they were suddenly convulsed into action by a fact or a phone call, which would turn out to be either a dud or a fulfilling Page One catastrophe.

There's a jumper on the George Washington Bridge, a copyboy would report; *Mr. Adams wants you to check it out.*

Or Frank Adams, now City editor, would walk over: *We need a quick obit of Everett Shinn, the last of the Armory Show rebels. Nine hundred words, a graf at a time please.*

Armory Show? Quick, Sammy, the clips.

Or the Brooklyn police shack would phone every few minutes with a trickle of detail that required a rewrite for each of the night's many editions until you had a prose poem worthy of Mike Berger:

> A 17-year-old boy rider wrestled valiantly for four hours yesterday to save his mud-frightened horse as it sank slowly to its death in a Canarsie marsh. . . . Deeper and deeper it sank, but the animal stood frozen as if posing for an equestrian statue.

Rewrite was combat—not only rapid-fire reporting but full-platoon newspapering. Arthur Gelb at the next desk would try to find the boy's family. George Barrett would interview some veterinarians to learn why a horse would refuse to swim to safety. Bernie Kalb would locate a book describing the ecology of Canarsie's marshes. Alden Whitman, the late man on the copy desk, would fit the pieces of prose together and persuade the Bullpen to hold the next edition for five minutes for a crucial update, then sweet-talk the composing room foreman to hold back one page from the engravers to await a new ninth paragraph:

Finally four patrolmen from Emergency Squad 14, attached to the Miller Avenue station, donned wading boots and borrowed a rowboat to get to the boy. They lifted Jerry from the horse and sent him in an ambulance to Beth El Hospital, where he was treated for exposure. The horse, though, by then was completely submerged.

We were the Rewrite Bank of the World's Greatest Paper, and when I finally took the army's oath, I carried a silver cigarette lighter inscribed with the slogan I had fashioned to express our pride: "From the Most Reliable Bank in the World—Interest Compounded Nightly."

I never imagined that my army career could compete in excitement with work at *The Times*. But it proved to be a high-voltage drama in three acts.

IMMERSION

They had no trouble drilling the fat and the fear out of me in basic training. As the sergeant at Fort Dix put it while we stood one dawn with bayonets affixed to our M-1 rifles, *Now this here ain't no child's game. There's a war over there in Korea, and you goofballs are gonna learn to defend yerselves. When you jab that blade into the sack, I want y'all to scream so they can hear it over in D Company. Then put yer foot under the blade, yank it out, and jab it in again harder, yellin' even louder, so as I can hear it back here: KILL! KILL! KILL! And we're gonna stay here till night if it ain't right, 'cause when those Chinks start comin' at you over the tops of the trenches, y'all better know how to jab it in quick and neat. Do ya hear me?*

Yes, Sarge.

Louder!

YES, SARGE!

I was good at bayoneting a straw man, screaming "Kill!" as he fell. I threw myself fearlessly across barbed wire to form a springboard for my squad, and I crawled unafraid under live machine-gun fire. My terror was the thought of scaling a high parapet, a test that I schemed for weeks to avoid with a well-timed offer to deliver the company's medical records to division headquarters. That errand equipped me with the army's most reliable armor: a clipboard; swinging a clipboard, you could wander around the camp for days unmolested.

In two months of basic infantry training, that was my only evasion of duty. In all other respects I absorbed the army's relentless brainwashing and bodybuilding. On my first weekend home I stared contemptuously at civilian stomachs, baggy trousers, and scuffed shoes. I swaggered in uniform among the loungers at the Wall in Washington Heights, transformed into a fascistic robot, a military zealot. More evidence of what a good Nazi I might have been. How easy it was, with persistent deprivations of sleep and liberty, to make me care for little else than the crease in my trouser, the sparkle of my boot, and the rust-free condition of my rifle, my "piece." I had been molded, of course, not just by sadistic sergeants but by the relentless stream of war propaganda.

Like most Americans, I approved of defending South Korea in 1950 just as in 1948 I approved of the airlift to feed Berliners when the Communists cut their supply lines. We worldly liberals thought it important to "contain" communism without yielding to the crazed advocates of a "preventive war." That meant protecting the lines that divided the postwar world into Soviet and American spheres of influence—roughly the lines that now ran clear through the middle of Berlin and Germany and along the Thirty-eighth Parallel in mid-Korea. The compulsion to resist Communist advances became even stronger after Communists won China's civil war in 1949. Senator McCarthy and his ilk blamed China's loss on Democratic "treason," but you did not have to be a fanatical jingoist or demagogue to support anticommunism abroad. It was unimaginable that North Korea would attack South Korea without Stalin's encouragement. And if the ghastly cost of defeating Hitler five years earlier had taught anything, it was that a tyrant's aggression fueled by an expansive ideology had to be thwarted in its earliest stages. This resolve to permit "No More Munichs!"—no more sellouts of little countries like Czechoslovakia—was reinforced now by the cry of "No More Chinas!" and produced a momentary national consensus. No one was fooled by President Truman's claim that the Korean conflict was a "police action"; though formally undeclared, it began as a popular war, questioned only by Stalin's stooges in the American Communist party and a shriveling roster of sympathizers.

Before I got into it, however, we were hand to hand with the "Chinks," as our sergeant emphasized. Chinese troops had intervened when General MacArthur, not content to settle for a brilliant defense of South Korea, persuaded Truman that he could easily liberate Communist

North Korea as well. At that, the Chinese intervened and drove him into bloody retreat, back to the Thirty-eighth Parallel, producing a stalemate that gradually sapped the public's tolerance for the war. Eisenhower virtually assured his election in 1952 by vowing with cynical vagueness that "I shall go to Korea" to end it. When he finally went, he settled for the imperfect armistice that Truman had already offered.

A year later, Ike also settled for half a loaf in Vietnam by bargaining to divide the country with the Communists who had routed France's Foreign Legion and colonial regime. That deal created the illusion of yet another frontier of Communist "containment," which Ike's successors, still obsessed by Munich and China, fought so catastrophically to preserve.

REDEMPTION

It was not to avoid combat but to cover it as a military correspondent that I had applied even before my army induction for eventual assignment to *Stars* and *Stripes*, the main military papers in Europe and Asia. The civilian manager of the *Stripes*'s New York office relayed my application to his superiors in Washington, but they feared that I would get lost in the army's labyrinth; after two months of basic infantry training, I would probably be shipped off for eight more weeks of training to acquire an arbitrary military occupation—maybe clerk-typist, but cook if they needed one. I would then be sent overseas, where my desire to join the staff of *Stars* and *Stripes* would be subject to veto by my company, regimental, division, and theater commanders. Instead of running all these risks, the Pentagon bureaucrats decided to requisition me to fill a clerk's job in their own office, the Army Newspaper Section, Troop Information and Education Division, Office of the Chief of Information, Department of the Army. That office did not exactly practice journalism, but close enough: it wrote rules for *Stars* and *Stripes* and all other newspapers printed or mimeographed by units throughout the world.

Thus it was, in a fit of carelessness that became an issue of great moment a year later, that the army spared me from the full sixteen weeks of basic training, pulled me out of Fort Dix after only seven weeks, housed me in a barrack at Fort Myer beside the Pentagon, and put me to work monitoring and servicing the journalistic output of troops the world over. It was humdrum work, but it carried the advantages of a most distinctive rank—private in the Pentagon.

The first of these advantages was the right to acquire a civilian wardrobe and an automobile, parked a few feet from my bed. Except when assigned to mess hall duties, I could drive to New York every weekend to court Carol Feinberg, a prim young Smith College graduate who duly announced, and a few months later broke, our engagement. I doubt that she was frightened off by the prospect of a garden apartment near the Pentagon. More likely she succumbed to the unrelenting warnings of her father that I faced a career that would never support her in the manner to which his dental practice had accustomed her. He often asked slyly what James Reston earned—not, of course, that every reporter could expect to become a James Reston. After returning my ring, Carol soon signaled yet another change of heart, which I should have respected as both courageous and flattering. But after mourning her loss for a few weeks, I had slammed the gates on our relationship, as firmly as I always slammed them against the past, against Weissenfels, Kraków, and Washington Heights, and the dreams of triumphant careers in opera and art. I passed too easily, even brutally, from one place to another, from one role to the next, unwilling, perhaps unable, to look back. I drove one Sunday morning through the still hills of Arlington Cemetery, my Plymouth vibrating to Verdi's *Requiem*, and all thoughts of Carol suddenly vanished.

The second advantage of being a mere private in the Pentagon was my personal Teletype link with Tokyo. Soon after I joined the newspaper section, the Pacific *Stars* and *Stripes* hired me as their "Washington Bureau," an off-duty job in which I provided coverage of special interest, from Pentagon news conferences ("50 Percent of 'Old Salts' Suffer from Seasickness") to the Army-Navy game in Philadelphia ("Cadets, Middies End Contact Drills"). As soon as he learned of this arrangement, Capt. Richard Taffe had another of his irrepressible ideas. Dick Taffe was a Massachusetts newspaper brat trapped in the army at a desk in the Newspaper Section by high family medical bills. He instantly embraced me as a professional colleague and generously shared his home, family life, and army smarts. He remembered at once that the Pentagon ComCenter was required at all times to keep an open line to General MacArthur's headquarters for urgent war messages. For long stretches every hour the center transmitted mere junk and gibberish. With just a few phone calls, Captain Taffe won permission for all dispatches signed "frankel" to be sent to Tokyo as part of that junk, a channel that soon became the envy of generals. Senior officers in our corner of the Pentagon discovered that instead of risking embarrassment with personal messages about their travel plans to the Pacific—which had to be typed in ten copies, encoded, and formally registered—they needed only to ask Private Frankel to relay requests for chauffeurs, billets, golf partners, and other amenities of wartime Tokyo. I normally confirmed arrangements within the hour.

I never exploited this communal telegraph service for private advantage, not even to agitate for relief from the once-a-month humiliation of KP duty in Fort Myer's mess. Those menial interludes only underscored the glamour of my desk duty on other days. But they rankled just enough to make me a most conflicted spectator at the great television brawl between the army and Sen. Joseph R. McCarthy. It took great restraint, and an overriding devotion to civil liberties, for me to pass up an obvious opportunity to rescue McCarthy at a crucial moment in that melodrama.

Most of the army brass around me had been devoted fans of the Wisconsin demagogue. Being at war against Korean Communists and training daily for World War III, they genuinely felt the ardor that McCarthy only feigned for cleansing the government of "subversives." Moreover, most army officers and their civilian bosses in the Pentagon were partisan Republicans. They welcomed the senator's smearing of Democrats and bestowed servile favors on him and his rabid counsel, Roy Cohn, notably including the promise to pamper Cohn's protégé, Pvt. G. David Schine, starting with exemptions from KP when he followed me to Fort Dix.

But the army brass refused to excuse Schine from a full four months of basic training. That was never done for anyone, they swore. And to avenge that modest resistance, McCarthy and Cohn set out to destroy the army high command.

A rich kid of twenty-seven, Schine was nominally the president and general manager of his daddy's hotel chain, but he thought of himself as a professional Communist hunter. After writing a primitive pamphlet about communism—and hospitably entertaining McCarthy's entourage at luxurious Schine residences in Florida and at the Waldorf Towers in New York—Schine was hired in early 1953 as the unpaid "chief consultant" to McCarthy's Permanent Senate Subcommittee on Investigations, the senator's personal chariot in the pursuit of "crime, corruption, and communism."

The public first heard of Schine when he accompanied Cohn on a boisterous tour of American libraries in Western Europe, where they claimed to have discovered an alarming number of "subversive" works by leftist and liberal authors. Their absurd demands of a book purge were widely mocked but nonetheless served McCarthy's claim that the American government could not be trusted to rid itself of disloyal elements. They fanned the fears of an already overanxious public.

The witch-hunters did not distinguish between the tens of thousands of Americans who had briefly flirted with communism in the 1930s, when capitalism produced the Great Depression, and the much smaller number who lent themselves to the party's conspiracies to infiltrate labor unions and government agencies in the service of Soviet interests. Americans who had long since severed their Communist ties were now expected to deliver abject confessions and to betray the names of other party members to keep the investigators in business. Private corporations and organizations anxiously purged their own ranks, dismissing and blacklisting people for reading the wrong publications, signing the wrong petitions, mixing with the wrong friends, or making the wrong enemies. Even a liberal and benevolent employer like *The New York Times* gradually inquired into the past and present affiliations of staff members and fired the few who refused to cooperate. The general hysteria left me hoping that Americans would never be tested, as Germans and Russians had been tested, by a despotism that practiced physical as well as psychological terror. The evidence suggested that we would fail the test.

McCarthy flourished in this atmosphere. Not even Eisenhower dared to resist him openly. The more reckless the senator's charges, the larger his headlines because a mindlessly "objective" press simply repeated and amplified his lies and defamations without insisting on evidence. The few publications that had the courage and resources to track down the truth found that their follow-ups rarely arrived in time to overcome the damage done by the original charges. And they were in any case drowned out by new sensations. McCarthy routinely rushed into print with information leaked to him from the raw personnel files of the FBI and other government agencies. His committee "hearings" would then claim credit for uncovering the suspects, even those few already marked for dismissal by a panicked bureaucracy. Where executive action was delayed out of respect for due process and the rights of the accused, McCarthy would complain about the prolonged "coddling" of Communists.

In July 1953, as I was entering the army, McCarthy's "chief consultant," Schine, was notified to prepare for his own induction later that year. He signaled a desire for an army job that would keep him hunting Communists, and in Cohn and McCarthy he had much more potent sponsors than I. They first called on the Pentagon to help Schine avoid the draft altogether by designating him an "essential civilian." That failing, they asked that he be instantly commissioned as an army lieutenant or given an equivalent rank as an investigator in the navy, air force, or CIA. Sensing that due regard for Schine's comforts would greatly enhance McCarthy's respect for the Pentagon's patriotism, the army brass gave elaborate consideration to these importunings. But after months of maneuver, they still judged Schine unqualified for the degree of special treatment he wanted. Army Secretary Robert Stevens consulted Defense Secretary Charles Wilson to see how far to bend the rules. He personally telephoned Schine shortly before his induction and promised a "good job" in which he could use "the knowledge and ability you have"—but only after Schine had completed basic training. Wilson and Stevens told him that he was "stuck with" the sixteen weeks that the army needed to mold *every* soldier.

Schine surrendered his body, but not his spirit. Once in uniform he generated even more insistent demands. In daily, sometimes hourly, calls, Cohn badgered the Pentagon to get Schine excused from KP, guard duty, and target practice. He won promises that Schine would not be punished for paying other soldiers to clean his rifle and barracks, for treating officers with insubordinate chumminess, and for disappearing from boot camp for days at a time to pursue McCarthy's "business" at the Waldorf Towers. After thus averting virtually all eight weeks of infantry training at Fort Dix, Schine fully expected transfer to a cushy assignment in January 1954. Instead, the army issued him what would normally be routine orders to report for eight more weeks of training at unglamorous Camp Gordon, Georgia.

This news struck Cohn as a declaration of war. He revived a demand, which the Pentagon had parried, that members of the Army Loyalty and Security Appeal Board testify before McCarthy about alleged derelictions of duty. His angry summons lit the fuse that exploded into the televised Army-McCarthy hearings.

Those hearings are vividly etched in the minds of older Americans, but most never knew the precipitating circumstances: the army's refusal to give Private Schine what it had amply given Private Frankel—a suitable desk job after less than eight weeks (and not sixteen) of basic training. Roy Cohn would never have persecuted the army if it had summoned Schine to Washington as it summoned me, directly from Dix. But the secretary of the army, Robert Stevens, and all his minions swore that they were obliged to treat Schine like any other soldier, by the rule book. To excuse him from a full sixteen-week course would have exposed them to charges of craven favoritism; Americans expect equal treatment for all. There were no exceptions. It couldn't be done. So help them God. Of course it had been done for me, and perhaps unnoticed others, whose skills happened to fit a bureaucratic need.

As we watched these pious perjuries in the Pentagon, I could barely contain my possession—my embodiment—of evidence to the contrary.

Several times a day, I mischievously asked the once fervent McCarthy fans all around whether I was not duty bound to march across town and present myself to the committee as living proof that a soldier could indeed be summoned to important work in Washington after only half of his basic training. Shouldn't I at least whisper the truth to Schine when I next encountered him at the Fort Myer movie?

I did no such thing, of course, as we watched dedicated Republicans, from the commander in chief down, finally acknowledge the McCarthyite danger, which they had long denied. As McCarthy and Cohn felt their wings being clipped, there's no telling what they would have given for my testimony. But the Eisenhower administration was at last learning the lesson I had absorbed from Professor Neumann's lectures about the rise of fascism in Germany: that a democracy must not tolerate an independent, "democratic" bureaucracy. When civil servants in the FBI and other government offices are allowed to transfer their loyalty and their files to members of Congress or other independent interests, the public loses control over its own executive, as happened in Weimar Germany. Giving McCarthy and Cohn access to the government's personnel files was tantamount to ceding them presidential power. Now that the army's files were under siege, even Eisenhower recognized the threat, and his White House urged the Pentagon to resist by compiling a chronology of Cohn's often obscene pressures on behalf of Schine.

The New York Times mysteriously obtained a summary of this chronology of the scandalous favoritism shown Schine at Fort Dix. And McCarthy, just as mysteriously, learned the name of a dentist who had been routinely drafted and promoted to the rank of major before the army discovered he was a Communist and marked him for discharge. "*Who promoted Peress?*" the senator cried. And when a decorated general refused under orders to betray the relevant personnel records, he, too, was denounced on television as "unfit" to wear that uniform. To retaliate, the army published the damning evidence, charging that Cohn and McCarthy had abused their authority to seek unwarranted privileges for their pal. The senator responded with a sheaf of dubious "documents" purporting to show that the pressure ran the other way, that the army had used Schine as a "hostage" to ward off his patriotic inquiries. The Senate solemnly ordered hearings to examine these rival accusations, hearings at which McCarthy displayed his boorish and unscrupulous tactics before the entire nation and prepared the ground for his eventual censure by the entire Senate.

As the country turned against McCarthy, so did the press, and I did my part with my silence. But I was deeply disappointed in my profession.

Even after McCarthy's demise, few journalists bothered to analyze how the conventions of the news business had allowed him to lie his way to fame and to inflame the nation's fear. Analysis and introspection were not then the vogue in American journalism.

APOSTASY

Having helped to preserve the army's rectitude, I was a logical candidate for an errand of disloyalty. I was summoned one day in February 1955 by the Office of the Chief of Information and asked the strangest combination of questions. Who were my friends in the West Coast press corps, and in particular, did I know Gladwin Hill of *The New York Times* and Bill Becker of the AP? The first very well, the second casually. And did I have dressy civilian clothes at hand? Yes, sir. Well then if I could get a Q-clearance—the government's highest test of trust to handle military secrets—I was the right person to be sent to break the rules and give some secrets away.

I was ordered to take a civilian flight to Las Vegas, my first plane ride ever, and driven to Camp Desert Rock, an army tent encampment that was only seventy miles away but had the barren look of a campsite on the moon. I was received by the commanding general, who assigned me to the camp's public information office, pending further orders. He said he was training 3,000 men for maneuvers with tactical nuclear weapons, an innovation in modern warfare worth bragging about in releases and recordings sent to the hometown of every GI. *Corporal Jones has been entrusted with an important assignment in this year's Exercise Desert Rock VI, which will give the Army firsthand knowledge of the effects of fighting with atomic weapons.* Unfortunately, the general explained, that was all the information the army was authorized to reveal. Everything else about the three nuclear devices to be exploded here in the Nevada desert in the next six weeks had been stamped "top secret."

The tests' main objective was to help the Atomic Energy Commission improve the nation's stock of atomic bombs and missile warheads. But to take full advantage of the test explosions, the army and other agencies were each assigned a pie-shaped segment in the circle surrounding Ground Zero to conduct their own experiments. The air force was using its slice to test the effects of atomic shock and dust on planes in flight. The civil defense people erected a village of flimsy houses to demonstrate the vulnerability of American cities to atomic attack. The army, by contrast, planned to huddle infantry troops in trenches very close to the blast to prove that they could employ atomic artillery to destroy enemy positions and then quickly and safely occupy Ground Zero and the surrounding terrain.

To justify their budget requests to Congress, all these agencies had been bombarding the public with rival and contradictory propaganda claims: *atomic warfare is controllable; no, it is devastating; the fallout is fatal; on the contrary, it is hardly perceptible.* The cacophony became such an embarrassing distraction that the Atomic Energy Commission angrily reclassified the entire operation as top secret and forbade any publicity about the detonations and their effects. The Pentagon's response to this clampdown was to fly in its own secret weapon, the newly promoted Corporal Frankel.

One dawn, after many rehearsals, a thousand of us were trucked to the test site, marched into shoulder-high trenches, instructed to crouch with eyes closed and heads buried in our arms, and warned that after sensing a searing bright light we were to count to ten before we stood up and prepared to move forward toward the site of the explosion, 1,000 yards away.

As I waited staring up at the tower that cradled the bomb, my mind summoned vivid images of Hiroshima, images from famous photographs and from John Hersey's extraordinary prose portraits of the victims. Suddenly a loudspeaker and its echoes counted down from sixty, and, as ordered, we assumed the crouch position. Ten . . . six . . . four, three, two, one. Silence. A measurable moment lapses before a fierce light penetrates clear through our closed and covered eyes and the earth throbs beneath our boots. Then a torrent of rocks and pebbles storming overhead. We count: eight . . . nine . . . ten, and when we peer over the top of the trench, the tower that bore the bomb is visible just for an instant as a grid of orange spokes, then disappears into vapor. A great fireball soars skyward, red, yellow, and purple, then drowns in huge clouds that slowly balloon into the familiar mushroom. Across the desert, ten thousand yucca shrubs are aflame, torches without bearers. A magnificent, exhilarating panorama beneath a radiant, predawn sky.

On command, we walked to where the tower had stood and marveled at its disappearance. Most of the debris that the bomb had sucked up into the mushroom was floating downwind, toward Las Vegas. What little fell on us was swept off with large whisk brooms that were passed around. And someone collected the little X-ray plates we wore on our chests—crude records of the radiation to which some of us would, years later, attribute grave illnesses, even death. For the moment, the troops felt cheerful, even privileged, to have done something more significant than cleaning tents and latrines.

Corporal Frankel, however, had a mission to perform. I was given a jeep and driver and sent to the Vegas casinos to find Gladwin Hill, Bill Becker, and other reporters who might be drowning their frustrations at the bar. They would have known about the blast that morning, of course; but I was to inform them in detail about the army maneuvers to prove the viability of atomic artillery. I was to describe the scene at the blast and the quick, safe troop deployments across Ground Zero and answer all other questions bearing on the army's preparations for nuclear combat.

I dumped my top secrets and promised to appear, same place, same time, after each of the next two shots. I assume that my divulgences helped the army to obtain millions more in appropriations for "tactical" nuclear weapons. My reward was less tangible. My three journeys of revel and revelation cost me ten dollars in the casinos, but I gained an entirely new appreciation for government "secrets"—top secrets and bottom secrets, too.

REPORTER:

Cold War East

1956–1961

13 · HAVE BYLINE, WILL TRAVEL

THAT FATEFUL DAY IN COLLEGE WHEN DAVE WISE AND I were handicapping a young reporter's chances of advancement and figured the *Trib* to be a better bet than *The Times*, we figured everything right except luck, fate, fortune, and the sinking of the unsinkable SS *Andrea Doria*. I returned to *The Times* from the army at age twenty-five, hoping that two years away had transformed my office persona from college kid to plausible adult. Yet in little more than a year, I was catapulted overseas to the front lines of the Cold War. Foreign correspondent. Trench coat. Third Man intrigues in Vienna and a life-altering sojourn behind enemy lines in the Soviet Union.

I had every reason to expect a long apprenticeship. The first time Pete Parke, as an assistant City editor, let me cover what turned out to be a Page One story, he was soundly chastised for such a careless tilt toward youth; front-page opportunities were reserved for the local staff's few byline writers.

Ah, the "by"line. Your name immortalized in the world's greatest newspaper, in bold type atop your own prose, and filed for the ages in the morgue. Before World War II, *The Times* gave bylines only to critics and star reporters—its correspondents abroad and a few in Washington. During the war, the risks run by combat reporters earned them bylines on virtually all dispatches, and they brought the honor home for national correspondents as well. Newsroom cynics thought bylines were compensation for the paper's low wages; "let them eat bylines" was presumed to be the first rule of management. But even then, *The Times's* City Desk hoarded its bylines for out-of-town assignments and for exceptional writing, like Mike Berger's. There was something to be said for this vestigial conservatism; it asked readers to put their trust in *The Times* rather than in any individual writer. But once even routine foreign and national articles were signed, the only reason for denying them locally was to teach the youngest reporters some humility. Which is why we would kill, or at least abandon hearth and home, for out-of-town stories and for features that let us stuff our prose with Bergeresque adjectives so that it might be mistaken for vivid writing.

Back from the army, I earned a half-dozen bylines for nothing more than flying to Syracuse and sitting through a tedious conference on juvenile delinquency. I truly earned a byline only when I was carelessly sent to cover a parade staged primarily for its photographic potential. When I finally finished one paragraph, I sent it to the editors without risking a mediocre second. Then I wandered repeatedly past the copy desk to see whether the city editor had penciled in the magical byline signal, "By ———." Someone had. Now I was condemned to hours of nervous nighttime pacing at a Times Square newsstand until the paper appeared. And there at the bottom of Page One, under a sparkling photograph, sat my first local byline and prose:

Eulogies were cheerful and eyes were dry yesterday as 25,000 Third Avenue residents bade farewell to their condemned El. In a rousing, polyglot wake for the quaint elevated structure, merchants and tenement dwellers who came from many lands to settle alongside the rattly railroad sang and drank sidewalk toasts to future, sundrenched days.

Just three days later, there I was on Page One again, with a confirmation of the complaint phoned in by Eugene William Landy. Though number two in his graduating class at the Merchant Marine Academy at Kings Point, New York, and fairly conservative in his political views, Landy had been denied a navy reserve commission because his mother had once been a Communist and still subscribed to the Communist party's *Daily Worker*.

Oh, how I relished that young man's misery! What a story! Tony Lewis had recently won a Pulitzer at *The Washington News* with just such a tale! They couldn't keep this off the front page! And they didn't.

Yes, as charged, we relish the misery of others. Our faith has always been that we do good by raking up the bad. We enjoy disaster, murder, riot, revolution. After me, an entire generation of cub reporters at *The Times* prayed that some distracted editor might one night ask them to investigate the first faint hint of an SOS at sea.

That's just how it happened, in July 1956. I was back on Rewrite, working the lobster shift from 8:00 P.M. to the start of the last pressrun at 3:20 A.M., when at midnight my life changed as suddenly as Cinderella's.

Barney Murphy was twirling dials back in *The Times*'s radio room after having sent out our nightly news summary for ships at sea. Suddenly he heard a faint SOS distress call from the *Andrea Doria*. She was the newest and most famous Italian passenger liner steaming toward New York, and now she was spewing a stream of Morse code cries for help. I was asked to check the Coast Guard, which had not yet overheard the drama, so with only Murphy's early transcriptions in hand, I suddenly owned the biggest sea disaster of the decade.

Between messages from the *Doria*, we picked up calls for assistance from the SS *Stockholm*. She had rammed the *Doria* in a dense Atlantic fog forty-five miles south of Nantucket. Then the *Ile de France* announced her presence close enough to try to help. Murphy's bulletins from all points of the compass began to pile up on my desk, along with wire service "urgents" now fed by the Coast Guard.

I wrote a cautious few paragraphs for a small Page One box in the delayed midnight edition. But the radio intercepts became thrillingly ominous: *"Here danger immediate—need lifeboats—as many as possible—can't use our lifeboats."* The shipping experts we consulted said that could mean only that the *Doria* was listing so badly she couldn't launch enough of her own lifeboats for 1,134 passengers and 575 in crew. And the nearby *Stockholm*, with 750 aboard, was taking water through a crushed bow. She had rammed the *Doria* amidships, but we found it hard to believe that a modern liner could sink swiftly, like the *Titanic*. We broke into the files of our locked ship news department and found the *Doria*'s brochures boasting of elaborate safety features. She was equipped with eleven watertight compartments and a "double bottom for greater stability *in the event of collision.*"

Seven times that night, I rewrote the ever-lengthening, ever more vividly imagined descriptions of the eerie Atlantic scene. We kept extracting news from the crackle of radio messages between the stricken vessels and among dozens of ships steaming to the rescue, firing flares, and fishing for lifeboats. All the top editors drifted into the office to follow the drama that their most junior reporter was stitching together with the help of many hands. We kept waiting for the ultimate scoop: an eyewitness report from Camille Cianfarra, *The Times*'s bureau chief in Madrid, who was sailing home on leave with his family aboard the *Doria*. One message soon after the collision had named Cianfarra's stepdaughter—"*Linda Morgan safe*"—but it came from the *Stockholm*, and we ignored it as some kind of mistake. Not until the next day, amidst celebrations of our work, did we learn that Cianfarra and another daughter were among the fifty-two people killed in the crash. The *Stockholm* had plowed straight into his cabin and plucked the sleeping Linda out of her berth. Moments after the collision, Linda Morgan was indeed "safe" aboard the *Stockholm*, lifted unhurt from one ship to the other as the vessels drew apart. The most amazing stories begin as "mistakes."

The last few thousand papers that morning were marked "7:30 A.M. EXTRA," a rare edition. Even rarer was the appearance of a rewrite man's byline beneath the eight-column banner: ANDREA DORIA AND STOCKHOLM COLLIDE; 1,134 PASSENGERS ABANDON ITALIAN SHIP. We reported mistakenly that while many were injured, "all" were saved. But thanks to Barney Murphy's radio room, we were the only newspaper with a graphic sense of the scene at sea:

For a few minutes, there was calm talk from the stricken vessels of "inspecting" and "surveying" damage. Soon, however, all the valuable radio time was devoted to the dire need for lifeboats and medical help.

The messages, as monitored by The New York Times, indicated that no offer of help, no matter how small, was being discouraged. Ships that at 1 A.M. promised to arrive at 5 A.M. with two or three lifeboats received a terse: "Okay. Thanks." . . .

The United Fruit Line's freighter Cape Ann was three miles away and the first to edge between the stricken ships. She lowered her eight lifeboats and was the first to take survivors aboard—at 2:24 A.M.

The Coast Guard said seas at the scene were "not rough." The Weather Bureau estimated, however, the visibility there at the time of the collision was "probably less than a mile."

The Cape Ann radioed at 3:55 A.M. that any attempt at searching the area by plane would be "suicidal," the fog was so dense.

My excitement over breakfast slowly ebbed into envy. Mike Berger and all the *Times* stars were deployed for the next day's stories, sent off to glean the human interest stories from rescued passengers while I could look forward only to more lobster-shift duty on Rewrite. But this one time the editors rewarded me with more than a byline in that last 7:30 extra. They also bestowed a twenty-five-dollar raise, to about eighty dollars a week, confirming the sense throughout the newsroom that I was no longer a cub.

I was pulled off Rewrite a few weeks later and sent flying around the country with one of a half-dozen teams of reporters to sample the mood of the voters during the Eisenhower-Stevenson rerun of 1956. This was the second national election since the calamity of 1948, when pollsters had unanimously predicted that Tom Dewey would defeat Harry Truman. Having lost confidence in polls, we went knocking on doors in the pivotal states to gather voter sentiment. I drove through odd precincts of Milwaukee and Austin, Arlington (Virginia) and St. Joseph (Missouri), feeding notes to William S. White, our Senate correspondent. Only his elaborate praise of my work to the editors in New York sustained me in lonely motel rooms, phoning nightly apologies to an abandoned young bride.

I met Tobi Brown at *The Times*, on my first day back from the army. She'd been the Barnard stringer and was saying farewells on her way to Harvard's Graduate School of Education. Dark and slender, sweet, smart, and flirtatious, she got my immediate attention, and we dated intensely that summer. But she was determined to get away from an overprotective home, to "credential" herself as a teacher. She also wanted space and time to compare me with other suitors, especially the prosperous proprietor of a plumbing business clearly favored by her parents.

The Browns were a struggling Brooklyn family, feeling left behind in Crown Heights by Tobi's uncle, an accountant, and other Jews whose wartime profits propelled them to Manhattan, Queens, or, better yet, Long Island. Tobi's father, Harold, was a graduate of Columbia College and Columbia Law School, but he had only modest success in private practice and kept waiting for Abe Beame and Stanley Steingut of the Madison Democratic Club to reward his humble partisan labors with a judgeship. But Tobi's friends were quickly exposed to her mother's deeper resentments. The youngest of seven children in a family from Odessa, Pauline Brown felt cheated of a college education, unappreciated for her frugal domestic management, tyrannized by an upstairs father-in-law, and starved for recognition, which she now expected mainly from the achievements of her daughters, Tobi and Marion, nine years younger.

How could these people subject me to such a humiliating rivalry for Tobi's hand? Were the plumber's suburban bathtubs and toilets a match for my worldly disasters and politics? Even as I delivered my "warnings" that a wife of mine would have to be portable and eager to share an unconventional life, I was determined to avoid rejection. Though only twenty-five, I lagged behind my college friends in finding a mate and often felt the terrors of loneliness, as in Chayefsky's *Marty*, of endless deferrals of sex, of the prospect of selling and reselling myself to women. I was in love with an attractive, intelligent Jewish girl who appeared to understand the tension between family values and journalistic excitements, who was obviously drawn to me, wishing only that I were two inches taller, a bit slimmer, and better paid. I pursued her relentlessly until she assented, in the spring. By June 1956 we were wed, at the Brooklyn Jewish Center on Eastern Parkway, whose cantor, as Tobi's mother emphasized, had once been the Metropolitan's tenor, Richard Tucker.

Fortunately, Manny Freedman, the foreign editor, had missed the announcements of our wedding in *The Times* and in its house organ. When Hungary exploded against Soviet domination in October and our Vienna bureau became a "listening post" for a restive Eastern Europe, Freedman thought himself lucky to have a German-speaking bachelor at hand to help out during the crisis. He found me ringing the doorbells of voters in northern Virginia, and I eagerly accepted his offer of "two or three weeks" in Vienna. But Tobi was braver than I. She chided Freedman for overlooking her, pleaded that *The Times* had already separated us for half our married life, and insisted on being sent along. Freedman protested that my assignment was only temporary, but she scorned his prediction. And because she won her point and won a leave of absence from editing textbooks for Macmillan, the months abroad turned into years, years of growth and unimagined adventure and professional achievements that were greatly enriched by Tobi's bold temperament and restless curiosity.

We flew in early November to the edge of a maelstrom, a storm of East European nationalism that proclaimed itself the unquenchable enemy of communism. Inspired by a newly assertive Poland, the people of Hungary bolted, in one fateful fortnight, from a Stalinist darkness into a fierce and blinding freedom. It was a portentous moment that foreshadowed the collapse of the Soviet empire three decades later. It taught me that tribalism and religious fervor are not always destructive, could in fact be a moral force for good. Yet in the end, moral values and Hungarian passions were made to yield to atomic imperatives, to the recognition by Americans that if conflict between East and West were not contained, and kept cold, it would consume the planet.

Americans at the scene felt a deep obligation to the Hungarians. For years, the CIA's broadcasts to Eastern Europe had kept alive the promise of "liberation." A boisterous Eisenhower administration came into office vowing to "roll back" communism in both Europe and Asia. But as Tobi and I were flying into Vienna's Schwechat Airport, Hungary's proud revolt was being crushed under the tread of Soviet tanks and abandoned by a mournful United States. Indeed, American and Soviet diplomats were at that same moment acting in ill-timed concert at the United Nations, bidding for favor throughout the Arab world by jointly compelling Israel, Britain, and France to retreat from their seizure of the Suez Canal from Egypt's charismatic Gamal Abdel Nasser.

Vienna that week was truly a "listening post." *The Times's* John MacCormac and Henry Giniger and dozens of other Western correspondents were risking their necks in the streets of Budapest to record the Soviet counterattack against rebels heaving Molotov cocktails. But a timorous American embassy, fearing that the Russians would cut its radio link to Washington, blithely appropriated the reporters' dispatches for its own reports to the White House and broke its promise to relay the stories to the newspapers for which they were written. Twirling radio dials around the clock in Vienna, we heard only the last gasps of Budapest's Radio Free Kossuth:

> This is the Union of Hungarian Writers! To every writer in the world . . . to the intelligentsia of the world: We ask all of you for help and support! There is but little time! You know the facts, there is no need to give you a special report. Help Hungary! Help the Hungarian writers, scientists, workers, peasants, and our intelligentsia!
> Help! Help! Help! . . . SOS! SOS! SOS!. . . .

Fittingly enough, the rebellion's last words were uttered by writers. Mere words, spoken earlier in 1956, had inspired the revolt—the remarkable words of the man emerging as Stalin's successor in the Kremlin, Nikita Khrushchev. He set out to rescue and reform communism by renouncing Stalinism. He thought he could legitimize its future, and his own, by shaking off the disgraceful past.

In three years of brilliant maneuver, starting the night of Stalin's death in 1953, Khrushchev had gained command of the Soviet Communist party and Red Army, disarmed the secret police, and freed millions of his citizens from Stalin's concentration camps. He spent 1955 becalming the Western powers and then, in February 1956, delivered a shocking "secret" speech to the Twentieth Party Congress in Moscow. Khrushchev recited an incomplete but chilling catalog of Stalin's crimes against Soviet society, emphasizing his crimes against the most devoted Communists, artists, scientists, and military elites, all of whom Khrushchev promised to "rehabilitate." And he blamed the obvious failures of Soviet industry and agriculture on Stalin's "cult of personality." By mocking the deification of his predecessor, he hoped to deflect blame from the Communist system, which alone sustained his own legitimacy.

Khrushchev's speech branded much of Soviet history a lie, Soviet law a sham, and Soviet theory a fraud. Alone among Stalin's henchmen, he confessed complicity in some of the horrors of the past. Most clearly among Stalin's heirs, he understood that terror could no longer hold the empire or stimulate a modern economy. Jet planes and radio broadcasts were penetrating the frontiers of totalitarian societies, bearing news and ideas of Western freedom and prosperity. Postwar industries needed an ever more educated, sophisticated workforce, not the slave labor that had once dug the mines and felled the forests of Siberia. "You can't whip people into paradise," Khrushchev declared.

Accounts of that sensational speech circulated around the world. To make sure they would reverberate in Communist societies, a text pronounced authentic by the Central Intelligence Agency was distributed in Washington. And its publication instantly discredited the Stalin clones who ruled Poland, Czechoslovakia, Hungary, Romania, and Bulgaria as Kremlin agents. They and their terror machines were promptly challenged by more moderate and patriotic Communists like Władisław Gomułka in Poland and Imre Nagy in Hungary, who were themselves survivors of Stalinist prisons.

Gomułka contained his people's restiveness and persuaded a panicked Khrushchev that he could keep Poland in "the socialist camp"—a vital corridor for the Soviet forces occupying East Germany. But Hungary's uprising, which started as a rally of support for Poland, spun swiftly out of control. Rebels who began by demanding Nagy's return to power propelled him, in just seven days, clear out of the Soviet orbit. They elicited his promise to create a multiparty democracy, to force the withdrawal of all Soviet troops, and even to renounce Hungary's military alliance with Moscow in favor of a new "neutrality."

A breakaway of such magnitude became a clear threat to Khrushchev's own hold on power. He never intended to yield control of the protective belt of countries that separated Russia from Germany, terrain that had been "liberated" in World War II at enormous cost in Russian blood. He stood for the moderation, not the liquidation, of Communist regimes. So at dawn on November 4, after flying through a storm to win the acquiescence of Yugoslavia's President Tito—then the most independent of Europe's Communists—Khrushchev sent his tanks to retake Budapest and other Hungarian cities. They routed the rebels in the streets, seized Nagy after luring him from the Yugoslav embassy with a promise of safe passage, and sent tens of thousands of Hungarians fleeing toward Austria.

I began my career abroad with no pretense of objectivity. I despised the Russians and sided passionately with their victims. No less than colleagues in Korea or World War II, I was a war correspondent tracking my side's progress against an enemy. I had no patience for any government's lies and propaganda, but I wrote unashamedly of and for "the free world," the half that did not censor its news or surround its populations with barbed wire.

At dawn the morning after my arrival in Vienna, Ben Welles, a *Times* colleague, drove me through Austria's frontier province of Burgenland, picking up the news that Prince Paul Esterhazy had been freed from the Hungarian prison to which he'd been condemned along with József Cardinal Mindszenty. When the rebellion collapsed, the cardinal took refuge—for the next fifteen years!—inside the American embassy, but the prince was smuggled out that week. An account of our futile search for him near his family castle in Eisenstadt, where Haydn once played, became my first overseas dispatch.

Every day for a week I returned to the frontier that had, alas, withstood America's threats of a "rollback." I watched the International Red Cross begging for safe passage for its convoys to carry $20 million worth of relief supplies contributed by guilty America. I wrote one sterile story after another: the convoys are in; no, they're stopped; they're back in business; they're off again. But I wrote with an unmistakable bias. All Americans in Vienna were ashamed of our impotence, shipping Band-Aids to a carnage.

Then one early morning an even stronger emotion seized me as I peered into a Hungarian fog across a *Schlagbaum*, one of those red-and-white barber-pole border barriers I had last encountered at the edge of another piece of European no-man's-land. This time, I carried a protective American passport, but I instantly recalled the helplessness of a stateless refugee as I watched thousands of people streaming across those bleak fields and out of Hungary. I made their plight my beat and used my *Times* dispatches to monitor the West's generosity in sending aid and opening doors. Some of my stories throbbed with autobiographical emotion:

SOME REFUGEES SWIM TO FREEDOM
Others Reach Austria Over Frozen Swamp
as Soviet Tank Shoots Down Span

ANDAU, Austria, Nov. 21—In Vienna they are refugee statistics. Here they are faceless shapes that trudge across the frozen swamp.

They come in groups of three and four, huddled against the cold and silhouetted against an amber harvest moon.

Their first taste of freedom is served up in plastic cups from what must be the most popular inn in Austria, a six-by-six wooden guard shack.

One slug of slivowitz to relieve the numbness, and the faceless shapes know they are now officially refugees.

As of 10 o'clock tonight, they were terrified refugees. Almost at once they talked of what happened at 4:40 this afternoon, when most of them lay pressed against frozen ground along the Einser Canal, a few hundred yards inside Hungary.

A Soviet tank rolled up to a bridge that crossed the canal, a bridge once obscure but now known all the way to Budapest as a bridge to freedom. The tank fired and the bridge collapsed.

Another bridge three miles to the east remained intact. Dozens of young men ventured again more deeply into the Soviet-patrolled terrain to try their luck. Others ripped off their clothes and waded and swam across. When they arrived here, the clothes they dragged along were starched with ice.

Once arrived, the refugees turned to the east and looked for other shapes. As each new group approached there was a wild shouting of names. Sometimes there were comradely hugs. Occasionally, a man and woman kissed.

As they waited, more stories poured out. "The Russkies" are clamping down. There are reports of shootings of refugees near the border. There are eyewitness accounts of arrests within sight of the headlight beams of a Volkswagen, which is the West's lighthouse in this swamp.

"Please radio my parents not to follow," cried a young student. "It's too dangerous. They'll never make it."

The next day I depicted the scene from Vienna:

AUSTRIA FLOODED WITH REFUGEES; PLEADS FOR HELP
Facilities Nearly Exhausted by 60,000 Hungarians—
6,000 Arrive in a Day

VIENNA, Nov. 22—Austria found herself today with an unmanageable and virtually uncountable number of refugees from Hungary.

Farsighted plans for their care have had to be abandoned. Makeshift solutions are proving inadequate. As coordination collapses, human problems are compounded.

I returned to Andau one more time to learn about the manhunts and shootings with which Soviet troops gradually closed the routes of escape.

This morning a woman came through the icy Einser Canal. Her two-month-old infant died in her arms last night while she lay pressed against snow-covered ground. . . . A student hobbled over the border with the help of two friends. His knee had been shattered by gunfire.

James Michener was there, too, asking questions for his fictional account of the revolution, which he called *The Bridge at Andau*. I bitterly resented his failure to acknowledge *The Times* article (or reporter) that caused him to focus his tale on that shattered span. Not even the idiotic egotists of the London tabloids, who would take one step across the border so as to write, "I spent two hours in Hungary this day," were so lacking in collegial manners. I resolved never to read a Michener novel.

One other visitor crossed my Burgenland beat to dip a toe into Hungary. Vice President Richard Nixon came to the border region and trotted awkwardly after puzzled Austrian peasants to thank them for their hospitality to the refugees. He kissed Hungarian babies as he delivered promises of more American visas. Commendably impressed with the relief efforts in Austria and West Germany, Nixon was also prophetically obsessed with the votes of a nation of refugees, past, present, and future. In his typically manipulative way, he stood at the border and pointed in the direction of Budapest until the photographers caught him just right. Then, on a train to Munich, he summarized his impressions for four reporters by artfully dividing them into two groups to assure himself of two sets of headlines. *Now fellas, that comment is for the A.M.'s, the morning papers*, he specified. *And this next comment will be for the P.M.'s.*

At the height of the Hungarian crisis, the Soviets expelled *The Times's* number-two man in Moscow, Welles Hangen, more for generally rude behavior than for the forbidden photography of which he was accused. Given the turmoil in Communist Europe, New York was desperate to replace him with a knowledgeable correspondent. The editors nominated Harrison Salisbury, our dean of Kremlinologists, but the Russians said *nyet. The Times* nominated Mike Handler and Hank Lieberman and others with a knowledge of communism, but Moscow rejected them all. To protect the size of their reciprocal press contingent in the United States, the Russians insisted each time that they were not denying *The Times's* right to a second reporter in Moscow. To test them, Freedman finally wired me in February 1957, while I was serving as a vacation replacement in Belgrade, to urge that I apply for a Soviet visa and consider going if it was granted. He thought it would take at least a month to get a reply.

Perhaps I had performed well enough in Austria to show some promise for such a vital posting. I had written well enough about the refugees and mastered the intricacies of American immigration law. But in six months, I had written only one sophisticated piece of genuine foreign correspondence, a "news analysis" of Austria's response to the crisis. It relied heavily on Tobi's shrewd observations of national character: the petty pricing that at the laundry differentiated between undershirts with short sleeves and without sleeves, or that charged extra for a postcard bearing too many words. I made a mark with that piece by producing a tone that was affectionately critical: "Even a foreigner must name all the parts of a car engine, in German, to get a driver's license, although no one seems to care whether a driver can recognize a pedestrian."

Still, I knew that when it came to Moscow, I was a choice of desperation, a Cold War neuter who probably lacked even a single entry in the KGB's files and who would finally test the Soviet promise of a two-man bureau. Freedman's call came just as I was writing home to my parents about my alarming ignorance of European politics and history, even in a place where I knew the language. "Every act of writing something enforces a discipline that quickly separates that little which you know from that which you don't. So here I am ending this first letter from Europe as I began it: telling you I don't know very much."

By the time of my next letter home, however, we were headed, more ignorantly still, for Moscow. We had hired a professor of Russian at the University of Vienna to teach us some basic vocabulary. The very day of our first lesson, the Soviet visas arrived. Grudgingly, New York gave us two weeks for an Italian holiday and a search for winter clothes.

Nothing suitable was available on Vienna's racks of ready-made clothing. Our colleague Elie Abel and the American ambassador, Llewellyn Thompson, urgently commended us to Adelbert Silhawy, a Hungarian tailor who featured the finest English fabrics and, for me, unprecedented prices. My three-piece suits, with extra lining at the chest and protective bindings at the pockets and cuffs, cost a week's wage, a horrendous $100 each. Never before had I paid three-digit prices for apparel. I protested bitterly to New York about this unavoidable luxury until finally *The Times* agreed to pay half the cost. I don't know how the company feels about its investment, but I was well served. I wore those suits—taken in a bit by the same Silhawy when I passed through Vienna seven years later—for twenty-six years.

Although fittingly dressed to represent America alongside Ambassador Thompson, who was also Moscow bound, I felt only outwardly prepared. Especially daunting was the prospect of dealing with Soviet censorship and a snooping secret police. I remembered how Mom and Pop had arranged to communicate past the Nazis who read their mail, giving political entities the names of fictitious relatives. In a letter home, I vowed to adopt the same code:

> You should know that Aunt Anna [the Soviet people] and Uncle Harry [the Soviet government] will now be resurrected from the correspondence you conducted among yourselves in the days of Uncle Adolf. The aunt and uncle will from time to time be variously described in our letters as thriving, depressed, rich, poor, good, or bad. . . . Whether Uncle Nikita resembles our Uncle Adolf or his own Uncle Iosef, we shall see. . . . Professionally, I am quite scared.

14 · THE DARK SIDE OF THE MOON

IT FELT LIKE A FLIGHT TO THE DARK SIDE OF THE MOON, far beyond the wire wall and wooden watchtowers and strips of sand that border guards raked each morning to find an escaping footprint. I was a lonely scout parachuting into the heart of a vast, hostile empire. Ten years had passed since Pop emerged from this forbidding land; almost twenty since the muddy villages where Mom and Pop were born had been wrenched from Poland and locked again inside the Russian shroud. And here I was, soaring freely across those locked borders, waving an American passport and an awesome press credential, come to hold the empire to account. And sort of settle a family score.

The year was 1957, the tenth year of what became a forty-year war. Though it was called the Cold War, the fears and passions that it generated were never cool. In the Southern Hemisphere, as old empires collapsed, the new conglomerates of East and West stirred ethnic strife to spread their domains. In the Northern Hemisphere, they fielded huge armies with ever more exotic, expensive weaponry. The war in Korea—which Americans called a police action to preserve the pretense of peace—had produced three years of combat and two of jousting and claimed nearly 4 million casualties, including 54,000 American dead and 103,000 wounded. The 100 million people of Eastern Europe—in Poland, Czechoslovakia, Hungary, Romania, Bulgaria, Estonia, Latvia, Lithuania, and Albania— were saddled with Communist tyrannies as oppressive as those already in place in Russia, Ukraine, Georgia, and the other "republics" of the Soviet Union. A paranoid Soviet oligarchy preached an irrational ideology to justify its exploitation of more than half the people of Europe. The Stalinist terror that Khrushchev had denounced wasn't the half of it.

A dozen years after Hitler's surrender, the Soviet and American armies still stood tank to tank in mid-Berlin, mid-Germany, and mid-Europe, stumbling into periodic "incidents" that enlivened their rehearsals for World War III. The western zone of Germany was being fed and refurbished by the United States to avoid breeding another Hitler and to add German muscle to the anti-Soviet alliance. Eastern Germany, by contrast, had been communized into a military buffer zone. The rival powers poisoned the air with tests of monstrous weapons. They mortgaged their economies to their armies. And they sustained the effort by preaching fear and hate.

I made no pretense of objectivity about the enemy. The Russians had sacrificed 20 million people to vanquish Hitler, yet the survivors seemed loyal to an even more pernicious tyranny. On Pop's testimony, they were capable of great kindness and generosity, and they were surely exhausted, weary of war. But victory had yielded them little, not even security, so they pushed their moats of sand and wire westward and enslaved millions more.

I came determined to record the brutalities of the Soviet regime. But I also came to discover ordinary Russians, whose loves and labors, dreams and anxieties belonged to the story of our time. Unadorned news about them had been rare in the West. At first, most American reporters had treated the Bolshevik revolution as not just a story but a cause. John Reed, the author of *Ten Days That Shook the World*, lay buried with honor in the Kremlin wall. And then in World War II, the American press was encouraged by our own government to celebrate the valiant Russian resistance, the Red Army, and "Uncle Joe" Stalin.

The New York Times's Walter Duranty, though no leftist, had been the most tendentious of all the prewar Moscow hands. A brilliant but callous self-promoter, Duranty invested his great reputation in energetic denials of the brutalities with which Stalin "collectivized" agriculture, inducing famine to kill off 7 million landowning peasants. Duranty employed so many elaborate sophistries to justify Stalin's purges that *The Times* finally caught on and eased him out of the paper and off the staff.*

Now, four years after Stalin's death, it was not sympathy for Communists but hostility toward them that colored everything. Most Western reporters in Moscow lived in well-policed foreign ghettos, were periodically denounced as spies, and were cut off from all normal contact with ordinary Russians. Their main occupation was to relay official Soviet proclamations and propaganda, into which they injected as much skepticism as the censors would allow. And their reports were supplemented back home by Soviet experts, like *The Times*'s Harry Schwartz, with openly antagonistic interpretations.

I came determined to break out of this sterile routine. I wanted to gather the shards of a shared humanity that our family had always detected, even in the worst places. I persuaded myself that I might actually help avert nuclear war by helping Russians and Americans to overcome their fears and to sublimate their rivalry in nonviolent competitions. Clifton Daniel had shown the way by producing some delightful accounts of daily life in Russia—making news even of a walk in a peasant market—until an ulcer forced him to quit the assignment after just a few months. William Jorden, who succeeded Daniel as Moscow bureau chief, tried from time to time to portray individual lives, but they were stilted stories and he was soon distracted by a collapsing marriage. At age twenty-seven, I was going to outdo not only my competitors in Moscow—at first a tiny band representing three wire services, the *Herald Tribune*, and the Baltimore *Sun*—but also the alumni and pundits who stood ready at home to second-guess every Moscow dispatch. I was going to illuminate this mysterious and menacing dark side of the moon and touch sensibilities that might tame the hatreds.

---

* When pressed fifty years later, *The Times* refused to renounce or "return" Duranty's Pulitzer Prize, telling critics that the misjudgment of his work was itself history that could not be undone. But a large asterisk adorns his portrait in the paper's gallery of Pulitzer winners, suggesting that he was probably unworthy of the honor.

15 · CENSOR, CENSOR ON THE WALL

A PORTENTOUS APRIL FOG FORCED OUR PLANE TO LAND first in Riga, the capital of an annexed Latvia then still closed to Western travelers. Tobi and I struggled down a wobbly stair to sip a lukewarm coffee in an ill-lit lounge. We seven passengers were soon outnumbered by an orchestra scratching out a succession of American pop tunes, and so the tension of this border crossing lifted sooner even than the fog. We danced. We were waltzing in Riga! The moment stays etched in my mind because it was here, only minutes after touching down on enemy soil, that a lovable Slavic slovenliness began to temper my fears of Soviet stringencies. As Pop had tried so often to explain, this Russia, no matter how brutally oppressive, would never attain the icy efficiency of Nazi Germany.

Our first Soviet home was charmingly seedy. We occupied a succession of rooms in the Metropol Hotel, trading up from a single to a room with alcove and finally to a suite. The hotel, facing the Bolshoi Theater and just two blocks from the Kremlin, was a barn of a place waiting for perestroika and Finnish millions before it could regain its czarist glory. Duranty had lived here a quarter century before, and the floors were still being waxed, as then, by a bristle brush strapped to the bare right foot of a gaunt and silent fellow skating through the halls. The clothes at the laundry were still pressed by a man who dampened the path of his iron with water noisily sprayed from his mouth. The hotel's chefs, as Art Buchwald would soon observe, had obviously all left immediately after the Bolshevik revolution in 1917; the waiters emigrated as soon as they took your order. A breakfast of tea and pumpernickel required the investment of at least an hour and a half. After a week of complaints to the management and bribes of our chambermaids, we were allowed to retain a few restaurant dishes and utensils so that we could prepare simple sandwiches in our room. A hot plate became our stove, the wardrobe our pantry, the toilet our garbage pail, the bathtub our dishwasher, and its wooden drip board our drying rack.

A mere stroll around the hotel presented a kaleidoscope of the old and new Russias. Out front, always, stood a knot of young men ogling the foreign cars at the curb and whispering "Dollar?" or "Fountain pen?" at their passengers. A few yards away, there labored a platoon of old ladies, each raking the sidewalk with a bundle of twigs tied to a broom handle. Beyond the weathered wall of the old Chinese quarter stood GUM, the glass-domed department store that faced the crenellated Kremlin and the candy-striped domes of St. Basil's Cathedral. The embalmed bodies of Lenin and Stalin lay at their feet.

Around the corner in the other direction stood the brooding hulk of Lubyanka, the headquarters and main torture chamber of the KGB. It faced the airy hulk of Moscow's newest building, Children's World, delivering the first installments of Khrushchev's promise of a wealth of consumer goods. Ill-mannered crowds surged along the streets past vendors who even in winter bore open trays of ice-cream cones. Acrobatic policemen twirled batons at major intersections to direct the modest stream of traffic, mainly flatbed trucks and Pobeda (Victory) taxis, all resembling 1939 Chevrolets. On the crowded sidewalks, foreigners were instantly recognized by the flair of the men's suits and the spiked heels of the women's shoes; if they spoke Russian badly, they might be mistaken as coming from annexed Latvia. The early American tourists amused themselves by searching out a smile in the sullen throng, bemoaning the misery of the population as if the urban crowds back home offered a panorama of joy.

We felt almost settled at the end of our second week when Turner Catledge, The Times's managing editor, paid a ten-day visit. He took Tobi on all his tourist tours of the capital, and she defied my deferential instincts by insisting that he interrupt his diplomatic luncheons and dinners with a Sunday brunch in our cramped room. With precious eggs borrowed from the *Herald Tribune*'s Carol Cutler and coffee imported from Copenhagen by CBS's Dan Schorr, we clearly impressed the boss. We never knew whether he was most affected by our storing the milk on the window ledge or by the sight of hundreds of Russians lined up at GUM to buy some eggs, but when he passed through Stockholm on the way home Catledge sent us a shiny rotisserie to replace the Russian hot plate and a huge refrigerator that was miraculously wedged through the door of Room 369 of the Metropol with half an inch to spare.

What really staggered our editor, however, was his encounter with Nikita Khrushchev and half the Soviet Presidium a mere ninety minutes after his arrival in Moscow. The ostentatiously collective Soviet leadership—they had changed the name of Stalin's Politburo to Presidium—began that very month to make a show of domestic harmony and foreign solicitude by appearing unheralded at virtually every embassy's "National Day" cocktail party. So there stood a baggy Khrushchev, wagging his finger at the Yugoslav ambassador and exposing the steel in his mouth to smile at his Japanese hosts. Across the room stood Anastas Mikoyan, the wily Armenian who had brought back *Yeskimo* ice cream from America and made himself the boss of consumer industries. In yet another corner, Vyacheslav Molotov, the stolid Stalinist, pretended that he approved of all this fraternizing.

I encountered the Soviet leaders on my third day in Moscow, while covering a diplomatic reception at the Polish embassy in honor of its visiting premier, Józef Cyrankiewicz. Khrushchev led half his Presidium into the ornate hall built by a czarist noble. He circled the room clinking glasses, with a special bow to America's ambassador, Llewellyn Thompson, and his vivacious wife, Jane. When he reached the guest of honor, he turned to make sure he had the attention of the ambassador and the American reporters and loudly warned Cyrankiewicz against accepting too much American aid.

"You are being wooed as a bride, but not because you are young," Khrushchev intoned. Then, more subtly, he issued a second warning to the Chinese, who were stoking Poland's bid for more independence from Moscow. "The Soviet Union is at least as good a friend to Poland as any other socialist country," he said.

"No, better," Mikoyan interjected.

"No, the same," Khrushchev insisted with mild annoyance.

"No, better," Mikoyan argued.

"You see," Khrushchev told the circle of American correspondents, "we have differences of opinion!"

That banal scene encapsuled the essence of my Moscow experience. Several times each month, the ruler of the Soviet empire exposed himself to scrutiny and interrogation by foreigners. He might banter aimlessly with the press corps, uttering cynical jests about conflict inside the Kremlin, or corner a diplomat to send a weighty message to the president of the United States. An exuberant patriot had succeeded the dark paranoid at the controls of the world's other nuclear arsenal, and he was eager to advertise the change.

I eventually encountered this man more often than any of his 200 million subjects. Over a period of three years, my only real Soviet acquaintances would be Nikita Khrushchev, a few of his fellow Presidium members, and a half dozen Muscovites who dared to defy the unrelenting warnings against contact with foreigners. Russia was not, as Winston Churchill famously declared at the start of World War II, a "riddle wrapped in a mystery inside an enigma." It was, in the succinct words of the previous American ambassador, Charles Bohlen, "just a secret."

We had no access to the vast bureaucracy of the ruling Communist party. Our contacts with the government were confined to the Press Department of the Ministry of Foreign Affairs and the occasional "press conferences" it staged to assail American policy or to boast of wheat and sugar harvests. Travel even to nominally "open" areas of the country required special permission, which the Press Department would obtain from the KGB after a delay of weeks, or months. Travel was attractive because it produced random encounters with Soviet citizens, but even these usually elicited some busybody's warning against CIA spies.

Our only unofficial Russian friends were a few curious and courageous souls who dared to stay in touch with Tobi, judging her to be at least once removed from espionage. Thanks to her rapid grasp of the language, she managed to sustain these trusting relationships, from which we pathetically squeezed some understanding of Russians' private lives.

Her first friend was Irina, an Intourist guide stationed at the Metropol Hotel. She gave us graphic accounts of the bureaucratic waste and corruption, compounded by the interference of the secret police. Zinovi Yuriev, a satirist at *Krokodil* magazine, risked irreverent evenings with us by stretching the license to fraternize possessed by his wife, Yelena, a translator for Reuters. Elsbeta Suritz, the daughter of a Soviet ambassador to Hitler's Germany, met us alone in public places; she wanted help in researching American ballet, but her husband could not cope with the tension of a meal in our company. Pavel Shikman, alias Paul, the translator for CBS's Dan Schorr and Paul Niven, did not really count as a native; as his speech made plain, he was Brooklyn-born and dragged back to Russia

Ancestral journeys more convulsive than any ocean crossing:
from Busk and Sokal in the east to Weissenfels in the west.

Mom and Pop, Marie Katz and Jakob Frankel,
after their engagement in 1927.

Biba in the first of his three innocent years.

Biba, Papa, and Opa Fränkel, three generations of merchants
three weeks before the Hitler storm in 1933.

First day, first grade, 1936.

A last portrait in Berlin, 1940.

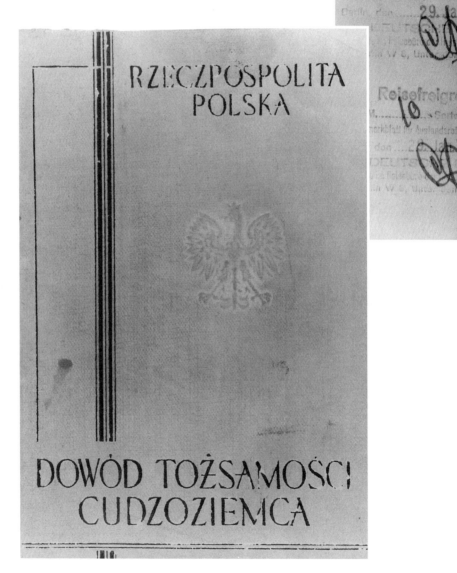

Mom's "stateless" passport and "Identity Card for Foreigners"
issued by the "Republic of Poland."

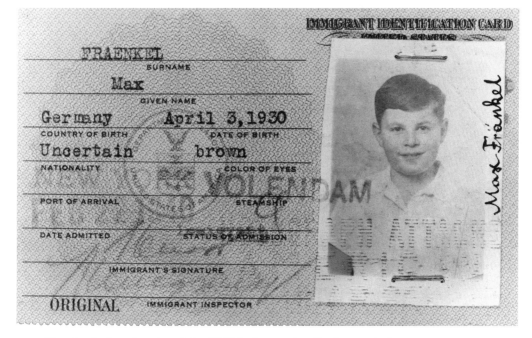

The precious exit visas from Nazi Germany for "Frau Maria" and "Child Mayer" (my Hebrew name), 1940.

First day in America, aboard the SS *Volendam*; nationality "uncertain."

Pop, when he finally reached the United States in 1946.

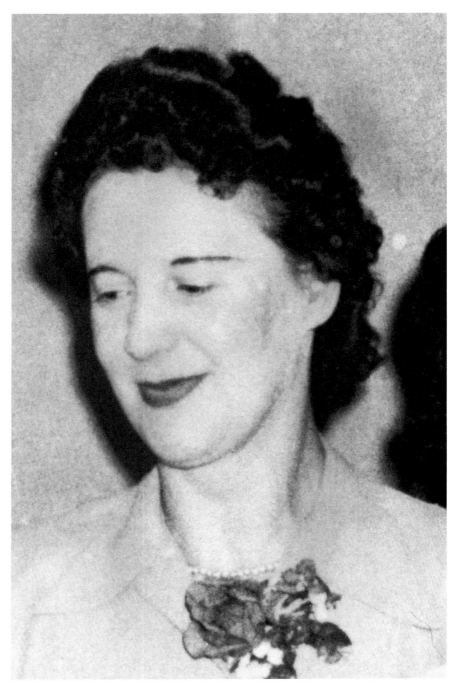

Elsie Herrmann, the teacher who taught reading through the excitement of writing.

An editor thrills at the touch of his first newspaper, the *Overtone* of New York's High School of Music & Art, in 1947.

The reporter, in regulation dress, at *The Columbia Daily Spectator* in 1951.

Corporal Frankel prepares to peddle atomic secrets, Camp Desert Rock, Nevada, 1955.

First dance with Tobia Brown Frankel, June 1956.

Mom and Pop at the wedding they never dared expect to see.

The Times's Rewrite Bank recording the SOS of a sinking *Andrea Doria*, 1956.
(Peter Whitney, The New York Times*)*

Leaving Vienna for the dark, Soviet side of the moon, 1957.

Hunting rare vegetables, and insights, at Moscow's peasant market, 1957.

in adolescence by parents who were sure that Stalin could run an economy better than Herbert Hoover. Paul had long since conquered the bitterness he felt about his fate. He had married a warm and hospitable Russian woman whose father was a card-carrying member of the Old Bolsheviks and was proud to share vivid tales of revolution, civil war, famine, purge, and Nazi invasion.

An entirely different view of Soviet society came to us through a young architect who designed the interiors of Soviet passenger jets. He met Tobi at a museum and shared a few afternoons in coffeehouses. But he stared clear through her one day when he and his mother found themselves next to us on a line to an exhibit of Czech glassware. Even in that shattering moment, of course, he was teaching us something about Soviet life. We learned months later that the KGB had thrown him off the Soviet delegation to the Paris air show and threatened, if he ever talked to us again, to cancel all his design commissions.

Only a few Soviet citizens had official sanction to work for us, and they were required to pay for the privilege by reporting regularly to the KGB. We were sure that Viktor, the office chauffeur, had to record all our movements when we were not directly followed around town. I realized that Svetlana, our translator, needed nuggets of information to secure her well-paid position when I caught her rifling through my dull correspondence with our New York office. Our only uncompromised and unlicensed "employee" was Stella Goz, who had served as translator for *The Times*'s Brooks Atkinson during World War II. She became our fervent teacher of Russian language and mores. An arthritic cripple, she felt immune to further punishment and revealed Soviet reality with a wicked tongue. Stella's family had taken her to Palestine after the 1917 revolution, but at twenty-one she had returned alone, like so many exiled children, "to help build the paradise." She married a pilot whose record-setting journeys, including one to Alaska, made him a national hero, but he was forced to abandon her during one of Stalin's anti-Semitic rages. Now, he occasionally brought her apples from his country dacha and shed tears of regret in her double-locked room. Stella lived in a typical communal apartment, where four families hung four toilet seats on the bathroom wall and brought their own matches to light the shared kitchen stove.

The rest of our social life was spent inside a cocoon of foreigners. Diplomats and correspondents lived in apartment blocks reserved for them, and those ghettos, "protected" by militiamen, were further segregated by ideology to separate Western foreigners from Communist and Third World foreigners. Only Henry Shapiro of the United Press and Edmund

Stevens, who contributed to *The Christian Science Monitor* (and formerly *Look*, *Life*, and *Newsday*), had real Russian neighbors. Both had married Russian women and were long held hostage by Stalin's refusal to let the wives depart. Now they were free to leave, but they must have made innumerable compromises with the authorities to ease their lives and had grown very deep roots. The Stevens's charming nineteenth-century log house near the Kremlin was the envy of every visitor, as was their daughter's enrollment in the Bolshoi Ballet school. The Shapiros lived among elite Muscovites in a spacious apartment that had been obtained for the United Press in the 1930s by Eugene Lyons, one of the many then sympathetic Americans in Moscow.

Our closest friends in the press corps were Dan Schorr and Bernie Cutler of the *New York Herald Tribune*, although both were more inclined than I to color their reports with Cold War polemics. Like passengers on a stormy voyage, we Americans felt drawn to one another, bonded by the hostility all around.

The American embassy let us shop in its commissary once a week for dry goods or leftovers from stocks shipped weekly from Helsinki. We also imported our own supplies of canned goods, wines, and spirits from Copenhagen; since the Russians generously charged duty only by the package or bottle, regardless of size, we favored restaurant-size cans of soup and three-foot-high display bottles of cognac and other liqueurs. But where possible, we fed off the local economy, paying extra at the peasant market for cucumbers and tomatoes in season and ordering gristly *bifstek* from GUM. Delicious breads and rich ice cream were always available in the state stores, but other produce appeared only randomly, advertised by a long line of shoppers. Many a time on our drive to the ballet or some diplomatic dinner, Tobi would shout "Stop!" to a taxi driver and dart across the street to fill the string basket that was always in her purse with a few precious oranges from Greece.

I did not match Tobi's persistence in studying Russian, concentrating instead on translations of the Soviet press. But I soon learned the sterile pidgin Russian that Soviet officials and journalists employed for political discourse. And I gave the impression of considerable fluency by rendering my limited vocabulary in authentic accents, slurring my endings to hide inevitable errors of grammar.

At work, I had to rely on Svetlana to spot politically significant essays in literary journals and to instruct me in the naughty dissent hidden in the plot of a new play or movie. She was generous with her explications so long as she found my interest in Soviet life to be genuinely curious rather than captious. The daughter of a high-ranking military man and the fiancée of a physicist engaged in some kind of secret work, she had an elite view of Russian society. Even so, she drove us to distraction with her typically submissive approach to all authority, a common trait that was always exacerbated by the double negatives so common to Russian idiom:

Comrade Ivanov, it's impossible, is it not, to get tickets to the play tonight? Slam. *He says it's not possible.*

No, Svetlana, you said it's impossible. He only said yes. Is it so hard to ask directly and make it harder for him to say no?

I don't understand.

———————

To improve my odds of encountering ordinary Russians, I filed endless requests at the Foreign Ministry to travel to allegedly "open" regions. These tended to be the major tourist centers that possessed reasonable accommodations and surplus cadres of KGB agents to keep track of us. Most of the country was off-limits, which made me a passionate advocate of reciprocal restraints on Soviet reporters in the United States. I held to this illiberal, unpopular view not because America had much to hide but because I wanted leverage to negotiate an occasional visit to forbidden Soviet terrain. I got to visit Yakutsk above the Arctic Circle in remotest Siberia, for example, by persuading the State Department to let a *Pravda* man into Detroit so he could wax poetic about our unemployed autoworkers.

I also badgered the Foreign Ministry for permission to visit kindergartens and colleges, factories and hospitals, anyplace where the tiresome boasts of new achievements might nonetheless offer a clue to how things really worked. Only a few of these requests were ever acknowledged; three years passed without an answer to my persistent plea to interview someone—any artist, musician, or writer—who could reliably define the approved Soviet aesthetic style called Socialist Realism. Responses usually came weeks late but with peremptory urgency. The phone might ring at noon, and Aleksandr Bessmertnykh, the meek-voiced English speaker at the ministry, was happy to report that the director of the Bolshoi Ballet would receive me this afternoon at four o'clock. Never mind that Khrushchev was that day threatening to expel the Western powers from Berlin, or offering a new proposal for "complete and general world disarmament." When Bessmertnykh called, you jetéed over to the Bolshoi, or packed for Tashkent. He had the right combination of intelligence and timidity to absorb our profane protests at the ministry's normal lack of cooperation. He went on to become a diplomatic star and genuine friend of America—first in the Foreign Ministry's America Department, then at the

Soviet embassy in Washington. Alas, in 1991, as Gorbachev's foreign minister, he momentarily entertained a request to join a plot against his boss and met the inevitable fate of a fence-sitter. He fell, in probably undeserved disgrace.

————

Normally, our search for news each morning began with a careful combing of the Soviet press, followed by frequent glances at the TASS wire in the afternoon and a hopeful search for the Khrushchev entourage at some embassy in the evening.

On the surface, the Soviet press dispensed only "good news"—remarkable harvest yields on the virgin lands of Kazakhstan, world-beating medical inventions in Leningrad, and unprecedented gratitude for Soviet aid in Indonesia. But behind the bluster and swagger, you could often discern some propaganda purpose from which you might infer some genuine problem or newsworthy discontinuity. Hadn't the Soviets been recently cool to Indonesia? Were they now displacing the Chinese Communists in Jakarta's affections? If the aid story in *Izvestia*, the government's organ, was followed later that week by an account of a military delegation's visit to Jakarta in *Krasnaya Zvesda*, the army paper, you could fairly safely take a leap of faith and piece together a story of considerable diplomatic consequence.

The first place to look each day for the most important news was the bottom of the last column of *Pravda*'s back page. That is where a single paragraph would announce the dismissal of a leading minister or high party functionary—"in connection with his transfer to other important duties" if he was still in good standing but without that fateful modifier if the man was departing in disgrace.

The back page checked, I would beg Svetlana to search the four inside pages for revealing feature articles and reviews that implied disfavor for some unfortunate writer or painter or gave colorful examples of the economy's creaks and groans. One of my favorite features dealt with the railway workers who earned huge bonuses for overfulfilling their "cargo quotas" by shipping empty freight cars back and forth across Siberia. Their quotas were reckoned in "cars hauled," not in the weight or value of the cars' contents, so they took to shipping barrels of water and finally perfected the fraud by shipping mere air. That silliness brought to mind another paper's disclosure about shoe factories whose productivity was measured only by the amount of leather they consumed; the bulkier the shoe, the greater the bonuses, even if the ugly product then languished on retail shelves. If the stores refused the ugly ducks, they would be denied a commensurate delivery of more attractive sandals. Mix and match such anecdotes, stir and heat slowly with some shrewd conjecture, and you had a yeasty yarn about the stultifying effect of Soviet central planning and resource allocation.

Besides studying Russian grammar and the vocabulary of Soviet politics, I also had to master the semaphoric codes by which the Soviet leaders communicated with Communists the world over—without truly informing the Russian man in the street. One of the simplest of these signals was the word *odnoko*—meaning "however"—which invariably appeared halfway down the page of an otherwise impenetrable treatise on forestry or oil production. *As is well known,* the article might begin, *owing to the wise and disciplined leadership of the Communist Party, our nation's glorious laboring class has, since the Great October Revolution, increased the per capita output of oil by 1,600 percent.* The article would celebrate this great advance paragraph by paragraph, until even the most patriotic reader could be expected to have tuned out. Only the cognoscenti would have known to run their eyes quickly over the page to the paragraph beginning *"Odnoko"* to learn that *However, the unfortunate failure to supply the Baku region with spare parts for its derricks last month threatened a woeful oil shortage that requires, starting immediately, severe rationing of gasoline throughout the country.*

Oh, how we chased the *howevers*! Every success or failure of the Soviet economic system was news now in the United States, of interest not just to university scholars and government analysts but to all alert citizens. The Cold War's competitions in productivity were as earnest as those in ideology and taken as seriously as the competitions in rocketry, basketball, and high jump. Hardly a day passed that the Moscow bureau did not land on Page One with such humdrum headlines as these:

SOVIET REVISING BONUSES TO REWARD COST CUTTING

**SOVIET PARTY ORDERS TIGHTENED CONTROLS
OVER THE COLLECTIVES**

**KHRUSHCHEV CHIDES A TOP AIDE FOR CONCEALING
FARM FAILURES**

MOSCOW DEMANDS NEW PROPAGANDA TO SPUR IDEOLOGY

Our readings of the Soviet press closely resembled the reading of tea leaves. Genuine Chinese tea leaves yielded the richest harvest of all: the unfolding story of the triumph of nationalism over communism, the shattering of the Communist commonwealth. Tobi and I had stupidly dismissed the first omens of the Sino-Soviet rift when we noticed the disappearance of Chinese artifacts from Moscow's International Book Store and the absence of China's Russian-language propaganda magazine at the hotel newsstand. Then, in mid-1958, we literally sat atop one of the century's great scoops and neglected to notice.

After eighteen months of pleading, and because the Soviets now needed every hotel room for a burgeoning tourist trade, we finally obtained an apartment large enough to house both us and *The Times*'s office. We were assigned not to a "Western" compound but to a cluster of buildings reserved for foreign Communists, out near the Riga Railroad Station on Prospekt Mira. Our sunny top-floor living room was double the normal size because, someone said, it had served as a mess hall for a commune of Chinese students. Those students, we eventually reasoned, must have been sent packing as relations between Moscow and Beijing deteriorated. We were the direct beneficiaries of the Sino-Soviet conflict and didn't have a clue. Only our ground-floor concierge, knitting beside the elevator like Madame Defarge, betrayed a hint of the Russian anxiety that surely underlay the breach. *Mad,* she'd say. *All mad. They used to appear half naked in the courtyard before dawn every day for calisthenics, even at twenty below! What kind of people are these Chinese?*

I did begin to report the friction when a long-planned international conference of orientalists attracted Asian scholars from all the world but none from China. Then I reported that Moscow's foreign policy pronouncements were no longer being issued in the name of "the Soviet Union, People's China, and the other nations of the Great Socialist Camp" but only "the Warsaw Treaty nations," meaning Communist Europe. And while Khrushchev continued, even in periods of East-West tension, to stress the importance of avoiding nuclear war, the Chinese were denouncing "those who exaggerate the consequences of the devastations" of war. As we learned years later, while Khrushchev had secretly ordered his diplomats and soldiers never to risk a military clash with Americans, the Chinese argued glibly that a superior Communist civilization would rise "on the debris of dead imperialism." Years passed before America's leaders, who lacked our faith in Kremlinological divination, accepted the evidence of the breach, a feud that eventually produced open competitions for influence in all parts of the world and even a few armed clashes along the Sino-Soviet frontier.

We burrowed for important news not only between the lines in

Pravda but, more absurdly still, among the portraits of Soviet leaders hung on holidays from the facades of Moscow's main buildings. If Pervukhin's mug hung closer to Khrushchev's than Saburov's, and the array of portraits was neither alphabetical nor somehow chronological, then Saburov was really on the skids. All Soviet displays of prestige and power had iconographic significance, especially those bearing on the Kremlin pecking order.

The pecking order was dramatically scrambled when a majority of the Presidium—all survivors of Stalin's purges—"voted" one day to dismiss Khrushchev as first secretary. But Khrushchev, invoking a broader "democracy," insisted on a vote by the party's full Central Committee, which he had stocked with his allies. Marshal Zhukov, the liberator of Berlin and Eisenhower's pal from World War II, provided the planes that assembled just enough loyal committee members to defeat the purge. Having observed only an ominous flow of black Chaika limousines around the Kremlin, we awoke one morning to Khrushchev's condemnation of the plotters—an "anti-Party group" led by Molotov, Malenkov, and Kaganovich—and a whole new (alphabetical!) display of Presidium portraits in *Pravda*, among them a beaming, bemedaled Marshal Zhukov.

The upheaval not only scrambled the Soviet hierarchy but also marked the beginning of a startling, humanizing turn in Soviet political life. For this was the first major purge of party luminaries that did not end in their execution.

At his very next embassy outing, an ebullient Khrushchev sought out the Western correspondents to assure us that his defeated opponents were "alive and well" and would soon be given employment for which they were "qualified." Indeed, their fate, though never revealed to the Russian public, had a comic dimension: Molotov, the Old Bolshevik who had traveled the world as Stalin's foreign minister, became Soviet ambassador to landlocked Outer Mongolia; Malenkov, an electrical engineer and once Stalin's designated heir, was assigned to tend a remote electric power station; Kaganovich, the scourge of Russia's peasantry and master builder of Moscow's subway, was sent to run a cement factory. Together with the release of most political prisoners from Siberian labor camps, these soft landings for Stalin's henchmen began to lift the heavy hand of terror from Soviet politics. Paradoxically, that emboldened a new generation of dissidents to challenge the party's authority and defy its orders.

To take full advantage of our embassy encounters with the Soviet leaders, the two dozen Western reporters in Moscow formed a rare alliance that must have confirmed the Russians' darkest suspicions about our CIA affiliations. Instead of all crowding rudely around Khrushchev and missing a chance to also interview Zhukov or Kozlov or Brezhnev, we agreed to go with the social flow and to reassemble after each party at the Central Telegraph on Gorky Street to pool our quotes for dispatch at a designated time. Most of us could be found at the Central Telegraph's foreign annex on other nights as well, because that is where we were required to let Soviet censors read every word we wrote.

I never met the censors. They were employees of *Glavlit*—the "Main-Lit" Agency that also monitored domestic Soviet publications. They sat behind a curtained glass door through which sleepy women condemned to twenty-four-hour shifts would carry our typed copy. Articles destined for cable transmission would be surgically but not always logically stripped of unflattering comments about Soviet life or whole paragraphs about Kremlin discord. Carbon copies were returned with faithful indications of all excisions so that repairs or even kill orders could be sent to our editors. Soon after my arrival, we gained permission also to read our dispatches to recording rooms in New York or London; the phone line was instantly cut if we were caught straying from the approved manuscript. Composing artful sentences from which negatives could be slurringly omitted during dictation became just another of the special talents needed for a successful Moscow career.

WRITE: There appeared to be no dissent from the premier's policy; none was reported by the Soviet press.

BUT DICTATE: There appeared to bemuchdissent from the premier's policy, yet none was reported by the Soviet press.

The censors' threshold of permissible criticism of Soviet life and politics shifted from night to night, and protecting the Soviet leaders was their main concern. The only correspondent ever expelled for eluding censorship was Roy Essoyan of the Associated Press. He once telephoned some speculation about an apparent diminution in Khrushchev's power, and Joe Alsop leapt to the false conclusion that the dispatch had passed the censorship and therefore signaled Khrushchev's imminent demise. Expelling Roy for bypassing the censor became the most effective way to get back at both men and to rebut Alsop's contention.

On other subjects, the censors were merely careful and petty. Articles based on reports in the Soviet press, even if highly unflattering to Soviet society, were routinely cleared. Dispatches based on less authoritative sources might be delayed for hours, even days, before passing virtually untouched. The censors obviously felt safer when given time to consult higher authority. Even Khrushchev's crude banter at an embassy party would be held up for hours until we took the hint and conveyed his meaning in more polite paraphrase.

Censorship at the sources of information was much more serious. On the rare occasions that I learned from travelers about food riots, wage strikes, or desecrations of synagogues in distant cities, I had to find a tourist to mail the facts to *The Times* for publication as an unspecified "report" from Moscow. Submitting such embarrassing news to the censor's certain veto would have made it unusable in any other way.

When time allowed, I tried appealing the censors' rulings by sending explanatory notes through the curtained door and took childish pleasure from a rare success. Denied permission one year to call the May Day parade a "charade" of civilian support for the Soviet leaders, I persuaded the censors to check the dictionary to satisfy themselves that *charade* was not a pejorative but rather a parlor game in which ideas and slogans are acted out in pantomime, just as the adoring crowds had done in their trek through Red Square.

Our circumlocutions often made us the censor's secret ally, pulling punches and avoiding sensitive subjects altogether. It was a Faustian bargain: to give the readers some close-up views of Soviet society, we had to withhold others. By and large, I felt I was reporting truthfully, to the limits of my available information. The tyranny of the censor sharpened my wits and my prose even as it deepened my bitterness toward the Soviet system. Journalism schools could do worse than teach "Writing Through Censorship" to hone the wits if not the prose of their students.

When I became the first American since World War II to be allowed to travel to Riga, I obviously could not write directly about the oppressive dominance of ethnic Russians over the native Latvians. But I could describe a factory where "in charge of production are Soviet men who impress the visitor as diligent and capable custodians of Moscow's trust." And as the first American allowed back into Lvov—Pop's old stamping ground, Lwów now Russified—I could not directly describe the bitter life of the few surviving Jews. But I could write that a Jewish woman cited the fables of Sholom Aleichem to describe her "comfortable" life, saying: "I don't mind your calling me a pot as long as you don't put me in the oven."

More direct sarcasm also worked in some circumstances. Describing

the Soviet airline for our Travel section, I had no censorship trouble with
passages like these:

> It is not true that Russian planes do not have seat belts. Most planes, even on domestic milk runs, have at least one or two sets, and the diligent passenger usually can find them before his trip is over. . . . It is not true, either, that Russian propeller-driven planes fly just over the tree tops. . . . When really bad weather threatens, the pilots climb high indeed, and the passenger, as he wrestles with his oxygen mask, quickly understands why he was flying low in the first place.

My most elegant construct to evade the censorship came at the end of a
two-week tour of Siberia, during which I passed through Birobidzhan.
Stalin had exiled a great many Russian Jews to that bleak Far East territory
in the 1930s in cynical reprisal for their Zionist desire to emigrate to
Palestine. Most younger Jews had long since abandoned the territory,
which was never much more than a penal colony dressed up with Yiddish
street signs, a Yiddish-language *Emes*—meaning "Truth," or "Pravda"—
and a few restaurants serving gefilte fish and *krem sodà*. After observing
these faint ethnic traces, I wrote that the Jewish Autonomous Region was
"about as Jewish as it was autonomous." To my continuing satisfaction,
the censor swiftly approved.

Only once, however, did a censor actually assist me in analyzing an
event—an event that one of my stories had unwittingly anticipated. The
subject was Marshal Zhukov, the minister of defense and savior of Nikita
Khrushchev. I had unexpectedly spotted him in Leningrad in July 1957,
cruising down the Neva River on Navy Day. He was waving from a white
launch at the head of a long parade of gray warships and was cheered from
the riverbanks by an idolatrous crowd of thousands. "Hundreds," I wrote,
"many with children on their shoulders, pushed through the throng, running and stumbling after his vessel for a second and third look at the
beaming military hero." There being little other news that Sunday, *The
Times* put the story on Page One and stimulated speculation among the
Kremlinologists back home, including our own Harry Schwartz, that this
newest member of the Presidium must be rising rapidly, achieving "unprecedented stature" for a Soviet military figure.

All this had registered in our minds when, three months later, Zhukov
returned from a routine visit to Yugoslavia to be greeted most unnaturally
by just a few military officers and no party or Presidium leaders. That fact
was buried in an account of his travels, but it was followed by one of those

ominous back-page paragraphs saying Zhukov had been "relieved" as minister of defense. There was no ameliorating reference about any "transfer to other important duties."

I was sure the general had fallen out of favor, but the entire corps of uncensored Communist correspondents told the world that a special plenum of the Central Committee had been convened "apparently to elevate Zhukov" to the prestigious position of head of state. The London *Daily Worker* said a promotion was imminent, and *Humanité* in Paris and *Unità* in Rome were even more confident. And sure enough, we all soon spotted the telltale black limousines around the Kremlin. *The Times*'s editors grew angrily impatient with my studiously noncommittal dispatches. I was writing that Zhukov had attained great prestige but perhaps also too much personal popularity "for the comfort of the Communist party leadership."

When another day passed without any further announcement, Harrison Salisbury, our preeminent former Moscow correspondent, berated me for resisting the conclusion of the world's Communist press about Zhukov's elevation. He said *The Times* could not afford to miss this possible dawn of a Soviet military dictatorship. If I demurred, Salisbury might write the story himself.

Angry but determined, I began to write yet another story sticking strictly to the known facts and preparing for telephone combat in its defense: "The fate of Marshal Georgi K. Zhukov, the hero of Berlin, was still not known here tonight. . . ." In a hurry to signal my intentions to New York, I sent that innocent sentence to the censor and was shocked, less than a minute later, to be summoned to retrieve the page. It bore a stamp of approval and only one minor change: the word "hero" was stricken.

Triumphantly, I rewrote the opening, waxing eloquent about the apparent disgrace of this "former hero" and assuring New York that I, perhaps alone among correspondents, now knew whereof I wrote. Someone nonetheless dampened down my prose and continued to give annoying credence to the Red rags in Western Europe. But at least I commanded a headline reading ZHUKOV REMOVAL SEEN IN MOSCOW AS DOWNGRADING. Note the "in Moscow"! Here I had the hated censor as my undisclosable but unimpeachable source, and still the "experts" at home withheld the last ounce of trust from their correspondent. An obviously infuriating experience. More than most Americans, I had learned that you could sometimes "do business" with the Communists, even their most despised agents. More memorably still, I had also learned that experts, too, can behave like censors.

16 · GHOSTS, GOULASH, AND SPUTNIK

ILYA EHRENBURG CALLED IT THE TIME OF "THE THAW"—
an unmistakable relaxation of the domestic tyranny and
opening of the dikes to foreign influence. Khrushchev's bold assault on Stalin released long-frozen energies, thoughts, and ambitions. And despite their rhetoric of hostility, the two biggest
powers to emerge from World War II were fitfully reconciling
themselves to a sharing of the planet, groping to contain the
threat of nuclear destruction.

One great question hung heavy over all our reporting from
Moscow: Could Americans trust these Soviet calls for coexis-
tence or were the Kremlin leaders hell-bent on communizing
the world? Although the Soviet Union and America had been allies in war and had no major claims on each other, their postwar
rivalry had sealed off minds as well as borders. A corrosive fear
festered in our mutual ignorance. If Russians had experienced
another famine in 1957, most Americans would have felt more
satisfaction than sympathy; they'd have gloated about the superiority of our capitalism. And if another depression had thrown

tens of millions of Americans out of work, Russians would have felt vindicated in their Faustian exchange of liberty for porridge; though poor and oppressed, they were, after all, cared for and minimally secure.

I arrived in Moscow full of contempt for the regimentations and dysfunctions of Soviet society and made no secret of my feelings. But I yearned to rise above the sterile propaganda wars. On May Day morning soon after my arrival, I saw the Kremlin bosses arrayed atop the tomb of Lenin and Stalin in Red Square, presiding over a fearsome parade of goose-stepping troops and hordes of submissive civilians. By nightfall, however, I encountered throngs of the same people strolling through the cobbled plaza, hungering to learn about the cost of a car in America, obviously weary of war and terror and yearning to make a better life for their kids.

A costly face-lift was preparing the Soviet capital for that summer's World Youth Festival and for the "cultural exchanges" that Khrushchev had negotiated with dozens of governments. The United States and the Soviet Union had begun to trade tourists—well-guarded "delegations" of Russians, each of whom had to leave a spouse at home as hostage, in exchange for rich Americans, most of whom forgave the hotel discomforts for the right to boast that they had penetrated the "Iron Curtain." In this traffic of exhibits, performers, and scientists, Americans slyly hoped to spread democratic values while the Soviets hoped to gain technological know-how.

Sol Hurok, the Russian-born impresario who managed most of the traffic in the performing arts, loved to throw his protective cape around Tobi and me, ply us with caviar in his suite facing the Kremlin, and whisper a wealth of gossip about intrigues at the Ministry of Culture and about the sprees to Bloomingdale's to which he treated the Bolshoi ballerinas. Visiting Americans spoke admiringly of the sounds produced by Russian orchestras with inadequate bows and reeds. American students at Moscow U told wild tales of Russian youth lusting to trade dormitory sex for jazz and pop recordings. I might be treated by day to a diatribe by Khrushchev against American militarists, but by evening I'd see him embracing a gangly Van Cliburn.

Cliburn's romantic renderings of Russian music at the first Tchaikovsky piano competition made him an instant idol of Russian audiences, but even such a wordless musical event was freighted with political and journalistic significance. The Soviet public celebrated Cliburn not only for his artistry but for his nationality; affection for him was a safe expression of affection for America. My account of his rapturous reception landed on the front page of *The Times* two days *before* Van was crowned the contest winner because I posed the obvious question of whether Soviet authorities would let an American beat out the finest Russian contestants. We now know that Khrushchev personally approved Cliburn's victory, making Van a hero at home and a symbol of a new maturity in relations between the two societies.

My Cliburn stories also affirmed *The Times*'s heady influence on Soviet-American relations. They made the pianist a star in the American media and inspired New York to prepare a ticker-tape parade for his homecoming. For the rest of the Cold War, the most famous living Americans in the Soviet Union were neither politicians nor capitalists. They were Van Cliburn and Willis Conover, who presented swing and jazz in nightly transmissions of the Voice of America.

The cultural exchanges brought a stream of prominent Americans to our home. Visitors like Leonard Bernstein, Arthur Schlesinger, Jr., Alfred Kazin, and Harold Prince came for unofficial briefings about Soviet politics and a few hours of unguarded conversation. Could they trust their interpreters? Was it safe to give dollars as gifts and to leave behind their American magazines and novels in dressing rooms? Where could they find more American cigarettes? Whom could they lobby to bring *West Side Story* to Moscow?

Every scrap of knowledge I had ever accumulated turned out to be helpful in covering this colorful beat. I could not have felt Moscow's excitement when Bernstein defied an official ban to perform *The Rite of Spring* if Sol Cohen had not filled my North Carolina evenings with Stravinsky's dissonances. I could not have understood the threat of modern art to Communist ideology if I had not studied the assaults on realism at the end of the last century. I would never have grasped Russians' vulnerability to Communist propaganda if I had not myself succumbed so easily to the U.S. Army's indoctrinations. I finally comprehended the "democratic centralism" of the Communist system when I recalled Mr. Graham's blackboard renderings of America's corporate "democracy" in which citizen-stockholders are allowed to "elect" slates of handpicked directors and, although celebrated as "owners," forced to accept policies decreed at the top.

The man at the top in my three years in Moscow turned out to be one of the most energetic and entertaining politicians of the century. Squat, paunchy, and steely eyed, Nikita Khrushchev sprang from the circle of Stalin's henchmen to rule with a peasant's wit, cunning, and vigor. Rash and belligerent, he struggled to lead a long-suffering people out of slavery and toward the Marxist promise of prosperity. He really believed that he could reform and rescue the Communist system by exorcising the ghosts of Stalin, serving goulash to his people, and turning sputniks into swords. I felt stimulated by his spectacular ambitions. And behind his mask of bluster, I thought I saw a face of decency.

GHOSTS

The Soviet Union at age forty was spooked by the ghosts embalmed in Red Square. Lenin bequeathed an ideology that made a lie of the past and a myth of the future. The regime he founded pretended to be a "dictatorship of the proletariat" and claimed to be evolving into a communal paradise of selfless, superior "new Soviet beings." Stalin braided these fictions into a totalitarian order that enslaved an empire and sacrificed even his most faithful servants. Whereas Hitler fed on the hate produced by economic collapse, humiliation in war, and domination by foreigners, Lenin and Stalin plied their people with an opiate, the promise of a distant Eden of inhuman innocence.

I could understand the Russians' fear of invasion along the routes that Napoleon and Hitler had followed to the outskirts of Moscow. I could understand a peasant nation's fascination with the technological triumphs of a forced industrialization. (*Don't shop with that straw basket, like a peasant,* the women would whisper to Tobi in the market; *a lady like you should have plastic!*) But I never understood how anyone could accept the promise of a "pure communism"—a time when no one would have to be paid to work, when no one would possess more than anyone else, and when the oppressive machinery of state would wither away. Every Russian child could see that where there was no property there was only poverty; things that belonged to everyone were tended by no one. Certainly Khrushchev saw as much and acted on his insight.

Slave labor could chop timber, mine coal, and erect dams, but only a creative and educated population could invent computers and manage robots. People might believe communist fairy tales, but they would work hard only if stimulated by incentives; there was no point even in paying workers well if their wages bought nothing worthwhile. Instead of resisting his people's admiration for American materialism, Khrushchev challenged them to "overtake America," starting with meat, milk, and butter production.

But Khrushchev's predicament did not yield easily to his slogans. He could afford to exorcise only half a ghost. To preserve the Communist regime and his place atop the party, he could denounce only Stalin's methods and "personality cult," not the system that had propelled them both to power. Khrushchev invented a new mythology featuring two Stalins—the master builder as well as the paranoid monster. And calibrating the twin images of Stalin quickly became a major Soviet industry. Whatever the issue of the day—whether to tighten controls on the secret police or to limit the spending of the military—conservatives would express their opinions by recalling Stalin as more good than bad whereas reformers would remember him as more bad than good. I could tell that one of Khrushchev's reforms was in trouble whenever he softened his portrait of Stalin from "criminal" to "tragic." I could feel another thaw in the wind with every discovery of a new Stalin flaw. Eventually, the struggle turned on the corpse itself: whether to remove Stalin's embalmed remains from the Red Square mausoleum. People joked that Khrushchev rejected Israel's generous offer to take the cadaver; he did not want to risk reburial in "the soil of the Resurrection."

Artists and writers also wrestled with Stalin's ghost. They fashioned images and memories of the dead tyrant to test the bounds of permissible criticism and dissent, confronting Khrushchev with impossible choices. He wanted writers to address social issues in ways that stimulated thought and creativity, but he drew the line at anything that undermined the party's authority. Vladimir Dudintsev's *Not by Bread Alone*, a novel about the party's stifling of a young inventor's ideas, was too much to swallow; its publication abroad and popularity underground caused the Kremlin to extract a hasty "confession of error" from the author. Yet not long after, Khrushchev personally approved publication of *One Day in the Life of Ivan Denisovich*, a searing portrait of a Stalinist concentration camp, thus arming the author, Aleksandr Solzhenitsyn, with a worldwide fame that he exploited brilliantly to excoriate the whole Soviet structure.

Spotting political trends in philosophical treatises and literary polemics became a special branch of our journalism: Kremlinology. When the military journals produced a stream of memoirs recalling Stalin's "morale-building" exhortations in World War II, we could surmise a bitter struggle between military commanders and the political commissars hovering over them in every unit. When the great Dmitri Shostakovich suddenly humbled himself to rail against "alien jazz" and composed an operetta glorifying Khrushchev's housing projects, we could be sure the composer was doing business with party apparatchiks—earning apology for Stalinist persecution and approval to perform his serious new compositions.

Kremlinology supplied the key to a fascinating paradox: Khrushchev was wielding Stalin's authority to dismantle Stalin's tyranny. Not until a decade later, in his memoirs, did Khrushchev admit the reason, as we had deduced, for the wild gyrations of policy. "We were scared," he wrote. "We were afraid the thaw might unleash a flood, which we wouldn't be able to control and which could drown us." The retired Khrushchev was particularly sorry that he kept the Soviet people locked inside their borders. He called travel restraints a "disgraceful heritage that lies like a chain on the consciousness of the Soviet state." His explanation was that "Stalin was still belching inside me."

Oh, how he belched! One notable day, Khrushchev appeared at the Manezh, the czar's old stable beside the Kremlin, to condemn the display of abstract paintings that he himself had approved a few days earlier:

> Those messy yellow lines, they look, if you will excuse me, as though some child had done his business on the canvas when his mother was away and then spread it around with his hands. . . . When I hear jazz, it's as if I had gas on the stomach. . . . Or take these new dances: you wiggle a certain section of the anatomy; it's indecent. . . . We should take down your pants and set you down in a clump of nettles until you understand your mistakes.

Anywhere else, such fulminations by a politician would be merely amusing appeals to primitive taste—Quayleries about *Murphy Brown*. In Moscow, they were desperate attempts to affirm the party's papal authority. Every hint of dissent engaged the highest leaders because every heresy inevitably inspired another. As the minutes of Presidium meetings revealed a generation later, the fate of even a single writer inspired agonizing debates over many months, even years.

I played a modest part in the most intense of those struggles, over Boris Pasternak and his epic novel *Doctor Zhivago*, which recounted the dreams and betrayals of the Bolshevik revolution. Pasternak's basic theme was not unsympathetic to Khrushchev's line: Russia had endured a brutal yet necessary upheaval, but the revolution had devoured too many of its own children. But the book's anti-Soviet overtones aroused the party's censors, and they prevailed on Khrushchev to block its publication. So Pasternak slyly consigned the manuscript to an Italian publisher, a major contributor to the increasingly liberal Italian Communist party.

In December 1957, before most Russians ever heard of *Zhivago*, Pasternak received me at his dacha outside Moscow to express a ritual "regret" over the excitement the book had stirred abroad. Despite his ascetic manner, however, he was acerbic about party dogma. "You know I am not a Socialist Realist, but I am grateful to Socialist Realism," he remarked, "for it has made me a realist!"

With equal sarcasm, Pasternak recalled his agreement to let the party help him "improve" the novel with a few cuts. It had assigned a "young and enthusiastic Communist" to the task, but nothing they jointly proposed satisfied the censors. Wasn't it amusing how some of the "mountains of gold" now being earned by this book in the West would be donated to Togliatti, the Italian Communist leader, who had belatedly joined the campaign to denounce its publication? Since I had not yet read the book, Pasternak gave me his own haunting summary of its subversive theme:

That the Marxist revolution in the Soviet Union has served its purpose and made great contributions to history and that a new epoch, a new era, is being born in silence, being born and growing like grass, like plants, all around; it is being born in children and in everything else; it will not be proclaimed, but it is coming, evolving.

Almost a year later, *The Times* heard rumors that Pasternak had won the Nobel Prize in literature, and I rushed back to his dacha to give him the news. This time he was festively surrounded by friends, scientists, and teachers, who exchanged seditious comments at such a pace that I had to keep running to the toilet to take furtive notes. Reinforced by the warm praise for *Zhivago* from Albert Camus, François Mauriac, Thomas Merton, and many other writers, Pasternak now had a much bolder explanation for its wide appeal. It recounted a society's "mythological passage," he said, reciting a drama that was "this century's *Faust*":

This book is the product of an incredible time. All around, you could not believe it, young men and women were being sacrificed up to the worship of this ox. . . . It was what I saw all around that I was forced to write. I was afraid only that I would not be able to complete it.

My censors held up those comments until after the prize was announced and a posse of hack writers had begun to heap venomous insults upon the author. They called *Zhivago* an "artistically squalid, malicious work replete with hatred of socialism." Pasternak "joyfully" announced acceptance of the prize, but he was vilified for taking the West's "thirty pieces of silver." The Moscow Union of Writers called him a "pig who dirtied his own pen" and urged that he be stripped of citizenship and expelled.

The inquisition took its toll. Like many other Russian artists, Pasternak dreaded exile and begged to live out his years among the birches of suburban Moscow. He would forgo the Nobel Prize, he told Khrushchev. "Leaving my country is tantamount to death for me, and I therefore ask you not to apply this extreme measure." He again offered a disingenuous "regret" that the novel had been read as an attack on the Soviet system.

Fifteen years later, it was Khrushchev's turn to utter regrets. He was ashamed to recall siding with the men who eventually overthrew him, resuscitated the KGB, and halted the de-Stalinization campaign. He had had enough support to allow *Zhivago* to be published, Khrushchev recalled. "But I did nothing and now I regret it. When dealing with creative minds, administrative measures are always most destructive and nonprogressive."

———————

I had a run of sordid scoops about the persecution of Pasternak, all brought to me direct from the Union of Writers and Central Committee by Viktor Louis. He was a mysterious, charming, Gogolesque rascal whose career became a caricature of the opportunities and corruptions inherent in the Soviet system.

I met Viktor in my first days at the Metropol, where he served as Ed Stevens's translator. He promptly placed himself in my debt by asking for a recording of *My Fair Lady* so that he could sell translations of the lyrics to a Moscow theater—without, of course, paying royalties. Born Vitaly Yevgenyevich Lui, apparently to a French father, Viktor was, genetically, a hustler who allowed no kind of ideology or tyranny to interfere with his commerce. He told me he'd been trained as a lawyer at Moscow University but sentenced in 1949, at age twenty-one, to a labor camp for black marketeering among foreigners. One of Solzhenitsyn's ardent friends and collaborators in smuggling books abroad, Natalya Stolyarova, knew Viktor from her time in Karlag prison and thought his behavior there "left something to be desired."

Viktor was among the camp's first parolees in 1956 and renewed his ties to Moscow's foreign colony. The American embassy shunned him as a KGB agent, but Viktor wooed and won a soul mate at the British embassy, a nanny from London named Jennifer. They were married in a lavish Russian Orthodox service and soon moved into two large apartments that had been merged for them. Within weeks, it was stocked with modern Russian art that could not be displayed or sold in any public gallery. Viktor and his artists made a fortune from his foreign clientele.

As he grew wealthy, Viktor crossed my path only to peddle pictures or news of particular propaganda value to the regime. His information was almost always accurate even if his interpretation of it was suspect. On return visits in later years, I found him proudly established in a huge country house in Peredelkino, with an indoor swimming pool and outdoor tennis court that converted to a skating rink. Viktor attributed his bountiful antiques, icons, and electronic gadgets to his income as a correspondent for the London *Evening News* and to the guide and phone books that he and Jennifer published for hard-currency customers in Moscow. But he must have had other paymasters who financed his luxuries, facilitated his extensive foreign travel, and sanctioned his commerce with foreigners.

Viktor alerted Western reporters to the news of Khrushchev's ouster in 1964 and played a mysterious part in auctioning the first volume of Khrushchev's memoirs in the West. Later he tried to sell an unauthorized manuscript of Solzhenitsyn's *Cancer Ward*, apparently to discredit the author. He also turned up with a film of Andrei Sakharov to support the official claim that the dissident physicist enjoyed good hospital care during his painful house arrest in Gorki. Among Viktor's last known transactions were his sale, in Germany, of the news that Anatoly Shcharansky would be released from prison and "exchanged" to the West and Victor's purchase, in Britain, of a liver transplant five years before he died in 1992.

I enjoyed Viktor's cynical exuberance. I recognized him as the prototypical victim and profiteer of the Soviet system. He used crass capitalist techniques to exploit the Communist system. Purged by Stalin, he was restored by de-Stalinization, enriched by re-Stalinization, and laid to rest just as the Soviet Union expired. He was survived by his widow and by a society of Viktors indulging their wildest entrepreneurial fantasies.

GOULASH

Malcolm Muggeridge dropped in one Sunday morning in 1959 and over blini and caviar offered one of his brilliantly wicked analyses. He had reported from Moscow for *The Manchester Guardian* in the 1930s, a time when he still hoped to devote his life to "socialism." But he soon discovered that the Soviet government, while lavishing food upon foreigners, was starving its own peasantry. Muggeridge had been among the first to report these atrocities and to mock the Western correspondents, notably

The Times's Duranty, whose pomposities and ideologies blinded them to the horror.

Inexcusably, I knew none of this history as I tried to compete with Muggeridge, then the editor of *Punch*, in witty commentary on the Soviet-American rivalry. Khrushchev and his puppet premier, Nikolai Bulganin, were off in India riding elephants that weekend and, to Americans' great annoyance, snatching an ally right out of the British Commonwealth.

Yes, yes, Muggeridge suddenly said with obvious contempt for both superpowers. *Those fellows are going to spread their influence across the globe and finish you off by the end of the century. But come to think of it, you may find some solace in the fact that when they've done with you, they will have everywhere implanted "the American way of life."*

Indeed, the American way of life was on elaborate display that summer out at Sokolniki Park. More than 50,000 Russians a day trooped through Buckminster Fuller's geodesic dome; past large collections of books, paintings, and sculpture; through a model home modestly furnished by Macy's and an RCA color television studio; and, of course, past cars and fashions galore. The main attractions were dozens of Russian-speaking guides, young Americans who spent hours fielding the questions of visitors and the taunts of party agitators. They provided colorful and credible accounts of American life, warts and all, and with their cheerful bearing demonstrated better than any exhibit the charm of speech not burdened by fear.

The exhibit was intended by Khrushchev to whet the appetite of Soviet consumers. But the party resented the public's enthusiasm. Soon the papers attacked the exhibit as "untypical" and wept for the unemployed Americans who could never afford these baubles. Instead of showing off robot vacuum cleaners and electric juicers, commentators asked, why not display the harvesters and combines and assembly-line technologies that made America famous? On the other hand, I complained in my coverage that the assembled consumer goods were inadequate props for the guides' responses to questions about family budgets, taxes, schools, and other aspects of daily American life. Why not use TV sets and mousetraps to demonstrate the virtues of competition and markets? Or a copying machine's usefulness in political protest?

Vice President Nixon came to open the exhibit and let Khrushchev goad him into a sophomoric debate about the quality of Soviet and American missiles and the achievements of our rival social systems. What became known as their "kitchen debate" actually began in the television studio, when Khrushchev pooh-poohed color transmissions while Nixon, still kindly disposed toward a medium that would cost him the presidency one year later, counterpunched with a paean to televised democracy. They continued sparring at the kitchen of the Macy's house, mixing boasts and accusations like adolescents comparing sexual exploits. I thought Nixon barely held his own against Khrushchev's crude belligerence; Nixon himself counted this visit as one of his "Six Crises" in a 1962 memoir: "I felt like a fighter wearing sixteen-ounce gloves and bound by Marquis of Queensberry rules, up against a bare-knuckled slugger who had gouged, kneed and kicked." But Nixon's fellow travelers in the press were predisposed to celebrate every American thrust and parry, and they inscribed his "victory" in the Great Kitchen Debate in the mythology of American politics. More than that, they made pugilistic prowess at summit meetings one of the necessary attributes of presidential candidates throughout the rest of the Cold War.

Nixon's need to define himself in combat was already chronic. But his fear of Khrushchev's belligerence was plainly excessive. When Khrushchev taunted that "your grandchildren will live under communism," he was just explaining what he had meant by "We will bury you!"—the cry that set all America trembling but was nothing more than a morale-raising vow to attend capitalism's funeral after it died of natural causes.

We were all inflamed by Cold War tensions and by our mutual vulnerability to nuclear attack. And those of us who lived under the constant surveillance of the KGB felt a special antagonism toward the Soviet authorities. But I had also experienced the daily deprivations of Soviet life and recognized the frailty of the Soviet system. I felt sure that Khrushchev's bombast was born mostly of envy and of insecurities greater even than Nixon's. Of course I had no license to psychoanalyze the Soviet leader, and neither the Soviet censors nor *The Times*'s editors would have let me publish my speculations.

Nixon conveyed an invitation to Khrushchev to visit the United States in the fall of 1959, which Eisenhower seemed to think was like inviting Eloise to the Plaza. I followed their encounter from Moscow, bouncing back the Soviet propaganda about Khrushchev's transcontinental tour. He was thrilled to be received as America's "equal" and went "a little overboard," as he later put it, in demanding protocol honors every step of the way. He was particularly frightened by Eisenhower's offer of a visit to Camp David, the president's mountain retreat. Hearing for the first time about this "camp," Khrushchev said, made him fear it was "the same sort of place where people who were mistrusted could be kept in quarantine." When he finally understood that it was not a *lager* but a *dacha*, Khrushchev let Ike take him there by helicopter—but not until he made sure that on his return to Moscow he would be flown from the airport to the Kremlin in his own new chopper.

Nonetheless, after he had seen something of America's achievements at the Moscow exhibit and on his coast-to-coast travels, Khrushchev acknowledged: "I had a feeling not only of satisfaction but to a certain extent of envy. But this is a good envy, envy in the sense that we would like to have all this soon."

Like Nixon, most Americans lacked the wisdom to discount more of the Soviet leader's defensive hostility, which beclouded his reformist impulses. Truly sophisticated coverage of the American exhibit would have done more than emphasize the obvious curiosity and consumer delights of Russian visitors; it would have asked why Khrushchev dared to expose his people to the subversive ideas, freewheeling discussions, and shiny baubles of capitalist society. No wonder he felt compelled to brag about his missiles in ways that Nixon and other American leaders took to be threats. More alert analysis would have made an even better story than the kitchen confrontation. It would have confirmed Muggeridge's sly jest about how the Soviet Union's emergence from isolation would in time make the Russians devotees of the "American way of life."

Permitting the American exhibit in Sokolniki Park was just one more daring effort to shift Soviet priorities toward the production of consumer goods. Khrushchev bragged simultaneously about his few new intercontinental missiles because, it turned out, he hoped that they would let him drastically reduce his standing army and navy and invest the savings in the production of food, clothing, and housing. He proclaimed assorted target dates by which the Soviets were going to "catch up with and overtake" America in the production of milk and meat and cement and, eventually, comrades, all other good things. "Catch Up with and Overtake America" became the slogan of his regime, and it hung from factory walls, village gates, and urban facades on holidays. As Khrushchev well understood, it was intoxicating news to the ordinary Russian that he was running on the same track with Americans. And never mind the jokes that people whispered in the market.

TEACHER TO IVAN: Tell about life in America.
IVAN: Millions of unemployed. Only millionaires in university. Negroes hang from trees. People very unhappy.
TEACHER: Very good. Tell about life in our country.
IVAN: Everyone has job. Schools are free. Discrimination is forbidden. People very happy.

TEACHER: Excellent. And what is Comrade Khrushchev's new slogan?

IVAN: We must catch up with and surpass America!

There was actually plenty of food at exorbitant prices in the private peasant markets, which the regime tolerated for the benefit of both the peasants and their elite customers. In a telling demonstration of capitalism, the tiny private plots that every farmer tended around his house were outproducing the huge collective farms that had to deliver their produce to the state at confiscatory prices. The luggage racks of sleek jet planes from southern cities were cornucopias of fruit and vegetables being hauled to private Moscow markets by farmers commissioned to return with boots, perfumes, and television sets from GUM. Forced by chronic shortages to barter their way through life, all Soviet citizens had paradoxically become shrewd traders, ferociously acquisitive and competitive in their material yearnings. In the citadel of communism I lived in a nation of bourgeois burghers.

I was introduced to these pent-up appetites in the summer of 1957, when the Red-tinged World Youth Festival was staged for the first time on Soviet soil. Khrushchev invited more than 30,000 youngsters from 102 countries to join 60,000 Soviet youths in the spruced-up dorms and streets of Moscow, trading coins, pins, and conversation with an exuberant citizenry in two weeks of carnival. Only about 150 Americans took part, including a few plants sent by the Central Intelligence Agency, which was a pity because all the foreign youngsters made a much deeper impression upon Russians than Soviet propaganda could ever make on them. Most notably on display were the material thirsts of Muscovites.

You are from America?

Yes.

I should like to ask you a question.

Please do.

How many hours would I have to work in your country to earn enough to buy a secondhand car?

Chorus of voices: *No, a new car!—A Buick!—An average car!—A well-working, old Chevrolet!—But what about Negroes?—And the unemployed?— Let the gentleman speak!*

Wherever I went for the next three years, Russians, Georgians, Armenians, Ukrainians all provoked the same litany, cleverly weaving safe smidgens of propaganda with their powerful curiosities. No amount of hostile propaganda could cure them of their veneration for America, its music, clothes, cosmetics, gadgets. Russian cars were made to resemble

American cars, even if that involved a senseless waste of chrome and a mindless devotion to rear-wheel drive. The best Russian cigarettes came with American-style filters, and in flip-top boxes.

Although he never allowed himself to fully define it, Khrushchev instinctively sympathized with his people's yearning for a more humane socialism featuring a decentralized, market-oriented economy. He constantly complained that paying workers a decent wage was not by itself a strong enough incentive to produce; there had to be decent goods to buy. Unless industry produced fashionable clothes and durable furniture, the production of steel and coal would also suffer. And what was fashionable in clothes and furniture, comrades, had to be determined at retail counters, not in the bowels of some Moscow ministry.

Khrushchev delivered these homilies at party meetings like a child displaying a new vocabulary. For me, the high point of these public didactics came the day he tried to prove to the party's Central Committee that money itself costs money. Yes, those massive dams on the Volga produce much cheaper electricity than coal-burning power stations. But, comrades, think of the fifteen years it takes to build such a dam—and of the billions of rubles we tie up unproductively during construction! The cost of that idle money must be added to the cost of waterpower!

As *Pravda*'s text then recorded: "Agitation in the hall."

To drag his society into this pragmatic new world, Khrushchev had to publish his lectures and tolerate a limited range of public debate and criticism. And while he had only contempt for genuine democracy, he was much less of a tyrant than his party wanted. One of my most memorable dispatches dealt with the consequences of a Khrushchev sermon to the collective farmers in his native village of Kalinovka. He used the place for instructive "experiments," all elaborately recounted by the Soviet press. One year he thought he would teach Kalinovkites the blessings of mass production. He predicted that they could greatly increase the yield of the single cow that each family was allowed to own if they would house and feed all private cows in a common barn and leave the milking in the hands of experienced professionals. Sure enough, one year later, the farmers reported a 30 percent increase in milk yields and the eternal gratitude of their wives, who no longer had to rise at dawn to milk the family cow. Yet a few weeks later, a front-page editorial in *Pravda* revealed that Communist officials everywhere had mistaken Khrushchev's "suggestion" as an order; they were conscripting all private cows into collective herds. *Give back the cows! Pravda* pleaded. *No one has authorized confiscation of private cows!*

I had come to Moscow, like Nixon, despising the "butcher of Budapest," the Khrushchev who had brutally suppressed the Hungarian revolution and executed its leaders to preserve the Soviet empire. Yet three years later, he was encouraging János Kádár, the Hungarian who rode the Soviet tanks to reassert Red power, to relax the harshness of Communist rule and to forget Marxist theory if he knew a better way to raise Hungary's standard of living. When Khrushchev finally dared to show his face in Hungary again, it was to declare: "After all, comrades, even a black cow gives white milk. . . . What is communism? Communism is goulash!"

I came to believe that Khrushchev was ready to overhaul not just Communist theory but also the Soviet political structure. The man who spent the first fifty-nine years of his life as an apparently faithful Stalinist was transformed by circumstance into a populist. Impatient with doctrine and hungering for goulash, he diluted the authority of the Communist party and tried to decentralize economic decision making. I should have realized, as I now believe Khrushchev himself came to realize, that he posed a direct threat to the elites that ruled the Soviet Union, that he was pointing toward a meritocracy in which talent, not patronage, would rise to the top, and that he was destined to subvert the party's power unless it overthrew him first.

I came close to grasping the essential meaning of my years in Moscow, but not close enough. In my valedictory articles, which ran under the deadly headline SOVIET NOW STRIVES FOR ECONOMIC MIGHT AND PROSPERITY, I concluded:

The story of the Soviet Union today is a story of the steady erosion of dogmatic ideology and of the preparation for transition from the painful stage of mass production to the promising age of mass consumption.

No one in Moscow appears to consider political freedom a requisite for material prosperity. . . . But in trying to make the system work, Khrushchev has encouraged appetites and unleashed social processes that tend to develop a logic of their own and on occasion limit the central Government's sphere of action. . . .

Communist textbooks did not make provision for the unpredictable whims of women who let ugly, clump-heeled shoes rot in Soviet warehouses. They did not anticipate the sudden overproduction of bicycles and cheap watches and a thousand other goods now plaguing the Government. They did not teach ivory tower planners that as more sugar went on the market, the jam would be stranded on the shelves. . . .

As a result, Soviet economists have been allowed to depart from orthodoxy and to prescribe practical solutions. They have flirted with new theories of value, interest and amortization. They have proposed such un-Socialist concepts as freedom for Government retail stores to reject the goods of Government factories.

Installment buying was introduced to move expensive goods and below-cost prices were set to move unwanted goods. Soviet economists have urged more private and cooperative house building. They have advocated unorthodox price formulas to spur production on the farm. . . .

These trends tend to act as a brake on the arbitrariness of the Government but they serve at the same time to increase the pressures against any meaningful "liberalization" of the Soviet political system. For to minimize the diffusion of real political power, to control the ever more complex society, Soviet Communists are drawn as before to the techniques of totalitarianism. . . .

Totalitarianism, having survived civil and world wars, famines, plagues, purges and crises of succession, has survived effective industrialization as well. It may not have been the best system for raising Russia from backwardness, but it has been adequate. Soviet Communists are determined to survive the challenge of mass consumption as well.

As I left Moscow in 1960, I asked *The Times* to mark me down for a return assignment a decade later, when Khrushchev's reforms, I felt sure, would have totally transformed Soviet society. That very prospect should have alerted me to the inevitability of a strong reaction from the Soviet oligarchy. By 1964, even Khrushchev's most trusted ally, Anastas Mikoyan, voted to depose him as first secretary and premier for "harebrained scheming, half-baked conclusions, and hasty decisions and actions divorced from reality." The real fear inside the Kremlin was that Khrushchev was shifting power from the Communist bosses in every farm, factory, and army unit to the technicians and managers who resented the party's interference.

Khrushchev's successor, Leonid Brezhnev, was a martinet lacking all conviction, but he restored the oligarchy to dominance, took Stalin's title of general secretary, and revived the KGB as a protective police. For the next seventeen years, the Soviet economy staggered under the weight of an outmoded system of central planning until Mikhail Gorbachev and a new generation picked up the reformist banner under the slogan of *perestroika*, reconstruction. More even than Khrushchev, they understood that genuine reform also required *glasnost*, or openness, so that error could be discovered and corrected.

This shift, from a closed and prophetic Marxist doctrine to what my philosopher-idol, Karl Popper, called the open, endlessly experimental society, led inevitably to the collapse of Communist rule. Indeed, the frustrations and deprivations of the twenty-year delay between Khrushchev and Gorbachev triggered an explosion that shattered not only the Bolshevik dream but the czarist empire. Khrushchev had preserved the realm with sputnik diplomacy, a largely defensive bombast that for too long terrorized the West. But his great gift to history was to redefine the promise of communism as nothing more than a full stomach—of goulash.

SPUTNIK

My most portentous dispatches from Moscow stoked the Soviet-American competition to create MAD—mutual assured destruction. It was a costly but simple game: build an arsenal of intercontinental weapons so secure they could survive an attack and still destroy the adversary. Every new threat to the survival of such a weapon required an improvement or the acquisition of so many more weapons that the survival of some was assured. So long as each side was certain to be destroyed in combat, each would be rationally deterred from striking a first blow. And since the missiles were never actually to be used, their only other function was to serve as "bargaining chips" in diplomacy.

A story that I wrote offhandedly in June 1957 turned out to be the first Soviet salvo in this competition. My story faintly hinted at the derision we Americans still felt for Soviet technology:

SOVIET TO LAUNCH FIRST "MOON" IN '58
Scientists Tell of Project—Suggest Satellites Will Excel Those of U.S.

MOSCOW, June 18—Soviet scientists said today that they would launch from somewhere in the Soviet Union before the end of 1958 the first of a series of artificial earth satellites. It will be of some undisclosed size and will circle the earth at some undisclosed altitude.

The scientists suggested their models would be superior to the United States satellite but insisted they had no desire to compete with Americans for the first launching.

Sharing my arrogance, the editors consigned this news to an inside page, and, like the rest of America, we went back to sleep.

Then it happened, near midnight of August 26. TASS, the Soviet news agency, hammered out an "Information" about a *mezhkontinentalnaya ballisticheskaya raketa*. My news was spread across three columns of *The Times*'s front page:

RUSSIANS ANNOUNCE FIRING INTERCONTINENTAL MISSILE
"HUGE DISTANCE" TO TARGET

MOSCOW, Tuesday, Aug. 27— The Soviet Union announced last night that it had successfully tested an intercontinental ballistic missile.

The announcement said the missile, flying at an "unprecedented" altitude, had "covered a huge distance in a brief time" and had "landed in the target area." It added that the results showed a missile could be directed "into any part of the world."

If the report is true, the Communist world has won what has been considered a crucial race for the perfection of a pilotless rocket capable of traversing the earth.

The announcement also said the Government had tested recently "a series of nuclear and thermonuclear [hydrogen] weapons" with success. No details were given on these tests except to say that they had been carried out at a "great height" to safeguard the populace. . . .

The Soviet government was speaking in a notably new tone of voice. But America's complacency lingered a few weeks longer, until October 4, when Moscow announced that the same multistage rocket had launched a *sputnik*—literally, a "fellow traveler"—the Earth's first artificial satellite, which everyone had expected to be an American invention. To rub it in, the Soviet press published a triumphant daily timetable of *Sputnik's* passage over Washington, New York, and other American cities, pointedly including Little Rock, where President Eisenhower was using the National Guard to escort a few Negro children into a public school.

Izvestia, the Soviet government's newspaper, aptly described America's reaction as "hysteria." With a mixture of fear and shame, Americans suddenly felt outgunned by the Russians in everything from ballet to ballistics, and especially in technical education. It did not help that the White House greeted *Sputnik* by feigning a lack of interest in "an outer space basketball game." With our rockets still collapsing on Florida's launching pads, Americans felt that our "missile gap" rendered us vulnerable to "nuclear blackmail." The Communist world, meanwhile, celebrated the fortieth anniversary of the Bolshevik revolution with the launch of an even larger Soviet orbiter carrying the first space passenger, a dog named Laika.

The truth was that America's nuclear forces all around the Soviet Union were more than adequate to avenge and therefore discourage any attack. The strategic balance of power, which had long favored the West, had not been altered. But America's psychological balance was severely shaken. Vast new sums were voted for the Pentagon and for education from kindergarten to university.

Nikita Khrushchev played our panic brilliantly, brandishing his new (and few) rockets to raise morale at home and to learn what diplomatic gains they might bring abroad. I could coolly admire his performance because nothing he said or did truly frightened me. I had stood face-to-face with the man at embassy parties, stared into his sparkling eyes, and followed the witty wag of his finger as he acted out the insecurities of his backward society. He proclaimed a maddening faith in the ultimate superiority of socialist economies, but it was capitalist achievements that he envied and market incentives that he longed to unleash. The Soviet censors would not let me call him a pragmatist, but I never doubted that a man who defined communism as goulash had no stomach for world conquest or pointless war against the United States.

Could I be sure? Well, I couldn't prove it, and I never dared to directly challenge America's impression of Khrushchev as a belligerent boor. Stalin had made *Soviet* a synonym for *aggressive*, and in the overheated atmosphere of the 1950s, my minority view that Khrushchev had a primarily domestic agenda could have marked me as the Communists' dupe. Americans were simply not ready to be reassured.

I nonetheless tried to reassure them by contrasting the spectacular success of Soviet rocketry with the pathetic poverty and inefficiency of daily life. And I tried to demonstrate that Khrushchev's most belligerent words could be traced to essentially defensive purposes. My speculations were tentative, to be sure. I had no access to knowledgeable Soviet officials or the information on which they based their policies. But the secretive atmosphere in which we had to work sharpened a reporter's sixth sense, the capacity to penetrate the deceptions inherent in all diplomatic and political discourse. A willingness to trust my analytical imagination proved to be the lasting benefit of my Moscow experience. It taught me to cope with a shortage of information.

Applied to Khrushchev's sputnik diplomacy, my hypothesizing gradually revealed a coherent pattern. Though an improviser and opportunist, spewing boasts and threats in all directions, Khrushchev projected ambitions that struck me as logically linked and farsighted: (1) Renounce the terror of the Stalin years and liberate Soviet society for creative labor. (2) Produce incentives for those laboring people by rapidly expanding the production of food and consumer goods. (3) Pay for these massive investments by reducing the size and cost of the army and navy and rely instead on a cheaper missile defense. (4) Reduce the need for large standing armies by inducing or forcing the West to accept Soviet sway over Eastern Europe as permanent.

The obvious restiveness of Poles, Hungarians, Czechs, and East Germans was a major source of Soviet insecurity because they looked upon communism as an alien as well as ugly force. Nothing so riled Khrushchev as American taunts about his "captive nations" and our vague threats to "roll back" communism from the heart of Europe. His tenuous hold on that region kept the Cold War boiling and, for decades, made Berlin a focal point of East-West tension.

Khrushchev's main objective in rattling his rockets was to secure his hold on East Germany—by ending the flight of its population through West Berlin, perhaps by driving the Western powers out of Berlin altogether. Once again my name appeared over his policy's first rattle. I was alone in Moscow in the fall of 1958, resentfully waiting for Osgood Caruthers to replace Bill Jorden as bureau chief. I failed to understand how I could be trusted with every kind of story in the Soviet capital but not with running our small office. Maybe the editors could not find anyone under twenty-eight to be my subordinate and did not want me bossing an older colleague. Whatever the reason, their decision further burdened our already difficult working conditions. Caruthers turned out to be a gentle man in his fifties, with only a superficial interest in diplomacy or communism. He, too, was resentful, because he had been dislodged from a luxurious life beside the Nile in Cairo. Once he had spread his Egyptian brass tables in an otherwise drab Moscow apartment, he refused to be distracted from his ritual afternoon martini. And he hated having to choose each day between the humiliation of seeking my instruction and that of ceding the big stories to me.

The biggest story, by far, broke just before his arrival. Khrushchev simply declared that the postwar four-power occupation of Berlin was null and void. He intended in six months to sign a peace treaty with Communist East Germany and to force the West to negotiate with that puppet regime for any residual rights of access to West Berlin. He wanted to make it a "free city," essentially severed from the West and therefore doomed to gradual absorption into Communist Europe.

Yet again Khrushchev stirred up fears of war to disguise a weakness. The real issue was refugees. West Berlin stood as a brilliant lighthouse deep inside Communist territory, attracting millions of East Germans who had only to take a subway to freedom. The exodus was crippling the East German economy, the Communist world's strongest. Khrushchev desperately wanted its frontiers sealed. He kept the crisis boiling by disrupting traffic on the West's vulnerable air and land corridors through East Germany to Berlin. But he so frightened his own people that he soon had to promise "no unilateral action" so long as there was negotiation about his proposal. Within two months, he was inviting Eisenhower to Moscow to discuss it.

———————

Deep down, Eisenhower understood Khrushchev's insecurity and tried repeatedly, though ineffectively, to engage him in a search for accommodation. The president knew that no conceivable deployment of long-range Soviet missiles could ever knock out the American triple threat of short-range missiles, bombers, and missile-bearing submarines that were poised to retaliate massively for any attack. And Ike felt certain, as McGeorge Bundy has documented, that the Soviet leaders would never risk an attack unless they faced some catastrophic danger to themselves.* But Bundy concluded sadly that Ike, "the man with the rank, the record and the personal understanding to make this argument fully and persuasively, appears to have made it, as far as the record now shows, only to himself." Eisenhower let Americans grow frightened about a developing "missile gap" and let inferior generals, like Curtis LeMay, talk recklessly about the possibility of a "preemptive" first strike at the Soviet Union.

"Too many of these generals have all sorts of ideas," Eisenhower said—but only in private. And the Soviet censor would not let me send out Khrushchev's comparable crack at an embassy party about *his* military leaders: "Give a general any situation and he will find strategic significance in it. I don't trust generals' appraisals of strategic significance."

So while Eisenhower and Khrushchev were publicly emphasizing their power to avenge an attack, both felt sure that they would not be attacked, if only because neither could expect to land a knockout blow. In a perverse regard for Soviet sensibility, Eisenhower withheld the evidence that underlay his own sense of security. The amazing photographs taken from five miles above the Soviet Union by the CIA's U-2 planes showed no alarming missile deployments. The Russians bitterly protested the flights, but only in private, and Ike refused to humiliate them further by disclosing their findings. He spared the Russians even after Sen. John F. Kennedy disingenuously accused him of tolerating a "missile gap" in Russia's favor during the 1960 presidential campaign. Scotty Reston, *The Times*'s Washington bureau chief, had learned about the U-2 flights in 1959 but was persuaded, probably with false appeals to military security, to keep them secret.

———————

* McGeorge Bundy, *Danger and Survival: Choices About the Bomb in the First Fifty Years* (New York: Random House, 1988).

Khrushchev took shameless advantage of these courtesies. His rockets were still rattling in all my stories about his 1959 journey to the United States, clear up to the day of departure:

RUSSIANS FIRE ROCKET AT MOON, EXPECT IT TO HIT TARGET TODAY; SHOT TIMED TO KHRUSHCHEV TRIP

and again,

KHRUSHCHEV ON HIS WAY TO U.S. TO BEGIN TWO-WEEK TOUR TODAY; BRINGING MEMENTO OF MOON SHOT

Only gradually did Khrushchev reveal the earnest purpose of these childish boasts. On January 14, 1960, the Western press and diplomats were all invited to the ornate hall of the Supreme Soviet to hear him announce a one-third reduction of the Soviet armed forces. The country's "formidable" stockpile of atomic and hydrogen weapons, its "concealed" rocket bases and lead of "several years" in rocket development assured its "unassailability." One week later, he announced the firing of a missile over a distance of nearly 8,000 miles to within "a mile and a quarter" of its target in the Pacific Ocean. Khrushchev was sure he would be seen as "an equal" at the four-power summit in Paris in mid-May and by Eisenhower when the president came calling in June.

Imagine Khrushchev's horror in early May, therefore, when his own antiaircraft rockets forced him to confess that his missile bases were not at all "concealed." The Kremlin announced that Soviet gunners had shot down a U-2 spy plane and bitterly denounced the many previous U-2 penetrations of Soviet airspace. Khrushchev seemed still willing to let Eisenhower apologize and so rescue their relationship, but Washington mindlessly issued the customary cover story that an American "weather plane" flying near the Soviet border was overdue at its base in Turkey. Probably for the last time in the Cold War, American reporters assumed that their government was telling the truth.

Cunningly entrapped, the "representatives" of the American press were given unusually privileged box seats for another session of the Supreme Soviet at which Khrushchev dropped the other shoe. In a torrent of anger and delight, he announced that the U-2 plane, much of its equipment, *and Francis Gary Powers, the pilot—alive!*—had been seized in deepest Siberia.

A few days later a new American exhibit opened in a Moscow park—a display of the shattered U-2, its amazing cameras, and samples of the sharp photos they had taken. The pilot's maps marked out his route, clear across Siberia from Pakistan to Norway. We were shown his assortment of foreign currencies and false identifications in many languages; his poison pills and also his real personal documents and credit cards. As we examined the wreckage, Khrushchev appeared, balanced himself on a wobbly wicker chair, and delivered a bitter, hour-long harangue against Eisenhower for his refusal to call an end to the spy flights. This was genuine rage, confirmed by the bulging veins in Khrushchev's neck, and it was not hard to dope out its cause. If the U-2s continued to count his missiles, his generals would demand an alarming increase in their number, eating up all the savings he had gained from reducing his army. Say it isn't so, he kept begging Ike, to no avail.

So Khrushchev flew to Paris and angrily disrupted the summit, withdrew Ike's invitation to Moscow, and said the Berlin negotiations would have to await a new American president. Yet inadvertently he opened the way to a whole new ethic of mutual aerial inspection. For when President de Gaulle belittled the whole U-2 affair by observing that Khrushchev's sputniks were at that very moment flying over France fifteen times a day, the Soviet leader claimed to perceive a great distinction between the intrusions of aircraft and those of orbiting satellites. On the spur of the moment, he thus opened all his territory to detailed inspection from space, a far-reaching concession of sovereignty to technology which eventually brought great stability to the nuclear arms race.

Even as Khrushchev was reviling Eisenhower in Paris, I wrote emphatically from Moscow that his "hard-won decision to entrust Soviet military might to rocketry, his attempts to raise the standard of living of his people, his easing of the Russians' personal life at home and increase of contacts with the rest of the world will not be reversed." I felt safe with Khrushchev's finger on the Soviet nuclear button, even throughout the missile crisis that he recklessly provoked in 1963, which I covered from Washington.

I considered Khrushchev the most robust politician of my time. He was the first Soviet ruler with the wit and courage to expose himself to his own people and to the world; the first to rule using his own name instead of a pretentious nom de guerre, like Lenin and Stalin; the first to call off class warfare; the first to leave his domestic enemies alive; and the first to deny that war with the capitalist West was inevitable. Even Khrushchev's demagoguery betrayed a peculiar honesty. When angered, he could bang his shoe at the United Nations and threaten to push Russia's abstract artists bare-assed into clumps of nettles. But he also told off the Chinese, warning a bellicose Mao Zedong that

> to hurry into the next world is not recommended, since no one has ever come back to tell us that life is better there.
>
> It is a known fact, comrades, that if you want to kill a bedbug, you need not burn down the house. . . . What did we make the Revolution for? We did not fight to live worse after the working class won power. And we repudiate the "theory" according to which the socialist countries must allegedly unleash a war against the capitalist states in the interests of the world revolution.

Somehow, Khrushchev surmounted the cancerous cynicism of the Stalin years to preach a politics of redemption. "Here, so to speak, therapy was effective," he remarked on his seventieth birthday. But that was his last birthday in office. The reforms he sponsored threatened too many interests even as they made it safe for those interests to organize against him.

Wise and daring, confident and insecure, sentimental and pugnacious, Khrushchev struck me as ideally suited to engage the equally gargantuan Lyndon Johnson in what would have been the most stimulating encounter of the Cold War. But as he prepared to visit Johnson's Texas ranch, Khrushchev was overthrown. The anniversary of the Bolshevik revolution in 1964 found him sitting at home, reciting poetry to his niece, Yulia, whom he had raised like a daughter.

"Don't cry," she remembers him saying. "Of course, I've erred a lot. I'm going to be corrected and criticized. Who doesn't work, doesn't make mistakes. But you're never going to have to blush on my account."

What a proud epitaph for any leader.

———

Russia taught Tobi and me much more than how to dodge the censor. Planning, for one thing. Not until we moved from the hotel to an apartment in mid-1958 did we conceive David Marshall Frankel. And given the sad state of even the most prestigious Moscow hospitals—no sanitary napkins, no visitors whatsoever—we scheduled our firstborn's arrival to coincide with the home leave owed us after twenty-four months abroad. Encouraged by Arthur Gelb's wife, Barbara, to try the rediscovered techniques of natural childbirth, Tobi let a Russian midwife, a huge and powerful peasant woman, knead her belly once a week to demonstrate assorted techniques of breathing. That pounding must be why David emerged not a minute late in New York Hospital while fog forced his father, flying in from a tour of Siberia, to circle overhead in frustration before his plane was diverted to Montreal.

Our infant son was soon instrumental in teaching us comparative psychology—the difference between the ill effects of communism and ordinary New York cussedness. Until we went home to have him, every incivility in a Moscow bakery or the Metro struck us as a sullen claim of license by people denied other freedoms. Now, pushing David's carriage through New York, we knew better. Our education was encapsuled one afternoon on a visit to Macy's when we asked the coffee shop to take the chill out of his milk. We were brusquely refused and realized in shame that if that had happened in Moscow's GUM, we'd have blamed communism and the absence of competition.

We took David back to No. 74 Prospekt Mira (the Prospect of Peace, formerly First Bourgeoisie Street) with a one-year supply of then new paper liners for plastic Swedish diapers, a dozen crates of Gerber's baby foods, and several editions of Dr. Spock's manual of enlightened baby care. (One edition favored pacifiers, one objected to them.) An enterprising Russian friend, Yelena Yurieva, studied all our references and imitated all our child-rearing techniques, but only after she was assured that "even a Rockefeller baby" would be fed the same mush and allowed to crawl so freely. Thirty years later, when the Soviet Union collapsed, her son emerged as one of the first Russian multimillionaires.

David was also a decontaminant; he made us safe partners for sidewalk conversation, particularly on extremely cold days, when he lay smileless in his stroller, wearing what looked like a dangerously thin nylon snowsuit. Russian babies, by contrast, lay swaddled and immobilized in several layers of cotton and wool. So virtually every passerby would stop to scold us for risking frostbite, then bend to admire the novel nylon, and finally linger for random gossip. Tobi and I eagerly exploited all these contacts, and we were sure David's first words were bilingual; we assumed that his "da, da" meant both "daddy" and "yes."

The more we learned about the rigors of Soviet life, the more ashamed we grew about our boastings about American goods and gadgetry. The smug pride we felt at the daily sight of youngsters crowding around David's collapsible carriage and *The Times*'s imposing Chevrolet began to wane as we learned to picture those youngsters doing their homework in crowded communal kitchens. The fun of passing out ballpoint pens and seamless nylons gradually faded as we learned about estranged and even divorced couples sleeping in the same room separated by a curtain. In the Russians' daily forbearance, we gradually recognized a tolerance for genuine suffering. Even in our time, people still risked arrest and banishment for open political dissent. Our gadgetry finally struck us as a pretty stupid definition of American values. We began to emphasize our freedom instead, but most Russians did not understand.

Clearly, a remarkable intensity defined our life in Moscow. Although I wearied of it after three years, I despaired of ever drawing an equally stimulating post. Every aspect of Russian life had become newsworthy, directly relevant to American politics and diplomacy and, indeed, humanity's chances of survival. Every aspect of Soviet life churned up my value system at a still impressionable age, goading me to reexamine opinions about human nature and social equity. Did Americans really value freedom more than Russians? Would Americans who surrendered so cravenly to McCarthyism with only their jobs at risk defy a life-threatening tyranny?

To prolong my personal journey of discovery, I asked *The Times* to send me to Germany but was denied. And Washington was unavailable; although I had impressed Scotty Reston when he visited Moscow, he had already tapped Bill Jorden to cover Soviet and other foreign affairs in his bureau. Then, as now, there was pitifully little career planning at *The Times*. The ebb and flow of the news and the shifting needs of individual writers caused even the best-intentioned editors to function as merely creative opportunists.

Not once in my longings did I imagine my destination as we sailed to New York on the SS *Rotterdam*, a direct descendant of the ship that had carried me to America twenty years earlier.

The New York Times.

LATE CITY EDITION

NEW YORK, SUNDAY, JULY 10, 1960.

THIRTY CENTS

EISENHOWER BARS A RED CUBA,
TELLS RUSSIANS NOT TO MEDDLE;
KHRUSHCHEV WARNS OF ROCKETS

MOVE TO KENNEDY
NEARS STAMPEDE;
HIS RIVALS UNITE

SEIZURES PUSHED; PREMIER VOWS AID

PRESIDENT IS FIRM

ROCKEFELLER SETS
PLATFORM GOALS

Havana Calls for Data
on Inventories of
U. S. Concerns

Would Back Castro
if U. S. Intervened
by Use of Force

Says Soviet Attempts
to Make Havana Its
Instrument in Area

Long-Term Aid to Panama
Weighed to Protect Canal

17 · BEARDING FIDEL

*C*UBA, SAID MANNY FREEDMAN, THE FOREIGN EDITOR. *WE need you in Cuba. All America wants to know whether Fidel Castro is a Communist. There's no one better equipped to find out.*

That was two fibs and a lie. *The Times* had two people better equipped than anyone. They were Ruby Hart Phillips, our Havana correspondent, and Herbert Matthews, veteran foreign correspondent and editorial writer, who practically invented Fidel Castro for the American reader. What Freedman meant was that no one trusted *The Times* to resolve the growing doubts about Castro because Ruby railed at him from the right while Herb was shielding him from the left. Since I had made such a success of my ignorance in the citadel of communism, the editors thought they would toss me naked into the swirl again. The truth was, they didn't know what else to do with me. I belonged to a possessive Foreign Desk, but it had no other opening.

My first reaction was to quote Scotty Reston: "Americans will do anything for Latin America except read about it."

I read the news from Latin America only when aborigines or Nazis were discovered there. My knowledge of the continent's economy never went beyond the public-school scrapbooks into which I pasted coffee beans at Ecuador and beefy cows at Argentina. As for Cuban history, I knew only about the suspicious sinking of the *Maine* in Havana harbor in 1898 and how Hearst and Pulitzer had exploited it and a Cuban uprising to drive up the circulations of their yellow New York rags, the *Journal* and the *World*, goading America into an imperial war that saddled us with the Philippines.

But Cuba lay so close to our shores that it had long ago become embroiled in our domestic politics. Once it was almost admitted, or rather annexed, as a state of the Union. It was muscled into giving the U.S. Navy a magnificent all-weather base at Guantánamo—"in perpetuity." And the whole island had been treated as a convenient base by North American gamblers, rumrunners, drug merchants, and pimps.

In their rise to power, Fidel Castro and his band of rebels shrewdly played upon Americans' guilt to help create their revolution's Robin Hood romance. Starting with just a few score men, they had toppled the fragile Batista dictatorship, vowing to create an American-style democracy and to inspire liberal revolutions throughout the hemisphere. At the dawn of the fateful 1960s, these bearded ones in khaki fatigues summoned young rebels everywhere to storm the barricades of suited establishments. Castro cursed the Yanqui colonialists, but he also admired the New York Yankees. He droned at his rallies like a drunken tyrant, but he also charmed his interviewers with New Deal dreams. By frightening the pants off American conservatives and charming them off American liberals, he embarrassed us all.

By the time I encountered Castro in mid-1960, his veneer of glamour had already worn thin. His disdain for free elections, alienation of the middle class, and confiscation of Cuban and American property had disillusioned his admirers and driven even close allies into exile. Now, as Freedman said, most Americans wanted to know only whether we had misplayed this revolution and driven Castro toward the Russians or whether Fidel had been a Communist all along. Was he a victim of America's moneyed interests, or had he been plotting from the start to impose a Soviet-style dictatorship and perhaps even a Soviet base only ninety miles from Key West? There was a lot of talk about the Monroe Doctrine and how no European power could be allowed to establish a colony in "our" hemisphere.

I soon learned that America's obsession with Cuba was not informed by much knowledge. *The Times* gave me six weeks to study conversational Spanish and a month for political briefings, but I could find only a single

North American scholar who had devoted his career to the study of Cuba. And then there was Herb Matthews, a student and admirer of Fidel, eager to brief all Cuba-bound diplomats and journalists from his perch on the editorial board of *The Times*.

An austere romantic, Herb was never content to just analyze events. He was one of those journalists who yearn to give history a hand by directing society toward the good and the beautiful. He made his reputation covering both sides in the Spanish Civil War—the great morality play of his generation—and went on to become a scourge of all Hispanic dictators. He had cheered the rise of Castro and his *Fidelistas*, and at one crucial moment in 1957, when the Batista dictatorship claimed to have decimated their ranks and killed Fidel, Matthews allowed himself to be smuggled into the mountains of eastern Cuba to prove that Fidel was alive and gaining strength. Writing on the front page, in violation of *The Times*'s vaunted separation of the news and opinion pages, Herb also vouched for Castro's idealism and was fooled by Fidel into exaggerating the size of his rebel army. Matthews's articles recharged the batteries of the opposition to Batista throughout Cuba. They also gave rise to the painful jest, after Castro came to power in January 1959, that Fidel's face belonged on one of our subway posters promoting the paper's Help-Wanted ads—posters made famous by the slogan "I got my job through *The New York Times*."

Sustained by his mountain adventure and new notoriety, Matthews persisted for too long in his hero worship and apologias for the Castro government. In mid-1960, after even radical *Fidelistas* had been displaced by Communists or jailed, Herb still wrote respectful, though no longer uncritical, editorials about Castro. He claimed to understand Fidel's revolutionary imperatives and was sure that, if properly encouraged, he would still change direction. Our news columns, meanwhile, were filled with ever more disturbing dispatches from Ruby Phillips about the Cuban people's losses of liberty and property. She had inherited a once sleepy bureau from her husband and was emotionally aligned with the dispossessed middle and upper classes now fleeing to Miami. She was widely accused of not recognizing the revolution's good works, in new housing and medical care for the peasant population.

The editors of *The Times*, like their readers, were obviously confused. I was being clumsily inserted between feuding writers, both old enough to be my parents and vastly more experienced in the subject. So that I could function freely on Ruby's turf, I was to be called "Caribbean correspondent," based in Havana but looking in on the despots in Haiti and the Dominican Republic and, if ever there were time, also on Puerto Rico and the islands curling down toward South America. Ruby was most gracious about this tortured arrangement, which established me to second-guess her judgments. Matthews tried to preempt her influence over me by sending along warm letters of introduction to his Cuban friends. I felt ill used, and ill suited for the assignment, and my distaste grew by the day. But if my destiny required a tour in Cuba, I could not have chosen a better time. Castro evolved into a Marxist before my eyes, and American efforts to deal with him crashed around my feet.

––––––––––

Ruby Phillips fumed too much about Castro's seizures of private property, notably the Havana villas of her friends. But on the central question of whether Castro had jumped or been pushed into the Soviet orbit, her sneering opinions were more perceptive than most. The insults and injuries being exchanged by Havana and Washington still left many Americans in doubt about the true cause of the conflict. Castro was gradually seizing both Cuban and American businesses with no credible promise of compensation, while Washington was rapidly cutting his sugar quotas and virtually halting all trade. So the Russians stepped in, offering a reliable new supply of oil in exchange for Cuban sugar, which they did not need.

I soon concluded, however, that in Cuba, as everywhere, the decisive influences on events were not foreign but domestic. Governments, like individuals, tend to resist outside pressures; they are moved mostly by inner compulsions, many of which are hard to detect from afar. When I first arrived in Havana, Castro had let a whole year go by without uttering a word of criticism of Cuba's Communists, the Johnny-come-latelys to his revolution. Communists were replacing his old comrades throughout the government, including the army, led by Fidel's brother, Raúl. *Fidelistas* who protested the trend were jailed or driven into exile. Castro's lofty promises of a new constitution, a multiparty system, free elections, free media, free labor unions, and free land for the peasants were not only broken but openly disowned as "petit-bourgeois prejudices." And the Eisenhower administration, having seen its faint but not unfriendly overtures rebuffed, had long since turned to secret efforts to organize a counterrevolution against him.

––––––––––

I finally met Castro in New York, in September 1960, during a gathering of world leaders at the United Nations, an unruly event that marked the beginning of Soviet efforts to exploit the organization for anti-American propaganda. After Khrushchev, at the peak of his world prestige, announced his intention to revisit New York as head of the Soviet delegation to the General Assembly, virtually every other head of government rushed to join him. And there they were, the cocky Communists, the self-righteous Non-Aligned, and the pained Capitalists, served up as a fortnight's feast for the media. By far the most interesting of these strutting visitors were the ones needing the most intensive police protection—Russia's Khrushchev, Egypt's Nasser, Yugoslavia's Tito, and Cuba's Castro.

Because no hotel wanted to admit his ragtag delegation, Castro became one of the stars of the week's melodrama. Not until he threatened to pitch a tent in Central Park did the United States government force the second-class Shelburne Hotel, at Lexington Avenue and Thirty-seventh Street, to give the Cubans some rooms. But a few nights later, the hotel's owner threw them out, claiming that they had messily plucked chickens and roasted dinner in the halls and suites. Since he produced no feathers or other evidence, I decided that Castro had more likely invited ejection by balking at the Shelburne's exorbitant prices, knowing by then that he could stage a delicious propaganda triumph by leading his bearded warriors to the Hotel Theresa at Seventh Avenue and 125th Street in the center of Harlem.

Thus it was that Herb Matthews's energetic effort to introduce me to the *Líder Máximo* was consummated in the Theresa's coffee shop. I was able to ask Fidel one routine question, evoking an hour-long recitation of soothing platitudes. The key words of every paragraph appeared two or three times, so that even with my Berlitz Spanish I could claim to understand. *Amigo . . . mi amigo, también.* Any friend of Herbert's was also his friend. He looked forward to our travels together, around Cuba. I would find much to teach the American people about *La Revolución. 'Ta luego, amigo.*

A few hours later, while I stood outside the Theresa idly listening to Malcolm X explain the cosmic significance of Castro's movement, a limousine pulled up and disgorged the only other reigning ruler of my acquaintance. Fidel appeared at the hotel door and strode with outstretched arms toward a beaming Nikita Khrushchev.

Despite their embrace, Matthews begged me to keep an open mind about the color of Fidel's revolution. Herb struggled hard against the smug certitudes of people who thought that anticommunism was the only political attitude that mattered. He was one of those good people who cling to bad thoughts because good thinking has been preempted by bad people. I was glad to be professionally obliged to suspend judgment, or at least to bury my opinions so deep that I was unaware I held them. Where Cuba was concerned, my ignorance became a handy shield, protecting my stance of neutrality.

I could not, however, avoid the conclusion that Castro's blatant praise of the Soviet Union and unrelenting hostility toward the United States resembled the slavish conduct of the Kremlin's stooges in Eastern Europe. I could see that the Soviet leaders had overcome their doubts about Fidel and decided to exploit this windfall of anti-Americanism. They could hold up Cuba as proof of a doctrine they had already come to question—that the tides of history favored communism. Here was proof as well that Soviet influence could spread beyond the American wall of "containment." Fidel's revolution was an inspiration for all anti-colonial "wars of liberation," a chance to humble the "imperialist" powers at low risk and low cost. Although Khrushchev had in fact been forced to draw in his military horns, support for Fidel and similar adventurers allowed him to pretend that the Kremlin was still a bright beacon of revolution.

I stayed in New York to cover Fidel's ostentatious applause for Khrushchev's percussive attacks on the United States, which the Soviet leader punctuated one day by pounding the table with his left shoe. Castro himself followed with a four-hour tirade, having that morning declined an invitation from Egypt's President Nasser to join the camp of the "nonaligned." Clearly Castro's alignment with the Soviet bloc had instant cash value. Soviet aid would let him continue to seize American assets without having to fear Washington's economic retaliation. I was still far from convinced, however, that Fidel had all along been a secret Communist eager to turn Cuba into a Soviet satellite and base.

While I packed for Havana in October 1960, the wives and children of Americans there were hurriedly evacuated. Escalating its war of nerves against Fidel, the Eisenhower administration expressed a fear of imminent "civil war." Three months earlier it had secretly authorized the CIA to begin training Cuban expatriates in Florida and Guatemala for an eventual invasion of the island. The October issue of *Hispanic American Report*, a Stanford University journal, carried the first public reference to invasion plans. The week I reached Havana, *The Times* carried a front-page warning by Cuba's foreign minister that an invasion was imminent. Nixon and Kennedy poured oil on these flames with their campaign rhetoric. *The Times* and other newspapers uncovered all sorts of Cuban refugee plots. Exiles in Miami jockeyed for cabinet jobs in a "post-Castro" regime. Fidel's young soldiers patrolled the beaches waiting to repel an invasion and, that failing, to wage a war of attrition from the hills.

Pan Am still flew twice a week between Havana and Miami, mainly to bring out refugees. The émigrés described an island on full military alert. Young men and women carried loaded weapons on every street, and dissidents set off grenades in sidewalk litter baskets to sow confusion. Even movie houses were unsafe as stray bullets careened down the rows of seats from rifles carelessly cradled in lovers' laps.

That was hardly a suitable environment for Tobi, four months pregnant with Margot, or for our romping eighteen-month-old, David. So we rented a garden apartment near the University of Miami, hoping to spend every other weekend together. But that only compounded the strain of our return to the United States. We were splitting up not just a family but a professional collaboration, a marital partnership in foreign adventure. Not only would I now be absent for two weeks at a time, but our separate experiences would lose much in hasty translation. Life in Miami/Havana, though we vowed to make it brief, became a sad, poorly understood prelude to the rest of our marriage. Our exhilarating teamwork abroad remained a proud memory, but it could not prevent the gradual disengagement of our domestic lives.

Guitar-strumming minstrels still met planes in Havana, but the bitter glances of Cubans huddled behind glass caused me to hurry out of the way; they had waited for months and paid small fortunes for their chance to flee. I needed only my American passport for admission to Fidel's Cuba, a hangover from the bad old days when nothing was allowed to impede a tourist's path to the casinos. I moved into the empty Havana Hilton, whose roulette wheels still spun for a few Polish and Bulgarian tourists. The next day I fled into the welcoming home of Harold Milks, the AP bureau chief, whom I knew from Moscow and who once again became a protective friend and mentor. I scattered my letters of introduction from Matthews among glum government clerks, and I shared a strange poolside collegiality with correspondents from Warsaw and East Berlin, who could hardly contain their delight to be swimming in such American luxury.

Over the next five days, Castro delivered almost daily alarms about the danger of American attack, a danger he no doubt thought real but also found convenient. It made it easy to justify the restraints on political and economic freedoms. As I wrote on November 5, under the headline CUBAN TENSIONS RISE:

The militia forces were regrouped and supplied with new Soviet-bloc weapons and drilled in overtime and weekend sessions. Hospitals were ordered to clear beds for the wounded and to stock up on plasma and drugs. Even sacks were ordered collected to be used as sandbags. The lines at the United States Embassy grow longer each day.

The Cubans kept repeating one of Khrushchev's vague summertime declarations that Soviet "rocket forces" were among the troops standing ready to help defend their island against American attack. And on November 7, the forty-third anniversary of the Bolshevik revolution and my eighth day in Havana, I heard the first firm answer to the question that had brought me there:

SOCIALISM HAILED AS HAVANA GOAL

The word *socialism*—in the Soviet sense—was used here last night for the first time by an official not known to be a former member of the Popular Socialist (Communist) party. The word was proudly proclaimed by José María de la Aguiléra, secretary general of the Federation of Bank Employees, at a labor rally honoring the Soviet Union.

Cuba's Acting Foreign Minister, Carlos Olivares, and the Soviet Ambassador, Sergei M. Kudryavtsev, were among the prominent guests.

"It is time to say without fear, without weak knees, without a trembling voice and with head high that we are marching inexorably toward socialism in our country."

Understandably enough, that revelation was lost in the paper of Election Day 1960. And Kennedy's narrow victory over Nixon produced not only a great domestic distraction but also a new Cold War dynamic. Khrushchev had been waiting to put his Berlin demands before a new American leader; those demands were of far greater importance to him than the defense of Cuba. That is why I was sure that as Kennedy prepared his presidency, Moscow would order Castro to stop boasting about Soviet missiles. And after only a few days of close monitoring of Cuban speeches, I could see how quickly Havana now obeyed its Soviet masters:

SOVIET CAUTIONING HAVANA TO SOFTEN ITS ATTACK ON U.S.
Warns That Relations with Washington
Top Cuban Problem in Importance

HAVANA, Nov. 18—The Soviet Union has been urging a course of "prudence" and "moderation" on the government of Premier Fidel Castro in recent weeks.

With some apparent effect, it has told the Cubans to quit rattling Soviet rockets against the United States and has warned them that Moscow's relations with Washington, especially with the new Administration of President-elect John F. Kennedy, counted for more in the Kremlin than the Cuban problem as such. . . .

On Nov. 8, as the election returns were being tallied in the U.S., Premier Castro told the Cuban people that they must defend themselves and not go to sleep with the comfortable knowledge that Soviet rockets would rain upon the United States following any attack on Cuba.

There has been no more talk here of the "symbolic" offer of Soviet rocket aid.

Once again logic had served me as a substitute for sources. No one told me what the Russians had said to the Cubans. Even if I enjoyed greater access to Soviet and Cuban officials, none would have dared openly to confirm my hypothesis. But by putting myself in Khrushchev's shoes and listening closely to Castro's new message of "self-help," I was able to reach conclusions that Soviet reporters—or agents?—found it impossible to deny. Their sympathetic nods were all I needed to write an important story of obvious interest to the Kennedy crowd. My article also made me a bit player in the trilateral diplomacy; both Cubans and Americans suddenly wanted to speak to me.

———————

Like Stalin, Carlos Rafael Rodríguez, the leader of Cuba's Communists, gave interviews at midnight. But he looked and sounded more like Lenin, with his goatee and gold cuff links and intellectual airs. He was a highly educated Marxist and a proven opportunist. Only forty-four, he had served as education minister in an early Batista regime. Like all of Cuba's Communists, he almost missed the Castro bandwagon. It was Rafael Rodríguez who was given the delicate task of climbing the hills of the Sierra Maestra in late 1958 to apologize to Fidel for the party's disdain for him and to offer its belated support. Nonetheless, just a few weeks after Fidel's triumph, Rafael Rodríguez emerged as master of the revolution's ministries for propaganda and education. Suave and secure, he would one day serve as Cuba's vice president and also its most accomplished secret nego-tiator with both friends and foes.

He invited me for 11:00 P.M., and we talked until dawn. He knew of me through Herb Matthews's letter but also from my writings. He thought we "spoke the same language," and sure enough, despite my weak Spanish, I understood most of what he said. Besides, his central message was so startling that I never dared to interrupt for explanation or transla-tion. He was eager to tell the world that the fish was hooked, that all his painful tutoring of Fidel in the catechisms of Marxism-Leninism had fi-nally paid off. He even patronized the great Fidel: the Communist party had made itself so indispensable to Castro that it now had the power to "control or restrain" him.

As we sipped our last coffee, I said I had gained the impression that while flattering Fidel's ego and proclaiming his authority, Cuba's Com-munists were now shaping his thoughts and assuming the day-to-day management of his government.

"Perfectly correct," Rafael Rodríguez replied.

After a mere three weeks in Cuba, I had fulfilled my mission, and *The Times* ran the report atop the Sunday paper:

EXTENT OF RED GRIP IN CUBA IS RELATED BY A PARTY CHIEF
Communist Says His Group Has Power to "Shape" Premier Castro's
Thoughts—Drive to Solidify Gains Under Way

HAVANA, Nov. 25—The leaders of Cuba's Communist movement are confident that they have won the battle for Fidel Castro's mind and are striving, under his protec-tion, to convert the Cuban people to their ideology.

After a bitter fight within their own ranks, the Communists have decided to consolidate their posi-tion of great influence here and to forgo an open bid for total power. . . . The disciplined Com-munist party, which counts itself a true member of the international Communist movement, is content to stand behind the banner of Cuban nationalism and to lend its considerable organization and po-litical talents to Premier Castro.

The Cuban Communists who ad-vocate this strategy do so because it conforms to their estimate of the progress of history. But they also fear that a premature bid for greater power would alienate the Cuban people, possibly arouse the wrath of the Fidelistas and almost certainly cause military interven-tion by the United States. . . .

In their short struggle with weakly organized non-Communist revolutionaries, the Cuban Com-munists have persuaded Premier Castro that anti-communism was really anti-revolutionism, that they were not only loyal but also essential to the consolidation of the power that he won without them.

I was expressing ideas that barely fit the conventions of newspaper language. But I remembered from my apprentice days in the newsroom how Scotty Reston and Abe Rosenthal muscled even speculative ideas past the copy desk if they were cast in a "Timesian" style. Having obtained impressive confirmation for a highly controversial hypothesis, I was determined to use every news peg to reassert the message: The Communists needed the charismatic Castro to impose their dogma on Cuba's peasantry. And because Castro possessed no ideology, party, or bureaucracy of his own, he needed the Communists. Only they would let him function as *Líder Máximo*, without democratic restraints. Only with their cadres could he be Cuba's caudillo. His choice of a new political philosophy had its roots in his congenital personality.

Much literate and liberal opinion in the United States was still too smitten with Castro to accept this news. Fidel's American fans found it hard to forgive the United States for a century of ineffectual meddling in Cuba and exploitation of its economy. They also found it hard to believe that Castro fully intended to deliver his people into a Soviet dependence that would only perpetuate their poverty.

I was sure, however, that I had found my answer and that I would not be welcome much longer in Havana. So I drove the length of Cuba for one good look at the interior, a journey that evoked many childhood memories of how readily people rationalized their submission to tyranny. The schools and clinics that Castro built did for him what timely trains had done for Mussolini and slick autobahns for Hitler. People said life was hard and confusing, but at least there were jobs to be had and the beaches were now open to the poor.

The report of my journey, in *The Times*'s Sunday Magazine, ended on a note of guilt and frustration:

There are Cubans who want United States aid and trade and there are Cubans who want the Marines, at once. Some ask just to be let alone. A great number asks just a word of hope: That this thing that is enveloping them isn't really communism, that their island is rich enough to survive whatever it might be, that this man Kennedy will surely think of something, that Cuba had to change anyway and won't the good remain long after the bad is forgotten? . . .

Neither Coca-Cola nor baseball nor a billion dollars in U.S. investments had secured this island against want and strife, nor had they taught it the real meanings of the slavishly imitated constitutional phrases. . . . Can our desperate, albeit true warnings of communism still be heard? Do we have an answer other than the Soviet answer to Hungary?

And if only Fidel Castro went away, would we retravel that road from Havana with anything worthwhile to say?

After these guilty musings I sent a follow-up, CASE STUDY OF A POLICE STATE, but it did not appear in our magazine until the end of April, as if written to justify the Bay of Pigs invasion. It was actually written in January 1961, and was obviously shaped by the experiences of my youth:

Long, long ago—last December— . . . Cubans both for and against "Fidel" were witnessing the gradual interment of their right to dissent, the ugly emergence of neighborhood spies and roughneck "policemen," and they would remark, "The Cuban people are not European peasants and automatons," or "Our undisciplined religious people will never stand for communism." . . .

The vise had begun to tighten only a few weeks after it was suddenly and excitingly opened by Castro's triumph over Batista. Each turn of the screw was firm and irrevocable. Each new departure from law and from civil rights was accompanied by elaborate explanations of allegedly special circumstances and by deafening shouts of "democracy." . . .

At first, the sport-stadium executions and kangaroo trials were only for Batista's "war criminals." Only the newspapers and radio stations of "corrupt millionaires" were seized and who did not agree that they were "reactionary" and not very good papers and stations at that?

If there had been elections, Fidel would have won anyway, so why waste time? If there were a Parliament it would approve everything anyway, so why waste money? . . .

Only student committees were democratically and independently purging the ranks of their professors; was this not the ultimate in "academic freedom"? Only those labor unions that extorted unduly high wages for their members while peasants went hungry were being forbidden to strike; was it not fair to let others climb the economic ladder for a while? . . .

Under the spell of [Castro's] oratory in the infectious atmosphere of the mass meeting . . . and eventually with armed patrolmen carting off the less than enthusiastic, decisions were heard and ratified by acclamation. . . . A Cuban with no alternate source of information—and very quickly there was none—could only believe that everything was going the regime's way and that his private reservations were only unhealthy aberrations. In any case, he did not dare withhold his signature from the petitions and declarations thrust under his nose at work and in his home. Not to be with them was to be against them.

As I was writing those words, the Cubans ordered the American ambassador to shrink his staff to just a few clerks and demanded visas for all future American visitors. Understandably edgy about the open preparations for an attack on Cuba, they wanted to reduce the number of CIA agents on the island. Eisenhower retaliated by breaking off diplomatic relations altogether. The Swiss assumed America's consular business in Havana and relayed the welcome news that my application for a visa had been "irrevocably denied."

I had done my duty and found the answer: Fidel was a despot by nature, a Communist not so much by conviction as by conversion and convenience. He so despised Cuba's oligarchy of wealth that he drove out its talent and settled for an equality of privation. He so resented Cuba's exploitation by North Americans that he delivered the country for a pittance to their Soviet adversaries. A brilliant orator and a genius in mob psychology, Castro turned out to be the most durable autocrat in a time of autocrats because he was blessed with a foolish enemy.

18 · AT BAY

T HE SUMMONS TO PALM BEACH WAS ALMOST DEFEREN-
tial: *If convenient, please join a few reporters for a chat with the
President-elect. He wants to learn about Cuba.*

We saw nothing wrong in those days about sharing reportorial impressions with politicians and diplomats, even CIA agents.
Especially in hostile countries, our functions overlapped and our
experiences were often complementary. Reporters, diplomats,
and politicians were all panning for information and, in
a sense, "representing" our nation, even what was called our
"way of life." So a flattering summons from a minister, ambassador, or president-elect quickened our steps. Some Washington
reporters flew a little too close to the honey pot and fell in, losing their independence and credibility. But the younger reporters who nowadays piously shrink from all social contact with
people in power are overreacting to earlier excesses. They are
right to beware of the seductions of political intercourse, but information is a commodity, and to prosper in the market you have
to give as well as get. Getting to "know" a premier or president

or president-to-be promises journalistic gold: the unguarded moment or comment that will enliven a story and sometimes even illuminate history. Access to the powerful also brings bragging rights which can be bartered among lower-ranking officials: *From what the president told me last week, he seems determined to negotiate with Khrushchev but never with Castro, don't you agree?*

I will never know whether Kennedy really gave a damn about my experiences in Havana. Three of us were admitted to his father's Palm Beach estate shortly before Christmas 1960, but we never got past Pierre Salinger, the press secretary in waiting. The president-elect was most grateful that we'd come, he said, and was eagerly awaiting Pierre's report. There are hints in the history books that John Kennedy still harbored doubts about the government's plans to have Castro killed and his regime overthrown. He was heard to wonder occasionally why Eisenhower hadn't embraced Fidel instead of letting him drift toward the Russians. But where Cuba was concerned, as I finally understood some thirty years later, Kennedy's head was no match for his gut. Nothing that we could have said in Palm Beach would have offset the agitations of his family, his friends, and his virile ego.

Salinger asked what the United States should or could do about Castro, and we were fairly uniform in our responses. We talked about little else during our lonely nights in Havana.

You mean what should the United States do for the exiles whom it has led to believe they can recapture Cuba?

Well, yes.

Persuade them that not even the U.S. Army could defeat Fidel's forces without a long guerrilla war. The Fidelistas would head for the hills and turn the population against the "Yankee occupiers."

You mean we have to tolerate a Communist regime ninety miles from our shore?

Well, yes. We have to tolerate the Soviet Union less than ninety miles from Alaska. And the Russians have to tolerate American bases in Turkey and Iran, a mere nine miles from their border. There's no significance in these trivial distances.

We can hardly claim to be "containing" the Commies if we can't keep them out of our own hemisphere. That's what the Monroe Doctrine was all about.

Well, the choice is between waging a long and ugly war of attrition and a long cultural war of education.

Educate whom with what? Salinger asked.

Educate the Cuban people in the joys of democracy. They already worship baseball and Hollywood, drink Coke, and smoke Camels. Why suddenly cut them off? We're desperate to sneak a few magazines and newspapers through the Iron Curtain and to enmesh the Russians or Romanians in our commerce. To do the same with Cuba, we need simply to keep lines open, keep them from reading only Pravda.

And just pretend Castro isn't there—isn't stirring up revolution all over Latin America?

No, just accept the fact that revolutions are not "exported," they're home-made. Cuba wasn't communized by the Soviet Army, like Poland or Hungary. It was ripe for revolution because we indulged its dictators, as we're doing next door in Haiti and the Dominican Republic and all over "our" hemisphere. Until Fidel appeared, we never gave a damn for Latin American democracy.

You want us to ignore him?

It's okay to ignore Castro if you address the problems that created him.

———

The rational JFK was planning at that very moment to address the hemisphere's problems with what his inaugural speech would call an Alliance for Progress. Even Castro admired the plan for its promises of economic aid and development. But Kennedy could address Cuba only with his viscera.

As most of us did not learn until decades after his death, John Kennedy visited Cuba two or three times *in the year before* Castro came to power. He went not to study conditions there but to go whoring around Havana with Sen. George Smathers of Florida, a glib reactionary who, in his youth, had worked for and performed similar procuring missions for the senator's father, Joseph Kennedy. Smathers and JFK had become buddies in the U.S. Senate, and now, in the court of the president-elect, Smathers was the ambassador of the American mobsters and sugar barons dispossessed by Castro. When Smathers needed reinforcements, he would call upon Earl Smith, another Palm Beach pal of the Kennedys, whose wife, Florence Pritchett, had been *the* flame of JFK's youth and remained his lifelong friend. Smith had been Eisenhower's ambassador to Cuba, and Kennedy now tried to make him ambassador to Switzerland. But Smith was such a blatant apologist for Batista that the Swiss, who were now representing American interests in Havana, refused to receive him. A furious Kennedy then ordered his diplomats to stiff the Swiss throughout his years in the White House.

Reporters rarely learn about such private influences on the public's business. But it helps to get close enough to the mighty to figure out with whom they sometimes dine. And sleep. It also helps to keep in mind, always, that "policy making" is not a disinterested science. It is driven by political calculation, passion, and prejudice. My generation spent a lifetime wondering what Kennedy would have ultimately done about Vietnam, yet we still don't understand what moved him to such unrelenting pursuit of Castro, a pursuit that nearly wrecked his new administration and provoked the gravest crisis of the Cold War.

We do now know that while I was chasing Castro and Khrushchev around Manhattan in the fall of 1960, Vice President Nixon was imploring Eisenhower and the CIA to let the exile army of Cubans they'd been training launch its attack in October. Nixon was sure that such a triumph over communism would guarantee his election; he seems not to have reckoned with the possibility of failure. Kennedy was briefed on these preparations and feared just such an "October surprise," so he went Nixon one better by *publicly* urging an immediate invasion. Kennedy was not convinced that the plan was wise or workable, but he and Nixon had stirred up so much anxiety about the Cuban menace that they were compelled to compete in militancy. Besides, Kennedy enjoyed repaying the Republicans for burdening Democrats with the "loss" of China in the 1950s; he slyly implied that Nixon's team was "losing" Cuba. So he called for action and vowed to support the exiled "freedom fighters," well aware that Nixon could not responsibly acknowledge the administration's secret invasion plans.

Nixon, enraged, redoubled the cynicism. He denounced Kennedy for urging American involvement in what would surely be a bitter Cuban civil war—the very policy that he himself was promoting behind the scenes. Whereupon Kennedy met lie with lie, contending that he was *not* advocating American involvement; he meant only to express "sympathy" for the freedom fighters.

I treasure that campaign episode, well recounted by Michael Beschloss.* It bears repetition whenever politicians put a stamp of "top secret" on the record of their skulduggeries and piously berate the press for treasonous disclosure of them.

I can respect statesmen's occasional shading of the truth, provided they are not simply advancing personal ambition. Diplomacy, like politics, is the art of reconciling conflicting interests, each of which wants to hear that it is yielding less and gaining more than others. In simultaneously ad-

---

* Michael R. Beschloss, *The Crisis Years: Kennedy and Khrushchev, 1960–1963* (New York: Harper-Collins, 1991).

dressing allies and adversaries, statesmen can almost never speak the whole truth about their motives and intentions. Yet even presidents ought to be made to respect the moral difference between lying for their country's advantage and their own. It is rarely wrong to assume that they usually confuse the two.

As our statesmen don't dare to admit, United States "intervention" in the nations of the Caribbean has always been unavoidable. The island people live in poverty in the shadow of our wealth, dependent on and exploited by our investors and tourists. They have been routinely abused by our politicians and occasionally even occupied by our marines. But we also "intervene" when we neglect them. The United States damaged Cuba's independence both when it bought too much of its sugar and when it bought too little. Castro's annoying leap into the Soviet orbit made it all too easy for Americans to forget that until he appeared we never offered the Cubans or their neighbors in Haiti and the Dominican Republic a better life inside our sphere of influence. In facing Cuba, Kennedy did not have to decide whether to "intervene"; he had to answer, Intervention for what? To improve the standard of living in a virtual colony? To implant democracy? To restore the Mafia mobsters to their Havana casinos? To reimpose the sugar quotas by which Congress had enriched America's sugar barons?

Our leaders in 1960 were choosing diplomatic policies not for their effect on the lives of Cubans—or even Americans—but on the deadly game of encirclement being played against the Soviet Union. Rescuing turf from communism—"reversing the Red tide"—counted most in our domestic politics. We had virtually conceded half of Europe and half of Asia to Khrushchev, so Latin America, by God, was going to be ours, for keeps. So soon after the Korean War, America's politicians were not yet ready to spill American blood in Havana as Khrushchev had spilled Russian blood in Budapest. Kennedy promised that "I am not going to risk an American Hungary." He was going to intervene but not get involved—a distinction that promised a fiasco.

The Times, similarly conflicted, wanted to report the government's invasion plans but not so boldly as to risk blame for a failure. We thought that "national security" was best served by a free press; the government thought that national security required press "responsibility." The controversy flared bitterly for more than a decade. *The Times* stood in the thick of the battle. And so did I.

Starting with Eisenhower's lies during the U-2 affair, the American press slowly learned to question its government's credibility in matters of national security. A great many of its secrets seemed to be serving not the nation's safety but only the political security and convenience of government officials. Else why could secrets be leaked with such abandon when it suited the army during atomic tests in Nevada or the navy during budget battles in Congress? The trust and teamwork that had defined relations between the press and government in World War II were eroding. Our perceptions of the public interest were becoming incompatible.

But it was a gradual, fitful estrangement. Even after the U-2 experience, *The Times* was slow to shake the old habits of "responsible" reporting, which often meant little more than deferring to officials in positions of responsibility. When it first heard reports about a secret American training camp and airfield in Guatemala, *The Times* gave much more credence to the lies of Guatemala's president, Miguel Ydigoras—that he was preparing defenses against a Cuban attack—than it gave to the testimony of his political opponents that Americans in Guatemala were preparing an attack against Cuba. *The Times* reported but plainly disbelieved the alarms being sounded by Cuban diplomats at the United Nations. We woke up only when Tad Szulc, passing through Miami at the end of March 1961, heard without even asking about the invasion plans from Cuban and American friends.

Surely Castro's agents were hearing the same accounts in the same Miami restaurants, but still our editors hesitated. Scotty Reston, who would usually run over his grandmother, as he put it, for a scoop, counseled against premature disclosure of any invasion plans. He thought *The Times* should not risk incurring blame for the high casualties or total failure of a military operation, or for its cancellation. He put great faith in the judgment of Arthur Schlesinger, Jr., the scholar turned White House counselor, who opined that our disclosure of the invasion plans would cause an ambivalent Kennedy to cancel them.

The editors rushed me to the Guantánamo naval base, but the only abnormal activity there was difficult to decipher. A ninety-six-foot schooner and cable repair ship called the *Western Union* had sailed too close to Cuba's eastern coast and, when challenged by one of Castro's gunboats, refused the urgings of navy warships to make a run to safety under their protection. State Department officials lied that the vessel was working on the "Barbados-Miami cable," but my civilian telegrapher at the naval base assured me, his now regular customer, that no cable in the area needed repair. Armed with that knowledge, we learned within hours that the ship had refused to risk a gunfight because it was carrying 180,000 gallons of flammable high-octane gasoline. Only weeks later did we understand the schooner's mission: she'd come to refuel a flotilla of defecting Cuban patrol boats that Castro had deliberately kept on short fuel rations.

Szulc meanwhile flew back to Miami, where Stuart Novins of CBS and other reporters were gathering unmistakable evidence that the invasion was imminent. And that is what Szulc tried to write in an article describing the CIA's nine-month training program for Cuban exiles, the location of their camps, and the expectation that their arrival in Cuba would trigger uprisings and military defections all over the country. Crediting the exaggerations he heard in the streets of Miami, Szulc put the size of the exile army at more than 5,000, though it was never more than 1,400.

His article was headed for the front page of Friday, April 7, 1961, under a large four-column headline, when, in a rare intervention, Orvil Dryfoos, *The Times*'s publisher, ordered the tale toned down and moved down the page "in the interests of national security." A myth arose at once that the publisher had killed the story at the behest of President Kennedy. But he was really responding to Reston's misplaced patriotism: that signaling the imminence of a military action risked damaging the operation and therefore both the country and the reputation of *The Times*. Reston was surely right to believe that the paper would have been blamed for yet again "saving" Castro, but not by fair-minded observers. You only had to read the speeches of Raúl Roa at the United Nations to see how fast the Castro regime was getting information about the exiles from its own agents in Miami.

Contrary to legend, Szulc's article was not killed; its headline was reduced to the width of a single column, and references to the CIA and the time of attack were deleted. The dispatch as printed merely described the exile army as in a state of "adequate preparation." Editors who resented their publisher's order then did their best to undermine it: To the bottom of Szulc's long article, they appended a brief summary of Stuart Novins's simultaneous radio report—from an unnamed source—that the invasion plans were in their "final stages" and that the Cuban troops would be "given" naval artillery and air cover. A careful reader could easily decipher these clues. But the drama of the tale was obviously muffled.

In any event, the imminence of invasion now informed our coverage even as we coyly pretended to know less than we knew. I reported on the mysterious cable repair ship and the beefing up of defenses at the naval base without saying they were probably coordinated with the invasion plans. The day after his toned-down scoop, Szulc reported how prominent Cuban exiles were openly bidding good-bye to friends and flying off to Guatemala to prepare for the seizure of a Cuban beachhead and the proclamation of a new democratic Cuban government. And the editors of *The Times*, virtually thumbing their noses at their own publisher, made a front-page story out of a wholly propagandistic boast by the head of the exiles' political council that a revolution inside Cuba—"not a revolution through invasion"—was (note the forbidden word) "imminent."

The Times was being written and edited with knowledge that it refused to fully share with its readers. Next day, a Sunday, the exiles' call for an uprising, without invasion, got a conspicuous two-column headline beside another Szulc special about political rivalries in the "final stages" of planning for a Cuban landing. By Monday someone had managed to throw Szulc off the track and gotten him to predict multiple small landings instead of one major invasion. On Tuesday, Reston produced the main Cuba story out of Washington, describing a major policy dispute about how much help the administration should give the anti-Castro army—an article that implicitly, but only implicitly, confirmed the imminence of an attack.

The lesson of this experience should have been simple: A secret can be secret only so long as it is secret. Information once lost by the government will seep out in uncontrollable and unpredictable ways. And government lies that are meant to protect an ill-kept secret will only compound the government's eventual embarrassment and the public's inevitable anger and skepticism.

When the landings at the Bay of Pigs were finally revealed, Reston was misled into depicting the attack as a mere pinprick by fewer than 300 Cubans. But Szulc's full-throated account, buttressed by the text of messages from the battlefield, suggested a much larger operation. Also on Page One were reports of the now highly credible complaints of Cuba and the Soviet Union about an American-sponsored aggression.

The invasion was, of course, an ill-conceived and only halfhearted American effort. It was a bitter failure, as was the still secret government effort to have Mafia mobsters avenge their Cuban losses by murdering Castro on the eve of the attack. Kennedy stoutly refused all appeals to dispatch American troops to rescue the exiles; he risked only one feeble effort by American planes to resupply them. Within twenty-four hours 114 of the exiles lay dead on the beach and 1,189 were locked in Castro's prisons. Kennedy struggled for months to get them freed and to recover from his conspicuous deceit and defeat.

From my post at Guantánamo, I monitored the reactions inside Cuba, reporting the mass arrests of "suspicious elements" during the battle and

Castro's TV proclamation, in the flush of victory, of an openly "social-ist"—that is, Communist—state. Khrushchev celebrated Fidel's victory and began to look for new ways to exploit Kennedy's weakness, while the president and his brother, Attorney General Robert Kennedy, looked upon Castro's survival as an intolerable, even personal affront. They took full responsibility for the fiasco, but they also lashed out at the CIA, the Joint Chiefs of Staff, and the press, notably *The New York Times*.

President Kennedy asked newspapers to learn to censor themselves when the national security was at stake. With no apparent awareness that *The Times* had done just that, he complained about our first feeble and gullible coverage of the secret training base in Guatemala. But when a delegation of editors came to the White House to express concern about his scape-goating, the president whispered a contradictory message to Turner Catledge: "Maybe if you had printed more about the operation you would have saved us from a colossal mistake." For years to come, some editors piously invoked that wry comment to justify the publication of govern-ment secrets. But they were either disingenuous or victims of Kennedy's self-deprecating charm. He didn't mean it. And neither did any of his suc-cessors as the government's relations with the American press tumbled from bad to disastrous.

A further consequence of the Bay of Pigs disaster was recognized by Robert Kennedy in a prophetic memo he wrote to himself just hours after the defeat: "If we don't want Russia to set up missile bases in Cuba, we had better decide now what we are willing to do to stop it." They did not de-cide, of course, until nuclear missiles were actually detected in Cuba eigh-teen months later, to everyone's shocked surprise. By then, I was covering the Cold War from the other side, our side, an assignment for which I was now haphazardly but spectacularly well prepared.

REPORTER:

Cold War West

1961–1972

19 · SCOTTY'S BOY

THE GALLING REWARD FOR MY ADVENTURES IN CUBA was condemnation to the United Nations to record the ventriloquy of governments speaking through helpless delegates. At least it served my vanity to be a "correspondent" on the East Side of Manhattan rather than a mere "reporter" on the West Side. After three months, which included Margot's birth at New York Hospital, Scotty Reston called.

He sympathized with my boredom at the UN, and he thought he had a remedy. He well understood the travail of having to move yet again, especially for a wife who was being dragged from place to place in the service of my ambition. But now hear this: Bill Jorden, your old sidekick in Moscow, was about to defect to the policy planning board of the State Department. If the Frankels, new baby and all, could muster the energy to pack up once more, I could have Jorden's job covering diplomacy—the job Scotty himself had once held—at the start of a dynamic new administration.

Reporting news that really mattered—as one of Scotty's boys! Back to lovely Washington, where the army had shown me the living was easy. The promise of a house and backyard was enough to entice Tobi, too. We were thrilled.

Scotty insisted, however, that his probe remain confidential. The formal offer had to come from Turner Catledge, the managing editor, because I was now the "property" of a New York department. Here began my tutelage in bureaucracy. *There's nothing you can't get done at* The Times *if you don't insist on the credit for it*, Reston said. *Your move to Washington will be Turner's great idea. Wait for his call. Just don't take delivery of that Danish furniture you've got coming!*

Scotty Reston was the most admired newspaperman of the day, the last to achieve true celebrity in print, before the Age of Anchors. He was always at the center of events. Just a month before I reached Washington, Reston stood waiting inside the American embassy in Vienna for a quick word with Kennedy about his meeting with Khrushchev when the president staggered in, depressed and exhausted, slouched onto a couch, tipped his hat down across his face, and moaned aloud into the darkened room. Reston had only to describe that scene to capture the essence of the summit. Khrushchev had bullied the young president to test his mettle, and Kennedy had failed the test. Now there would be confrontations in Berlin, a cold winter ahead, Kennedy said. To Reston, but to no one else in the press corps, the president predicted that he would have to prove himself somewhere else in the world, mumbling that it would probably be Vietnam.

Reston's scoops were not the factual kind that could be quickly verified and duplicated with a few phone calls. His dispatches were nuanced narratives, analytical diaries. He flattered officeholders by sympathizing with their burdens, incidentally getting them to confess their deepest anxieties. Yet he could also pierce their pretensions with wit and charm. Reston knew what he didn't know, and he knew how to make smart people tell him. He worked the Town, as he called the capital, the way a bee works a garden, ferrying ideas and gossip from Foggy Bottom to Capitol Hill, from Embassy Row to the White House. Welcomed everywhere for the sly questions he asked, the flattering motives he presumed, the tales he bore, and the readership he commanded, Reston truly earned the right to generalize, as was his habit, about "the mood in Washington this morning" or "the reaction of this capital tonight."

Reston's articles rarely spoke the telegraphic patter of ordinary newswriting. They read like melodious conversation:

Talking to Premier Aleksei N. Kosygin of the Soviet Union is a little like pitching batting practice to the New York Yankees. You throw a question, then duck.

Or:

Eisenhower was a good man in a wicked time; a consolidator in a world crying for innovation; a conservative in a radical age; a tired man in a period of turbulence and energetic action. He avoided war and depression, the two things he feared most. He broke the isolationist tradition of his party, which is why he sought the Presidency in the first place, and he presided over an era of prosperity and good feeling within the nation.

With insights like that, Reston forced the editors in New York to print his articles even when he failed to name "sources." They had to tolerate his style even when it violated every hoary newspaper convention. His depictions of mood and motive seemed out of place in the news columns. Yet they were so compelling that they demanded to be published. So over the protests of Arthur Krock, the pompous head of *The Times*'s Washington bureau, the publisher and editors had let Reston share in the bureau chief's privileged rubric, labeling his interpretive dispatches "News Analysis" and giving them a conspicuous double-column display among the single-column tombstone headlines on the inside pages. That distinction preserved the pretense of that time that "objective" political and diplomatic news, the headline stuff on Page One, was unsullied by reportorial judgment.

Reston had perfected his colorful, probing style as a sportswriter and war correspondent, describing the bruises and burdens of battle. Now, having succeeded Krock, he was leading a long struggle to open all sections of *The Times* and the front page itself to equally vibrant analysis. His purpose was to explain, not to opine; to portray the motives of political actors, not to vent his own prejudices. He was a patriot, but not a partisan. If anything, he was too elaborately evenhanded and generous in assuming that most men in power had a nobler purpose than personal ambition. Never, however, did his predilection for analysis diminish his zest for legwork. On the contrary, the man who'd scooped the world with the plans for the United Nations and the records of the Roosevelt-Stalin accords at Yalta would run all over town to learn the subject of the president's next speech or the name of the next ambassador to London. Scotty prized every kind of scoop because he relished creating the impression that he and his staff were privy to every government design.

Just as formidable were Reston's talents as a bureaucrat. Building on the sovereign privileges that Krock had amassed for the Washington bureau and capitalizing on his own close relationship with all the Sulzbergers, Scotty ran an independent fief inside *The Times*. He was the only department head who designed the size and shape of his own staff, re-cruiting young reporters from all corners of the country with barely a nod to New York. He favored elegant writers with a special aptitude for Wash-ington's subjects—the pageantry of politics (Tom Wicker), the subtleties of the law (Anthony Lewis), the complexities of economics (Edwin Dale, Jr.), and the foibles of all humanity (Russell Baker). After the formality of my "release" by New York, I, too, became one of Scotty's boys, a member of the A-team covering the seat of empire for the world's greatest news-paper at the height of the American century.

In the New York office, they considered service in Scotty's army as marching for the Confederacy, an act of rebellion if not outright seces-sion. Reporters even mocked me for imitating Reston by wearing bow ties and smoking a pipe. The fact is, I had taken up bow ties in Moscow be-cause I routinely slobbered food on four-in-hand silks and saw them de-stroyed by Soviet cleaners. I took up the pipe in Russia as well, at Tobi's insistence that it was healthier than two packs of cigarettes a day. But I did imitate Reston's prose and, eventually, his mannerisms. I learned to amble through the halls of government with his nonchalant gait and to phrase my questions with his unction and historical pretension. Scottish Calvin-ist and Polish Jew, we were nonetheless soul mates who shared the ag-gressions and curiosities of assimilating immigrants. When years later it actually came to civil war between Washington and New York, I was ready to lay down my professional life in Reston's defense.

Feeling rescued after only three months in UN purgatory, Tobi and I jumped at Catledge's proffer of Reston's summons. For the third time, we purchased wall-to-wall green Karastan, this time for a five-bedroom brick colonial in Chevy Chase, a Maryland village whose convenience to Roman Catholic churches and schools, as the real estate agents were no longer allowed to point out, had endowed the neighborhood with spa-cious homes on modest plots. Protestants and Jews were moving in now, but as in most of northwest Washington, they were all white. We did not join the agitations to integrate the neighborhood until after young David one day remarked on seeing a black woman, "Look, Mom, here comes somebody's maid." We didn't succeed until we sold that very house to a foreign service officer who in turn rented to an African diplomat. The poor man felt compelled to wear a "University of Kenya" T-shirt when-ever he raked the lawn or went for a run.

We didn't know it then, but our purchase of that home, at the outer limits of our budget, would eventually yield an obscene profit that we could parlay through a series of real estate booms into luxurious housing for the rest of my days. None of us who worked for newspapers ever dreamed of assets of such magnitude. Whether such comforts also skewed my sensibilities became a serious question in later years.

More good fortune struck quickly in Washington to help me adjust to its intoxicating and intimidating ways. Abroad, mere ambassadors were kings. Now I sat among reporters who golfed with senators, swam with White House aides, and called cabinet members by their first names. For my inaugural lunch in his garden, Scotty invited Felix Frankfurter, who gossiped freely about his fellow justices of the Supreme Court and reminisced about his daily walks to work with former Secretary of State Dean Acheson.

My first days at the bureau were equally daunting. Wally Carroll, Scotty's deputy who monitored the copy and coordinated with New York, was himself a distinguished student and graduate of government with amazing contacts among the intelligence agents among whom he'd served in World War II. To watch him work the phone to confirm a hot tip about strife in the Congo or inside the FBI was a humbling experience. And so were my first briefings at the State Department, where my competitors turned out to be people like Murray Marder and Chalmers Roberts of *The Washington Post*, Phil Potter of the Baltimore *Sun*, and John Hightower of the AP, writers I had admired since my army days in the capital.

What a relief, therefore, when fate dealt me the one international crisis that I understood so well I could instantly make the story my very own.

Wandering the halls of the State Department in the first week of August 1961, I learned from diplomats I had known in Moscow that the simmering crisis in Berlin had become a major preoccupation of the Kennedy administration. Khrushchev had warned at Vienna that he intended to force the West to recognize Communist East Germany by the end of the year, making East Berlin its capital and leaving West Berlin to wither as an isolated enclave. Although they vowed to resist this pressure, administration officials appeared remarkably sympathetic to Khrushchev's "German problem." Nearly three million East Germans, a fifth of the population, had fled to West Germany, mostly through the open portal of West Berlin, and they left behind an economy that was bleeding to death. Unless the borders of East Germany were somehow sealed, its impoverished people were bound to stage strikes and revolts that only Soviet tanks could put down. Such a slaughter would tempt West Germans to rush to the aid of their countrymen and force Washington to choose between supporting a dangerous intervention and standing aloof in humiliating fear. Even without an East German revolt, the chances were that Moscow would sooner or later have to replace the lost workers by moving in Russians and other East Europeans, thus altering the ethnic mix and destroying all hope for Germany's eventual reunification.

Instead of lusting for a "rollback," therefore, the Kennedy men were quietly hoping that the Russians would find a way to stop the population hemorrhage, provided only that the remedy did not interfere with the West's access to Berlin. Ambassador Thompson had speculated from Moscow that the Russians might be planning to cordon off East Berlin, preparations that might explain Khrushchev's latest threats of massive destruction "in case of war." As only Kremlinologists understood, Khrushchev's most bellicose rhetoric usually disguised a new sense of insecurity. He had indeed secretly authorized the erection of a wall around West Berlin but insisted that the East German Communists test the West's response with barbed wire before they turned to brick and cement.

My account of the Kennedy team's trepidations about instability in East Germany became my first substantial front-page story from Washington. Just days later, during the night of Saturday, August 12, came the news of the feverish unrolling of the barbed wire. It was being strung clear across the middle of Berlin, even down the middle of streets that separated the eastern and western zones of the city. East Berliners wept as their escape routes were sealed. West Berliners trembled in fear of isolation.

I stalked the halls of the State Department that Sunday, hoping for a clue to Washington's reaction. Given the administration's concerns, it should have felt relief that the Russians were looking to stop the flight of East Germans without having to evict the Western powers from Berlin. But no one dared to confess any such relief or say anything except rail against the cruelty of incarcerating 16 million East Germans behind a new iron curtain. By accident, I encountered Foy Kohler, a fellow Kremlinologist then in charge of the Berlin "task force," as he rushed from one meeting to another. "It kind of solves a problem, doesn't it?" I whispered.

Kohler responded with just one quiet, wistful yes. Hypothesis confirmed: Once vague longings were now policy. Without any further comment from any official, I was able to write that although the division of Berlin would be loudly protested by Washington, it would not be militarily challenged—provided only that the West's access to Berlin continued to be undisturbed. By dint of my anticipatory conversations, I was able to explain this acquiescence in a way that no official could ever concede in public: as a desire to help East Germany retain its labor force and stabilize its economy. It was a far more accurate dispatch than the scores of articles

I had to write in succeeding weeks, recounting the administration's protests, threats, and demands for "negotiation." Those theatrics were deemed necessary to buttress the morale of shaken West Berliners and to defend the president against domestic critics. But as we learned years later, Kennedy instantly saw that the Berlin crisis had passed. Khrushchev would not have needed a wall if he intended to take West Berlin.

Reston was duly impressed by my swift reading of the situation and my Reston-like confidence in reasoning my way past misleading policy pronouncements. That was the essential trick in covering politics and diplomacy, where public statements so often conceal private calculations. Deciphering the verbal codes in *Pravda* and the pecking order of Soviet Presidium portraits proved to have been excellent preparation for observing the Cold War through the other end of the telescope.

True to form, Reston thought that one good scoop only deserved another. He urged me to press ahead, shrewdly predicting that government and embassy doors would now swing open for this seemingly well-informed new boy in town. One good catch always yielded bait for the next. Reston cheered us on and tapped his sources to help us when asked, but he rarely told us how to do our jobs. Unlike most of the editors in New York, he dared to presume that we knew our territory. When he had a question, he posed it in a way that let us pretend we'd thought of his angle ourselves. He almost never complained about gaps in our stories; he just sat on your desk, puffed his pipe, and chewed the fat until you secretly blushed about a blatant oversight in that morning's article. And unlike many star reporters, Scotty never stole a subordinate's story. On the contrary, he used his extraordinary access to high officials to nail down our missing facts. We'd repay him with analytical hunches that occasionally enriched his columns. It was an effective collaboration among very large egos.

Typical of the way Reston worked with us was his response one night when I rushed into his office with the scoop that Bobby Kennedy was flying to Indonesia.

Hmm. Let's think about that, Scotty said—*always* said, no matter how late the hour. *Why do you think the president would waste his brother's time on a tinhorn like Sukarno while he's toe-to-toe with Khrushchev in Germany?*

Yes, I finally allowed. *Indonesia could be a feint, to justify a secret visit to Moscow.*

Reston picked up the phone and, to my amazement, the attorney general promptly took the call.

Can't give him time to deny it, Scotty whispered. *Good evening, General,* he said, signaling for me to listen on an extension. *What on earth do you think you can accomplish by going to Moscow?*

Kennedy's shocked silence confirmed my guess. We now knew his travel plan no matter what else he might say. My little back-page paragraph was suddenly front-page news—although the publicity ultimately led Kennedy to cancel the Moscow stopover.

Reston also taught us not to fret about that kind of interference with government operations. We had no right to "play God," to pretend that we could accurately foresee the consequences of either publishing or withholding a piece of news. Where secrets are concerned, it's for the government to keep them, if it can, and for us to learn them, if we can. Except in the rarest circumstance, what we know we owe to the reader. Publish and be damned.

Reston's own decision not to reveal the U-2 spy flights over Soviet territory was probably a mistake, he allowed; the flights were embarrassing to the Russians but hardly a secret from them. On the other hand, not revealing the *imminence* of the invasion of Cuba, he thought, was probably a good idea, if only to protect *The Times* from the charge of endangering lives. There simply were no rules for deciding these hard cases, each circumstantially different from the next. But our main business was to print the news, not to ration it.

Nonetheless, just as we were not directly told everything we printed, we did not print everything we were told. We respected confidences, not merely as a matter of ethics but as a transaction of commerce: Protect your sources and they'll see you again, perhaps even tell you more the next time. Officials spoke to us because they wanted to explain and sell government policy to the public—or because they wanted to expose a policy that they opposed. To protect the identity of a source, we took care not to rush from any official's desk straight to the typewriter; better to make a decoy run through a half-dozen other diplomatic and congressional offices. Another defense was to take information from one source and build it into the questions put to others, leading several people to think they merely confirmed what a reporter knew all along. In extremis, we would pass sensitive information to a colleague on a different beat, throwing everyone off the scent.

Since virtually every diplomatic document in Washington was stamped "confidential," "secret," "top secret," or "eyes only," almost every conversation between a reporter and an official working on "national security" was a potentially treacherous transaction. But officials and diplomats cannot justify their actions without sharing some of those secrets. So they insist on speaking "for background," meaning "don't quote me." Their anonymity might also shield hypocrisy, but reporters have no obligation to print what they are told until convinced with more reporting that they have the truth. The gist of background conversations vitally informed our coverage of military and diplomatic affairs. Even so, the temptation to violate the rules was sometimes hard to resist. I felt burdened for many years by the confidentiality of a passionate "off-the-record" comment that Secretary of State Dean Rusk made to me in our introductory meeting, long before the military escalation in Indochina.

"Laos," he said, leaning forward across his desk and staring coldly into my eyes, "Laos is not worth the life of a single Kansas farm boy."

It was a searing pronouncement, virtually writing off the strategic importance of Southeast Asia. Rusk went further: he wished there were a painless way to scrap the Southeast Asia Treaty Organization (SEATO), the treaty that he repeatedly and disingenuously invoked in later years to justify the ground war in Vietnam. Implicitly, Rusk's comments contradicted even his subsequent claims that America was honor bound to defend Southeast Asia against "the Chinese hordes." Rusk became a hawk on Vietnam and sacrificed a huge number of Kansas farm boys, but I knew from just that one confidential conversation that he did so mainly to make good on presidential threats and commitments, not out of concern for South Vietnam's territory or freedom. I made frequent use of that insight over the years without betraying his confidence. Why? Because periodic chats with the secretary and other high-ranking officials were more important to my work, and to my readers, than one colorful quote that would foreclose access to them.

"Off-the-record" meant not for publication—at least until memoir time. As even Supreme Court judges found it hard to understand, however, information is not a tangible object that can be safely locked away or given back, like the White House silver. Off-the-record could never mean out-of-mind. Off-the-record information that had evidentiary value could, even if unpublished, inform a reporter's research and writing. If you believed it, you could hardly forget it. The knowledge could also guide you to someone else who was willing to provide the same information in printable form. Off-the-record, therefore, was a condition that we grudgingly accepted to gain otherwise unattainable access. But there were times when I refused such a limitation because I thought I could get the information elsewhere on better terms.

Off-the-record, in any case, was the least confusing of the codes that governed press traffic in Washington. Trickier by far were the conditions surrounding interviews and briefings held explicitly, and sometimes only implicitly, "on background" or, more stringently, "deep background."

"Deep background" meant we could use a piece of information but without any attribution to anyone. That was the only way to get the CIA to disgorge a biography of a new African leader or the Pentagon to admit that its military attaché in Poland really did photograph Soviet army installations before he was expelled. When employed with a single reporter, "deep background" could shield an official who was willing to betray a secret he was obliged to protect, or *his* sources of information. But when sprung on a crowd of reporters at a virtually public meeting, "deep background" was only a propaganda weapon, a way to induce the media to disseminate a government line on their own authority. It took a lot of courage to refrain from reporting such a "briefing" when you knew that other papers next morning would be stating flatly that "President Kennedy is unimpressed by the latest Soviet disarmament proposal" without revealing who said so. I remember Walt Rostow, President Johnson's national security adviser, claiming the veil of "deep background" to denounce Sen. William Fulbright for lending aid and comfort to the North Vietnamese. He did not go on the record until I threatened to print a wire service report of his remarks and to identify him as the speaker. Only a major paper like *The Times* could afford to make such a threat, and even I was not entirely sure that my editors would have approved.

My all-time favorite piece of "deep background" news was acquired at the very deep end of our Chevy Chase neighborhood swimming pool on a very hot Sunday afternoon in June 1964. The Frankels were there and so were Madie and Marvin Kalb of CBS and other reporters and quite a few government officials. Treading water after a lap or two, I encountered Tom Hughes, the head of intelligence and research at the State Department and a close associate of soon-to-be Vice President Hubert Humphrey. Hughes could hardly contain his amusement at a cable the night before from Henry Cabot Lodge, the liberal Republican then serving as Lyndon Johnson's ambassador to South Vietnam. Obviously eager to get home to contest the nomination of Barry Goldwater, Lodge was asking to be relieved within thirty days and allowed to plead not politics but reasons of health.

Wow! Can I use that? I asked.

Just leave me out of it, Hughes replied.

Not knowing whether we'd been observed in the pool, I rejoined our family circle in the grass and played conspicuously with all the little Frankels. Not until an hour later did I amble to a phone, dictate a lengthy story direct to New York, and dive happily back into the pool. The story— LODGE RESIGNING; EXPECTED HOME FOR CONVENTION—led *The Times* the next morning, and, much to my surprise, all hell broke loose.

The White House denied receiving any such communication. Johnson obviously warned Lodge that his request would be honored only if he let the president announce it in an orderly manner in his own good time and with a successor in hand. Cleverly, though dishonestly, Lodge said in Saigon that it was "totally false" to suggest he had to quit for reasons of health. He didn't say he wasn't quitting, but envious rival reporters eagerly focused only on "totally false" so that even *The Times* felt obliged to print Lodge's statement. We, at least, added that his quitting *for political reasons* remained an "unresolved" question. Johnson hated to be scooped or rushed. He wanted the leaker caught and punished. He may have been hoping also to delay Lodge long enough to damage the anti-Goldwater movement; he obviously wanted Goldwater as his opponent in November.

Are you sure? Scotty asked without asking for my source.

One hundred percent, I said. *But I'm mystified by the denials. Lodge's request definitely arrived, so our story was absolutely accurate. But maybe Johnson intends to talk him out of it.*

New York is nervous, Scotty observed.

Well, let's keep printing the denials—but keep them short and unconvincing, I urged.

For nine long days, Johnson left Lodge—and me—twisting in the wind. And I, of course, had to stay far away from Tom Hughes. *Time* magazine was particularly snide, and typically fanciful:

> Even as Frankel's story appeared, people began assailing its verisimilitude. . . . In Saigon, Ambassador Lodge swam ten laps at the Cercle Sportif pool before facing inquisitive newsmen. "I'm supposed to be sick, am I?" he grinned and, with that, disavowed the story of his resignation. "There's no truth in it at all."
>
> As it turned out, Frankel himself had not really considered his own story hot news. He wrote it several days before its appearance, slugged it "hold for Monday release" and then went picnicking all day Sunday with friends.

On the very day that this fiction appeared, the White House announced that Lodge was being replaced by Gen. Maxwell Taylor. McGeorge Bundy alerted Reston to give me the satisfaction of covering the White House announcement. My proud account of it said the Republican was "hurrying back from South Vietnam to help Gov. William W. Scranton's bid for the Republican Presidential nomination." And, I hinted, perhaps his own. *Time*, of course, never apologized, but my stock in Washington soared. "Deep background" had its uses.

And then there was plain-envelope "background," which required a reporter to fudge the source of a piece of news and relieve the speaker of direct responsibility for his words. Plain "background" information could be attributed in some generalized form—to "a high State Department official" or "a White House aide" or "Administration aides" or a "Communist diplomat." One obvious value of any "background" briefing was to let the White House augment, say, a presidential speech with explanations, facts, and figures without risk that the briefer would upstage the boss in the morning paper. A Bundy explanation of an arms control proposal was certain to be more precise and meaningful than a presidential speech, but it would not be offered if an assistant's name and fingerprints wound up all over Kennedy's pronouncement. Secretary Rusk liked to brief reporters on "background" over Scotch on Friday afternoons. He used our questions to infer the public's mood, and he hoped to influence the tone of our Sunday think pieces. He insisted, however, on being a "high official" rather than the secretary of state so that he did not have to guard against a sloppy phrase or a shorthand expletive. Disguising his voice was the price we paid for a chance to probe his thoughts.

When we withheld a name, we tried at least to suggest the bias of our source. Was the unnamed informant military or civilian, American or foreign, ally or adversary? Just "an official" was irresponsibly vague. "A reliable source" was a common but dumb locution; it implied that a reporter might also quote an *unreliable* source. Crediting just "a source" is even more absurd—as vapid as writing "someone told me."

When there was no honorable way even to hint at the source of our information, Scotty's remedy was to report the news on his own authority, without attribution. *Joe Jones will be named ambassador to Paris tomorrow*, or *The President is known to be considering Jones and Fitch*. But whenever I tried that approach, itchy pencils in New York always inserted a meaningless "officials said"—as if that somehow relieved *The Times* of responsibility for error. I was sure that if one day I wrote, *The sun came up this morning*, the copy desk would add, *officials said*. Some editors saw such meaningless evasions as a requirement of "objective" writing; it preserved the pretense that our news was devoid of human judgment and interpretation. They would rather lie than shatter that myth, preferring to write, *Cuba appeared to be retaliating for President Kennedy's trade embargo, observers said*, when in fact we had consulted no one. "Observers" became a silly synonym for ourselves.

The petty, often destructive editing that greeted analytical articles in New York became a major irritant. Every writer needs editing. The best *Times* editors have not only saved me from countless errors but also have improved much of my writing. Yet many editors were plainly confused about the permissible range of analysis in our dispatches. Our rebellions against some of their mindless "rules" produced a nightly combat. Then, almost every morning, a handful of us would bombard Scotty with plaintive memoranda and annotated clippings that documented New York's destructive deletions and erroneous insertions. In imitation of Ted Bernstein, the assistant managing editor, who published an in-house critique of our writing called *Winners & Sinners*, we took to producing a critique of the editing, matching our original prose against the mangled version in print. We called it *Sluggers & Muggers*.

Some days, while reading your own story, it was hard to hold down breakfast. More than once, some of us were driven close to resignation. Reston was sympathetic but ill suited to this trench warfare. He blamed Turner Catledge, the managing editor, for making lofty pronouncements about "objective" writing but then, in Reston's phrase, neither managing nor editing, neither controlling his bureaucracy nor involving himself in the editing process. We Washington reporters looked enviously each week to *The Economist* for its brilliantly concise and dispassionately analytical coverage of our beats. One winter, we went so far as to enlist Sol Linowitz, of Xerox fame, in an effort to raise money to create an American imitation of that British journal. It was galling to learn from Nancy Balfour, the late editor of *The Economist*'s American section, that her best articles were merely rewritten from *our* dispatches. For a time I was actually promised that my stories would not be changed without consultation. I kept a diary of New York's compliance with that deal and did indeed gain more freedom to inject analysis into our diplomatic reporting. But I never knew whether I earned that accommodation by analyzing well or simply by screaming long and loud.

Our struggles over editing at *The Times* were just one manifestation of the broader transformation of American journalism. Newspapers were ceasing to be mere expositors of government policy. More and more, even our misnamed "paper of record" was reporting events from an independent vantage. We were beginning to shun intimacy with people in power. We saw ourselves as more accountable to our readers than to our sources.

In the generation before ours, it was enough for Arthur Krock to interview President Truman to qualify for a Pulitzer Prize. In our time, the prize went to Woodward and Bernstein for planting dynamite under Richard Nixon's throne. In the years between, Scotty Reston scored notable scoops by making himself part of the government's decision process. When the men around Harry Truman decided after World War II that only huge sums of American money could rebuild Western Europe and rescue it from communism, it was to Reston that they confided the plan to provide the unheard-of sum of $18 billion in aid. Giving *The Times* a beat was their way of drumming up public interest and congressional support. The news appeared on a Sunday morning, and by ten o'clock, Sen. Arthur Vandenberg of Michigan, the chairman of the Foreign Relations Committee, called Reston at home to say, *You must be out of your senses; no administration would dare to come to the Senate with a proposal like that.* Of course it was Truman's sanity, not Reston's, that Vandenberg questioned. But it was through Reston—and his influential readers—that presidents and senators often negotiated in those days.

By the 1960s, however, Reston stood a respectful distance from power. Unlike Walter Lippmann and Joe Alsop, he was content to give advice in full view of his readers. He did not like it when William S. White, a Texan covering the Senate for *The Times*, drifted into Lyndon Johnson's coterie or when Tony Lewis, besides brilliantly covering the Supreme Court, became too conspicuously a member of Robert Kennedy's social circle. It was tough to keep your balance when you were expected simultaneously to get the inside scoop and to remain a disinterested witness of events.

Because Franklin Roosevelt and World War II still haunted the capital, most of us retained a special respect for the president, the commander in chief. We treated the chance to question him as an act of high purpose. On the mornings of Kennedy's news conferences, Scotty assembled the staff and urged us to look at the world through the president's eyes to determine which questions might produce the most rewarding insights. As we sharpened the wording of those questions and decided their order of importance, we conscientiously ruled out trick phrasings. Our job was to inform the readers, not to entrap the president. Scotty himself often used his follow-up questions to untangle a presidential syntax, asking whether Kennedy "really meant" to leave this or that impression. That is why even a decade later, in the 1976 campaign, it came as second nature to me to throw a lifeline to President Ford after his catastrophic gaffe during a debate against Jimmy Carter. Responding to my challenge that he justify the signing of what were called the Helsinki Accords with the Soviet Union, Ford clumsily tried to protect himself against Ronald Reagan's recent

charges that he had thereby ratified the Soviet Union's domination of
Eastern Europe:

> Thirty-five nations signed an agreement, including the Secretary of
> State for the Vatican. I can't under any circumstances believe that
> His Holiness the Pope would agree by signing that agreement—that
> the thirty-five nations have turned over to the Warsaw Pact nations
> the domination of, uh, Eastern Europe. It just isn't true. . . . There is
> no Soviet domination of Eastern Europe and there never will be
> under a Ford administration.

The next questioner had already begun when I hastily interrupted:

> I'm sorry . . . I wanted . . . Could I just follow? Did I understand you
> to say, sir, that the Russians are not using Eastern Europe as their
> own sphere of influence, occupying most of the countries there and
> making sure with their troops that it's a . . . that it's a Communist
> zone?

Ford replied, reasonably enough, that the Yugoslavs and Romanians had
wriggled free of total Soviet domination. But he doggedly spurned my
help and dug himself an even deeper hole:

> I don't believe that the Romanians consider themselves dominated
> by the Soviet Union. I don't believe that the Poles consider them-
> selves dominated by the Soviet Union. Each of those countries is in-
> dependent, autonomous. It has its own territorial integrity and the
> United States does not concede that those countries are under the
> domination of the Soviet Union.

Ford's rhetorical liberation of all Eastern Europe invited ridicule that may
well have cost him a very close election. I was widely praised not only for
exposing Ford's intellectual failings but also for trying to help him recover
his balance. But I was not looking to expose. I had responded instinctively,
with no partisan purpose. On Scotty Reston's team, you did not rush to
exploit the misstatements of a responsible official. You made sure that he
actually meant whatever you understood him to say.

Paradoxically, it was not the effrontery of my follow-up question but
the excessive deference of Ford's staff that caused the greatest political
damage. From Henry Kissinger down, they were so quick to praise his de-

bate performance that they failed at first to alert him to the Polish mistake and for too long delayed the necessary amendment of his remarks.

A further reason for our elaborate respect for the president of the day was that he alone among Americans held the power to blow up the planet. The nation felt itself so vulnerable to surprise attack that he was stalked, day and night, by a military officer carrying "the football"—a black case containing the codes and options by which presidents, starting with Eisenhower, could in minutes order land, air, and naval forces to unleash nuclear weapons against predetermined Soviet targets. That awesome reality deified a presidency that was already imperial in scope and paternal in aspect. And the Kennedys, John and Jacqueline, played their royal parts divinely.

They were young and handsome, apparently healthy and in love. They wore elegant clothes, refurbished the White House with exquisite taste, and gave glittering parties that celebrated art and intellect. They were elected to govern, but they also reigned, to popular acclaim. At formal events and private dinners, public servants stood and sat like nobles at court, their importance reckoned by their distance from the throne. And the press corps reveled in this spectacle of glamour and romance, fawning and deceived.

Reporters gossiped about John Kennedy's premarital affairs and about his summoning stenographers to dance with him and Peter Lawford, his brother-in-law, upstairs at the White House. But no one imagined this wily and witty president to be so wantonly stupid as to bed Mafia molls and movie stars between meetings of heads of state and tours of flood disasters. It was not out of deference, as later generations of reporters thought, but simple ignorance that we failed to report Kennedy's promiscuity. Not even the president's friend and recent neighbor Ben Bradlee, then of *Newsweek*, knew about the sexual escapades.

Nor did we suspect the gravity of Kennedy's chronic illnesses—Addison's disease, a failure of the adrenal glands, and the persistent backaches from either a spinal or a muscular infirmity. Kennedy lied about his health, admitting only to back problems that he ascribed to various football and wartime injuries, and he claimed to have conquered them under the care of Dr. Janet Travell, a back specialist. We now know that she kept the president on a lifesaving diet of cortisone and procaine, which he supplemented with amphetamines surreptitiously supplied by Dr. Max Jacobson, an eccentric New York physician whose mysterious

potions brought him the moniker Dr. Feelgood. The cortisone conspicuously puffed and reddened the president's cheeks, a symptom, we were
told, of painkillers and occasional sunlamp treatments. Yet Kennedy's
ostentatious displays of coatless vigor and touch football agility kept us
all from the truth. We never knew that he was in almost constant pain.
We never understood that his drugs could cloud his mind, impair his
judgment, and stimulate his libido. Our ignorance, not deference, sustained his stoic cover-ups.

———————

Kennedy himself became America's Dr. Feelgood. He vowed to defeat
Communist aggression even as he offered to negotiate East-West accommodation. He reduced taxes to stimulate the economy. And he tapped the
idealism of young Americans eager to serve the disadvantaged at home
and abroad. But until too late in his abbreviated term, Kennedy also underestimated the pent-up demands of black Americans and grievously
misjudged Khrushchev's largely rhetorical threats to spread communism
around the globe.

Although he campaigned for president by cynically accusing Eisenhower of incurring "a missile gap" in Russia's favor, Kennedy entered office convinced of precisely the opposite. He knew that the United States
was capable of such "massive retaliation" that it could reliably deter any
direct nuclear attack. It was "conventional" nonnuclear warfare and guerrilla insurgencies for which he thought us unprepared and ill equipped. By
misreading a Khrushchev speech in early 1961, Kennedy came to believe
that the Kremlin had a "master plan" for gaining world domination, by fo-
menting rebellions and inspiring "wars of liberation" throughout Asia,
Africa, and Latin America.

Addressing Soviet propagandists in Moscow on January 6, two weeks
before Kennedy's inauguration, Khrushchev had indeed vowed to support
all anticolonial movements. But he did so defensively, firmly rejecting
Stalin's prophecy that world communism would triumph over capitalism
in an "inevitable" major war. World wars and even "local wars,"
Khrushchev argued, had become "unthinkable"; they would only lead to a
nuclear holocaust. But as usual, the Soviet leader disguised his ideological
retreat by predicting new victories. He boasted that nuclear missiles had
made Soviet communism impregnable, while the "imperialists" were daily
losing ground to "national liberation" movements, as in Cuba, Algeria,
and Vietnam. In other words, the Soviet Union could safely rely upon nuclear weapons for its own defense, drastically reduce the size of its army

and navy, and still perform its international Marxist duty by lending aid and comfort to whatever forces happened to be waging anticolonial "wars of liberation."

As Ambassador Thompson reported from Moscow, that speech—"*if read literally*"—was a kind of declaration of Cold War. But Thompson and Eisenhower knew from long experience that Khrushchev's bluster could never be read literally. Kennedy lacked that experience and made a literal reading of the speech compulsory throughout his new administration. Defense Secretary Robert McNamara, a master manager but political naïf, remembered study of that speech as a "significant event in our lives."

By the time I arrived in Washington six months later, the capital's anxiety had been further exacerbated by the Bay of Pigs fiasco and by Khrushchev's Berlin bluster at the Vienna summit. Kennedy responded by increasing the Pentagon's missile budgets and insisting on a simultaneous expansion of the army's "Special Forces" to prepare for overseas guerrilla wars. Not only Castro but pro-Soviet rebels like Patrice Lumumba in the Belgian Congo were targeted for assassination by the CIA. And Kennedy was heard to say more than once what he had said to Scotty Reston while slouching on that couch in Vienna—that besides standing firm in Germany he needed to prove himself to Khrushchev. If not in Laos, then surely in Vietnam.

Though new to Washington, I was highly skeptical about these alarms. I had experienced Khrushchev and also benefited from the weekly tutelage of Ambassador Thompson and his expert staff in Moscow. As Michael Beschloss, a historian of the Cold War, discovered decades later, Thompson told Kennedy at the very start of his presidency that Khrushchev, for all his bluster, was by far the most pragmatic of the Soviet leaders. He was making his country a more normal society and struggling not only against hard-liners in the Kremlin but also against those in Communist China, who had hoped to lure him into conflict with the United States. Khrushchev obviously wanted most of all to raise the standard of living of his people, Thompson concluded, and those people were "becoming bourgeois very rapidly."

Those of us who had had to cope with Russian plumbing, food lines, and crumbling masonry simply could not believe that Khrushchev would sacrifice his ambitious domestic program to costly conflicts against high-tech America. But the cocky captains of the New Frontier had no patience for such intuitive testimonials to Khrushchev's sobriety. In these early months, they considered the Soviet leader a dangerous adversary and cast a suspicious eye at any diplomat or reporter who dared to discount his bluster. And of course no one could be sure that Khrushchev's reforms would take root and steer the Kremlin's foreign policy in benign directions. *Sputnik* proved what extraordinary resources the Soviet system could extract from an otherwise inefficient economy to neutralize America's military might. Despite his denunciations of Stalin, Khrushchev commanded the same awesome powers over the vast Soviet empire. And his pursuit of Soviet interests, even if defensive and born of insecurity, had certainly become aggressive.

In Washington, as in Moscow, fear seemed to me to color all discourse and distort all analysis. The men in the Kremlin were unnerved by the ring of American nuclear bases around their territory, bases commanded by generals like Curtis LeMay, the air force chief of staff, who made no secret of his desire for a "preemptive" first strike against the Soviet Union. The Russians also feared the gusts of freedom and individualism that propelled American culture across the globe. In Washington, the Kennedy men feared not only the growing Soviet influence in underdeveloped nations but also the domestic consequences of any sign of weakness. After his narrow victory over Nixon, Kennedy had no votes to give to Republicans poised to prove him soft on communism. So Kennedy and Khrushchev spoke to each other in the language of force.

Yet the superpowers wanted very little from each other. The main danger, as Kennedy eventually acknowledged, was miscalculation on either side. Besides Khrushchev's speech, Kennedy also urged study of Barbara Tuchman's *The Guns of August*, which recorded the clumsy steps by which the European powers had stumbled into war in 1914. For me, the Tuchman book was one more reminder that officials with big titles, lavish offices, and luxurious limousines were capable of ghastly misjudgments.

The sterile posturing of the two superpowers gave me a run of tiresome stories—Page One "news" that soon drifted far from reality:

U.S. BELIEVES MOSCOW SOFTENS TONE, IF NOT IDEAS, ON GERMANY.
But Speech by Khrushchev Elicits No Immediate Words of Optimism—
Address Encourages French

RUSK RULES OUT TROOP PULLBACK IN GERMAN CRISIS.
Says Reduction of Forces in Europe Might Be Studied in Disarmament
Talks. Acts to Reassure Bonn

RUSK SAYS STRONGER U.S. IS READY TO MEET RUSSIANS

**WEST STILL SEARCHES FOR A BASIS FOR NEGOTIATION
WITH SOVIETS**

ADENAUER TO SEE PRESIDENT NOV. 20–21 ON BERLIN CRISIS.
Chancellor, Re-elected, Accepts a Bid for "Thorough Review"

U.S. DISCOUNTING REPORT IN SOVIET OF A BERLIN SHIFT.
Capital Sees No Perceptible Advance over Earlier Russian Proposals

RUSK HINTS WALL NEED NOT BLOCK TALKS ON BERLIN.
He Indicates Its Removal Is Objective Rather Than Condition for Parleys

Over drinks one Friday afternoon, Rusk confessed that aimless maneuver had become the central aim of American policy in Europe. While giving lip service to the goal of German reunification, he said it was his fondest hope that after eight years of service as America's chief diplomat, he could pass the problem of Berlin to his successor "in exactly the form in which I inherited it."

Yet virtually every Saturday morning, when my editors in New York looked over their schedule of articles for the Sunday paper, they could think of nothing more suitable for the "lead" story than something more on Berlin. Week after week they would call the Washington bureau with a plea that Frankel "move Berlin forward, even an inch or two," or at the very least "review the bidding" of the nonbargaining players. After a while they simply issued a standing order: let's be sure to have a Berlin story every Saturday afternoon.

Stalking the halls of the State Department or Pentagon on Saturday mornings became one of my favorite rituals. High officials were at their desks in sport shirts, almost never guarded by secretaries. They enjoyed being interrupted for some lively banter and, besides a meaningless nugget for the weekly Berlin summation, often produced a useful bit of background information about a less conspicuous situation.

I protested the standing Berlin order, of course, and one Saturday rashly proclaimed that I could throw a dart at the State Department phone book and come up with something more interesting. Al Shuster, our mischievous Washington weekend editor, accepted the challenge and, lacking a dart, used a paper clip to spot the name of the desk officer for Iceland. I called the poor man at home and chastised him for not tending to the "crisis" on his turf, whereupon he revealed, in utter seriousness, that the British had promised to stand down for a week and to permit no more confrontations at sea with Icelandic fishing vessels. Was there a new incident? Was anyone hurt?

No, I reassured him; I was just checking an obviously wrong rumor. But maybe he could tell me more about America's behind-the-scenes mediation. He did, and I had the pleasure of writing for once about a real war, the fishing war in the North Sea.

The New York Times.

SOVIET ORBITS MAN AND RECOVERS HIM;
SPACE PIONEER REPORTS: 'I FEEL WELL';
SENT MESSAGES WHILE CIRCLING EARTH

20 · TOBI'S PATH

JOHN F. KENNEDY'S WASHINGTON WAS GLAMOROUS AND quaint, sexist and arrogant, and those of us caught up in its warp found the combination intoxicating. Whether you were in the White House, commanding imperial carriages and letterheads, or pressing your nose to its windows, begging for anecdotal scraps, you were a player in a pageant of power. Fortunately, I arrived long after the bondings on the 1960 campaign trail, too late to become a pal to America's new governors. I never met Kennedy alone, and I saw his closest colleagues only through the prism of their official rank. So I consoled myself by claiming to be a student of the issues, not of personalities, although that was no defense against my own swelling sense of importance.

When the secretary of state, Dean Rusk, poured you a drink on his veranda overlooking the Washington Monument and quietly mocked the foreign minister of France, you felt yourself looking down upon all mankind as if from Heaven's gate. When the president's national security adviser, McGeorge Bundy, returned your phone call and assumed he could speak confidentially in the arcane vocabulary of arms control, you could easily confuse comprehension of his policy with enthusiasm for it. Distance and disinterest were not easily preserved, though I was probably more conscious than many other Washington reporters of the duty to try. I kept reminding myself of the evidence in *The Guns of August* that officials just like those I was now covering turned out to have been historic fools.

My experience of Moscow helped to keep me balanced in Washington. My private sense of the Communist world and its complexities protected me against the simplifications and panics of the Kennedy entourage. I never learned whether it was President Kennedy himself or his secretary of defense, Robert McNamara, who first presumed that Washington's bargaining power against Moscow could be greatly enhanced by a massive program of civil defense, a demonstration of our ability to absorb a nuclear attack. But I knew at once that it was hysterical nonsense to stampede Americans into digging up their lawns to install fallout shelters. The shelter mania was exacerbated by the obviously false claim that all Muscovites had been trained to find refuge in the city's deep but ill-provisioned subway stations. I well knew that there was not even a candy bar to be had in those gorgeous caverns. The shelter mania also produced a hilarious debate, duly dissected in Sunday sermons across America, about whether a family taking cover in its small backyard shelter had the right in an emergency to shoot an intruding neighbor who had failed to prepare his own underground nest. I argued earnestly at dinner parties that we could fashion a much more reliable guarantee of survival by sending several hundred members of each country's leading families to live as hostages in the rival capital.

Those dinner parties were ritual extensions of the workday. Insulated in the northwest quadrant of the capital from the city's black majority, the movers and shakers and their chroniclers in the press not only worked and lunched in close proximity but also spent their evenings and weekends together, discoursing on the fate of Laos, the risks of Negro sit-ins, the obstructions of de Gaulle, and the ballooning of the Treasury's surplus. The social protocol rarely varied. After highballs and martinis, people were seated for dinner by rank, and they turned dutifully to the left and right for three courses of small talk with the opposite sex, sharing complaints about the help, reminiscing about less humid and more cultured capitals, and exchanging naughty asides about the hosts and their decor. Then the women would be led to safety while the men took cigars and brandy and watched two or more gladiators debate the legislative and diplomatic crisis of the week.

The rebellious decade that lay ahead did not intrude on these salons until Katharine Graham, who had inherited the chairmanship (her word, always) of the Washington Post Company, refused one night at the Averell Harrimans' to depart "with the ladies." She thought she had as much to teach and learn about the Congo as any male and threatened to leave the party if denied. She left soon after anyway, but the postdinner demitasse segregation was soon abandoned, and even women of lesser rank were allowed to listen deferentially to the wisdom of the anointed males.

For most women it was a cruel town. Few had the face and wardrobe of the president's wife, yet they were expected, like Jacqueline, to be the adornments of their husbands. More insistently even than the rest of America, the capital cared only for what you did and the title or rank you held and hardly at all for what kind of person you really were. At countless dinner parties, the opening question to Tobi was simply, *What does your husband do?* When she finally gained the courage to return the insult—*And what does your wife do?*—she always encountered surprise that she should be so offended. *You're not ashamed of your husband, are you?*

Tobi weathered Washington better than most of the wives of its fiercely ambitious young men. Though only twenty-seven when we arrived, she managed a home larger than any she had ever known with a confidence awakened during five merciful years beyond the reach of a domineering mother. She had tackled two strange languages and learned Russian well enough to qualify as a teacher and translator. She had mastered driving a car and staging a formal dinner party, with or without help, and given almost effortless birth to two children, upon whom she now lavished love, learning, and Jewish lore. Before a third pregnancy temporarily grounded her again, she helped to run a cooperative nursery school and a community pool and tennis club. She went on to edit a magazine, to teach history to high school girls, and eventually to write a young person's book about Russian artists.

But she deeply resented the lack of a clear career path of her own and the intellectual separation of our two lives. In Moscow, she'd been a full partner in the business of foreign correspondence. Her observations in the market and conversations at the theater had hugely enriched my dispatches, as had her friendships with assorted Russians. She had pushed her way into Moscow University's language program for foreigners and organized venturesome tours to nearby cities. She'd soothed my nerves after I'd battled the censor and, thankfully, failed to mail my resignations when I felt ill served by *The Times*.

Now, in Washington, I disappeared each day in a downtown office until past many dinner hours and came home to speak, if at all, with haughty certainty about mysterious places like Phnom Penh and Da Nang. More than I understood, Tobi felt unjustly excluded. More than I realized, her frustration inspired her often rough handling of our three children. The reluctance of one or another to be toilet trained at the age predicted by Dr. Spock struck her as part of a larger conspiracy to humiliate her talents and to hobble her career. My resentment of her high-decibel and violent disciplines—which I often sabotaged—only enlarged her sense of loneliness inside a family that she nonetheless prized.

We lacked the skill to talk out these tensions. Yet over time, Tobi gave even that aspect of our relationship educational force. Her search for a more purposeful life prepared me better than any polemics for the gestating feminist revolution. From the depth of her own frustrations, she anticipated its main themes. She inspired me to shop for groceries, to scrub the pans, to be the nocturnal prosecutor of the children's matinee misdemeanors, to shift my conversations with female dinner partners from maids to Marx. She led me to understand how the needs of educated women would gradually reshape American institutions. More than she knew, she again became my eyes and ears to the real world around us.

Most tellingly, Tobi thought masculine Washington was mad to be going to war in Vietnam. And she thought her husband and other Washington reporters were dupes to be giving serious weight to the Kennedy administration's reasons for its creeping intervention in Indochina. From the first American exertions in that alien terrain, Tobi dismissed Vietnam as a macho obsession, perhaps even racist in its faith that American technology could prevail over a peasant people. Among friends, we would joke that I had an evenhanded front-page approach to these issues whereas Tobi projected a fiery editorial conviction. In private she refused even to hear my recitations of the official logic. More than I ever confessed to her, she fed my doubts about our escalations of the conflict, doubts that must have shone through my coverage of the government's pronouncements. Either that, or Tobi's declamations on Vietnam were recorded in my FBI file. For when I finally succeeded in having my assignment changed from diplomacy to the presidency in 1966, Lyndon Johnson was convinced I'd been sent to his White House for the sole purpose of fueling the opposition to him and to the war.

Tobi spoke her mind, but more than that, she felt a persistent compulsion to confront. Her challenges to me and the children, though grounded in sound values, became increasingly harsh. So did her run-ins with colleagues at work and even with offending strangers. She grew not only restless about the incoherence of her career but wildly confused about the direction it should take. She turned virtually every social encounter into a search for praise and application for employment. She lectured random acquaintances and guests at our home about their business, all in the pathetic hope that some corporate executive or museum board member might suddenly desire her services. Not that she lacked for opportunities. In Washington, she edited a Jewish monthly, taught Russian and history at the National Cathedral School, and wrote educational pamphlets for the Smithsonian Institution. After we moved back to New York, she edited *Newsday*'s Op-Ed pages but quit when promotion came too slowly. In her midforties, she underwent the torture of statistics to earn a master's degree in business administration from Columbia but was unsatisfied as a management consultant. At forty-nine, after her steamy temperament caused her dismissal as marketing director for the New York City Opera, she went back to Columbia a third time to enroll heroically in its law school.

Tobi periodically resented the children for having delayed her return to professional life, or me for having uprooted her to head overseas. Most vehemently she berated me for not resolving her career crises by getting her a job with *The Times*. The publisher, Arthur Ochs "Punch" Sulzberger, did in fact agree to recommend her to the women's magazines owned by *The Times*, but Tobi rejected them as beneath her.

Secretly, she combined these manic pursuits with long, lonely labor at her typewriter, filling drawers with tearful and repetitious monologues. She wrote page upon page to no one in particular, dwelling on her remorse about her misfired ambitions, her failures with friends, and her anger at me. She typed streams of consciousness at odd moments of the day and night and augmented those compositions when away from her desk by scribbling the same thoughts into notebooks, calendars, even law school texts.

Many years later I saw in these notes how she passed from frustration to desperation, from anger into deep depression:

> I come on too strong; I press too hard; too full of hostility; I am stubborn, inflexible, intractable. . . . I always have this eruption problem. There is the studied, masked, controlled exterior of parties and in answering the telephone but the other me forcibly reveals itself much to my damage. . . . The insecurity, the need to show off, the

little girl, the look-at-me, notice-me syndrome. . . . I am not wanted. . . .

I do not believe I have lacked opportunities; on the contrary, I have muffed them all. . . . In every job I was unhappy, lusting after more—more prestige, more power, more position. . . . I am played out, burned out. Success is what I want, in any form. . . . Max offers no help; he will give me money but he will not leave his job and New York and help me find a newspaper somewhere that I can run. The tennis court is a place of acting out all my hostilities and aggressions. Is Max my mother?

None of us suspected that these communions often approached suicide:

I hunger for approbation, for external corroboration. Oh, God, I need release from that demon. . . . Feel so alone, can't shake it. Want to feel good inside. Don't even feel good with Max. He has to be reminded [to make love]. . . . Oh, God, give me some pleasure, make someone call and want me. Oh, please please please. I can't be sweet.

I, too, yearned for release. I despised myself for my hostile responses to many of Tobi's provocations and unfair assaults upon our kids. My job did take me away too often, but our division of labor seemed then like the natural order of things. I responded to Tobi's rages by retreating into sullen silence. Sometimes I sided openly with our children against her strictures, or compensated them with furtive kindnesses. I was ashamed of their shame in refusing to bring friends into such a volatile home. I knew that my inability to go on loving such a temperament only confirmed Tobi in her resentment and drove her to seek love elsewhere. Though I demonstratively packed my bags on a few occasions, I could not leave. I dreamed of a peaceful embrace in loving arms, but I dreaded a public brawl to claim custody of the kids. And what cowardice if I left them with her! Then again, perhaps these were just rationalizations for the inconvenience of a split.

I suspected all along that Tobi was sick, rather than malicious, but after one obscene drubbing for saying that, I could never again raise the subject directly. And Tobi refused, for years, to take my indirect suggestions that she consider analysis and therapy. She had been raised to treat not just emotional disorder but even the tiniest physical ailment as a shameful blemish; her childhood loss of hearing in one ear and the scaly patches of psoriasis on her scalp and arm could not be mentioned even to close friends. Although she barely heard conversation on her left side, she preferred appearing rude to confessing a defect. She had to remain the perfect specimen her mother had wanted her to be.

When she was finally persuaded at the age of fifty that depression was treatable, Tobi was given medicines that in just a few weeks restored her cheerful, youthful temperament. After years of stormy conflict, she could again delight in her family, strike up friendships at law school, and ignore the rudeness of strangers. The drugs worked such a miraculous change that when Tobi took seriously ill a year later, my first fearful question of the doctors was whether she'd have to stop taking them. The answer was no, and the pills kept her mercifully balanced. They also helped our children to understand that the tempests we had all endured were neither flaws of character nor denials of their mother's love. Tobi's chemistry was for too long her destiny.

21 · DECEPTION WITH HONOR

LIGHTS AT THE PENTAGON AND STATE DEPARTMENT blazed too late one Tuesday night in October 1962. We figured wearily that the farcical coalition of three Laotian princes might be coming apart again. Most unusually, however, officials refused to tell us much, even "on background." The closer we looked, the greater the frenzy we observed. Jack Raymond heard that the Joint Chiefs of Staff were canceling speaking dates and travel plans. Maggie Hunter saw foreign service officers fleeing from dinner parties, one of them his own birthday celebration. But the State Department's Asia desks were dark, so our suspicion shifted to Berlin.

Ominously, Robert Kennedy refused to answer calls even from Tony Lewis, his favorite contact at *The Times*. And the loosest gossips in Congress knew nothing. On the second day of our pursuit, the president's national security adviser, McGeorge Bundy, told Scotty Reston he was sorry that he couldn't discuss the problem, but he hinted that Berlin was a good guess. The next day the White House press secretary, Pierre Salinger,

called Reston with a two-part message from the president: Kennedy knew
we were smelling a problem and was sure we'd figure it out soon enough;
when we did, he wanted to be called before we published anything. Reston
agreed, and spurred us on.

The administration's European experts looked to be very busy. But
when I tracked the West German ambassador to his home at about 10:30
P.M. Friday, he'd gone to bed!

Can't possibly be Berlin, I shouted even before the ambassador came to
the phone and sleepily confirmed that he knew of nothing unusual back
home.

On Saturday, the president cut short a campaign trip in support of
midwestern Democrats running for Congress. He said he had a mild cold.
We concluded he had a major crisis.

If not Asia and not Berlin, it had to be Cuba. A crisis in Cuba could
mean only one thing: Sen. Ken Keating was right. The Republican senator from New York had seemed to us to be taking cheap shots throughout
this political season, warning that Soviet nuclear missiles were being in-
stalled in Cuba. The president and all his men kept insisting that the senator was wrong, that all those ships from Soviet ports carried only
"defensive" weapons. Didn't the senator know that the Soviets had never
stationed nuclear missiles outside their territory? Never! To put the matter finally to rest, the president had issued a blunt warning: If the nature
of the buildup in Cuba were to "change" and turn the island into an "offensive" base, the "gravest issues would arise" because "the United States
would act." Both on and off the record, however, his experts were sure it
wouldn't happen.

The sudden discovery that it had in fact happened was the only apparent explanation for the weeklong agitation in government. And whatever the military significance of such a shift in Soviet policy, the affront to
a president who had warned that it must not happen was self-evident.
Kennedy faced humiliation abroad and a political disaster at home.

Sure enough, by Sunday we detected extraordinary activity in offices
dealing with Latin America. Scotty told me to start writing what we knew
and what we suspected, all pointing to the unavoidable conclusion that
nuclear missiles had been discovered in Cuba. He interrupted only to let
me listen on an extension while he placed the promised call to President
Kennedy. Their exchange went something like this:

So you know what it is?

*Yes, sir. We struck out on Berlin and by a process of elimination figured it had
to be Cuba, offensive missiles in Cuba.*

And do you know what I'm going to do about it?

Scotty looked at me, and I shrugged a negative.

No, sir, we don't, except we know you promised to act and we hear you've asked for television time tomorrow night.

That is right. I'm going to order a blockade—a blockade of all Soviet shipping to Cuba.

Just like that, matter of fact, the president revealed that his threatened "act" would be an act of war. He didn't even bother to call it a quarantine, the less provocative euphemism that he had decided to use in public in the days ahead.

Of all the excitements and anxieties I felt at that moment, the main one was, What a story! But the president quickly punctured our scoop.

If you reveal my plan, or print that we discovered their missiles in Cuba, Khrushchev could beat us to the draw. He could make some preemptive move or counter with an ultimatum that would force us to take more violent action.

You're asking us to suppress the news?

I'm asking you not to disclose what we've discovered in Cuba until I have a chance to address the country and the Russians tomorrow night.

Well, that sounds like a reasonable request, but we down here only report the news. This is a decision the publisher will have to make. I'll pass on your request immediately.

Give Orvil my regards and tell him to call me if he disagrees.

———————

Even at that grave moment, the name of an important publisher, Orvil Dryfoos, came easily to the president's tongue. And as McGeorge Bundy remembered in his memoir of nuclear diplomacy: "He surely did not think that taking such calls was a distraction from his work on the crisis. It was part of that work, and not a small part. No one but the president himself could have stopped the [*Washington*] *Post* and the *Times* that Sunday."*

Reston summoned the reporters who were working this story to recount the president's request and said he would urge the publisher to honor it. I suddenly heard myself begging Reston to delay the call to New York and to let us discuss the matter further. Even if we didn't betray the president's obviously confidential reference to a blockade, didn't we have a right to report the discovery of the missiles, which we'd doped out ourselves? Why hold out on the readers? What if other papers had made the same deduction?

---

* McGeorge Bundy, *Danger and Survival: Choices About the Bomb in the First Fifty Years* (New York: Random House, 1988).

Other papers were the president's problem, Scotty replied. Besides, the most likely competitor was *The Washington Post*, and Kennedy would have no trouble persuading its publisher, his friend Phil Graham, to hold back. *The Times* in any case had to be responsible for its own conduct.

But weren't we sorry that we had held out vital facts about the Bay of Pigs invasion just eighteen months ago? And *that* was just a proxy war, Cubans against Cubans, not a conflict between us and the Russians. Were we going to let the president go to war against the Soviet Union without any notice to the country or discussion in Congress?

Hearing murmurs of agreement around the room, Reston reached for his telephone and told Pierre Salinger he needed to speak with the president again. He was put through almost instantly and again beckoned me to listen in.

Mr. President, one more question, if you will: We all remember the Bay of Pigs and our belief that more advance publicity might have spared the country that humiliation and spared our Cuban friends many casualties. If we hold out on our readers now, are we going to be in a war against the Russians before we print another edition? Some of us wonder whether you are asking for secrecy until after the shooting has begun.

Scotty, we've taken a whole week to plan our response. I'm going to order a blockade, it's the least I can do. But we will not immediately attack. You have my word of honor: There will be no bloodshed before I explain this very serious situation to the American people.

Though his words were often devious, the president's "word of honor" struck us as a genuine and generous gesture. We were impressed not just by the fervency of his response but by his willingness to submit to our presumptuous cross-examination.

We did not then realize that in this fleeting exchange on a tense Sunday afternoon, we had stumbled up against what would become the major constitutional issue of the decade—whether a president had the constitutional authority to commit the country to war in the nuclear age. Our private little deal with the commander in chief both acknowledged and limited that power. We had agreed to let him *risk* a shooting war without first informing Congress and the public, but not to wage it.

The next morning's *Times*—and *Washington Post*—did indeed reveal less than we knew. We fashioned sly hints of crisis activity around Washington, but even if the Soviet embassy caught our drift, it could not learn from our articles precisely what the United States had discovered about the missile buildup, when Kennedy planned to act, or what he would do. In fact, the Soviet ambassador, Anatoly Dobrynin, was himself ignorant of the missile deployment; like the president and all of us Kremlinologists, he thought Senator Keating's warnings were the fantasies of Cuban exiles and America's right-wingers.

I wrote *The Times*'s article that Sunday night but insisted that it not carry my byline. I wanted our deception of the readers to be a collective responsibility:

CAPITAL'S CRISIS AIR HINTS AT DEVELOPMENT ON CUBA; KENNEDY TV TALK IS LIKELY
TOP AIDES CONFER
U.S. Forces Maneuver off Puerto Rico—Link Is Denied

WASHINGTON, Oct. 21—There was an air of crisis in the capital tonight.

President Kennedy and the highest Administration officials have been in almost constant conference all weekend, imparting serious agitation and tension to official Washington.

Mr. Kennedy is expected to give the country an explanation in a radio-television address in the next day or two, but he has wrapped a tight veil of secrecy around the source of his concern so far.

Meanwhile, the Navy and Marine Corps are staging a powerful show of force in the Caribbean not far from Cuba, which has been the site of a large Communist military buildup in recent weeks. About 40 ships are heading for the island of Vieques off Puerto Rico.

The Administration denies that there is any connection between the anxious mood here and these maneuvers, which involve about 20,000 men, including 6,000 marines.

But the speculation in Washington was that there had been a new development on Cuba that could not be disclosed at this point.

The maneuvers near Vieques were indeed unrelated to the missile threat. Kennedy had ruled out another invasion of Cuba, but he had agreed to all sorts of plans, from sabotage to assassination, to cripple the Castro regime. The maneuvering Marines were trying to unsettle the Cubans by ostentatiously rehearsing amphibious landings in a mythical Caribbean country led by a dictator named Ortsac (read him backwards). They certainly caught the attention of Havana and Moscow, but those maneuvers in October did not inspire the Soviet missile shipments. Those had been planned since May.

To the end of his life, Khrushchev explained his nuclear buildup in Cuba as primarily a defense of the island against invasion by the United States, and Soviet records of the period give weight to that motivation. That rationale helped to persuade Castro to accept the missiles in the first place. It also helped Khrushchev to rationalize their humiliating withdrawal after Kennedy gave him a public promise never to invade Cuba. But I believed from the start and have grown more certain over the years that defending Castro was never Khrushchev's main purpose.

As we now know, the Cuban missile ploy was cooked up in the spring of 1962 by Khrushchev and his defense minister, Rodion Malinovsky. They faced a growing "missile gap" in America's favor and realized that catching up in the production of intercontinental missiles would take years and cost a czar's fortune. Quickly building nuclear bases in Cuba would let them deploy their abundant stocks of short-range (1,000- to 2,000-mile) missiles and instantly multiply the number of American targets in their nuclear sights. In a stroke, they would increase the Soviet attack potential by perhaps 40 percent.*

There was no question that missiles aimed at two thirds of American territory had an "offensive" capability of the sort that Kennedy had warned he would not tolerate. That is why Khrushchev deployed them in such haste and secrecy, with many deceptive assurances that his armada of freighters was carrying only "defensive" weapons to Cuba. He intended to lull the American public and government until after the November election, when he planned to visit the United Nations and Cuba to celebrate his new striking power as a fait accompli. Surprise! Now let's negotiate as equals!

It was a desperate effort to match Kennedy's missile buildup and to approach strategic parity without ruinous new ruble investments. From the day the Soviets launched the first sputnik, Eisenhower had tolerated Khrushchev's public pretense of military "equality" with the United States, and even "superiority" in some weapon categories. Kennedy helped to perpetuate that fiction when he campaigned against the "missile gap" that Eisenhower had allegedly incurred. But after the Bay of Pigs and new tensions in Berlin, Kennedy felt compelled out of weakness to speak the truth, unwisely boasting of America's vast superiority and continuing buildup. He was challenging the very rationale by which Khrushchev had hoped to shift Soviet investments from weaponry to consumer goods and agriculture.

---

* My reasoning here has been amply reinforced by information in an excellent book that nonetheless leans (unconvincingly) toward a different conclusion. The book, citing many previously closed records, is by Aleksandr Fursenko and Timothy Naftali: "*One Hell of a Gamble*": *Khrushchev, Castro, and Kennedy, 1958–1964* (New York: W. W. Norton, 1997).

Having already reduced his army and navy, Khrushchev must have come under severe pressure from his military and other Presidium members to answer the American buildup. The Cuba gambit was his response. What looked to us like recklessness was more likely desperation. With boasts and measures that were meant to reassure domestic critics, Khrushchev and Kennedy managed only to whip themselves into the most dangerous confrontation of the Cold War.

Were we at *The Times* wise enough to inject this kind of historical perspective into our coverage of the crisis? Decidedly not. Newspapers flatter themselves by pretending that they produce "the first drafts of history" when history is their weakest suit. Even the best reporters lack the skills and memories needed to evoke the past. The evidence for our short memories lies each night on the obituary page, the one page frankly devoted to the past. In its commemorations of important lives, even *The Times* regularly cheats those whose fame was achieved when they, and we, were young. Journalism is shaped and defined by the virtues and vices of youth.

In accepting Kennedy's "word of honor" and preserving his secret for another twenty-four hours, we were obviously reacting as patriots and not just as dispassionate reporters. There really was a danger that Sunday night that writing a fully truthful report could lead to violence in the Caribbean. If Khrushchev knew his ships were about to be challenged at sea, he might have preempted Kennedy's move with irretrievable threats to run a blockade. He, or the Cubans, might have declared Cuba's airspace inviolate and begun to shoot down the U-2 spy planes that were keeping watch on the missile deployments. Since Kennedy had resolved to remove the missiles, by force if necessary, he had good reason to hope that the surprise of a blockade would suffice to have the missiles dismantled.

I never doubted the president's "word of honor" and never regretted our honoring his request. There can be no fixed rules for dealing with such appeals from responsible authorities; they have to be evaluated one at a time. Only the gravest circumstances can justify withholding important news from the public, but on rare occasions those circumstances appear.

Contrary to the alarms of that October, however, we had not helped to save the world from nuclear war. There was never much danger of a nuclear exchange in the Cuban crisis, and those of us with some experience of Khrushchev felt sure of it throughout. We were wrong about his intentions in Cuba but not about his sanity. Khrushchev believed in nuclear diplomacy and bluff, never in nuclear war.

My day-to-day analyses of the crisis in *The Times* closely resembled those that we later learned Kennedy was getting from Ambassador Thompson. Less brilliant but also less arrogant than George Kennan and less assertive than Charles Bohlen, Thompson was nonetheless their equal in his grasp of Soviet reality and desire to improve East-West relations. He had lived longer in Moscow than any other American diplomat. In 1941, when the Soviet government and diplomatic corps fled to the interior from Nazi tanks, a young Tommy Thompson was left in cold and lonely charge of the Moscow embassy. In the 1950s, he spent several years negotiating the Soviets out of Austria, an exercise that first demonstrated the willingness of Stalin's heirs to pay the price of retreat for stability on their Western front. As ambassador in Moscow, Thompson strongly urged that Khrushchev be invited to the United States, accompanied him from coast to coast in 1959, and came to understand the interests and obsessions of this complicated Soviet leader better than any other American. He knew how to balance Khrushchev's belligerent boasts against his wily humanity and understood his desperate desire to be accepted in America as an equal. Thompson taught me to see that, beneath their maddening belligerence, the Russians were usually cautious and fearfully defensive, qualities sustained by a deep-seated sense of inferiority.

Throughout the missile crisis, Thompson never doubted that a deal could be struck to resolve it. Neither did I. But while I merely scoffed at the people who suddenly wished they had really built fallout shelters, Thompson channeled his confidence into daily advice to the president. He kept Kennedy focused on the idea that Khrushchev needed the appearance of some reciprocal concession to justify a Soviet retreat. This was crucial advice that offset the more impetuous counsel of the older, anti-Stalin generation led by Dean Acheson.

As the crisis became public, Kennedy framed his challenge to Moscow with great precision. He objected not only to the threat of seeing nuclear weapons so close to the Florida coast but also to the deception with which they had been deployed. He did not merely deplore the presence of the missiles, he demanded their removal under a reliable inspection routine. But his threats of further action were deliberately vague, leaving ample room for still other nonviolent maneuvers. Only his rhetorical embellishments were overblown, carelessly creating the impression that there was imminent danger of "worldwide nuclear war."

Still, the confrontation lasted for a week, and the risks of a clash near Cuba—or some Soviet military challenge elsewhere—could not be entirely dismissed. On Tuesday, the morning after Kennedy's speech,

Moscow ritually objected to the blockade. But as so often before, it carefully defined the American challenge as a challenge to Cuba, not the Soviet Union. My training in close readings of Soviet syntax spotted that evasion. By applying the same close scrutiny to the informal words of American officials, I was able to report on Tuesday that while the West's position in Berlin would never be traded for the missiles in Cuba, it was "conceivable" that the United States "might be willing to dismantle one of the obsolescent American bases near Soviet territory" in exchange. Officials were in fact thinking of trading away the bases in Turkey that pointed Jupiter missiles at Soviet targets. They called the Jupiters outdated and claimed they had been kept active only to symbolize a commitment to the defense of Turkey. What a convenient symmetry of purpose! By Thursday, Walter Lippmann's column explicitly suggested an exchange of the Cuban and Turkish bases. Moscow took quick notice of these hints.

Kennedy's naval "quarantine" did not take effect until Wednesday morning, and by Wednesday afternoon all the Soviet ships carrying military cargoes had turned aside or completely around. We recorded the retreat under a banner headline across the entire front page: SOME SOVIET SHIPS SAID TO VEER FROM CUBA, and the president's men breathed easier. As Secretary Rusk whispered backstage, invoking the memory of a childhood game in his native Georgia, "We are eyeball-to-eyeball, and I think the other fellow just blinked." To keep things cool, the president allowed a Soviet oil tanker to pass through his blockade unmolested, and the next day he challenged only a leased vessel that he knew to be carrying innocent cargo. While much of the country and much of the world continued to tremble, the two leaders struggled for three more days, mainly to find a formula that would let Khrushchev yield to the president's demand and take his missiles back home with some kind of face-saving "compromise."

By Saturday, Khrushchev had sent two separate offers to pull out his missiles as part of a deal. One asked Kennedy to promise never again to invade Cuba. The other proposed a reciprocal dismantling of bases in Cuba and Turkey. Kennedy took the no-invasion pledge, but he also promised, orally and secretly, that he would soon scrap the Jupiters in Turkey provided no one in Moscow ever linked that withdrawal to the Cuban settlement.

That little codicil, known to only eight other American officials, remained secret for many years. It may have helped Khrushchev cover up his humiliation among his Kremlin colleagues. Our ignorance of that secret promise surely encouraged us to exaggerate Kennedy's triumph. Although the president cautioned his aides not to gloat in public, they took full credit for brilliant "crisis management" and also for the "moral achievement" of limiting the loss of life to that of a single U-2 pilot, Maj. Rudolph Anderson, Jr. The press helped the Kennedy crowd heap scorn upon those officials who had originally favored the use of force against the missile sites and also on those few who had wanted only to issue a diplomatic protest. The winners in politics are rarely charitable to the authors of advice they rejected. That is one reason leaders so rarely get honest advice.

It was not secrecy or spin, however, that most distorted our chronicle of this Cold War moment. Our daily coverage of the crisis and our "ticktock" (minute-by-minute reconstruction) of it a week later were exemplary feats of *Times* reporting. We failed, as we usually do, only in setting the confrontation into a broader frame. I was more remiss than most of my Washington colleagues because I never found enough ways to emphasize my conviction that Khrushchev's aggressive gambits, in Cuba as in Berlin, were driven by feelings of weakness and inferiority. My judgment, based on my long exposure to Soviet politics, deserved to be shared with our readers. But that kind of analysis was always the most difficult to deliver within the discipline of "objective," nonideological journalism. At a time when Kennedy was condemning the Soviet leaders for their nuclear duplicity, it would have taken more courage than I—or *The Times*—possessed to explain Khrushchev's conduct in a way that would not seem to be excusing it.

Emotionally, my competitive instincts ran in precisely the opposite direction. My next big scoop in that crisis week was getting the evidence for the president's charge that Andrei Gromyko had directly lied to him about the missiles. By challenging the White House to prove it, I obtained the president's permission to have someone read me the complete record of his minuet with the Soviet foreign minister, a dance in which Kennedy never let on that he had detected the missiles while Gromyko kept reading from a cagey note that authorized him to state that Cuba was getting only "defensive" weapons.

It is futile, but not entirely pointless, to speculate on the course of history if Kennedy had been more sympathetic to Khrushchev's predicament and accepted the presence of nuclear missiles in Cuba. They did not greatly diminish America's strategic advantage; Soviet targets were abundantly threatened from American bases and submarines all over the globe as well as by long-range missiles on American soil. Instead of being condemned and, a year later, deposed for his "harebrained schemes," Khrushchev might then have been a hero to his Kremlin colleagues, and allowed to save money by further reducing the Soviet army and navy. He'd have tried also to capitalize on his success by forcing the pace of negotiations over Berlin and reforms at home. Kennedy, of course, might have been seriously wounded, accused of truly "losing" Cuba, and driven to step up the arms race and to deepen his commitment to resist the Communists' "war of liberation" in Indochina.

As it is, the Soviet leaders vowed in retreat never again to be caught short of missiles capable of avenging an American attack. Khrushchev's cuts in military budgets were reversed. And for the next two decades, the superpowers invested vast sums in the perpetual quest of a nuclear balance.

Even more costly was the now reinforced American impression that the Soviet Union aspired to "world domination" by sponsoring proxy wars, revolutions, and insurgencies on every continent. With his missile diplomacy, weapons sales, and "anticolonial" agitations, Khrushchev seemed to have rejected Kennedy's invitations to ratify the status quo—to more or less freeze the existing spheres of influence and slowly bring the arms race under control. For the World War II generation of Americans, the Soviet probes and thrusts were all too reminiscent of the early aggressions of Germany, Italy, and Japan, which the major Western powers had failed to resist when they might have done so at tolerable cost. They were a generation determined never again to "appease" dictators as Britain and France had done when they fed pieces of Czechoslovakia to Hitler at Munich in 1938. "No more Munichs" had become the imperative object of American foreign policy, and thus, seduced by history, we slid carelessly and disastrously into the morass of Vietnam.

22 · WEATHER VANE

I BLUNDERED MY WAY INTO VIETNAM WITH THE SAME cocky ignorance that propelled the Kennedy administration. It had been spoiling for a "conventional"—i.e., nonnuclear—fight from the day the president misread Khrushchev's speech about the promise of "wars of liberation" in Asia, Africa, and Latin America. From his first days in office, Kennedy demanded that the Pentagon and CIA prepare to fight in such "proxy" wars with "special forces" and "counterinsurgency" teams. Khrushchev's presumed "proxies," and Mao's, had to be resisted with our own. That would either defeat a localized challenge or force the Communists to expand and escalate the battle to the point where America's superior wealth and technology would always prevail. Under the tutelage of his favorite army generals, Maxwell Taylor and James Gavin, the president ordered the army to concentrate on antiguerrilla tactics. British veterans of guerrilla war in Malaysia and American advisers to antiguerrilla forces in the Philippines were celebrated at the White House and at Georgetown dinner parties. The green beret became the most treasured army headgear, and the old soldiers who had vowed after Korea "never again" to engage in battle on the Asian mainland were shoved aside as anachronisms; they did not understand the modern struggle for the "hearts and minds" of poor peoples. On to Vietnam!

In our collective ignorance of Southeast Asia, the media failed to mount a timely challenge to a myth created by the Eisenhower administration in 1954. After the defeat and withdrawal of the French from Indochina, the United States sponsored the creation of a non-Communist South Vietnam and persuaded itself that the line dividing it from North Vietnam was as sacred a frontier as the lines drawn after World War II through the middles of Germany and Korea. The press failed to challenge the extended myth that by continuing to struggle to unite all Vietnam, the North Vietnamese were the agents of an expansionist Sino-Soviet alliance. And while we didn't all believe it, we dutifully parroted the further myth that a Communist victory in South Vietnam would threaten the stability not just of Laos and Cambodia but also of Malaysia and Thailand and even distant Indonesia, India, and the Philippines. They would fall "like dominoes."

Scotty Reston wrote a column in February 1962 saying that the United States was now involved in an undeclared war in South Vietnam, a fact well known "to the Russians, the Chinese Communists, and everyone else concerned except the American people." And so it remained for three more years. When *The Times* sent Homer Bigart to Saigon for six months in early 1962, he was the first newspaper correspondent to join a few American wire service reporters. Homer immediately smelled trouble and soon predicted failure. He was succeeded in September by David Halberstam, who thought that the war was worth winning and going well—until a month later he ventured out of Saigon: "It should be reported that there is considerably less optimism out in the field than in Washington or in Saigon and that the closer one gets to the actual contact level of this war, the farther one gets from official optimism."

With America's eyes riveted on missiles in Cuba, no one paid much attention. Halberstam and also Mal Browne and Neil Sheehan of AP and UPI kept sending bad news, so bad that Kennedy tried to have Halberstam recalled. The president had now committed 16,000 American military "advisers" to South Vietnam, and his response to the bad news from the field was to let McNamara and Rusk pump up the Washington press with hopeful fantasies. I was so inexperienced in Southeast Asian affairs that I had no independent view of that distant conflict. I became, for too long, just a weather vane registering the winds of Washington's false optimism.

––––––––––––

At *The Times*, we were particularly distracted by a four-month printers' strike, which closed the New York plant and left us with only the modest circulations of our California and European editions. I sided emotionally with the company and against the printers, whose featherbedding and rejection of labor-saving machines had severely damaged other New York papers. But I honored my compulsory membership in the Newspaper Guild and, like two-thirds of the news staff, refused to cross the printers' picket line. To replace the lost wages, I took freelance reporting assignments, including a far-afield study for the Ford Foundation about the denigration of good college teachers who fail to publish original research. After the strike ended in March 1963, we were further encumbered by the tensions between strikers and scabs, by the unexpected death in May of our publisher, Orvil Dryfoos, and by the scramble to adjust to his successor, the thirty-seven-year-old "Punch" Sulzberger. All this drew us far from Vietnam and off the trail of most other stories.

I returned to my desk determined to tolerate no more inhibitions on my interpretations of government policies. To report only what officials were willing to say, as some copy desk pedants preferred, was to rob the reader of context and to take the sport out of reporting. To know what Kennedy was saying, people could read his texts in *The Times*, or watch television. My job was to discover *why* he said what he said in the way that he said it. When I found the answers, I wanted my paper to rely on my informed judgment and to trust me to render an accurate explanation, even if I was unable to cite sources.

Some timely blows for more analytical journalism were being struck by our foreign correspondents and also by our competitors at the *New York Herald Tribune*. As Dave Wise and I had anticipated, the *Trib* favored younger talents and indulged its brightest and brashest raconteurs, like Jimmy Breslin and Tom Wolfe. It featured sprightly writing and delighted in taunting *The Times* with ads boasting that "a good newspaper doesn't have to be dull." Ted Bernstein, *The Times*'s arbiter of style and tone, actually agreed with that premise and devoted the bulk of his biweekly in-house bulletin, *Winners & Sinners*, to favorable mentions of witty leads and bright passages. But Bernstein's grip on *The Times* also symbolized the primacy of "the desks," the authority he gave editors to guard against error, murk, and bloat, and to rewrite and even restructure with scissors and paste the often mediocre and temptingly triple-spaced copy set before them. As Bernstein himself eventually realized, pencils unsheathed to attack bad writing tended from habit to attack good writing as well. His *Winners & Sinners* belatedly deplored some of the damage done by "itchy pencils," but most of us thought the only true remedy was to put good writers in charge of the desks, a revolution that was already under way. Like all revolutions, it would, inevitably, go too far by demeaning the job of copy editor.

Despite its fading resources, the *Herald Tribune* was a colorful competitor almost to the day of its demise. And with its dying breath, the *Trib* bequeathed to me a new birth of stylistic freedom. In its desperate search for revenue, it made me a head-turning offer to write a syndicated Washington column on foreign affairs. The *Trib*'s syndicate would peddle the column to papers around the country along with another new entry, by Rowland Evans and Robert Novak, who were to succeed Joseph and Stewart Alsop. I would be "the next Walter Lippmann." If even modestly successful, I might quadruple my salary of $13,000 a year. And I could write as I wanted.

The itchy pencils at *The Times* had struck again that very morning, insisting that newswriting had to be—or at least pretend to be—devoid of all reportorial judgment. I had written about the challenges that the world's two superpowers were facing from allies like China and France, observing that "both the United States and the Soviet Union are adjusting to limitations on their power." On the way into print, that innocent passage was amended to read, "Both the United States and the Soviet Union, *it is thought*, are adjusting . . ." A petty insertion, to be sure, but typical of the constant, disingenuous effort to "attribute" even commonplace observations to mysterious, unnamed observers. "Who thought? Anyone but you, Big Shot," was *The Times*'s answer. As Chock Full O'Nuts coffee shops guaranteed with their food, we were serving stuff "untouched by human hands." I was sure ready for my own column, I told Reston in my customary morning-after protest.

Well, he said, puffing his pipe, *I'm going to make it hard for you to leave, so you should not trust my counsel. If you want to be the next Lippmann, go ask Lippmann's advice.*

Lippmann was the capital's reigning pundit. Three mornings a week, he composed chillingly crisp columns that illuminated the most difficult issues of the day. He lunched at the Metropolitan Club with no one below the rank of senator, general, or ambassador. Then he'd return to his home office on Woodley Road to read the press of the world, field phone calls, nap, and prepare to debate the fate of nations at his dinner table with foreign ministers, cabinet secretaries, and White House aides. Emulating Lippmann seemed like a pretty good deal. He was a philosopher king who had written brilliantly for decades about American democracy and world instability. He was also a shameless policy meddler, telling presidents what to do and writing their speeches when they let him. He was a conservative in the old sense, who wanted to preserve elitist government and an international balance of power among great nations, each with its sphere of influence. But inside him there also lived an insecure demon who was ashamed of his Jewishness and probably also of his early respect for Hitler and contempt for Franklin Roosevelt. Still, Lippmann's elegant essays commanded the attention of all thoughtful Americans, and I eagerly sought his advice about the life of a columnist.

It was the only time I ate at the then all-white Metropolitan. Lippmann flattered my Washington work but warned that to write a successful column I would have to choose between two paths. I could be a one-man newshound, competing for scoops with hundreds of reporters like myself. Joe Alsop was the best of that breed, Lippmann remarked, adding condescendingly that even Alsop wound up lunging for every crumb of gossip that rolled off Washington dinner tables. More sensibly, I could aspire to write like Lippmann himself, as a preacher, running events through the prism of my "philosophy of life."

I hated Alsop's self-importance and melodramatic inflation of any problem that concerned him. But did I have a "philosophy of life"? Did I embrace an ideology that would rescue my analyses from on the one hand this and on the other that? I was happiest, I realized, as a disinterested student of affairs, eager to comprehend the thoughts and passions of others, not to promote my own. By temperament, I was a reporter and student of theories and causes, not their author—a weather vane, not a hatching hen.

Reston encouraged my new self-awareness by arranging with just one phone call for a raise of more than 50 percent, to $20,000 a year. More important still, he pushed New York to confer upon me his old title of diplomatic correspondent and to promise me greater stylistic latitude. Paraphrasing my own memo to him, Reston used my complaints to advance his own quarrel with Turner Catledge's narrow definitions of news:

It is important that we agree on what this job is and what it is not. There is, I think, a suspicion that Max really wants to write a column and that, if he stays with us, he does not want to write "news" but merely do Q-headers. This is totally wrong. If there is a difference between Washington and New York it is on the question of what "news" is in this rather unusual period. Ideas, attitudes and judgments in the diplomatic field are the things we commonly regard as "interpretation," but our point here is that they are really the big "news," often bigger than the movements and pronouncements of officials (which of course also have to be covered). If we wait to report attitudes, ideas and judgments of officials until they are announced as policies, we shall be very late with the news, indeed.

I mention this because, unless there is agreement on the desks about the nature of this intangible kind of news and a willingness on the desk to regard these things as news, we'll be in constant trouble with each other and it would be better to let Max go his way. . . .

For example, one of the biggest stories of recent months is the gradual reconstruction by the U.S. and Soviet Union of the uneasy, pre-Cuba nuclear truce. This has been done by a kind of sign language and with gentlemen's agreements that no one defines and which everyone would deny. But these tacit understandings govern our relations in Berlin and in Cuba, the crisis points of recent years, and they are greatly affected by the Soviets' problems with Peking and ours with Paris. No one says all this, there are no documents, negotiations or events to be covered to prove it. . . . This means, in my judgment, giving Frankel scope to gather this kind of diplomatic news as well as covering the big spot stories.

I stayed. And I gained a considerably broader range of expression, in my news articles and in almost weekly essays in the Week in Review. The Review was the creation of Lester Markel, *The Times*'s irascible Sunday editor, who also presided imperiously over the Magazine, the Book Review, and the Arts & Leisure and Travel sections. A Jew and therefore not eligible in his day to become the paper's top editor, he ruled jealously over these "supplements" and steered them toward sharply critical, analytical writing. Though they sometimes bordered on pomposity, his features were always more ambitious and sophisticated than anything then available in other American newspapers. Markel was so jealous of his mandate to interpret the news that he insisted there be no "News Analysis" or "Man in the News" profiles in the Sunday "straight news" pages outside his jurisdiction. This artificial wall between "facts" and their "meaning" burdened *The Times* for another generation. Tearing it down became one of my abiding ambitions.

Markel was a mercurial, often abusive boss but, like most bullies, an easy mark for those of us who could afford to resist his aggressions, or at least repel them with humor. His demands for rewrites of magaziners to make them address his curiosities and prejudices were legendary. Brooks Atkinson, *The Times*'s theater critic, refused after a while to contribute to his Magazine. When finally importuned to relent, he wrote a special message across the top of his manuscript: *This article has already been rewritten.*

For all his achievements, the Sunday editor was easily mocked because his grasp of events tended toward the mechanistic. A typical Markel request for an article would read: "Please explain (a) the three main U.S. objectives in Western Europe; (b) the reason for opposition, especially in France; (c) the consequences for East-West relations and (d) what this teaches about how foreign policy is made. 800 words. Copy Thursday night. Please confirm. Regards." Still, he was incurably curious and the proud patron of the best *Times* writers and analysts, reporters like Abe Rosenthal, Abe Raskin, and Tom Wicker. Markel's Sunday sections became a refuge for those of us who felt suffocated by the daily paper's constraints. Now, as diplomatic correspondent, I had won the right to emulate Reston with an occasional weekday News Analysis. But more important, I received Markel's regular invitations to contribute Sunday articles ranging far beyond anything the daily would admit.

In the Sunday *Times* I could write that our European allies no longer enjoyed being "wards of the United States." I could observe about Canadians that "just about the only thing that makes them *them* is their persistent claim to be different from us." And I could define a Soviet-American "détente" on my own authority: "Though no one ever quite said so, it was to be the product of an unmentionable division of the world into clear spheres of influence."

———

Even more remarkable than the tone of my writings in those years was their preoccupation with European affairs. Like much of Washington, I averted my eyes from the remote and ill-understood struggle in Vietnam. We awoke briefly in May 1963, when Buddhist monks set themselves aflame in the streets of Saigon to dramatize their hostility to our ally, the Diem regime. Not until July did I try to explain the administration's reluctance to speak much about its growing problem:

It is a politically embarrassing war in which the United States finds itself allied with the authoritarian South Vietnamese regime, whose methods it doubts and whose popularity it questions. . . .

Every military triumph must be balanced by social and political progress. The results have rarely been better than mixed. . . .

To hold southeast Asia against pressure by North Vietnam and

Communist China, the Administration says, it must hold South Vietnam. And to hold South Vietnam, it must "sink or swim with Diem."

Preferably, therefore, official Washington wants to say nothing on what is obviously a tender subject. When the Administration's displeasure over Saigon's mistreatment of Buddhists was reported recently, newsmen were denounced as saboteurs of the war effort and their sources were investigated like subversives.

Explaining his anger, one official remarked: "What do you want us to do? We're in a box. We don't like that Government but it's the only one around. We can't fight a war and a revolution at the same time, so lay off."

And not until October did *The Times* fully describe the extent of America's accelerating commitment to Vietnam. Typically, it did so best in Markel's Review, when it paired a prescient dispatch from David Halberstam with my account of a raging debate about overthrowing Diem:

Halberstam's view from Saigon:

There is now a fear that this can turn into an ugly meat-grinder war, where one side's military superiority is matched against the other side's political superiority. . . . The sophisticated anti-Communist Vietnamese now fear that the Americans may be setting the stage for a frustrating, elusive type of war where more American prestige is involved than American control.

And my report from Washington:

President Kennedy this week tried to decree that the war over Vietnam inside his own Administration ought really to yield to the war in Vietnam. . . .

The "militarists" . . . see South Vietnam today not as a country to be built or reformed or made viable or prosperous, but primarily as a battleground in a global contest with Communism.

The "political" view of South Vietnam harbors serious doubt that the war against the insurgents can ever be won by military action alone. . . . It is based on the theory that . . . Communists would not seriously menace the country if they did not regularly find new recruits among disaffected peasants. . . .

And some [officials] believe that the United States should abandon the Ngo family altogether by encouraging any number of young and educated Vietnamese to seize power at the first opportunity.

No "according to" or "sources say" or "observers think," just the truth as learned through dogged legwork. When the much-debated coup against Diem occurred, on November 1, our long struggle to explain the news, and not merely to parrot official pronouncements, produced a genuine breakthrough. Past practice would have required me to write a lead quoting the official denials of American involvement in the plot and only dimly hinting at evidence to the contrary. Now I was permitted to cut through the fog to the essence of the story, and on Page One:

The Administration welcomes the coup d'etat in South Vietnam, assumes that its policies helped to bring it about and is confident of great progress now in the war against the Communist guerrillas.

There were, of course, no public statements to this effect even after the success of the coup appeared certain this morning. Officials denied any direct involvement in the military plot and are likely to deplore the deaths of President Ngo Dinh Diem and his brother Ngo Dinh Nhu if reports of their deaths are confirmed.

It is conceded here, however, that the United States Government had created the atmosphere that made the coup possible.

Markel then asked for a definition of the stakes in Vietnam, and I sent him the full domino doctrine—just barely hedged to hint at its most obvious exaggerations. I was analytically liberated but still doctrinally compromised:

[The coup] was, in the end, welcomed not because South Vietnam is small and weak and defiant of its colossal sponsor but because it figured prominently on the world's strategic map. . . .

It is easy to exaggerate the argument and to distend the logic by which the Presidential Palace in Saigon has suddenly become the center of Washington's universe: As the palace goes, so goes Saigon and all of South Vietnam—either to responsive, responsible rulers who can really lead their people to a fight against Communist-led guerrillas or to petty tyrants who would lose South Vietnam to North Vietnam, in the peasant field or at the bargaining table, and to Asian Communism, which is becoming, increasingly, the front for Chinese nationalism.

And as Vietnam goes, so would Laos, and Cambodia, and Burma, and so could Thailand, Malaya and Indonesia, and what then, for India, the Philippines, and Taiwan, and Japan, and all the rest of the continent that is the home of half of mankind?

Never in all my analytical glory did I anticipate or properly prepare *Times* readers for the grim Vietnam slaughter ahead. The "diplomatic correspondent" of *The Times* should have visited Vietnam, all the more since he lacked understanding of its history and people. Like Kennedy and his equally ignorant counselors, I had come to think of Cold War battles as symbolic "games," fought with proxies and with diplomatic feints and parries inspired by Harvard's "game theorists." In the heady air of our imperial capital, I came dangerously close to forgetting that its officials and journalists were waging the game with real lives, and deaths.

23 · THE MOTHER DID IT

BACK BEFORE OLIVER STONE, BEFORE WATERGATE, BE-
fore the riots of '68, and before Ashbury and Haight, Americans could still believe in chaos where foreigners saw only
conspiracy. Americans believed what the Warren Commission
told them a year after Kennedy was shot: that Lee Harvey
Oswald did it, and did it alone, and that Jack Ruby alone did
Oswald in. We all saw Ruby lunge and fire in that unruly Dallas
police corridor as they paraded Oswald past the cameras. ("Hey,
Sarge, when ya gonna walk 'im?" is the universal cry of the
American police reporter.) We all understood how Oswald
needed love or fame and found neither at home or far away. We
knew he needed no conspiracy to write away for that gun, delivered by the U.S. mail; anyone in America could write for a gun.
And we had faith in the judgment of Earl Warren, the humane
chief justice, and his fellow commissioners, among them the
straightest shooters in Congress—Richard Russell and John
Sherman Cooper, Hale Boggs and Gerald Ford. Those of us
who digested and dissected the Warren Report for our readers

knew in great detail that none of the counterclaims and conspiracies hatched by shameless profiteers fit *all* the indisputable facts of the case—or all the loose ends. The assassin flourished in America's chaos. Those who could not accept that lived in dark and alien lands.

The pattern of disbelief was both geographic and ethnic. The U.S. Information Agency discovered that only the newspapers of Great Britain and the British Commonwealth, optimistic democracies like our own, accepted the Warren findings. Most of the rest of the world did not.

Why not? Americans kept wondering. Why must they have conspiracies to sustain them?

Well, I'd say, imagine this sequence of events: Khrushchev travels to the Republic of Georgia in his southland and is shot, we are told, by an anti-Communist recently returned from a thirty-month defection to the United States. The Soviet leader is immediately succeeded by Georgia's leading politician. Before he can be questioned and tried, the assassin is himself killed two days later in the arms of his jailers in a Georgian police station in full view of the television audience. And his killer turns out to be a sleazy two-bit gangster who somehow knew when the assassin would be walked through the station and gained easy access to him.

Given such a tale, would we believe the bland assurances about a string of crazy coincidences or would we conjure a Kremlin conspiracy? Would we accept Freud's explanation that a loner so starved for mother love and wifely sex could resort to such a deed to find a place in history? Or would we turn to Marx and conclude that the exploiting classes found themselves a drone to kill off their liberal nemesis?

––––––––––

I had just arrived at Arden House, Columbia's conference center forty miles north of New York, for a meeting of Kremlinologists, opened my suitcase, and turned on the small radio atop my underwear. Kennedy had been shot in the head, Walter Cronkite said. I phoned the Washington bureau, where Al Shuster, almost by rote, was composing a long assignment sheet. His reporters were scattered for lunch, but this list wrote itself; the greater the disaster, the more coldly efficient our newspaper machine: *Dallas lead-all*, Wicker; *Capital mood*, Reston; *Congress react*, Morris . . . I told Shuster I'd be back by seven o'clock: *Diplo effect*, Frankel.

The government briefly put itself on alert for a possible foreign plot, then settled into grief. Television transported us all to the important places, announcements, and ceremonies that did not just illustrate events but made them a shared experience, more vivid and immediate than anything radio and newspapers had ever achieved. We could study the faces of Johnson and all the Kennedys, and we could attend the police briefings about how Oswald had murdered a policeman before he was seized in a movie house. Once exposed to the minutest details of the case, few of us doubted the official accounts of events.

As the memory of those vivid pictures faded and as more of our leaders fell to assassins, America gradually changed its mind and embraced the darker visions of its nature. A belief in chaos survived as the crutch of optimists, but conspiracy became the faith of pessimists, and after Vietnam and Watergate they became the majority. As a mama's baby bathed in the love that Oswald craved, I know that no conspiracy took Kennedy from us. Oswald's mother did it.

24 · ROOTS

I WAS THIRTY-FOUR, IN EXCELLENT HEALTH, AND HAD JUST fathered Jonathan, our third child, with a capable and attractive woman who was a diligent if restless partner. I saw my name on the front page of the world's best newspaper several times a week atop articles that increasingly met my standards. I commanded the presence of politicians and policy makers at my home to debate the issues bestirring the world's most powerful nation. I was important, well paid, and well liked, and, inexplicably, discontented. While the storms of war were agitating the Gulf of Tonkin in August 1964, Tobi and I took our kids to the Outer Banks of North Carolina to give earnest consideration to Max Ascoli's siren song to come and be the heir apparent of *The Reporter* magazine.

I would be the Washington editor, writing and ordering articles as successor to Douglass Cater, who was joining Lyndon Johnson's White House staff. *The Reporter* was a well-regarded political journal, domestically liberal and internationally anti-Communist. Ascoli had nourished lively and influential writers, like George Bailey, Marya Mannes, Meg Greenfield, and Robert Ardrey, and a succession of well-known editors, including Harlan Cleveland and Irving Kristol. Above all, however, the magazine was the private preserve of Max Ascoli, an imperious Italian Jew who had married Marion Rosenwald and a piece of the Sears, Roebuck fortune. He had also endowed the magazine with a few monopolistic enterprises, like TV relay antennas and the annual lubrication guide to new car models, which, he promised, would keep it afloat well beyond his lifetime. Cater had been the most recent in a long line of favorite sons who were encouraged to think of themselves as his heirs. Now it was my turn.

I had received many admiring letters from Ascoli and, when my duties at *The Times* allowed, written for him about Russia, Cuba, and Washington. He caught me in another of my chronic moments of restlessness. I had begun to inquire about jobs at CBS and PBS and revived the effort to finance my own magazine. There seemed to be no chance of succeeding Reston anytime soon; now that I had ruled out column writing, I lusted for the large audiences of television or the self-expression offered by a small magazine. Mom's explanation was probably right: You've gone too far too fast for your own good.

Whatever the cause, I was highly vulnerable to Ascoli's "once-in-a-lifetime" proposition, and after overcoming a damnable, persistent fear of leaping from heights, I agreed. My letters of resignation to *The Times* left no room for further conversation. They evoked warm letters of regret while *The Reporter* sent out a flattering press release.

That very day, to my total surprise, Scotty Reston announced his resignation as bureau chief so that he could devote himself to his thrice-weekly column, and he named Tom Wicker to succeed him. As we would soon learn, Turner Catledge, Scotty's former rival in Washington, had won the bureaucratic lottery in New York. Having generously befriended Punch Sulzberger when no one else paid him much mind, Catledge became the new publisher's most trusted counselor, and he now applied his Mississippi charm to achieve total dominance over all the News departments. He was being promoted from managing editor to the new position of executive editor and, with the exception of the editorial page, taking command of all parts of the paper. Lester Markel, the indomitable Sunday editor, was being kicked upstairs, and Reston, instead of allowing himself to sink lower in the chain of command, was stepping aside into his own orbit.

Though envious of Wicker, I thought his advancement appropriate. Tom was a boyish Carolina liberal, a novelist with a keen eye for Americana and a shrewd grasp of American history and politics. He was much better prepared than I for managing coverage of the mainly political stories in the capital. But because I had not told anyone of my negotiations with Ascoli, it was widely assumed I had quit in pique over Wicker's promotion. The obsessive desire I felt to erase that impression was the first clue that I was not really comfortable with the decision to leave. I paraded my respect for Wicker and listened intently to his regrets that we would not be working side by side.

I had sealed the *Reporter* deal on a Friday, and it was to be announced on Monday. On Sunday, as had become his custom since we began our negotiation, Ascoli called after breakfast to discuss the week's news. But he spoke now in a new tone, or so I thought. He was imperious instead of inquisitive, suddenly less interested in my views than in delivering his own.

"He thinks he owns me," I said to Tobi.

"He does," she replied.

In the rush of metaphors that defined my confusion, the break with *The Times* suddenly seemed indigestible. I wasn't becoming a big fish in a small pond; I was being swallowed by a whale. In any case, was a small pond really preferable to an institutional stream? Was I surrendering *The Times*'s great megaphone just to sing more solo parts? Or did I want the security of being defined by *The Times* and luxuriating in a fur-lined rut?

After one sleepless night, I had conquered the awkwardness of retreat. I decided that one day's embarrassment was preferable to a lifetime of regret. Actually, the toll was greater than that. My editors took me back, but they judged me impetuous. My colleagues still considered me petulant. And my apologies to Ascoli could not preserve our friendship:

THANK YOU FOR YOUR GENEROUS WIRE BUT YOU OWE ME NO REIMBURSEMENT FOR MY LOSS HAS SAME WORTH AS YOUR HONOR—MAX ASCOLI.

Harrison Salisbury was the most comforting. An indefatigable reporter, he had covered Russia in Stalin's final years, acquiring a romantic fascination with the place and, of necessity, a powerful imagination about the motives that shaped the tyrant's actions. I'd seen Harrison cut some sharp corners by hyping rumor into fact, perceiving unprovable conflict inside the Kremlin, and predicting all-out war between the Soviet Union and China. But I understood his weakness as an extension of the Moscow correspondent's strength: the talent to imagine yourself inside the shoes of the Russians. Salisbury's acknowledged fictions, his novels about Russian and Chinese history, were fascinating and popular, and his anticipations of news, as national editor and now as assistant managing editor, were formidable. At every stage of my career, he accurately imagined *my* frame of mind. Now an assistant managing editor, he wrote: "There's going to be plenty of room around here for you to realize your dreams and work out your restlessness." And to make good on his promise, he waited only a month to show me how. He rushed me over to Eastern Europe to report its reactions to Khrushchev's ouster.

I hated missing election night and a Thanksgiving at home. I didn't share Salisbury's expectations of a great upheaval in the Communist world and felt less urgency about my tour. But he pressed hard, and I accepted the consequences of my new commitment to *The Times*. I had now made my peace with institutional life. Good thing, too, because my trip climaxed with the most emotional journey of my reporting career.

From East Berlin I detoured down through Saxony to spend a day in Weissenfels. It was an experience that left me pacing a Berlin hotel room for two sweaty nights while composing a brief memoir of my hometown for the daily paper, coyly disguising my connection to it. But the editors of our Magazine spotted the autobiographical angle and urged me to blare forth, writing for the first time in *The Times* with the pronoun "I" a report they aptly titled "You Can't Go Home to Weissenfels."

I was quite prepared to surrender the lovely illusions of childhood, which had made of this dinky town of 40,000 something of a modern metropolis. I granted without remorse that the lofty old castle on a distant mountain was actually a chunky hilltop relic brooding right in the middle of town, that the grand portals and hallways of the old apartment house were just dark and narrow passages, that the trim, modern buildings downtown were really quaint old Germanic stuccos faced with wooden beams and Saxon carvings, that the town's great shopping center had shrunk to a double row of bedraggled storefronts, and that the distance from our store on the Markt Platz, now become the Marx Platz, to Hahn's bakery, which I had often boldly traversed in pursuit of cookies, was about a hundred feet. I was prepared for the unmistakable signs of Communist rule in our town, for the shabby displays of shoddy goods, for the claustrophobia of people who lived knowing that within 150 miles in three directions there was only barbed wire. But I was not prepared for my response.

I had come to brandish my American passport and to gloat at my triumph over Germany, but I mainly saw Weissenfels as a victim. Soon after the extraction of the Jews, the best young men of the town were shipped off to war. And as the casualty lists arrived from Smolensk and Kiev, their fathers too were drafted, most never to return. And then it was the young women's turn to defend the weary town; American troops commandeered the best homes and apartments and saved the people from starvation by paying with cigarettes and chocolate bars and cans of beef for the girls' favors. Next, under postwar agreements, came the Russians, to claim the same good homes and the same women, and they couldn't even pay. The surviving Nazis disappeared into West Germany or into jail or, miraculously, into the emerging Communist bureaucracy. Party hacks arrived to take over the police and the politics, and they forced the remaining few socialists into bogus coalitions, arrested them on fake charges of corruption, or encouraged them to flee, like traitors, to the West. And then it was the turn of the big and little businessmen; they were destroyed by a few cleverly devised taxes or persuaded by carefully timed arrests to beg the state to "nationalize" their shops. When the workers at the Leuna chemical plant called a strike in June 1953 to improve their wages, the Soviet tank division garrisoned in Weissenfels fired a few rounds into the crowd and hauled the leaders away. That left only the farmers, who were gradually dispersed to cure their attachment to the land and herded into collectives.

Wherever I turned, our family's acquaintances had run off to the West. My old teachers. My nursemaid's daughter. The druggist. For one reason or another, someone was missing from every house. Instead of finding the sources of my life, I found a museum piece of a town populated by sad people, just other victims.

I ended my visit in a back-alley town hall where at least a thousand perspiring, beer-swilling youngsters, many wearing the gray uniforms of the new East German Army, were squirming and stomping through a raucous twist that a frenetic jazz band and a hefty blond had adapted from the *William Tell* Overture. A Russian lieutenant and his gun-bearing escorts were enthralled by this spectacle and expressed regret that duty barred them from joining in. We talked about Washington and Moscow, and then the lieutenant wondered whether it was also duty that kept me from dancing. I said yes, in a way it was.

"Do you know Weissenfels well?" he asked.

"I was raised here," I said, "but I was lucky enough to be thrown out."

"And I," he said, "was lucky to be sent in."

———

I have wondered all my life about my refusal to condemn all Germans and mere Germanness for the horrors I so narrowly escaped. By counting many Germans among the century's victims, I have been accused of dishonoring the dead, my own grandparents no less. People say I risk forgiving the unforgivable.

I do not forgive acts of horror or indifference to them. But I cannot believe that evil resides in the genes or culture of any one people. The Germans who acquiesced in the persecution of the Jews had more to fear than the many peoples elsewhere who paid no attention. If there were such a thing as ethnic guilt, how guilty are we Americans who feed off lands seized from an annihilated people and partake of the wealth created by slaves? If our sins are genetic, cultural, or national, none of us can be born or buried innocent.

The New York Times.

LATE CITY EDITION

NEW YORK, THURSDAY, JUNE 30, 1966

*U.S., EXTENDING BOMBING, RAIDS
HANOI AND HAIPHONG OUTSKIRTS;
CITES REDS' DISPERSAL OF FUEL*

HEAVY LOSS SEEN

Oil-Storage Capacity
Is Reduced by 50%,
Pilots Indicate

25 · WHITE HOUSE TREATMENTS

L YNDON JOHNSON GREETED MY ASSIGNMENT TO THE
White House as a hostile act. *That fella's been prying secrets
out of the State Department, pushin' bad news about the war. Why
would they send him here except to do a job on his president?*

Within the week, the president sent word that he would
grant me an off-the-record interview. I put him off.

———

The time was September 1966, a thousand days into a most
remarkable presidency. Lyndon Johnson's Rabelaisian ambition was to eliminate poverty in America, to confer equal
rights and power on American blacks, to amplify the New
Deal's Social Security with medical care for the aged, and to
commit vast new resources to the education of the young.
Cunning yet insecure, imposing yet ungraceful, Johnson was
our Khrushchev, the shrewd peasant come to shake up a nation and rule a superpower. And he came with a legacy that
he could neither resolve nor shed; his Stalin was Vietnam.

U.S. TARGET: Burning fuel storage facilities three-and-a-half miles northeast of Hanoi are shown
taken from American plane after raid yesterday. Flames rose 12,000 feet. Bomb craters are visible

I had begged to cover the White House, to erase New York's impression of me as an insipid diplomatic theorist and to engage this most intriguing political figure of our era. Johnson was the first southerner elected to the presidency since the Civil War, and he knew that by championing the aspirations of blacks he was relinquishing the Democrats' century-long, ill-gotten hold on the South. Johnson was the first populist to reach the White House in this century, but he knew that he was exhausting the intellectual energies and resources that had produced the New Deal. He was the most effective legislator of his time, who led a reluctant Senate into censuring Joe McCarthy and passing the first, faint Civil Rights Act in 1957. Yet his preoccupation with deal making in Washington left him out of touch with the shifting moods of the electorate; Johnson thought a handshake with a labor leader like George Meany was still tantamount to securing the support of laboring people.

As for the world overseas, Johnson approached it with two typically American opinions. He bore the isolationist's contempt for foreigners and the interventionist's desire to reform the world. Like Kennedy, he was reluctant to commit the country to a ground war on the Asian mainland, particularly where the Chinese could again intervene, as in Korea. Yet, like Kennedy, Johnson was scared of the charge that he had "lost" a country to the Communists, that he had appeased aggression, betrayed an ally, let the Red tide wash across the Pacific. And most fatefully, Johnson kept Kennedy's foreign policy team, led by McNamara, Rusk, and Bundy, who lacked a realistic plan to rescue South Vietnam but judged the stakes to be so high that their commitment to its defense became unconditional.

With the notable exception of Under Secretary of State George Ball, who privately shared his dissent with Reston, the top Kennedy men treated the defense of Vietnam as a strategic interest of the United States. They believed that a nuclear superpower could not afford to bluff; its failure to keep a promise to assist an ally in a "conventional" war would destroy its credibility in a nuclear confrontation. Even a rash commitment in Vietnam had to be honored, the theory went, to avoid a future miscalculation by the Soviet Union.

Kennedy holdovers like McNamara and Bundy spent the rest of their lives trying to prove the unprovable, that JFK would have pulled back in time to avoid a grave waste of American blood and treasure in Vietnam. They sought solace in the retroactive faith that Kennedy would have resisted—perhaps never even entertained—their further counsels of step-by-step escalation. Unconvincingly, they blamed Johnson for lacking the wisdom and courage somewhere along the line to reject their advice and turn tail.

I think their complicity in the disaster distorted their perception. I have always believed that Kennedy, too, would have followed them into the Vietnam muck. He was already in for 16,000 combat "advisers." To avert defeat, he, too, would have sent more planes and helicopters, which needed bases, which needed to be defended by marines, who needed more army units to secure the perimeters. Kennedy's responsibility for the coup that took the life of President Diem of South Vietnam would have surely increased his own sense of commitment. We will never know, of course, because within the month Kennedy, too, was shot dead.

Preaching "continuity" but aiming to prove his superior skills, Johnson moved Kennedy's stalled legislation through Congress and set out to win a landslide election in his own right. During that campaign year of 1964, he rarely mentioned Vietnam except to denounce Barry Goldwater, his Republican opponent, for itching to enlarge the conflict and risking nuclear war. Month by month, however, my reports recorded a growing frustration and stiffening resolve inside the administration:

> The poor progress of the war . . . has caused increasing concern here in recent months. (February 22)

> And thus ended another period of anxious re-examination here. The boasts of early victory were quietly put aside. The threats of deeper commitment were quietly shelved. The talk of negotiating a way out was again dismissed as visionary. (March 21)

> Some officials insist it is already too late for subtle hints and diplomatic maneuvers. They cite analyses that the situation in Vietnam will deteriorate even more sharply in the coming months. They say the use of American force in some direct fashion is inevitable and the sooner the better if the doubters in Asia are to be held. (May 20)

> The highest diplomatic and military officials of the United States gathered . . . with increasingly discouraging estimates of the position of non-Communist governments and troops in South Vietnam and Laos. (May 31)

> In the minds of officials here the United States' commitment to the security of Southeast Asia is now unlimited and comparable with the commitment to West Berlin. (June 19)

Johnson did not want a war to cloud his election prospects. He promised never to send "American boys" to do what "Asian boys" ought to be doing. Only a few intimates knew what he really believed, or felt to be his duty. As he said to his Senate mentor, Richard Russell of Georgia, "I don't think it's worth fighting for and I don't think we can get out." Even winning the war was not worth the casualties it would take, he added, but "they'd impeach a president, though, that would run out, wouldn't they?" So while pledging peace, he called for planning for more war, hoping eventually to frighten Hanoi into backing off.

The military escalations began furtively in 1965, and to Johnson's obvious annoyance, my articles in *The Times* undermined his constant claim to have made "no change in policy" in the war. I reported that he "now sanctions [air] attacks on North Vietnam, even without further specific provocation." I reported that American crews were flying combat missions in South Vietnam, not just "assisting" the South Vietnamese, as claimed. Then one day I even "burned" a source to get a scoop on the indisputable expansion of the war.

To justify the more aggressive American tactics, McGeorge Bundy invited me to the White House to read the draft of a new government pamphlet documenting the long history of North Vietnam's aggressions against South Vietnam. But the typescript that Chester Cooper of the Bundy staff showed me was more than a propaganda brochure. It was an unmistakable rationalization for the all-out bombing of North Vietnam.

A fever propelled my pen. Copying the portentous passages in a windowless closet, I kept thinking of a legendary Pulitzer scoop obtained in just such a closet in the very same Executive Office Building by Anthony Leviero, *The Times*'s White House correspondent in 1951. Truman had fired Gen. Douglas MacArthur, his supreme commander in the Korean war, for publicly criticizing the president's refusal to bomb Communist "sanctuaries" inside China. MacArthur came home to a hero's welcome and promptly lied to Congress about his failure to anticipate the intervention of the Chinese Communists in Korea. Leviero was left alone with a secret document, the transcript of conversations on Wake Island in which the general had blandly assured Truman that China's army would not, indeed *could not*, do what it had now done: cross into Korea and send our forces reeling.

President and press—who uses whom? The truth is we use each other at every important turn. Officials use the press to influence public opinion, to win support in Congress, and even to communicate informally with other governments. The press, meanwhile, employs its access to hold government accountable, to spot deceptions, and to provide an outlet for dissenters and whistle-blowers. That I was being used by the White House to convey its propaganda did not diminish the importance of the knowledge I was gaining. Indeed, I thought the imminence of attacks on North Vietnam justified my stretching the rules by which I was shown the document. Without asking the permission of my informants, I turned their "background" briefing into a screaming front-page article whose first sentence—"The Administration is about to issue a long indictment of North Vietnamese 'aggression' against South Vietnam to justify air attacks against the North"—promptly produced a multicolumn headline:

U.S. WHITE PAPER BRANDS HANOI AS AN "AGGRESSOR" AND HINTS AT AIR ATTACKS
Policy Is Altered
Washington Now Feels Military Effort Must Go Beyond South

I knew that I was surrendering a valuable White House source—Cooper for sure and maybe even Bundy. But news bearing on war and peace altered *my* rules of engagement. I think I got Cooper into some difficulty; I never had the decency or courage to contact him to find out. Long after, he wrote an astute and scholarly book about the war that I praised in public and also in a warm private note that bemoaned our having had to play on competing teams.* The point of this story is not to demonstrate my cleverness or deviousness. It is to show that my personal opinions about events rarely shaped my sense of the news. A good story was a good story, and being the first to figure it out was what mattered most.

When even the bombing of North Vietnam proved ineffective, Johnson finally yielded to the Pentagon's demand for massive infusions of American infantry. Once again he tried to hide the escalation and left us hunting for clues to his purpose. As I wrote on June 9, 1965:

Despite some semantic hedging at the White House today, private and public official comments here leave little room for doubt that American marines and soldiers are not yet actively supporting the South Vietnamese in battle but are likely to be soon.

The number of United States troops in Vietnam is rapidly growing past 50,000 and toward at least 70,000. The majority are "advisers" but an ever-growing number are poised for combat. . . . The fine line between backing up the South Vietnamese and joining them will probably disappear in many places during the expected Communist ground assaults in the current rainy season.

Bundy and other officials responded to my scoops by insisting that the new tactics were merely "continuations" of the old. Among themselves, they rationalized this deception as necessary to avoid triggering a possibly

---

* I read in 1997, in an account of Cooper's visit to Hanoi, that he told the Vietnamese he had resigned from the White House in 1966 "in quiet protest" and shifted to the State Department to work "on negotiations only"—until he concluded in late 1967 that our diplomatic feelers were "a charade."

secret treaty that might require a Chinese or Soviet response to our attacks. Although I reported those concerns, I gave them little weight; I was sure that Beijing and Moscow would be guided by our actions, not our words. The pathetic claim that the Communist powers would let semantic legalities force them into war against the United States was every bit as fanciful as the administration's lawyerly contention that a few vague phrases in the SEATO treaty required our plunge into Vietnam.

As Johnson feared, his decision to wage a prolonged and undeclared war soon produced a wave of anxiety radiating out from university campuses and church pulpits. The opponents staged contentious "teach-ins" about Vietnam's history, its anticolonial struggle, and its grievance about getting only half a loaf after defeating the French in 1954. The critics argued that what our government was calling aggression across an international boundary was more aptly seen as a civil war. Against Johnson's better judgment, many administration officials joined these debates, if only to defend their personal reputations. "After all," Bundy said of the campus critics, "these are my people."

The opponents were also disproportionately *Times* readers, which meant that they had an oblique influence over the tone and scope of our coverage. Even professional students of the press overlook this phenomenon; they think the mainstream media practice only one-way communication. Perhaps the most important thing I have learned about journalism is that the opinions and prejudices of the consumers of news inevitably affect, even infect, the producers of news, particularly at times of stress. To some undiscernible degree, our news will influence the views of readers, but readers' perceptions also influence the shape and scope of our news.

If that sounds strange, consider the most obvious example from sports. Newspapers cover sports as partisans of the local teams because they are writing for passionate fans. Even the proudly objective *New York Times* covers its Yankees and Mets, Giants and Jets from the point of view of the home team—How is it doing? Why are *we* losing?—because the readers want to relish its victories and repair its deficiencies. Yet when the locals play against each other—when the Giants meet the Jets or the Yankees oppose the Mets—our coverage suddenly becomes studiously impartial for the obvious reason that the sympathies of our readers are now divided. In covering the Olympics, or a popular military enterprise like World War II and the war in the Persian Gulf, the American media make no effort to disguise their cheerleading for the home team. Are we winning? Hooray if yes; if not, why not? But when a sizable part of the audience wearies of a war, as it did in Korea and Vietnam, the coverage will gradually respond to that split opinion. No editor or TV producer has to order such a change of perspective. Perceptive journalists quickly sense and respond to the shifting loyalties of their readers and listeners.

It was not the willful propaganda of the media that soured a large part of the American public against the war; it was public opinion that gradually shifted the media's focus from scoring gains and losses to questioning the wisdom of the entire enterprise. Television images of the bloody, inconclusive struggle certainly eroded public support for it. But it was not until a large number of Americans openly protested our involvement in Vietnam that the press felt emboldened to really cover the critics. And only then did many politicians dare to raise their voices against the war, venting doubts that further spiced the media coverage.

"I can't fight this war without the support of *The New York Times*," Johnson remarked in one of his many off-the-record conversations. He was no doubt thinking fondly of his experience in Texas, to a time when publishers and writers could be charmed—or paid—to support any course of action. What Johnson should have realized was that he could not long fight a major war without the support of the *readers* of *The Times*. Once enough educated and affluent Americans turned against him, criticism of the war ceased to be "radical" and the president had to vie with his critics for attention in the news.

Having cast *The Times* among his enemies, Johnson naturally assumed that I came to the White House to press the attack at close quarters. He assumed that I was the agent of an "Ivy League establishment" that resented his usurpation of the Kennedy crown and was using Vietnam to bring him down. *The Times*'s editorial page, although appreciative of his domestic agenda, was insistently demanding negotiations to end the war on terms that the president, knowing his weakness in combat, considered tantamount to surrender.

I saw more tragedy than perfidy in the Vietnam situation. As I moved to the White House in the summer of 1966, my attitude was best revealed in my *Times* review of Bernard Fall's impressive history of Vietnam:

A dozen years and a quarter million troops too late, we are beginning to learn something about Vietnam, and about ourselves. Teetering now between an unwanted war and an unpalatable peace, we ask frantically how such a choice was ever forced upon us. Beholden to an inscrutable ally and beleaguered by an insidious enemy, we berate ourselves almost as much as we do them. "Get it over with!" is one cry, or "Get out!" yet we are unable to do either. . . .

What we are beginning to sense, of course, is tragedy: the inexorable yet continually surprising march of incidents, evoking almost predictable responses, driving the drama along. Aid to sustain the land. Weapons to guard the land. Advisers to demonstrate the weapons. Helicopters to bear the advisers. Troops to guard the helicopters. Planes to protect the troops. More troops to build the bases. Still more troops to defend the builders. Shoot when shot at. Shoot to keep from being shot at. Shoot to protect. Shoot to destroy. Bomb to kill. Kill.

These were grave and grim words, to be sure, but I recall writing them with sympathy for a president in torment. I was obviously of many minds about the war, but I did not deem it my mission to preach to our readers, only to represent their curiosities. Lacking a name for that fiduciary function, the press kept tripping over the word *objective*, pretending that we were immune to "subjective" influences. As our critics routinely countered, genuine objectivity was unattainable even in the science laboratory. We were striving always to approach events from the different perspectives of different readers, but we did not have a good word for our function until the dawn of the computer age. Our typewriter journalism was, subtly, interactive.

Johnson, of course, would have sneered at such theorizing. My assignment to the White House was just one more symptom of ignorant opposition to him. And whatever the opposition, Johnson hurled his giant hulk against it. Whatever the obstacle, he favored motion, even mere commotion. "We don't know how to unpollute the water and desalt it," he would say. "We don't know if rent supplements are the answer. We don't have a complete program on how to clean the air. The main point is that we are not standing still, we are moving forward!" And if an obstacle was human, he'd curl his tall frame over the top of it and pour down a stream of crude, shrewd argument. The Treatment, we called it.

All key members of Congress had experienced the Treatment, and they responded by enacting his Great Society program. But the media had begun to depict him as a six-gun Texan riding the range well past "Credibility Gap." His reputation for gross exaggeration began with little fibs, like the one about his grandfather fighting at the Alamo. Then came the intervention in the Dominican Republic, to avert "another Cuba"; he had panicked when the Dominican military sounded the alarm against "radicals," and he told ridiculous stories about his ambassador cowering beneath a desk to report that "the blood of 1,500 heads was running in the streets." No one in the press corps could ever again fully trust Johnson's judgment, or even his facts.

Yet Johnson professed to enjoy the company of the White House correspondents. Unlike the Kennedys, he did not bribe us with favors or punish us with ostracism as long as he felt he was getting a "fair shake." But he thought fairness included sitting still for the Treatment, or at least calling him directly before committing criticism to print.

"When you hear that I'm going to rape someone at 7:00 A.M. tomorrow on the White House lawn, you call! And when I tell you I'm not, don't print it! Because I'm not!"

So didn't I want to talk to the Man in private? his aides kept asking.

Not yet, I kept saying.

I wanted to wait until I knew enough to ask him tough questions. And I hoped he would reveal himself more if he first learned to respect my reporting. As he should have understood, *The Times*'s policy on the war had nothing to do with my assignment. In fact, I had to beg for the White House beat to advance my own ambition; I wanted to prove myself at politics, not just diplomacy. Though I had studied *American* politics, all my editors thought I was good only with foreigners. They could imagine me in striped pants but not in overalls at weekend barbecues on the banks of the Pedernales or chasing Lyndon and Lady Bird Johnson from ranch to church in little Fredericksburg. Even after assenting to my redeployment, the editors wanted to split the White House job into "domestic" and "foreign" halves, with me once again playing the alienist. I insisted instead on a truly versatile colleague so that one of us could stand guard at the White House while the other roamed the town to learn something meaningful about its occupant. I was sure there was more to be learned in a few minutes from a senator or cabinet officer who'd been sparring with the president than from a week of deadly bivouac in the White House lobby. I finally prevailed and was paired with Roy Reed, a wise and fluent writer from Arkansas. Like so many of our best southern reporters, he yearned to return home to witness the South's evolution and eventually quit *The Times*, much too early in a promising newspaper career.

Roy and I took turns camping in the West Wing lobby, which the sprawling reporters, photographers, and broadcast technicians turned into a Greyhound waiting room. We sat idle between the morning and afternoon feedings—"briefings," they were called, though they were rarely more than routine announcements interrupted by the bilious questions that bespoke our boredom.

The President will sign the Clean Air Bill next Tuesday and then address the Philadelphia Junior Chamber of Commerce on Wednesday.

Philadelphia, George? Does that mean he'll be snubbing the governor of Pennsylvania, or has he forgiven his speech at that Vietnam teach-in?

Normally, we were free to wander no farther than the press secretary's office to deliver a question, to fence for "guidance" on some issue, or to charm a typist into betraying a clue to the president's always top secret travel plans. By appointment, we were sometimes escorted to meet with Bundy in the basement or with upstairs staffers like Bill Moyers, Joe Califano, Jack Valenti, and Harry McPherson, from whom we might glean an explanation of some presidential action and a colorful anecdote. Even if fruitless, such visits broke the monotony and unnerved an envious competitor in the lobby. Mostly, though, we just sat on our haunches until the press secretary announced a "lid" on further news, which meant that we could depart, safe in the knowledge that we would be personally summoned in case the president suddenly called a news conference or chose to leave the White House grounds. Most major news organizations kept a "death watch" on the president, insisting on having someone close wherever he went. Thus we could savor the pretense of being "with" the president and reporting with false authority "from" the White House. But most days, we led duller lives than the reporters waiting for a good murder at police headquarters.

To make the most of the job, *The Times*'s Washington staff let the White House correspondent function as its broker on major stories, putting important questions to the president's assistants and urging them to squeeze the answers from departmental offices all over town. But away from Washington, the White House correspondents suddenly found themselves inside the presidential bubble, members of a privileged entourage that flew first-class and traveled behind police sirens. Even on weekends and holidays, when Johnson retreated to his West Texas ranch, we could mingle informally in an Austin or San Antonio hotel with members of his staff, encounter his friends and family, and accompany the president to some church service or barbecue. On a rotating basis, some of us always flew as "pool" reporters aboard *Air Force One*, and a few of us were sometimes summoned to the ranch itself, for a massive dose of the Treatment Plus.

I took over the White House beat in the fall of 1966, just as Johnson felt his vaunted powers ebbing. As he confessed to a group of us on a street corner one day, now that Goldwater was not weighing down the Republican ticket, the Democrats were destined to lose the bonus House seats they had gained in Johnson's landslide two years earlier. The Great Society was over, he remarked, even before the war's inflation sapped its energy. Indeed, his party's likely losses soon persuaded the president to abandon the election campaign and to flee abroad. Off we went to Honolulu for a council of war; to Australia and South Korea, to thank their governments for sending conscripts to the war; and to the Philippines, from where the president flew unannounced to visit "my boys" at Vietnam's Cam Ranh Bay.

The war had already claimed 4,000 dead and nearly 24,000 wounded. The casualties touched the president deeply, and he boasted, in great detail, of the heroic helicopter and hospital routines that saved the lives of virtually every GI found alive. The sight of the GIs, however, also overheated his rhetoric. "If the people in Moscow, Peking, and the other places ever discover that the promise of the United States does not mean what it says," he told the troops, "then the world goes up in smoke. It's as simple as that. . . . Now go out there and nail that coonskin to the wall."

On the flight out of Vietnam, he remarked, "It's better to do it there than in Honolulu," and for an emotional moment it seemed as if he really believed that.

I myself no longer knew what to believe about the war's progress, so I remained behind in Asia to visit Tokyo, Hong Kong, and Saigon. Even without the distraction of a presidential inspection, a week in Vietnam was hardly license to draw conclusions. But I did encounter a disturbingly obsessive General Westmoreland, pawing his map with open palms to illustrate his game of hide-and-seek with North Vietnam's General Giap. "That's 'his'—this here's 'mine,' but he won't stand and fight like a man!" And Johnny Apple arranged a scary scurry down toward the Delta in our bureau's Volkswagen, an excursion that let me taste the pitiful course of the conflict:

> The enduring impression is that at close range the war bears little resemblance to its statistical representations at home.
>
> Fundamentally, this war is seven men and a radio set holed up in a shack about as far from Saigon as the George Washington Bridge is from Times Square, talking about the two ambushes in two weeks on the road to the city and talking about how maybe enough can be learned in a few months to help ease the load on the next seven Americans who come to crawl in under the mosquito netting behind the mound of sandbags.

I returned home just in time for my first Treatment, a tour of the LBJ Ranch one December morning after church, for newcomers on the beat, including the man from TASS, the Soviet news agency. We saw a cluttered but tasteful ranch house, a kidney-shaped pool, a family graveyard, airplane hangars, and residences for pilots and agents who'd been thoughtfully asked to bring their wives. We listened to a stream of presidential anecdotes deploring greedy neighbors who were raising the price of the land he wanted to "square off" his holdings, and complaints about Lady Bird Johnson's opposition to his development projects—"she'd like to keep everything in the most natural possible state." But we heard only praise for his parents and other ancestors, his ranch hands and neighbors, and even the Mexican officials whom we had briefly visited across the border the previous day. "Good people, the Mexicans. They take an independent 'neutral' line 'cause they have to demagogue it a bit—now that's off the record, you understand, I don't want to be calling them things; you might say 'they have to appeal to their own electorate,' that would be the way to say it—but they really help us out, on Cuban things, in their quiet way when we need them."

The most lavish praise was for the Secret Service agents who functioned as watchmen, drivers, and gatekeepers as the president drove us around the ranch looking for Clarence, the buck named for an agent and trained by Johnson to sidle up to his station wagon to be fed a cigarette or two. *I like to listen to music, Strauss waltzes and things, and I like to look at pictures, like that Wyeth I showed you in the house, and I like to read. But there's nothing that'll take your mind off that missile coming so much as this watching the deer.*

Good neighbor, loyal employer, model family man, with just a little weakness for improving the land and some harmless pranks, an eye for a pretty girl and the mating habits of deer. Nothing that this president said, and very little of what he thought, lacked a self-serving, self-flattering purpose. Yet the sum of it also betrayed a self-consciousness and deep insecurity, like an immigrant struggling to prove his worth. When I finally went for my first private interview, in March 1967, Johnson explained why he had flown all the way to Guam to confer with General Westmoreland: *The most important thing for a president in the middle of a war is to have the understanding of the heroes . . . to get the man on top of the heap to get me the things I need. . . . In every town there's a man on the top of a hill in a big white house who can get things done. . . . Right now, that's Westy.* Johnson seemed to have forgotten that we were seated inside a very big white house. His.

A month later Johnson showed Tobi and me around that house after a small dinner with Mrs. Johnson and the Humphreys, two Senate couples, and Eric Sevareid of CBS, a tour that featured a visit to his bedroom toilet and a demonstration of its proximity to a wall safe containing his late-night bathroom reading of top secret documents. It was the same toilet that after other dinners Johnson actually put to use while some of the wealthy men of his cabinet, like Douglas Dillon and Robert McNamara, had to watch and carry on conversation. The decidedly unwealthy and southern secretary of state, Dean Rusk, told me he'd heard all about those indignities and believed them, all right, but honest to heaven, *he'd* never been shown that side, or part, of the president.

When Johnson heard in late May 1967 that I was writing a magazine article about his staff, he insisted that he was the only reliable source on the subject and commanded my presence at lunch with George Christian and Tom Johnson (no relation), his loyal and effective press secretaries. The president began, as usual, with an ingratiating gesture. He described the home movies he'd watched the night before of him leading the three Frankel children on a Shetland pony when we'd visited the ranch the previous weekend. *Beware of Greeks bearing gifts,* he said, *but maybe you could borrow the film for a family showing.*

Well, he continued, *what do you know that's good for the country?*

How are things going in Vietnam? I asked.

With some pleasure, Johnson described the most recent air raid on Hanoi, which had "surgically" knocked out all the city's lights and also some of the water supply. He was glad to make them "feel the war"; he could just see some people scrambling out of an elevator in the dark. He only wished they would stop feuding and hold elections in South Vietnam; he didn't care who won so long as the vote was fair and free. *I don't think the North will stop because they're winning in all the capitals of the world. They want to punish me—of course they can't do that until November '68. I think our doves just want to get out altogether but are afraid to admit it. I just can't understand how they want to injure the man who might have to negotiate for them. If you had Ed Williams as a lawyer and then went out and told everyone he's a liar, you can't trust him, and so on, he couldn't do a very good job for you, now could he?*

Would he now like to talk about his staff?

Yes. There are no buddies from Texas, just loyal, pure, clean, efficient, and intelligent aides. One or two have been too ambitious, but not mean. Most are very good—I'd give them A's. One or two I'd rate B-plus. One C.

Even Bobby Baker, his top Senate aide, though *"not a protégé,"* had been loyal to the end and testified, as he went off to jail for fraud, that *"Lyndon told me not to do it—he told the truth."*

Johnson had resentful praise for Bill Moyers, who'd left his almost filial position at the White House a few months earlier to become Captain Guggenheim's heir as publisher of Long Island's *Newsday.* Moyers was an excellent press secretary, Johnson allowed, except that *the lower the president slides in the polls, the higher his press secretary goes in the esteem of you re-*

porters. Odd, don't you think? When handling the legislative program, Moyers did a very good job—as did Califano. *Either one about as good as anyone who ever did that job. I remember getting briefings from Sorensen in Kennedy's day—lousy, piss poor.*

Walt Rostow, who had succeeded Bundy as national security adviser, was too professorial and loquacious but a great patriot who was scrupulous in specifying that Rusk thought this and McNamara thought that and *occasionally appending some of his own thoughts but never pressing them.* He therefore had the president's trust and great influence, *but the idea that Rostow is some kind of hawk peddling a single line is a great injustice. Mac Bundy was equally good and could have stayed. When he came to leave for the Ford Foundation he said he would of course stay if the president felt it was important. I figured that meant he wanted to be secretary of state. He was just a little too flip and clever. I wish he'd been in a college fraternity a little longer and worked that off.*

John Roche had taken the professorial chair passed down from Arthur Schlesinger, Jr., and Eric Goldman. *Provocative and sharp; I take only half of what he produces, but I always enjoy it and profit. There's nothing he touches that doesn't come out better than when he got it—memos, speeches, ideas. Of course, I have to Johnsonify it, if that's the word, because there's a lot of difference between Roche of Brandeis and Johnson from Johnson City. . . . I just don't see as much of him as the others because, well, because of that damned mustache.*

McPherson: *Naive, gentle, decent . . . too trusting. Bobby Kennedy could have a knife between my shoulders and run off with his wife and Ol' Harry wouldn't know it. . . . But a very good man who earned his first marks by writing a civil rights amendment that Kennedy and Pastore bought.*

George Christian had left the room, and so the president let fly the superlatives about his "unflappable" press secretary: *When the president asked him why he should waste an evening at the White House correspondents' dinner sitting through a lot of small talk by dull people and dull speeches, Christian said there were two reasons. He said, "First, it will do you good. And second, it will do me good to be able to deliver you up there." Well, when any man is that honest and forthright, I do it.*

Rummaging through his storehouse of influential aides and friends, Johnson dwelt at length on only two more. Most surprising, one was Sen. Wayne Morse, the Oregon maverick who had told Johnson from the beginning that he opposed the war in Vietnam and was denouncing it at every turn. *I keep asking how he can be so wrong and still so brilliant and supportive of me on labor, education, and everything else. And he says pupils always feel that way about their teacher and he's just trying to teach me something about foreign affairs.* Over and over, the president spoke of Morse with affection,

and he wondered why Bobby Kennedy could not similarly separate his opposition to the war from support for the Great Society programs. It was
Bobby's relentless carping on *domestic* issues that Johnson shrewdly took as
proof of Kennedy's as yet unarticulated intention to run against him. He
saw him as a threat and an ingrate. *Look what I did for them: I gave them*
Cape Canaveral. I gave them Idlewild Airport. And I gave them the half dollar!
Nothing's enough until another Kennedy sits here.

And finally, at greatest length, there was Abe Fortas, the New Deal
lawyer from Memphis, who had masterminded the legal defense of
"Landslide Lyndon's" victory over Coke Stevenson by eighty-seven votes
out of nearly a million cast in the Texas Democratic primary for senator in
1948. *Fortas was the best thing to hit this town since Frankfurter and maybe*
without Frankfurter's occasional meanness. He could cut a fellow's pecker off, and
so can Fortas, but he'll do it clean and neat and wrap it up nice and tie it with a
ribbon and pour perfume all over it.

Actually, it was Johnson who had amputated part of Fortas's anatomy
to make him accept the Frankfurter-Goldberg "Jewish seat" on the
Supreme Court. And like his predecessors, Fortas kept right on advising
his president. Johnson checked with him on almost everything, he said,
having just that morning consulted on a new assistant secretary of state for
Latin American affairs. Fortas came elaborately to mind that day in May
because Israel was on the verge of going to war against Egypt to break a
blockade of the Gulf of Aqaba, and Fortas had "remembered his Memphis
roots" and performed so well with the Israelis when it came to the jenny
mule. *You know what a jenny mule is: a sterile mule sometimes used for a young*
man to gain experience.

Fortas and the mule played a central role in his diplomacy with Israel,
Johnson said. *They sent in the ambassador, Abe Harmon, to ask for a military*
alliance, and we told him that so long as the Russians and Egyptians understood
the president's commitment to Israel there was no need to write a treaty. So then
Harmon wondered whether there couldn't at least be a confidential alliance, or at
least a secret letter that no one would know about. And I said to Fortas, "Tell him
about the jenny mule, Abe." And Abe told him about the fella who came to a
Memphis whorehouse with just two bucks in his pocket, not nearly enough for the
going rate. But if he was desperate, the madam said, two bucks was enough for
the jenny mule out back.

The man winced, but he was desperate. So he said, "Okay—I'll go for the
jenny mule if it can be absolutely confidential."

And the madam promised: "Absolutely confidential. No one will ever know
except you and me—and the four guys it takes to hold 'er down."

I never stopped marveling at the joyous vulgarity of this president as he sank into a military morass. Despite all temptation during the Six-Day War, I honored his coarse confidence about the treaty, and I think he detected a touch of commiseration in my smiles in the days that followed. Nothing else can explain the still deeper insights into his psyche that he allowed me that summer, in even stranger settings and circumstances.

26 · DESCENT FROM THE SUMMIT

I CALL IT THE NASSER SYNDROME: A POLITICIAN WHO makes a bad war can't make a good peace. The thought occurred to me in 1967 as I watched President Nasser of Egypt struggle to regain his footing after being whipped by the Israelis in the Six-Day War. He enjoyed dictatorial power at home, weapons and financial aid from the Soviet Union, and the adulation of Muslims everywhere. Yet his humiliation in battle sapped his strength and dulled his creativity. Although the Israelis stood ready to return his Sinai desert, which would let him reopen the profitable Suez Canal, he could not bring himself to engage them in serious negotiations. It was left to his successor, Anwar Sadat, to fight a few good rounds against Israel in 1973 so that he could lead Egypt to accept Middle East realities.

Make a bad war and you'll never make a good peace. Within just a few months of the Six-Day War, Lyndon Johnson made that aphorism into an axiom. I had come to the White House just in time to cover the demise of his presidency.

AFTER THE MEETING: Premier Kosygin takes leave of President Johnson. Between them is Secretary

JOHNSON IN WEST | Big Day in Glassboro | TOWN'S R

Johnson knew in 1967 that he was beaten. "Ho's outlasted me," he would say, meaning that Ho Chi Minh had matched or survived all the American military escalations for a full presidential term and was now waiting for the American electorate to vote for a halt. Ho would not again, as in 1954, accept the half loaf of a divided Vietnam. He was willing to negotiate only a disguised American surrender. Having made a bad war, Johnson lacked the stature to bargain for a satisfactory peace.

In a last bid to finesse the Vietnam failure, he hoped for help from Moscow, maybe even Beijing. And he wanted me, which is to say *The Times* and its internationally minded readers, to pay close attention to his desperate diplomatic gambits. I thought at the time that he was looking to salvage his reputation as a statesman. But I now think he really tried to circumvent the Vietnam muddle, perhaps in time to revive his political fortunes for the 1968 campaign.

Johnson perceived his opportunity in the fallout from the Six-Day War. Americans marveled at Israel's swift knockout blows, the rush of its armies to the Suez Canal deep inside Egypt, up over the Golan Hills into Syria, through the walls of Old Jerusalem to the Temple Mount, and across the West Bank to the Jordan River. Hardly anyone remembered in the glow of David's triumph over the Arab Goliath that Israel was forced to fight only because the United States, the world's greatest naval power, had failed to resist Egypt's provocative blockade of the Gulf of Aqaba, an Israeli lifeline. To Washington's great relief, Israel took matters into its own hands and humbled not only its neighbors but their patrons in Moscow.

To recover from that setback, the Soviet president, Nikolai Podgorny, flew to Egypt and the Soviet prime minister, Aleksei Kosygin, rushed to the United Nations. With Kosygin in New York, Johnson smelled a chance to stage his own summit meeting at last, to make a pitch for a major Soviet-American arms agreement, and thus to give the Vietnamese some cause for anguish about the wartime fickleness of their Soviet ally. The rival motives of the two leaders turned Johnson's quest for a meeting into comic opera. The president refused, of course, to consider meeting Kosygin on the neutral turf of the United Nations; Kosygin refused to come calling at the White House. It took a week to agree to meet halfway, and for the governor of New Jersey to steer them to Hollybush, the home of the president of Glassboro State College, right off the New Jersey Turnpike.

Flying to and from his two meetings with Kosygin, Johnson made sure that I was appointed to the small "pool" of reporters aboard his plane. He was full of the "Spirit of Hollybush," a hokey tale of two grandfathers conspiring to prevent their grandchildren from shooting at one another. "We reached no new agreements; that does not happen in a single conversation. But I think we understand each other better. . . . Kosygin came to posture to the Arabs, but he's not tried to crowd us. I let him see what kind of man I am. I wanted to show him that 'I'm not afraid of you, not afraid to look into your eyes.' . . . I knew things about foreign relations before Jack Kennedy even got on the Foreign Relations Committee. . . . The Russians are obsessed with China. But I don't want that written—that we're over here carving up China."

I thought these long disquisitions pretty well exhausted the Hollybush pretensions, but two weekends later, I was summoned to a "strictly confidential" meeting at the LBJ Ranch. George Christian and I came upon the president standing neck deep in his swimming pool, a yellow visored cap and huge sunglasses shielding his face from a searing July sun. Two large speakers at poolside were delivering the local Austin news as the press secretary and I were sent to rummage for bathing trunks in the pool house. We found scores of trunks but could not fill even the smallest, which were obviously chosen to fit the amplitudes of Texas tycoons. Johnson enjoyed our ill-clad discomfort and compared our condition with that of Mary Slater, who was supervising the preparations for lunch. Whoever chose *her* swimsuit, he said, "obviously skimped on fabric."

If you ever breathe a word of this to anyone, I'll kill you, the president began. He then described his intercepts of Kosygin's conversations with his fellow Soviet leaders in Moscow and Cairo, relishing their displeasure over Kosygin's embarrassing chumminess with Johnson at Glassboro. Now that the Russians were beginning to understand him better, maybe Senator Fulbright and other American critics of Vietnam would understand, as well, he argued. *I'll stop the bombing to start negotiating as soon as I get the word that those five North Vietnamese divisions won't move down into South Vietnam—or even if it's understood that if they move, I bomb again. Why is that so unreasonable? . . . They used to say they wouldn't negotiate under "the threat of force." Now they say they won't talk under "the pressure of force." Maybe that change means I can threaten to bomb so long as I stop when we actually meet?*

Pretty fine distinctions, I mumbled, and Johnson nodded a sad agreement. Not until the ice cream came to conclude a Mexican lunch did he return to diplomacy and the purpose of my summons. He had decided to tell a "responsible correspondent" about his interest in opening a dialogue with the Chinese Communists—or at least having it reported that was what he wanted, I was never sure which.

All the things he'd achieved at home were important, he said, but they were still "small potatoes" compared with relations with the Soviets and Chinese. Once the Chinese were given some responsibility in the world, they'd behave more responsibly. And it wouldn't hurt for the Russians and North Vietnamese to notice us doing business with China. He was going to reestablish relations *with a quarter of the human race, and, after Vietnam, ain't nobody gonna call me an appeaser!* He'd had a visit from Romania's Premier Maurer a week ago and urged him to convey Johnson's feelings to the Chinese. He was to say that Americans had no desire to change the Chinese system of government and wanted to work out ground rules to avoid a war.

I was hearing the very gambit that Nixon and Kissinger pursued for the very same reasons to wide acclaim four years later. After double-checking the Romanian visit with Washington sources, I led the paper three days later with a wholly unattributed story:

JOHNSON REVIVING BID FOR CONTACTS WITH RED CHINESE
Seeks to Convey His Views Through Romanian Chief
and Other Visitors

Thus did politicians deal with diplomacy marked "secret." And thus did reporters lend themselves to errands of state. In serving our separate interests, we were, at least incidentally, serving the public, disclosing a few more of the devious stratagems of politics.

I grew to admire Johnson the president without much liking the man. He encompassed a dozen human natures, from scoundrel to statesman, and relished every role. He was a fellow immigrant who never ceased to hunger for acceptance by those who had arrived on an earlier boat. He carried the twin banners of Democratic welfarism and internationalism and dropped them both. He legislated benefits for both the poor and the middle classes and hugely advanced the civil rights of blacks. Yet he broke the tranquillity and morale of the country he loved in what he knew from the start to be an unwinnable war.

To round out my perceptions of the Johnson presidency, I spent two weeks in November 1967 traveling through Iowa, Colorado, Oregon, Texas, Georgia, and Ohio, just knocking on doors and loitering in shopping centers to ask people about their lives and opinions. I found only discontent. People resented the war, as either pointless or simply too long and costly. People felt prosperous, but instead of crediting the government they considered it profligate. The implications for Johnson were devastating. Those who most vehemently opposed the war were the warmest supporters of his Great Society programs. Those who most fervently supported the war were the most vehement critics of his domestic record. And both groups belabored their dissatisfactions. Johnson sent word that he agreed with my findings, which should have prepared me for the drama of the first hundred days of 1968.

They were weeks of self-pity and self-righteousness in the Oval Office. Sen. Eugene McCarthy led a youthful army of war dissenters into the first presidential primary in New Hampshire and ran a close second to Johnson, which was tantamount to beating him. McCarthy became the Pied Piper of the antiwar movement without ever conceding that he favored simply abandoning South Vietnam to its enemies. Like the editorials of *The Times*, he held out "negotiation" as a feasible alternative to war, sliding past the bitter terms that a weakened United States would have had to accept. Because Johnson had failed to articulate a plausible rationale for his massive military commitment, the war's opponents were relieved of any obligation to debate his war aims or terms for peace. Like the president, they played to patriotic passions, with songs of peace and paeans to flower power.

Envious of McCarthy's success, Robert Kennedy leapt into the campaign. He proclaimed himself the more genuine, more professional peacemaker, or at least the more electable rival of Lyndon Johnson. Not to be outdone in self-esteem, Johnson blamed his growing vulnerability on his excessive magnanimity. *If we've made a mistake*, he told me in early March, *it's being too restrained. Maybe we misled Ho Chi Minh about not having the will, the guts, the power to destroy him. I don't have any MacArthur or LeMay on my staff threatening him with nukes.*

It was not McCarthy and Kennedy, however, who were the most effective in persuading Johnson to reverse course in Vietnam. That job fell to the new secretary of defense, Clark Clifford. A counselor to Democratic presidents since Truman and a peddler of influence to all who could afford his outrageous legal fees, Clifford was tapped by Johnson to replace the wobbly McNamara at the Pentagon. He took over soon after the Vietcong's demoralizing Tet offensive at the end of January. The Vietcong's casualties were enormous, so great that Walt Rostow and other hawks argued that the Communists had suffered a huge defeat that only the American media transformed into a triumph. But by taking the war inside the walls of the American embassy compound in Saigon, the guerrillas visibly unsettled the American public, and the Saigon command's follow-up request for an additional 200,000 American troops propelled Clifford into action.

Clifford laid siege to the president's mind, starting with an extraordinary "background" briefing over lunch at *The Times*'s Washington bureau. Manicured fingers cupped before him, he declared in a prayerful whisper that America was wasting lives and treasure in a war that had become unwinnable. He was urging Johnson to reject Westmoreland's bid for reinforcements. And no, he didn't mind our reporting his views—if we included his exit strategy. It was to somehow stiffen the South Vietnamese Army to fend for itself so that America's gradual withdrawal might still be traded for a tolerable political settlement. We could "Vietnamize" the war and then leave behind a face-saving, not *entirely* Communist coalition regime.

Unknown to us, Johnson was simultaneously composing declarations of abdication. He prepared one version for the end of his State of the Union message in January. He'd asked Clifford about Truman's timing with a similar refusal to seek a second term. He'd asked Westmoreland's judgment about the effects in Vietnam if he chose not to run again. He'd submitted a withdrawal text for editing by his wife, Lady Bird. But no one believed that he meant it. Equally incredible murmurs of withdrawal were heard from Johnson in 1964, at the peak of his popularity. The sheer political lust of the man, and his prodigious mastery of presidential powers, made it unthinkable that he would surrender them voluntarily. Not once but whenever he heard a reporter mention McCarthy or Kennedy, Johnson would recite the arithmetic by which he expected to win both renomination and reelection later that year.

Hardly anyone was prepared, therefore, for the stunning announcement that Johnson slipped onto the end of a television address on March 31, containing an appeal to North Vietnam to negotiate "face-to-face" to end the war. The text distributed to us in the White House pressroom before his 9:00 P.M. telecast featured the news that Johnson was again halting the bombing of most of North Vietnam to prove his good faith. It ended with a typically pious pledge that he "should not permit the Presidency to become involved in the partisan divisions" of a political year. But in delivery, he drove that coda to its logical conclusion. We suddenly heard him saying that with America's sons dying in fields far away he would not devote even an hour to personal partisan causes. "Accordingly, I shall not seek, and I will not accept, the nomination of my party for another term as your President."

Chairs tumbled as we raced for telephones and broadcast booths. And Johnson savored his command of the news, even though it contained his political obituary. Confronting us shortly before midnight, he testily dismissed all probes for a hidden motive. He was stepping down simply to remove suspicion that he was acting for selfish reasons, to keep faith with "the men out there."

"Sir, then you are sacrificing yourself?"

"No, I am not sacrificing anything. I am just doing what I think is right, what I think is best calculated to permit me to render the maximum service possible to the country in the limited time that I have left."

Early the next morning we flew off to Chicago, with truth and bunkum, pride and hurt pouring out of Johnson in a jumble of monologues aboard his plane:

Everything I did was always suspect, even when I'd gone to see the pope on Christmas Eve to see whether we could negotiate an exchange of prisoners. (We had flown around the world in thirty-four hours on December 24, 1967, so that Johnson could attend the funeral of Prime Minister Harold Holt of Australia, visit more troops in Vietnam, confer with Ayub Khan in Pakistan, and then summon helicopters from Wiesbaden to Rome to bear him over the heads of Communist protesters into the Vatican. Flying westward with the sun, we met Christmas Eve at every stop, and we almost missed the holiday at home because the choppers were mired in the mud of the pope's garden.)

If I put out the Lord's Prayer, people would still find fault with it. People even wondered why we circled the globe westward instead of eastward. I just couldn't be effective in such a cussed divided country. It wasn't easy to be pulling out. But I've had a full and productive life. I could be happy doing almost anything, and I'd give a good show of liking things like bridge or bowling or movies with Mrs. Johnson. It's a good feeling now to be able to go to Chicago and say what I want without all this political suspicion attached. I won't have to carry that sack of cement around anymore. If I'd had my druthers, I would have stayed on as Senate leader. I didn't really run for president in 1960; I only made a minimal effort that I knew couldn't work. By running in a few Democratic primaries I was just proving Kennedy's popularity, helping to save him from the impression he was the pick of the bosses. And I wanted to be vice president about as much as I wanted to be pope of Rome. Friends told us through tears not to do it. Sam Rayburn, though, said it was important to beat Nixon—Nixon, who'd called Rayburn and Truman and other Democrats traitors. I didn't agree with Kennedy on the Bay of Pigs, and on cutting taxes, but only the president knew it. In public, as his vice president, I always carried the flag. And as president, I felt like a trustee for a partnership in which one partner died; I felt obliged to take care of the family and the employees. Everyone who wanted to stay was kept on.

There is no indispensable man. I'm not vindictive. I feel no hatred and, I hope, no pettiness. There's not much in life that anyone who came from Johnson City could have had that I haven't had. But the country ought to be careful; it's playing with fire. If the U.S. goes down in South Vietnam, there go Laos, Thailand, Cambodia, Indonesia, the Philippines, and soon we'd be worrying about our own territory. Most important, soon you're no longer the number-one nation in the world, you're number three, or something.

Most people want to see a president do well, especially at the beginning, when he's learning. After a time, he develops barnacles and we turn on him. If I felt that I ought to have run, say, for the sake of the boys in battle, I would have. But this'll be better for y'all, for your children and grandchildren.

The text of the previous night's press conference was being distributed, and Johnson grabbed my copy to write, "For Max, my best always." He handed it back, asking, "Well, Max, do you still believe in the First Amendment?"

———————

I did not understand that cryptic thrust until a month later, after the murder of Martin Luther King, Jr., had set the cities aflame. The White House entourage was flying to Missouri to visit Harry Truman when Johnson visited the press pool on *Air Force One* to bemoan the nation's latest trauma. Suddenly he remarked: "The only difference between my assassination and King's and Kennedy's is mine's a live one—more tortuous—more sadistic."

And in his final appearance at the White House Correspondents' Dinner, Johnson cast the same bitter sentiment in the occasion's obligatory, self-deprecating humor: "Once you step aside, things start happening. Mary McGrory may even call you a statesman. Walter Lippmann may think so, but can't quite bring himself to say so. And y'all have had some real surprises to report. Who would have ever thought that Scotty Reston would have left Washington before Lyndon Johnson?"

"All the News That's Fit to Print"

The New York Times

LATE CITY EDITION

VOL. CXVII..No. 40,240

NEW YORK, MONDAY, APRIL 1, 1968

10 CENTS

JOHNSON SAYS HE WON'T RUN; HALTS NORTH VIETNAM RAIDS; BIDS HANOI JOIN PEACE MOVES

ROCKEFELLER URGES ALBANY LEADERS TO SPEED BUDGET

Liberals Designate Javits; Nickerson Race Confused

TAX RISE PUSHED

DMZ IS EXEMPTED

SURPRISE DECISION

President Steps Aside in Unity Bid—Says 'House' Is Divided

27 · MUTINY

A S THE PRESIDENCY AND AMERICA CAME UNHINGED IN the early weeks of 1968, Scotty Reston and his boys barely had time to notice. We were consumed by a bitter domestic feud that Abe Rosenthal called a mutiny. I stood squarely with the rebels belowdecks. In fact, I wound up carrying the crew's beef over the heads of the officers to the paper's commander in chief. It provoked Punch Sulzberger to assert himself in the management of his newsroom and marked a fateful turn in my career.

Abe Rosenthal stood third in line in the News Department hierarchy, gathering his forces for the ascension. He had been a masterful foreign correspondent and an innovative, self-promoting City editor. In the service of his superiors, Turner Catledge and Clifton Daniel, Abe adopted their disdain for the Reston mystique and the independent authority that it conferred upon the Washington bureau. The New York triumvirate thought it had blunted if not extinguished that mystique in 1964, when Catledge became executive editor. That was when

Reston took himself out of the line of bureaucratic fire and made Tom Wicker bureau chief. Scotty nonetheless tried to preserve some of the bureau's independence by brokering a friendship between the Sulzbergers and the Wickers. But Tom's fiery temperament did not mix easily with Punch's equanimity. Worse, Tom was an indifferent administrator for a publisher who prized managerial neatness. He emulated Reston's relaxed leadership style and devoted himself more and more to the editorial-page column he had inherited from Arthur Krock. He left a void that Catledge, Daniel, and Rosenthal set out to exploit, determined to take control of Reston country.

These personal and bureaucratic ambitions were never openly acknowledged, of course. They were piously sheathed in a lot of sanctimonious concern for the reader and the reputation of *The Times*, sometimes even the fate of the Republic. No political party ever pleaded the national interest more passionately than the competing factions at *The Times*. All I learned about the functioning of government was a projection of my backstage *Times* experience.

There was certainly room for improvement in Washington's performance and in relations between the bureau and New York. Both Reston and Rosenthal had encouraged me to believe that I would one day succeed Wicker because I would know how to reduce these debilitating tensions. All at once, however, Catledge, Daniel, and Rosenthal became persuaded that no one could simultaneously write and lead, as Reston had done. So they ruled out all of Reston's boys and, in great haste, decided to replace Wicker by sending down James Greenfield.

Greenfield had been hired by Rosenthal just a few months earlier to help plan an afternoon edition of *The Times*. They were chums from their days as correspondents in India, where Greenfield wrote for *Time* magazine. A man of great intelligence and wide experience, he had served as an assistant secretary of state and Dean Rusk's spokesman in Washington, where he was admired for balancing the interests of government against the curiosities of the press. He then worked unhappily as a public relations executive at Continental Airlines until Abe rode to the rescue. All the younger reporters welcomed the prospect of an afternoon paper that might be looser and livelier than *The Times* itself; we lobbed ideas at Abe and Jim for their dummies and future staffs. But the project was ultimately abandoned as unprofitable. Rosenthal had to reconcile himself to years more as an assistant managing editor, and he had to find a compelling new assignment for Greenfield. Overnight, he had an idea: Greenfield to Washington. At last New York would have a trusted agent in that alien precinct. Wicker could be told to find glory in his column. Punch Sulzberger, who had grown fond of Jim, cheerfully ratified the plan and personally carried the news to Tom.

Wicker exploded, and so did his Washington bureau. We felt demeaned to see his chair passed to someone not only new to *The Times* but also lacking significant newspaper experience. We all thought that Wicker deserved a more dignified transfer; if he needed to be replaced, why not wait ten months for the customary changeover time after Election Day? And why pass over Max Frankel or Tony Lewis or another accomplished Washington correspondent? Why indeed.

Reston felt rudely snubbed on a matter affecting the staff he had lovingly assembled. He thought New York had delivered a discouraging message to me and other *Times* reporters who aspired to leadership jobs. He thought the publisher had carelessly ratified a plan that alienated talented men of his own generation. Even after Greenfield's appointment was announced, at the end of January 1968, Reston and Wicker continued to petition Punch Sulzberger to reverse himself.

When Scotty cited my profound unhappiness, he was authorized by Catledge to suggest, if not exactly to offer, some palliatives. I should think about becoming chief of the Paris bureau, or perhaps reporter-at-large in America, or editor of the Week in Review or the Book Review. The suggestions struck me as even more cynical than the maneuvers that provoked them. I barely spoke high school French and was an ignorant Francophobe. Given my reading habits, I would have been an embarrassment at the Book Review. I still longed to engage the issues, politics, and people of Washington. If my advancement was to be blocked at *The Times*, I was sure I would be welcomed at *The Washington Post* or some other strong paper. And if Wicker's replacement might yet be postponed, I wanted to remain in Washington, poised to succeed him.

There would be no postponement, Reston reported. Even his own veiled threats of resignation left Sulzberger unafraid, or at least unmoved. There was nothing left to do but to walk the last mile by spending a day in New York to demonstrate my discontent to the powers that be.

I stumbled through brief meetings with Catledge and Daniel, insisting that if even Reston and Wicker could be humiliated, I saw no future for myself at *The Times*. They argued that I was barely thirty-eight and had a fine future; they'd heard such grumbling before. When I phoned Reston to tell him that the editors failed to credit my resolve, he said I still owed the publisher a calm account of my feelings. "Don't leave New York without seeing him."

When my call to Punch was patched through to his home, I was surprised to find his wife, Carol, eager to take a knowing hand in the affair. Carol had formed a deep attachment to a handful of *Times* staffers, notably the Wickers, and she did not shrink from pressing their ambitions on her husband. Arthur, as she always called him, was on his way home to celebrate his forty-second birthday. If I would show up for dessert, she was sure that he would want to sneak away with me for a quiet little chat. Whether or not Punch really wanted to rehearse the affair yet again, Carol forced the issue. Thus do small twists of fate shape lifelong relationships.

Although I confidently cruised the halls of the White House and Congress, I was still enough of a refugee to feel awkward in the Fifth Avenue home of the publisher during a private family celebration. I was afraid the setting would blunt my message and leave me vulnerable to some blandly reassuring nostrum. And sure enough, Punch proved to be full of familial goodwill when Carol chased us into their leathered den. She did not join the discussion nor ever reveal her interest in the controversy.

Punch and I drank two tumblers of vodka each and exchanged pleasantries. The publisher, surely well briefed by Catledge, thought that I was overwrought. He was confident that good things awaited me at *The Times*. I said that I was always prepared to take my chances on merit, but that the mistreatment of Reston, Wicker, and their aspiring successors left me doubting that merit had much of a chance. Punch sent me away hoping I would get over my hurt. I left his home convinced that my fifteen-year career at *The Times* was near an end.

I do not know what other maneuvers occurred that night. A birthday dinner graced by his mother must have awakened in Punch some of the paternalistic or, more accurately, maternalistic values that always figured large in his life. And he hated confrontations. By the time I reached Washington the next afternoon, he had decided that he wanted more time to sort out the rivalries roiling his stable. He ordered Catledge to reverse course and to keep Wicker in place in Washington, at least until Election Day.

Catledge, facing retirement at year's end, wearily bowed to this decree, but Daniel, facing ten more years as managing editor, protested the publisher's turnabout with a vehemence that fatally poisoned their relationship. A talented and debonair correspondent, Daniel had gained added luster through his marriage to Margaret Truman, the president's daughter. But as editor, he seemed to lack fire, devoting himself to improving society news and other peripheral features and complaining oddly about his lack of authority over the staff. His suddenly haughty response to being overruled by Punch sent him down a slippery slope.

Rosenthal, ten years younger than Daniel, scrambled for terra firma. He loudly advertised the pain of *his* humiliation and shrewdly extracted new assurances from Punch that he was still loved and prized. Jim Greenfield, too, was assured that his talents had never been in question, but having lost his seat in a deadly game of musical chairs, he quit the paper without even emptying his desk.

Within weeks, Punch summoned Reston to New York to prepare to replace Catledge as executive editor. And Reston encouraged Wicker to prepare to retire as bureau chief with dignity in November. He told me the publisher had painfully cast his lot with the young, turning even against Turner Catledge, his most valued mentor at the paper. So it was imperative for the young to commit themselves firmly to him. If I could do that, and devote the rest of my career to this great institution, then come November 1968 he would name me to succeed Wicker as both head of the Washington bureau and chief Washington correspondent. He did, and with a lifelong ambition realized, I thought it would be my last job at *The Times*.

28 · ALMOST ABOVE THE FRAY

ONE NIGHT BACK IN THE 1950s, AN ANXIOUS WOMAN called *The Times*'s newsroom to say she'd heard nuclear war was imminent. *The Russians are firing up their missiles,* she shouted. *We're all going to die!*

Yes, ma'am, my colleague Jack Roth replied.

Well, what are you going to do about it?

The Times, he said, *will provide the usual thorough coverage.* That was our motto, our promise to stand apart from the passions of the moment, to coldly record even our own demise. The bitchy beauty of journalism was that it cordoned us off from the strife and strivings of ordinary people in the paradoxical hope that we could better discern and depict the world's pain and injustice. There are truths to be found in more partisan journals that write with boiling blood instead of ink, but *The Times* commanded us to be spectators even at the most calamitous events. And so I watched the tumults of 1968 with dutiful but dumb dispassion.

The night Martin Luther King, Jr., was murdered, I watched from a rooftop as Washington's ghetto consumed itself in flames, then helped to shovel our colorful accounts to the wire room. I felt no guilt over my detachment. Since my first days on the police beat, I'd carried my press card as a shield against pain and sentiment. I became so accomplished at describing shock without myself feeling it for very long that I easily understood how presidents, priests, doctors, and other masters of emergency function with numbed sensibilities. There's a show-biz bond between politicians and reporters: the audience awaits, life must go on.

The night Robert Kennedy was murdered, I studied the televised scene for clues that would preoccupy yet another presidential commission reflecting yet again on violence in America and issuing yet another futile cry for gun control. And even before he was buried, my mind assayed the political consequences: by default, Humphrey was now his party's nomi-nee. And when Mayor Daley's cops rioted against yippies, hippies, and peaceniks in Chicago's streets and parks that August, I watched the may-hem as I would a TV movie while typing cool dispatches on a platform high above the din of the Democratic National Convention. It was not an entirely admirable perch.

There are reporters who climb so high above the battle that they can only look down upon a struggling humanity with indifference and loathing. And there are political combatants who resent our professed neutrality as just upper-class snobbery. Daniel Patrick Moynihan was ahead of his time, as usual, in declaiming against the elitist, Ivy League bi-ases of journalists no longer capable of empathy for the common bloke. Moynihan was right to observe that newspaper jobs once occupied by blue-collar offspring and high school dropouts were now filled by college graduates. But he neglected to note that he, a Harvard professor, and most other government officials were also far removed from the laboring ranks. And so were most of *The Times*'s readers. It is the insulation, not the edu-cation, of journalists that threatens to dull their experience of life and to blind them, as it blinds privileged politicians, to injustice.

I was secretly ashamed of my detachment through much of 1968. Friends were marching against the war, and a few were off fighting or cov-ering it. Yet my emotional balance produced some of the best writing of my career.

I had come to believe that the war in Vietnam, however just the initial impulse to resist a Communist advance, was inflicting unjust suffering on both Americans and South Vietnamese. And I was convinced at the start of the year that Lyndon Johnson was emotionally incapable of leading a retreat from the war. I thought that Sen. Eugene McCarthy, a sly romantic with little interest in governance, was temperamentally unsuited for the presidency. But I thought he had served a laudable purpose by channeling antiwar passions into political action. By contrast, I thought that Robert Kennedy, though perhaps the ablest potential president, was still practicing the crass opportunism he had once displayed by joining the staff of Joe McCarthy's unsavory committee.

The campus revolts seemed to me to lack any serious purpose. Unlike the civil rights confrontations staged by young blacks, they had no program for reform. The upheaval at my alma mater, Columbia, was ignited by a minor dispute over the location of a new gymnasium, and it left a decade's residue of chaos. The *Daily Spectator*, my valued training ground, lost its sense of community and independence to the cavorting rioters. Most tragically, the revolt destroyed two of my most caring teachers. David Truman, an enlightened political scientist and then Columbia's provost, was only months away from being chosen president of the university, an office crying out for his gifts and values. But when the rebels struck and paralyzed the outgoing president, Grayson Kirk, Truman had to speak for authority without wielding any. As peace was restored, he was sacrificed to the student mob and driven into exile, to the presidency of Holyoke. Uglier still was the fate of Prof. Charles Frankel (no relation), the philosopher who had so cheerfully championed the "open society" against all its enemies and had been consistently voted Columbia's most popular teacher. As reason and merit fell into disfavor in campus governance, he turned sullen and bitter and took his great talent elsewhere.

After Labor Day in 1968, I looked in briefly on the campaigns of the "New Nixon" and the wily George Wallace, but I was principally responsible for covering Hubert Humphrey's candidacy. That meant covering the demise not only of the Johnson administration but of the New Deal coalition that had once united northern liberals and southern populists. As I wrote at the end of the convention mayhem in Chicago:

> After 35 years of majority status, the Democrats finally confessed their inability to coalesce. They spoke proudly of how the "real issues" of white versus black and war and peace came before their party, and not the Republican convention of three weeks ago. They did not even pretend, however, that conflict on those issues was still consistent with election-year collaboration. . . . Because it had become so many things to so many people, the party could no longer accommodate so much conflicting passion.
>
> That discovery has been a blow more severe than any inflicted by Chicago's free-swinging police, and the Democrats were in no shape today to think about its consequences and implications.

Humphrey came within a hair of holding the White House, but only be-cause of the country's deep mistrust of Richard Nixon. Humphrey was the most openhearted and ill disciplined of our national figures, incapable of hiding an emotion or ending a speech. Although he spoke for unions, farmers, and the urban poor and wanted federal programs of Marshall Plan scale, he was easily outmaneuvered by the Kennedys in 1960 and re-duced to the humiliations of the vice presidency by Lyndon Johnson. He had come to deplore the war in Vietnam, yet that war had now given him an unexpected last shot at the White House. Unlike Nixon, however, Humphrey could not pretend to be a shrewder peacemaker than Johnson.

By October, with Humphrey closing fast on Nixon in the opinion polls, Johnson proposed to halt all bombing of North Vietnam if Hanoi would admit South Vietnam's regime to the peace talks in Paris. The North Vietnamese agreed, but President Thieu of South Vietnam refused to come to the bargaining table in time to boost Humphrey's prospects. Apprised by Henry Kissinger of the Democrats' secret diplomacy, Nixon had sent word to Thieu that he could expect a better deal if he waited for the Republicans to capture the White House. Intelligence agencies recorded these Nixon intrigues, but Johnson did not tell Humphrey until five days before Election Day. By then, the president counseled, there was nothing to be done. Johnson waited three more days before telling Nixon that he'd been overheard in his plotting—a sly maneuver for which John-son obviously hoped to be rewarded if Nixon ended up winning.

Many years passed before historians exposed the full story of these sordid maneuvers, more cynical by far than the motives reporters nor-mally suspect in politicians. Why would Johnson want to damage Humphrey and assist the Nixon he'd so despised eight years earlier? LBJ hinted several times that he thought Nixon was more likely than Humphrey to justify the war, to persist in it and rescue something of John-son's reputation. But I discerned a still deeper motive. Johnson, like all presidents, developed an egocentric view of his office, and he found Humphrey lacking in Johnsonian tenacity and guile. He showed his con-tempt one morning early in the campaign when the vice president entered Johnson's bedroom to ask for the services of Larry Levenson, a respected White House aide. Johnson, according to a witness, feigned rage and asked why Humphrey didn't just take the president's right arm. Hum-phrey abjectly backed out the door. If Humphrey had only argued that the president should give up the man for the president's own good, Johnson said afterward, he'd have relented. *You just saw evidence*, he concluded, *of why Hubert's going to lose.*

Johnson not only withheld Levenson but piously insisted on the "neu-

Kremlinologist, 1958.

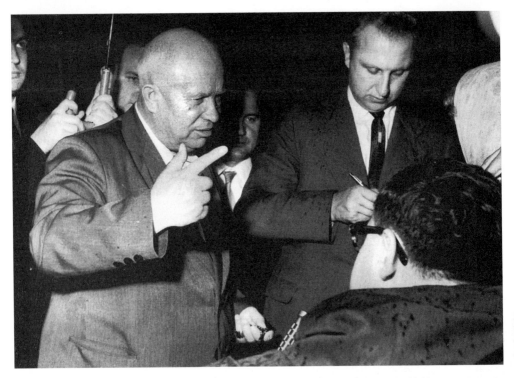

Nikita Khrushchev lectures an old acquaintance on Park Avenue, 1960.

Fidel Castro lectures a new acquaintance in Harlem
(with Herbert Matthews looking on).
(The New York Times)

Scotty Reston, role model extraordinary, in Beijing, 1971.
(Sally Reston)

The Times's diplomatic correspondent in Washington, in regulation dress, 1963.
(The New York Times)

Bringing analytical reporting to television on PBS, with
Tom Wicker and Lester Markel, 1962–1968.

A White House correspondent lectures his occasional source, 1967.
(White House Photo)

Abe Rosenthal, *The Times*'s new managing editor, in 1968.
(The New York Times)

A poster advertising "Supermax," a Washington bureau
chief, on a thousand trucks in 1969.

Trailing a president
to India, 1969.

Trailing a president
to China, 1972.
(William F. Buckley, Jr.)

With Turner Catledge
at Washington's
Gridiron Dinner
in 1975, long after
the end of our
bureaucratic wars.
(Arthur O. Sulzberger)

Punch Sulzberger
and Sydney Gruson
sharing an award for
having published
the Pentagon
Papers, 1974.
(The New York Times)

Punch at the start
of my executive
editorship in 1987.

Punch as he passed the
publisher's chair to his son
Arthur Jr. in 1992, before a
portrait of the founder of
the modern *Times*, Punch's
grandfather Adolph Ochs.
(Burk Uzzle from
A & C/Anthology)

Joyce Purnick, City Hall
bureau chief and secret friend
of her editor, 1987.
(Fred Conrad, The New
York Times*)*

The editor and the editorial
writer, now married,
at Fire Island, 1989.
(Suzanne Grossman)

David, Margot, and Jonathan Frankel experiencing a Johnson Treatment at the Texas ranch, 1966.

David, Jon, and Margot at the Sundance premiere of David's film, Park City, Utah, 1994.

Passing the baton to Joe Lelyveld, as Joyce leads the newsroom applause.
(Suzanne Grossman)

With Punch, Joe, and Arthur Jr. on retirement day, 1994.
(Suzanne Grossman)

With my successor and predecessor, in a display of harmony.
(The New York Times)

Joyce, *The Times*'s first woman Metropolitan editor, 1998.
(*Andrea Mohin*, The New York Times)

trality" of all his appointees. While Humphrey ran us back and forth across the continent, desperately chasing big-money donors, Johnson hoarded the then considerable sum of $600,000 in his "President's Club" and competed with Humphrey by simultaneously tapping the same sources for money for a Johnson Library in Austin. His pettiness was as great as his ambition.

The price of Johnson's obstruction of Humphrey was not evident until very late in the tallying of votes. Nixon's popular vote margin was barely 500,000 out of a total of more than 73 million. It fell to me as the new Washington bureau chief to record Nixon's triumph, or, more accurately, to write the ten or twelve leads through the night that described the close race.

Richard Milhous Nixon emerged the victor yesterday in one of the closest and most tumultuous Presidential campaigns in history and set himself the task of reuniting the nation.

Elected over Hubert H. Humphrey by the barest of margins—only four one-hundredths of a percentage point in the popular vote— and confronted by a Congress in control of the Democrats, the President-elect said it "will be the great objective of this Administration at the outset to bring the American people together."

He pledged, as the 37th President, to form an "open Administration, open to new ideas, open to men and women of both parties, open to critics as well as those who support us" so as to bridge the gap between the generations and the races.

Why do we print such noble nonsense? Just because they speak it? Because the audience yearns for a romantic new beginning? The answer is that at certain solemn moments in the nation's history, readers want their reporters and analysts to stand aside and let the media function as mere community bulletin boards. By the weekend, in Markel's Week in Review, I was back down to earth:

It's been a long time since a real live, partisan and combative Republican came to town to claim the White House.

In fact, counting Dwight D. Eisenhower as a gentle and non-partisan monarch who reigned above the din, it hasn't happened since the election of Herbert Hoover in 1928. No wonder everybody here wonders what it will be like, and no wonder no one knows.

I wondered intently. I had realized my fondest journalistic ambition only to be facing four or eight years of a White House crowd that despised the press, especially *The Times*. My best government sources were departing, and their replacements were swiftly silenced by a Queeg in the Oval Office. Our fun was almost over.

The New York Times

"All the News
That's Fit to Print"

LATE CITY EDITION

NIXON WINS BY A THIN MARGIN,
PLEADS FOR REUNITED NATION

NIXON'S ELECTION
EXPECTED TO SLOW
PARIS NEGOTIATION

GOAL IS HARMONY | ELECTOR VOTE 287

President-Elect Vows Lead in Popular Tally
His Administration | May Be Smaller Than
Will Be "Open" | Kennedy's in '60

Soviet Bids U.S. Confer;
Calls for 'Normalization'

REPUBLICANS GAIN
SAFE ALBANY EDGE

Senate's Liberal Coalition
Survives Gains by G.O.P.

29 · ENEMIES

R ICHARD NIXON WAS A CLUMSY, GRACELESS, AND IN MANY
ways despicable man, but he was a cunning politician and
diplomat whose presidency profoundly tested our capacity for
fair and sophisticated reporting. I believe that Nixon so despised
his own warped nature that he found it difficult to perceive
virtue in anyone else. But ever so briefly, he tried. He entered
the White House as a "new" Nixon, who would "bring us together" and build a stable peace with foreign adversaries. He appointed moderates to manage social and economic policies in a
constructive spirit and, despite the animosities of the past, the
press extended the customary first-year courtesies. Reviewing
Nixon's first year, I was embarrassingly generous, if not naive:

He is trying to be a temper-
ate President in intemperate
times, a moderate man coping
with extravagant problems, a
modest figure upon a gigantic
stage. He is trying to get out
of Vietnam and away from inflation as fast as his sense of
prudence will allow. For the
most part, he has lowered his
voice, just as he promised at
the inaugural a year ago; in
fact, he has said virtually
nothing memorable. . . .

> After a lifetime of sly and aggressive partisanship, he is slipping into the habits of a judge, presiding over policy debates that are systematically inscribed on his calendar and resolving them—plausibly, practically or even compassionately.

But Nixon's only real interest was in diplomacy, a sport without rules and with few congressional restraints, which he and his brilliant cohort, Henry Kissinger, thought they could pursue in imperial isolation. They set out to succeed where Johnson had failed, to exploit the Sino-Soviet dispute by offering both Communist powers a cordial new relationship, hoping thus to isolate and weaken North Vietnam. They insisted that America's prestige required defending South Vietnam until it could defend itself—or at least until it could survive, it was whispered, for a "decent interval" after our withdrawal. But unless Hanoi grew suddenly serious in the Paris negotiations, that meant the movement of American troops out of Indochina would be as gradual as had been their movement in. It left Nixon hoping that Soviet pressure and American bombings would compel Hanoi to compromise and that an early end of the military draft would persuade the home front to tolerate continuing casualties.

Nixon and Kissinger labored in such secrecy that they badly misjudged the country's tolerance. Unlike his predecessor, Nixon kept aloof from most reporters and denied us access even to his White House intimates, Bob Haldeman and John Ehrlichman. He tried as well to control Kissinger's contacts, particularly with liberal writers and academics, but Kissinger was too nimble to be caged from his natural peers, and too important to be punished. Of the White House figures in daily contact with Nixon, only Kissinger preserved his individuality and thus survived the Watergate fiasco.

The political operatives, like Vice President Spiro Agnew and Attorney General John Mitchell, were rarely available to us. The cabinet members who dared to lunch or dine with *The Times* were those with independent pasts, like William Rogers and Melvin Laird, or independent futures, like George Shultz and Elliot Richardson. Like Kissinger, they instinctively understood the role of the Washington press in vetting and explaining government policies, and they learned to handle the inevitable tensions between us. For all his cunning, Nixon never did.

A president and his top aides enjoy almost unchecked powers of communication to define and defend their policies and to attack their adversaries. They can shape the agenda of public discussion, commanding the airwaves and headlines with the slightest hint of crisis. They can bury their mistakes by sealing their files on the pretext of national security. The

Washington press, in turn, feels so dependent on government information and so dutiful in disseminating official propaganda that it grows desperate to prove its mettle by also exposing error, hyperbole, hypocrisy, and abuses of power. Thus are government and press condemned to a symbiotic relationship, a precarious balance of collaborations and antagonisms.

Within months of his inaugural, however, Nixon destroyed that balance. As the high cost of his policy in Asian and American casualties became evident, the bitter rifts in public opinion reappeared, and the president blamed the messengers.

Long before we realized it, Nixon was agitating to discredit the press with cynical stratagems, including wiretappings and FBI investigations. He was capable of the most Machiavellian intrigues. While outwardly sponsoring a progressive and expensive welfare reform that Patrick Moynihan developed in his White House, Nixon instructed Haldeman to make certain not only that it was defeated but that the defeat was accomplished primarily with Democratic votes. When Mrs. Nixon angrily deplored his failure to nominate a woman for the Supreme Court, the president proposed circulating the name of at least one female candidate who was sure to be judged "unacceptable" by the American Bar Association so that he could blame the lawyers for his sexist failure. When George Wallace was shot by a lone gunman in 1972, Nixon's first reaction was to get his agents to strew the man's Milwaukee apartment with McGovern literature so that the crime would look like the work of a "left-winger." A president stooping that low to betray his own policies, to deceive his own wife, and to obstruct the FBI's investigation of a political crime was not likely to flinch at smearing the press.

And Nixon waged war not only against the press and the permanent government, whose loyalty he questioned, but against some of his own cabinet and staff. By the spring of 1969, after our man at the Pentagon, Bill Beecher, revealed the secret B-52 bombing of Cambodia, Nixon and Kissinger ordered the FBI to tap the phones of Kissinger's aides as well as those of reporters and even the principal aides to the secretaries of state and defense. Nixon and Kissinger not only spied on Rogers and Laird but froze them out of major policy discussions and plotted to actively mislead them at important junctures.

Over time, we smelled the intrigue. Civil servants whom we had known as keen interpreters of world affairs were suddenly terrified of expressing an opinion or even bumping into us on the street. Ranking diplomats and military officers took to begging us for information about White House decisions that was being withheld from them. The most damning evidence came from Kissinger himself, who muttered disdainfully about the ignorance, prejudice, and backbiting all around him.

Though we had never met before he entered Nixon's White House, Kissinger and I shared an interest in diplomacy and respected each other's writings. We also shared an intangible bond: We were two Jewish refugees from Nazi Germany and New York's Washington Heights, charmed by the circumstances that led us to meet in the citadel of American power, a White House led by a president whose values we each secretly deplored. We met four or five times a year to review his diplomatic objectives on a "background" basis. Only rarely could I lure Kissinger into indiscreet asides, most of which expressed contempt for the secretaries of state and defense and their "bureaucracy." Just once, while safely conversing out of doors, did Kissinger dare to go further. He responded to a mention of his refugee roots by bemoaning the anti-Semitism that he was forced to endure—"in the highest places." That clue was dropped long before the world heard the tapes of Nixon's vulgarities about rich kikes whose presumed hostility he would avenge on their tax returns.

No doubt because of our biographical kinship, the impression spread that Kissinger and I were in constant secret communication. I did nothing to dispel that false assumption; it helped to open the doors of other officials. I was making shrewd use of *The Times*'s recognized influence, as Scotty Reston had taught. But I called Kissinger only when he had an obvious interest in addressing a situation, and our contacts were rigorous, never chummy, and often tense. For example, when he and Nixon decided in the spring of 1970 to prove that they could intensify the war to improve their bargaining power with Hanoi, they announced the invasion of Cambodia. But it was left to us to discover and reveal that they had simultaneously resumed the massive bombing of North Vietnam. That bombing was a clear violation of the deal by which Lyndon Johnson had brought Hanoi to the negotiating table in Paris.

Nixon greeted our report of that bombing with a massive FBI investigation and a wave of new wiretaps on officials at the White House, State Department, and Pentagon. Our first clue about the bombing, however, came not from a leak in Washington but from a terse Associated Press dispatch from Southeast Asia, which recounted Radio Hanoi's reference to a raid by "more than one hundred" American planes. I called Bill Beecher to ask about an obvious anomaly. Just a day or two earlier, Secretary Laird had threatened a resumption of the bombing of North Vietnam under only two conditions: if its army crossed openly into South Vietnam or as a "protective reaction" to North Vietnamese air attacks against the South. Could it be that the North Vietnamese were avenging the invasion of Cambodia by invading South Vietnam through the long-demilitarized border zone?

A Pentagon spokesman assured Beecher that Hanoi's complaint about an air attack must have been an exaggerated reference to a relatively modest "protective reaction" flight. Gen. Al Haig, Kissinger's deputy, laughed off the report as "the usual Radio Hanoi stuff." But within an hour Beecher learned from a high-ranking military officer that there had indeed been a massive raid, by 128 aircraft to be exact, against North Vietnamese supply dumps and logistic lines. So back we went to Kissinger's office, where our new knowledge caused General Haig to stop laughing and to pretend he had not been "working the problem." He would have to check.

Now Kissinger called me to say it was "a Defense Department matter" and the Pentagon would have to deal with it. His refusal to deny our information was actually all the confirmation we needed. With an early Sunday paper deadline looming, I told Kissinger the United States looked foolish not to be explaining a major policy change that was no secret to the North Vietnamese. We were calling him because the Pentagon refused to help. He suddenly said firmly, "It will help—even if I have to call Laird off the golf course."

Kissinger called yet again to report that the Pentagon would be talking soon. I asked whether our story was wrong, whether he was disputing our facts. He said, "I would prefer you not to use the figure, because the numbers in these things are always conjectural." I asked again whether our number—128 planes—was wrong. He said printing that number "would not be right." I caught the distinction; his "not right" did *not* mean incorrect.

Finally Dan Henkin, a Pentagon spokesman, called to speak "on background." Without giving the number of aircraft involved, he said the raid had been a "reinforced protective reaction" against antiaircraft installations. If supply lines were hit, he implied, they were not the intended target. Henkin was a friend from his days as a reporter for the *Army Times*, and I did him the courtesy of saying I was not convinced. And he did me the courtesy of saying, "You're obviously onto something."

In our final exchange of the day, Kissinger asked if he could make a "private" comment, one that he did not want published in *The Times* and one "definitely not inspired by the president." More guarded than usual, I said, Okay.

Max, if you blow this up, you will be doing a grave disservice to the national security—with all that is going on. He obviously meant the invasion of Cambodia and the negotiations in Paris. I told Kissinger I was not impressed by the need for secrecy about a raid first publicized by the enemy, but I would pass on his appeal to my superiors. Scotty Reston's response was "nuts." In fact, he called Kissinger, chewed him out for wanting to suppress the news, and, ever the scoop artist, chided the White House in the Sunday column then running through his typewriter for trying to suppress our scoop.

On Monday, a reporter for Jack Anderson's syndicated column called me to ask about the attempted "suppression," but I refused to discuss it. Not so Henry Kissinger.

At the ungodly hour of 7:00 A.M. on the following Friday, a frantic Kissinger called me to explain that he had been "trapped by inexperience" into reading from his "notes of our conversation" when the Anderson man called. He had denied ever asking us to suppress a story, "only the number of planes involved." And he was hoping now that "this matter will not escalate." As Tobi indicated by passing me the morning paper, a clever selection of Kissinger's verbatim remarks during our "private" conversation was reproduced in an Anderson column and arrayed to dispute Reston's complaint about White House pressure. I told Kissinger I remembered every word of that conversation, including his request to make "a personal and private" appeal. Having agreed to listen, I said, I felt honor bound to keep our conversation private, even if, sadly, he did not. On an empty stomach, that was not a bad riposte.

Even when we had lunch our exchanges were similarly taut. Conversations with Kissinger were always so subtly nuanced that I refused to invite him to dinner at our home. Whenever Tobi pleaded for a chance to meet this international superstar, I told her that I could not joust with him by day and beckon him to pat our children's heads by night. His deceptions and my probings were best confined to purely professional contacts. I did not relent until our farewell dinner from Washington, when Tobi sat herself next to Henry and promptly told him he had not previously been invited for an evening because he lied to me by day. He soon appeared at my side demanding to know when he had lied and refused to let me soften the charge to a merely "clever but stressful use of words."

Kissinger's gift with words was formidable. He persuaded adversaries on every continent that he understood their true interests and knew how to promote and protect them. He disguised selfish national interests as beneficent concessions to others and crafted statements and agreements that satisfied so many diverse audiences they seemed to reconcile the irreconcilable. He believed that in a lawless, nuclear world, survival was ethic enough for a diplomat.

Kissinger's most important achievement was to tame the rabid anticommunism with which Nixon and other Republicans had infected American foreign policy. It was their ugly charges that the Democrats had "lost" China and otherwise appeased communism that drove Kennedy and Johnson into their calamitous interventions in Cuba and Southeast Asia. Finally, Nixon encouraged Kissinger to negotiate in Moscow for some limits on nuclear missiles and in Beijing for a way around our troublesome support of a separate "China" in Taiwan. Those deals, and the Middle East disengagements that set Israel and Egypt on a course toward peace after the Yom Kippur War in 1973, were the main achievements of the Nixon years. They were fully appreciated by the American people, despite the continuation and escalation of the war in Vietnam and the obsessive secrecy with which Nixon and Kissinger conducted their business. But what a bitter price they paid for their mistrust of press and public. The furies descended upon them on the very day that Tricia Nixon was wed in the White House.

30 · THE PAPERS

I ENJOYED THE JOB OF BUREAU CHIEF, THE LICENSE TO apply myself to every sort of newspaper problem. How to train more blacks and Hispanics for reporting. How to get good photographs from dull congressional hearings. How to coordinate the coverage of legislation in Washington and its effects on the country. How best to deploy thirty-five reporters, and how to make reporters rather than remote editors the originators of ideas for articles.

Bob Phelps was my indispensable deputy, the selfless stage manager without whom no journalism could succeed. As news editor in the Washington bureau, he deftly managed assignments and copy flow and with steely patience coordinated our labor with the volatile demands of a half-dozen departments and a hundred temperaments in New York. We worked out a conceptual blueprint that seated the staff in clusters, forming teams of reporters assigned to related subjects, like foreign and military affairs, and the relevant buildings, like the State Department and Pentagon. We also created teams for urban affairs and social policy, for Congress and politics, and for business and economics, and we expected each group to fix its own priorities in covering both daily events and long-term trends. The system encouraged planning and let good ideas flow up instead of down.

So long as Scotty Reston served as executive editor in New York, I had almost free rein to recruit talented outsiders, like Jack Rosenthal from *Life* and Jim Naughton from the Cleveland *Plain Dealer*, and *Times* insiders like Johnny Apple and Neil Sheehan. I also felt a duty to atone for the managerial neglect of my predecessors. The three lowest salaries on our staff turned out to be those of our three women reporters, obvious victims of discrimination and the shibboleth that men needed higher wages to support their families. More amazing still by 1968, there had never been a black reporter in our Washington bureau, not only because blacks were still rare in our business but because of the outrageous notion that some bigots in government would not give a black reporter the time of day. The few accomplished black reporters in the capital were discovering their market power and charging a "black tax" as major newspapers bid for their services. Phelps and I bid for and hired Paul Delaney, a dedicated corre-spondent, from the Washington *Star* for our urban cluster. But we de-cided we had an obligation not just to raid other staffs but to open a path into our business for promising youngsters. We hired trainees as news clerks and persuaded Nan Robertson, our union rep, to let us violate the contract by employing those minority clerks as reporters. Phelps took their work home each night and provided tough but loving instruction every morning. We promised to sponsor the trainees for reporting jobs in New York if they met our standards, or for smaller papers if not. In three years, we placed four recruits with *The Times*. More important still, our furtive deal with the union was eventually sanctified in the paperwide con-tract, but New York never produced a teacher so wise and devoted as Phelps.

Thanks to Phelps, I was able to lead the bureau while also writing news analyses that augmented our coverage without stepping on the toes of col-leagues. Reston, however, never achieved that kind of balance in New York. Unwilling to surrender his column, he kept a writing office in the newsroom, a full city block from his executive office, and shuttled between them without ever learning the names of many of the people in his path. He lost touch with the editing hierarchy while producing only mediocre "Washington" columns. After just eighteen months, he fled back to the capital. He had sidetracked Clifton Daniel, promoted Abe Rosenthal to managing editor, and now left the executive editorship vacant.

After the Greenfield affair, Rosenthal and I restored a respectful relationship, but trust and friendship, which I always hoped for in a boss, proved irretrievable. Abe still felt himself a stranger in Washington, where he'd never worked, and so he left us ample managerial freedom. He was generous in his praise of my writing, and he often posed incisive questions to sharpen our coverage. But his manner was too often confrontational or condescending, and his calls were unwelcome. I was not alone in feeling estranged. It was to put some daylight between Abe and his circle of pals that Punch insisted he take Sy Topping rather than Arthur Gelb as his deputy. And that, paradoxically, opened the job of foreign editor for Jim Greenfield, whose return to *The Times* gave me a welcome, soothing buffer against Abe's temperament. Just in time, too, for the three of us were destined to collaborate in *The Times*'s historic printing of the Pentagon Papers.

One afternoon in early March 1971, Neil Sheehan brought me a brown paper bag containing a small sample of the Pentagon Papers' 2.5 million words. Neil was still looking to find his rhythm in our bureau, after heroic service for UPI alongside David Halberstam and Mal Browne in Vietnam had led him to *The Times*. Despite his ease among the military, he did not want to cover the mere daily doings at the Pentagon. But he was excruciatingly slow at producing deeper reports. We had already encountered both the tenacity and the dawdling that led him to take sixteen years to produce his masterful history of the war, *A Bright Shining Lie*. It was only on projects related to that war, and especially those condemning it, that Neil sprang to life, overcoming the back spasms that regularly found him prone on the office floor.

Now he was ablaze with conspiratorial fever. He had learned about the existence of a massive Pentagon archive, a top secret history that used government archives to trace the decisions that had led four administrations ever deeper into the Vietnam muck. Neil's secret sources wanted us to publish most of the forty-seven volumes, and, in my temporary absence, Neil had asked Scotty Reston to consider whether our book division, Times Books, was interested. Reston asked Ivan Veit, a company vice president, and they decided, well, sure, maybe, but not sight unseen. Neil then asked my advice, and I urged him to obtain at least some sample pages.

Once those pages were out of the paper bag, their portent was self-evident. They combined historical documents and interpretive narrations that had the makings of one helluva big story: a tale of reckless military gambles and public deceptions as recounted by the government itself—history to be sure, but front-page history, with or without a companion book. I urged Neil to get as much of the material as his sources would release. Afraid to discuss the matter on the phone with New York, I asked Reston to tell Veit to go immediately downstairs to brief Abe Rosenthal.

An understandably frantic Abe called within minutes. *What's this all about? What's going on? What's Ivan Veit got to do with the news? What the hell is Reston up to now?*

In what became a ritual reply over the next few months, I had to say, *Sorry, I can't tell you.* I wasn't sure what we would finally get. And what little I knew was not fit for phone conversation in our bugged, paranoid capital.

Neil went "up" to see his sources without telling us where and has never, to this day, spoken their names to me. Of course we all learned eventually of Daniel Ellsberg, a man of incisive, devious intellect and volatile temperament. While married to the daughter of a marine colonel, he had enlisted in the corps and became an exemplary platoon leader. Then, as a hawkish civilian, he served a think tank and the Pentagon as a policy analyst. When his marriage fell apart, he returned to Vietnam to design counterinsurgency programs. But like Sheehan and others, including his dovish future wife, Patricia Marx, Ellsberg now recognized the complexity of the struggle and the futility of America's involvement. Along the way, Ellsberg had taught crisis management and decision making, even lecturing once in Henry Kissinger's Harvard seminar about "the political uses of (feigned) madness" in diplomatic negotiations—a tactic that Kissinger freely employed in White House duties, using Nixon as his madman. But once he became an opponent of the war, Ellsberg loudly attacked Kissinger for prolonging the conflict.

During his transition from hawk to dove, Ellsberg had been recalled to the Pentagon to join a team led by an assistant secretary for diplomatic affairs, Leslie Gelb, to write a history of the United States' involvement in Indochina. The work was commissioned by Secretary McNamara in 1967 to instruct posterity in the making of a catastrophe and, I suspect, to shed and share some of his guilt for producing the disaster. When the work was done, Ellsberg copied one version of all forty-seven volumes, blotting out the stamps of TOP SECRET—SENSITIVE at the photocopying machine. He spent much of 1970 looking for a way to publish the material to stimulate opposition to the war. But he did not want to go to jail for violating his security clearance. He was hoping to enlist a legally immune member of Congress, but the available candidates, like Senator Fulbright, insisted on seeking the administration's permission, which was denied. So Ellsberg took to dangling the material before *The Times* without fully relinquishing it. He teased and tortured Neil, until in late March Sheehan fled back to Washington in disgust.

The next night, a Friday, Neil's wife, Susan, called to say he'd been suddenly summoned back to I-would-know-where. I said okay. And on Saturday, around midnight, an outraged Gene Roberts, our national editor in New York, called and demanded to know, *What the hell is going on in New England?*

New England was news to me, and I asked what he meant. He said Bill Kovach, our Boston bureau chief, had been awakened by Neil Sheehan, urged to rush over with $600 in cash to help in a vital endeavor, and warned not to tell either the National Desk or Gene Roberts. Roberts was more furious even than he was curious.

Oh, I think I know, Gene. Please relax. I can't tell you about it on the phone, but in any case it's a Foreign Desk matter.

Foreign Desk, hell! It's up in New England! That is my *correspondent who is calling me for advice!*

I'm sorry, Gene, I can't talk about what Neil is doing. I don't know the specifics either. Just let him have the money and anything else he wants.

We got through that weekend with a lot of bruised feelings and an outlay of $2,000. Though I was not told the whole story at the time, Ellsberg had finally left Neil alone to "read" the archive, and Neil packed it into a suitcase and ran off to one duplicating shop and, when its copier broke down, another, until he had a complete copy to stash away at the home of his mother-in-law in New York. At the nexus, Neil was never *given* the material, and Ellsberg never *authorized* its duplication. This was not the kind of deal anticipated in Journalism 101, but it was hardly shocking to me and other reporters who had often trafficked in top secret military and diplomatic information.

But go tell that to a judge as, sadly, we had to.

————————

Once I was able to show Rosenthal and Greenfield some of the papers and we were sure of their authenticity, we had to digest the full set and figure out what was really new and important. Gerald Gold, one of the Foreign Desk's best editors, came down to work with Neil. It was a tense collaboration, and two weeks passed before we distilled the essence of maybe half the material and prepared a report for the top editors—and lawyers—in New York.

I had casually mentioned our cache to *The Times*'s chief counsel, Jim Goodale, when he attended the annual Gridiron Dinner in Washington a month earlier. He soon concluded that we risked an injunction forbidding publication of the archive and demanding its return to the government. Now Goodale and other top executives and editors heard the dimensions of our scoop: reams of documents bearing on virtually every important decision about Vietnam, from 1945 to 1968, along with chronologies of relevant actions and a narrative evaluating the significance of the documents. There were private memos to and from the secretaries of state and defense, the joint chiefs, the White House, and the American team in Vietnam. The archive lacked only the relevant presidential papers, though these were mostly deducible from the rest. Of the forty-seven volumes, Neil's sources had withheld only four, dealing with diplomatic efforts to end the war through channels that were possibly still active and therefore vulnerable to publicity.

The Pentagon Papers proved that every administration after World War II had enlarged America's commitment to the defense of South Vietnam and secretly intensified attacks on North Vietnam. Yet at every stage the government had hidden the true dimensions of the enterprise and its own abundant doubts about the prospects for success. Although by 1971 the terrible cost and length of the war were obvious, no one who believed that government was accountable to the governed could fail to recognize this history as explosive news: the government analyzing and bemoaning two decades of its own Vietnam operations.

Reston and Rosenthal wanted more proof that the papers were not a hoax, but the tone, detail, and context of the material left no doubt. The papers' revelations were easily checked against the record of public statements and actions; a private suggestion to "plant" some propaganda in a national publication, for example, was easily tracked to show that the plant had been accomplished. Many of us, and particularly Greenfield, a former assistant secretary of state, had seen enough government documents to recognize their authenticity. Moreover, many of the texts bore scribbles and markings that correlated with the covering narratives. Those markings, and the photocopy patterns, might also reveal the documents' trail to our sources, so Neil warned that they must never be surrendered or reproduced in the paper. He thought that parts of the archive had been given to Marcus Raskin, a think-tank analyst, and mentioned by Raskin to Random House for possible book publication. He also thought several members of Congress were still being urged to make the archive public. But no other newspapers were at work on the material, which meant we had time to study it while staying poised to print in case a competitor suddenly appeared.

We reached a consensus that we would present the material as a government history, without adding our own interpretations. We also felt from the start that the Pentagon's narrative, while itself fascinating, gained force and credibility from the huge annex of supporting documents.

We assigned a dozen writers, editors, and researchers to the project and moved them all to suites at the New York Hilton, where they could come and go unobserved even before we had final "permission" to publish from Neil's sources. Extra copies of the material were made on Punch's private photocopier and scattered in many safes; one set was stashed under Jim Greenfield's bed. We were well aware of the paradox of taking elaborate security precautions as we set out to defy the government's. We feared a leak that would force us to print prematurely or bring the FBI storming the Hilton to seize our material. If there was going to be a legal battle, our lawyers preferred to argue for our right to publish and not against the government's right to reclaim top secret documents.

And Jim Goodale still reserved judgment about the project until he could further study the legal implications. He was eager to see the story in print, but full of foreboding about a court injunction or criminal action under the Espionage Act. The act forbids "communication" of information about "national defense" where there is reason to believe that it will "injure" the United States or "advantage" a foreign nation. No newspaper had ever been censored or prosecuted on these grounds, but this enormous cache could trigger quite a fight. We could, of course, avoid an injunction in midseries by printing everything on a single day. But that, I argued, was a disservice to busy readers; it would be demeaning to dump an indigestible mass of the material with one eye on the sheriff.

As the work dragged on, still more ominous rumbles came from *The Times*'s fourteenth floor, where Reston learned that Punch Sulzberger was unhappily casting about for advice on the project. He was hearing a lot of skepticism from the Editorial and Sunday editors and firm objections from *The Times*'s Wall Street lawyers at Lord, Day & Lord. Louis Loeb, the family's friend at the firm, thought it was unworthy and unpatriotic as well as illegal for *The Times* to publish secret documents. Even more adamant was his senior partner, Herbert Brownell, who had been attorney general under Eisenhower and remained an influential Republican. He refused even to look at the papers, lest he feel compelled to turn us in.

Abe Rosenthal was hoping to devote ten pages a day for ten days to the story, but in early June, Punch said he was not going to jail for something he hadn't read. And he was now determined to read and decide before leaving for London on Monday, June 14. I saw the publisher once in this period and heard an uncharacteristic vow: *I am going to be the publisher on this thing. . . . I don't like this business about ten pages a day. And why not just tell the story? Why do we have to print the documents?*

Reston was concerned not about the obviously political motives of Neil's sources but about the objectivity of the Pentagon historians. Once shown that they were not at all judgmental and had followed the threads of decision with scrupulous attention to detail, Scotty urged Punch to "publish and be damned." But he grew pessimistic about what he thought was the publisher's low interest in the substance of the material. He said Punch spoke respectfully about his editors' judgments, and he didn't want to tell his managing editor what to run and not to run, but he really couldn't see why everybody was so excited about this story.

Now that he could read some first-draft material, Reston, too, was disappointed, and the naysayers around the publisher were in full throttle. On the Tuesday before his Saturday deadline, Rosenthal phoned me to say, *This is the call for the reserves. . . . Better come up here and run this through your typewriter. I've bargained for one more reading by the publisher.* We had been given until Thursday to present him with the entire first-day package of two articles and supporting documents. We would go to press on Sunday, or not at all.

The main problem with the Hilton product was that it lacked an overture, a sweeping introduction that set the stage for the drama of our revelations and the mass of material to come. I spent a day reading our distillations, wrote a new introduction of about 1,500 words, and promptly encountered the same tensions that the hotel crew had nursed for nearly two months.

Oh, yes, we need something like that if this is going to be the first article in the series, said Neil. *I'll run it through my typewriter.*

He ran it through four times, changing perhaps four of my sentences, but with each retyping, the new lead felt more like his own prose. But his slow pace left Gerry Gold screaming and Jim Greenfield pacing and Abe Rosenthal warning that Punch would be up before seven o'clock and certainly at his desk by eight! *Thank God you've arrived,* Gold told me. *Now we're all on speaking terms again because you're the son of a bitch who's tampering with the copy.*

Still, by breakfast time, we had our package:

A massive study of how the United States went to war in Indochina, conducted by the Pentagon three years ago, demonstrates that four Administrations progressively developed a sense of commitment to a non-Communist Vietnam, a readiness to fight the North to protect the South, and an ultimate frustration with this effort—to a much greater extent than their public statements acknowledged at the time. . . .

Though far from a complete history, even at 2.5 million words, the study forms a great archive of government decision-making on Indochina over three decades. The study led its 30 to 40 authors and researchers to many broad conclusions and specific findings, including the following:

—That the Truman Administration's decision to give military aid to France in her colonial war against the Communist-led Vietminh "directly involved" the United States in Vietnam and "set" the course of American policy.

—That the Eisenhower Administration's decision to rescue a fledgling South Vietnam from a Communist takeover and the Administration's attempts to undermine the new Communist regime of North Vietnam gave the Administration a "direct role in the ultimate breakdown of the Geneva settlement" for Indochina in 1954.

—That the Kennedy Administration, though ultimately spared from major escalation decisions by the death of its leader, transformed a policy of "limited-risk gamble," which it inherited, into a "broad commitment" that left President Johnson with a choice between more war and withdrawal.

—That the Johnson Administration, though the President was reluctant and hesitant to take the final decisions, intensified the covert warfare against North Vietnam and began planning in the spring of 1964 to wage overt war, a full year before it publicly revealed the depth of its involvement and its fear of defeat.

—That this campaign of growing clandestine military pressure through 1964 and the expanding program of bombing North Vietnam in 1965 were begun despite the judgment of the Government's intelligence community that the measures would not cause Hanoi to cease its support of the Vietcong insurgency in the South, and that the bombing was deemed militarily ineffective within a few months.

Punch promised a decision by Thursday afternoon, and it was grudging at best. *Well, the first couple of thousand words read okay,* he said. *I'm not yet impressed by the way we've written it, but I'm sure you'll fix it up some more. What concerns me is this documents business. I'm against it, it's against my better judgment. If you insist, you can go ahead, but I wish you'd reflect some more.*

We've got a go-ahead—I think, Rosenthal told Greenfield, and those are the words that reached the Hilton, where the editors begged the writers to stop polishing the introduction and to finally start on the still unwritten articles three through ten.

But Rosenthal also insisted that he was now honor bound to confer yet again about the documents, and we assembled at Jim's home at midnight Thursday as he was rudely dismissing dinner guests. "It's off," Greenfield whispered when I arrived, and when I smiled at his jest he came back gravely, "I'm not kidding!"

Punch had left the office saying his decision just wouldn't go down well, and he had once again "reserved judgment" on printing the documents. He would decide Friday morning.

We agonized until Friday dawn. Abe was badly torn. He knew that the publisher wanted *him* to decide against printing the documents, without making it an order. So Abe dutifully mustered every conceivable challenge to our arguments in favor of printing them. Were we just on an ego trip? Were we risking the reputation of *The Times* for pages of material that only a few readers would bother to read?

Greenfield and I stood firm. *No documents, no story. If we can't do it right, don't do it at all. We can't say to the reader, "We've got this fantastic history and we know it's right because we have the documents, but we're not going to show them to you." We can't call presidents of the United States liars and withhold our evidence. Better just say, "National security prevents us from running the story," and close shop—though God only knows what kind of explosion* that *would cause on the staff and around the country.*

Exhausted, we left to take a nap, although I kept jotting notes for a memo I planned to write to appeal Punch's ruling against us. At 8:15, Rosenthal called and said he urgently needed help at the office; Sydney Gruson, the publisher's friend and assistant, said his boss—a marine, after all, with service in two wars—felt like we were "waving a bloody shirt in the face of the U.S. government." Gruson said he now sided with the publisher against the documents.

You're a new voice for them, Max, go over what we concluded during the night.

What did you *conclude, Abe? You never finally said.*

I came out more firm than I went in. No documents, no story. But he's the publisher, and my nightmare is that if he insists, I come damned close to the point of having to decide whether I quit.

Abe began recounting his shaky personal finances and leading us all into weary, fearful hallucinations. But we mustered the arguments yet again for Gruson, and we were encouraged to find him suddenly grabbing the napkins that came with our black coffee to scribble down some of our points. We allowed that the consequences of publishing might well be serious, but those of *not* publishing would be unbearable: The Pentagon Papers would emerge somehow, and we would lose the faith of our readers and our staff and be shown to have betrayed every journalistic value we cherish. *And for what, Sydney? For refusing to print documents that don't blow a single military secret?*

Gruson seemed startled and scribbled faster. *Are you serious? There are no military secrets?*

Incredibly, we had determined as much so early in the game that no one had ever said it outright to Punch and his fellow executives. Sydney said we were turning him again, and he would summon us upstairs as soon as possible. Punch, with his marvelous equanimity, had gone off shopping for London. Did that mean he had resolved it in his own mind? Abe wondered. Do we really say all or nothing? In the elevator, finally, he said, *Max, he hasn't heard you yet—you talk first.*

I felt like Moses stuttering at the burning bush through the opening jovialities. I was groping so hard for coherent speech I never caught the sudden jest in Punch's voice:

"I've decided you can use the documents," he said.

Pause.

"But not the story."

When this joke finally pierced our brains, Punch laid before us an already neatly typed memo, as fastidious as the numbered government texts we were about to dump into the public domain. Punch's document said that (1) we would proceed as he had originally decided on the previous day, but with documents and texts limited to six pages a day; (2) Harding Bancroft and Sydney Gruson of his office would look through each installment to satisfy themselves that they contained no live military secrets; and (3) some trivial thing that in my excitement I promptly forgot if, indeed, I read that far.

Being a marine also meant that when you've surmounted one hill you look not back but ahead to the next. As I would often discover in the years ahead, Punch Sulzberger hated conflicts, loved their resolution, and delighted in breaking tension with wit and humor.

31 · TRIAL BY FURY

JIM GOODALE, OUR COUNSEL, WAS RIGHT. NIXON COULD not resist the ultimate smear. He would convict *The Times* of violating the Espionage Act, expose the traitors at last, and, in the process, create a new presidential power. He would use our prosecution to win for presidents the right to prohibit publication of any piece of paper that he or anyone else in the vast federal bureaucracy had stamped "secret."

No such censorship—"prior [to publication] restraint," the lawyers called it—had ever been attempted in American history. Early in the century, Congress had explicitly refused to authorize prior restraint even in wartime. Like the authors of the Bill of Rights, it preferred the risk of losing a few secrets to the risk of letting government edit what Americans read. Some democracies, like Britain, legislate against the publication of "official secrets," but they lack our history of mistrust of the sovereign. They also lack a First Amendment.

So once again, in 1971, *The Times* stood on the ramparts, beating back a sinister assault on press freedom. Seven years earlier, at great expense, it had fought to prevent the use of libel suits to intimidate critics of government. Thanks to that victory in the Supreme Court, public figures can obtain libel judgments only if they prove that the press has maliciously or recklessly disregarded the truth. In asserting the right to publish the Pentagon Papers, *The Times* risked not only more money than in the libel case but also its good name and reputation for patriotism. Nixon knew, from long experience, how to play the treason card.

We published the first installment of the papers in *The Times* of Sunday, June 13, 1971. To avoid enraging the government and to emphasize the material's historical nature, Abe insisted on a modest Page One display headlined,

VIETNAM ARCHIVE: PENTAGON STUDY TRACES THREE DECADES OF GROWING U.S. INVOLVEMENT

He sat at his desk when the paper went on sale Saturday evening, and I sat at mine so that we could at last explain the project to a curious but still ignorant majority of the staff. But no one in government made a move; the capital's first reaction was an annoying indifference. If they saw the paper at all Sunday morning, the Nixons no doubt reveled in the article and photograph that appeared right next to our big scoop—a celebratory account of their daughter Tricia's White House wedding the previous afternoon. The Washington press corps was so lulled by our quiet packaging that none of the reporters interviewing Defense Secretary Laird on television Sunday morning asked a single question about the huge spill of Pentagon documents onto six pages of *The Times*.

After the second installment appeared on Monday, other papers carried brief references to our series, but I doubt that many readers had yet studied our documents and summaries. We learned later that President Nixon's first reaction was to welcome this massive leak. Since the Pentagon history ended in early 1968, it reflected mainly on the Kennedy and Johnson administrations. Indeed, the president was inspired to order a search for *other* secret files that he could similarly leak to the press to further damage the Democrats during his coming bid for reelection.

But Kissinger had little patience for the political benefits of such disclosures. He kept secrets not only from the public but from much of his own government. Any breach of secrecy—except of course his own—drove him frantic. His sense of the national interest and of his own convenience were barely distinguishable.

This time, Kissinger's anger became manic. It was fueled, I'm sure, by the fact that suspicions about the leakers first fell on members of his own staff and then shifted to Ellsberg, a man known to have once enjoyed his trust. As we finally learned from Bob Haldeman's *The Ends of Power:*

> Kissinger told the President he didn't understand how dangerous the release of the Pentagon Papers was. "It shows you're a weakling, Mr. President." Henry really knew how to get to Nixon. . . .
>
> The Pentagon Papers affair so often regarded by the press as a classic example of Nixon's paranoia was Kissinger's premier performance. . . .
>
> I was in the office when one of the angry speeches was made. As I remember, it ended with charges against Ellsberg by Kissinger that, in my opinion, go beyond belief. Ellsberg, according to Henry, had weird sexual habits, used drugs, and enjoyed helicopter flights in which he would take potshots at the Vietnamese below. . . .
>
> By the end of this meeting Nixon was as angry as his foreign affairs chief.

Nixon ordered an all-out attack on *The Times.* The Justice Department was to seek an injunction to prohibit further publication of the papers and, eventually, a criminal indictment under the Espionage Act. Moreover, *The Times* was to get no more information from any White House official without the president's consent. In the courts, Haldeman recorded, "the Administration's interest here is in the violation of Top Secret classifications rather than in the release of this particular material." Although George Shultz shrewdly wondered whether the material should have been classified to begin with—wasn't this the kind of top secret material routinely published every day?—Nixon thought he could extract a double benefit. He would use the case to rough up both the Democrats and the press. And he hoped to emerge with judicial rulings that gave him what Congress had explicitly rejected: the right to forbid and punish the publication of anything that the executive branch—particularly the president—chose to brand as "classified."

Attorney General John Mitchell deferred as usual to the president and to his own deputy for internal security, Robert Mardian, a zealot who shared Nixon's lust for prosecuting a liberal newspaper. Mitchell telephoned *The Times* on Monday evening, barely two hours before the third installment went to press, to ask that we stop writing about the papers and arrange for their return. He warned that he planned to seek a court injunction to compel compliance. In a follow-up telegram he said that the publication of "national defense information" was directly prohibited by the Espionage Act and our articles were causing "irreparable injury to the defense interests of the United States."

After some discussion and a call to Punch Sulzberger in London, the editors and executives of *The Times* "respectfully" declined the government's request. We ran the third of our ten articles, promising "of course" to obey court rulings.

Mitchell buttressed his threat with a call to Herbert Brownell at Lord, Day & Lord. Having advised us not to print the papers, Brownell angrily refused to let his firm defend *The Times*, thus stranding us without counsel just twelve hours before we were due in court. That left our house counsel, Jim Goodale, an embarrassed graduate of Brownell's firm, scrambling through the night to assemble a new legal team. Because of a chance encounter earlier in the day, he turned to Floyd Abrams of Cahill Gordon, who in turn proposed engaging his former teacher at Yale, Alexander Bickel, a distinguished constitutional litigator.

"You better get out of town," Goodale told me in a call to my Washington home early Tuesday. I had written that day's lead story, MITCHELL SEEKS TO HALT SERIES ON VIETNAM BUT TIMES REFUSES, but that was the end of my journalistic involvement with the papers. Bickel and Goodale were afraid of being tried in a Washington courtroom. They thought— wrongly, as it turned out—that the capital promised less sympathetic judges than New York. They also wanted to avoid receiving a temporary restraining order to halt publication of the papers until they had a chance to argue against its issuance. So I jumped out of bed and flew to New York to pursue a brief yet exhilarating legal career.

As one of the few *Times* people who knew his way around the mass of documents and also knew how they compared with the revelations in other histories and memoirs of the Vietnam War, I was invited to brief our new legal team. The lawyers had never seen the material from which our articles and documents were drawn, and, as upright citizens, they assumed that "secrets" were really secrets that had to be kept from foreign eyes. I was shocked to discover that Bickel and his crew assumed we had in fact done something terribly naughty, if not actually criminal. Was it not true that we had printed "top secret" government documents in wartime? The first line of defense, they said, lay in acknowledging that fact and getting prominent public figures to testify that publication of these particular papers, though perhaps embarrassing, was not really damaging. So our reporters were sent to approach likely candidates.

Although the former secretary of defense, Robert McNamara, had privately told Reston that he saw nothing damaging in our published articles and documents, he refused to assist our legal defense. So did McGeorge Bundy, Cyrus Vance, and other establishment figures who thought we were wrong to expose the record of their misjudgments. I suspect that they also wanted to protect their own future access to government secrets, without which they could never again render public service. The exception was Ted Sorensen, President Kennedy's White House aide, who agreed to testify for us and demonstrated a faith in open government that probably contributed to his failure to be confirmed, six years later, as head of the CIA.

Our difficulty in finding support reinforced our lawyers' suspicions that they had an outcast for a client. At the least, we were guilty of civil disobedience. Perhaps they could show, they said, that our conduct did not directly offend any statute and that the whole process of classifying secrets was an administrative procedure, binding on government employees but not anyone else. Though vaguely worded, the Espionage Act was clearly intended to prohibit only the *furtive* dissemination of defense secrets to foreign enemies. And the only kind of "prior restraint" that any Supreme Court justice had ever held to be permissible seemed to be only metaphorically relevant to the Pentagon Papers. In a 1931 decision that strongly upheld freedom of the press, Chief Justice Charles Evans Hughes had held that no freedom was "absolutely unlimited" in wartime: "No one would question but that a government might prevent actual obstruction to its recruiting service or the publication of the sailing dates of transports or the number and location of troops."

Bickel said that he, unlike Justices Black and Douglas, was not a First Amendment "absolutist." By granting the validity of Hughes's "troopship exception," he would have a better chance of winning over the conservative centrists on the current court. He would translate the Hughes exception to mean that the government had a right to prevent only the publication of information that *directly, immediately, and irreparably* imperiled human life and national security. And he would argue that the heavy burden to prove such peril fell entirely on the would-be censors in government.

Our case seemed strong, but our lawyers still lacked the fire of conviction. They kept harping on the fact that we were claiming a right to publish hundreds of top secret documents, some only three years old, bearing on both military and diplomatic calculations in the middle of a bitter, costly war. I could almost hear them thinking, Is nothing sacred?

Of all the men who were plotting our defense that day, only Jim Greenfield and I knew how casually the government wielded its top secret stamps. And only we understood what a lively commerce in such secrets occurred in Washington every day. If our lawyers found that difficult to comprehend, I despaired of their explaining it to judges. In a fit of passion, I sat down that night to write a memo to try to educate our attorneys in the facts of Washington life:

> The Government's unprecedented challenge to *The Times* . . . cannot be understood, or decided, without an appreciation of the manner in which a small and specialized corps of reporters and a few hundred American officials regularly make use of so-called classified, secret and top-secret information and documentation. It is a cooperative, competitive, antagonistic and arcane relationship. . . .
>
> Without the use of "secrets" there could be no adequate diplomatic, military and political reporting of the kind our people take for granted, either abroad or in Washington, and there could be no mature system of communication between the Government and the people. . . .
>
> I know how strange all this must sound. We have been taught, particularly in the past generation of spy scares and Cold War, to think of secrets as *secrets*—varying in their "sensitivity" but uniformly essential to the private conduct of diplomatic and military affairs and somehow detrimental to the national interest if prematurely disclosed. By the standards of official Washington—Government and press alike—this is an antiquated, quaint and romantic view. For practically everything that our Government does, plans, thinks, hears and contemplates in the realms of foreign policy is stamped and treated as secret—and then unraveled by that same Government, by the Congress and by the press in one continuing round of professional and social contacts and cooperative and competitive exchanges of information.

I showed our lawyers how presidents make "secret" decisions only to reveal them for the purpose of frightening an adversary nation, wooing a friendly electorate, or protecting their reputations. I gave examples of how the military services conduct "secret" research in weaponry only to reveal it for the purpose of enhancing their budgets or demeaning a rival service. I wrote that for the vast majority of "secrets," there had developed between the government and the press a rather simple rule of thumb: The government hides what it can, pleading necessity as long as it can, and the press pries out what it can, pleading a need and right to know. I recalled

President Kennedy's leaks to me during the missile and Berlin crises, President Johnson's swimming-pool revelations about the Glassboro summit, and Dean Rusk's private contempt for the SEATO treaty, stopping just short of my official army orders to leak atomic secrets during the Korean War. And I listed the many raw disclosures of much more recent secrets in the histories written by insiders like Ted Sorensen, Arthur Schlesinger, Jr., and Robert Kennedy.

I succeeded so well that the lawyers instantly retyped my memo into the form of a legal affidavit. And they had me hurriedly dig up seventy-five examples of the "routine" publication of obvious military and diplomatic secrets in newspapers to be attached to my brief.

The case of *United States v. New York Times Company et al.* careened with lightning speed through the judicial system clear up to the Supreme Court. Though they resented the rush, judges at every level well understood that *The Times* had been silenced virtually in midsentence after the third of ten installments and that merely taking the time to hear the government's argument required them to tread on the liberty of our readers. Yet their haste magnified the risks of error and miscalculation and an onerous outcome.

Our first judge, in Manhattan's Federal District Court, was a new Nixon appointee hearing his first case ever. And like our lawyers, Judge Murray Gurfein approached it with respect for the government's need to protect secrets bearing on war and peace. He stopped our presses, at least long enough to hear the evidence, and even granted the government's request to stage a "secret" hearing. That retreat to a sealed basement courtroom was a theatrical diversion. We had already published eighteen full newspaper pages from the papers, any of which the government could have safely cited in open court as "evidence" of the "irreparable damage" we were allegedly causing.

The secret, in camera hearing further propelled my legal career. Our lawyers expected to confront a cascade of citations from the Pentagon Papers, which they had never seen. So they persuaded the judge to admit me to the sealed chamber as their "adviser." I was thus able to watch the government radicalize the Wall Street attorneys at our table—and finally even the one sitting on the bench.

Instead of bedazzling the initially sympathetic Judge Gurfein with an index of dangerous disclosures in the papers, the government witnesses ended up offending him by refusing to cite any. Responding to the cryptic hand signals of Robert Mardian, the Svengali seated in the jury box, they parried the judge's increasingly plaintive pleas for just a few "samples" of damaging information. In desperation, Judge Gurfein speculated from his own experience as an army intelligence officer in World War II. Maybe, he guessed, the government's codes were at risk because our published texts could be matched against recordings of their encrypted transmission. But an obviously embarrassed Adm. Francis Blouin confessed at that point, "You and I, Judge, are the only ones who remember those days." As we had come prepared to prove, in modern cryptography, every coded message is sealed with a separate key.

On the way into court, we had learned that *The Washington Post*, then scrambling to achieve national stature, had obtained a good part of the documents from Ellsberg and, trusting *The Times* to have verified their authenticity, began immediately to publish summaries of them. We therefore clamored to be released from restraint to keep up with the competition, forcing the government to move against the *Post* as well. But as it fell silent, Ellsberg managed to send some of the documents to still other newspapers. In place of our careful, coherent, but dense narrative, three months in the making, the government had unwittingly produced a flood of half-baked sensations all over the country. It kept referring to the papers provocatively as "stolen" property that had to be returned, but it had proved dramatically that a secret once lost is truly irretrievable. Once the reporters and editors and secretaries and researchers and printers and art directors and copyboys of even one newspaper had read the papers, there was nothing left to "return" or protect. All that the government could now achieve in court was to create a radical code of censorship for future cases. A president who had come into office arguing for "law and order" and "strict construction" of the Constitution was asking the courts, without benefit of law, to enlarge his authority as commander in chief to include the right to censor.

Though he had only one night to write his opinion, Judge Gurfein produced not only a judgment in our favor but a fervent affirmation of First Amendment rights:

> The security of the Nation is not at the ramparts alone. Security also lies in the value of our free institutions. A cantankerous press, an obstinate press, a ubiquitous press must be suffered by those in authority in order to preserve the even greater values of freedom of expression and the right of the people to know. . . .
>
> These are troubled times. There is no greater safety valve for discontent and cynicism about the affairs of Government than free-

dom of expression in any form. This has been the genius of our institutions throughout our history.

The *Post* won just as easily in Washington. But the appellate court in New
York received a new government affidavit purporting at long last to pin-
point damaging secrets in the papers, and it therefore asked Judge Gurfein
to hold another hearing. In the Washington Appellate Court, blackout
curtains were drawn across the courtroom doors—"to prevent lipread-
ing"—as the government delivered a pretentiously sealed briefcase containing an allegedly devastating piece of evidence: a passage in the
Pentagon Papers that revealed the United States had intercepted North
Vietnam's codes. By dumb coincidence, the *Post* was immediately able to
produce a copy of the identical information as already published by a committee of Congress! So by Friday, June 25, the tenth day of our enforced
silence, the Supreme Court cut short the arguments below and agreed to
hear the case on Saturday morning.

Friday evening at six o'clock, contrary to all permissible legal procedure, the government injected entirely new facts into the case. It filed a
secret "annex" to its public brief listing forty-two allegedly injurious passages in the papers. But instead of quoting the offending secrets at meaningful length, it gave only vague descriptions of them, keyed to volume
and page numbers that did not match the numbering in our copies of the
Pentagon history. Then, without telling us, the government's solicitor
general, Erwin Griswold, decided that he could not in conscience argue
for the validity of thirty-one of those new citations. So he pegged the government's entire case to just eleven "secrets"—some of which appeared
only in the four volumes of diplomatic negotiations, which he knew the
newspapers had never received.

But we were left struggling through the night to identify and dispute
forty-two allegedly damaging disclosures. Thus it happened that the most
feverish piece of writing of my entire career—a dissertation rebutting the
government's secret annex—became the body of a top secret brief to the
Supreme Court. All copies were immediately sealed and, it seems, eventually lost.

The government's annex began with a catchall list of what it claimed
were taboo subjects, ranging from "details of bombing in Indochina" to
"confidential information relating to peace negotiations, assets or tactics."
We replied that if those broad subjects were declared off-limits to the
press, the government would have succeeded in promulgating a dangerous code of censorship. Besides, we showed that those very subjects had
been routinely addressed in the writings of present and former govern-

ment officials, in open testimony to Congress, and in daily press coverage of the war.

We also argued that the government had no standing to fret about the publication of "national intelligence estimates" and the "deployment times" of troops to Vietnam. Intelligence estimates were openly debated in the capital, and Nixon himself regularly boasted about the pace, size, and timing of troop movements *out* of Indochina. Most deliciously, we were able to parry the government's demand that the Court protect "the sanctity" of Ambassador Thompson's confidential advice to Nixon about Soviet affairs. We showed that four separate examples of Thompson's analyses of Soviet policy and confidential advice had been published less than two years after they were rendered—in *Six Crises*, by none other than Richard Nixon.

William Hegarty, the attorney who signed our secret reply, told me years later that Griswold credited it with winning the case. I did take great satisfaction from my role, but it was Bickel's strategy that clinched the essential fifth and sixth votes on the Supreme Court—those of Justices Stewart and White, who joined the predisposed Justices Black, Douglas, Brennan, and Marshall. The administration's tawdry tactics persuaded Stewart and White that, as Hegarty put it, "you can't fairly try such a case with the government as the other party endlessly throwing up unrebuttable claims of dire consequences."

Aiming at the two centrists, Bickel was careful from the start to avoid arguing against *all* prior restraints; he openly refused to let Black and Douglas lure him into their corner. Instead, he invited the Court to allow that the government could in extremis censor a newspaper. The justices needed only to find that it had failed to prove a need to do so in our case. As a result, the law ever since has been as Bickel framed it: prior restraint is, at least in theory, conceivable under the Constitution, but only with proof that something headed for publication is *certain to cause immediate, direct, and irreparable* damage. Merely *contributing* to harm, or producing an *eventual* risk of damage, or doing damage that is not discernibly grave are insufficient pretexts for censorship. In practical terms, those conditions are almost impossible to meet, and prior restraint will hardly ever prove justifiable.

Legally speaking, the troopship has long since sailed away. As Erwin Griswold conceded *eighteen years* after our trial:

> I have never seen any trace of a threat to the national security from the publication [of the Pentagon Papers]. Indeed, I have never seen it even suggested that there was such an actual threat. . . .

It quickly becomes apparent to any person who has considerable experience with classified material that there is massive overclassification and that the principal concern of the classifiers is not with national security but rather with governmental embarrassment of one sort or another.

In fact, one year *before* the publication of the Pentagon Papers, while the Soviet Union remained a formidable adversary and Vietnam was still aflame, a Defense Department task force had concluded that "more might be gained than lost if our nation were to adopt—unilaterally, if necessary— a policy of complete openness in all areas of information." Yet a quarter century later, the government was still stamping "secret" on 5 million additional papers each year and elaborately and expensively investigating more than 3 million Americans to "clear" them to read those papers.

—————

Most remarkably, our great and swift legal struggle did lead—*immediately, directly, and irreparably*—to the demise of Richard Nixon's presidency.

In Nixon's perverse view, mere failure loomed as an intolerable defeat. For every defeat he needed to avenge himself upon an enemy. Usually, he fancied his enemies to be liberal elitists, and so he lusted to replay his great triumph over the eastern elites in the case of Alger Hiss. And Hiss, he now recalled, was brought down not by the law but by calculated leaks to the press. No irony there; the press, Nixon's nemesis, now became his preferred weapon of revenge.

In Nixon's paranoid imagination, Ellsberg was the leader of an alien conspiracy that had to be convicted, at least in the court of public opinion. That was how he broke Alger Hiss, he kept telling his staff: cleverly planted leaks to the press had baited the man into committing perjury. We need to dig up dirt on Ellsberg, leak it, then give it to the same Un-American Activities Committee and destroy him. We can't just trust the FBI and Justice Department to develop a good criminal case. We need a "nonlegal team." Tie Ellsberg to the Communists. Do it ourselves.

As Haldeman remembered:

For the out-in-front-smash-them-over-the-head approach, he naturally selected me. I was called into his office and ordered to confront personally every single Cabinet officer and agency head, brutally chew them out and threaten them with extinction if they didn't stop all leaks in the future. . . .

For a more devious approach than mine, Nixon . . . told

Ehrlichman, "If we can't get anyone in this damn government to do something about the problem that may be the most serious one we have, then, by God, we'll do it ourselves. I want you to set up a little group right here in the White House. Have them get off their tails and find out what's going on and figure out how to stop it." . . .

John's two men [Egil Krogh and David Young] set up shop in a little office in the basement of the Executive Office Building and were soon dubbed the "Plumbers" because of their assignment to fix leaks. . . .

Not to be outmaneuvered or left in the cold from anything as potentially juicy as this appeared to be, Chuck Colson hastily got involved, too—recommending the hiring of Howard Hunt to augment the Plumbers' staff.

On the very day that the Supreme Court ruled in our favor, Nixon spurred his White House staff to root out the multiple conspiracies that he imagined to be operating in Ellsberg's shadow. He urged Haldeman to organize a team to break into the Brookings Institution, a liberal think tank whose vaults, he thought, contained Vietnam documents somehow damaging to his presidency. One team of Plumbers actually concocted a plan to firebomb Brookings so that it could ride a fake fire truck to the scene and in the confusion make off with the desired documents. To smear Ellsberg with the depravities that Kissinger had ascribed to him, Nixon also inspired Colson to have Hunt and the Plumbers break into the office of Dr. Lewis Fielding, Ellsberg's psychiatrist. That caper, in September 1971, yielded nothing of interest, but it so clearly broke the law that the government was eventually forced to abort its criminal prosecution of Ellsberg.

The Plumbers, however, carried on with their dirty labors. In the summer of 1972, the Nixon White House sent the same team to bug and discredit Larry O'Brien, the chairman of the Democratic National Committee. And it was to cover up that break-in at O'Brien's office in the Watergate that Nixon committed the massive obstructions of justice for which, had he not resigned, he would certainly have been removed.

The story of Watergate triggered another heated competition between *The Times* and *The Washington Post*. Only this time the *Post* ran well ahead of us. I had better alibis for our Watergate failures than the president had for his, but much as I welcomed his disgrace, my frustration was so great that I could never fully savor it.

The Plumbers were caught stumbling around the Watergate before dawn on Sunday, June 18, 1972. It seemed at first like a story for local police reporters, but to their credit, the *Post*'s locals had a keen eye for the political implications. They quickly established that the perpetrators were no ordinary burglars. Four of them were Cubans with ties to the Miami exiles that the CIA had trained for the Bay of Pigs invasion; one, as the *Post*'s Bob Woodward and Carl Bernstein learned at a court hearing, was a former CIA man. The AP discovered Sunday that this CIA alumnus, James W. McCord, Jr., was the "security coordinator" for CREEP, the Committee to Re-Elect the President. We all came to suspect a political operation, but none of us yet imagined that it could be traced to the White House, much less the president himself.

At *The Times*, we first assigned the story to Tad Szulc, who knew all the Bay of Pigs actors in several countries. By Tuesday the *Post* had found a connection between the Watergate suspects and a White House "consultant"—the very same Howard Hunt who would eventually be exposed as Colson's agent in the pursuit of Ellsberg. Szulc knew Hunt, and although he couldn't find him, he became convinced, as Nixon now schemed to mislead us, that the burglary was an anti-Castro plot, a "national security" operation.

Our Washington bureau had no ties to the capital police or courts. Even so, we only narrowly missed the trail that eventually led Woodward and Bernstein to their spectacular series of stories tying the burglars to the White House. In collaboration with ambitious Miami prosecutors, our bureau's Walter Rugaber tracked large sums of money in the account of one of the burglars to a Mexican bank that was obviously laundering funds sent from the United States. What he missed, but inadvertently led Bernstein to find, was that the source of some of that money had been the Republican campaign chest at CREEP headquarters in Washington.

It was a pivotal breakthrough, linking the Nixon campaign team to the break-in, and it helped the *Post* to outscore us in Watergate scoops by at least five to one. We were too sluggish even after the White House was implicated. Not even my most cynical view of Nixon had allowed for his stupid behavior. There he sat at the peak of his power; why would he personally get involved in tapping the phone not even of his opponent but of only a Democratic party functionary? For once, my habit of hypothesizing my way through a story slowed me down.

I was so envious of the *Post*'s lead that I allowed myself to be skeptical of some of its revelations. That was because it failed to cite credible sources for much of its information, as we would have demanded. I still doubt the *Post*'s claims to have had two independent sources for every published Watergate fact. But it was seriously wrong only once or twice that fall as Woodward and Bernstein gave us a humbling reminder of the essence of great reporting: dogged detective work that confronts and badgers sources until they cough up the clues that transform suspicion into evidence.

It was said for the rest of the century that Watergate had transformed the press from a dutiful monitor of public affairs into a cynical prosecutor and persecutor of public officials. That may be. The *Post*, with Hollywood's help, glamorized the role of investigative reporters and inspired many others to make a career of pursuing villains in high places. But it is nonetheless true that the press's strong streak of skepticism is rarely misplaced.

Our press has been mistrustful and disrespectful of executive authority since the earliest days of the Republic, as were the framers of our Constitution. The wistful wish for a more pliant press that was heard after Watergate expressed a nostalgia for a time of only short-lived patriotic collaborations between press and government during World War II and in the first years of the Cold War. If anything, that era of good feelings left the press too timid in its pursuit of government scandal. Though sometimes too eager to pry into the personal habits and sex lives of public officials, the media even after Watergate have been lazy about misconduct in office, about the corruption and waste in Pentagon procurement, and about the influence of money in American politics. Only rarely has the press uncovered the costly ways in which those campaign debts are repaid with bountiful expenditures of the public's treasure. And after President Clinton's misuse of his office and staff to satisfy and cover up his sexual longings, it may be that even this one last zone of privacy can no longer be safely granted to people in power.

Most of the "reforms" inspired by Watergate to reduce the need for riches in our elections were quickly diluted and evaded. The misuse of executive power—by the FBI, the IRS, and also by the "independent" prosecutors empowered to investigate wrongdoing—has gone unchecked. The massive "classification" of government secrets continues without much restraint. And altogether too few news teams are left with the resources to protect the public interest against the predations of government.

32 · THE PRIZE

RICHARD NIXON CARRIED HIS PETTY VENDETTA AGAINST *The Times* all the way to China and unwittingly stoked all my reportorial embers.

America's resumption of relations with mainland China was long overdue in 1972. The Republicans, Nixon prominent among them, had immobilized our Asian diplomacy for more than two decades. They had accused the Democrats of "losing" China to the Communists in 1949 and politically barred all moves toward "recognizing" the mainland government. They cast our lot with the Nationalists, who lost China's civil war and took refuge on the island of Taiwan. The Communists claimed Taiwan as part of their China; the Chinese on Taiwan claimed the mainland as part of theirs. Both believed in only one China, but the United States had maneuvered itself into behaving as if there were two.

On his way to the White House in 1968, Nixon, like Johnson before him, signaled a readiness to deal with Chairman Mao Zedong's Communist regime, reckoning that both could benefit from a coming together that would frighten the Russians. By late 1969, I detected and reported that "the Nixon Administration is not so much interested now in formal diplomatic relations with China . . . as in some initial exchanges of scholars and businessmen and the beginning of trade relations. In recent days, Peking appeared receptive, or at least interested." The Chinese soon proved their interest by inviting our touring Ping-Pong team to be humiliated by theirs.

The main obstacle to any kind of relationship was Taiwan—not its disposition, merely its definition. When Henry Kissinger paid his secret visit to Beijing in 1971, his assignment was to find a face-saving formula by which the United States could keep its promise to defend Taiwan without offending the principle of "one China." At the same time, a way had to be found for the Communists to take China's seat at the United Nations without the United States openly joining in the expulsion of Taiwan. We allowed ourselves to be stripped of the right to veto the Nationalists' expulsion, and that cleared the way for Kissinger's journey.

He returned from Beijing with an invitation for Nixon to visit Mao and with much admiration for his host, Premier Zhou Enlai. After the Pentagon Papers battle, the president had ordered Kissinger to avoid all contact with *The Times*, but the high-flying national security adviser could not resist sharing some of his achievements with the country's only truly international newspaper. He was really taken with Zhou Enlai's dignity and sophistication. If you dropped a nickel while negotiating with the Russians, Kissinger told me, they would stomp on it and claim it as their own; if you drop a dollar in front of Zhou Enlai, he'll bend and pick it up for you. Although he was without any embassy support in Beijing, Kissinger was impressed to find a sheaf of Western news reports at his door every morning so that he would not feel disadvantaged in discussions with his hosts. *Classy*, Kissinger said, *aristocratic*.

We were still a useful channel for Kissinger because *The Times* had established its own connections and reputation in Beijing, most notably through the efforts of the Canadian ambassador, Chester Ronning, whose daughter Audrey was married to Seymour Topping, our managing editor. After Top's own ice-breaking visit to the mainland, the Chinese invited Scotty Reston at the very same moment they were entertaining Kissinger. Reston scored his own front-page scoop in Beijing by submitting to the then exotic craft of acupuncture during an attack of appendicitis. After recuperating, he made the front page again by interviewing Zhou Enlai, a conversation in which Reston wondered how the Chinese felt about dealing with a president who had so recently been America's leading Red-baiter.

Nixon read the text of that interview as evidence that *The Times* wanted "clearly to sabotage" his trip. In a new burst of paranoia, recounted by Haldeman, the president vowed that no one from *The Times* would be allowed to accompany him to China.

Had I known of this curse, I might have been grateful six months later when the White House press office allotted *The Times* a single seat on the press plane to Beijing. But in my innocence, I argued furiously for at least one more seat for our White House correspondent, Bob Semple. I cited the historic nature of the trip, *The Times*'s preeminence in diplomatic news, the awkward time difference between China and New York that would require writing through the night, and the massive competition we faced, especially from live, round-the-clock telecasts made possible by a relay station that Nixon had sent ahead and donated to the Chinese. I was told I was lucky to be going at all.

My anger turned to rage when I encountered vice presidents from all the television networks and other obvious tourists among the one hundred "journalists" boarding the press plane. I vowed to outdo not only the other newspapers but all the networks that the White House was courting so elaborately at the start of this election year.

From the moment we landed, I saw myself outgunned by cameras, so I labored to paint verbal pictures into my interpretive commentaries in ways that television could not match.

Mr. Nixon grasped the hand that Secretary of State John Foster Dulles spurned at the Geneva Conference in 1954, when the memories of conflict between China and the United States in Korea were still raw and their contest over Indochina had just been joined. . . .

Peking has been spruced up for the Presidential party, but all the repainting and restocking of supplies has been accomplished in the name of the just concluded spring festival marking the Lunar New Year. Most—but not all—of the slogans denouncing American imperialism have been replaced by less directly challenging wordings on the billboards. . . .

Mr. Mao's portrait stares down upon visitors from prominent positions at both the Shanghai and Peking airports and from many of the prominent buildings of the capital along the drive to the Government guest house, where the Nixons will be staying. Also in view in several places are portraits of the universal giants of Communism—Marx, Engels and Lenin—plus the figure no longer worshipped in his own country, Stalin. . . .

The huge red Gate of Heavenly Peace stands to the right, the stark 100-acre Tiananmen Square to the left, flanked by the Great Hall of the People and other big modern buildings thrown up by the new regime in the 1950s, before it rebelled against Soviet thought and design.

Because Beijing's clocks run twelve hours ahead of New York's, I was able to cover events all day and write all night, sleeping only an hour or two. In my desire to capture the texture and mood of events better than any camera, I invented—and Abe Rosenthal eagerly featured—yet another kind of article that has since become a staple of *Times* coverage: a "Reporter's Notebook" that mixed informal observation and commentary in ways not usually countenanced in conventional newswriting:

The dolls in a department store are uniformly Caucasian in appearance. The toy AK-47 rifles look very real and the Ping Pong balls are pink and blue and yellow as well as white.

The dominant sound of this city seems to be silence, even as mobs of people shuffle along the sidewalks and thousands of bicycles pass in the streets. Only the steady tinkle of a hundred faint bicycle bells suggests movement, until a lone bus or delivery motor tricycle comes along honking a vicious rhythm.

And the dominant colors, well reported by every previous visitor but still startling to behold, are blue, blue and blue—in hats, jackets, coats, shirts, pants. Add the pitch black hair to virtually every face and some brilliant red windburn to the cheeks of many girls and children and the picture is virtually complete. Khaki canvas shoulder bags serve civilians as much as soldiers and white gauze masks, in increasing number, cover many lips and noses against dust and cold.

Premier Chou appears no livelier in his gray and blue tunic suits. But up close, as he greeted the Presidential party and posed with the American press and technicians for group photographs in his Great Hall antechamber, the Premier was a well-tailored figure, in the style of a man who does care.

These "Notebooks" let me twit both the president—

It was the Nixons' evening at the theater yesterday, and there was the First Lady sitting beside Chiang Chin (Mrs. Mao Tse-tung)—both women with modest stage experience—watching the flaming red banners triumph in ballet over the black running dogs of capitalism. . . .

Miss Chiang was the radical mentor of the Chinese arts during the recent Cultural Revolution. She was also the inspiration for radical challengers who are thought to have opposed Premier Chou En-lai during much of that revolution. But last night, walking purposefully and graciously into the auditorium of the Great Hall of the People, she was the hostess for the couple from Whittier, Calif., whose taste in ballet and politics had not been pointing all these years toward the saga of Wu Ching-hua in the den of the landlords.*

---

* I have retained the English spellings of Chinese names as they appeared in *The Times* but, like *The Times* in more recent years, use the current pinyin transliterations in my own text.

—and the massed legions of television—

The greatness of the Great Wall of China, obviously, is that it can survive anything—even an American political extravaganza.

Perhaps the whole idea started in the President's private briefing book on China, which observed that the monumental ruin in the craggy Pa-ta Mountains 35 miles from Peking had been rather ineffective for defense but very good for communications.

The briefing-book writers meant that the wall, in its heyday, could accommodate 10 men abreast moving inland from the sea with their carts and chariots over a span of 2,484 miles. The record needs to be amended with the news that only two of the wall's two-story towers can accommodate three rival network anchor men with full crews, several tons of gear, including remote color cameras, several miles of cable and several hundred camera-toting extras dangling from the battlements. . . .

The American Commander in Chief . . . moved confidently past the firing slits in the wall for several hundred yards, showing by his gaze that he knew the position of every major camera emplacement. . . . There was a momentary threat of mutiny in the air among the media camp followers struggling for a picture of the visitation. In fact, catastrophe was only narrowly averted after the Presidential party inadvertently sealed Walter Cronkite's escape route to the departing film courier.

I dwell on these paragraphs because they demonstrate the full range of journalistic expression that so many of us fought so long to bring to *The Times*—not just to our house organ, as of old, for the amusement of our colleagues but to all the readers of the paper. From this success I drew the inspiration, years later, to welcome ever more colorful and meaningful writing into the paper.

––––––––––

Writers were at last in full command of the tone of *The Times*, and Abe Rosenthal, long one of our stylistic models, put even my "Notebooks" on Page One. I became more certain than ever that full and fair newswriting not only allowed but required a deft weave of fact and analysis, drama and humor. Three examples make my point—the tops of long articles that I filed during one single, sleepless day in Shanghai.

The "news" story:

President Nixon and Premier Chou En-lai concluded a week of unusual negotiations here today and parted with an American pledge to arrange a gradual withdrawal of United States forces from Taiwan and a joint pledge for a gradual increase in American-Chinese contacts and exchanges.

Mr. Nixon, contending that "This

was the week that changed the world," headed home with a conviction that both governments were committed to "build a bridge" across the Pacific and 22 years of hostility.

The "News Analysis":

President Nixon returns from his "long march"—an arduous retreat that in Chinese Communist history became a legendary victory—urgently offering the American people the claim that he is, after all, the great peacemaker, that he has found his mission for four more years in the White House, that he has overwhelmed the agony of Vietnam with the promise of reconciliation in China and that the youth of America, which never suffered his own fierce hatred of Communism, has reason to celebrate the new China lobby led by the new Nixon.

And the "Reporter's Notebook":

The last glimpse of China for the American voyagers is through weary eyes. They felt the excitement of Marco Polo, but they had only days where he had years. To be precise, they had eight days to fill a hunger of decades—one day for every 100 million Chinese, most of whom were babies when Americans last strolled these streets. The streets leave a drab memory—clean drabness, to be sure, and blue drabness when the people are milling in the streets in their ultramarine suits, which is almost always. But how can you call anything drab that has so much life and so many unknown ambitions and misfortunes and adventures and dreams?

A year later, thanks to Nixon's vindictive challenge to make *The Times* cover his big story with a single reporter, I was honored for my week's labor in China with a Pulitzer Prize. I would have much preferred a prize for day-in, day-out coverage of Moscow or diplomacy in Washington instead of the feat of composing 35,000 words about the mostly superficial theatrics of a presidential journey. But they don't usually give prizes for routine excellence. The most favored stories are those "with consequence"—a correspondent's expulsion or a malefactor's imprisonment. Abe Rosenthal deserved a prize for his brilliant correspondence in India but got one only after Poland's Communist regime threw him out for "prying too deeply" into its affairs. Many remarkable investigations of crime and corruption go unrewarded by Pulitzers because the perpetrators are not prosecuted quickly enough to impress the juries in the year of publication.

Like all subjective judgments, the Pulitzer awards can be unfairly generous or cruelly blind to real achievement. If the Pulitzers were recognized as just one measure of excellence and not ranked so far above all other journalism prizes, they would serve the intended purpose of inspiring our craft and setting standards of distinction. But *The Times* and the other major winners have overdone the promotion of the Pulitzers, giving them much more coverage and status than comparable honors. A Pulitzer is attached to names in the news almost as regularly as a Nobel. Pulitzers are overvalued by publishers and circulation managers; even those won decades ago are held out as marks of current excellence. So editors and reporters covet and celebrate Pulitzers much more intensely than they do any other professional achievement. At *The Times*, we gather hundreds of staffers in the newsroom to toast the winners with champagne, and we permanently display huge photos of them on the walls passed by company guests. We are disappointed when we win only one of the fifteen journalism Pulitzers in any year; we feel defeated when we miss altogether.

These exaggerations can distort the practice of journalism. There are editors who undertake massive projects mainly to impress the Pulitzer juries, even if they produce reams of copy that readers find indigestible. While there is plenty of second-guessing in newspapers about the National Book Award, or the Oscars, Tonys, and Emmys, there is hardly ever any critical examination of the Pulitzers and their administration. Critics who lack a prize can only sound envious. Critics like me, who've won one and benefited from the honor in renown, speak with ill grace. Prizes can enrich our craft, but like all institutions, they could use more honest assessment.

I did not dare demur when the honor came to me at the very end of my reporting career. The news immediately raised my stock and meant a permanent place for my portrait in the *Times* pantheon. And in Russell Baker's immortal observation, it meant an automatic adjective in the lead of my obituary. Pulitzer Prize winner Max Frankel ended his reporting career by burying his reservations, enjoying the irony of Nixon's favor, and hoping that the laurel would enhance his status in the corporate wars that lay ahead.

EDITOR

1972–1994

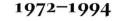

The New York Times

VOL. CXXIII...No. 42,566   NEW YORK, FRIDAY, AUGUST 9, 1974   15 CENTS
LATE CITY EDITION

NIXON RESIGNS

HE URGES A TIME OF 'HEALING'; FORD WILL TAKE OFFICE TODAY

'Sacrifice' Is Praised; Kissinger to Remain

The 37th President Is First to Quit Post

SPECULATION RIFE ON VICE PRESIDENT

POLITICAL SCENE SHARPLY ALTERED

Rise and Fall
Appraisal of Nixon Career

JAWORSKI ASSERTS NO DEAL WAS MADE

---

33 · UP, UP, AND AWAY

REPORTERS ARE HUNTERS WHO THRILL TO THE CHASE, but sooner or later they yearn for relief from running, from chasing rumors, from careening down blind alleys. They become physically exhausted and spiritually defeated. Middle-aged dignity rebels at being so relentlessly manipulated or shut out, misled, and deceived. There is, however, no easy escape to more adult duty. Management, which journalism calls editing, is the only visible destination in the newsroom. Yet reporters are not well trained or well suited for the managerial arts; they are not naturally organizers, problem solvers, budget plotters. So when the time comes to abandon the beat, a crisis beckons. The juvenile joys of reporting cease to satisfy, but, unlike cops or soldiers, midcareer reporters are not lured into other lines of work with generous pensions. Even reporters who qualify as potential editors face a steep pyramid on which colleagues suddenly loom as competitors.

One of the few benefits of growing up in Hitler's Germany was that I became skilled at peering around corners for routes of escape. I learned habitually to reconnoiter the future, and, on reaching the crisis age of forty, I thought I had already finessed the reporter's midlife miasma. I was *the* Washington correspondent as well as chief of the Washington bureau—both writer *and* editor, actor *and* director, bohemian *and* bureaucrat. I had landed the only job I ever wanted and intended to hold it until another generation swept me aside. I figured they'd have to make me a columnist to pry me out of my chair, like Tom Wicker and Tony Lewis, and let me roam the globe with a generous expense account. I led the most talented newspaper team in America and held the best job on that team. Even the hostility of the Nixon White House would pass. In another administration, I would again enjoy the company of colorful, maybe even admirable politicians. I wished for a lighter hand than Abe Rosenthal's at headquarters in New York, but I had the benefit of a 200-mile buffer zone between us. No professional anxiety disturbed my sleep in the spring of 1972 as I prepared to follow Nixon to Moscow and into his campaign against George McGovern.

Out of the blue, Sydney Gruson appeared with an unsettling proposition. Gruson, the publisher's dapper friend and conscientious assistant, said I was wanted in New York at the end of the year, to be *The Times*'s next Sunday editor and, by definition, a member of the publisher's inner circle. It was a flattering but not immediately tempting offer. I had all the executive perks I wanted. I hated the thought of moving back to the frenzy and filth of New York. And I sensed, albeit dimly, that the Sunday editor occupied a most anomalous position.

The Sunday *Times*, which then sold 1.5 million copies nationwide, had nearly double the circulation of the weekday paper. It was actually a hybrid produced by two antagonistic departments. The Sunday editor controlled the five sections that the imperious Lester Markel had managed to invent or wrest away from the "Daily": the Magazine, the Book Review, the Week in Review, and the Arts & Leisure (alias Drama) and Travel sections. The rest of the Sunday paper—the Main News, Sports, Business, and Real Estate sections—was produced by the seven-day staffs that owned the enviable title of "News Department." The "Sunday Department" labored on the eighth floor of the Times building, a hushed world high above the clatter and romance of the third-floor newsroom.

For many years, while the News Department was resisting analysis and interpretive reporting—mistaking them for opinion—the Sunday editors had a distinctive mission. They looked back into history, past the events of "yesterday" and over the horizon to the destination of trends. The Magazine, Week in Review, and Arts & Leisure sections allowed

Times writers to reflect on events in stylish essays. But now that the Daily itself welcomed analysis and valued polished writing, the need for a rival team of editors was fast fading. The Magazine, Book Review, and Travel sections still had the distinction of relying heavily on freelance writers. But the Week in Review depended on staff correspondents, and Arts & Leisure featured the views of *The Times*'s regular theater, film, music, dance, and art critics.

When Markel, the Sunday editor for forty years, was pushed into retirement in 1964, Punch Sulzberger gave Turner Catledge the title of executive editor and command of both the Daily and Sunday staffs. But Catledge—and Reston briefly after him—showed no interest in breaking down bureaucratic walls; they did little more than visit the alien, arty precincts of the eighth floor and let Markel bequeath his independence to his mild-mannered deputy, Dan Schwarz. When Abe Rosenthal succeeded Reston as head of the News Department, he was initially denied the title of executive editor, leaving at least a theoretical opening for someone else to be inserted over him. More likely, as Mom always wished for me, the publisher wanted to leave Abe "something to look forward to."

My political antennae, like most reporters', had been trained outward from *The Times*, blithely ignoring office maneuvers that did not directly affect my work. When Gruson delivered his surprising offer, I had only the faintest awareness of the Sunday Department's history and condition. And I gave little credence to his whispered sales pitch that the publisher wanted me in New York as a potential rival to Abe Rosenthal, at least as a spare tire for future advancement. I had assumed that only inertia preserved the independence of the Sunday Department and shared the general expectation that Abe would gain control of it by sponsoring his closest friend, Arthur Gelb, for the Sunday job. Gelb's raging curiosities and enthusiasms ran naturally toward feature writing and cultural news. But Gruson insisted that the publisher was unwilling to yield control of the whole paper to the homogeneous team of Abe and Arthur. I should have recognized that report as a portent of unpleasant rivalry if I took the job. That did not, however, figure seriously on my many lists of pros and cons as I weighed Gruson's summons.

Reasons to reject the offer: No more writing, except memos; the loss not only of a byline but of the stature it conferred as a political and diplomatic commentator. The move to New York, a tough and expensive place to raise a family. Remoteness from events, depleting rather than enlarging my store of knowledge. *Reasons to accept:* The breadth of the Sunday sections, the mandate to plumb every field of human interest. The parochialism of life in Washington, where no dinner in seven years passed without a wrenching discussion of Vietnam. My commitment to *The Times*, a unique institution whose success I had come to regard as a patriotic cause.

The Nos seemed selfish. They embodied the subtle corruptions of Washington, the home of so many people who came to do good and stayed to do well. Didn't the job in New York fulfill my long-buried dream of running my own magazine? *Five* magazines, no less. And if Tobi showed little fear of returning to New York, how could I use the family pretext to cling to the capital's comforts? If writing for *The Times* was so satisfying, wouldn't actually shaping it be exhilarating?

I accepted the Sunday job in July—for announcement in September—and headed off to cover the 1972 presidential campaign. While stalking the voters, I wondered how I would relate to the *next* campaign, four years hence. As it turned out, I played a briefly prominent role in that next election, but no longer as Sunday editor. And as Gruson intimated, I was indeed being stretched and held in reserve as a potential successor to Abe Rosenthal. I had firmly closed out one twenty-year career and begun another, one that taught me more than Washington ever could about the world and, finally, myself.

―――――

After six months of hellish weekend commuting to wait out the end of the school year, I brought the family to New York for a refreshing adventure. We bought a huge house in the Riverdale section of the Bronx, commanding a majestic view of the Hudson River. Having poured our savings into this behemoth, we could afford only a few new pieces of furniture. But we were proud that the frugal habits of many years, the explosion of realty values in Washington, and their depression in New York could yield such luxury.

Still, this bountiful environment yielded only fitful contentment.

David, Margot, and Jon adjusted easily to the Fieldston School, which we favored for its close resemblance to Washington's Sidwell Friends and my memory of Music & Art. They all landed in private school after we refused to have a visibly bored David skipped far ahead of his peers in his Chevy Chase public school. We were ashamed to pass up the New York public schools that both Tobi and I had attended, but so many middle-class New Yorkers had withdrawn not only their children but also their political energies and financial resources from the public system that it had been seriously damaged. We thought our only responsible choice for three bright children was between private school and migration to the suburbs. I decided that an executive of *The New York Times* owed his taxes to New York City but not his kids.

Our children were rapidly defining themselves as individuals. David early on made his mark with words, not only by excelling in his studies but by teaching us all to deflect tension and anxiety with disarming humor and inventive irony. The film writer-director in him was visible at an early age. Margot, a conscientious student, battled her athletic brothers by also pursuing a dozen varsity letters. She was recognized as a leader by her peers but, like her father, showed an early tendency to retreat from confrontations into lonely hours of drawing and painting. Her love of reading and design led straight into a career in magazine art direction. Jonathan scrambled for recognition by shortening his name to Jon and showering smiles upon all humanity. Of the three, he had the roughest time with academics; his early schooling was too loose and his mother's pressure too burdensome. In the search for structure, we moved him from Fieldston to Horace Mann, but the school itself was a pressure cooker and Jon's only reliable support system became the football team. It endowed him with passions and friendships that still serve the alert, articulate television broadcaster he eventually became.

Tobi finished her book for young people about Russian art and artists, wrote tour pamphlets for the Smithsonian Museum of Natural History in Washington, besieged the museums of New York for similar contracts, and finally shocked us all by enrolling in Columbia's business school. Dazed by the study of statistics, she became a management consultant and eventually the marketing director for Beverly Sills at the New York City Opera. But her combative spirit and hunger for recognition left a trail of tension wherever she went. Her next, quite unpredictable stop was the staff of the Op-Ed page of Long Island's *Newsday*, and when there, too, promotions came too slowly, she returned to school yet again, this time to her father's alma mater, Columbia Law.

No matter what psychological demons were driving Tobi, I deserved some of the blame for her restlessness. We had drifted apart emotionally as well as professionally. I yearned for a harmony and balm that seemed alien to her nature. She yearned for achievements commensurate with mine and for the romance of our younger years. I misread her depressions as moods, though they ranged all too typically from the volcanic to the morose.

More than I realized at the time, I greatly added to our unhappiness by lugging home the anxieties of an unhappy executive. The ride atop the Sunday *Times* taught me a lot about the business side of newspapering and about the difficulties of steering an unwieldy staff of creative people. But the profits of *The Times* were too meager to permit the aggressive innovations of which I had dreamed. Even in recessions, the paper allowed its News Department to spend quite freely to pursue the news aggressively. But the Sunday sections were "profit centers," expected to generate maximum revenues at minimal costs. If they were not profitable, their very existence came into question. The edict from on high was that we could recruit new talent only to the extent that we streamlined functions and retired unproductive editors. I brought Jack Rosenthal from Washington as my deputy, but that was the limit of my refurbishing. In three years, we managed to negotiate severance deals with only six of our one hundred staffers, which, laughably, caused us to become known in the leering pages of *The Village Voice* as Jack the Knife and Max the Ax. But the modesty of these personnel shifts defeated many of my editorial ambitions.

I also had to contend with the hostility of an obviously competitive Abe Rosenthal. He had tried to obstruct my recruiting of Jack, making much of his annoyance that a second Rosenthal now appeared on *The Times*'s masthead. More injuriously, Abe resisted giving staff writers time off from the Daily to pursue Magazine projects. He encouraged the culture critics to feel overburdened by their Sunday obligations. He even told political writers that he did not want to read ideas in the Week in Review that had not first appeared in his Daily pages. Although he commanded a third-floor division of 1,000, he treated our eighth-floor platoon of 100 as a threat and repelled bids for cooperation.

For all these reasons I staggered through my term as Sunday editor. To be sure, I began to think strategically about journalism, about the necessity of matching aspirations to resources. I learned to respect the anxiety of writers and editors whose only bottom line was my subjective judgment of their work. I learned to apply a former painter's eye to typography, photography, illustration, and page layout. I learned to live with the antagonisms between the business and editorial departments. The most difficult adjustment was to my own transformation from performer to conductor. Like the sections of an orchestra, the Sunday publications each sang in a different voice and rhythm, and the success of the whole demanded separate attention to the parts.

THE MAGAZINE

The *Times Magazine* was in many ways a historical accident. Begun soon after Adolph Ochs, Punch's grandfather, purchased the moribund *New-*

York Times in 1896, the Magazine evolved largely in response to technological improvements in paper and printing. It became a showcase for news and feature photographs and richly illustrated advertisements. Its editorial content was always entirely discretionary, yet severely constrained by the fact that most of the customary features of a weekly magazine, particularly political comment and cultural reviews, were preempted by other sections of the Sunday *Times*.

After chafing for years under Lester Markel's black-and-white view of the world—weighty reportage and opinion at the front, food and fashion and the famous crossword at the back—Dan Schwarz brought in not only editorial color but also more subtly shaded articles on a broader range of cultural themes. For my inaugural week at the start of 1973, for example, he had assembled a Merle Miller account of the conversion of Cord Meyer, Jr., from a romantic world federalist into the cold-blooded spymaster of the CIA; a portrait of Woody Allen and his neurotic films by Richard Schickel; an essay proposing limits on the presidential war power by Arthur Schlesinger, Jr.; a profile of a Korean poet; and an (insufficiently skeptical) account of the "death" (more aptly "suicide") of Nixon's welfare reform.

That was a rich diet, matched perhaps by monthlies like *Harper's* and *The Atlantic* but by no other weekly except *The New Yorker*. But *The New Yorker* drew on the generous and well-paid output of seasoned correspondents, critics, and cartoonists; the *Times Magazine* employed a staff of only editors. It was widely resented for its low fees for articles—a few hundred dollars for three or four weeks' work—and for the excessive rewrites it demanded as ideas and manuscripts traveled up our hierarchy. Most frustrating of all was the Magazine's production schedule. Though a weekly, it went to press nearly two weeks before distribution, which meant that articles were needed more than a month in advance, inspired by ideas or events that were three or more months old. It took more imagination and talent than we possessed to present a mix of articles that was fresh and topical yet more deliberative than those in every other part of the paper.

I thought each week's Magazine could claim success if every serious reader found even a single article of interest. But it was being sold to advertisers as a magazine with a shelf life of at least a week, not just a newspaper supplement. And by that standard we almost always fell short, lacking a heavy cover, enough open pages for generous color illustrations, and the columns and other staples of a weekly journal.

Walter Mattson, the astute general manager of *The Times*, moved as fast as he could to upgrade the quality of our Magazine's paper and color, but I managed to make only modest improvements, starting with a modest raise for our writers and illustrators. We created a lighthearted "End-paper" next to the rear cover and persuaded Russell Baker to move one of his Op-Ed page columns into the front of the book. When he wondered which of his ideas were most suitable for the Magazine, I glibly demanded the best, whereupon Russ delivered a memorable lecture in editorial wisdom: "To get the best of Russell Baker," he said, "you also have to print the worst."

Unable to leaven the French bias of Craig Claiborne, our haughty food columnist, and the haute couture pretensions of our fashion mavens, I tried to compensate by broadening the appeal of our bylines, attracting authors like James Q. Wilson, Martin Mayer, Andrew Greeley, Don Barthelme, Robert Lekachman, Joseph Brodsky, Carlos Fuentes, Irwin Shaw, Norval Morris, Willard Gaylin, Gaddis Smith, Anthony Burgess, Garry Wills. We strained for attention by devising special issues, notably a book-length recapitulation of the Watergate drama by J. Anthony Lukas and an account of a week at President Ford's elbow by John Hersey. We had fun, once even mocking *The Times* by inviting Jules Feiffer to invent a comic strip suitable for our august pages. He produced "Hodgkins of State," the tale of a foreign service officer who triumphs over a diplomatic rival by maneuvering to sit a few inches higher at a negotiating table. In a single year, we doubled the Magazine's mail from readers and its sales of reprint rights to other papers.

But the freestanding national *Times Magazine* that I envisioned never got beyond the mock-up stage. I wanted to collect articles from *all* our Sunday sections and, with the new computer technology, to churn out a separate journal offering, "The Best of *The New York Times*," for sale in all the cities then unable to get the regular Sunday paper. By recycling our best features and most important news analyses, I was sure that we could compete with *Time* and *Newsweek* and earn enough new revenue to pay for an ever-higher quality of writing, photography, and illustration. The enormous national appeal of the Sunday *Times*, now that it can be distributed almost anywhere in the United States, vindicates the promise that I foresaw in that 1970s project. But our company lacked the confidence to risk the sizable investment that would have tested our prototypes.

THE BOOK REVIEW

Adolph Ochs thought a literary journal, first offered on Saturdays, would quickly enhance *The Times*'s appeal to educated and affluent readers. And as he soon discovered, the news of ideas could be as interesting and important as the news of politics and finance.

Over the decades, the Book Review became an influential showcase for New York's publishing industry and the only newspaper supplement able to attract large volumes of its advertising. Even after some book publishers concluded that ads in *The Times* were not always worth their cost, they felt obliged to buy them to appease the egos (and contractual demands) of their most valued authors. An ad in *The Times* proclaimed a book's seriousness, to the trade as well as the public, and a prominent review, especially on the Review's cover, itself became a promotable achievement.

Even more marketable was a book's appearance on *The Times*'s bestseller list. Although other publications learned to compile their own rankings, none achieved *The Times*'s national influence among sellers and readers. Authors' contracts began to promise special rewards for books that reached our list and bonuses for a book's longevity near the top. A prominent review in *The Times* or a solid best-seller ranking could bring a book generous shelf space and display, exponentially multiplying its success.

No part of becoming Sunday editor promised as much fun as joining in the evaluation of books, authors, and the people invited to review them. Nothing turned out to be more disappointing than my discovery that a Sunday editor barely had time to read the Review, much less any books. Like my predecessors, I was virtually irrelevant to the editing of the Book Review.

I did not like much of what I read there, although I admired the writing and taste of the Review's editor, John Leonard. As a Daily book reviewer, he had been fair, learned, and witty, but in editing the Review he had trouble rising above his own political opinions, especially about the war in Vietnam. It is admittedly difficult to be simultaneously interesting and evenhanded in a magazine that serves up the judgments of an eclectic, random roster of reviewers. And as Leonard brought me to understand, "we sell reviews, not books." Still, I felt that *Times* readers deserved to get the news of books and an appraisal of their value without drowning in a sea of disputation. Leonard and his associates could not resist the temptation to champion the intellectual counterculture and the most passionate voices of the antiwar movement. And for too long, I failed to restrain them.

My ignorance of fiction made it even harder to discourage the Review's indulgence of long and learned treatises by Ivy League scholars who labored to compete with the more academic *New York Review of Books*, which had sprung to life during the long New York newspaper strike of

1963. My constant pleas for shorter, more accessible reviews were airily ignored, as if I were a philistine who preferred the drivel then dominating the best-seller lists—*Jonathan Livingston Seagull* and *Dr. Atkins' Diet Revolution*.

The Review was admirably dogged, however, in searching out promising first novels and other unheralded books worthy of notice. It employed a half-dozen editors as "pre-reviewers" to scan through 20,000 titles a year, pick the 2,000 we had space to review, and nominate suitable reviewers for Leonard's selection. Yet here, too, there was room for improvement. Too many of our reviewers turned out to be novelists promoting their own literary achievements or scholars parading their own expertise at a rival's expense. I often found the in-house memos from our pre-reviewers more informative and dispassionate than the criticisms we ended up purchasing from contributors.

I gradually learned that my main job was not to second-guess the editors of the Book Review but to defend them against the agitations of our accounting department. Since the advertising revenue that the Review attracted consistently failed to cover the costs of its production and staff, the "return-on-investment" crowd foresaw profit in its elimination, or at least significant shrinkage. They never bothered, of course, to measure the contribution that even an "elitist" Review made to the sale and cachet of the whole Sunday paper. Nor did they dare to openly propose its elimination. They knew that all Sulzbergers were genetically programmed to decide any direct confrontation over the quality of the paper in favor of the editors. But the company's profits in the early 1970s were approaching zero, and the Review was whispered to represent a "drain" of up to $5 million a year. Its critics refused to consider it a "loss leader" that brought customers to the rest of the paper.

I wanted us to broaden the Review's appeal to nonacademic readers, but preaching financial realities to its editors would have merely confirmed their view of me as a vulgar bureaucrat and sent them gossiping to *The Village Voice* and other guardians of our morality. So I decided to wait out the always restless John Leonard until he moved on and limited my interventions to mostly cosmetic issues of design. Leonard finally left to write a delightful personal column, which gave me the chance to replace him with Harvey Shapiro, a poet and an incisive senior editor at the Magazine. But he took over late in my term as Sunday editor and wound up compromised in Abe Rosenthal's eyes, like many others, by my favor. Another decade passed before my responsibilities again embraced the Book Review, and it was, fortunately, still being allowed to "lose millions" in the service of its worthy mission.

THE WEEK IN REVIEW

The Sunday section that I was most qualified to manage proved to be the one least suitably situated in the Sunday Department. The News of the Week in Review, as it was then called, employed too few good writers to give analytical weight to its summaries of events. And it lacked the authority over the News Department's correspondents to compel their best contributions.

Now that news analyses were commonplace in the daily paper, the Week in Review had to outsmart the News Department in the themes it stressed. And it could afford to pay only modest fees for their timely execution. We radically redesigned the section on the assumption that its closest readers were news junkies rather than people looking to catch up on news they had missed during the week. We concentrated on interpretive essays by *Times* correspondents, devoting separate pages to The World, The Nation, The Region, and Ideas & Trends. That basic approach and design served the Review for more than a quarter century, but it could not fully realize its promise until the section was integrated into the News Department.

ARTS & LEISURE

Paradoxically, the Sunday Department's most profitable supplement became the straw that broke my bureaucratic back. Arts & Leisure had been much too long in the custody of Seymour Peck, a sensitive editor whose devotion to the Broadway theater left him reluctant to reckon with the shifting tastes of the film and television generation. With the Shuberts howling in protest from their alley across the street, I encouraged his successor, William Honan, to emphasize the movies, and to treat both light and serious music and art and photography as the equals of theater. And over the protests and obstructions of the advertising department, we added a decent listing of the week's cultural events that matched the guides long available in *The New Yorker*, *New York*, and *Cue* magazines. When the cultural critics delivered lazy Sunday essays, we risked their further alienation by daring to offer editorial suggestions, a novel experience for most of them. Also galling was the section's production schedule; it went to press on Mondays, making it impossible to cover the week's major cultural events. In both form and substance, Arts & Leisure was completely divorced from the Daily's cultural coverage, a dumb and debilitating arrangement.

In early 1975, after only two years as Sunday editor, I told the publisher that the very existence of a separate Sunday Department ought to be reconsidered. My realm was illogical and expensive, without much redeeming journalistic value. He seemed to agree but did not act on the idea until a year later, after I had occasion to repeat it to Walter Mattson, our general manager. A tall, smart, stubborn, and secretive Swede, Mattson had devised a strategy that would force our craft unions to let modern computers and automated printing processes slowly erode their jobs and wages. Without automation, labor costs were bound to kill off *The Times* as they had strangled so many other New York papers. But even generous terms could not quickly persuade printers and pressmen to permit the elimination of their jobs.

While pursuing Mattson's goals, the paper passed through very hard times. So Mattson and his team looked for ways to attract new readers and new categories of advertising, a search that led them to want to print the daily paper in four rather than two sections and to make one of them a daily "magazine" devoted to rotating subject matter. The News Department had long wanted a four-section paper for more conspicuous display of national and sports news, but economic pressures dictated a different course.

Mattson informed me in early 1976 that he'd been working with the News Department to begin the conversion to a four-section Daily with a "Weekend" magazine in the Friday paper. Movie ads looking to attract customers for Friday and Saturday nights would support the section, which could also focus on other "going out" attractions in New York and gain a whole new revenue stream without, he hoped, damaging the Sunday business. His question was, could our Arts & Leisure staff be creative enough to hold its own against the new Friday Weekend section?

No, I insisted, we could not. An augmented Daily staff would now jealously withhold its best material from Sunday and, insult to injury, go to press Thursday nights in competition against a Sunday section already distributed on Wednesday. This was dramatic proof of the illogic of separating the Daily and Sunday staffs, and things were bound to grow worse with the invention of other weekday "magazines."

A few weeks later, in mid-February, the deal was done. Punch told me that he intended to merge the Daily and Sunday departments, that he had chosen Abe to head the merged operation and hoped I would prepare myself to succeed his cousin, John Oakes, as editor of the editorial page at the end of 1976.

I recoiled with envy of Abe, contempt for editorial writing, and a genuine alarm that there was little appreciation for my strategic thinking about *The Times*. I was not appeased by Punch's warm assurances that "somewhere in our chemistry and future" a role would emerge for me in shaping the newspaper. I composed a hurt and hurried creed to display my managerial talents. But Rosenthal easily outbid me by taking a week in the Caribbean and crafting what must have been a compelling summary of his considerable achievements as managing editor and his hopes for the paper's future.

In my distress, I spoke with rare candor about the lack of vision and planning in his News Department. Besides sloganeering about our being a "New York newspaper," I discerned no effort to cope with the dispersion beyond the city of our readers, readers who now had suburban interests. I complained of the difficulties of navigating through a paper still growing larger by the day. I bemoaned the failure to keep up with the business coverage of *The Wall Street Journal* and its inevitable effort to add to its national circulation by appealing also to *Mrs.* Executive. I deplored our unimaginative sports coverage. Most of all I bemoaned the poor planning that left much of the initiative for innovation to Mattson and the business side of the paper.

Not until many years later did I learn from a tearful John Pomfret, in his cups at a birthday party for Gruson, that Punch had in fact seriously considered me for executive editor at that point. Pomfret had been a close friend and colleague in the Washington bureau, where I succeeded him as White House correspondent. He had befriended Punch when both worked for the *Milwaukee Journal* and the publisher summoned him to New York to apply his knowledge of labor affairs to our union problems. In time, when Mattson became president of the company and second only to Chairman Punch, Pomfret succeeded him as general manager. And now, he drew me aside and wept through a "confession" that he had strenuously argued *against* my promotion to editor.

Why? Because I had once too fiercely resisted his efforts to appease some Magazine advertisers. As I barely remembered, he and Mattson had asked me to give them early notice of any negative Magazine articles about cigarettes. They did not directly request that I suppress such articles; they only wanted "fair warning" of anticigarette copy so that cigarette ads could be moved from the offending issue to a later week. I had to struggle to recall the encounter, which was provoked by our publication of a sardonic Endpaper cartoon featuring a "Non-smoker's Gas Mask." Soon after, I was asked to postpone an article about cigars that emphasized the link between cigarettes and emphysema because several cigarette ads were already locked into page forms. Our timing was especially unfortunate because the offending Magazine would be appearing on the eve of a Pomfret business trip to Winston-Salem.

I vehemently refused to delay the smoking piece, holding firm to the principle that editing with one ear cocked to the advertisers would inevitably pollute all our decision making. Mattson thought me rigid and uncooperative, even though he agreed with the slant of the article; his own father had died of emphysema. I had not yet understood that *The Times*'s feature supplements operated under a looser standard than the regular news pages. Although rigorously honest in what they carried, they were nonetheless expected to be more pliable at the margins, in both the material they published and that which they avoided.

The Sunday Travel section, for example, obligingly devoted inordinate space to a single subject—skiing or cruises—for the simple reason that doing so creates an attractive "environment" for the advertisers of the travel industry. Whereas Macy's, Bloomingdale's, and Citibank must risk having their ads land next to starving Africans or feuding Bosnians in the news pages, the Sunday travel ads are assured display in a sea of upbeat copy.

The same desire to sell a favorable "environment" led eventually to the creation of the Living and Home sections to attract the ads of supermarkets and furniture marts. I do not doubt the effectiveness of a sales pitch that promises to segment the readers by specific interest, but in a newspaper, the compartmentalizing of ads is easily overdone. For many years, *The Times* refused to let the Book Review admit a furniture ad, even for a bookcase! And we were always at risk that the sheer volume of food, movie, or travel ads would distort our priorities and commit too much staff and space to those profitable subjects.

Whatever the effect of these tensions between us, I never believed Pomfret's antagonism counted for much in Punch's choice of Abe as executive editor. Rosenthal offered a much longer record of newsroom experience. I had distinguished myself as a manager mainly by recommending my department's demise. And I was much more easily reassigned and kept in the publisher's circle once he decided to persuade his first cousin once removed, John Oakes, to yield control of the editorial page at the age of sixty-three.

The only trouble was, as I put it in a memo to Punch, that "I am not an editorial writer, and I don't understand why others wish to be. I don't believe in group-think on weighty public issues. I don't believe that any one person can know enough about enough to assert responsibility for meaningful opinions 365 times a year, not to mention three or six times a day." My resistance was honest, but my argument was not. I had grown up worshiping E. B. White's anonymous essays in *The New Yorker*, which addressed the most complex moral and political issues with uncommon horse sense and ironic detachment. I delighted in the crisply reasoned "leaders" of *The Economist*. I had greatly valued the courage and conviction with which both *The Times* and *The Washington Post* editorially assailed McCarthyism and beat the drums for Nixon's resignation. And in my years in Washington, I had particularly admired the *Post*'s change of editorial tone, from heated declamation to cool deliberation. The best editorials were those that taught me *how* to think about a subject even if I found their bottom-line conclusion unsatisfactory. My problem with *The Times*'s editorials was that I generally agreed with their point of view but did not often enough find them surprising or instructive. They pulsed with a predictable liberal passion that often lapsed into immodest certitude. They were more virtuous than useful, more right than readable. I wanted no part in their production.

To my surprise, Punch let me know via Gruson that he, too, hoped for a different tone on his editorial page. Neither of them ever explained what changes of voice or policy they favored. Gruson stood several degrees to the left of Punch's centrism, and I stood instinctively between them, but there never arose any discussion of our political values. We all knew that *The Times* would always defend humane capitalism, enlightened internationalism, civil liberties, and the environment and that it would always oppose tyranny, waste, fraud, and indolence. But values alone could not determine the tone and skill with which they were expressed.

Slowly, I began to see the challenge of the job but not the tools to meet it. Changing the editor of the editorial page was not going to change the style or content of many of its essays. Even a reduced agenda of twenty or twenty-five well-researched and -reasoned opinions a week could tax the energy of a dozen writers. I would never attempt it, I said, without the chance to bring in a half-dozen new writers of my choosing—fully expecting that such an overhaul was unmanageable and that I would be sent off to write a bylined column on the Op-Ed page, a perfectly satisfactory banishment from my sawed-off executive perch.

But Punch persisted. And I realized that my reluctance about becoming a know-it-all editor argued even more tellingly against becoming a know-it-all columnist. As Walter Lippmann had counseled, a newspaper column has value only to the extent that it views events through the prism of a distinctive ideology. More than ever, I disdained ideology and remained a skeptical pragmatist.

In the end I yielded, on one condition: that the newly merged News and Sunday departments absorb five or six of our editorial writers to allow me to recruit replacements.

Punch agreed to the deal and never wavered in his commitment. But we did not explain it properly to John Oakes. While I hid in the shadows and set about educating myself in alien subjects like Latin America and the New York City budget, Punch pushed his cousin toward early retirement and then had Gruson deliver the further blow that half the editorial board would be traded downstairs to the News Department. Even a less prideful man than Oakes would have resented this urge for rapid overhaul. And even a more articulate publisher than Punch would have had trouble calibrating his policy differences with Oakes—differences arising from his struggle to prevent *The Times*'s financial collapse, his less demonic view of the profit motive, and his more muscular, marine chauvinism.

Punch was thirteen years and an entire generation younger than his cousin, but he was born to the trunk of the family tree, not just a branch. Punch was Adolph Ochs's grandson and felt more surely entitled to lead *The Times* even than his father, Arthur Hays Sulzberger, who only married into the family. By contrast, John Oakes was a Rhodes scholar out of Princeton with many more years of journalistic training. He was certainly not hampered by being the son of George Ochs, Adolph's brother, but he always felt that he had earned his lofty *Times* rank. He respected Punch's prerogatives as publisher but felt himself to be intellectually superior and philosophically purer.

Having inflicted the pain of early retirement, neither Punch nor Gruson wanted to add to the discomfort of this principled man by demeaning his accomplishments. Oakes had employed *The Times*'s great prestige to denounce the escalation of the war in Vietnam and to support negotiation and arms control with the Communist world. He had passionately argued for every environmental cause and championed New York even as he raised alarms about the city's reckless financial accounting. He stood for civil rights, abortion rights, and divorce rights and against every kind of lawlessness, especially Nixon's. The end of such a laudable career was no time to begin finding fault with the jabbing style of many of his editorials or with the quality of his staff. He was simply told that Max preferred to bring in some of his own people, and Oakes, understandably, grew so resentful that he forbade me from meeting with his writers "during working hours," gave me only the most cursory transitional counsel, and fanned hostility even among the writers whom I expected to retain.

No one was fired. Punch compelled Abe's cooperation to offer good positions to most of the editorial writers designated for rotation—positions like chief of the United Nations bureau and Washington correspondent. But several found it so demeaning to return to reporting and to move from cloistered offices to a cluttered newsroom that they quit. Their cries of anguish were heard throughout the building, and my cold reason yielded cruel consequence. On the afternoon of December 31, 1976, I found myself staring at two empty editorial columns and presiding over the disheartened remnant of a decimated staff whose departing leader did not speak to me again for many years.

The New York Times

LATE CITY EDITION

VOL CXXVI...No. 43,383

NEW YORK, WEDNESDAY, NOVEMBER 3, 1976

20 CENTS

CARTER VICTOR IN TIGHT RACE; FORD LOSES NEW YORK STATE; DEMOCRATS RETAIN CONGRESS

Moynihan Defeats Buckley For New York Senate Seat

GEORGIAN WINS SOUTH

Northern Industrial States Provide Rest of Margin in the Electoral Vote

Atlantic City Casinos Approved

Election At a Glance

8 Senators Lose Seats, but Lineup Of Parties Stays About the Same

---

34 · PULPITEER

MY DESIGNATION AS THE EDITORIAL VOICE OF *THE Times* prompted much clucking around New York about how rapidly this Frankel, an agnostic apparatchik, would betray the muscular liberalism of John Oakes and bare the conservative fangs of Punch Sulzberger.

Actually, Punch never tested my opinions about the issues of the day. He knew, of course, that I was intensely pragmatic and civil even in disagreement. Although I agreed with most of the opinions fervently expressed by John Oakes, I obviously did not exude the same pious certitude. I deemed Oakes excessive in his allegiance to every environmental cause, no matter how small the benefit or great the cost to society. I was no more trusting than he of capitalist greed and political ambition, but I could also find amusement in human knavery. And I particularly enjoyed challenging liberal as well as conservative dogmas.

I was delighted, for example, to be among the dozens of commentators invited in the summer of 1976 to tell *Commentary* magazine how I understood the terms *liberal* and *conservative*.

These excerpts fairly well encapsule the credo of skepticism with which I mounted *The Times*'s pulpit:

It is liberal to wish to conserve our resources and conservative to wish to spend them liberally.

It is liberal to tolerate monopolistic prices for foreign oil and conservative to tolerate monopolistic prices for domestic oil.

It is liberal to expect corporations to behave like the Government. It is conservative to expect the Government to behave like corporations.

It is liberal to risk high-priced failure and costly overruns in almost every Federal department except the Pentagon. It is conservative to risk them only in the Pentagon.

It is liberal to subsidize buildings in which people live and conservative to subsidize buildings in which people work.

It is liberal to oppose international boycotts on grounds of principle, except against Rhodesia. It is conservative to oppose international boycotts as ineffective, except against Cuba.

It is liberal to perceive humanism among the Communists of Italy. It is conservative to perceive humanism among the fascists of Chile.

It is liberal to think that the United Nations has become an alien and anti-democratic force hostile to United States interests. It is conservative to say so aloud.

It is liberal to favor food stamps in New York. It is conservative to favor food stamps in Des Moines.

It is liberal to favor government subsidy for the Metropolitan Opera. It is conservative to favor government subsidy for the New York Mets.

It is liberal to believe that inequality results primarily from inequity. It is conservative to believe that inequity results primarily from inequality.

By and large, it is middle-aged to find anything peculiar or paradoxical in these formulations and it is youthful to find them unremarkable. So while the key words may have lost most of their value and no longer define coherent political philosophy, they still serve, like neckties, as useful symbols of pretense or identification among the fashion-conscious majority of us. . . .

Now that we are done with Marx—I'm sure—and almost finished with Freud—I hope—what can be the harm of debasing our political definitions à la Einstein?

It is liberal, in Wall Street, to work for *The New York Times*, and conservative in Greenwich Village.

––––––––––

The first editorial I ever wrote for *The Times* was also the last that had an immediate, demonstrable effect on events. Only that first exhortation scored a direct hit on the body politic, yet my hand in it was not only anonymous but also a secret.

It happened in September 1976, four months *before* I formally succeeded John Oakes. Sydney Gruson popped in one day to ask what I thought of a draft editorial urging a vote for Daniel Patrick Moynihan in the Democratic primary for U.S. senator. I said I warmly approved of the choice but strongly disliked the writing.

Good, he said. *That means you can rewrite it for us. This is Punch's draft because Oakes prefers Bella Abzug, as do most of his board members—except one or two who want to endorse Ramsey Clark.*

I begged off the job, wanting no further quarrels with Oakes. I imagined myself in his place, being roughly overridden on a highly visible political decision. He had already deferred to the publisher's preference for Moynihan by deciding to make no endorsement of anyone in the primary.

Punch has made up his mind, Gruson insisted. *I've rarely seen him so determined. He wants to help Pat.*

I was surprised by the publisher's willingness to humble his cousin—and afraid also for myself. I surmised, weeks later, that Punch found reinforcement in Scotty Reston's good report on Moynihan. I suspect that he was further energized by a nasty cover profile of himself in a recent *Business Week*. *The Times*'s stock in the 1970s had dropped from $53 to $15, but the magazine gave Punch no credit for his already promising plan of recovery. And it must have rankled to have *The Times* accused in a business journal of becoming "stridently antibusiness in tone."

Either you write a better editorial or he'll go with this one, Gruson persisted.

So I wrote, but I demanded that my involvement be concealed. I had come to know Moynihan in the Kennedy and Johnson years as a passionate sponsor of welfare legislation and, with the stimulus of midday wine, a glib and entertaining raconteur. He had been widely slandered as a racist for pointing with alarm to the disintegration of poor black families a full decade before most Americans came to share his concern. Democrats could not forgive his joining Nixon's White House staff, even though he tried there to reshape the welfare system. Oakes and others persisted in misreading a leaked memorandum in which Moynihan told Nixon: "The time may have come when the issue of race could benefit from a period of benign neglect. We may need a period in which Negro progress continues and racial rhetoric fades." Liberals insisted on treating that as a call for "neglect" of Negro needs. And they totally washed their hands of Moynihan after he insisted at the United Nations on talking back aggressively to the anti-American regimes of the underdeveloped world.

I also knew his main opponent in the primary, Rep. Bella Abzug. She had belatedly abandoned her irresponsible leftism and Cold War pacifism to become a tough advocate for New York and a prominent feminist. But I thought Moynihan had a stronger claim to advancement and, as a centrist, a much better chance of unseating the right-wing Republican incumbent, James Buckley. I pegged my rewrite of Punch's editorial to that practical argument and predicted that Moynihan would add "spice as well as distinction" to the Senate. I also took oblique notice of both Oakes's concerns and misperceptions:

> We choose Daniel P. Moynihan, that rambunctious child of the sidewalks of New York, profound student and teacher of social affairs, aggressive debater, outrageous flatterer, shrewd adviser—indeed manipulator—of Presidents, accomplished diplomat and heartfelt friend of the poor.

Oakes was at the end of a Martha's Vineyard vacation on September 9 when his deputy reported the publisher's ambush. Oakes begged Punch to sign the editorial, so as to dissociate his editorial board, but the publisher refused. He offered instead—against the established policy of his father—to let Oakes publish a personal dissent as a Letter to the Editor.

As Arthur Hays Sulzberger once put it to his successor, Orvil Dryfoos, when it came to editorial policy, "ownership, which you represent, must have the final voice, and disagreements are not to be publicized." The editor, he wrote, "merely edits the page but does not make any public statement as to the difference. We are not going to have *The New York Times* changed into a *New York Post*"—a reference to the public brawl between Dorothy Schiff and her editor, James Wechsler, when she suddenly decided to switch the *Post*'s support from Gov. Averell Harriman to Nelson Rockefeller in 1958. But a *Post*-like breach now began to haunt my editorship even before I assumed it.

Oakes used the publisher's offer of a public dissent to compose a long and angry letter that he wanted published beside the editorial I had ghosted. It agreed that Moynihan would be better than Buckley but denounced him as an "opportunistic showman" who had produced the "infamous" phrase "benign neglect" and defended Nixon's retreat from social programs. After further telephonic debate, Punch killed that letter, ran the endorsement on September 10, and permitted Oakes to publish only forty words on the following day:

As the editor of the editorial page of *The Times,* I must express disagreement with the endorsement in today's editorial columns of Mr. Moynihan over four other candidates in the New York Democratic primary contest for the United States Senate.

Three days later Moynihan defeated Abzug by fewer than 10,000 votes—less than 1 percent of the 917,000 votes cast for all five candidates in the race. All of them agreed that Abzug would have won with *The Times*'s support, perhaps even if *The Times* had stayed neutral.

Weeks later, when asked in public about the affair, John Oakes bravely defended his publisher's right to decide endorsements and called him "honorable" for having published his own curt dissent. Such are the bonds of institutional life. I expected, however, that I would never settle for such a bone. I resolved to avoid collisions by giving Punch early warnings of my political preferences, leaving ample time to negotiate disagreements. That failing and with a major issue at stake, I thought I would have to resign rather than leave my name on a page that betrayed my best judgment. Owners have prerogatives, but the owned have reputations.

As it happened, a year later Punch let me turn right around and, against *his* better judgment, endorse the "flamboyance and sometimes rough ways" of Bella Abzug. In a race in the publisher's own district, we urged her return to Congress as preferable to the election of the then inexperienced Bill Green. But she couldn't transfer her West Side popularity to the East Side's Silk Stocking electorate and lost, much to Punch's satisfaction.

In a decade, Punch and I veered apart over only two election endorsements.

The first time was 1980, when Jacob Javits, a seventy-six-year-old Republican senator, insisted on seeking a fifth term. I had followed Javits's career since the 1940s, when he campaigned for the House in my old Washington Heights district, dashing by limousine from synagogue to synagogue on Yom Kippur without even removing his prayer shawl. Republicans were grateful to have found someone willing to run so zealously against the dominant Irish and Italian Democratic clubs. With his strong appeal to Jews, liberal voting record, and eventual alignment with Nelson

Rockefeller, Javits became his party's strongest vote getter in the city and state. He befriended all influential New Yorkers, most particularly Carol and Punch Sulzberger, and he took *The Times*'s endorsements for granted.

In 1980, however, Jack Javits was a mere shadow of his ebullient self, suffering from the early stages of Lou Gehrig's disease. He also faced a primary challenge inside an increasingly conservative Republican party from a Hempstead town supervisor, Alfonse D'Amato, who did not hesitate to advertise Javits's age and infirmity. The senator begged for Punch's promise of support clear through November, hoping that would help him beat back D'Amato in the primary. When I argued against surrendering our vote two months in advance, the publisher said he would not abandon Javits so long as he felt able to serve. He invited him to an off-the-record lunch at which the two of us could demand a true accounting of his health.

Javits insisted in his already hoarse voice that he was mentally sound and had his doctors' blessing to seek another six-year term. Punch said he was inclined to endorse him but invited me to express my doubts. In the most difficult conversation I ever had with a prominent official, I said the combination of Javits's frailty and his party's rightward drift was likely to give D'Amato the Republican nomination. Then, I predicted, a hurt and angry Javits would stay on the November ballot with just the Liberal party line, drain off votes from a liberal Democrat, and end up losing his seat to a man whose conservative doctrines he professed to abhor. Javits found it inconceivable that he would lose to a "hicktown pol." Then he turned to Punch with beseeching eyes and said, *On my word of honor, if Max is right and my presence on the ballot points to a D'Amato victory, I will get out of the way.*

With that promise in hand, we endorsed the senator "above all" other candidates of both parties, announcing that "as long as he remains fit, Jack Javits has our vote." But when, four days later, he lost badly to D'Amato, I subtly recalled his secret promise in print:

> Senator Javits deserved better than to be rejected for a suburban administrator. But the progressive Republicanism that he personifies is a spent force hereabouts. . . . Mr. Javits now looks to the Liberal line to save him. . . . So we suspect the Senator will take some time to decide whether he can really prevail in November or would only divide the center and lose his seat to Mr. D'Amato, whom he calls "intellectually unfit." It is a poignant choice in the twilight of a brilliant career.

But the senator broke his word, perhaps, as he later rationalized, because the Democratic nominee, an acerbic, prideful Elizabeth Holtzman, failed to ask for his support. We had sponsored "Javits Above All," but in the last week of the campaign I finally won Punch's consent to call on Javits to "free his supporters from sentimental loyalty" and end his career "with a selfless, principled withdrawal." He never did, and when it came time to recapitulate our endorsements on Election Day, we were left stranded with no Senate vote, only an explanation: "Jacob Javits (Liberal) is the superior candidate, but we regret that he is now dividing the moderate vote with Elizabeth Holtzman (Democrat), to the benefit of the least desirable candidate, Alfonse D'Amato (Republican-Conservative-Right-to-Life)."

It was a futile gesture. D'Amato won. But so did I, in the publisher's eyes. He never again pressed me to go against my best judgment. Luckily, six years later, when he next insisted on imposing his political will on the page, I was no longer in charge of editorials. By that time D'Amato, a demagogic hack, had wormed his way into the establishment's favor, running petty but profitable errands for New York, including subsidies for its Metropolitan Museum of Art, whose grateful chairman was Punch Sulzberger.

One strong reason for clinging so long to Javits was that we were eager to demonstrate our independence by supporting worthy Republicans as well as Democrats. It was bad enough that New York City was a one-party town, largely taken for granted by state and national Democrats. We didn't want *The Times* to be taken for granted or seen by readers as a mere partisan; since 1960 we had endorsed only Democrats for president. That is why in 1984 I strongly urged sticking with Rep. William Green, the Republican then seeking reelection in a race against the Manhattan borough president, Andrew Stein, the Sulzbergers' unusually frequent dinner companion. Punch squirmed when he heard my counsel but let me have my way, making sure only that our editorial reached Stein's door at the same time as the Sulzbergers' gift of a dozen roses.

I came to doubt the wisdom and value of election endorsements. We coolly supported Jimmy Carter and Walter Mondale against Ronald Reagan in 1980 and 1984, but I'm sure we changed nobody's vote.

"The old joke still applies," is how Jack Rosenthal began the Carter endorsement. "Someone chases a voter down an alley, points a gun to his head and demands an answer: 'Carter or Reagan?' After thinking for a moment, the voter replies, 'Shoot.' " We opposed Reagan again four years later, even though he had "in some ways done a good job," because he wildly expanded the deficit, punished the poor, and failed to stabilize the arms race. Yet now that voters were able to watch the major candidates perform on television, we knew they neither needed nor wanted a newspaper's warrant.

If at all, readers looked to us for advice only about the candidates for minor office, especially judgeships, but our impressions of them were gleaned from cursory research and only brief interviews. We had to play hunches and rely on hearsay, so to ease our conscience, we tended to support incumbents until given strong reason to unseat them. And we endorsed judges only while simultaneously confessing our ignorance about them and protesting that judges should be appointed, not elected.

Only once did I have an opportunity to measure the size of our influence in minor election contests. In 1983 we took exception to one of a dozen arcane proposals to amend the City Charter and State Constitution. The voters approved all the amendments on the ballot, but the one that we alone among the major media had urged them to reject received about 50,000 fewer votes than the rest. I seized upon this evidence to argue ever after that our influence was marginal and minimal.

I once urged Punch to let us stop "endorsing" political candidates altogether. We could write about them extensively, and harshly if necessary, I said, and then let readers draw their own conclusions. We would thus avoid the temptation to pull our punches on behalf of someone we planned to endorse. Candidates would no longer be able to litter the airwaves with misleading citations of The Times's "support." And our news pages would be less burdened by the impression—the false impression—that they were influenced by the paper's endorsements. But the publisher disagreed. He acknowledged that endorsements carried little weight in major races but thought readers badly needed help at the bottom of the ballot. My deputy and successor as Editorial editor, Jack Rosenthal, also disagreed. He thought endorsements tested our value system by forcing a choice among imperfect candidates.

My reluctance to endorse, I now realize, betrayed a deeper uncertainty about the whole editorial process. I never fully accepted the legitimacy of editorials in the modern newspaper. For whom, really, do these disembodied voices speak? Whose values do they invoke? Why not let the editorialists write signed opinion columns?

The anonymity of editorials certainly gives them weight, but it is heft earned over many decades by the labors of the *news* reporters and editors; they are the ones who daily produce and preserve the paper's reputation for fair and reliable judgment. Why let a dozen other people spend that reputation? To ask that question is to realize that an editorial is, in a sense, a brazen deception: the opinion of one or two individual writers masquerading in institutional dress. The editorial We yelps and declaims in the name of "*The Times*," but there exists no mechanism to achieve a "*Times*" consensus. John Oakes and his staff of twelve editorial writers never even met as a group; each one had a field of interest and sat alone with the editor to exchange ideas and frame opinions. I insisted on regular meetings of our "board" but did not take votes on the issues before us. I wanted only a continuous airing of our values, to help set a rhetorical tone, and an in-house testing of our arguments to expose their weaknesses. At the end of the day, our editorials had to satisfy only their author and me, or my like-minded deputy.

Yet we never stood entirely alone. We functioned as surrogates of the publisher, who expected never to be surprised by significant shifts of opinion. I well knew his attitudes on major issues. In our banter and gossip over frequent lunches, it was not hard to discern his discomfort with, say, our declared opposition to the death penalty, our sympathy for some striking union, or our reluctance to erect trade barriers to punish Japan's mercantilism. He could squirm and sometimes declare himself unconvinced, but he amply rewarded our respect for his outlook and temperament by never asking us to embrace conclusions we did not share. Punch himself occasionally wrote a short editorial to complain about New York's miserable taxi service or the courts' abuse of citizens called to jury duty. More cheerfully than most writers, he accepted our editing and even total rejection. But he would not casually let us lead him down some radical path. He balked, for example, at our advocating experiments with the legal distribution of drugs, not because he firmly opposed the idea but because he, too, felt an institutional restraint; it seemed wrong to sign *The Times*'s name to such an unconventional and easily misunderstood position.

Editorials deliver opinion, and I had been paid for twenty-five years never to have an opinion in print. Our news ethic required reporters to suspend most moral judgments and to interpret events through other people's eyes. Could I now distill my life experiences and expound social principles and policies that served a public need? My buds of conviction ripened slowly, mainly through the tireless instruction of gifted colleagues and articulate petitioners. Despite my doubts about the legitimacy of unsigned editorials, their daily preparation extended my journey of self-discovery.

HIGH COURT BACKS SOME AFFIRMATIVE ACTION BY COLLEGES, BUT ORDERS BAKKE ADMITTED

PRESIDENT TO ISSUE ORDER TO LIBERALIZE RULE ON SECRET DATA

BELL HAILS DECISION

Calls Ruling a 'Great Gain'— Plaintiff Is 'Pleased' and Others Express Relief

GUIDANCE IS PROVIDED

Medical School Racial Quota Voided, but Advantage for Minorities Is Allowed

South Africans Reported Ready For Nuclear Ban

A Plateau for Minorities

Most College Programs Expected to Continue, But Ruling Is Seen as Brake on Rights Efforts

35 · WE

THE EDITORIAL WRITERS OF *THE TIMES* LABOR IN A hushed tenth-floor oasis of large, austere offices arrayed in cloister style around the paper's superb little library. My clumsy maneuvers to repopulate the board made the floor even lonelier than usual when I took possession on New Year's Eve 1976, planning to change not only the staff but also the editorial page's design and tone of voice.

The most straightforward, unswervingly liberal voices were suddenly stilled: John Oakes and his deputy, Abe Raskin, had retired; Jim Brown had angrily resigned; Peter Grose, Graham Hovey, and Herb Mitgang had sullenly accepted transfer to the News Department. They were fervently righteous and predictable liberals, and while I agreed with most of their conclusions, I rarely found their instruction surprising or enjoyable. I hoped, in time, to serve up much the same liberal values in essays that were less predictable and more fun. Those were also qualities that I thought Punch Sulzberger would value, but that was only a guess.

Punch accepted my judgment that our Op-Ed columns were already too liberal and insufficiently "op" to our own points of view. Accordingly, he refused to give columns to two survivors of my purge, Leonard Silk and Roger Wilkins, and they, too, moved to the News Department. When William Shannon was similarly turned down, he got Jimmy Carter to make him ambassador to Ireland. Fred Hechinger became president of the Times Foundation, and Ada Louise Huxtable and Bob Bendiner stayed, as before, on a part-time schedule. The only full-time holdovers from the Oakes staff thus became the two men whose transfer out I had most ardently desired—Robert Kleiman, a pretentious and vexatious expert on arms control, and Harry Schwartz, a scholar on Soviet affairs whose once useful Kremlinology had long since degenerated into dull harangues. It was not a felicitous transition.

My sanity in those early, lonely days was preserved only by an unexpected gift from Abe Rosenthal. He had scotched my desire to hire Robert Semple, Jr., then London bureau chief, as my deputy; *Well, I'll see you in the elevator sometime*, was the career advice he gave to Semple. In the same spirit Abe woefully undervalued the talents of Jack Rosenthal, my deputy in the Sunday Department, whom I had left in charge of the Magazine. When Punch alerted me to the skids under Jack's feet, I cheerfully recruited him to join me yet again. Both friend and neighbor, Jack had been understandably eager to run something by himself; he'd been an assistant altogether too long at the Justice and State Departments in Washington and to me in the Sunday Department. Curious, energetic, and fastidious, Jack was a keen policy analyst and an elegant stylist. Thanks to Abe's mistrust of him, I was blessed for an entire decade to have him as a partner, an alter ego in managing and editing the editorial page, notably including the prose of its editor.

Together, we gradually replenished the staff. Since we could employ only one writer for most major subjects, we paid a heavy price for any miscasting. The hardest thing was to find writers who shared our centrist values and yet brought diverse viewpoints to our table. We engaged Walter Goodman, a cultural essayist, from the old Sunday Department to help edit copy. We hired Roger Starr, a city housing expert and neoconservative; Peter Passell, a refreshing young Columbia economist; Philip Boffey and later Nicholas Wade, accomplished science writers; and, as the first of a succession of foreign affairs writers, Richard Ullman, a Princeton scholar with government experience in both diplomacy and military affairs. Soma Golden, a *Times* reporter, signed on to write about business and economics and became the first woman to write editorials full-time. During her maternity leaves we gave visiting chairs to Jerry Goodman, better known as Adam Smith, and Lester Thurow of MIT, outsiders whose perspectives were especially rewarding.

Anne O'Hare McCormick had sat on the board a generation earlier but wrote mostly foreign affairs columns under her own name. Ada Louise Huxtable also sat on the board only part-time while she continued to write architecture criticism for the Sunday paper. It was three years before we hired a second full-time woman member—Mary Cantwell, who cast a wise, witty, and decidedly feminine eye on the human condition.

We practiced the affirmative action that we preached. And I learned at once that the effort benefited from numerical goals—goals that bespoke a purpose even though they were in no sense "quotas." There has been much confusion about the difference between goals and quotas, and I found later in my executive career that the use of statistics as an administrative device often produced misunderstanding and hurt. But even in managing a staff of just twelve editorial writers, numbers mattered. When Roger Wilkins left for the News Department, for example, I decided that having at least two black board members would relieve them of the burden that Roger always felt to "represent" an entire race; two or more black colleagues could function as individuals, even disagree, and so help us to overcome stereotypical attitudes.

My theory was instantly rewarded when we were joined by Hugh Price, the human resources administrator of New Haven, and Robert Curvin, a political scientist at Rutgers. Their inexperience as writers was more than offset by the distinct life experiences they brought to our discussions. Our collaboration reinforced my faith in affirmative action and what, in commenting on the *Bakke* case, I had called "Reparation, American Style." I think now that I was wrong in that case to endorse not only laudable acts of "affirmative action" but also California's strict set-aside of sixteen seats for racial and ethnic minorities at a state medical school. The social goal of producing more black and Mexican doctors should have been pursued with more flexible numbers, taking account of the community's shifting needs and the size of the applicant pool. But the resolve to recruit minorities surely is more valid than the routine set-aside of places and scholarships for football players, alumni offspring, and political payoffs.

Our personnel deals with the News Department, unfortunately, moved in only one direction—from the tenth floor down to Abe Rosenthal's third. He never understood that reporters could stretch their journalistic muscles by writing editorials for a year or two; he thought the experience would taint them ideologically, a humorous objection since many of his political passions and prejudices were better known to the world than mine. Reporters can greatly benefit from writing editorials;

besides sharpening their style, the process exposes the inadequacy of much newswriting. Our editorial writers had to do a lot more of their own reporting to supplement the information in the paper before they could reach a reasonable opinion.

On entering the editorial monastery, I learned to reexamine not only my private opinions but also my private conduct. Barely two weeks at the task, I found myself lecturing three nominees to President Carter's cabinet who were hurriedly resigning from social clubs that discriminated against blacks, Jews, or women (or all three). "Quitting is not acquitting," I wrote; prominent people like Griffin Bell, Cyrus Vance, and Harold Brown should have protested club bias much earlier in their careers. In the future, I urged, Congress should not let federal appointees purge themselves with last-minute resignations. Even before those words were set in type, I realized that I had better take my own advice. I had recently accepted membership in the Century Association, a convenient luncheon club down the street, on the promise that the members were getting ready to admit women. But it hadn't happened yet. So although John Oakes and many other *Times* men appeared comfortable in an all-male Century, I felt obliged to quit that very day. The club insisted that reform was "imminent." But it took many more votes, more resignations, and even official threats of dire tax consequences before the Century finally admitted a few women—six years later.

We did not shrink from telling politicians and institutions what to do or stop doing. But we learned that perceptive analysis did not have to be prescriptive. The ideal editorial addressed readers, and its mission was to instruct, not to incite. I looked upon editorials, no less than news articles, as primarily educational. Indeed, I treated the editorial column as a pony to the world's news, a crib sheet for busy readers who could not follow every twist and turn in arms control negotiations or tax legislation. They could rely on our page to signal noteworthy developments.

Every day's headlines were our most obvious sources of inspiration, but my favorite themes were those that blossomed from small nuggets of news. One day in January 1977, for example, a single sentence seemed to signal America's passage from one era to another:

Something Cleansing, Something Final

It just sits there on Page One, pretending to be news, like yesterday's temperature low. But it sears the mind. It isn't just news; millions have known it for many years, some painfully, some righteously. It isn't just politics; nobody's fate or income or reputation required it. It isn't even significant history; the lessons and consequences can be only dimly calculated so far. Still, there is the sense that something momentous has been uttered, something cleansing, something final. The speaker was the next Secretary of State of the United States. The time was 21 months after the final American evacuation from Saigon at the end of a 12-year war. He said: "Let me say, in light of hindsight, it was a mistake to intervene in Vietnam."

Over the years, that modest idea grew wings. The healing of America became a major preoccupation of my editorial page. So did the desire to dampen America's imperial urges and to promote a prudent patriotism. I felt destined, and qualified, to becalm the Cold War fears and fantasies I had encountered in both Moscow and Washington—and at our table when Ronald Reagan came calling during the 1980 campaign. He was convinced that an air-raid shelter accommodating millions had been dug under the Moscow subway and that the Soviet leaders dreamed of delivering a knockout blow at the United States. Starstruck on a Star Wars missile defense, he became a useful foil for my preachings.

"Forget the *Maine*" and other jingoistic doctrines, I wrote in 1983, when Reagan threatened armed intervention in hapless El Salvador:

Even Cuba will not forever be a Soviet ally. Much depends on what the United States has to offer Latin Americans, including its revolutionaries. Fidel Castro's renown owes as much to our hysterical opposition as it does to his own accomplishments.

Revolutions are unsettling, but not inevitably Communist. If Communist, they are not inevitably pro-Soviet. If pro-Soviet, they are not irreversible. Only the Red Army keeps Eastern Europe Communist; the Chinese and Yugoslav Communists have become America's friends. The idea that the whole world is tilting from right to left and threatening to bury the Americans in a Marxist avalanche is a dangerous delusion—just one more doctrine.

And when later that year Reagan invaded tiny Grenada to compensate for the loss of 200 marines in Lebanon, I inveighed against "The Grenada High":

After all is said and done, the real inspiration and justification for the Grenada invasion lies in those false feelings of impotence— fanned by years of deceptive politicking about American re- treats, defeats and even nuclear inferiority. . . . As Soviet history shows, the worst thing about a national inferiority complex is that it induces conduct that really is inferior.

In speaking for "*The Times*," I had to define myself as never before. I had spent my whole life fleeing from ideology, hiding comfortably behind the reporter's mask of impartiality. I paid for that detachment with a measure of loneliness; just as I cried in childhood at being left out of *Hitlerjugend* parades, I pined in middle age for the camaraderie of a cause. But I hungered for understanding more than faith. My exposure to fascism and communism must have inoculated me against all doctrine, no matter how appealing its pageantry. My religion was American pragmatism, Popper's piecemeal social engineering, the daily struggle to combine creative individualism with a humane social ethic. "Secular humanism" some called this derisively, and I gladly embraced the term. It well describes a civil society that refuses to enshrine any of its citizens' gods or greeds.

But pragmatism is to ideology what an instruction manual is to poetry; it speaks to problems but rarely sings. The more dispassionate our sermons, the wilier and wittier they had to be. First day on the job, I redecorated the page, displaying the editorials in a horizontal mode. Our design gave us the option of delivering just two or three opinions a day where there had previously been five or six. We also invented three new editorial features that appeared in rotation: a collection of short jabs and jests called "Topics"; an "Editorial Notebook" recording the personal views and experiences of board members; and a special "Letter to the Editor" that quarreled with us in an important or effective way.

We could wish that the letters regularly selected for the other half of the page were equally compelling. But the dozen that we published each day from a weekly stream of more than a thousand (and soon nearly two thousand) were often tedious emendations of news articles or rebuttals to Op-Ed opinions. To be sure, our letters were widely read, yet try as we might, we could not attract the tart polemics that were regularly featured in *The Times* of London. And in the era before fax machines and E-mail, most of our letters appeared long after readers had forgotten the articles that inspired them.

The editorials, by contrast, were not put to bed until eight every evening and could be updated through the night, if necessary. We preferred to rush into print only with our most obvious and banal opinions, figuring that the less we had to say, the sooner it needed to be said. Expressions of horror that President Reagan had been shot or of satisfaction that an electrical blackout had evoked the public's good behavior were best delivered the morning after, along with everyone else's trite sentiment. But a considered judgment about airline deregulation or missile reduction was useful only when our evidence was sharp and our writing clear. It took many days of discussion in 1979 to produce "How to Save Social Security" and to present the then ill-understood problem in Peter Passell's incisive metaphor:

Social Security is a sort of chain letter with socially redeeming features. For decades, the system paid the expenses of relatively few retirees by lightly taxing relatively many workers. But now the chain letter is running out of new addresses; a slowly growing work force will be pressed to pay the bills of a rapidly growing pool of pensioners.

When the Reagan administration proposed to build monstrous MX missiles with the promise that they would slow down the arms race, it took some days to recognize the policy's resemblance to "voodoo economics," George Bush's term for Reagan's claim that lower taxes would produce greater federal revenues. We introduced our long campaign against the MX in 1983 with an essay entitled "Voodoo Arms Control": "The people who brought you the biggest tax cut ever as an exercise in revenue raising now present: the biggest American missile ever as an exercise in arms control."

"The False Choice of Bitburg" came very late in the controversy over Reagan's promise to visit some Nazi graves in Germany, but it brought a revealing clarity to that emotional issue:

It is finally clear how President Reagan came to his Bitburg blunder and why his defense of it grows more repugnant by the day. His perception of the planned tribute to Germany's war dead begins and ends with a false dichotomy, bitterly expressed this week by one of Chancellor Kohl's closest aides.

"What are we?" the aide asked. "Are we primarily friends and allies or are we primarily the children and grandchildren of the Nazis? At some point one has to decide."

Why? Why must I decide, the President should have replied when Chancellor Kohl proposed the same choice last fall, no doubt more subtly.

Why are today's Germans good friends and allies? Because some of them, and most of their fathers and some of their grandfathers, having brought the world to ruin 40 years ago, then accepted America's tutelage and generosity and made much of them. What is most admirable about the new Germany is the moral distance it has traveled from the old. To ignore the old is to ignore what is so remarkable about the new.

Childhood memories of black shirts and swastikas obviously danced before my eyes as I wrote those words. But reasoning my way past hate had become an adult duty, and I always felt cleansed by its exercise. Journalism—a word literally derived from *diary* (via *diurnal* and *journal*)—gave me a daily ritual for exorcising the common demons of life: hatred, envy, prejudice, fear. Some of our readers mistook such sublimations of rage for indifference. They perpetuated a myth that *The Times* considered all issues "on the one hand, and on the other." The myth took root even inside *The Times* and led Howell Raines, one of my successors, to promise rashly that his page would print only "one-handed" opinions. His fist did rattle the china for a while, but if he had read more of yesteryear's papers, he'd have recognized that mere invective is no substitute for vigor and verve. We had plenty of both.

We campaigned relentlessly against Reagan's attack on government safety nets for the poor. Jack Rosenthal led that effort in 1981 with editorials that won him a Pulitzer Prize:

The Reagan Paradox

That the President's plan will revive the economy remains to be proved. What is no longer in doubt is that his economic remedies mask an assault on the very idea that free people can solve their collective problems through representative Government.

One day soon, Americans will rediscover that their general welfare depends on national as well as parochial actions. And then they will want not just a powerful President but one who cherishes the power of Government to act for the common good.

Even before Reagan, we campaigned just as lustily against misuses of governmental power, urging the deregulation of the oil, gas, airline, trucking, banking, and communications industries. Lending our liberal credentials to what were then presumed to be conservative objectives was an especially satisfying exercise. Long before it became a prominent issue, we offered blueprints for genuine tax reform, ideas to restore the citizens' trust in fiscal fairness and to enable anyone with a high school education to complete an income tax return. And we chastised New York's Democratic Governor Mario Cuomo as we would chastise President Clinton a decade later for ignoring the essential "prerequisite for workfare: work."

We were tough on Senator D'Amato's ethics when his financial kickback schemes were revealed on Long Island. We were acutely personal, some said rude, when our new cardinal, Archbishop John J. O'Connor, began his ministry by comparing abortion to the Nazi slaughter of Jews. But we were no less firm in appraising the conduct of leading liberals. When Sen. Edward Kennedy decided in 1979 to run for president, we refused to forgive or forget the manner in which he had abandoned a woman passenger a decade earlier when he drove a car into a pond on Martha's Vineyard:

The Legacy of Chappaquiddick

The issue that lingers is not whether the Chappaquiddick party was as decorous as claimed, or where the Senator and his passenger were headed that night. His failure to seek competent help, out of panic or cruel calculation, was much more serious. And the Senator's success in avoiding tough cross-examination remains, politically, the most serious matter of all.

More important now than the loose ends of his unsatisfying accounts are the reasons they were left so loose. . . . As we know from Watergate, there is no graver question for a President than whether he can be trusted to respect the law. All those who had anything to do with the Chappaquiddick affair and its aftermath owe the nation an accounting that in a decade, for some reason, they have never had to give.

And when Jesse Jackson drew attention to his campaign for president by demonstrating influence with foreign tyrants, we wrote:

Mr. Jackson's Prisoner Dealing

The Rev. Jesse Jackson's burgeoning traffic in prisoners from dictatorships is not, as President Reagan suggests, a prosecutable crime. But neither is it, as Mr. Jackson asserts, a moral enter-prise. It is political opportunism in reckless disregard for American diplomacy. . . . That a few individuals incidentally benefit from this show-manship does not relieve its cynicism.

Writing editorials required me to sacrifice virtually all the respectful relationships with public officials that I had built up as a reporter. An evaluation of Henry Kissinger's eight years of service in 1977—as a flawed strategist but a brilliant diplomatic tactician—still strikes me as balanced and fair, but it brought a pained rejoinder that ruptured our fragile bonds of experience. Kissinger believed that the accommodations he achieved in Moscow and Beijing amply justified the Nixon administration's costly persistence in the Vietnam War and were, in fact, a direct result of that persistence. Understandably, his conscience could not abide our denial of that premise.

Two years later, our commentaries provoked an even angrier missile from President Carter, which his staff tried but failed to intercept. He complained about one columnist—obviously Bill Safire—"who is generally known to prevaricate and habitually to distort the truth," and also about "errors" in news articles and editorials that allegedly damaged the nation and libeled the president. The letter was a delayed reaction, I think, to Safire's attacks on the banking practices of Bert Lance, Carter's friend and political financier, and to our editorial distress about the president's responses to the oil crisis and economic stagnation. One summer day a few months earlier, Carter had included me in a helicopter load of editors flown to Camp David, where he and his wife, Rosalynn, had gone to ponder the nation's predicament. They decided during this "retreat" that the root of the trouble lay not in any of their policies but in the public's unwarranted "malaise." This lame effort to shift the blame for governmental failures onto the public evoked only further ridicule and contempt. And although we eventually supported Carter for reelection, we did so with obvious reluctance and mainly from mistrust of Reagan's values.

Our proud realism did at times make us passive. Instead of bemoaning the only available choice in 1980 between an ineffectual Carter and an insensitive Reagan, the greater public service would have been to rail against both of them before their nominations were secure. Our opposition had no chance of derailing their campaigns, but it would have more effectively registered our standards for leadership. We were more grievously negligent, along with the rest of the American press, in failing to sound the alarm about the rape of the nation's savings and loan banks.

Among my major mistakes I also list a 1981 editorial denouncing Israel for its "surgical" air strike against an Iraqi laboratory working on nuclear weapons. I have never felt comfortable about the effort of the so-called major powers—meaning China, Russia, France, Britain, and the United States—to monopolize the world's supply of nuclear arms; if they have behaved more responsibly than some lesser powers, it is precisely because they possess those weapons and have good reason to fear their use. When Israel, an unacknowledged nuclear power, staged a surprise attack on Iraq to disrupt Saddam Hussein's nuclear program, it seemed to me to be invoking an impermissibly aggressive right of "self-defense." Should a Pakistani attack on India have been similarly tolerated and celebrated? My principle was sound but also piously unrealistic, as Iraq's invasion of Kuwait and unprovoked missile attacks against Israel demonstrated ten years later. As I should have remembered from reading E. B. White in high school, it is folly to hold nations to a standard of "law" in an anarchic world. Better to acknowledge the jungle until we reach a higher stage of civilization, or at least a world government.

Our most painful editorial comments were the ones we felt compelled to aim at our colleagues in the media, to compensate for the shortage of responsible criticism of journalism. The most persistent faultfinder at the time was no critic at all but rather a right-wing ideologue, Reed Irvine, who ran an enterprise called Accuracy in Media. He did sometimes find factual errors or evidence of bias in national newspapers and on television, but it was right-wing ideology, not "accuracy," that mainly concerned him. He dwelt invariably on those claims of error that sustained his own formidable prejudices; he agitated for mass mailings and personally confronted media executives at stockholder meetings. In self-defense, Punch Sulzberger made a Faustian deal to meet Irvine privately from time to time if he would stay away from *The Times*'s annual meetings. But that gave Irvine an access granted to no other stockholder, and he regularly boasted about it in his propaganda sheet. Despite my protests, Punch held to the deal.

In the absence of more enlightened media criticism, we dared on a few occasions to offer our own. We deplored *Time* magazine's arrogance in refusing to correct a libel against Israel's Gen. Ariel Sharon even though he deserved, as a public figure, to fail in his quest for a jury verdict. We saw even less merit in Gen. William Westmoreland's suit against CBS for a television documentary whose distortions of history, we emphasized, were nonetheless palpable. More enjoyably, we punished the editorial page of *The Wall Street Journal* by ignoring it. We refused for two long years to respond to its taunts of *The Times*'s failure to acknowledge that the Communists had used poison gas in Indochina. Although that charge was cynically echoed by two secretaries of state, military intelligence, and other apologists for *our* use of chemical weapons in Vietnam, we refused to credit the evidence for poison gas. We ignored the *Journal* even when we were finally proved right. As Nick Wade had written on our page, the rash-producing "yellow rain" allegedly supplied by the Soviet Union and poured over the jungles of Indochina was not gas after all. It turned out to have been bee excrement.

And I don't remember a more satisfying moment than the day in 1984 when I raised a hand against the gods of my adolescence down the street at *The New Yorker*. It had allowed Alastair Reid to publish fictions about Spain in the guise of nonfiction and, when caught, attempted to defend the deception. To break free from that magazine's mystique was worth even a collateral credit to *The Wall Street Journal*. It was one of the most heartfelt essays I ever composed:

The Fiction of Truth

The end of the world seems near now that our colleagues at *The New Yorker*, that fountainhead of unhurried fact, turn out to tolerate, even to justify fictions masquerading as facts. Quotes that weren't ever spoken, scenes that never existed, experiences that no one ever had—all are said to be permissible in journalism, provided they're composed by honest reporters to illustrate a deeper truth.

"Facts are only a part of reality,"

avers Alastair Reid, the fine writer whose poetic inventions in *The New Yorker* over the decades were reported this week by *The Wall Street Journal*. "If one wants to write about Spain, the facts won't get you anywhere."

So Mr. Reid has routinely imagined Spanish taverns and characters and conversations, palming them off as real because "there is a truth that is harder to get at and harder to get down toward than the truth yielded by fact."

And the editors and legendary "fact-checkers" at *The New Yorker* seem unperturbed. "He's not trying to deceive anybody, including me," says the top man, William Shawn. "He's a man of utter integrity and that's all I have to know."

Then why not simply publish everything as fiction, which is just as highly prized in *The New Yorker*?

The answer, as Mr. Shawn would be the first to teach, is that fictional speculation and factual reporting provide radically different reading experiences. Fiction thrills by analogy, by the knowledge that unreal events can illuminate truthfully. Nonfiction excites by experience, by extending a reader's knowledge of reality and quest for understanding. Why should not writers, like carnival barkers, pretend that fictions are facts? First, last and always, because the reader lured into the House of Facts, poor sap, has paid to experience facts.

The tritest truth is that truth is more than facts. You may read that President Reagan has called the Soviet Union an "evil empire" but you will not then know the truth of what he means or whether he really believes it. That he said it is true, a fact. But grasping the statement's truth requires knowing the President's standards of good and evil, his historical understanding of empires and his motives for making such a declaration.

Journalists and historians can aspire to perfection only in recounting the fact of what a President has said. After that they are reduced to groping imperfectly, speculating along with others, for the surrounding truth. A fact is a true phenomenon; truth is the ideal explanation of a fact.

That is not a particularly difficult distinction. Yet too many people find profit in blurring it. Some mongers of mere fact, notably salesmen and politicians, routinely pretend to be revealing truth. And some mongers of opinion, claiming like Mr. Reid to have hold of a singular truth, are openly contemptuous of fact.

When either type shows up in our own ranks—or pages—we feel both cheated and devalued. Wrong truths are always correctable, with facts. Fictional facts are forever counterfeit.

The New York Times

"All the News That's Fit to Print"

LATE CITY EDITION

VOL. CXXVIII   No. 44,188   NEW YORK, TUESDAY, MARCH 27, 1979   20 CENTS

EGYPT AND ISRAEL SIGN FORMAL TREATY, ENDING A STATE OF WAR AFTER 30 YEARS; SADAT AND BEGIN PRAISE CARTER'S ROLE

OPEC PARLEY WEIGHS NEW OIL PRICE RISES AND CUTS IN OUTPUT

CEREMONY IS FESTIVE

Accord on Sinai Oil Opens Way to the First Peace in Mideast Dispute

Mood of Peace Seems Somber And Uncertain

Treaty Impact Still Unknown

'Hopes and Dreams' but 'No Illusions' for Carter

36 · Bist ah Yid?

TO CLIMB PROPERLY INTO OTHER PEOPLE'S SHOES, YOU need first to get out of your own. The best reporters and editors normally have no race, sex, or religion. They may charm or muscle their way into strange places, but they try not to *think* male or female, black or Jewish. Still, there always comes a time for exceptions. I remember reliving the shudders of refugee life at the sight of Hungarians trudging across a frozen frontier swamp. I never totally banished that twinge of smug American security when interviewing high-ranking Germans. And there's no denying the conspiratorial bond that suddenly appeared when an old man on a park bench in Kiev whispered, *Bist ah Yid?*

Are you a Jew? was a question often put to me, and with decidedly different inflections. In Communist countries, it came from Jews who meant thereby to ask whether they could trust me with seditious conversation. In Israel, it was asked to discover whether I would ever put my feelings for the Jewish state ahead of my journalistic mission. Now that I had charge of editorials in *The Times*, the question was usually hurled with contempt; I was obviously a Jew, but in the eyes of many Jews, an unworthy one for daring to criticize Israel's government. So whenever I turned to the subject of Israel, there was no escaping my skin. Most of *The Times*'s editorials on the Middle East during a fateful decade in that region were written by a proud, defiant Jew: proud of the chance to sound off about my people's fate and defiant of the majority of American Jews, who believed that a people so horrendously victimized could never do wrong.

Not, of course, the circle of Jewish immigrants around Mom and Pop. They conferred great honor and status on my parents for their son's prominence and overlooked his actual performance. One of their German refugee boys from Washington Heights had grown up to be the voice of *The New York Times*, the world's greatest newspaper. Most ungratefully, I resented the boasts in the old neighborhood, not because I shied from notoriety or begrudged my parents their pride, their *nachas*, but because I refused to think of myself as a *German* Jew. Except for my place of birth, I was a Galicianer, dammit, an *Eastern* Jew just one generation out of the shtetl. The Nazis obliterated that Yiddish world, a constellation of townlets that stretched from Lithuania to Romania, but the shtetl culture kept on fiddling in the hearts of millions of us, in Israel and America. No matter how aggressive our assimilation to new worlds, we Galicianers always juggled a kind of dual citizenship. Unlike many German Jews, we wanted to retain our Jewishness, our *Yiddishkayt*. And after the Holocaust, not even the starchiest Americans dared any longer to demand that we shed it, as they had demanded of striving Jews in the 1920s and '30s—compliant German Jews like Walter Lippmann, Felix Frankfurter, and Arthur Hays Sulzberger.

Adolph Ochs, too, was born to German Jews. But with a father who fought for the Union and a mother whose family sided with the Confederacy, he seems to have been comfortable with cultural ambivalence. He married a rabbi's daughter, and once established in New York, he refused to join clubs that welcomed the owner of *The Times* but no other Jews. Yet he, too, felt the sting of anti-Semitism and heard *The Times* condescendingly called a "Jewish newspaper."

Long before Hitler and Goebbels, the myth of an omnipotent "Jewish press" had been spread by bigots like Henry Adams and Henry Ford. Yet in the first half of the twentieth century, journalism was so inhospitable to Jews that some of its most successful practitioners, like Walter Lippmann and Arthur Krock, hid or denied their Jewishness. Ochs and the son-in-law who succeeded him at *The Times*, Arthur Hays Sulzberger, were openly supportive of the Jewish religion and never disguised their ethnic roots. But they treated Jewishness as a faith, never as a secondary nationality or aspect of personality. They were American Jews, not Jewish-Americans, and they felt none of the shtetl Jews' transcendent bond with Jews the world over.

Accordingly, Ochs discouraged extensive coverage of the plight of Europe's Jews in World War I. And while *The Times* in the 1930s distinguished itself in recording the rise of the Nazis and their atrocities, it was plainly reluctant during World War II to feature the early reports about the mass slaughter and gassing of Jews. There is no evidence that *The Times* set out to suppress such reports. Some of them surely struck the editors, as they struck even Jewish observers, as unbelievable wartime propaganda designed to demonize the Germans. Even Jews trapped in Nazi-held territories long doubted the whispered news that they were being uniquely and systematically exterminated. After the murder of millions was finally undeniable, prominent American Jews were nonetheless reluctant to engage in "special pleading" for the rescue of the remnant lest they be accused of damaging the war effort and delaying Hitler's defeat.

Still, though I cannot prove it, I suspect that some of *The Times*'s news judgments in those days were infected by the owners' palpable fear of appearing to favor Jewish causes. Even after the war, Arthur Hays Sulzberger was careful to "never put a Jew in the showcase," as he once remarked, meaning he never wanted a Jew as his editor and final arbiter of content—not because he mistrusted the available candidates but because he feared the devaluation of *The Times* in Gentile circles. He did not prevent the rise of many talented Jewish journalists, but the vast majority were kept working in and around New York and found it harder than it should have been to draw assignments abroad and in Washington. Although *Times* bylines gradually came to include names like Weiler, Raskin, and Rosenthal, these writers were somehow all persuaded to render their first names as A. instead of Abraham.

Editorially, before World War II, *The Times* aligned itself with the moneyed German Jews who opposed the formation of a Jewish state in Palestine. They thought that Zionism confused the Jewish religion with a superfluous nationalism (and socialism!) and feared that it would only exacerbate doubts about every Jew's ultimate loyalty. They were not, to be sure, the only anti-Zionists among Jews; some of the poorest and most devout Hasidim from Eastern Europe refuse to this day to recognize Israel's statehood because the Bible foresees an "ingathering" of Israelites only after the appearance of the Messiah. Eventually, after the Holocaust, *The*

Times acknowledged the need for a state in which Jews could control their own destiny. It even assigned Irving "Pat" Spiegel, a Yiddish-spouting New York reporter, to write inane articles about every Zionist fund-raiser and convention of Jewish committees and congresses, as if to atone for its past neglect. But that past hung over us for decades.

By the time Punch Sulzberger occupied his father's chair in 1963, American society had shed many of its anti-Semitic prejudices and permitted the rapid advancement of Jews in professional life and corporate suites. The general revulsion against fascism turned into a revulsion against bigotry itself, as demonstrated by the election of the first Catholic president, John F. Kennedy. Exploiting this atmosphere, and Gentile guilt about the Holocaust, American Jews of my generation were emboldened to make themselves culturally conspicuous, to flaunt their ethnicity, to find literary inspiration in their roots, and to bask in the resurrection of Israel.

My Jewishness proved to be excellent preparation for my Americanism. I had learned in childhood to follow, indeed to lead, every sort of religious ritual and service, even though I understood only a few of the Hebrew words that I read so fluently. Typically tardy at shul, like every other shawled and shaking worshiper I needed to hear only a few cantorial phrases to spot my place in the prayer book. Another feature of Jewishness was a vigorous individualism, because our deity had a decidedly democratic spirit; rabbis were teachers, not priests. And so to the paradox: Encouraged by my Jewishness to devise my own ethical codes, I drifted after my bar mitzvah into agnosticism.

I could stray from God but not from Torah, that rich collection of laws and fables that had been my earliest literature. So I gladly inflicted Bible study on our children even as I angered the more faithful Tobi with my obvious inability to pray. The Torah, our Declaration and Constitution combined, urges a faith in law as the only reliable restraint on human behavior, the only alternative to violence and war. And the democratic codification of law requires debate and dissent. Instead of idols and passions, I worshiped words and argument, becoming part of an unashamedly Jewish verbal invasion of American culture. It was especially satisfying to realize the wildest fantasy of the world's anti-Semites: Inspired by our heritage as keepers of the book, creators of the law, and storytellers supreme, Jews in America did finally achieve a disproportionate influence in universities and in all media of communication.

Punch Sulzberger unconsciously abetted this movement. He felt born to the publisher's chair and had none of his father's hang-ups about being

Jewish. Israel's ambassadors to the United Nations lived just a few floors below his Fifth Avenue apartment and always enjoyed easy access to him and to his table at *The Times*. Within a few years of Punch's ascendancy, there came a time when not only the executive editor—A. M. Rosenthal—and I but *all* the top editors listed on the paper's masthead were Jews. Over vodka in the publisher's back room, this was occasionally mentioned as an impolitic condition, but it was altered only gradually, without any affirmative action on behalf of Christians.

Because my name was Max and because I produced editorials that disapproved of some of the hawkish policies of Israel's prime minister, Menachem Begin, many Jewish readers leapt to the conclusion that I was just another German assimilationist who, like *The Times* of yore, accepted Israel only grudgingly and was "bending over backwards" to impress Gentile establishments. Even modest criticism of Israeli actions inevitably provoked angry articles in Jewish weeklies, demands that I meet for remedial instruction with the heads of Jewish organizations, and a flood of angry letters, many condemning me as a "self-hating Jew" who had abandoned his people to curry favor with the goyim. I was denounced for being ignorant of the Holocaust and indifferent to the damage done by disharmony among Jews. To the most sober of these assaults, I sometimes responded with a hurt biographical note, stressing my roots in the shtetl, our family's taste of both Nazi and Soviet anti-Semitism, the disappearance of my grandparents, my sojourn among relatives who had survived the death camps to settle gratefully in Israel, and my intimate familiarity with every liturgical variant of Jewish ritual. Mostly, however, I would simply retort that my only remaining Jewish friends were Israelis, to make the point that many Israelis also found fault with their government and also favored accommodation with the Palestinians, as they eventually proved in the Peace Now movement.

I was much more deeply devoted to Israel than I dared to assert. I had yearned for a Jewish homeland ever since learning as a child in Germany that in Palestine even the policemen were Jews! Like most American Jews, however, I settled on a remote brand of Zionism, which rejected all importuning to move to Israel to share its hardships and dangers. With their guilt thus compounded, American Jews poured energy and money into synagogues and organizations whose main purpose was helping Israel, both directly and through vigorous political lobbying of presidents and Congresses. Israel became so crucial to the definition of Jewish identity that most Jews gave unqualified support to its governments. They brooked no criticism of Israeli society or policy. Especially after Israel's lonely and remarkable triumph in the Six-Day War of 1967, any editorial disagreement with either the Labor or Likud regime came to be read as not just unhelpful but treacherous. And I was cast as turncoat in chief.

I did indeed have many close Israeli friends, not only relatives and journalists but high officials, ranging from Yitzhak Rabin to Lova Eliav. That is why I well understood the full range of Israeli opinion on all of that country's vital security issues.

Lova Eliav was secretary-general of the Labor party until he resigned over Golda Meir's refusal after the Six-Day War to negotiate with or even recognize the existence of Palestinians. He went on to secretly befriend some leaders of the PLO when doing so was still considered treasonous, and he became a valued intermediary when the hawkish Prime Minister Begin needed to negotiate prisoner exchanges and other accommodations with Yasir Arafat.

Lova and I had become friends in Moscow in the late 1950s, when he toured Russia to rekindle some *Yiddishkayt* among Soviet Jews. Operating out of the Israeli embassy, he distributed prayer books and shawls and Hebrew dictionaries to awaken Jewish consciousness, dissidence, and a desire to emigrate to Israel—an enterprise that I ignorantly deemed vain and quixotic. Lova turned up later in Managua, helping the Somoza dictatorship to recover from a devastating earthquake in exchange for badly needed weapons, and in Teheran, where he helped to rebuild devastated towns for the ayatollah's regime in return for the secret release of Iranian Jews. He wrote four or five books, sat in Parliament as a one-man party, shook the American money tree, and organized desert settlements for new immigrants. Lova was a passionate Zionist who resented the drift of tens of thousands of Israelis and even Soviet Jews to Brooklyn and Queens. When I once observed that Israel's expatriates nonetheless rushed home to join their army units in the Yom Kippur War of 1973, he replied scornfully that his father did not split rocks in the desert to prepare the way for two divisions at Kennedy Airport.

Because he instinctively understood the weakness of the Soviet Union, Lova knew that however much the Russians tried to stir the passions of Arabs against the West, only Israel could give the Palestinians a place in the sun and so unlock the doors to regional peace. For that heresy, he spent most of his life in the political doghouse, but many Israelis slowly came to agree with him. Their hopes, and mine, that a militarily invulnerable Israel would find the confidence to recognize the Palestinians' Zion-like aspirations found little sympathy among American Jews. They pilloried Tony Lewis, whose sensitive Op-Ed columns dreaded Israel's drift toward a kind of South African apartheid. And they were fortified in their fears by the tough talk they had heard from Israel's ambassador to Washington in the late 1960s, the man who eventually and grudgingly returned to Washington as prime minister to extend a hand to Yasir Arafat—Yitzhak Rabin.

Fresh from his triumphs as chief of staff during the Six-Day War, Ambassador Rabin had been more than a good source for the Washington correspondent of *The Times*. On many an evening he was my stimulating sparring partner in debates of world affairs, although he clearly preferred lecturing to listening. He could be simultaneously pontifical and brilliant, describing the ancient Sinai battlegrounds at our Passover seder or the current vulnerabilities of Arab armies in his living room. But he could also be shortsighted about American society. Instead of struggling to reinforce Israel's ties to young American Jews in the antiwar movement, he was openly partisan toward President Nixon, contending that only Americans who honored their commitments to allies—even in a losing and badly managed war—could be relied upon to defend Israel in a time of peril.

Right or wrong, Rabin was always strategic in his thinking, never ideological. He insisted that Israel needed more geographical depth on the west bank of the Jordan River for military defense, but he opposed creating vulnerable settlements there whose defense in war would waste precious lives. And he knew that Israel's ultimate line of defense ran not along the Jordan but through the heart of the Oval Office.

I watched in amazement as Ambassador Rabin described and then carried out his own strategic plan to make himself Israel's prime minister. But I am sure that he never dreamed of one day conducting a more daring version of Nixon's China turnabout by leaping to the front of the Peace Now parade. Once the Soviet Union collapsed and exposed the Arab nations' dependence on the United States, Rabin instantly understood the value of risking concessions to Arafat and pursuing economic as well as diplomatic relations with key Arab countries.

Fortified by my knowledge of Israel and my friendships there, I myself wrote most of our Middle East commentaries. As more Arab than Jewish readers recognized, I wrote them from a pro-Israel perspective. And I wrote in confidence that *The Times* no longer suffered from any secret desire to deny or overcome its ethnic roots. Besides freely and frequently lecturing Israel on its diplomatic opportunities, I dared near the end of my first year to speak *to* America's Jews *as* a Jew. Entitled "The Jews and Jimmy Carter," the editorial was one of the longest I ever ran, and it began like this:

As Norman Mailer says, only the unsayable is really worth saying. And one of the unsayable things in our political life these days is that most leaders of the American Jewish community are acting as if President Carter is risking Israel's survival for an illusory Middle East settlement. Meanwhile, Administration officials and other influential citizens are increasingly annoyed by the formidable resistance the President's diplomacy is getting from the American Jewish community.

Translation: Jimmy Carter had set out to broker a peace between Israel and its neighbors and, not so incidentally, also to protect America's alliance with Egypt and oil-rich Saudi Arabia. But like other Americans who had walked that path, he despaired of getting Israel to grant the Palestinians some kind of "homeland" so long as American Jews used their political clout to defend Israel's intransigence. Democrats, especially, depended heavily on "Jewish money," which was offered them at early and decisive moments of every political season. They also depended on the concentrated voting power of Jews in the largest states. But Jewish support was firmly tied to Israel's interests. Even fervent friends of Israel, like George McGovern and Ed Muskie, used to complain to me during their campaigns for president that they had to "clear" their statements on the Middle East with Jewish censors. Although the purchase of influence is a common feature of American politics, I found it disheartening to see Jewish organizations spending their influence uncritically on behalf of every twist and turn in Israeli policy.

It was with affection for Israel that I became its critic after the Six-Day War, when it refused to use its military triumph to offer the Palestinians honorable terms. The territories that Israel won in that war housed more than a million Arabs, many of them refugees from the Israeli heartland. To retain that land, no matter how sacred to some Israelis, required the subjugation of an already embittered people. As I argued to Rabin and others, the Palestinians would either be deprived of political rights or rapidly multiply and outvote the Jews. Unless it found a way to rid itself of the West Bank and Gaza territories, Israel would become either Jewish and undemocratic or democratic and un-Jewish. Or, as Meir Kahane wanted, it would disastrously yield to the temptation to drive the Palestinians off their lands altogether, some for the second time in twenty years. The occupied lands of Gaza and the West Bank offered the triumphant Israelis a false sense of security, and their awed friends in America were too busy celebrating military triumph to think for themselves.

After yet another costly war in 1973, which clearly demonstrated Israel's dependence on American diplomacy and weaponry, there appeared a Likud government that favored a Greater Israel not just for security but for biblical ideology. Led by Begin, it reopened a Zionist schism that Ben-Gurion thought he had resolved by offering to partition the land with Palestinians after World War II. And American Jews blindly switched their allegiance to the new Israeli regime. They rationalized its annexationist doctrines and failed to see that American and Israeli interests were beginning to diverge. They were hooked on the myth that Israel was a "strategic asset" for the United States, when it was more a burden born of a moral commitment—a commitment that had to be constantly nourished with moral conduct. I felt not only qualified to challenge the slavish propaganda of American Jews but secure enough in my *Yiddishkayt* to do so from my once tainted pulpit. Mom did not enjoy the obloquy now heaped upon her son by other Jews, but she offered only encouragement for *talking takhlis*, confronting tough truths, saying the unsayable.

"The Jews and Jimmy Carter" sprang from the deepest feelings of the Frankel family—our feelings for Israel, for America, for journalism. And after Punch went out of his way to welcome its publication and a point of view that we had never really discussed, I knew that I had also tapped his deepest feelings. Fortuitously, the editorial appeared in November 1977, only one week before President Anwar Sadat of Egypt stunningly gave added meaning to my message by offering to visit Jerusalem to begin making peace. Most appropriately, I had stumbled upon a closing theme that implored the Jews of both Israel and America to liberate themselves from their "siege mentality":

Such a siege mentality runs two grave risks for both American and Israeli diplomacy.

The first is that the spokesmen of American Jews, while always respected for their political strength, could cease to be taken seriously in Washington on the merits of the issues. If, at every turn, the most that a President hears from them is a dutiful echo of Israeli policy, he must be forgiven if he seeks more sophisticated instruction elsewhere.

It is a fact of recent history that politically difficult but valuable Israeli concessions have come only in response to American pressure. The President who manages that pressure must judge from day to day which resistance protects a vital nerve and which only an expedient interest. If ever there is an unwitting American betrayal of Israel it will be due to miscalculation on this point. The credibility of the American Jewish community is the best defense against such ghastly error.

The second danger is that the spokesmen of American Jews might cease to be taken seriously in Israel, too. If their considerable influence in the United States can be played too easily, it will be taken for granted—and even misplayed for unworthy goals. Political divisions in Israel have enfeebled the diplomacy of all its recent governments, causing it too often to be pegged to the lowest common denominator—the most zealous of its parties. If the views of American Jews are also reduced to that level, they will surely lose the capacity to instruct Israelis in the perceptions and imperatives of American opinion and policy, on which, above all, Israel's security depends.

Israel's ultimate defense line runs through the conscience and political stature of an American President, whose help in a moment of peril would be vital. That help is assured so long as the failure of any negotiations is perceived in the United States as the failure of the Arab nations to respond to a truly forthcoming Israeli diplomacy. The best link between that Israeli diplomacy and American perceptions is a credible, independent and influential American Jewish community.

In the protracted negotiations that followed, the Begin government had no choice but to exchange the wasteland of the Sinai for Egypt's recognition, but instead of offering comparable terms to the Palestinians, it exploited the peace on its southern front to lay claim to ever more territory in the east. I no longer felt so isolated when other Jewish voices, including Saul Bellow, Daniel Bell, Seymour Martin Lipset, and Leonard Fein, joined in protest against some of Begin's policies. But it was not until Begin and General Sharon engineered a bloody pursuit of the Palestinians, all the way to Beirut and at a huge cost in lives, that a full-throated protest movement finally emerged inside Israel. Peace Now was patterned after America's antiwar movement in the Vietnam era and spawned a sizable following in the United States. But the leading Jewish organizations refused to publicly condemn Begin's aggressive course. They preferred to accuse protesters like me of suffering from a "ghetto mentality."

I realize now that our conflict played out the contradictory impulses that shtetl Jews have always carried inside themselves. As discerned by a remarkable anthropological study, that heritage was the product of competing forces, from within and without Yiddish society.* From outside came the pressure to stand united always against the goyim, in a federal hierarchy of obligations:

---

* Mark Zborowski and Elizabeth Herzog, *Life Is with People: The Jewish Little-Town of Eastern Europe* (New York: International Universities Press, 1952).

Individual may react against individual within the family, but the unit is solid in facing the community at large. Similarly, the community presents a solid front. . . . Each town criticizes and ridicules the next. Yet the towns of one region display a common bond and loyalty opposite another region.

But from inside the shtetl came an entirely different commandment, which I always took to be the higher imperative:

The shtetl recognizes no absolutes. Even God's authority is subject to check, question and criticism. The only absolute authority is the spirit of the Torah. . . . The authority of the leader is limited also by the right and duty of each man to try to understand and interpret for himself.

In that confluence of ethnic and religious legacies I recognized the source of my devotion to rationality and reasonableness, my attraction to individualism and relativity, my faith in debate and democracy. Like my forebears in the shtetl, I understood my God to be an abstraction, without image, and I defined godliness as the pursuit of knowledge and good deeds. In my editorial combat against fellow Jews, I realized why I grew to define myself through journalism: because I shared the faith of the shtetl that "the word is threshold to the deed," and because I wanted always to escape the irrationality of the herd. Although I am sentimentally faithful to the tribe whose genes I carry, I know that my culture has been both diluted and enriched by a dozen other tribes. If my *Yiddishkayt* is to survive in America, it will be as a value system, not in a taste for bagels and lox or a guilty twitch at the sight of bacon.

37 · TOWARD A HAPPY PLACE

ONE DAY SOON AFTER I TOOK CHARGE OF EDITORIALS, *The Times* received a full-page ad, costing perhaps $40,000, in which a company processing plutonium denounced our editorial against processing plutonium. Since I used to hear complaints around the paper's business office that some articles I put in the Magazine were chasing away advertisers, I thought it amusing to ask the publisher for "credit" now that our editorials often attracted advertising. Punch's memo replied, "No. Not only is it a one-way street, it's filled with tow-away zones and potholes." We could jest about such things because even in the bleakest times our publisher never ceased to protect our journalism from commercial pressure. From time to time, Punch Sulzberger had to humble himself to woo back an advertiser who disapproved of something we printed. But he never burdened me with knowledge of such a boycott. Never.

For a man with Punch's burdens, that took remarkable restraint. During most of his early years as publisher, he had to prove to his family, to his corporate peers, and to the stock market that he could restore the profitability of *The Times* despite the collapse of other New York papers, the decline of the New York economy, and the dispersal from the city of many of our readers, industries, and advertisers. Punch cared deeply about his reputation as a manager and businessman. He spent more time with corporate executives than journalists and must have pined to blame us for things gone wrong. Yet he never lost his bearings or sense of purpose. *The Times* existed to practice great journalism. It needed to make money—not to enrich the Sulzbergers or even the stockholders but because profits were the only guarantee of the paper's honesty, independence, and survival. If mismanaged or misdirected, the paper could not look to any private fortune for rescue. So while he might curse the troubles his editors could cause, particularly when we carelessly erred, squandered money, or gratuitously insulted advertisers, Punch took most of the guilt and obligation upon himself. When he thought I needed to be reminded to respect the rich, the most he would do was tell an anecdote, usually the one about the goddam reporter who in writing about a notable charity of the Annenberg family felt compelled to recall that its wealth originated with transactions that landed a forebear in jail.

Punch grew up among the rich and famous and knew them as human beings, not icons. He disdained the populist prejudices of most reporters, who tend to treat all wealth as suspect. His childhood homes were routinely visited by prime ministers, explorers, executives, and generals. He inhaled history at the family table. Yet he was also an indifferent student, plagued by dyslexia, more attracted to gadgets and machines than to abstract ideas. Only after service in the marines in World War II did he buckle down to some serious reading at Columbia.

As the only boy among four children, Punch was reared for a career at *The Times* and fitfully exposed to its news and business operations. But until the sudden death of the fifty-year-old Orvil Dryfoos, his sister Marian's husband, everyone thought it would be at least fifteen years before Punch was "ready" to command the family business. Even at Dryfoos's death, there was resistance to him until Iphigene Sulzberger put an end to the loose talk about her son needing a "copublisher" or "regent."

Still, the misperceptions of him never ceased. Punch continued to be underestimated, not only because of his youth but because of his genuine informality. People were forever astounded to discover that the publisher of the awesomely powerful and austere *New York Times* was a man totally lacking in pretense and pomposity, a man who on weekends packed his own car, broiled his own steaks, and washed his guests' dishes. Then again, that informality left others equally unprepared for the steely clarity with which he could make swift decisions, to abandon the California and

European editions of *The Times* and to jettison a succession of senior managers too proud or hidebound to accept his leadership.

I often found Punch to be brutally abrupt and disarmingly droll, in
quick succession. One night during the Pentagon Papers siege, he trashed
some of my writing one minute, then lovingly prepared his back-room bed
for my overnight stay, drawing jolly arrows to guide me to assorted toi-
letries and naughty literature. When our embittered Soviet expert, Harry
Schwartz, embarrassed Punch at a stockholders' meeting, I experienced the
full range of his temperament within a single hour. Schwartz tried to
avenge my pressure for his retirement by accusing me of employing a subversive—an editor who taught an after-hours course at a frankly Marxist
institute. That was, admittedly, an impolitic affiliation, and Schwartz did
his best to create the impression that I was harboring a Soviet spy. Angered
and embarrassed by the surprise attack, Punch sent word through interme-
diaries, without further inquiry, that he wanted the young man fired. He
became even angrier when I resisted; the editor had served me scrupu-
lously, without a trace of ideological bias, and had in fact drafted some
sharply anti-Soviet editorials about the Solidarity uprisings in Poland.
Punch finally acquiesced and just an hour later ended the affair in typical
fashion. He returned a memo in which I asked whether he minded my joining the search committee for a new dean at Columbia's journalism school.
"Not at all," he wrote across the bottom. "How about Harry Schwartz?"

Punch was above all honest with himself and those around him. When
urged from many sides in the 1970s to give up cigarette advertising, he
made no pious claims for the rights of a legal industry; he said he and *The
Times* were hooked, financially. When urged to prohibit smoking throughout the company, he insisted that we devise exemptions for our North Carolina affiliates—and his own after-lunch cigar. (The remedy was to allow
smoking in "private offices.") Punch seemed always to know what he did
not know and never hesitated to appear ignorant or innocent. He thought
nothing of asking a high-ranking government guest why we could not
avenge Japanese trading practices by letting their goods rot on the docks.
He wondered out loud whether other societies were right to chop off the
hands of chronic drug dealers. He refused to believe that New York taxi
drivers could not be forced to speak English, wear clean shirts and caps,
and pass a test in city geography. Obsessively tidy, he had a clear sense of
corporate direction. While his acquisitions of a newspaper here and a magazine and TV station there were opportunistic, they served a shrewdly designed strategy that produced a remarkable and insufficiently noticed
turnabout in the paper's commercial fortunes.

When Punch took charge, *The Times*, like other urban newspapers, was breathlessly chasing its readers and advertisers to the suburbs and sinking under the weight of escalating labor costs. So he set about attracting new readers and advertisers by augmenting *The Times*'s traditional foreign, national, and local news. He pressed for a greatly expanded business report and for the evolution of daily magazines, in newspaper format, devoted to food, furnishings, the arts, science and technology. Yet these improvements only increased the costs of creating and printing the paper. And *The Times*'s blue-collar unions refused to admit laborsaving machines into the building. On the contrary, the typesetters and pressmen used their power to halt publication of New York's newspapers to impose all sorts of featherbedding—at least double the number of men needed on every press, proofreaders who checked for errors *after* the paper was printed, and typesetters who filled predetermined work quotas by setting and discarding nonsensical dummy type. The unions alone were hardly to blame for all the newspaper failures in New York, and they correctly foresaw the computer's threat to the hoary arts of typesetting, platemaking, and printing. But instead of looking for a graceful and prosperous path out of existence, they held the whole industry hostage to their costly old ways.

Punch's answer was cannily combative as well as generous. He would let the endangered workers share the savings if they would negotiate for a decent pace of automation. But he also intended to wear them down. He abandoned the shibboleth that history could not afford to have *The New York Times* silenced even for a single day. Only by proving that he could survive a long strike would he get the negotiations he needed. And to survive a strike, he realized, he needed sources of income beyond the unions' reach. Automation required diversification, the purchase of media properties that *The Times* would know how to run and whose profits exceeded the printers' war chest. And diversification required going public—creating a special stock that could be used to pay for acquisitions of other companies but not to seize control of *The Times* from the Sulzberger family.

The strategy was as complicated as it sounds—more so, given the internecine battles among the unions and the outright gangsterism at the top of one or two of them. But Punch stuck to his battle plan. He kept control of *The Times* in a family stock but sold second-tier common shares to the public in 1969 to facilitate the purchase from the Cowles family of *Family Circle*, a mass-circulation supermarket magazine, some TV stations, and smaller magazines and newspapers. He was now chairman of a budding conglomerate, all the while protecting the family's grip on the enterprise and remembering the purpose of it all: to engage the New York unions in painstaking dialogues so as to persuade them to let their members share in the profits generated by the computers that would send them into retirement.

Logically enough, the man best placed to execute this strategy was the executive in charge of manufacturing the paper, Walter Mattson. Step by step, Punch and Mattson revitalized *The Times* and made it profitable. It was an achievement as noteworthy as the paper's continuing journalistic progress, but business journals that had been quick to recount the paper's difficulties could never bring themselves to write about this managerial triumph. Given Punch's modesty and refusal to make a show of his anxieties along the way, even those of us who labored close by failed at the time to appreciate the magnitude of his undertaking and success.

I could sometimes detect the publisher's innermost concerns from the way he closely questioned corporate executives who came to lunch about their management styles and organization charts. But he never imposed a business interest on our editorial policy—never even discussed a pecuniary issue except to bring his own actions into line with the principles we preached. He was careful, for example, to solicit our editorial views about communications policy before he joined in the newspaper industry's campaign to keep telephone companies out of the advertising business. He wanted, as a good citizen of Times Square, to throw the ads of porno movie houses out of the paper but accepted our plea that he not become a censor; we decided instead to make their ads conform to *Times* standards of appropriate hemlines and cleavages—a hedge that mercifully caused them to abandon us voluntarily. Punch quit a corporate association formed to promote the sale of United States Savings Bonds when he learned of our desire to condemn the low interest rates that the government paid to small savers. He made sure to square our opinions with his votes as a Columbia University trustee on such matters as affirmative action and disinvestment in South Africa. And in an obviously galling surrender, he let me talk him out of suing *The Washington Post* for ruining our syndication profits by prematurely publishing the news in H. R. Haldeman's book about Watergate. He understood my point that as a newspaper we should wish to lose the suit that as a syndicate we would seek to win. Indeed, whenever an ancillary business, like publishing books or pharmaceutical magazines, threatened to confuse or compromise the values of *The Times*, Punch never wavered about his priorities and let even profitable sidelines lapse.

Punch was fiercely loyal to people as well as the paper. For some good deed in the distant past that was never revealed to me, he was maddeningly tolerant of the self-promoting agitations of Federal Judge Irving

Kaufman. Punch recognized him as the pest he was, and agreed with our judgment that Kaufman was pathetically panting for favorable notice all his life to overcome his guilt for having sent Julius and Ethel Rosenberg to the electric chair. Nonetheless, Punch kept all our doors open for the judge even as he tolerated our resistance. Another favored petitioner was Jean Mayer, the chancellor of Tufts University while Punch's son, Arthur Sulzberger, Jr., was a student there. But when once I hesitantly proposed to censure Mayer for selling a university honor to the hateful President Marcos of the Philippines, Punch did not hesitate to send back a firm "Yes!"

Loyally, Punch entrusted the day-to-day management of *The Times* to the most willful talents at hand, the secretive Walter Mattson and the volcanic Abe Rosenthal. But he protected himself by preserving a balance of power, or at least the appearance of it. For the longest time, he pretended that Mattson had a genuine rival in James Goodale, our chief counsel, just as he kept Abe Rosenthal looking over his shoulder at my hovering presence. And he annoyed both Mattson and Rosenthal by having Sydney Gruson as confidant and freewheeling adviser.

It was Gruson who had urged Punch to bring me to New York and who recruited me for the editorial page. Starting in 1985, Gruson awakened me, and presumably also Punch, to the tensions boiling up in the newsroom as Rosenthal, in a Lear-like tempest, began to confront his executive mortality. Abe's immediate deputies, Seymour Topping and Arthur Gelb, were roughly the same age, and when Punch urged him to plan for an orderly succession, Abe staged ostentatious but patently ineffective "tryouts" of younger editors. His obvious unhappiness at the task left him moodier than ever, curt and arbitrary in ways that disturbed even his closest friends. He felt that no one was ready to take his place, I least of all. But Gruson suggested that if I wanted the job, the time had come to tell the publisher. I did, offhandedly, believing that Abe had at least two more years before reaching retirement age.

———

Why did I want to be executive editor? Well, because it was there—the highest peak in serious journalism. It was also the nearest that I, a lifelong employee, would ever come to running my own enterprise, commanding my own environment. An institution that had identified me throughout my life might now for a time be identified *with* me.

Most of us lifers at *The Times* think of the paper as the only worthy medium of communication. It reaches the most influential, interesting, and powerful people on earth. It is the "house organ" of the smartest, most talented, and most influential Americans at the height of American power. And while its editorial opinions or the views of individual columnists and critics can be despised or dismissed, the paper's daily package of news cannot. It frames the intellectual and emotional agenda of serious Americans. Television and a few magazines may have larger audiences, but none speak so immediately, constantly, and simultaneously to the White House and Wall Street, Broadway and Berkeley, Macy's and General Motors, Cape Cod and Cape Canaveral, Madison Avenue and MIT—with the Kremlin and the Elysée Palace listening in. To have the chance to inspire and to instruct that news report promised me the greatest thrills of an already thrilling ride through the twentieth century. To enhance the appeal and success of *The Times* for another generation struck me as the ultimate public service.

In July 1986, almost a year before Abe turned sixty-five, Punch contrived to have me at lunch alone in his private dining room and quietly announced that he had persuaded Abe to step down and write a column at the end of the year. And he wanted me as his next executive editor.

Although I had expected to be his eventual choice, I was caught completely off guard. I managed only to mumble a few embarrassed words of gratitude. Even after drinking in the news, I could not properly express my surging pride and excitement. I said I hoped he knew what this moment meant for a refugee kid from Germany. Despite his demand for secrecy, I simply had to tell my parents as well as my ailing wife.

Not knowing what else to say, I haltingly asked him to define my "mandate"—what the next editor most needed to accomplish.

Punch answered instantly, with memorable clarity: "Three things," he said. "Make a great paper even greater. Help to break in my son Arthur as the next publisher. Make the newsroom a happy place again."

38 · MALIGNANCIES

THANKS TO THE PILLS, TOBI COULD FEEL GENUINE DE-light at my advancement. The envy had disappeared. "My wonderful husband," she said, even to me, with hardly a hint of self-pity about the cancer eating her brain.

Two years earlier, heading into her second year at Columbia Law, Tobi had finally found a psychiatrist she was willing to trust and agreed to experiment with antidepressants. She soon found the right formula; it dried her mouth but oiled her emotions. It let her feel affections and joys that she had not known for decades. It caused us to wonder whether we could heal our bruises and renew our marriage. But barely a year later, in mid-1985, another demon struck.

The first signs were more comic than alarming. In what the family took to be a new idiosyncrasy, Tobi would stop play after every point on the tennis court to insist on ostentatious recitations and repetitions of the score. We thought she was taking excessive precautions against cheating. Then, biking along the wooden walkways to our beach house on Fire Island, she pedaled in constant dread of collision with some careless child and feverishly jangled her bell at the approach of every intersection. She lobbied for public meetings to address the town's tricycle menace.

We found nothing remarkable in such willful conduct. One previous summer, simply to prove that a sunny beach day was no time for television, Tobi had insisted on a long walk in the sand just as Björn Borg and John McEnroe began their historic tiebreaker at Wimbledon. David and Jon leapt frantically from cottage to cottage to learn the outcome of each point, bitterly insisting that they were not "watching" the match. But those had been days, and years, of resentments now apparently vanquished by the pills. We dared to mock Tobi's new anxieties, and she took no offense. With a judicial clerkship and solid job awaiting her after graduation, we tasted a strange serenity—a new delusion.

On a Tuesday in late October 1985, after gulping a muffin and coffee, Tobi felt so nauseous that she tried in vain to induce vomiting. Unable to make it to the law school's nurse, she was taken a few blocks by ambulance to St. Luke's Hospital, where she suffered a momentary convulsive seizure, her back arched, her arms flailing, her open eyes rolled crazily to one side. A shot of Valium halted the attack, and by the time I reached her, she had passed all preliminary neurological probes. She even remembered parking her car in a metered spot on the west side of Amsterdam Avenue that morning to unload some heavy law books but angrily insisted that the car was therefore pointed northward. She was suffering no mere headache.

The next day she delayed her CT scan to apply her legal training to challenge four paragraphs of the consent form. So it was not until Thursday that we learned of "the infection or growth," the euphemism of choice for a sizable tumor, on the right frontal lobe—a "good" location, we were assured, because tunneling to it threatened "only a few" sensory and vision channels.

My quest, through friends and relatives, for the "best" neurosurgeon to test and remove or "debulk" the tumor revealed that even this delicate, exacting craft is actually a personality-driven art. The best surgeon for us meant one with the necessary tactile skills but also a compatible temperament. Did we want a surgeon who might pursue every millimeter of necrotic tissue—"I got it all!"—even at the risk of impairing more physical functions? Or did we want the kind who would defer to a fatal diagnosis and foreshorten a doomed life? Or was there a compromiser who would try to balance the length and the quality of life? The ranges of medical strategy were as great as the ranges of skill.

Largely on faith I chose New York Hospital, and on hearsay I chose

Dr. Richard Fraser to cut and Dr. Frank Petito, a neurologist, to manage Tobi's care. She wondered, "Why me?" but she asked them good questions, all premised in optimism. She was told that the price of entry over the right ear would be some peripheral loss in the upper left quadrant of vision—"the area of a backhand lob," Fraser explained; she might have to rotate her law books slightly to the right to compensate. But the doctors gave me access to all their brain cancer literature, and I quickly learned that the condition they suspected from CT scans was inevitably fatal within eighteen months, sooner if surgery was not followed by radiation and chemotherapy.

The pathology report was bad: a glioblastoma multiforme and anaplastic mixed glioma. I sent the slides to be independently read by an expert in Virginia, and he offered his best judgment only orally: take a six-month cruise together to spare your wife the agonies of "treatments" that would, at most, extend her life by a year. But I could not bring myself to abort her law school enrollment or to make her confront death so directly. We cried together one long evening as if to say a premature good-bye, but as Dr. Fraser predicted, Tobi never asked about her life expectancy. So we chose the treatments, and their misery. I informed David, Margot, and Jon about their mother's dim prospects but insisted, also for her sake, that between frequent visits they resume their independent lives.

Tobi came home from the hospital after eighteen days with bottles of Decadron, phenobarbital and Dilantin, Tarfenel and optional reserves of Tylenol with codeine, Halcion and Mylanta. I counted out the dosages each night to be administered by our support team. Evie Hall, our housekeeper, had the early day shift; my parents or Tobi's relieved in late afternoon; and I stood guard evenings and through the night. For her daily dose of radiation in the first six weeks, Tobi was escorted downtown by Mom-Pop, as David had named my mother, and sometimes Pop Jack, my father, in a limo provided by Punch so that I could come to work without guilt. But the pain was always with us, and the side effects were horrendous.

A droll wig could cover the indignity of a bare scalp, but Tobi's fatigue became chronic. A severe pain in the left leg turned out to be phlebitic and required the first of eight hospital admissions in sixteen months. The moment the radiation ended, doctors discovered a detached retina and, to avert multiple operations, devised a single three-pronged intervention: to repair it, to implant a gas bubble whose expansion would smooth it out, and to surround the eye with a silicon belt to prevent a recurrence. The next two operations reopened the brain, to reattach and then again to reposition a shunt through which to drain the fluid from the swollen wound. After a round trip to Syracuse to witness Jon's graduation from college came three more hospital tours to fire chemical poisons at the tumor, another pursuit of a phlebitic clot, and a fourth round of chemotherapy at home. The tumor retreated long enough to allow us a relatively calm summer in 1986, encouraging Tobi to plan for two fall and two spring courses to finish law school the following May. No longer afraid of Fire Island intersections, she tootled around Saltaire atop a large tricycle, almost unaware of how much steroids had bloated and skewed her face.

That July, Punch tapped me to be his next editor and inspired Tobi's displays of pride. Fully aware of our domestic tensions, Punch never even asked whether I could manage both the cancer and the paper. He just assumed I could, as he himself soon had to do when his wife, Carol, was attacked by a slower but equally fatal cancer.

In the fall, Tobi staggered heroically through her daily class at Columbia. She walked reasonably well in sneakers but soon needed our housekeeper's support. Stumbling around the halls of the law school, she became a familiar and beloved figure and found true friendship among her classmates at last. But the steroids overpowered the antidepressants, and her moods swung wildly again. She scrawled desperate notes in texts and notebooks and on scraps of paper:

> I think so sadly about how I have wounded the kids. . . . I feel lucky that I am not in pain, yet sleeping to avoid emotional pain is such a sad future, and it is no solution. . . . I know I've been depressed for years, wanting love, and to give love. I have no joy in my breast. . . . That's why I cuddled with a pillow, imagining it's love and its great successes. . . . So now some of the dreams have come true. I did marry a man who became successful and well known (it was only later that I realized that I couldn't feed off Max's fame—that's all that people wanted you for was your name). . . . Please, God, help me. I cry when I anticipate my death, but it is what I want.

Fifteen months after the surgical debulking, in January 1987, the tumor resumed its growth at a quickened pace. There was nothing left to do except to comfort Tobi with nightly readings, mostly from E. L. Doctorow's *World's Fair,* which describes a Bronx youth outwardly resembling her young years in Brooklyn. I hated the medical knowledge that made me feel superior to my patient and that kept me asking whether she wanted to move back to the hospital. Tobi resisted, as if she knew she would not again come home, and her resistance left me ashamed. One day, after a rough struggle with the paraphernalia of home care, she did ask to be returned to the hospital, and there a few days later, in the first minutes of March 16, 1987, she died.

Through the formalities of burial and shivah, the kids and I talked at length about the different malignancies produced by chemical imbalance. We recalled that pitifully brief year when Tobi's healthy nature had shone through, and we wondered why it took so long for us to learn that an ill temper can be no less an infirmity than an ill cell.

39 · PERSPECTIVES

THREE THINGS, PUNCH HAD SAID. MAKE A GREAT PAPER greater. Which I took to mean create a still loftier vision of news. Make the newsroom happier. Which I took to mean create harmony and a climate that rewards achievement. And help break in a new publisher. Which I took to mean stand up for newsroom values in the commercial strategies of the future.

The assignment suited my temperament. I approached the editor's chair with undiminished faith in the power of news to enlarge and enrich readers' experience, to remedy wrong, to relieve public anxiety, and to cultivate community. *The Times* in my years had opened its columns to more vivid writing and cogent analysis. It had defeated government censors. It had transformed itself into a national institution with international influence and invented new ways to pay the high costs of good journalism. What fun it would be to shape these values for another generation, to inspire the staff with respect and affection, to enlist the sensibilities of more women and minorities, and to justify still greater investment in our tasks.

How gentle the slopes appeared before I began their ascent.

My biggest secret on taking command of *The Times* was that I often still had trouble in reading it. I caught myself skimming the news pages despite the obvious risk of missing something important. Many days I felt more welcome in the bright, frothy pages devoted to food and furniture than among the news accounts of public issues I cared about.

Some of the obstacles to enjoying *The Times* were physical. I always resented the midsentence, even midword interruptions of front-page stories as they jumped to the inside. Once inside I grew even more resentful if the continuation sprawled over many columns, demanding more time than I had for the entire paper. I was annoyed when the foreign report bled inconspicuously into national news, which would run for a few pages, then suddenly leap from Section A to B or even D. Still more frustrating was the daily search for Sports and Obituaries, which floated from one section to another as ballast, to satisfy the demand of our presses for two pairs of sections of equal size. And while the front pages of our four sections were invitingly designed, most of the inside pages were gray landscapes relieved only by photographs whose relevance was often obscure. Not even the Culture pages possessed the glitter of their subject matter.

Other obstacles were conceptual. Too many Page One stories belabored the obvious, predictable subjects. They delivered only incremental crumbs of information—another advance or setback for percolating legislation or diplomacy, another round of cross-examination at a trial. These dollops of news were strung out with dutiful repetitions of background information, honoring a hoary *Times* command that every reader be presumed a cognitive virgin. To be sure, there were some readers who wanted a daily account of the dullest trial or legislative debate. But they knew the background and did not need our relentless rehash. Other readers surely wished, with me, that we save our percussive blasts for climactic moments.

The Times too often observed another shibboleth of American newsrooms: that the later any bit of news, the more compelling it must be. I suspect that this false premise was born in the days of clipper ships, when couriers raced across the Atlantic bearing bulletins from distant wars and kings. It was obviously reinforced by the telegraph and then the wireless, which operated in constant peril of interruption; they put a premium on "bulletins" of new information and became the enemies of coherent narrative. Whatever was learned "today" always trumped what had been learned yesterday or the day before. And any event that overtly *happened* was more easily captured than the news of things that were quietly *happening*. Given those pinched definitions of news, "events" staged by politicians and propagandists were regularly accorded greater prominence than the most significant undercurrents of life. And the most banal utterances of authorities were automatically assigned greater weight than the wisest utterances of the unheralded. The importance of words was too often confused with the importance of their source.

The Times was especially burdened by its false reputation as a "paper of record." Because it had always printed more official texts, wartime bulletins, and lists of stock prices, fashion buyers, high tides, and barometer readings, it fell victim to the myth that a newspaper's primary function was to present "just the facts." People assumed from the paper's heft and its microfilmed presence in every library that *The Times* was a daily almanac of everything worth knowing. And true enough, despite lapses, like the unforgivable neglect of the Holocaust in World War II, *The New York Times* did become the most comprehensive American diary of the twentieth century. But it was no almanac or mere record of facts.

Like every other newspaper, *The Times* was shaped by the wandering interests of its readers, editors, and, yes, advertisers. In my decades on the staff, I saw us constantly shifting interests and priorities. We gave up reporting the sermons at New York's bigger churches and synagogues and switched to covering religious practice and institutions. We retired from massive war correspondence to almost total neglect of military science, weaponry, and procurement. We abandoned lists of academic promotions and honors but found room to record the comings and goings of corporate vice presidents.

We prided ourselves on offering the best coverage of issues agitating the public—from elections to recessions, from shipwrecks to shoot-outs—without neglecting the quieter realms of Latin America or archaeology. We gloried in the knowledge that Americans looked to *The Times* to learn what *really happened* when terrorists struck the World Trade Center and when our soldiers were sent into battle against Iraq. But big-bang coverage was always the easy part. The hard thing was to remember in quieter times that journalism was a narrative art, connecting past to future, cause to consequence. Our job was to choose, to apply judgment to events, and to transform mere information into understanding. Facts don't inform. Reporters and editors do.

All this I understood at the start of my editorship. What dawned only gradually was the drag exerted by our amateurism. The best of us knew what we did not know; we prided ourselves on learning fast. But to protect the reader against the manipulations and prejudices of people making news required more than our customary skepticism. It required enough significant knowledge of medicine or law or statistics or sociology to frame shrewd questions, to select among sources, and to synthesize their instruction.

Contrary to the complaint that education and affluence had dulled our sensibilities, I soon found us struggling to overcome ignorance and mere opinion in vital areas. We were pathetically thin in talented writers and editors who truly understood such disparate subjects as health care, outer space, and the traffic in illegal drugs, or even such staples as polling and campaign financing. The days when savvy police reporters could be glibly converted into foreign correspondents or social analysts were over. Even this greatest of newspaper staffs lacked sufficient resources to realize my dream of turning every major article into a piece of incisive analysis. Yet in our corporate offices, the newsroom was usually seen as more of an expense than an asset. Our most talented writers were unfairly underpaid compared with corporate executives. And as profits slipped after the stock market crash of 1987, we came under great pressure to cut corners, skimp on staff, dilute our wares. There were tough days ahead.

The Noriega Fiasco:
What Went Wrong

By ROBERT PEAR
and WARREN V. LEWIS

REAGAN AND GORBACHEV BEGIN SUMMIT PARLEY IN THE KREMLIN; 'STRIKE SPARKS' ON RIGHTS ISSUE

CORDIALITY FADES

Soviet Leader Annoyed
President Even Raised
Religion, Migration

By STEVEN V. ROBERTS

Reporter's Notebook

Presidential Stroll: Chaos and Applause

By BILL KELLER

---

40 · NOT-ABE

AFTER ANOINTING ME AS HIS NEXT EXECUTIVE EDITOR, Punch held the last of several difficult conversations with Abe to arrange his retirement at year's end. And after equally protracted negotiations with Walter Mattson, the company's president, it was decided that Arthur Jr. would be named deputy publisher, reporting to both of them but assuming command of all the newspaper's executives. Arthur's advance toward the top also required delicate conversations with Punch's three sisters, some of whose children had their own ambitions in the family enterprise. So it was with understandable relief that Punch outlined the year-end package to the board of directors on Thursday, July 17, 1986, just as Abe, in a final display of executive passion, flew off to Communist China. He was rushing to demand the release of our correspondent, John Burns, who had motorcycled far afield without permission and was being held in a dismal prison awaiting trial. Punch observed that Abe's only chance of success was to offer himself as a hostage in Burns's place; not expecting that, he applied some typically quiet diplomacy instead, enlisting former Secretary of State Cyrus Vance, a member of our board, to solve the problem.

On his return, Abe soon wearied of life as a lame duck. He had Punch announce my appointment in September and wanted to be relieved as soon as the carpenters and painters could finish his new office among the columnists on the tenth floor. When I reported to the newsroom in mid-October, I asked to watch for a few days while Abe conducted the front-page meeting. He responded by leading me to the presiding chair, uttering a quick "good luck," and departing for the elevator. In front of an amused assembly of editors, Arthur Gelb had to show me how to take notes on the dozen or so stories that were being pitched by department heads for Page One display so that I could circle my favorites for a subsequent layout discussion.

Abe had left with only one request: that I hire his talented son, Andrew, who was serving as a correspondent for the Associated Press while waiting for his father to get out of his way at *The Times*. Even in our family enterprise, only the royal family itself could safely practice nepotism. Andy Rosenthal was a most valuable first recruit.

The newsroom greeted my arrival with relief and pity. There was relief that Abe Rosenthal's unsettling endgame had finally ended. Unscathed by the succession battles, I took command of a staff that clearly preferred the novelty of me to Abe's more familiar but bloodied heirs apparent. Yet I also heard clucks of pity. People whispered that I was a mere nine years from retirement, destined to be only a "transitional figure" in their lives. Some began at once to speculate about *my* successor.

The best-known *Times* editors, it is true, had all served double-digit terms. The legendary Carr Van Anda, whose curiosities hugely enlarged the paper's definition of news, reigned for twenty-one years, starting in 1904. Edwin James, the World War I adventurer and cane-wielding boulevardier, returned from Paris to preside over a rapidly expanding but fractious News Department for nineteen years, until 1951. He was followed by Turner Catledge, who in seventeen years gained control over the competing fiefs of Scotty Reston in Washington, Cyrus Sulzberger in Paris, and Lester Markel in the Sunday Department. Abe Rosenthal held sway for another seventeen. Nine years did seem a short time to make my mark, particularly since my years spanned the slow-motion passing of the Sulzberger family torch from father to son. Still, as I said reassuringly to the skeptics, I had the prospect of one year longer in office than Ronald Reagan, and he claimed to be making a revolution. Actually, I had no plan except to be not-Abe.

Abe Rosenthal left the newsroom with a reputation for brilliant, instinctive news judgment coupled with an intimidating, self-centered management style. Most of his values were admirable, and many of his tactics were therefore forgivable. He had had to struggle harder than many of us to get abroad and on his return had to fight all over again to establish his authority as an editor. His predecessors, Turner Catledge and Clifton Daniel, were too often content to critique the paper after it appeared; Abe commendably refused to be a chronic second-guesser and closely monitored the paper *before* it went to press. Abe also had to wage combat against the paper's ascendant budgeteers to obtain the staff and space needed to cover the news in profitless years. The trouble was that Abe displayed his angers and affections in ways that often terrorized subordinates and left him constantly wondering why he was not better loved. His innermost judgments of people depended not just on their value to *The Times* but on their regard for him and his ideas. His closest friends were his closest associates. His infatuations with people and causes were often transparent. He boasted of keeping the paper "straight," but his measuring rod was not.

I was chronically reluctant to be so clearly silhouetted. Although I had hurled opinions at the world every day for ten years, I finished the decade, as I began, ideologically ill defined and determined to stay that way. In a carefully crafted memo for my first day in the newsroom—October 14, 1986—I told the staff:

> From this moment on, as in my first 25 years at *The Times*, I have no editorial opinions, and I find the transition no more peculiar or difficult than that of a lawyer appointed to the bench. A passion for fairness dominates even our opinion pages, but partisanship and special pleading have no place in *The Times*'s newsroom. All else is welcome, most particularly good fun. . . .
>
> I bring only one commitment: that we remain a family newspaper in every sense. We are led by a family devoted to fearless reporting and peerless quality. We address a family of readers whose trust and devotion we must earn anew each morning. And though grown huge and multifaceted, we best serve those families by honoring our kinship to one another, in an exciting and creative but always collective enterprise.

In thus distinguishing myself from Abe's domineering personality, I had the luxury of his achievements. I could shed power and share command without really dissipating much of the authority he had struggled to amass. To display my confidence, I parachuted onto the third floor alone, without a retinue of handpicked staff. I made myself widely accessible and gathered my own intelligence. I asked indiscreet questions, hoping to trade candor for trust. Eyes popped when I dropped into the Sports Department, which had not seen an executive editor in many moons. Tongues wagged for weeks after I appeared at a Metro reporter's rooftop beer party to get better acquainted and pick up revealing gossip. I moved out of the cavernous conference room that executive editors had always made their office, keeping a smaller space for myself and creating a place for others to meet without me. In free moments, I strolled the aisles of the newsroom, hoping to overcome reporters' obvious reluctance to just chat with power. Fortunately, in that October of 1986, I could bubble with genuine excitement about the triumphs of the New York Mets, which must have helped to offset my unfair reputation as a sober intellectual.

It was hard, however, to shed the executive editor's imperial garb. When I told the department heads in my first meeting to prepare to give out their own merit raises, they didn't really believe me; nor did they entirely welcome the responsibility of also turning down requests for raises. I asked them for memos that defined their missions and deployments of staff, with estimates of how they would adjust to a budget increase—or decrease—of 10 to 20 percent. Instead of welcoming this invitation to discuss significant change, many new colleagues became alarmed and sadly defensive of the status quo. No matter how tender my tone, my question marks were often misheard as exclamation points. "Why do we do that?" produced a careening echo down the chain of command that "Max wants" to do something else.

I could never recognize myself in the puissant figure that others saw as they fell silent at my approach or hung upon my every nonchalant word. As a playing manager in Washington and on the editorial board, I had shared the vulnerability of other writers even while functioning as their leader. Now there was no way to preserve that camaraderie. I soon learned that to be both fair and demanding, I had to keep some distance after all. In ways I never anticipated, life as a leader became unavoidably lonely.

Eager to avoid major mistakes, I spent many days drawing elaborate organization charts to see how the managing editor, Arthur Gelb, and I and a few assistant managing editors could relate to twenty distinct departments and sections. Some departments commanded large armies of reporters, others were staffed mostly by editors who relied on freelance writers. Some had nightly deadlines; some looked mainly weeks ahead. Each department faced different competitors and had different definitions of success. I thought it had been presumptuous for Abe Rosenthal to centralize authority over this vast enterprise and staff of 1,000. Creativity had to flow up as well as down. I was going to be deliberative and methodical. I was going to take my time shaping my team. I was going to hang back and think.

In less than a fortnight, that bubble burst and my entire oligarchy unraveled. Bill Kovach, the Washington editor, quit to begin an ultimately unhappy stint as editor of *The Atlanta Constitution*, and with my encouragement, John Vinocur, the Metropolitan editor, was named editor of the *International Herald Tribune*, a Paris enterprise jointly owned by *The Times* and *The Washington Post*. Both Kovach and Vinocur had hoped to succeed Abe Rosenthal and were doubly disappointed not to be immediately summoned to my side as assistant managing editors. I barely knew the plausible candidates who might replace them but could not afford much delay in filling such central positions. The now headless Washington bureau was panting to keep up with the Iran-Contra scandal; I was hearing daily warnings, inside and outside the paper, that I risked another Watergate embarrassment if I did not immediately hire Seymour Hersh and other investigative hotshots and fervently devote myself to the pursuit of this one story.

I was most immediately charmed by Craig Whitney's offer to accept demotion, from assistant managing editor for administration, to replace Kovach in Washington. He had been a first-class correspondent in Vietnam, Russia, and Germany and an effective foreign editor. Though he lacked experience in domestic politics, he would have as his chief Washington correspondent the fervently political R. W. (Johnny) Apple, Jr. Abe had wearied of the pomposity and gluttony that now defined Apple, once one of his prized recruits. But I had worked closely with Johnny for many years and welcomed the challenge of reigniting his career.

A further attraction of Whitney's offer was that it made way for several other constructive shifts. Warren Hoge seemed especially well suited to be our administrative chief, to oversee recruiting and personnel management, and to monitor Jim Terrill, the "alien" I brought in from our corporate staff to be our business manager. That in turn let me bring Joe Lelyveld out of virtual exile in London to be the next foreign editor. I wanted him to run international news without the customary close involvement of the executive editor, and I wanted to place him among the candidates to succeed Arthur Gelb as managing editor in two or three years. That done, I flew to Washington to persuade an obviously hurt, passed-over Howell Raines, Kovach's deputy, to broaden himself by succeeding Lelyveld in London. In the tradition of many talented southerners like Turner Catledge, Clifton Daniel, Tom Wicker, Claude Sitton, Gene Roberts, and Bill Kovach, Raines had risen rapidly on the strength of his vivid prose and political savvy. But with the notable exception of Daniel, all these veterans of America's racial wars lacked experience overseas. When Raines finally yielded to my well-meant pressure, I set about searching for a new Metro editor and settled on John Darnton, Hoge's deputy on the Foreign Desk. When first dealt, the cards of a fresh deck feel deceptively smooth. Not all these cards, however, played well.

Nor even then was I able to stop shuffling. All my appointees were white men, and I felt a strong obligation to advance more women and minority staffers. I saw an opportunity in the expansion of our National Edition, but it, too, required more sleight of hand than I anticipated. Instead of shipping papers all around the country from New York, *The Times* was moving to print its National Edition on rented presses at eight remote sites equipped to receive satellite transmissions of pages composed in New York. I thought the National Edition had enormous potential for growth and needed its own senior manager. Dave Jones, our national editor, was the perfect choice and most eager to move on. He had been trapped on the national desk for seventeen years because Abe refused either to promote or disappoint Jones's deputy, Paul Delaney, the man I had hired years earlier as *The Times*'s first black reporter in Washington. Abe warned me that if Jones were moved, I would have to make Paul national editor or risk an explosive backlash from black members of the staff, who had only recently and reluctantly settled a discrimination suit against *The Times*. Jones, too, counseled against promoting Delaney; he said Paul was good at organizing coverage of spot news but less effective in discerning the social and economic trends that I wanted to feature in our national pages. Having brought Paul to *The Times*, I thought I had credential enough to steer him in a new direction. I was deeply committed to the advancement of minorities, but I had seen that cause betrayed by too many merely sentimental decisions. I urged Delaney to try life as a foreign correspondent in Spain, and off he went with my gratitude and promise to keep him involved in our efforts to recruit and advance black journalists. It was only my first tense taste of the racial politics that had become an unavoidable part of newspaper life.

After passing up Paul, I was especially determined to give an encouraging signal to women and chose Soma Golden to be national editor. Soma had left my editorial board to develop and edit a lively Sunday Business section. With Carolyn Lee in Photos and Nancy Newhouse in Style, she became the third woman to lead a department and the first to head a major news desk (not counting Sports). But the progress of women only emphasized our lagging effort with blacks. For the moment, there simply were no suitable black or, indeed, Hispanic candidates for promotion.

There was, however, yet another "minority" in a state of sore neglect. Though not definable by sex or ethnicity, our copy editors as a class were virtually shut out of top management jobs. They labored at night and anonymously, without the glamour showered on reporters. They guaranteed the quality and timely production of our news report, yet they were uniformly presumed too narrow to rise above the middle ranks. To break that barrier, I gave an instant promotion to our most brilliant and successful copy editor, Al Siegal, from head of the News Desk to assistant managing editor, a name-on-the-masthead position. Al was the newsroom's Pooh-Bah, not only because of his great girth but for his recruiting, testing, and supervision of copy editors; his mastery of typography and computer technology; his guardianship of our writing style; and his management of makeup and production, which entailed the pursuit of diplomatic relations and complex written treaties with the advertising, circulation, and production departments. He was closer than any of us to being indispensable, yet he had left himself without fully trained deputies in most of his realms. Quite a few careers for editors could be envisioned in his considerable wake. Al became an enthusiastic ally in improving the appearance and readability of *The Times* and he soon nominated my next major appointment, Tom Bodkin, to be our design director and head of the art department.

In a mere dozen weeks, I had moved, replaced, and advanced more than a dozen top editors and shaken up four of the five major news desks—Foreign, National, Metro, and Washington. Although I was careful to brief Punch and Arthur Jr. on all major personnel shifts, it must have seemed to them as if a new conductor had not bothered to play a single concert before he changed the leading players in his string, brass, woodwind, and percussion sections. I thought, therefore, that it was my unavoidable haste that inspired Punch to blow a cautionary whistle one morning early in 1987 when he noticed all the jump lines on Page One transformed from boldface type to italics. Overnight, they came to read *Continued on Page 28, Column 1,* instead of **Continued on Page 28, Col-**

umn 1. The publisher liked the change, he said, but he did not like to be surprised by change. I thought at first that this was only a metaphorical warning; I couldn't believe that I had greater license to replace my top editors than to replace a small element of type. But no, the publisher of *The Times*, like its readers, felt most possessive about the appearance of his paper. I could think of our talented staff as an orchestra over which I wielded awesome authority. But I had to learn that the paper itself was more like a supermarket, exactingly arrayed so as never to disorient the customer.

41 · HEADLINES AND HEMLINES

THE *TIMES* IS A GIANT MART STOCKED WITH INFORMAtion—more than 100,000 words on weekdays, half a million Sundays. The goods should be arrayed in well-marked sections and navigable aisles that allow the customers to wander efficiently. The shoppers come knowing what they want and where to find it, but they also delight in brief diversions. Each pursues a different route, keeps to a different schedule, and departs with a different load. The ideal newspaper, like the ideal supermarket, combines order with dazzle, the comfort of familiarity with the pleasure of surprise.

Thus conceived, a newspaper serves contradictory impulses. It should continually enrich its wares to prolong the reader's passage. But it needs navigational aids to speed that passage, to help customers choose with confidence and ignore without regret. It must serve both skimmers and diggers. It must not solve its back-room problems out front, at the consumer's expense.

These objectives have obvious commercial value. A more congenial *Times* could hold or regain the many readers who admired its heft but found it too gray and too daunting. I implored our business department to mount aggressive promotions to teach people *how* to read *The Times*—where to find what and when. Readers needed encouragement to pursue their individual tastes and deserved relief from guilt when they left a lot unread. We did finally produce some house ads explaining the layout of the paper and some television commercials echoing Frank Sinatra—"I Read It My Way." But our marketers preferred their own ideas for sales slogans. And the quality of our news concerned me even more than its display.

News is anything new, anything you didn't know if knowing it matters. It may matter to your well-being, awareness, or education, or it may be entertaining or diverting. Fear and anxiety are the most persistent stimulants of news—fears of war, crime, and sickness will always attract a crowd. News by definition, therefore, is the unusual and unaccustomed—what you rush to tell your neighbor. A plane has crashed. A bank was robbed. A politician died. But news is also something that is only quietly happening—what you reflect upon over dinner: people eating out more, having fewer kids, living longer. One of the most harmful habits of journalists has been to venerate discrete events as "hard news" and to denigrate the news of long-term trends as "soft." Although *The Times* favored government news more than police news, it tended to draw the same false distinctions between "hard" and "soft" and was not easily cured of the habit.

Especially over the din of television, it was difficult for many of my colleagues to realize that there was no such thing as "the news" of the day; there was only "our news" as we chose to define it or, more precisely, as we thought our readers defined their needs and interests. As I grew comfortable in the editor's chair, I pressed the departments to nominate less conventional news as worthy of Page One and to make certain that all our articles quickly explained their relevance to a busy reader's life. But defining our own firm standard of news proved an elusive goal.

We knew pitifully little about our readers and their reading habits. Like most journalists, we so feared the taint of commerce that we often prided ourselves on this ignorance. We did not just give people "what they want," we would sneer. We aimed to tell them "what as citizens they need to know, whether or not they want to know it." But how did we know what they needed to know?

Our reader surveys were designed mostly to help sell advertising and were disdained, for good reason, by the News Department. For our alleged benefit, the surveys asked such questions as "Do you read at least one article on Page One?" Yes, 90 percent. "Which news is most important to you?" Foreign, 35 percent; National, 50 percent; Local, 80 percent. Well, then, should we print fewer movie reviews because they draw only 10 percent of the readers? Heavens no, replied the advertising staff. And that was that. The faddish "focus groups" that we were invited to watch through one-way glass were even less helpful. Half their blather came from people who never read *The Times*, although they qualified for coffee mugs by holding it in high regard. Those who did read it were asked such broad questions that their true interests were indiscernible.

But lo, one morning at the end of my first year as editor, a remarkable gift from our marketing crew fell into my arms, like manna. Having heard of my desire to spy on the reading habits of unsuspecting readers, they had devised an experiment that amounted to the next best thing. They brought me more than a hundred large manila envelopes, each labeled with the sex, occupation, income, and address of a confirmed but un-named reader and containing a marked-up copy of *The Times* of September 21, 1987. These randomly chosen readers had been approached on the morning after, handed a red crayon, and told to mark the spot at which they had begun their reading of each section and to circle the precise por-tions of articles, headlines, graphics, and photographs that they had taken in. After examining only a few of these revealing envelopes, I knew that we faced a cognitive crisis: Almost none of our readers read the paper the way we did, or the way we thought *they* did.

No two readers read the paper in the same way. Each followed his or her own trail and strategy. Most scanned the front page and then pursued one or more special interests—a few stock quotes, perhaps, or the obituary headlines, a movie review, an Op-Ed column, the Crossword puzzle. A fair number of readers skipped the outside pages altogether and began inside, with the culture report or sports news or stock tables, and thumbed quickly forward or backward from there.

Hardly any reader even looked at more than half the articles on Page One. Most read the front-page portions of only one or two dispatches. The readers' starting point on Page One was not usually our designated "lead story" at the top of Column Six, which that day offered the customary and cramped one-column headline:

SENATE COMMITTEE
THREATENS DELAY
OF NEW ARMS PACT

Many more eyes landed first on one of the multicolumn headlines at the middle and bottom of the page or on one of three large photographs and their captions.

Most readers ignored invitations to "continue" an article past Page One.
They simply stopped reading where we interrupted the story, in midsentence, even midword. At most, a reader might follow only a single article
to its "jump" portion inside.

Only a few readers looked inside all four sections of the paper. A large number skipped even the front pages of some sections.

*Readers thumbing through the paper stopped primarily for eye-catching ele-
ments like photos, maps, graphics, and headlines.* Only if seized by one of these
distinctive elements might they then glance at a related article.

Collateral interviews with the crayon brigade revealed that readers
spent anywhere from ten minutes to an hour with *The Times;* the average
was thirty-seven minutes. Even with a full hour, someone able to read at a
breakneck pace of 400 words (a page in this book) per minute and willing
to skip all the advertising and small-type sports and financial tables would
be able to consume less than a quarter of the more than 100,000 words in
the normal weekday paper. At a more typical speed, and with time out for
a sip of coffee and a glance at a few photographs, thirty-seven minutes
with *The Times* would let a person read through only 8 or 9 of the 135
major articles presented each day. Ten minutes would barely get you
through the prose on Page One, although, as Walter Cronkite was fond of
observing, that was still more efficient than watching TV; he would need
his entire broadcast of twenty-two minutes to read our front page aloud.

Most startling of all was the discovery that none of us came remotely
close to correctly guessing which of the articles in our front-page mix of
local, national, and foreign stories was the most thoroughly read by the
largest proportion of readers that day. Besides the lead about the Antibal-
listic Missile Treaty, the top of the page featured a dramatic photo of Lech
Wałesa demanding free trade unions in Poland, a report that President
Reagan opposed a law banning discrimination against AIDS sufferers, and
a most unusual photo of Pope John Paul II "emerging from a tepee in a
fringed vestment before saying mass for 4,000 Indians" in northern
Canada. The middle of the page carried an analysis of the effect of the
pope's orthodoxies on American Catholics and the news that the United
States would probably raze and rebuild its heavily bugged new Moscow
embassy. At the bottom were reports that Nicaragua would let the opposition's paper reopen without censorship, that New York City had the nation's worst record for building-site accidents, and that TRAPPED AT THAI
CAMPS, CAMBODIANS DESPAIR.

Incredibly, crayon after crayon circled that dull headline in the bot-
tom-left corner of the page and the dispatch beneath it, recounting "that
Cambodia's human misery has entered a new phase."

It was mainly from a sense of duty that we had put that story on Page One. Not one of us would have predicted such universal interest. Even more surprising was the now obvious explanation for that interest: the crayons that encircled the entire story, clear through its continuation inside the paper, also drew the number 1 across the accompanying photograph, meaning readers were first attracted by the pathetic sight of a Cambodian boy and girl framed by a dark doorway and a caption reporting that their father hanged himself after despairing of ever being released from a refugee camp. It was that haunting photo that hooked the readers; it was the relatively dry story that "accompanied" the picture. What a dramatic demonstration of the role of newspapers in the era of television! Not only were pictures important, but they could be preeminent. Accounts of human cruelty fascinated readers, even if they concerned alien peoples in distant lands.

Almost as compelling was a merely explanatory article that we had briefly flagged on Page One as appearing on Page B14. It contrasted the past opinions of Judge Robert Bork with his recent testimony at hearings to consider his nomination for the Supreme Court. The televised inquisition into Judge Bork's philosophy, far from exhausting public interest in the drama, had greatly enlarged the audience for our story and put a premium on the kind of analysis that is rarely available on the screen.

Did we properly absorb these lessons? Some immediately and some over the years. But we have not fully absorbed them yet.

I realized at once that newspaper photos should not so much "illustrate" the words of an article as represent an event or the mood surrounding it in their own visual vocabulary. Thanks to our gifted photographers, and Carolyn Lee, Mark Bussell, and Nancy Lee, our (unrelated) photo editors and Design Director Tom Bodkin, we gave increasing prominence—and precious space—to striking images. We forbade the use of black borders around photographs, which had become a crutch for weak images, and the random splaying of multiple photos. "When it comes to pictures," I lectured, "let the eye and the heart have at least equal voice with the head." And the response was encouraging. Richard Avedon wrote: "Something amazing has happened at *The Times*. In the past you published pictures, now you're publishing photographs. Hardly a day passes without my clipping photographs from the paper." In time the photos grew so large that I accused Bussell of imperialism. "You call it imperialism," he replied. "I call it Manifest Destiny."

Siegal and Bodkin also responded astutely to make *The Times* more "user friendly." Some of our innovations sat so comfortably that it seems quaint now to think of them as new. Since many readers turned pages randomly and even backward, we labeled each page to identify its location in International, National, Metro, Sports. Since readers' eyes fell first on larger type, we broke up gray columns of prose with magazine-style blurbs that expressed some essential aspect of each tale. Since readers looked at photos and their captions before they read the stories, we learned to write captions that moved beyond identifying the pictured subject to an explanation of the photo's relevance to the news. We highlighted the names of books, plays, and films under review by our critics. We divided the sports pages into segments for each major sport. While awaiting new printing plants that would let us create separate sections for Sports and the Arts, we created faux "front pages" for them, and also for National News, inside the paper.

To spare the busy reader the shock of finding a brief Page One element "continued" in a page-long mass of type on the inside, we labeled our long narratives "A Special Report," hoping to train readers to recognize that signal as meaning "Save this for when you have the time." And we divided such long articles into clearly marked chapters so that writers would organize their material more logically and let readers skip to the subheadings of greatest interest. We applied our desire to facilitate scanning even to the little weather ear atop Page One by boldfacing the words "Today," "Tonight," "Tomorrow," and "Yesterday." And in imitation of *The Wall Street Journal*, we created a Company Index that identified and located the corporations mentioned in that day's news.

Since computer graphics could often portray events more succinctly and vividly than either words or photos, I skimmed the budgets of other departments to let Richard Meislin quickly build a staff of artist-reporters, a new journalistic breed. Their clear renderings of why Interstate 880 collapsed while the skyscrapers just swayed in the San Francisco earthquake of 1989 marked the day, as I put it to them, that graphics came of age at *The Times*. It was the day when the art of conveying pictorial information in a hurry took its place beside newspaper writing and photography. They produced amazing work, day after day, most notably when they turned New York inside out to locate the original architectural drawings that made possible unique front-page illustrations of the damage done by the bomb at the World Trade Center in 1993.

All our readers obviously knew about that explosion before *The Times* reached them. In the modern age, we were no longer first with big news of disasters, wars, and elections. We were often obliged to satisfy curiosities aroused by others, to add perspective to the headlines of the day. Yet paradoxically, the more that radio and television usurped our function of being first with the news, the greater the public's desire to have it explained, investigated, and amplified as only we could. Cameras attended presidential speeches and Pentagon briefings and could convey even the "full text" of them. They could transport people to distant battles and political uprisings, floods, quakes, and other convulsions. But as we all know from personal habit, the ball games or storms that we experience are the ones we most want to read about analytically and relive reflectively.

Instead of supplanting newspapers, cameras and other instant delivery systems actually whet the appetite for newspapers. Even the best, however, have been slow to embrace their new function. Print journalists still yearn for the fun of shouting out bulletins and do not easily find the same glamour in dissecting events and exploring their meaning. We used to "leg" a story. Now we must leg and think at the same time. Many of us instinctively understood this change of function and found it congenial to our styles of reporting. But as editor I had to articulate our changed mission and transform the impulses of a huge organization. If we remained enthralled with the traditional news of violent crime and airplane crashes, presidential journeys and politicians' speeches, we would not only fail our readers but lose them to the faster media. Our new function was to add unique value to widely available information. As much as news, we sold judgment and expertise. And that had far-reaching implications for every facet of newspapering.

Judgment and expertise are expensive commodities. They require a staff drawn from an elite talent pool plus training and experience and time for research and reflection. Above all they require a willingness to break with convention.

There was much uneasiness in the room at a Page One conference in January 1987 when I wondered aloud whether President Reagan's much-heralded State of the Union address had really delivered the most significant news of that day. We and others had ballyhooed the event, writing reams about his struggle to regain the public's trust after the Iran-Contra mess. Now "the Great Communicator" was appearing on the Capitol Hill stage and on all major networks. Tens of millions would hear him declare that "serious mistakes were made" in his White House and how he regretted his failure to have Iran arrange the release of American hostages in Lebanon. But faithful to my own experience, I kept bringing the discussion back to the Moscow bureau's report of a most surprising speech by Mikhail Gorbachev. Emboldened by my special knowledge of Soviet rhetoric, I sensed a historic shift in the making. The Soviet leader was deploring "stagnation" in his Communist party and demanding secret ballots to choose among truly competing candidates. I insisted that Gorbachev trumped Reagan for that night's "lead." And while we actually gave the two speeches almost equal billing on Page One, for those who understood our sign language, and especially my colleagues, I was challenging conventional judgment. *The Times* had to seek its own unique understanding of events and resist the superficial excitements generated by others.

A few weeks later came a moment that symbolized our obligation to be alert to the unadvertised tides in human affairs. Just days before, I had made room on the front page for an account of changing tastes in popular music: FOR COUNTRY MUSIC, A NEW SOUND ENDS 5 YEARS' STAGNATION. Now I thought I detected an even bigger change, in women's fashions. Our Style Department responded with an article mercifully free of the customary fluff in fashion writing. It focused on the cultural and economic implications of observable taste and for the first time in many years put Bernadine Morris, our lead fashion reporter, on Page One:

Women Are Stealing a March on Short Skirts

Although nobody has used the word, the miniskirt is definitely back. For the first time since the 1960s, women who follow fashion are shortening their skirts, or rolling them up at the waist to see how they look and feel with more leg showing.

In a rare display of unanimity, designers in the world's leading fashion centers here and in Europe focused on short skirts in their recent showings of collections for fall. Most of them, deciding to forget about "choices" and "options"—catchwords for the last few years—showed hemlines that bared the knee in most cases and frequently half the thigh as well.

No one had announced this news or published a poll about the public's response. We were offering our cumulative, reportorial judgment that after a decade of fashion anarchy, women were heeding the designers' summons to a display of legs. The alteration orders in New York department stores were running at record levels; the next wave of Hollywood films was showing skirts well above the knee. Women faced a choice between resisting fashion or starting to clear out their closets. Even for a paper that kept its eyes fixed on arms control, were not hemlines significant news?

For months there was much sneering about my lack of seriousness, my weakness for "soft" news. The commentators tracking my direction of *The Times* mocked my apparent desire to compete with *Vogue* and *Women's Wear Daily*. Instead of grasping my point about the news value of important and interesting trends, they suspected me of chasing younger readers with trivia. And for a time, the critics slowed me down. A full month passed before I dared to give front-page display to Einstein's love letters and to a large picture of Rita Hayworth famously kneeling in her negligee, to advertise her obituary inside. It took another year before we were all comfortable with a less predictable Page One and no longer startled anyone with headlines like WOMEN: OUT OF THE HOUSE BUT NOT OUT OF THE KITCHEN and NEXT OFFICE REVOLUTION: "VOICE MAIL."

My redefinition of news also found expression in many subtle changes of the paper's design—at a pace that addicted readers, starting with Punch, would not find unsettling. One of the most satisfying was the gradual elimination, one section at a time, of the distracting vertical lines that used to appear between all columns of type. Rules now appear only *between* articles, separating one from another and reducing clutter. But I failed to reach the promised land in which there would be no more annoying "jumps" from Page One and other section fronts to inside pages. We did it at the Book Review and for all but one article in the Magazine. And we began to use photographs, graphics, and tiny articles as billboards for articles found "inside." My ideal newspaper, however, would use its section fronts as posters containing elegant summaries of the most important stories with signposts pointing to the details and related articles. That idea struck Punch and most colleagues as too radical, but the multiplication of sections has only made the problem worse.

Still, near the end of my run as editor, we gave those busy crayon-wielding readers the ultimate gift of legibility: we took a 14 percent loss in wordage to enlarge the size of *The Times*'s body type and the white space between lines. As intended, hardly anyone noticed. After all these changes, conceptual and typographical, large and small, my greatest satisfaction was to hear the frequent comment that *The Times* had become *more readable— but I'm not sure why!*

The New York Times

JOYOUS EAST GERMANS POUR THROUGH WALL; PARTY PLEDGES FREEDOMS, AND CITY EXULTS

42 · LOVES LOST AND FOUND

MEANWHILE, AS REPORTERS USED TO WRITE WHEN leaping narrative gaps, the private me was not nearly so cool and contained as the editorial I. Besides grieving during Tobi's long decline, I had also pined for release. And, guiltly, I had dreamed of another chance at love. A widower in the prime of life, I fantasized about the delights awaiting an eligible New York bachelor. Would I favor socialites on Park Avenue or poets in Greenwich Village? Worldly or domestic? My age or younger? Did I have the energy to manage a career and courtships? Did I have the patience to reveal myself to a succession of strangers? With remarkable speed and audacity, several women, some known to me, some not, presented themselves. Some apologized for the unseemly haste but said they knew from experience that in just a few months I would be "taken." I marveled at these predictions, not realizing that I already was.

How does a boss become involved with a colleague? Neither of us knows precisely when it happened.

I knew Joyce Purnick's name from her savvy political reporting before she came to *The Times*. But we had met only once, at an editorial board meeting with a New York schools chancellor at which I fell asleep. When I became executive editor, Joyce was our City Hall bureau chief, and I sought her views, among many others, about the Metro operation. She returned from a vacation in London equally eager to meet the new editor, whose welcoming memo she had admired from afar. She flung her coat, a mink from her father's workshop, across a chair and addressed me with notable ease and candor, qualities that also distinguished her writing. But months passed before we talked again, at the Inner Circle gala at which New York politicians and journalists roast and flatter one another. Tobi was close to death, and this was my only evening out in a very long time. When asked to approve the seating arrangements, which put Joyce and me at a table with three couples, I casually remarked that she was my designated date for the evening. I don't think I intended her to read anything into that locution, but she did. She also took note of the progressive warmth of notes I sent complimenting her work. If these were pointed messages, I was not consciously devious. I wrote many encouraging memos in those early months to connect with our writers, and I thought it a safe form of correspondence. At that Inner Circle dinner, Joyce and I chatted routinely as colleagues, but I remember thinking that she was more attentive to her notebook jottings for an article about the affair than to any of my conversation.

She was taking notes again when we next met at a similar bash, the Gridiron Dinner in Washington. Without my knowledge, Joyce had been assigned to compare the two political events and had wangled a rare ticket. I was alone now, several weeks after Tobi's funeral, and felt an unmistakable spark of pleasure at her unexpected appearance. I made sure after the long and tedious show that we landed at the same postdinner cocktail party, and we conversed in the center of a dense crowd for several hours. Even then, however, I never imagined that I was drifting into a relationship with a member of my staff. Neither then nor in the wondrous weeks that followed did I ever stop to consider that Joyce, lacking the benefit of rank, was venturing into even deeper water.

Smart, sensitive, and attractive, Joyce had reached the age of forty without finding a mate and without the fulfillment of children. Her most prized possessions were the career she had painstakingly fashioned and her reputation for fierce integrity. She kept nourishing her hopes for a chance to love and to be loved, but did she imagine a widower sixteen years her senior and the boss of her bosses? Not even Mary Tyler Moore's Mary Richards, the idol of her youth, ever tossed the dice with such daring.

The sparks between us struck tinder one day in April when Joyce was covering the resignation of Bess Myerson, New York's commissioner of consumer affairs. A former Miss America, Myerson had been Ed Koch's invaluable prop when he first ran for mayor of New York and needed to ward off suspicions of homosexuality. Koch was obviously pained to have to force her off his team. But Myerson, who never made good use of her intelligence and statuesque beauty, had carelessly done a kindness for a judge who was at that moment presiding over a divorce proceeding involving her imprisoned, mob-connected lover. So the Metro Desk asked Joyce for a "news analysis" to go with her front-page report, a separation of news and explication that I regarded as burdensome to the reader. Merge the two articles, I insisted at our front-page meeting, an order that caused Joyce to fume noisily that she wished editors would not change their minds so close to deadline. I sought her out to explain my reasoning and, guessing at the cause of her anger, apologized for disrupting her dinner plans. As she told me months later, she had no such plans, and once again thought she was hearing a strangely personal message from her boss. Even stranger, therefore, was the call she received in the City Hall pressroom the next morning. I thanked her for the deft and hurried merger of her two articles and again apologized for disrupting her evening plans. Testing her antennae, she said:

"It seems to me, Max Frankel, you owe me a dinner."

"I accept."

"You do? When?"

"How about tonight?"

She called time out to catch her breath, then called back to nominate a place, halfway between *The Times* and her apartment in Brooklyn Heights. I let my secretary make the reservation, still perhaps regarding it as a quasi-professional encounter. But I announced at the start of dinner that it was not professional. That meal never appeared on my expense account.

Joyce and I both knew the next morning that our lives had taken a dramatic turn. We spent the next weekend together, and more time, still thinking that we were leaving ourselves a way out. We thought of many reasons, beyond the office complications, to hesitate and draw back. I was too raw a widower, perhaps too vulnerable for Joyce's enveloping warmth. My children might understand their father's momentary needs, but they would not soon appreciate his rush into another lasting relationship. Moreover, at fifty-seven, I was selfishly unwilling to endure another round of child rearing, whereas Joyce, at forty-one, might still have a chance at motherhood with someone else. We tried to pause, and at Joyce's suggestion I even attempted a few other dates. But the attraction to her was over-powering, so we embarked on a secret affair that was really an unspoken engagement, an act of uncharacteristic daring for both of us.

Like me, Joyce normally respected all the conventional values of a striving New York Jewish family. Her father, Jack, then still a vigorous and handsome man at eighty-four, was brought to America as a child, had his unpronounceable Russian name subsumed in Purnick, and slowly made that name a sign of quality in his fur market salon. He fathered two sons in a disastrous marriage, then found happiness in a second to Charlotte, a tall and lovely redhead who had modeled his coats and swum in the World's Fair water ballet. They reared Joyce in two strong streams of love, that of a father for his only daughter and of a mother for her firstborn. Joyce was clever, pretty, ambitious, and persevering, an honor student and newspaper editor at Jamaica High and again at Barnard. She was a city girl, unpretentious but never reticent about asserting her own conclusions about things. Her outstanding quality, which seemed to scare some men, was a rigorous honesty in word and deed. She struggled her way up from television lister to political reporter at the *New York Post* but quit on principle with no job in sight when Rupert Murdoch opened the *Post's* news columns to partisan propaganda. She finally reached *The Times* in 1979 but had to prove herself yet again in the tough Rosenthal years. Her values and her spunk appealed to strong men, like Ed Koch, who enjoyed sparring with her at City Hall, but most of the strong men in her path were not suitable or available for romance. I was.

We sneaked about like giddy adolescents, hoping to avoid discovery in crowded museums, distant parks, darkened theaters, and remote diners of the Bronx and Brooklyn. We shared our secret early on with David, Margot, and Jon, and then with Arthur Gelb, who bathed us in a supportive enthusiasm. We were spotted here and there by colleagues but, most remarkably, they respected our privacy. Punch responded to my bashful confession with a quick hug and genuine joy at my happiness. Arthur Jr. seemed at first to be silently disapproving.

By coincidence, Joyce had contracted months earlier for a share in a beach house just minutes from mine on Fire Island, so we revealed ourselves all summer to mutual friends, half expecting city tongues to begin to wag. We drove off to the beach Friday evenings after Joyce jumped into the car a few discreet blocks from the office. In the fall, when we wearied of the pretense and thought some gossip would soon reach print, I leaked our news to Liz Smith, who thrilled over our romance in her column in *New York Newsday*, *The Times's* formidable city rival. It was a unique example of the benefits of competition.

Our engagement was announced in *The Times* in September 1988, by a single paragraph—"Joyce Purnick to Marry"—a coyness that amused many. We were married at the small but elegant Lotos Club on December 11 by Rabbi Alexander Schindler, then head of Reform Jewry and a friend since the early 1970s. My kids' former piano teacher, Nat Rand, brought a dance band that carefully and uniquely permitted conversation over lunch among our seventy-five relatives, friends, and colleagues. But in most respects I again slammed the gates on my past, not so much regretting or denying it as fleeing with the abandon of a refugee and yet again hurling myself at the future.

Tobi's mother so resented the speed of my new love affair that she could not accept Joyce for many years. With Joyce's generous help, I made certain not to let this breach estrange Mom Paul from her grandchildren, but I was glad to be distanced from her. I only regretted losing touch with her husband, Hal Daddy, a pliable but sweet man whom I encountered thereafter only at funerals, and finally at his.

My mother, in glorious contrast, quickly accepted Joyce and overcame her unexpressed doubt that any woman was ever truly deserving of her son. Mom never wholly sympathized with wives who pursued their own careers, but she soon pronounced Joyce *haimish*—the highest possible accolade, meaning cozy, warm, and, above all, unspoiled. More than that, she recognized herself in Joyce's loving nature, in her common sense and worldly spunk, a combination that she had obviously made her son's ideal of womanhood.

Punch resolved the only remaining awkwardness in his newsroom's most conspicuous romance. He appointed Joyce to the conveniently vacant job of writing about New York for the editorial page, the only page, besides Op-Ed, which did not report to me.

When I first joined *The Times*, only one pair of foreign correspondents, Ray Daniell and Tania Long, were known to me as a couple. The company's true feelings, however, were expressed in its relentless refusal to let Flora Lewis, a first-rate foreign correspondent, come on staff so long as her husband, Sydney Gruson, was also writing from abroad. With the coupling of more and more reporters working for rival papers in the 1980s, Abe Rosenthal reluctantly employed spouses like Marlise Simons (wife of Alan Riding) and Felicity Barringer (wife of Philip Taubman) as "contract writers" to sever their ties to *The Washington Post*. It was not until my term as editor that we learned to accommodate equally talented husbands and wives in the same bureau.

Even though Joyce and I had pretty well managed not to let our relationship interfere with work, the potential difficulties went well beyond the risks of undesirable competition, collusion, or favoritism. Joyce, a widely admired colleague with a healthy disdain for executives, suddenly found herself excluded from disrespectful gossip or targeted as a conduit for complaints. Although a fair number of couples now worked in the News Department, and although Punch's son and nieces and nephews were scattered throughout the company, my exalted status created an unmistakable awkwardness that argued for our separation.

Joyce quickly learned the craft of editorial writing and every autumn heroically interviewed hundreds of boring candidates for local political office to select those *The Times* would endorse. But she did not enjoy the editorial board debates among policy wonks and missed the camaraderie of the newsroom. Joyce spent more than five years writing editorials out of love—for me. Only after I retired did she return to the third floor, where she wrote a powerful, often moving column on New York affairs and eventually became the first woman to serve as *The Times*'s Metropolitan editor.

Happy though we were to have found each other, we also endured a succession of personal traumas. The least of them turned out to be my abandoning a beloved but now absurdly outsized house in Riverdale. Joyce spent a year gently coaxing me to consider relocation and another year looking for a midtown apartment that might satisfy my desire for generous space. We should have known we'd finally find the right place not through the many agents we engaged but in the ads in *The Times*'s Magazine. It was a triplex on West Sixty-seventh Street, just off Central Park, with access to a rooftop that Joyce turned into a glorious garden.

But moving was the least of our burdens. Throughout that year of relocation, Pop grew progressively weaker and temperamental, isolating Mom from their few remaining friends and treating her to tantrums that finally forced her to violate a lifelong resolve not to burden her son with appeals for help. Pop just wasted away and finally died as we were closing on the new apartment, in October 1990. He had borne the cruelties of Hitler and Stalin and the worst indignities of the twentieth century with stoic dignity for all but the last two of his eighty-eight years.

Twenty months later, Mom was felled by a stroke that left her with the worst possible combination: a mostly clear mind and a crippled body. A helpless right leg and arm sentenced this proudly self-reliant woman to life in a wheelchair. We kept her in her home with round-the-clock care, which, amazingly, she could afford from her own resources after a lifetime's frugality. But weekly visits and periodic outings only deepened my frustration at my inability to give Mom a happier endgame. Her conversation dwindled to only two questions: *What's new?* and *What will be?* The former meant *I have no interests anymore; tell me anything to relieve the boredom.* The latter meant *What will become of me?* She kept asking even when, after three unhappy years, she began to force the answer—by starving herself. Five months later, in May 1996, in her ninety-second year, Mom succeeded in her final ambition.

Pop's misery and Mom's suffering at life's end were, I now realize, their final gifts to me. Their unhappiness made them want to die, and painful though it was, it made me wish them on. Their deaths rekindled my admiration for the burdens they bore in life, including the ultimate sacrifice of seeking fulfillment only in the life of their son.

Before I knew her, Joyce had had to witness the even more painful decline of her mother, the central figure of her life. Joyce had temporarily moved back home to nurse her through a cancerous agony and ugly death at the age of sixty-eight. Now, soon after Pop's death, Joyce's father was found to be losing strength to lymphoma. Jack Purnick at eighty-nine continued to amaze us with his travel lust and gift for attracting female companions. But he needed Joyce to look after his housing and comforts. Six months after my mom's stroke, at the end of 1992, he was hospitalized in Palm Beach, where Joyce assembled the family to say good-bye.

Only six months later, in June 1993, Joyce and I raced from one hospital to another trying to cope with her diagnosis of breast cancer. The latest of her mammograms, which she had had taken since age forty, led her radiologist to call attention to some ambiguous X-ray specs, a caution rewarded by a mercifully early detection.

The lumpectomy and subsequent treatments dominated our lives for nearly a year. It also deepened our appreciation for whatever time we were destined to have together and kept our love at the center of our lives.

Yet again I fulfilled Mom's wish. I encountered good luck in the midst of bad.

43 · THE FEMININE MYSTIQUE

ALTHOUGH JOYCE WAS PROBABLY THE BEST POLITICAL reporter in New York, she might have never reached *The Times* in the late 1970s if the paper had not promised to vigorously recruit women to settle an embarrassing discrimination suit. As I had already discovered in other jobs, *The Times* had not paid women as well as men, had been slow to hire women in significant numbers, and therefore had few women available for promotion to senior positions. Things were even worse in the advertising and circulation departments, so the *Times* women who had dared to sue held out not for large fines but for a commitment to equal pay and urgent efforts to hire and promote more women. No fair-minded person could deny the need for "affirmative action" to overcome the habits of the past.

   The Times's sexism had been no worse than that of other newspapers and, indeed, the rest of American society. In Adolph Ochs's time, even the great Anne O'Hare McCormick could work only as a freelance stringer; she became the industry's most notable exception in 1935, when she was hired as a correspondent by Arthur Hays Sulzberger and eventually promoted to the editorial board and foreign affairs columnist.

I became *The Times*'s stringer at Columbia University in 1949, when my predecessor, Nan Edwards, was put on staff to write wedding and engagement notices. That was still her job when I got my first press card in 1952. Outside the "Women's News" and Society departments, there were only four or five women reporters on the staff. The most conspicuous was Lucy Freeman, who had created a new beat and fame for herself in the field of mental health. As Nan Robertson recalled in her book *The Girls in the Balcony*, the only path open to her in 1955 was as a "temp" in Women's News, where she wrote fashion items designed to please advertisers. She finally made it to the City staff in 1959 and to Washington in 1963; there women covering speakers at National Press Club lunches were still penned in the balcony, with no food and no right to ask questions.

When women finally dared in 1972 to form a caucus to improve their conditions at *The Times*, they were still only 10 percent of the News Department's professionals, including just three foreign correspondents and three members of my Washington bureau. No women served as photographers, columnists, or editorial writers; only four were copy editors. So eighty-four women from all departments publicly accused *The Times* of discrimination in hiring, pay, and promotions. That led to some hurried remedial hiring, but the other grievances were ignored. Thus in November 1974, six truly bold women, later joined by a seventh, filed suit in federal court and provoked four years of litigation. The depositions and discovery proceedings revealed huge discrepancies in the salaries paid to men and women for similar work, a fair amount of condescension toward women, and even some coarse and insulting memos among male editors appraising women by their dress and sexuality. Since some of the crudest examples were dug out of the files of my predecessors in the Sunday Department, Punch acknowledged his awareness of the company's guilt by sending me a typically naughty comment on unmarked stationery—author unidentified:

JUDGE: Mr. Sulzberger, please take the stand, and in your own
      words tell the court why you hired Miss Jones. What really were
      the final criteria?

SULZBERGER: I should like to proclaim to Your Honor
             That I followed the usual rules
             And availed both myself and my office

> Of the latest of management tools.
> I broke down and coded her answers
> In their logical pieces and bits,
> And then I discarded them fully
> And went out and hired her tits.

Judge: I'm a leg man. You're guilty.

That satiric doggerel, alas, was uncomfortably close to some realities. By 1977, the suit against *The Times* had become a class action, and the publisher, unwilling to defend conduct that he abhorred, ordered the case settled. He paid a nominal sum of $350,000 to cover legal fees and back pay but promised an energetic and sustained affirmative action program.

Yet a decade later, when I took command of the News Department, no women had reached the masthead list of news executives. None were even in line to lead the Metro, National, Foreign, or Business staffs. Many talented young women had surged through the opening gates into journalism, and they now made up about 15 percent of our news professionals. But the shortage of promotable women continued, and it was not entirely the paper's fault. One promising candidate for Metro editor, Anna Quindlen, had been reassured by Abe Rosenthal that she would not lose a shot at promotion while on maternity leave, but at the sight of her first baby she decided to stay home. She was only the first of many who chose to combine family obligations with writing rather than more arduous executive duties.

I probably have Mom to thank for the fact that I was always a sympathetic listener to women. Even in adolescence, girls confided in me more than they did in other boys. And Tobi found me a good student for her lectures about the sexist habits of American males. As boss of the newsroom, I instantly understood the frustrations of women, who saw almost no one of their sex among the top decision makers. I shared their belief that our responses to events and our definitions of news were probably skewed as a result. Why, for instance, should news pertaining to family relations and child care be segregated from general news on "women's pages"?

Fortunately, during my editorship, women came to fill more than a third of the professional jobs. The applicants who knocked on our door, and those we sought out for special expertise, were as often women as men, and we hired women in almost equal numbers. Soma Golden and Carolyn Lee eventually qualified to become assistant managing editors, but the pool of experienced women was still not large enough to find department heads for the principal news divisions. Some proved disappointing in leadership roles. Some rejected the more erratic work schedules and administrative burdens as incompatible with child rearing. Some deferred to their husbands' careers. Even after a decade of remedial effort, we were still not comfortably integrated in the upper ranks.

An emphasis on sex in recruiting—as also on race and ethnicity—is often condemned as a violation of standards of "merit." But in a creative enterprise like journalism, which relies heavily on individual judgment, biography shapes ability; who you are and where you come from inevitably influence what you see and how you perceive it. As a reporter who once crawled to safety across the muddy borders of Eastern Europe, I was bound to respond differently than other writers to the sight of refugees streaming out of Hungary in 1956. As the son of a man trapped in Stalin's gulag, I was bound to feel a deeper respect than others for the relief that Khrushchev's thaw brought to the Russian people. Yes, we are all supposed to be dispassionate professionals, but we can never fully escape who we are.

I had gifted women writers and editors to thank for front-page articles like Sara Rimer's "Women, Jobs, and Children: A New Generation Worries"; Gina Kolata's "Cancer Experts See a Need for Caution on Use of Birth Pill" and "Why a Drink for a Woman Acts Like Two for a Man"; Alison Leigh Cowan's " 'Parenthood II': The Nest Won't Stay Empty"; Felicity Barringer's "Divorce Data Stir Doubt on 'Trial Marriage' "; and Alessandra Stanley's "Romance Novels Discover a Baby Boom—Heroines Want Mr. Right to Be Also Mr. Mom." Could men have found, written, and featured such stories? Certainly. Were they likely to in the absence of female colleagues? No. These were the real rewards of staff diversity. They also discredited the mechanical habit of obsessed feminists who judged us only by the number of female bylines on Page One or, worse, the number of women pictured and quoted on the front page.

The first of my self-inflicted crises as editor grew out of such an exercise in feminist bean counting. Exploiting the fame of Betty Friedan, a group of women decided in 1990 to shame the national print media by counting the number of stories about women on their front pages. Naturally *USA Today*, with its heavy emphasis on entertainment and sports news, scored high on the survey and *The New York Times* very low. In view of our great progress in hiring women and, more important, our featuring much news of interest and importance to women, I denounced this survey and promised that "as soon as Mr. Gorbachev lets Mrs. Gorbachev do his deciding, or even speaking, we will be quoting or photographing more women on Page One." Why, I asked, did the group generate such mischievous publicity without differentiating among the clearly different missions of different newspapers?

When interviewed about my protest by Eleanor Randolph of *The Washington Post*, I tried to explain without publicly belittling *USA Today* as a frothier newspaper than *The Times* and glibly remarked, "I mean that if you are covering local teas, you've got more women on Page One than *The Wall Street Journal*." Male editors cheered my saying "what had to be said." But as Joyce was quick to warn, my example provoked a storm in the newsroom.

Nancy Lee, our photo editor and a favorite of mine for her combination of warmth and candor, condemned my remark as "chilling." She said it revealed to her that I saw Raisa Gorbachev "only in the context of a man" and that while "men rule the world, women have tea." She thought that my one-liner had undermined everything we had accomplished:

> You put a woman on the masthead, you purposely look for different kinds of pictures for Page One to show a more varied world, you support and promote women in the newsroom. I think I know what you were trying to get at through your comments: We are a global newspaper, men do run the world, therefore we quote more men than women. And I think you've done quite a bit (visually, at least) . . . to equalize our treatment of men and women. But when I read these kinds of quotes, I'm concerned about our true commitment.

The next day Nancy and every other woman in the office, with the merciful exception of Joyce, appeared wearing tea bags as earrings. But their good-humored reproach, itself a tribute to the relaxed atmosphere of our newsroom, did not erase the hurt of what I thought was an unwarranted response to a flip remark. The tension persisted for days until there came a petition, repeating that I had "undermined" my own achievements and begging for an explanation. I finally wrote a letter to the petitioners, apologizing for giving offense with what I called a chronological rather than an ideological sin:

> In my formative reportorial years, teas were a respected, predominantly female activity and were widely used to facilitate diplomacy— so much so that younger foreign service wives felt deserving of

greater recognition and pay for the service they were rendering. That all sounds quaint now that we have happily reached a time when the spouses of diplomats (and foreign correspondents) are often male. . . . I am angry with myself both for giving offense to some colleagues and for obscuring my real point. . . . I deeply resent the implication that we discriminate in our coverage and that we are somehow "last" in our coverage of women and news of special importance to women. All of us are owed an apology for that implication.

Barely one month later, I took solace from our own bean counting. To raise my spirits, a few women remarked that four of the seven articles on our front page of May 28, 1990, carried the bylines of women. And a year later, they sent me the front page of May 26, 1991, on which five of six articles were written by women, all on serious political and financial subjects, with a note saying, "Some of us suspect this is a historic page." It was a particularly touching gesture because we had just passed through the bitterest controversy of my editorship over the article that named and described Patricia Bowman, the woman who filed a charge of rape against William Kennedy Smith.

Luckily, at that critical moment, Soma Golden's female sensibility stood guard over national news, sparing us the charge that only piggish males would have dared to explore the character of Smith's accuser. But I alone bore responsibility for publishing Ms. Bowman's name. I had demanded a profile, never intending to use her name. It had long been our practice to withhold the names of rape victims for the express purpose of serving a social objective—to spare women the stigma of having been violated and thus to encourage them to report and prosecute sex crimes. The only comparable restraint commonly observed in news coverage was the anonymity we accorded some juvenile offenders and, when requested by the courts, jurors in some criminal cases. Early in my editorship, I reviewed this policy and reaffirmed our intention, as good citizens, to protect the privacy of rape victims. But I specified that "this cannot, obviously, apply to any name that becomes public, or is somehow unconcealable." I also concluded that the policy obliged us not to name anyone suspected of a sex crime on the word of an anonymous accuser; we had to be sure to wait for an official charge or indictment. Yet for two weeks, and only because of his middle name, William Kennedy Smith was daily accused of rape in *The Times* and other papers without facing any charges from the Palm Beach police. At the very least, I kept insisting, our readers deserved to know the nature if not the name of the person who was making these accusations.

The article produced in response to my urgings was accurate and by no means unsympathetic to Ms. Bowman. The headline read WOMAN IN FLORIDA RAPE INQUIRY FOUGHT ADVERSITY AND SOUGHT ACCEPTANCE. It described her as coming from a working-class family whose life had been transformed a decade earlier when her mother married a wealthy industrialist, a blunt-spoken man used to getting his way and fiercely determined to prosecute his stepdaughter's complaint. We learned that Ms. Bowman, then twenty-nine, was thought in high school to have had "a little wild streak." In tenth grade, she suffered a broken neck in an auto accident, but despite the continuing pain she became an aggressive, often careless driver who had had her license suspended ten times in the last twelve years. She was known around Palm Beach for having "fun with the ne'er-do-wells in café society." Judging by the children's books we could see through her window, she was a conscientious mother of a two-year-old child, by a man she had not married. "This wildness you have heard about, it wasn't the same kind of wildness as other people," an acquaintance told us, explaining that the accident and resulting arthritis left Ms. Bowman feeling that "her time clock was much more fragile than yours or mine." The article gave a cool but hardly hostile portrait.

Yet when it appeared on an inside page on April 17, 1991, the staff of *The Times*, and especially the women, went wild. They read into it an old-fashioned sexist bias and even a desire to blame the victim for her misfortune. There's no telling how much the anger was fanned by the last-minute decision to include Ms. Bowman's name. The discussion of her wild streak and single motherhood sounded particularly prosecutorial once it was directed at an identified person. But I know from hundreds of angry letters that most people outside *The Times* were much more upset about our use of the name—until, that is, Anna Quindlen, without asking my view of the matter, used her Op-Ed column to condemn my "mistake" and denounced the profile as both irrelevant and punitive. Arthur Sulzberger, Jr., then deputy publisher, poured fuel on the fire by ostentatiously congratulating Anna in the newsroom.

Like Soma and Al Siegal, who read the profile before it went to press, I found it on first reading to be a solid, if hurried piece of investigation, a pretty good reporting job considering that Ms. Bowman's family and lawyers had tried to obstruct our inquiry and refused to answer our questions. But I gradually understood why the article was seen to be inflammatory and wished we had toned it down further. Although not "irrelevant" by the normal standards of our profiles, some of the details about Ms. Bowman's life were hardly necessary to assess her personality and credibility.

I continue to believe, however, that we were right to use her name—and wrong, after the uproar, to withhold it again throughout the trial of young Smith. Ms. Bowman was known as the accuser all over Palm Beach. Her name was printed first in a British tabloid and then by an American supermarket gossip sheet, both of which were unlikely to reach the homes of most *Times* readers. So we held back even then. But the night we were preparing the anonymous profile, Ms. Bowman's name was broadcast nationwide by NBC News. I was sure that every paper in America would—and should—now print the name, and ordered that we do so. Yet only a few other newspapers joined us. The holdouts were no longer protecting Ms. Bowman's privacy; it had been shattered. They were withholding now public information to make a political statement: to shame NBC and to appease their staffs and offended members of the public. However high-minded, such sentiments were improper guides to news coverage. I have always regretted that during the uproar I lacked the courage to keep using Ms. Bowman's name.

My only excuse is that the pressure became intense. More than 100 colleagues signed a petition of protest, and 300 appeared at a meeting that quickly turned confrontational. I was berated not only for the tone of the profile but for failing to balance it with a similar biography of Smith. We were in fact preparing such a profile, but our curiosity about his unknown accuser quite logically took precedence. I printed an Editors' Note, regretting that some parts of the Bowman profile left the impression *The Times* was challenging her testimony. And we printed a long news article describing our staff meeting and the uproar elsewhere. I insisted that *The Times* had not abandoned the policy of protecting the privacy of sex-crime victims so long as that privacy had not been effectively breached. But in the excitement of the moment, I betrayed that vow by not again printing Ms. Bowman's name until others did, many weeks later.

To my dismay, no one shed a tear of sympathy for Sen. Edward M. Kennedy, who was damaged much more substantially than Ms. Bowman by the publicity surrounding the affair. The day we printed her profile and used her name deep inside the paper, our front page featured a three-column photo of a brooding senator over an article headlined, "For Kennedy, No Escaping the Dark Cloud." He had been drinking late with young Smith at the bar in which they encountered Ms. Bowman, creating some doubt in the early stories about which of them was being accused of rape and reviving all the ghosts and television jokes about the senator's irresponsible behavior at Chappaquiddick two decades earlier.

I found little comfort in the fact that I had created an atmosphere in which my *Times* colleagues felt so free to air dissent and grievance. I was angered most by the critics who not only refused to engage my reasoning but found a connection with our improved sports coverage and livelier writing and concluded that they were witnessing the "tabloidization" of *The Times*. I took solace only from the fact that our policies and practices drew so much attention precisely because our standards were widely esteemed. It was flattering to realize that we were seen to be the principal custodians of journalistic ethics even when we stood accused of betraying them.

44 · Black and White

MY EXERTIONS FOR RACIAL INTEGRATION AT *THE TIMES* were not just affirmative but prodigious. Yet my achievements at work and in my personal life were modest. Like most Americans, I did not live or play close enough to blacks in early life to grow up genuinely color-blind. Nor did I have to depend on blacks the way my son Jon did on the football field, an experience that left him easily comfortable in interracial settings. But black colleagues have often had to depend on me, and I am aware of the duty imposed by that imbalance. Duty may not be the noblest inspiration for human conduct, but it does represent a response to reason. And in twentieth-century America, whites and blacks still had to reason their way out of prejudice, resentment, and imbalance, usually without benefit of much honest interracial conversation.

I learned that the hard way one day in 1990 at a forum about the progress of women in newsrooms. I was asked whether I could be content with a staff not yet half female. And I said yes, that though 50 percent or even more, given the mommy track, was the ideal target, the most important thing was to reach a "critical mass." That point is reached, I explained, when enough women are succeeding and being promoted to high positions, making it no longer a politically sensitive act to demote or replace one of them with a man. Gratuitously, but truthfully, I added that our news staff had not yet attained such a critical mass of blacks. "They're still a precious few. If they are less than good, I have to hesitate before removing them too quickly."

The heavens thundered all around. I was denounced for feeding the stereotype that blacks needed "special treatment." *The Times*'s black reporters angrily deplored my "double standard" and denied that firing a black would have "political overtones." Yet whenever some black reporter or editor quit because he or she felt unappreciated or found greater opportunity elsewhere, the same staff members would denounce our "inhospitable" environment for blacks. As the *Journal of the National Association of Black Journalists* once put it, "*The New York Times* has been hit by another exodus of black journalists, forcing the nation's most prestigious newspaper to acknowledge it still has a problem keeping people of color." The truth is that we did have a problem, shared by many institutions: The most successful blacks were repeatedly tempted by opportunities elsewhere and the least successful were often left wondering whether they were the victims of prejudice or "cultural" alienation.

Responding to these pressures, *The Times*'s corporate management kept insisting that all editors and managers submit to assorted programs of "diversity training," many of which were delivered by shameless charlatans. Their insistence that white managers needed special instruction to appreciate the talents and cultures of nonwhites was, of course, the ultimate double standard. Yet to avoid being branded as racist, we had to humor these peddlers of pop psychology and sit through their lectures about racial habits, mannerisms, and patterns of speech. Having myself passed through the travails of assimilation, I felt emotionally that minorities needed to bend to conform to majorities. But having also witnessed the shameful rejections of blacks throughout American society, I knew that my own smooth path to success was not available to most people with dark skin. In the tension between that feeling and that knowledge I found my affirmative action policy.

I was eager to build the most diverse possible staff, and not just to ward off protest or to satisfy my social conscience. *The Times* desperately needs a staff that matches its diverse ambitions. The more women and blacks, Asians and Catholics, immigrants and natives, midwesterners and southerners, the greater our reach, the better our grasp of the news. Although good reporters and editors learn to transcend their own experience and to deal with alien peoples and strange surroundings, a newspaper nonetheless often encounters conditions in which a woman or a black or an Arab or a Spanish speaker can best get at the news and the people making it. The greater the tensions surrounding a newsworthy situation—tensions of race in our cities, religion in India, ethnicity in Israel—the greater *The Times*'s need for reporters who can gain the confidence of contending factions. I insisted on affirmative and aggressive recruiting of blacks not to serve some legal requirement or political obligation or just to offset Jesse Jackson's implied threats to picket our front door. We had to seek out minorities to do our job. We had to seek aggressively because they were hard to find. And we had to seek honestly because we could not afford to settle in haste for mediocrity. When three black men were severely beaten by whites in the streets of Howard Beach, causing one of them to be killed by a car as he fled across a highway, we soon felt the shortage of black reporters to help monitor the city's tensions and enough black editors to help shape our judgments. Too often, we found ourselves discussing articles about racial strife without a single black face in the room.

I could think of only one way to demonstrate the urgency of change and to enlist every editor in a new recruiting effort. I took personal charge of employment decisions and served notice that we would hire white reporters only at the same pace at which we hired blacks—one for one. No desk would be allowed to hire whites unless it had helped to recruit blacks, at least for another department. Even if the Foreign Desk found no black with experience abroad, it could use its correspondents around the world to scout the staffs of other papers.

As the shoes began to pinch, I certainly got everyone's attention. I did not apply the one-for-one stricture to copy editors, who were already in such short supply that we endured chronic production delays. But we did pass up or delay hiring some highly desirable white reporters to sustain the drive. And to withstand the predictable pressure that we bend our standards and take excessive risks, I conspicuously vetoed the hiring of some black recruits who presented doubtful credentials or prospects.

In the first year of this intense effort, we succeeded in adding four black reporters, two trainees, and one photographer while hiring nine nonblacks, for an accounting deficit of two. In the second year, we added six more blacks and thirteen whites because I relented and allowed credit for six other blacks who received hard offers but had them matched or trumped by their employers. The restraint on total hiring caused some hardships, but it also placed a premium on acquiring the best possible white as well as black recruits. The know-nothings outside *The Times* who denounced my "quota system" showed no real interest in our needs or progress. As the numbers proved, I was using the one-for-one formula not to guarantee a fixed result but as an administrative device. In a large organization, there is simply no way to measure good-faith management efforts without some numerical accounting of results.

Heading into my third year, I set out to repair our shortage of Spanish speakers by including them in the minority count. I brought Paul Delaney back from Spain to devote himself full-time to minority recruiting. We pressed Brent Staples, a gifted writer and student of literature, to give up a position in the Book Review to try his hand at helping to run the Metro Desk. And I set out a special, fast-track training program by which Gerald Boyd, our White House correspondent, could prove himself capable of leading a department and perhaps more. All three not only made creative contributions but gave us vital protection against racial conflict when we had to dismiss one black reporter for delinquency and insubordination and when we had to disappoint the ambitions of others. For despite the denials when I dared to mention it in public, the political problem of dealing with the failure of a black colleague persisted.

The benefit of nurturing black reporters and editors became evident in our handling of the news, notably the case of Tawana Brawley, which inflamed race relations and politics throughout New York State. Our integrated team reported what a seven-month grand jury investigation eventually confirmed: that Brawley, a fifteen-year-old black woman, had fabricated a shocking tale of abduction and assault by whites to cover up her extended absence from home. She had smeared herself with feces, written racial slurs on her body, and faked a traumatized daze just to deflect the wrath of her parents. Black demagogues, led by Al Sharpton, C. Vernon Mason, and Alton Maddox, seized on the case to promote themselves and to assail the criminal justice system. The idea that any black teenager would go to such extremes was, admittedly, hard to believe at first, and our early suspicions of fraud provoked heated interracial debates among our own reporters. But the credibility we achieved when blacks and whites reached a consensus about the evidence was powerful proof of the value of fielding an integrated team.

Hardly a month passed without some demonstration of the need to recognize black sensibilities. When a gang of black teenagers rampaged in Central Park and raped and bashed in the brains of a white woman jogger, one article about the gang's Harlem neighbors—as it happened, by a white writer—evoked an immediate reaction that taught us to keep pursuing public opinion. "My whole neighborhood is up in arms," Rosemary Bray, a black editor in the Book Review, reported, "and it was wonderful to see my paper treat something so tragic and confusing with the seriousness and lack of hateful diatribes that it deserves." Similarly, Howard French, a black reporter on our Metro staff, recorded his "pride" when we explicitly compared a gang rape by white youths in New Jersey with the case of the Central Park jogger.

To be sure, not all the racial consciousness on our staff was positive. After a gang of whites beat the black Yusuf Hawkins to death in Bensonhurst, Brooklyn, in 1989, black colleagues and readers bitterly complained that we had failed to capture the emotions expressed at his funeral service. We refused to apologize for having assigned a white reporter, who was meanly barred from the church by a cordon of black toughs. There was also a great deal of fuss the next year when we printed a balanced account of the benefits and flaws of black history courses around the country. Black colleagues resented our citing some ludicrous teachings—that Africans had preceded Columbus to the Americas by 2,000 years and that a black man had "drawn up plans" for Alexander Bell's telephone. And there were occasions when our sensitivity about race caused our coverage to be much too deferential to poor black people, as if their poverty automatically excused bad conduct. After a particularly contentious conflict in Crown Heights in 1991, I felt compelled to urge our reporters to suspend the customary impulse immediately to analyze the motivations of people in the news:

> When passions run high and blood is being spilled, let us concentrate first and foremost on who is doing what to whom. That's the time to check our customary desire to explain and analyze—until we know what it is we need to explain and analyze. Whether we're sick in the head, Officer Krupke, or criminal or deprived are questions that should be held in abeyance—no matter what the columnists are yelling—until we're sure we know what actually happened.

Ultimately, the newsroom could not avoid the passions and prejudices roiling all American communities. Some blacks wanted me to forbid all racial identifications, even in our descriptions of criminals at large. I had one sad request from a valued editor to put an end to all the idiomatic negative uses of *black*, as in *black magic, Black Monday, film noir.* And as in other contexts, political propaganda inevitably crept into some of our articles. I was shocked to read in *The Times*, more than once, that whites had become "the electoral minority" in New York. They had indeed slipped from being a majority to a plurality, but the sudden invention of a majority called "people of color" glibly made all Hispanics "colored" and assumed that Hispanics, Asians, and blacks had a common political interest, which they decidedly do not.

Still, the frictions caused by integration were preferable to the tensions of imbalance. The sad fact is that we could not hold some of our most valued black colleagues. Gwen Ifill jumped from covering presidential politics for us to covering the White House for NBC. Crystal Nix left a promising reporting career with a leave of absence to attend Harvard Law School and to clerk for two Supreme Court judges, and never returned. Larry Olmstead was lured by an administrative vice presidency in the Knight-Ridder organization. Mary Curtis was offered a department of her own plus a job for her husband by *The Charlotte Observer*, and Rosemary Bray got a huge advance for her autobiography. E. R. Shipp, a much-admired reporter, used my recommendation to Columbia's history department, where she, too, wanted to concentrate on tracing her family roots. But she soon turned up as a columnist for the *Daily News* and denounced our newsroom as a "plantation," aggrieved apparently because we failed to assign her to cover the Supreme Court. A senior black editor whom we had wrongly promoted too far (but never demoted) wound up suing *The Times* for discrimination. Most regrettably, my valued colleague Paul Delaney felt himself at a dead end in personnel work and reluctantly left for the deanship of Alabama's School of Communications.

Our progress, in short, was fitful and slow, so slow that we felt ourselves in constant danger of letting impatience in recruiting betray our judgment. That was one reason for my reluctance to give pressure groups a census of our staff defined by race, sex, and ethnic group. To have refused would have implied that we were making even less progress than was the case. But I resented the scorekeeping that reckoned the black population of our newsroom to two decimal places and assigned no value to recruiting efforts and to the qualifications of the professionals that we and others needed. Compared with other metropolitan papers, *The Times* offered relatively few entry-level jobs and demanded much wider experience in national, cultural, financial, and foreign correspondence. It is absurd to expect any newspaper, especially a paper like *The Times*, to employ blacks in the same proportion that blacks occupy in the general population. Blacks do not attend college in the same proportion as whites, and even fewer have shown any interest in working on college newspapers, an important training ground for print reporters.

I left behind a staff that was about 85 percent white—only a few points less white than when I arrived, not counting Anatole Broyard, who was born to black parents but disguised himself as a very white *Times* book critic. During my editorship, the portraits of our Pulitzer Prize winners came to include the black faces of Gerald Boyd, who led the team that covered the World Trade Center bombing in 1993; Isabel Wilkerson, who wrote illuminating reports on poor children, flood victims, and other human dramas; and Margo Jefferson, a literary critic and stylist with enormous range and insight. Yet I clearly failed in my effort to reach that critical mass.

We had stars who happened to be black, but too few to assure the advancement of blacks to top editorships. We had so few blacks in various sections that editors were reluctant to face up to some of their inadequacies. We had so few coming along in the next generation that recruiters were tempted to relax their standards. And as elsewhere in American society, these distortions aroused bitter resentments among some whites. Despite the best will in the world, and the strongest possible commitment to integration by the Sulzbergers and their top editors, I doubt that we will achieve harmonious integration any sooner than other professions and institutions. Until then, we must go on wobbling between well-intentioned favoritism and hardheaded realism, recognizing, I hope, that policy cannot be fashioned from mere sentimentality.

45 · FINALLY GAY

UNTIL I STUMBLED INTO LEADING ONE, I THOUGHT REVolutions had to be planned. The truth is that the most significant upheaval inside *The Times* during my editorship occurred almost by inadvertence. Without any declaration of emancipation, gay and lesbian members of the staff felt emboldened to take their rightful places in our business, some ostentatiously, most quietly. After decades of stealth and fear, anxieties amplified by the devastation of AIDS, they could, at least at the office, breathe free. I was declared their hero, pathetically honored merely for accepting them as normal colleagues and for letting the paper fully address the issues agitating their lives.

I couldn't possibly have planned or even anticipated a gay revolution at *The Times*. I never dreamed that so many homosexuals were hiding in newsroom closets, awaiting the trumpet call. I never wondered even to myself how many colleagues might be gay. Women speculated about unmarried men because they were always hunting mates for their friends, but even after I began dating Joyce, no such gossip reached my ears. I had

never heard the suspicions that Rich Meislin lost his foreign correspondency because he was gay. It never occurred to me that Jeff Schmalz
fought hard against my sending him to Miami because we might be disrupting his sex life. I did not realize that promoting Nancy Lee to head the
Picture Desk was a historic day for colleagues who thought they were forever barred from executive positions. When I retired as editor, I still did
not know who on my staff was gay or lesbian unless they deliberately revealed themselves.

My innocence bespoke much ignorance. Not knowingly acquainted
with many homosexuals, I only dimly understood their struggles and aspirations. Somehow, over the years, I had shed the typical prejudices of my
generation, but it was a slow and private journey. I used to wrestle eroti-
cally with a boy named Murray when we were eleven or twelve, and
I looked back on that as a normal rite of passage, one of the stages of
emotional growth. I thought it was a psychic passage comparable to an
embryo's passage through the stages of evolution. I concluded that homosexuals failed for some reason to outgrow that prepubescent phase and
thus failed to attain heterosexuality. In my untutored fantasies, I cast them
as incomplete and unfulfilled, but not therefore sick or homosexual by
choice.

In adolescence, I was twice propositioned by gay men; as it happened,
both were drama coaches whom I admired, and both quickly honored my
flustered resistance. I then imagined that homosexuals belonged to a tiny
minority of men—only men—who were peculiarly attracted to "sensitive"
professions like the arts. But I also thought of sex acts between males as
distasteful. In the army I heard many ugly expressions of contempt for effeminate males, and I acquiesced in the cruelty of that barracks humor.
And throughout much of the Cold War, I found validity in the government's discrimination against homosexuals; since they had reason to fear
exposure, they were obvious targets of blackmail and therefore "security
risks" legitimately barred from sensitive jobs, including newspaper jobs in
delicate places like Moscow. It never occurred to me that Roy Cohn and
Joe McCarthy and J. Edgar Hoover, the most unsavory exploiters of this
persecution, might themselves be homosexuals sublimating their self-
hatred.

Heterosexuals, of course, were also drugged and photographed in
compromising poses by the Soviet secret police, but we all thought "normal" sex was easier to survive, and we were probably right. As we learned
only thirty years later, Joe Alsop had secretly proved a homosexual's vulnerability when he was lured into compromising acts by the KGB in

Moscow, photographed, and offered protection if he would become a spy in Washington. An ostentatious anti-Communist, Alsop managed to disarm the weapon he had handed the Russians only by confessing his homosexuality at the American embassy and thus becoming forever a captive of his own government.

My travels in Europe exposed me to Britain's lively debates about homosexuality, but that only gave me the false impression that England, like ancient Greece, had for some reason produced an abnormally large gay population. The echoes of these debates in America totally escaped my attention. *Time* magazine wrote about homosexuality in 1966 as "a pernicious sickness." Not until two years later did the American Psychiatric Association reject the view that homosexuals were mentally ill, and not until 1973 did it judge them free from a "psychiatric disorder." On becoming a *Times* editor that same year, I had no inkling that the paper employed a sizable number of homosexuals. I still did not question the general assumption that noticeably effeminate men—like heavily bearded men—were poorly suited to be reporters; too many sources would regard them as disagreeable "representatives" of *The Times.* By the 1980s, I managed a less benighted outlook when Margot counted a few gay men among her close friends at college. But I still recoiled when I read the ads for openly gay dances in college newspapers.

Given this history, I am astonished to discover in my files how I responded as Sunday editor to the flap provoked in April 1975 by an article on the front of our Travel section. It was a mature, low-key description of an ocean cruise for 300 homosexuals, and it described the growth of similar group travel as organized by gay clubs and agencies. The article sent tremors through the Times building, down to its reinforced foundation. In the publisher's office and in the advertising department, I was denounced for giving offense to our readers and risking the loss of vast revenues. And while I might be forgiven, I heard suggestions that I dismiss Bob Stock as Travel editor. To my continuing surprise, I wrote what is probably the toughest memo I ever sent to Punch Sulzberger:

> You ought to know that Bob Stock recognized the subject as sensitive, even though the story was maturely and responsibly written, and he had my approval to proceed.
>
> My reasoning was simply that the homosexual culture, all but totally open now in New York and a few other major centers, is a major phenomenon in American society, deserving of both medical and sociological examination. We did not make it happen and I don't think

we should champion its cause, but I cannot see how we can pretend it does not exist.

We will respect your wish to avoid the subject "for a long time," but I think you are wrong.

As ordered, we avoided "the subject" in other Sunday sections, as did Abe Rosenthal in the daily paper. Indeed, throughout his editorship, perhaps unnecessarily, homosexuals in the News Department trembled to be found out. When given charge of editorials in 1977, however, I did not ignore homosexuality altogether. Like John Oakes before me, I supported local legislation that would outlaw discrimination against homosexuals, notably including teachers. My editorial page vigorously denounced the Supreme Court's 5–4 decision permitting states to declare sodomy a crime even in the privacy of the bedroom. And we dared to refer to "anal sex" as a major source of AIDS infection while the News Department was still squeamish about the subject.

Like most American newspapers, however, *The Times* was inexcusably indifferent to the early evidence of epidemic in homosexual ranks. The first front-page article about the disease appeared in May 1982, by which time 1,450 cases and 558 deaths had been reported throughout the United States. *The Times*'s interest in AIDS did not pick up until after Rock Hudson died of the disease in 1985.

––––––––––

We published a series about the AIDS epidemic in Africa in late 1985, but by the end of 1986, when I became editor, there had been nothing comparable about the United States. We were constantly and properly reproached by the Gay & Lesbian Alliance Against Defamation for ignoring the epidemic and crimes against homosexuals. We took little notice of the distress and emerging cohesion of the gay community in Greenwich Village, just two miles south of our office. The rest of the American media did no better, but it was *The New York Times* whose negligence inspired the greatest rage. As GLAAD observed in resentful tribute:

The Times is the nation's most influential newspaper, the supreme journalistic court that legitimizes trends, events, and people in our society. Presidents and senators, scientists and philanthropists, editors and opinion makers all read it, and then often act on what they read. Sadly, if it isn't in *The Times*, then it isn't actually real to many in power.

We prided ourselves on precisely that influence, which well defines *The Times*'s responsibility to all Americans, whether or not we approve of their conduct and causes. Indeed, we arrogantly take it to be our responsibility to the world. But we can usefully cover only what we understand, and I began my editorship understanding almost nothing about homosexual health and society. As always in my journalistic life, I was just lucky to know what I did not know. And in one of my first projects, I summoned our science and medical writers and key editors and demonstrated to them that we were ignoring an epidemic of catastrophic proportions. I said we had to overcome whatever restraints of prejudice or fear or bureaucratic rivalries held us back. We listed some ideas worth pursuing and put a single editor in charge of AIDS articles. Within six months, we managed not only to increase the tempo and sophistication of our coverage but also to produce a lengthy series of articles summarizing experience with the disease to that point.

I am sure that the memory of the Holocaust and its unforgivable neglect by *The Times* intensified my concern. I remember the bell that rang in my head in early 1987, when Jon Nordheimer of our staff sent me a particularly poignant memo about "the plague." He wrote passionately about the "flames of paranoia" surrounding homosexuals, who feared that AIDS testing was only the first step toward the concentration camp, and among bisexuals, who were even more extensively hidden. I sent his list of suggested articles to our new committee, saying, "This is as sound as it is sensitive. But it's still only another alarm bell to wake us up. We need still more articles that dramatize and explain the problem—for others to 'solve'—so that years from now we shall be seen to have done our duty."

A particularly great goad was Larry Kramer, the cofounder of Gay Men's Health Crisis, a service agency, the author of plays and essays that screamed in fear of AIDS, and the founder of ACT UP, which practiced the propaganda of rage. Although we never met, Kramer and I exchanged dozens of letters between 1987 and 1990. His diatribes alternately scolded and thanked *The Times* for its AIDS coverage. I replied respectfully, sometimes helpfully. I may have paid him extra mind because, unknown to Larry, his brother Arthur Kramer had been unusually kind to Tobi when she served as a summer intern at his firm, Kramer, Levin, Nessen, Kamin & Frankel (no relation).

"At last," Larry Kramer wrote in response to our first big series of articles, "*The New York Times* is finally writing about AIDS in a compassionate way. Thank you, thank you." The next month, he proposed himself as an AIDS columnist, citing an offer from *The New Yorker,* but not long after there arrived a succession of denunciations not only of our medical writers but even of Jane Gross, an elaborately sympathetic reporter. I welcomed his "brilliant polemics" and said our staff welcomed his instruction and stimulus, so "please don't make them hostile with unfounded and unsubstantiated accusations." That evoked the customary 3,000-word missive about our continuing failures, about his desire to make *The Times* "perfect" and his wish to correspond on a first-name basis.

In August 1988, Larry suggested that we use the concluding section of his book, *Reports from the Holocaust*, as a magazine article. I rejected it as much too long and also deplored his slur upon our Magazine editor, who had struggled through the first seventy pages of its tough prose. But soon after came a note of congratulations on my engagement to Joyce and an invitation to his play, which, because Frank Rich had a convenient scheduling conflict, was unfavorably reviewed by our assistant critic. After months of silence, Kramer returned to the attack.

> Dear Max: *The Times*'s reporting of AIDS continues to be awful and your coverage of the Montreal Convention sort of became a laughing stock. . . . I have stopped writing you—which I am sure you must consider a blessing—because it seemed to do no good. . . . I hope you are well. I hope you are happily remarried.

> *Dear Larry: I am happily remarried but never happy to receive your professional disapproval. . . .*

> Dear Max: I am so tired of writing [these long] letters to you, Max. I know you read them, and I know you answer them, and I know you "conscientiously steer all valid ideas to the responsible desks." I also know, Max, that in *The Times*'s heart of hearts, nothing really changes. You still shit on us, Max, and your AIDS coverage still shits. . . .

> *Dear Larry: We do the best we can and I think our best is very good now. I'm sorry you disagree.*

> Oh, Max, what are we going to do? I now know that I am HIV-positive myself. (I finally had the test.) . . . Could I bring a group to talk to you? If you can't stand me, could I put together a group to send to you? Quite frankly, we grow increasingly desperate, and increasingly exhausted. And *The Times* is so important.

Dear Larry: We were all distressed to learn of the diagnosis you received and wish you the best in your fight against this awful disease. . . . With the addition of Phil Hilts to our Washington staff, we are also stepping up our coverage of the Federal response to AIDS.

Dear Max: Forgive a sentimental letter, but I am crying for several reasons, not the least of which is the fine article about us in *The Times* this morning. . . . Watching [Governor Cuomo's sympathy for the dying], reading today's *Times*, I was so proud of ACT UP, just as I was last week when Gina [Kolata of *The Times*] wrote about our AZT-dosage story. We have fought so long and so hard, for many things of course, but especially to be treated seriously in and by *The Times*.

Dear Larry: Sometimes the stars we all pursue do cross, just as minds or hearts sometimes touch. Now, after tears, bring us cause to smile.

It must be impossible for anyone not suckled on *The Times* to comprehend the emotion that its lifelong readers invest in the paper's triumphs and failings, real and imagined. To its faithful readers, as Kramer so sadly affirmed, *The Times* represents the only meaningful reality because it bonds Americans of thought and power. Our ink assumes the force of blood and joins us to our readers in a perpetually loving, feuding family.

Only days after our first big meeting about better AIDS coverage, one of our copy editors appeared hesitantly at my office door, introduced himself, and asked permission to plant an idea. He said he was sure there were many subjects concerning homosexuals besides AIDS that were also newsworthy, and if I ever wanted suggestions he stood ready to offer them. In my silly innocence, I said, "Sure, just write me a memo anytime." And he did, promptly. Months passed before I began to understand that I was being entrusted with a hitherto dark confidence, being invited to enlist the help of an editor who was almost ready to reveal himself as homosexual. I was being tested for my tolerance of a coming out.

Still unwitting, I passed the test. Other gay staff members gradually revealed themselves to colleagues, sometimes even to me. Nancy Lee, then assistant photo editor, returned from a nine-month leave of absence in mid-1987 and found that the atmosphere for homosexuals had been completely transformed. In time, she felt emboldened to display pictures of her partner beneath the glass on her desk. And eventually she and others dared to bring same-sex partners to *Times* functions. I stared at them once or twice, the way I briefly stared as a child when two women rose to dance at a café. I still recall Mom's quick reassurance: *Just because they don't have a man, why shouldn't they dance and enjoy themselves?*

As the climate changed, Al Siegal, the arbiter and conservator of our style, asked me to review some policies. First, in December 1986, he wondered how hard we should press family members to declare AIDS as the cause of any death in obituaries. We decided to press, particularly for obits of well-known persons, but without harassing the bereaved. Where we suspected a misleading response, we would omit the cause of death altogether; if told what sounded like a partial truth, we would print it with a pointed attribution to the source. Next came the question of whether our obits should mention "live-in companions" of the same or opposite sex. We decided they should, but not count them among the "survivors," like other relatives. And what of the word *lover?* We judged that to be an unwarranted invasion of privacy—and also unverifiable. Obviously, we took our usage seriously, particularly at the juncture of sex and politics.

Six months later Siegal asked me to consider lifting the ban on the use of *gay* as a synonym for *homosexual.* Barely a year had passed since Abe Rosenthal, in the closing weeks of his editorship, finally agreed to sanction the use of Ms. as a substitute for Miss or Mrs. Back in 1974, when Punch solicited our opinions, I had argued in favor of Ms. on the ground that Miss and Mrs. were to many women no longer neutral honorifics but an unwarranted, unwanted advertisement of their marital status, a discriminatory act that did not apply equally to men. "I fail to see why accepting that corrective and fashion is any more difficult for us than the manner in which we gradually shifted from 'Negro' to 'black,' allowing the two terms to coexist where desired." But Punch voted no at Abe's behest; they thought Ms. was still shorthand for feminist propaganda and would offend as many *Times* readers as it satisfied. So it was not until mid-1986 that Abe decided Ms. had become socially acceptable usage, although we had all routinely used it for years in our correspondence. With similar reasoning, reinforced by Punch's discomfort with homosexuality, Abe prohibited the use of *gay* except in quoting others or citing the official names of organizations.

Dutifully briefing me on this history, Siegal asked whether I thought *gay* had lost its propagandistic and provocative ring and—implicitly—whether I had the authority to get the publisher to relent. Hoping not to be countermanded, I simply informed Punch that we would begin to use *gay* and *lesbian* as adjectives in social, cultural, and political contexts, while continuing to use *homosexual* in references to sexual, psychological, or clinical activity and orientation. He acceded by acknowledging that whatever we did, the straight meaning of *gay* was already regrettably lost.

I looked upon the change as a belated adaptation to popular usage, one that required a review of other hoary habits. It was time to abandon thoughtless sexisms like writing about a basketball team of women employing the "man-to-man" defense. Only by accepting modern locutions like *chairwoman* could we defend our strong desire not to call such a woman a *chair*. Only by calling some lifestyles *gay* could we persist in our dignified refusal to call a group of gay men *gays*. Precious but meaningful. For the gay and lesbian members of our staff, our acceptance of the adjective was another important step toward acceptance of them.

Our stylebook could not, of course, settle all the issues posed by social upheaval. A storm of protest broke over our heads in early 1989 because of a few sentences deep down in an article entitled "Lesbian Partners Find the Means to Be Parents." You would think our attention to that issue would have been welcomed. But no, we were condemned for including some speculation by anonymous "clinicians" that the hostility of some lesbians to men might burden their children. There was no peace until we published an Editors' Note blaming an editor for the injection of this idea and claiming that it did not fairly reflect "the spectrum" of scientific opinion.

After the mayoral election of 1989, the agitators of ACT UP condemned our "exclusion" of gays and lesbians from the categories of voters in our political polling. The *Daily News* had found them to have contributed an obviously undercounted 4 percent to David Dinkins's margin of victory. Since he won by only 1 percent, the same credit could of course be claimed by every other segment of the electorate. I replied that we had written many articles about the role of homosexuals in the campaign but were not about to ask all poll respondents what they did in the bedroom. That was marked down as a "clearly homophobic response." So was my refusal to "out" homosexuals without their consent—the refusal to report the "discovery" by *OutWeek* that Malcolm Forbes was gay and that the Pentagon, while dismissing homosexuals from the military, employed a gay civilian as its top spokesman.

Other storms brewed largely out of sight, in our editorial councils. A furor erupted after we published a four-month-old photo of a well-known Connecticut legislator kissing another man. On the day he proclaimed his homosexuality, Rep. Joseph Grabarz, Jr., had kissed a supporter in full view to encourage passage of an antidiscrimination law. When the law was finally enacted, he recalled that kiss, observing that the photograph of it had aroused much greater hostility than his stepping out of the closet. Since the photo now figured in the news, our Picture Desk pulled it from the file and put it in the paper, greatly upsetting Punch Sulzberger and a fair number of readers. I, too, winced when I saw the picture in print, because I feared the fuss it was bound to provoke. I feigned annoyance that I had not been consulted in advance. And Arthur Sulzberger, Jr., a strong supporter of our new attitudes toward homosexuality, pretended annoyance that we would so needlessly disturb his father. But even if I had been consulted, I could hardly have objected to the publication of a highly relevant photo. Most appropriately for a newspaper, we were saying, "Look, dear reader, does this upset you as much as it upset some voters in Connecticut? If so, ask yourself why—and prepare yourself for more such displays." When historians come to reflect on the customs of our time, I realized, that picture and the events surrounding it would tell them more than a lot of long articles about the struggle for gay rights. I pointedly refused to forbid the use of such pictures on other relevant occasions.

In this same period of vaulting consciousness, a valued reporter announced that he had been offered the job of spokesman for a group of gay activists and that he would stay at *The Times* only if we let him "pioneer a gay rights beat." He was ready with proposals for articles about homosexuals needing family health benefits for their partners and adopted children, about their exclusion from the military and from churches, and about the bias against them in the media. These were indeed newsworthy subjects; they sounded radical in straight ears at the time but became downright ordinary within a year or two. Still, we decided that this reporter's declared readiness to shift his whole career to political action defined him as such an ardent partisan that we could not trust his pioneering the issues for *The Times*. We let him leave, never imagining that our resolute "objectivity" would be emotionally overwhelmed in just a few months.

The agent of our ultimate enlightenment was Jeff Schmalz, a gifted reporter who had started to run newsroom copy in his college years nearly twenty years earlier. He was a true member of *The Times*'s family, having served impressively as a Metro reporter and regional editor before he became Albany bureau chief in 1986 and, reluctantly, head of the Miami bureau in 1988. Jeff returned to New York two years later and had barely settled in as deputy national editor when one December afternoon he suffered a grand mal seizure at his desk. I returned from lunch just minutes before the arrival of an emergency crew. Jeff was shouting in confusion as he regained consciousness, so I took his hand as he was borne through the newsroom past startled colleagues. I told him that I had learned a great deal about seizures after Tobi suffered one five years earlier and that the range of possible causes was vast. He needed to be-calm himself and prepare for a full round of tests. Unaware that Jeff was gay, I was worried most about brain cancer and whispered my fears to top editors. But the gay men on staff immediately feared AIDS and, without my realizing it at the time, found a pain-relieving symbolism in my grasp of Jeff's hand.

Not until he suffered a second seizure, in his mother's living room, was Jeff tested for HIV and found positive. He was stricken with full-blown AIDS shortly after, and exploratory surgery discovered an untreat-able brain infection that was typically fatal within months. He came to the office to tell us individually, and we cried together. I not only held his hand but insisted on holding Jeff's job open during a medical leave. But when he returned to steal a precious two years from death, he found no suitable work until Joe Lelyveld urged him to look closely at the 1992 presidential campaign. Taking a range of medicines, including AZT, Jeff managed to crisscross the country, discovering purpose and excitement in the assignment, especially whenever that year's politics touched on AIDS and homosexuality.

Tough questions arose. Should we tolerate this reporter's emotional involvement in his subject? Did we want a condemned man reporting on the circumstances surrounding his own predicament and fate? At first, we let mere sentiment dictate our response: Jeff was a pro, he knew the limits of news, he understood the requirements of fairness. Besides, we rational-ized, Jeff was just one more voice among dozens of reporters covering the campaign for *The Times*; he added a unique perspective that we would be crazy to pass up or suppress.

Jeff responded maturely to our trust: "I feel better that when I do get sick [*sic!*]," he told an interviewer, "I'll be able to look back and say that I really did what I could do, that I really stayed in there for the fight, and I really made my contribution not just to the gay cause but to *The New York Times*—that I really gave them terrific stories on this issue. I didn't give them maudlin stories. I didn't give them editorials." And so he did, although he oversimplified the issue with the further claim that his writing about AIDS was no different than blacks writing about blacks or Jews about Israel. It was like blacks writing about *being* black or Jews writing about the invest-ment of their very identity in the state of Israel.

Repeatedly challenged by Jeff's performance to define our standards, I was surprised to find my consciousness raised not so much about homosexuality as about journalism. Had I not reported about Hungarian refugees' pursuit of visas to America with the passionate memories of childhood yearnings for such a visa? Did I not report on Soviet tyranny and German democracy with the memory of family traumas? Did journalistic "objectivity" require us to banish feelings from the human experience, to deny our own innermost values? Did not the shrewdest reporting require crawling into the shoes and skins of other people?

Jeff's sentient correspondence clearly ran the risk of lapsing into partisanship and sentimentality. But for the most part he avoided them. He helped us raise reporting to yet another level, at which, admittedly, only a few masterful writers could be trusted to function fairly. With rare honesty, he told readers how it felt up there at this new level, in a first-person essay that was itself a stylistic innovation in the Week in Review in December 1992:

To have AIDS is to be alone, no matter the number of friends and family members around. Then, to be with someone who has H.I.V., be it interviewer or interviewee, is to find kinship. "I'm so glad they picked you to do this," Mary Fisher said in an interview just before she spoke at the Republican National Convention as a woman with H.I.V. With her, as with Magic Johnson and Bob Hattoy and Larry Kramer and Elizabeth Glaser, who spoke at the Democratic convention, the talk was the same: of anger and courage and politics. We talked of that deep nausea, in the pit of your stomach, when even cancer patients pity you and when a doctor, who should know better, puts on latex gloves just to shake your hand.

I concluded that Jeff was taking his readers deep into the world of gay politics and AIDS in forthright and revealing ways that no healthy reporter could match. His scoops were the rarest kind, looking at the scourge from the inside out and also from the outside in. He was always as accurate, sharp, and honest as we had a right to expect and obviously labored to restrain his emotions:

Now I see the world through the prism of AIDS. I feel an obligation to those with AIDS to write about it and an obligation to the newspaper to write what just about no other reporter in America can cover in quite the same way. . . . Some people think that it is the journalism that suffers, that objectivity is abandoned. But they are wrong. If the reporters have any integrity at all, it is they who suf-

fer, caught between two alle-
giances. . . . At times, I think my
fellow AIDS sufferers are laughing
at me, looking up from their beds
with eyes that say, "You'll be here
soon enough."

Only after he died, in November 1993, at the age of thirty-nine, did Jeff
let fly his editorial anger, in an article he left behind for the *Times Magazine*. Its cover honored his dying request:

There is a phrase that I want
shouted at my funeral and written
on memorial cards, a phrase that
captures the mix of cynicism and
despair that I feel right now and
that I will almost certainly take to
my grave: What ever happened to
AIDS?

President Clinton read his message and interpreted it for an audience at
Georgetown University:

Basically what the article said was AIDS is sort of receding in the
public consciousness as a thing to be passionate about . . . not only in
our Administration but in the community at large and even in the
gay community. . . . He was saying that people were just frustrated
dealing with what they considered to be a perpetually uphill battle . . . that there just seemed to be no payoff. And so . . . he challenged us all with these words in the article: "I am dying; why doesn't
someone help us?"

The flood of opinion generated by Jeff's journalism fell into two distinct
categories. The shallow response of neoconservatives who can find "objectivity" only in their own prejudices was most clearly expressed by John
Leo in a column entitled "Tribalism in the Newsroom?" The question
mark, of course, was disingenuous; he knew *his* answer:

O.K., so Schmalz was a courageous man and a good reporter, under
great stress, who was allowed to violate just about every rule of conventional reporting. . . . Personally, I don't want reporters to be af-
firming beacons for any ailment or any cause.

Strange thoughts from a patriot like Leo. He seems never to have detected
pain and passion in American reporting about lynchings and Jim Crow
laws, about apartheid in South Africa, dissidence in China and the Soviet
Union, or, indeed, about the travail of the homeless, the poor, the imprisoned, and the insane in America. What a neutered world some of our critics conjured from their own politics.

With us stood many ordinary readers like Andrew Behrendt, who honored Jeff's memory with a contribution to charity and wrote:

> I appreciate that you ventured with him into that important territory where objectivity and subjectivity lose their ordinary definitions. This phenomenon is better recognized in the science/philosophy of physics than journalism. . . . I still look every day for his articles. His words are still there even if one has to read between the lines.

We had certainly come a long way, to an understanding of the reflexive nature of truly incisive observation. Just as our generation won the battle to give readers the analytical tissue that renders facts meaningful, so the best minds of a new generation were enriching that tissue with infusions of experience. The best reporters always employ intuition and experience to guide them through the murk of events. That is why we need staffs of such great variety. Could we trust the average reporter, even at *The Times*, to weave personal experience and values into our news reports? Of course not. Most had to be held to overt tests of sourcing and documentation. But for the greatest reporting, we had to trust the innermost values of an Abe Rosenthal walking the grounds of Auschwitz, of a Joe Lelyveld wandering the streets of Soweto, of a Linda Greenhouse perceiving the hidden conflict over abortion inside the Supreme Court.

We were growing in large matters and in small. In mid-1992, mindful of Jeff's passage toward death, we relented further in the matter of obituaries. As the Siegal-gram to the staff explained:

> It has been more than five years since we began including references to unmarried companions in obituaries upon request. That practice has clearly been accepted by readers. Now we would like to embrace widespread usage and apply the terms "survived" and "survivor" to unmarried companions of the same sex or the opposite sex. In other words, when we learn that a companion is among the survivors, we list her or him as such, along with family members and without differentiation.

Inevitably, we were then asked to record the "marriages" of gay and lesbian couples. I demurred, believing that the majority of readers had not yet accepted such unions as the equal of male-female weddings. New York City was getting ready to take official notice of gay unions, and our publisher, Arthur Sulzberger, Jr., commendably extended health benefits to live-in partners. But I decided that we would not open our society page to same-sex weddings until they had full legal sanction—and also a legal mechanism for signifying divorce. I then realized, however, that "engagements," which we were reporting slavishly every Sunday, were similarly self-proclaimed and unofficial. Before anyone had time to catch my inconsistency, I killed the engagement notices, taking credit for saving us space, paper, and endless lobbying from the betrothed.

Jeff's obituary in *The Times* listed no same-sex survivors, but we all counted ourselves among them. As I commented in his obit: "The healthy Jeff was an outstanding correspondent and editor, with a great future in American journalism. Jeff in illness plumbed the depth of his experience and applied it brilliantly to his coverage of the plague, producing a remarkable bequest to American journalism." Jeff's performance while healthy was an essential prelude to the trust we invested in his performance while ill. First and foremost, he belonged to our journalistic family. When the gay community clamored for his replacement by another gay or even AIDS-afflicted reporter, I resisted. I did not want to enshrine Jeff's precedent or reserve the homosexual beat for only gay men. And I certainly did not intend to honor the regressive demand that I ask staff members to leave the closet or reveal they have AIDS to qualify for the assignment.

Jeff was unique for his time, and so was our trust in him. The changes he personified deserved the gay community's reciprocal trust in *The Times*. No matter how uplifting, revolutionary storms must also subside.

46 · Press Runs, Hits, Errors

THE NEWS THAT TOOK UP MOST OF MY TIME AS EDITOR was the news of something gone amiss in our own operation. At breakfast each day, I would nervously hunt through competing papers for important stories that had failed to make it into *The Times*. Finding one was galling enough, but it was often only the prelude to wrestling with colleagues who would rather belittle a rival's scoop than chase it. By the time I reached my desk at about 10:00 A.M., an undertow of other troubles would drag me far from journalistic concerns. A board member might have been calling since dawn to protest our article on breast implants; he manufactured the silicone. A photographer might be demanding a formal protest to the police commissioner; she was roughed up by a cop. Our correspondent in Beijing had had her accreditation canceled. A reporter in Washington needed an immediate leave of absence to accept a sizable book advance. A clerk needed help and sympathy because a fire destroyed his home last night. And, by the way, the paper had closed twenty minutes late last night for no obvious reason.

Whatever talents had propelled me to this job seemed only incidental to the performance of my daily chores. In Jack Rosenthal's phrase, I was for much of the time carrying the piano, not playing it.

Moreover, soon after the invention of the printing press, it must have been decreed that readers address all their praises to the writers and all their complaints to the editor. The chief occupation of an editor in chief turned out to be fielding whines, whimpers, and laments.

The slightest disturbance of his ego always inspired New York's Governor Cuomo to spray the newsroom with angry phone calls, leading up to an assault on me if I failed to take evasive action. Senator D'Amato fired way over our heads, straight at Punch Sulzberger, with reminders of the favors done for the publisher's business and charity interests, notably the Metropolitan Museum of Art. Mayor Koch sent letters rebutting even the most trivial imputations of error—Herzogian missives that had to be judiciously answered because all would be reprinted in his self-satisfying memoirs. Koch, at least, could be appeased with a jest, or a correction if necessary. Not Mayor Dinkins. He maintained a calm facade but seethed within, particularly at our failure to be impressed with the significance of his red-carpet receptions on overseas junkets.

Most days, I could not even refuel over lunch. I was expected at the publisher's table to help flatter or subtly assuage some importuning public official or corporate executive. When I ducked and sent deputies, Punch understandably took offense; he promised assorted big shots or advertisers a meal with "the top editors," and he was a man of his word. Lunch became an honorable but often tense or tedious duty.

No businessmen wept as profusely as show-business men, most notably our neighbors, the moguls of the Shubert Organization. They knew better than to complain directly about a bad review of a mediocre show. Instead of blaming us for every empty seat, they lobbied tirelessly for compensating favor—better placement of their ads, more publicity for their stars, less attention to their ticket prices, more appreciation for their good works in the Times Square neighborhood. When they encountered Punch and Carol Sulzberger at dinner parties, however, Broadway's angels really let fly, trashing our critics and baiting the publisher to condemn his employees. The producers pined for the critics of yore until we finally armed Punch with research demonstrating that the venerated Brooks Atkinson and his predecessors were condemned with equal fervor in their time.

Every mail brought a new tide of objections. I dutifully pursued all allegations of error and answered every letter—except the many from prison inmates that bore implausible tales of unjust incarceration. But even some prison complaints merited attention. One such came from Jean Harris, the Madeira headmistress who in a jealous rage had killed her lover, Dr. Herman Tarnower, the peddler of the Scarsdale diet. Mrs. Harris wrote that her son, in renewing her subscription, had ordered only a weekday *Times*, but she was getting *two* copies every day plus one on Sundays. When she complained to the circulation department, she was told that was impossible—there was only one subscriber at her address: the prison rabbi. Moreover, her son had just received notice that the subscription was about to lapse when he had paid for an entire year! A second problem, while she was at it, was that she had not received the customary $150 fee for her recent Op-Ed essay, even though it was plainly not subject to the "Son of Sam" law, which forbids prisoners to profit from their crimes. She had promised the money to a Catholic nun who cared for the children of inmates; if we could not pay a prisoner directly, would we please send the check to the nun?

> Dear Mrs. Harris: I'm told your problems have been solved—at least your problems with *The Times*. If not, please let me know.

Little did she know how many New York politicians at our luncheon table had asked our opinion about the campaign to commute her sentence. I never answered and, in fact, never made up my mind. Professional neutrality was one of the few perks of my office.

The most common complaints in the mail dealt with conditions I could not repair, like a distributors' refusal to deliver the paper to some remote suburb and the damage done to clothes and kitchen counters by our ink. *The Times* had despaired of ever finding a "no rub-off" ink, and until chemists finally produced a "low rub-off" variety, the smudging was so great that novelty stores sold gloves "for reading *The Times*." Barbara Bush complained from the White House that bedding fashioned from *The Times* had turned her beautiful white puppies gray and forced her to revert to the hated *Washington Post*. I sent her a column from the *Post* that proved our rub-off was much less than theirs or *The Wall Street Journal*'s; if her puppies smudged our pages beyond legibility, I added, she might consider ordering a second copy.

The entire Bush family scrimmaged against *The Times* in 1992, when a front-page article suggested that the president had failed to recognize a bar-code scanner at a supermarket checkout counter. The story reinforced the possibly unfair impression that George Bush was out of touch with people's daily concerns, but I always thought that presidential candidates had ample means to defend their own imagery. None ever approved of our campaign coverage, particularly our preference for news over trite promotional material. In 1992, for example, we focused heavily—and most critically—on Bill Clinton in the spring, when he first gained national attention, producing among other things the earliest hint of his Whitewater finaglings. By early summer, we shifted our attention to the little-known Ross Perot because he suddenly loomed as a credible challenger. Not until late summer did we recapitulate George Bush's largely familiar record, which led him to conclude that we were unfairly targeting him in the campaign's decisive weeks. In any case, you do not have to be a politician to wince at your portrayal in print. I can attest that an editor not running for anything often found it difficult to recognize himself in articles written about him.

The complaints of some readers, however, hit home and inspired instant innovation. A letter deploring our "elitist" restaurant reviews made me realize that we gave no credit for good food achieved at modest cost. I thought that an excellent $30 meal—my speed—might well be more deserving of three or four stars than an admittedly better one produced for $100. But that populist heresy offended Bryan Miller, our restaurant critic, who argued that we should no more judge a meal by its price than we would a book or a Broadway show. Out of his resistance came the idea for a separate "$25 and Under" column of restaurant reviews. And when Ruth Reichl replaced Miller, she met my concern partway by often commenting on the relationship of price to quality at the finest places.

Other readers taught me to be aware that our wedding announcements were vital sociological documents. For example, historians could use our nuptial notices to spot a growing number of interfaith marriages or a generational shift from mercantile to professional occupations. In a direct response to feminist emotions, I had already opened the society pages to photos of grooms as well as brides. But it took a reader to remind me that we were failing to record the tendency of young people to marry much later in life than their parents. Over the protests of a few late bloomers, we began to ask newlyweds to reveal their ages to *The Times*.

––––––––––

The most persistent complaints from the staff dealt with the condition of our newsroom. Its maze of carpeted cubicles bore little resemblance to the linoleum-lined warehouse in which I first labored, but it was overcrowded, ill lit, ill ventilated, and infested by mice. It took me almost my entire term as editor to persuade the company to invest more than $30 million to rebuild. For too long, our intolerable environment greatly exacerbated the tensions and even physical injuries caused by computer typing in cramped spaces.

The most painful days were those on which harm befell a colleague, and these were mercifully few. No story is ever worth undue risk of injury; we refused to let staff members venture into the chaos that was Lebanon, and we readily consented to give the foolhardy John Burns an armor-plated car in Bosnia. We had a top secret plan for dealing with the kidnapping of *Times* personnel, but it was never needed. I had a bell hidden under my desk in case some lunatic threatened violence in the newsroom, but the only time our security men came running in response, my knee had brushed the button accidentally. Our greatest emergency occurred far from my desk, when a sniper's bullet randomly struck John Tagliabue in the spine in rebellious Timişoara, Romania. Our bureaus in Moscow, Berlin, and Bonn scrambled to fly a medical evacuation team into that anarchic war zone so that Tags could get to Munich for surgery and a long psychological as well as physical convalescence. The saddest day by far was when Jim Markham fired a shotgun into his mouth at the end of his tour as Paris correspondent. He was due in New York, to repair relations with his wife and children and take up duties as deputy foreign editor. Much of the staff knew nothing of Jim's private torments and entanglements abroad and blindly blamed "management"—me, that is—for creating career pressures that would drive a man to such extremes. I had to be prodded by Arthur Sulzberger, Jr., into holding encounter sessions with our traumatized staff, a ritual which struck me as superfluous and patronizing but for which I received much praise. The most sophisticated journalists seemed unaware that suicide was often an act of aggression.

I fled from all managerial chores at 4:30 every afternoon, when I shut my door to read the summaries of the day's major stories in preparation for our climactic five o'clock Page One conference. I let nothing take precedence over this forty-minute discussion among all the top editors of the twenty-odd stories that department heads nominated for possible front-page display. I invited all their opinions before choosing six or seven articles and two or three photographs and then presiding over the page's design. But I kept firm command of the discussion, viewing it as my main chance to engage the news intellectually and, by the case method, to define our values and refine our judgments throughout the paper. I hoped to set a tone that would filter down through every section's chain of command:

Is this truly a critical moment in the evolution of the new tax law? I might ask.

No, Max, but it's an important hurdle, might be the reply of the national editor or of the disembodied voice of our Washington editor on the speakerphone.

Well, how many hurdles do we cover on Page One before we bore the reader?

Not every one, but this was the crucial hurdle in the House.

I didn't see that explanation in the summary.

Relax, you will see it near the top of the story.

Well, I certainly hope so.

Getting stories to advertise their own importance and relevance was a constant objective. Another was to educate ourselves in the long-term implications of any single day's events. If the foreign editor reported on new violence between Soviet Armenians and Azerbaijanis and also between Israeli soldiers and rock-throwing Palestinians, I might ask him to choose:

If we can take only one of those outside, what's your preference?

Well, both. One points to the possible dismemberment of the Soviet Union, and the other may portend Israel's weariness with the intifada.

Are those just your opinions, or will we offer those interpretations in print?

The Moscow bureau will, but Jerusalem doesn't want to go that far.

So you put the Soviet story first?

But we haven't stressed the obvious Israeli frustrations often enough.

Well, then, let the story emphasize the frustration, not a few more kids throwing rocks; let's help the reader get to the point.

It's right there in the fourth graf.

Why delay the punch line?

My baitings and imperious rulings were not always welcomed around the table. But I thought the editor in chief ought to behave like the reader in chief, a surrogate for all *Times* readers. Even if they shared my views, editors often felt protective of their writers and reluctant to blame them for inadequate analysis. At other times, they themselves had been inattentive or distracted. To encourage candid conversation, I admitted only a few visitors to these meetings, but they frequently included Punch and Arthur Jr., who enjoyed the preview of the next day's paper and perhaps the combat as well. For me, these daily devotions to the front page were restorative. They took everyone's mind off the day's managerial chaff and enlarged our comprehension of events across departmental lines. Sometimes they also exposed procedural and ethical issues requiring lengthier study—such as how to deal with racial identifications or blind attributions. I favored debate without concern for rank, ego, or turf, a blurting out of ideas and easy acknowledgment of error, and sometimes we actually reached that weightless condition. I turned down scores of requests from writers and filmmakers who wanted to record these conferences. They were right to consider them edifying, but I was afraid that their intrusions would be inhibiting. The public's right to know, which I loudly proclaimed in every other venue, did not extend to *my* office.

———————

There was no predicting the sources of our best ideas. Some came from solitary contemplation of the news, as happened one day when I read consecutive summaries of articles from Russia, China, Cuba, Italy, and Nicaragua. I suddenly realized that our use of the word *Communist* in all those places no longer made much sense. Although this now sounds like a banal awakening, American politics and news coverage had by no means absorbed that reality. After months of coordination among all our foreign bureaus, we produced a distinguished series of articles that let Communists the world over demonstrate their divergence in their own words. Beyond embellishing my thesis, those articles focused attention on the cultural, religious, economic, and nationalist forces then undermining Marxist totalitarians. Although we did not directly predict the quakes that finally shattered the Soviet empire, we prepared ourselves and alerted close readers for the cascade of events that redefined the twentieth century.

Other good ideas had to be teased out of long, contentious meetings, the most difficult of which considered the inadequacy of our coverage of racial tensions in American life. But our best effort on the subject was produced independently, at the inspiration of our National and Metro staffs. They spent months seeking out poor kids of all races and, in interviews over many weeks, got them to portray their families' struggles with poverty and racism. The heartrending "Children of the Shadows," a project that sprang to life entirely from the ranks below, was probably the most important series of my years as editor.

I did not give enough prominence, however, to the rioting in 1991, when bands of black youths, shouting "Kill the Jews!" ran wild in Crown Heights. They accosted Hasidim and policemen and fatally stabbed a rabbinical student from Australia who had the misfortune of crossing their path. The mob was avenging, or at least exploiting, the death of a black child who had been crushed in an accident caused by the speeding motorcade of the Lubavitchers' chief rabbi. The two deaths and three nights of turbulence inflamed New York for many years and contributed to the de-

feat of the city's first black mayor, David Dinkins, in 1993. The mayor and
his black police commissioner had sorely underestimated the force needed
to contain the violence, and many Jews accused them of coddling the rioters. Not until forty-eight hours into the disturbance, after mobs menaced
the mayor himself, did the cops produce an adequate show of force. Many
blacks, however, thought it was the Hasidim who always benefited from
official favoritism, and some excused the rioting as an expression of justified resentment.

Our reporting of those terror-filled nights was thorough and fair.
But we were distracted from those symbolic events close to home by the
simultaneous and fateful coup in the Soviet Union. When the authorities later bungled the trial of the man charged with the Hasid's murder,
outraged Jews extended their anger to *The Times*. They thought we un-
derplayed the anti-Semitism that was spreading in black communities
with the encouragement of demagogues like Louis Farrakhan. The truth
is that the information gathered by our reporters in those fields of rage
was better than City Hall's and never disputed. But we should have followed up by exposing the inflamed emotions of the rival communities—
as was ultimately done by the brilliant Anna Deavere Smith in her
one-woman drama *Fires in the Mirror*. Crown Heights proved again that
even courageous reporting can fail to penetrate the filters in readers'
minds and that creative journalism needs to deal with perceptions as well
as realities.

The other major news failures of my editorship were common to the
entire American press. We woke up much too late to the bleeding of savings and loan banks at the taxpayers' expense. The politicians of both parties took huge bribes in the form of campaign contributions to tolerate the
frauds—if they even understood them. We did not catch on until the cost
to the public exceeded a half-trillion dollars. Nor did we adequately pursue the frauds of both major parties in their fund-raising for the 1992
presidential campaign. We did not expose enough of the theft and waste
resulting from chummy collaborations among weapons manufacturers,
Pentagon procurement officers, and their protective politicians. And we
stupidly donated our own staff's dollars to crooked charities like the
United Way.

Our failures were especially harmful because only *The Times* and a few
other papers, like *The Wall Street Journal* and *The Washington Post*, were
willing to invest the energy and money that multiple investigations require. The editors at smaller papers could afford one or two local projects
at most. Television news, though it pretends to defend the public from

chicanery, has only recently shown an interest in investigations for its "magazine" shows, and these tend to shun the biggest frauds, which are rarely telegenic.

Sins of omission are hard to spot. Our sins of commission, both grand and silly, were simply hard to confess. Although the work of reporters and editors is highly visible, they are no more disposed than other people to acknowledge even obvious error. That the prompt and conspicuous correction of error can actually enhance a newspaper's credibility has not noticeably reduced the urge of most newsrooms to appear omniscient and infallible. Most papers are content to print some letters of complaint, which even if noticed rarely overtake the original error. Even the best television news programs and magazines rarely bother to correct mistakes or the inadequacies of previous reports.

The Times has been far ahead of other media in confessing error and repairing unfairness, but we could do still better. Abe Rosenthal began the practice of correcting errors of fact in a predictable and conspicuous place—at the bottom of our daily news summary. Though modest in size, these corrections serve to amend the record, and they are electronically attached to the *Times*'s data bank to help reporters and scholars avoid repeating an error in the future. It is unlikely, for example, that anyone will ever again refer to the lightweight boxing match listed in our television schedule for April 15, 1992, as pitting Angel Hernandez against Sera Anunciado. As we sheepishly confessed, *será anunciado* is Spanish for "to be announced." And it is unlikely that anyone but *The Times* would have bothered with this correction, of December 11, 1992:

> An article on Nov. 26 under the heading "New England Journal," about the resurgence of wild turkeys in New England, misstated the history of turkeys bred to be eaten. They are descended from turkeys domesticated by Aztecs in Mexico, not by the Incas, whose homeland was Peru. The article also misidentified the period in which turkeys were introduced to Europe by returning Spanish explorers. It was the 1500's, not the 1300's.

Still, not all our mistakes are spotted or conceded. Reporters and editors are rarely gracious about owning up to anything more than a trivial slip. And our daily collection of corrections mixes the truly significant with the merely punctilious. The odds are always low that even an important correction can catch up with most of the readers of the offending article. Who knows what damage we caused before we got around to this confession:

An article on Nov. 25 about a recommendation by an advisory committee of the Food and Drug Administration that food be fortified with folic acid referred incorrectly in some copies to the amount that might be taken by people with vitamin B12 deficiencies. It is more than one milligram, not more than 1,000 milligrams.

In one instance the article also misstated the amount recommended for women of childbearing age. It is four-tenths of a milligram a day, not 400 milligrams.

Rosenthal's most original corrective, which appears occasionally beneath the Corrections, was called "Editors' Note" and designed to confess a significant departure from *Times* standards or sound journalistic practice. The Notes regret violations of our own policies, which forbid anonymous pejoratives, always require the source of accusatory information and comment about someone cast in an unfavorable light. Or, heaven help us, all of the above, as confessed on November 24, 1992:

An article about Marla Maples in The Home Section on Aug. 20 described her home life, her relationship with Donald Trump and her new career on Broadway. The article reported that Chuck Jones, who was then Ms. Maples's publicity agent, had been arrested in the theft of lingerie and shoes from her apartment, and that he had been videotaped "licking and sniffing" some of the shoes.

The article gave no source for those reports and offered no independent verification. The videotape mentioned in the report is held by the police, who will not release it for viewing.

The article should have attributed its account of the tape's content; it came from unsubstantiated press reports. *The Times* should also have included a comment from Mr. Jones. He telephoned the writer soon after the article appeared, to deny that he was videotaped licking and sniffing the shoes; he was referred to the editors, whom he called only last week.

The article should also have noted that Mr. Jones had pleaded not guilty to burglary, criminal possession of a weapon and criminal possession of stolen property. The charges are pending.

Amusing or not, these correctives amounted to a healthy advance in American newspapering. Yet while they helped to keep *Times* editors and writers on their toes, I doubted that they often enough overtook the impressions planted in readers' memories. Even when we felt compelled to prepare an entirely new article to correct a previous one, we were reluctant to recall the original as simply wrong. Ideally, I wanted such articles to begin with the phrase "Contrary to a report in last Tuesday's *Times* . . ." and I wanted to see the words "Correction" or "Times Error" in the headline. I was widely suspected of merely "showboating" when, early in my editorship, I demanded such an article and headline at the top of Page One:

A CORRECTION: TIMES WAS IN ERROR
ON NORTH'S SECRET FUND TESTIMONY

We had misstated the pivotal point of Oliver North's sworn testimony in the Iran-Contra affair. I took care to have the same reporter who made the error write and sign the corrective, but staff members nonetheless complained that I was exaggerating the offense and humiliating a colleague. They were not assuaged by the tributes he and we earned for "courage" and "credibility." We published a few more such front-page correctives in my time, but probably not often enough.

We should certainly have disowned a front-page sensation that appeared one weekend in April 1991. It was a long summary of Kitty Kelley's irresponsible and poorly sourced *Nancy Reagan: The Unauthorized Biography*, featuring a claim that Mrs. Reagan had had a long affair with Frank Sinatra. Such unsubstantiated gossip was not appropriate news for *The Times*, particularly not three years after the Reagans had left the White House and active politics. When I said as much at a meeting the next morning, I was overheard on our Washington tie-line by Maureen Dowd, the usually astute author of the piece. She fled the room in dismay and would not be consoled until, without my prior knowledge, Joe Lelyveld appeased her with a reassuring bouquet. I had protected so many of Maureen's incisive but acerbic articles against timid editing that I resented my colleagues' resistance to publishing an Editors' Note that would, for once, admit bad taste. We did print a long article a few days later calling into question many of Ms. Kelley's biographical techniques, but we neglected to mention that we were atoning for our own lapse. There are, alas, institutional restraints that keep even a captain from rocking his own boat.

The Ochses and Sulzbergers have always insisted on the paper's adherence to "family values." We felt obliged, even at the end of the twentieth century, to write "barnyard epithet" instead of "bullshit," having made only a few exceptions for Richard Nixon's "fucks" and "bitches" in the transcripts of his tapes—though not in our own articles about those tapes. We held ourselves out as defenders of polite discourse, which I rationalized publicly as a socially useful defense of the power of profanities. After all, when *The Times* finally began printing a cussword, like *hell* or *damn*, it quickly lost all potency and pushed society toward more outrageous expressions.

At times, however, our prudery risked cheating the reader. In covering the controversy about public subsidy of Robert Mapplethorpe's photography, we were content for months to call it "homoerotic" without explaining that it showed a man urinating into another's mouth or a man's hand and forearm inserted into another's rectum. The "detail" was surely essential to understanding the fuss. In a controversy over the rap lyrics of 2 Live Crew, we waited much too long before disclosing that a singer "brags about the physical power of his penis, refers to a woman in terms of her genitalia and commands the woman—usually addressed as 'bitch'—to gratify his desires for oral and anal sex."

In the era before Monica, our pretensions of decency also produced many comic evasions. After weighty deliberation, our Magazine once quoted Secretary of State James Baker telling Prince Bandar of Saudi Arabia that he was "sitting on your royal"—end of direct quote—*behind*. Wouldn't it have been better, I asked Punch, if we'd just this once let *The Times* accurately deliver a calculated crudity? He conceded that our circumlocution looked odd but said he always feared "opening the gate too much." He recalled his great relief at the Tony Awards one year when the tributes to *A Chorus Line* did not require a printed reference to the show's hit number, "Tits and Ass." Not until AIDS gave us a medical pretext did *The Times* accept ads for condoms, even though birth control the world over had long been a cause close to our editorial hearts. Suffice it to say that Eric Asimov of our staff had us just right when he composed "All the News That's Fit to Print":

> *The Times* tells the world what is doing;
> Who's winning, who's losing, who's suing.
> Who's striking, who's stealing,
> Who's dying, who's healing.
> But won't say a word on who's screwing.

Until, that is, six months into my editorship, when along came Gary Hart, who was then leading the race for the Democratic nomination for president. *The Miami Herald* caught him trysting with Donna Rice, a Miami model, and we were forced by the resulting tumult to recount the *Herald*'s adventure, chastely, on Page 16. But there was no keeping it off Page One once Hart's fibs and evasions proved hollow and forced him to quit the campaign.

A year later came a flood of stories about Rep. Barney Frank's homosexual encounters. Struggling to define a standard, I wrote this instruction:

We do not "expose" or pry into anyone's sex life unless a larger public purpose is served thereby. . . . One such public purpose might be
the exposure of a significant hypocrisy. That is why Gary Hart's sex
life became newsworthy—he himself had tried to make his family
values and marital status a political asset. Noting that a politician
who is actively denouncing homosexuals is himself homosexual
could be another such instance. But "exposing" a politician who
merely voted in ways deplored by gay groups would be insufficient
reason in my view.

When a Philadelphia man filed suit accusing the late Cardinal Joseph
Bernardin of abusing him sexually *twenty years earlier,* I held the story to a
few paragraphs that merely recorded the cardinal's denial. I also refused to
let news that we were shunning creep into *The Times* by the back door—
the sly coverage of the coverage of the subject in other media. We held to
that resolve when Gennifer Flowers described her alleged escapades with
Bill Clinton, printing only a one-paragraph story headlined, CLINTON AT-
TEMPTS TO IGNORE RUMORS. I personally believed that they had had a relationship but far enough in the past that it did not warrant our attention
or the enormous resources it would have taken to try to prove it. As far as
the 1992 campaign was concerned, the Clintons had given mature voters
all they needed to know when they responded on national television by
confessing that theirs had not been a perfect marriage.

We observed the same decorum when Democrats tried to counter the
Clinton gossip with plausible rumors of an erstwhile George Bush affair.
And when Paula Jones, abetted by Republican tutors, appeared to accuse
Clinton of having years earlier approached her lewdly, we were content to
let others traffic in the details while restricting our coverage to the legal
battle ignited by her suit.

We were simply and proudly reluctant to report on the sexual activities of consenting adults. And whenever we were somehow forced to delve
into people's private lives, we preferred not to be first with lewd and lurid
details. Our resistance to scandal was of course easier to proclaim than to
observe as we traversed the era of Anita Hill and Clarence Thomas, Jim
and Tammy Bakker, Mike Tyson, Michael Jackson, Joey Buttafuoco and
Amy Fisher, Lorena and John Bobbitt, Heidi Fleiss and half of Hollywood, and, in a climactic orgy, O. J. Simpson & Co. Monica Lewinsky
mercifully arrived too late for my attention, and I continue to hope that
The Times will always be late and sedate in pursuing scandals of sex.

To my delight, I discovered on the occasion of our centennial in 1996
that our fussy urbanity in these matters was in the best tradition of Adolph

Ochs, the founder of the modern *Times*. Looking over the very first issue
of his reign in 1896, I found that one of the longest articles concerned the
marriage of an obviously prominent and wealthy New Yorker to a woman
of obviously questionable pedigree. The story of her long pecuniary path
to his bed was rendered in elegant and enviable *Times* style:

> Elizabeth L. Blanc, a woman of many husbands and much mystery, added to the latter and apparently to the former yesterday when the morning newspapers published in their marriage columns this vague notice: WATERS-BLANC. . . .
>
> Mrs. Blanc has been for several years one of those whose doings cause people to talk about them a great deal. . . . Her [first] husband lost all his money and she left him. . . . Then she became the wife of the man from whom she took the pseudo title "Baroness"— Baron Frederick Blanc. Baron was his first Christian name, but he seldom used it. . . . The "Baroness" and her husband were not inseparable, and soon a detective was the principal witness in a suit for divorce. . . .
>
> Mr. Waters is said to be the possessor of several million dollars. He is a member of several prominent clubs.

The "tone of *The Times*" has always been the subject of lively debate in our
ranks. My goal was to keep us away from cruel and tawdry gossip without
discouraging shrewd observation and witty writing. The distinction was
hard to define and never static; mocking the ego of a politician or movie
star who labors inside a tightly controlled publicity bubble is not the same
as trashing the personality of a private person who figures only incidentally in the news. Bucked up to me in my last month on the job in 1994 was
Maureen Dowd's wickedly deft lead from Oxford, England:

> President Clinton returned today for a sentimental journey to the university where he didn't inhale, didn't get drafted and didn't get a degree.

I hesitated but approved. I knew that sentence on our Page One would
arouse a pious burst of criticism that we were "editorializing" in the news
columns. But that was no editorial; it was an apt spoof of an otherwise in-
consequential presidential photo op, an occasion of *only* biographical interest. I later confessed to colleagues that I was strongly influenced in my
decision by the bitter memory of *The Times*'s refusal to print *my* description, two decades earlier, of a president's similar diversion from the affairs
of state—when Richard Milhous Nixon journeyed to the city of Limerick
in a comic election-year search for an Irish forebear. I had filed a dozen
paragraphs in this vein:

He stayed in a millionaire's house—
Mulcahy, who often shoots grouse.
But the hunt on this day
Was for much bigger prey:
"A kingdom for just one Milhous."

"Don't care how he spells it," he said.
"Or whether he's living or dead.
"I need a relation
"In this mighty nation
"Lest the polls once again drift to Ted."

My verses were no match for Maureen's prose. But we were both right to look upon trivial presidential junkets as invitations to spoofs. I thought our readers had the wit to enjoy a joke in their news and that such small steps toward permissiveness would be giant strides toward sophistication. Long live Mrs. Blanc!

47 · LONG LIVE THE MONARCHY!

LIKE IT OR NOT, AN EFFECTIVE EDITOR MUST KEEP AN eye on the company's business ledgers, if only to know when to go lean and when to turn mean. Here is what I have learned about the business of newspapers.

Every newspaper enterprise uneasily unites three factions. One writes the paper. Another prints and distributes it. The third sells admission to readers and advertisers. Almost everywhere, this third faction has come to dominate the enterprise. The "marketers" bring in all the revenue and compel the other teams to help sell and reduce expenses. In management lingo, the marketers constitute "profit centers," whereas the production and news departments represent centers of "cost." And wherever that terminology takes hold, quality journalism is at risk.

The business is rife with slogans that camouflage the threat. *The only free and independent press is a profitable press.* True. But ever-greater profits do not make a paper more free and independent. Quite the opposite. The relentless pursuit of profit panders to commercial interests and causes informative news to be replaced with the inane.

Our first fiduciary duty is to the stockholders. True again. But providing for stockholders can shortchange readers; their interests can significantly diverge. Unless they are specially educated and restrained, stockholders care most about a company's customers—and readers are not a newspaper's main customers; advertisers are. Readers pay for only a small fraction of a newspaper's costs; they are, in fact, themselves a commodity that is routinely "sold" to advertisers—so many thousand readers per dollar.

The advertisers, stockholders, and Wall Street "analysts" who together decide a newspaper's commercial prospects generate a force that few news departments or publishers can withstand. Especially when profit margins slip and stock prices stagnate, emergency measures are invoked. News bureaus are closed. The space allotted to news is reduced. Reporters and editors are "bought out," and hiring is "frozen." Since most American newspapers no longer face any other paper's direct competition, this dilution risks no immediate reader revolt, only a slow erosion to which bonus-seeking managements and transient stockholders are usually indifferent.

In the struggle among a newspaper's three factions, the news team has been further weakened by two technological blows. Since computers replaced live printers, editors have had to assume the drone labor of preparing articles and photos for the press. Therefore newsroom tasks have increased even as newsroom budgets have been constrained. And with the dwindling of the blue-collar labor force, the newsroom staff and the price of milled newsprint are what loom as the costliest items—and targets—in the company budget.

The imbalance of power between earners and spenders has damaged news operations at all but a handful of American newspapers. The exceptions are obvious: instead of stockholder "democracies" they remain limited monarchies. They are family papers, like *The Times*, whose founders did well by doing good and who managed against the odds to pass both their values and assets to succeeding generations.

That explains why *The Times, The Washington Post*, and *The Wall Street Journal* head the lists of the best American papers. They are still substantially owned by wise, lucky, and public-spirited families. Even these great enterprises had to strain to survive the confiscatory estate tax laws that forced most other family papers into the chains of absentee owners. *The New York Times* itself has acquired a chain of subsidiary papers, to which it will never give the same affection and nourishment it gives to the family's own. The families that salvaged control of their papers did so by selling a gimmicky kind of stock, which promises dividends and growth to public shareholders but denies them sufficient voting power to challenge the monarchy for control. And that is why bloodline publishers are still able to resist the relentless pressure for ever-greater profit margins that is felt at entirely public corporations.

The families are not absolute rulers. They, too, must deliver dividends and ascending profit margins. But they can pursue a more distant and responsible vision of success than next month's bottom line.

Long live the monarchy!

———————

Although he took pride in his corporate success, Punch Sulzberger regularly invoked his royal authority to balance *The Times*'s pursuit of profit against the performance of public service. He has maintained the largest newspaper bureau in Washington and the largest number of newspaper correspondents around the United States and across the world. He spent a bundle—and risked the store—to defend publication of the Pentagon Papers and to challenge other government attacks on the press. He imposed budgets on his News Department, but when revolutions flare and empires collapse, no *Times* editor need hesitate before spending whatever it takes to chase the story at full throttle. No one upstairs dared to flinch when I would report at a year's end that "we came in under budget—*except, of course, for covering the tumult in Eastern Europe and the war in Iraq.*" The Gulf War alone cost the News Department an extra $3 million, not counting the cost of extra newsprint.

When I became editor, the regal scepter was passing slowly to Arthur Sulzberger, Jr., Punch's only son, a smart, energetic, and opinionated thirty-eight-year-old. Arthur was quick to leap to conclusions, but he soon learned to hear out those who dared to disagree. Like his father, he sheathed his authority in good manners and displays of informality. Like his father, he hated confrontation and yearned to lead a harmonious team. He was elaborately prepared for his princely functions through years of reporting, editing, marketing, and production duties at *The Times*. Alas, he also passed through one too many management courses and began his ascendancy by peddling their nostrums. For a time, we were subjected to the platitudinous mantras of W. Edwards Deming, an itinerant preacher who exhorted corporations to "drive out fear" by governing "cooperatively" instead of hierarchically. Sure.

Then came intramural meetings led by "facilitators" who demanded the composition of a corporate "vision statement," an undertaking rivaled only by the writing of the Constitution. We could not decide whether *The Times* had to be a good newspaper to be profitable or profitable to produce a good newspaper. The laughable compromise ("Editorial excellence and independence are essential to our profitability, and profit sustains them") was proclaimed to a puzzled staff and mercifully filed away.

Still, these misfired bondings had the salutary result of demonstrating to Arthur that he could not overcome all of our factional rivalries. The business departments were paid to make money; the news departments were paid to spend it creatively. We could respect each other, but not cease our tug-o'-war, and the publisher was destined to remain both rope and referee.

Despite all his infatuations with business-school devices, Arthur, like his father, did not define the family business as the making of money. He wanted to make money to underwrite great journalism, to enrich American life, and to take his place among the custodians of one of the world's great institutions. His sense of public service ran in the blood that passed from Adolph Ochs to his daughter, Iphigene, to her son, Punch, and daughters, Marian, Ruth, and Judy, and to a large cohort of Arthur's sometimes envious cousins. The ultimate irritant among our factions was the business team's lingering knowledge that, if pushed too hard, a Sulzberger would always end up on journalism's side. So when the day arrived in January 1992 to announce Arthur's elevation to the job of publisher, I cheerfully climbed atop a desk in the newsroom, raised a glass of champagne, and, to the obvious embarrassment of father and son, exclaimed to the entire staff, "I believe in the monarchy."

The assembled reporters and editors knew what I meant. And no matter how many wished—with me—that we lived in a society where more of us could still aspire to actually own a press, they cheered my meaning.

I was not, even then, prime minister to a wholly secure sovereign. As deputy publisher, Arthur had formed a kind of triumvirate of himself, Lance Primis, and me to preside over the paper. But we were all accountable to and manipulated by Walter Mattson, the corporation's president and chief operating officer.

Mattson, a production wizard, had earned his great authority by liberating *The Times* from the stranglehold of the printers' union and lifting the paper out of penury during New York's recession in the 1970s. In the recovering '80s, he won the board's blessing for a ten-year investment of $1 billion to build the country's most advanced four-color printing plants. He was assured by a grateful Punch that he would not have to report to the next Sulzberger generation and so stayed only long enough to complete his constructions and to sell off some misguided purchases of small newspapers. He retired young, at sixty, just as Arthur was named publisher. But until that moment, it was Mattson who guided Punch in defining the paper's priorities and profit goals, setting salaries and bonuses and staffing levels for all major divisions.

I came to admire Mattson's firm sense of purpose and obvious pride in the quality of the paper. I also felt his respect for my managerial style, which his stolid Swedish soul had not expected to find in anyone of my liberal persuasion. But I regretted his failure to create a forum in which the most critical corporate strategies could be more widely discussed and debated. My suggestions for new investments were normally welcomed only when justified with a predictable profit potential. All other ventures had to be largely self-financed from our own economies and even then fenced off from periodic pressure to retrench. My staffing needs were usually reduced to a foolish "FTE" census—a body count of full-time employees—which induced us to sacrifice clerks to hire reporters, even though Punch rightly fumed at our failure to properly answer the phone. Moreover, the annual budget review was less a rational planning exercise than a treacherous poker game. First time at the table, I no sooner confessed that we could do without the meager offerings of UPI, a then dying news agency, than Mattson pocketed the $1 million saving for his own disposal. With an obviously primed Punch nodding assent, he announced that he could not possibly share the windfall with the News Department. I never again turned up my cards so quickly.

In time, my petitions to Mattson became much more indirect. I might casually remark in a hallway encounter that I planned to add more business news, a cause close to his heart. Finding him enthusiastic, I would at once feel authorized to budget for additional reporters, maybe even including a couple of media writers under the "business" rubric. I think we both preferred these subtle collaborations to tiresome blather about managerial fraternity.

One of my proudest achievements began with just such a casual conversation. While reviewing the benefits, bonuses, and stock options available to managers and editors, I complained to Mattson in Punch's presence that we were unfairly denying such rewards to our most valuable writers. They were losing out simply because they preferred, to our benefit, to write rather than to manage. Since they had no supervisory duties, they were required to remain members of the Newspaper Guild, a now toothless union whose benefits, especially retirement pay, were disturbingly inadequate.

Mattson understood at once that a creative team should not be seen as a conventional hierarchy; the stars of every sports team were better paid than the managers. But he discovered that we were not legally permitted to select out some union members for special benefits. We were, however, free to pay them cash bonuses, I countered, so why not translate the managers' rewards into cash equivalents and urge the best writers and photographers to buy their own supplementary annuities, stocks, and life insurance? Arthur Sulzberger, Jr., eagerly took up this project to gradually designate about a tenth of our staff as senior writers and photographers, to augment their salaries by about 25 percent, or $20,000, and to counsel them on long-term investments. It took only a few weeks to draft the plan but an incredible three years to put it through. First the company dawdled, demanding a "consultant" who was paid $30,000 to translate my ideas into business-school jargon. Then the union called a halt, accusing us of plotting an "unfair labor practice." We were finally able to proceed in 1991, making a modest start on a vital bit of profit sharing with our most talented performers.

Still, my influence in company politics depended entirely on Punch's and Arthur's tilt toward news values. That proved to be crucial after the recession of 1987, which produced a paradox that haunted my entire editorship: a progressive loss of advertisers despite a steady gain in readers. The greater our appeal, the smaller our profit. The more exciting the news and the more accomplished our delivery of the paper, the greater the economic strain. We lost even more business than newspapers elsewhere because New York's giant retailers disappeared into bankruptcies and mergers. The stock market's decline depressed New York's real estate values, cutting our classified advertising in half. The company's operating profit as a proportion of revenues plummeted from 17 percent in 1987 to 5 percent in 1991–1993; we earned $2 per outstanding share in 1988, 61 cents in 1991, and *lost* 14 cents in 1992. As the company scrambled to adjust, my yearnings for tidy planning had to yield to shameless opportunism.

The paradox revealed itself the moment the market crashed on October 19, 1987. From the start, we subjected the news to sophisticated analysis, predicting the decline in the New York economy and reaching far beyond the obvious headline of STOCKS PLUNGE 508 POINTS, A DROP OF 22.6%. To add perspective and help avert panic, we ran a huge graph across the front page to show that while the market had surrendered more than a year's growth in a single day, it still held the gains of four prior bullish years. We featured two articles whose headlines addressed the readers' most anxious questions: DOES 1987 EQUAL 1929? ("The quick answer, many economists say, is no") and WHO GETS HURT? ("Most Americans . . . even those who own no stock at all"). For days, we later learned, the brass at *The Wall Street Journal* marveled at our performance on their turf. We greatly reinforced the prestige of our business coverage and gained new confidence for the analytical approach to big events. But we immediately felt a great strain on our staff and the frailty of our expertise. While our halls echoed with praise, I hurried to cash in by getting approval to hire the likes of Floyd Norris and Diana Henriques, Wall Street mavens who could keep *The Times* competitive in the exploding field of business journalism.

Readers were now expecting us to cover business with the same skill and skepticism we brought to coverage of government. Besides earnings statements and new stock offerings, they wanted to know about business failures and frauds. And a smart business section had become an essential element in our new National Edition, an obvious competitor of *The Wall Street Journal*.

I was always convinced that *The Times*'s destiny was to become America's foremost national paper. Our kind of educated, curious, and affluent readers could be found not only in Manhattan, Scarsdale, and Southampton but also in Grosse Pointe, Atlanta, Dallas, and San Jose. The proof came quickly after the market crash, when the rapid growth of our national readership concealed an actual decline in circulation in recession-struck New York. Yet the company clung to the doctrine that our fate was tied to the volatile New York economy.

Like all American newspapers, *The Times* was conceived as a purely local institution and only slowly followed its readers into the suburbs. Even papers that had spread their wings across larger regions, like the *Chicago Tribune* in the Midwest and *The Boston Globe* in New England, operated with a geographical state of mind. They reckoned success by their "penetration"—the percentage of homes they reached in a measurable region. But *The New York Times*, while similarly dependent on local advertising, was all along evolving a demographic appeal. Its readers were defined not so much by where they lived as by their place in American society.

Tugging against our own business department, we gave David Jones license to edit the National Edition to national tastes. We could not possibly cover California for Californians or Texas for Texans, but we featured the national, foreign, cultural, and business news that was shortchanged in most other newspapers, and we screened out parochial stories so that far-off readers did not have to be greeted on Page One by news of a Brooklyn subway derailment.

During my editorship, the weekday sales of the satellite edition increased by more than 100,000 while sales in the Northeast grew by only 50,000 and in New York City hardly at all. It was not until the 1990s that *The Times* capitalized on this success by daring to raise the price of the National Edition aggressively, to $1 on weekdays and $4 on Sundays, and getting all our readers to pay as much as a fourth of our total costs. And it was not until after I retired as editor, in the late 1990s, that *The Times* slowly overcame its view that a newspaper's fate is forever bound up with the local economy.

––––––––––

The strength we discovered nationally made it all the more remarkable that one of my main achievements as editor was the expansion of our local news coverage, notably including sports. Although two thirds of our readers lived and worked in the New York region, I inherited insufficient staff to keep up with the major news of a three-state area extending 100 miles in all directions. And our paper's design and deadlines left us badly trailing the vigorous sports coverage of three local tabloids—*New York Newsday*, the *Daily News*, and the *Post*. *The Times* was able to run a distinct sports section only on Sundays and Mondays. Most days, we offered 40 percent less sports news than other major papers, and we allowed the sports pages to wander unpredictably from section to section, as our press configurations required. Worse still, nearly half our readers received papers without any coverage of night games—meaning most games—because we had to start our presses before 10:00 P.M. to load trucks bound for New England and the mid-Atlantic states.

The conjunction of three circumstances now turned these deficiencies into strategy. Most fortunately, Lance Primis, our general manager, was a former minor-league pitcher, an ardent golfer, and an avid reader of sports news. He was palpably shamed by our cramped and always late sports report. Fortunately also, the *Los Angeles Times* was then investing heavily in a New York edition of its Long Island *Newsday*, hoping to become the city's lone surviving tabloid. In trying to put the *Daily News* out of its multiple miseries, *Newsday* had more reporters on the streets of New York City than I had throughout the metropolitan area. Most important, the Sulzberger family had learned from experience that bad economic times were the best times to reinvest in the quality of the paper, so that when good times returned we would be riding the crest of the wave in top form.

For the sake of sports news, but also the quality of our general coverage, the best thing we could possibly do was to narrow the gap between the time we went to press and the time our readers received the paper. So long as the first complete paper had to be finished at 9:00 P.M. in New York, a reporter in Washington would have to leave a hearing by five and a reporter in California would have to start writing at two o'clock local time. If we could send the paper by satellite to eight different plants around the country, why not also to Boston and Washington, and liberate ourselves from the truckings north and south? The potential benefit was startling: we could produce three distinct editions—Metro, Northeast, and National—advance our deadline by three hours to nearly midnight, and still deliver the paper to every door sooner than ever before. The force of my arguments deserves some credit for this strategy, but it was the Sulzbergers' determination to invest in the future and the devotion to this ten-year plan by our business and mechanical departments that brought it to fruition by the end of 1997.

Besides building two new local printing plants with color presses, the company had to purchase the cooperation of unions that did not lightly relinquish the Northeast truck runs or pressroom featherbeddings. Simultaneously, *The Times* was struggling to regain control of its delivery routes and wholesale distributorships, carefully navigating around the antitrust laws and the violent threats of unsavory union operatives. One of our major deals had to be concluded with drivers long suspected of the systematic theft of papers and led by Douglas LaChance while he was still on parole after serving five years of a twelve-year sentence for racketeering and extortion.

Until the ten-year plan could be realized, I also proposed an interim but by no means inexpensive expansion of city, regional, and sports coverage. It called for adding two pages of Metro news and two of Sports, separate Sunday sections for Metro news and for City neighborhood coverage, and an upgrading of the Sunday suburban weeklies for New Jersey, Westchester, and Long Island—all requiring the addition of more than fifty reporters and editors. At a further cost in newsprint, I insisted that we anchor the Sports pages in a predictable place, ideally the Metro section, so that we would have a genuine "New York paper" inside *The New York Times.*

This interim plan would have cost the News Department an additional $5 million a year, or more than 5 percent of my annual budget, not counting the cost of paper. It was approved in principle in early 1991, but with profits still declining, it was whittled down and parsed into stages for only gradual execution over thirty months. I lost the chance to upgrade the suburban Sunday sections and was allowed only about half the proposed staff expansion. I also had to accept delay in the reconstruction of our newsroom, settling for $350,000 in new carpeting.

Our high operating costs made it all the more remarkable that we spent the recession years plotting all these costly improvements. The Sulzbergers even heeded my plea to exempt the newsroom from the hiring freeze imposed on our commercial departments. They quickly understood that the accidents of illness and resignation during a freeze would dangerously distort the character of *The Times*. We would always replace a White House correspondent or food or fashion critic, which meant that most attrition would strike at the highly competitive Metro and Business staffs. Moreover, if we wanted to be ready with great reporters for Moscow or Tokyo or Washington six years hence, we simply could not interrupt the annual infusions of new talent in New York.

———————

One of the great joys in newspapering is that whatever misfires today can be set right, retired, or retried tomorrow. A newspaper is a furniture mover's heaven; one change always leads to another. And the pace of the business itself breeds experiment because ideas can be realized so quickly. Now that the local news was appearing Sundays on a page headed "Metro Report," it occurred to us that we could mimic a "front page" inside Section A to mark the start of a "National Report" and inside Section C to announce the beginning of "The Arts" section. We thus projected our hopes for the multisectioned paper that would, by the end of 1997, roll from four-color presses, packing all national news coherently into Section A and letting the Arts and Sports flourish in their own separate sections at last.

Like Moses, I was gone before *The Times* reached this promised land. And so, alas, was my favorite foil, *New York Newsday*. The family that once directed the *Los Angeles Times* had lost interest, and its many heirs, to cash out, summoned a new management that pursued a scorched-earth policy to drive up the value of the company's stock. The closing of *New York Newsday* promised new life to the *News* and the *Post*, but it deprived us of a vital and useful local competitor.

The New York Times as a whole confronts no single rival. The Washington bureau feels the hot breath of *The Washington Post*, but the Business section runs primarily against *The Wall Street Journal*, the Foreign Desk keeps a wary eye on *The Economist*, while the Book Review competes for writers and readers with *The New York Review of Books*. Even the advertising in various sections must be sold in competition against different media. And the time-consuming *Times* must ultimately compete with golf and travel and child rearing for the attention of affluent, busy readers.

The unpredictable rise and fall of our rivals and of the public's interest in news proved to be a draining distraction. We spent precious hours worrying about the upward creep in the age of our readers and our insufficient appeal to the young. We were improving sports, and we were good at pop music, TV, and computers; what else might infect young readers with the newspaper habit? At one point, when the *Daily News* was mismanaged into bankruptcy, we came close to losing our bearings altogether. Arthur Jr. asked Joe Lelyveld to consider which of its features, particularly its comics, we would rush to acquire if the *News* died.

Tossing that potato to me, Joe shrewdly observed that our desire to lure younger readers and the desirability of acquiring comic strips ought to be separate issues. And if we now wanted comics, after a century of scorning them, shouldn't we find our own? Everything else in *The Times* was original work.

For once, I felt unfit to reach a judgment. Most newspaper comics bored me, even "Doonesbury," the yuppie rage. Stumped by Arthur's inquiry, I punted to Punch, who set me right with a typically wise and witty response:

> I am very much from Missouri when it comes to introducing them in *The New York Times*. . . . We should nurture and strengthen the perception of *The Times* as a serious paper, and I am loath to discard it just to exploit the passing of the *News*. . . .
>
> I am a comics reader from way back. . . . I start my day with a blueberry muffin and the *News*. . . . "Calvin and Hobbes" is brilliant, and "The Far Side" nicely sick. To me, "Doonesbury" is turning into a bore, but it's still good. . . . "Hagar" is consistently amusing, as are "Blondie," "Herman," "Peanuts" (the best of the lot, bar none), "Grin and Bear It," and "Beetle Bailey". . . . But I would have great reservations about importing or starting our own strips—what would we do on Sunday? . . .
>
> Suppose all these comics and an editor cost us $500,000 per year. Is that where we would be best spending it? There must be a million ideas to capture new readers and still keep us in the news business— a business for which we are known and in which we excel.

The most important function of the family monarch is to resolve the inevitable conflicts between Advertising and News and to protect journalistic values from commercial attack. There is always one more ad or category of advertising to be gained if only, if only, if only. If only we would write more about cosmetics in the Magazine. If only we had a columnist salivating over automobiles. If only we could keep unpleasant international news out of the Travel section. If only we would give more space to the runway fashions in Milan. If only we gave advertisers a better "environment." Our kingdom for environment! Supermarkets want an environment of recipes, not famine in Africa. Airlines want an environment unsullied by news of a plane crash. Department stores don't mind Cambodian genocide, but keep them away from the ads of discount houses!

These strictures are easily mocked, but they derive from an undeniable fact of newspaper life. Environment pays. Book ads want to appear where book readers congregate. Computer ads flock to a technology section. Stockbrokers insist on the business columns. We would cover sports, concerts, and travel news even if they drew no ads. But a well-read restaurant critic certainly sells restaurant ads, just as a flood of movie ads every Friday stimulates *The Times* to write more about films than about gardens. We do sell "environment" where that benignly means creating a definable category or community of readers. The trouble starts when advertisers demand not just subject matter that complements their products but also influence over the words and images appearing beside theirs.

Not since Adolph Ochs's earliest weeks at *The Times* did any editor ever have to hesitate to print news that might offend a major advertiser. And when we did, no one so burdened in our advertising department would dare complain to News. Once, when our articles exposing a conflict of interest at Fidelity Investments provoked that company to withdraw all its ads, I was not even made aware of the loss until after the publisher managed to lure them back.

The only persistent whoring for advertisers in *The Times* occurs in our fashion supplements, which shamelessly feature the clothes of designers, manufacturers, and retailers whose business we seek. None of that coziness, however, blunts our news coverage of the fashion and retailing industries. Not even appeals to the publisher helped Ralph Lauren, a major advertiser, to persuade us to glorify him and his company on his company's twenty-fifth anniversary. Nor could the Pressmans of Barneys get us to ease up on chronicling their financial troubles on the way to bankruptcy. If anything, our sharp coverage served to warn our own accountants that some advertisers, like Macy's at one point, might face trouble paying some of their bills.

Some challenges to our independence arose inside the News Department itself. Our growing sophistication in spotting fraud in government, business, sports, and even science made us progressively aware of our own vulnerability to conflicts of interest, real and apparent. Conduct that had seemed unexceptional in the past came to appear questionable and caused us, case by case, to keep revising the posted rules for reporters and editors.

In the 1950s New York's politicians and Tammany bosses routinely showered reporters with liquor and luggage at Christmas, rarely buying specific favors but assuring themselves of "access" to a sympathetic ear. That was soon stopped with Punch's order to return any gift worth more than ten dollars. But it was not until the 1970s that reporters and editors began paying for tickets to sporting events and other attractions at which they performed no professional duties. That same decade I was deeply embarrassed by my service on the board of the German Marshall Fund of the United States, an apparently safe educational foundation that suddenly veered into subsidizing media ventures in ways that troubled me. We learned from other papers in the 1980s to guard against stock trades by members of our financial staff and to limit the frequency with which *Times* writers appeared in other publications or on television programs.

To eliminate all suspicions of insider trading, I and other top news executives annually reported all our personal investments to *The Times*'s chief financial officer. We had to forbid ill-advised book collaborations after a colleague who sometimes wrote about the auto industry thoughtlessly became Lee Iacocca's coauthor. We had long since forbidden endorsements of commercial products when we discovered that the greatest embarrassment could flow from the flip endorsement of a book. Marty Tolchin, a reporter then covering the House of Representatives, had carelessly offered a few kind words for the jacket of Speaker Jim Wright's *Reflections of a Public Man*, a book whose bulk sales turned out to be hidden subsidies from Texas fat cats. The trickery led to Wright's resignation from Congress and led me to quickly add book blurbs to the list of impermissible endorsements.

A great uproar followed my discovery in 1989 that the reviewers of other papers were engaged in blatant politicking over the annual honors awarded by the New York drama and film critics. Since our critics routinely listed their favorite films, books, and stage plays at season's end in *The Times*, I saw no reason why they should also join in a rival listing that provoked such unseemly behavior. Our first-string critics felt much relieved; our second-stringers resented losing their places at the table. Complaints about my "arrogance" and "pomposity" were heard around town, but I insisted that critics had no business distributing commercial favor. Responding to pressure, Punch begged me for an exemption so that our fashion writers could continue to vote for prizes given by the Council of Fashion Designers, but I persuaded him that those industry awards were especially suspect. By the same logic, I rejected the appeal of our leading sportswriters, who wanted to go on electing retired baseball players to the Hall of Fame.

Hardly a month passed without some such conflict question. Linda Greenhouse, our brilliant Supreme Court reporter, failed at first to see why I objected to her participating in a Washington parade in support of abortion rights. She thought her anonymous appearance in a huge crowd was not the same as signing her name to a petition. I argued that it was no different than wearing a silent campaign button to a White House press briefing. Fortunately, these indiscretions were nothing like the case of the reporter fired by Abe Rosenthal for having once taken up with a politician on her beat. In a memorably succinct rendering of our policy, Abe said, "I don't care if you fuck elephants as long as you're not covering the circus."

That still did not prepare me for the news in *Sports Illustrated* that Steven Crist, our outstanding racing correspondent, was an addicted handicapper who regularly multiplied his salary at the track. Our rules had somehow neglected to cover that contingency, and he swore that his job never exposed him to inside information. But the appearances alone were troubling enough for me to make him stop. He did, but he began at once to look for work with a more sympathetic employer. That same year ended with the startling news that Al Scardino, our media reporter, had been secretly giving David Dinkins and his staff his "perceptions" of their campaign for the mayoralty. To erase all doubt about such behavior, I felt compelled to denounce the deed even as he quit to become the mayor's press secretary. He called my reaction libelous.

None of our rules and guidelines, of course, could fully define the rights of the Sulzberger family—the only ones among us who, as A. J. Liebling put it, enjoyed real freedom of the press by owning one. Adolph Ochs had set an impressive precedent in his first year in New York, when he told a leading financial backer that "I cannot agree that any publication which is to appear in *The New York Times* or that is proposed for publication should be submitted for your approval." Ochs had just as stoutly resolved not to demand approval rights for himself, a policy normally honored by all his successors. But then again, publishers are human. They want their paper to serve their interests, and, as good citizens, their interests extend beyond the paper itself. Punch's greatest interests outside *The Times* were the Metropolitan Museum of Art, which he served as chairman; Columbia University and Mount Sinai Hospital, where he sat as a board member; and the Marine Corps, whose anthem always brought him to his feet.

Punch pressed us hardest only when he thought himself the agent of a worthy cause. He gave the heads of the Metropolitan, Columbia, and Mount Sinai special access to his editors but never ordered any stories about them into or out of the paper. The closest he ever came was an expression of nervousness after the temperamental Walter Annenberg gave (or had tentatively given?) his art collection to the Met:

> Please make sure that Mr. Kimmelman's review is devoid of zingers. I have no problem with him using his critical eye to determine which of Walter's paintings are world class and which may be of a more minimal nature. But there are ways of indicating this . . . without cutting off the balls of the owner. This is truly important for me and for New York.

An added cause of this concern, I am sure, was Frank Rich's drama criticism. Wherever they went, Punch and Carol Sulzberger had to suffer the bitter laments of the Shuberts and other Broadway angels whose productions failed to elicit a Rich rave. Producers called our critic "the butcher of Broadway" and blamed him for cruelly closing their shows—not, they insisted, because he had earned the trust of theatergoers but because he abused *The Times*'s unique influence with them. Punch relayed these complaints with obvious sympathy. He wanted me to restrain Rich's caustic prose and gratuitous blows at pop targets like Andrew Lloyd Webber. I, too, wished that Rich's negative opinions could be rendered more often in sorrow than in anger. But I felt duty bound to shield him from obviously commercial pressures—and from Punch's too tolerant taste in musicals. As I never dared to admit out loud, I trusted only Rich's pans; his praise often struck me as too generous.

Punch never demanded direct satisfaction in the news columns—not even for *Times* board members or his own acquaintances and business associates. A wedding announcement for the daughter of a friend or advertiser was the customary limit of our corruptibility. I might hear that Richard Gelb, a *Times* director, was dissatisfied with an article affecting his company, Bristol-Myers Squibb, or that William Scranton, another member, was eager to publicize a railroad museum in Scranton, Pennsylvania, to help it obtain a federal subsidy. Punch might ask me to "see what the trouble is," or "see if we can do something." But a fair response was all that he desired.

The greatest clash of interests occurred not between *The Times* and outside forces but among the factions inside our corporate structure. When Lance Primis succeeded Walter Mattson as company president, he virtually stopped peddling the paper to devote himself to pitching the company's stock. He exaggerated the promise of his trivial ventures into electronic journalism and preened in front of the staff about his pursuit of Wall Street's short-term, short-lived praises. The great newspaper at the heart of this enterprise seemed to strike Primis as merely a cost to be managed, squeezed for cash to fuel fanciful acquisitions like the Knicks and Rangers, whose management he knew nothing about. Primis wanted our chain of smaller newspapers to increase their profit margins to an obscene 33 percent, disregarding the effect on their quality. After leaving the triumvirate by which we had jointly managed *The Times* and fashioned our ten-year plan, he had not a single further conversation with me. And he treated Arthur Sulzberger, Jr., as an errant underling. Primis obviously hoped so to impress the stock market and the business moguls on our board that he would rise to become the first outsider to command the corporation. He dealt roughly with not only Arthur Jr., an obvious rival, but also the other family members working at the paper.

Happily, Punch and his sisters understood that the family's values were safe only if entrusted to family leadership. *The Times* was not just a profitable brand name to be stamped on lesser goods but a unique American institution that could not be allowed to become a subsidiary function in a media company. If drained of its vitality, this great newspaper would never be re-created. The ultimate power had to be retained for family members whose identity was firmly entwined with that of *The Times*. Arthur Jr. was the inevitable leader of such a family council in the next generation. Primis, having sought the throne for himself, became the inevitable loser. With a swift stroke in late 1996, Punch replaced him with Russ Lewis, a far less pretentious attorney imbued with *Times* values, and he quickly appointed Lewis, Arthur Jr., and his nephew Michael Golden to the board.

Long live the monarchy!

The New York Times

VOL.CXLI No. 48.808   NEW YORK, MONDAY, DECEMBER 9, 1991   50 CENTS

DECLARING DEATH OF SOVIET UNION, RUSSIA AND 2 REPUBLICS FORM NEW COMMONWEALTH

Frantic Moves Came to Light In Days Before Maxwell Died

As the Empire Was Crumbling

West Europeans Gather to Seek A Tighter Union

By ALAN RIDING

The New and the Old

TAKE OVER A-ARMS

Newborn Bureaucracy Is Inheriting Functions of Old Authority

By SERGE SCHMEMANN

"We, the republic of Byelorussia, the Russian Federation and Ukraine ... state that the U.S.S.R., as a subject of international law and geopolitical reality, is ceasing its existence.
— Brest declaration, Dec. 8, 1991

The Union Is Buried: What's Being Born?

Gorbachev's Vain Pleas Make His Rulings Clear

---

48 · STOP THE PRESSES!

ONE AFTERNOON IN MAY 1989, THE HUNGARIANS PULLED down a piece of the border wire at the very spot where I had watched them restring it in November 1956. I drove the Picture Desk crazy looking for a close-up photo of that barbed strand, as if I knew the cut would collapse an empire. I didn't know, of course, but I had been expertly trained, by the Nazis and the Communists, to know that totalitarians were no stronger than their weakest link.

What I should have known deep within me is that the coup de grâce would be delivered by refugees, refugees always searching for a path out; refugees, no less, from my zone of Germany.

Some Germans who happened to be vacationing in Hungary when the wire was rent simply rode to the border and walked into Austria, where they could claim the citizenship and passport that *West* Germany had always promised its countrymen in the East. Hundreds of other vacationers who did not want to trudge across borders by night then besieged the West

German embassy in Budapest and refused to leave until they, too, obtained the precious papers. Sensing opportunity, thousands more swarmed the grounds of the West German embassy in Prague.

The Communists in Moscow and their satraps throughout Eastern Europe had only a few hours to remember their totalitarian catechism, the lesson of Lenin and Stalin that you cannot preserve an irrational order with reason. Either smash disaffection or watch the order crumble. At the crucial moment, Gorbachev proclaimed himself a man of reason, and without his tanks the Polish, Czech, German, and Hungarian Communists stood naked and disarmed. They bowed to "humanitarian" demands to let the 10,000 camped on various embassy grounds entrain for the West. But as soon as the trains pulled out, tens of thousands more packed for Prague. The refugees poured across borders and jammed the highways for miles around until finally people all over East Germany assembled in nightly demonstrations to demand *their* right to travel in dignity, by any route. Directing our coverage, I felt myself to be conducting a grand opera finale.

A year had passed since I indulged my intuition and gave the lead position in *The Times* to an austere headline that read MOSCOW IMPOSES EMERGENCY DECREE IN ETHNIC CONFLICT / STRIFE IN DISPUTED AREA. I thought I recognized an important event, but a letter from Sen. Pat Moynihan woke me up to its truly historic significance:

> I venture to guess that [it] . . . will be recorded as one of the most significant headlines of the century. The undoing of the Czarist/ Soviet empire is surely at hand.
>
> When [Nathan Glazer] and I wrote *Beyond the Melting Pot* thirty years ago now, I was mostly going on about the old neighborhood. He had something much larger in mind. Namely, if we were right, Marx was wrong. Ethnicity would prevail; not class solidarity. . . . An astounding act of intellectual audacity in the New York of the time.

And astounding still in 1988. Moynihan was light-years ahead of our vaunted CIA analysts. And who ever thought that the Irish, black, and Puerto Rican gangs that had assaulted me in the old neighborhood embodied such a tribal force?

By the autumn of 1989, I understood. In Berlin, just yards from where Mom had begged and schemed for our visa to America, crowds of Germans pressed against the Wall that Kennedy had not dared to destroy. It crumbled into pieces, a few of which were brought to me as souvenirs. Serge Schmemann wrote:

| As hundreds of thousands of East Berliners romped through the newly porous wall in an unending celebration, West | German leaders today proclaimed this the moment Germans had yearned for through 40 years of division. |

And in an adjoining column, Craig Whitney deftly supplied the context:

| By the simple act of forcing their Communist rulers to open the Berlin wall and allow them to go wherever they wish, the people of East | Germany have irrevocably changed the way Berlin, Germany and all of Europe have defined themselves for more than 40 years. |

For the front of that paper of November 11, 1989, I chose a large photograph that showed not the happy faces of the liberated throng but the *rear* of the crowd surging against a half-opened gate toward a breach in the hated Wall. I chose it because that photo swept me autobiographically into the throng, funneling me once again from dark toward light.

In spring, Joyce, Margot, and I, with David as our cinematographer, inspected the Communist ruins in my old haunts—Berlin, Weissenfels, and Moscow. The shock of freedom was best explained to me by Dieter Matthes, who had lived one floor below us and was my best friend until we were eight. Dieter, a barber's son, had become the manager of Weissenfels's largest beauty salon and bestrode it now like an owner. Two dozen beauticians snipped and dyed under his supervision; a compact Trabant stood parked at the back door. But the prospect of free enterprise disturbed him; it was bound to give rise to smaller salons that would not have to carry the excessive number of employees forced upon him by the old regime. And he was terrified of retiring into a capitalist economy with a Communist pension.

No other familiar face or name turned up in my old hometown. Our store, facing the central square, sold motorcycle parts. The butcher a few doors away displayed a tempting array of sausages, the first tokens of open trade with West Germany.

In Moscow's butcher shops, the stink of rotten chicken drove us quickly back into the street. The elegant old National Hotel could not even produce a cookie or sandwich to go with my coffee. As I walked along Gorky Street chewing on a roll that I had spotted in a bakery, a dozen people anxiously stopped to ask where I had found such treasure.

I came home to propose entirely new themes for our coverage:

We who live in a "system" of laws and relationships cannot imagine the psychic and physical disorientation and dislocation that occur with the disappearance of the Communist system.

Germany, at least, has a memory of "property" and of laws relating thereto and an example and bankroll in West Germany to help support the transition.

But the Russian people are left without any theology, philosophy, or pragmatic social system and institutions. What's it mean to move to a "market" system when there's not even a theory about who owns land and buildings, when private contracts have no tradition or model, when there are no lawyers to draft them and no courts to adjudicate the system?

And yet "entrepreneurs" step into the void and make up rules. Who runs an enterprise and by what right? or a newspaper? or the Bolshoi? It's endlessly fascinating—a real-life illustration of rootlessness, if not anarchy.

Maybe you can figure out how to cover this.

But my career as a Kremlinologist was not yet done. Shortly before midnight on Sunday, August 18, Joan Nassivera, our night editor, phoned to read me a portentous decree just issued in Moscow. A cabal of military and KGB men who called themselves "the Soviet leadership" proclaimed a state of emergency, pronounced President Gorbachev unable "for health reasons" to perform his duties, and blamed him for steering the country into a "blind alley." I needed no Soviet censor to help me decipher that message. The "blind alley" was Gorbachev's decision to enter a liberal new era of power sharing with the nation's republics. His silence about his own health meant he was being deposed. It was a coup; the hard-liners were in revolt.

I raced to the office and prepared to reclaim my old chair as lobster-shift Rewrite man until we finally established phone contact with Frank Clines in Moscow. The two of us quickly agreed that "apparently ousted" was the correct reading of Gorbachev's fate, and while Frank dictated a few explanatory paragraphs, I had my first chance to give the legendary command:

STOP THE PRESSES!

But I, too, had to confront hard-liners:

Tell him our orders are not to stop the run after midnight.

For God's sake, tell them I know their pressroom rules, and I also know when rules have to be broken!

I think, sir, we have to get that order from a production executive.

Stop the goddam presses, and I'll get you the publisher himself in three minutes. Just stop dickering and let us remake Page One!

Well, you know, this has never been done before.

You'll never forget it if it isn't done right away!

The next morning, though basking in commendations, I had to humbly ask Arthur Jr. to certify me as possessing authority in the future to "stop the presses." Of course I never needed it again.

On the following day, Boris Yeltsin stood atop a tank staring down the coup d'état. And even as Gorbachev returned to Moscow to reclaim his office, we fortunately possessed the expertise to dig deeper than other papers and produce a prophetic headline: GORBACHEV BACK AS COUP FAILS, BUT YELTSIN GAINS NEW POWER. Punch called that August 22 paper "a classic" and wrote, "I'm setting aside seven copies for my grandchildren."

Throughout 1991, he could have set aside thirty-eight *Times*es with banner headlines—more big-type urgencies than *The Times* had printed in any year since 1945 to record the end of World War II. The first, on January 9, 1991, had Bush asking Congress to support the use of force against Iraq. The last, on December 26, recorded Gorbachev's resignation and America's recognition of the independence of each of the former Soviet republics. Serge Schmemann composed the front-page obituary:

The Soviet state, marked throughout its brief but tumultuous history by great achievement and terrible suffering, died today after a long and painful decline. It was 74 years old.

Conceived in utopian promise and born in the violent upheavals of the "Great October Revolution of 1917," the union heaved its last in the dreary darkness of late December 1991, stripped of ideology, dismembered, bankrupt and hungry—but awe-inspiring even in its fall. . . .

There was no ceremony, only the tolling of chimes from the Spassky Gate, cheers from a handful of surprised foreigners and an angry tirade from a lone war veteran. . . . The reaction depended somewhat on whether one listened to the ominous gunfire from Georgia or watched spellbound the bitter if dignified surrender of power by the last leader of the Union of Soviet Socialist Republics, Mr. Gorbachev.

Most people vacillated. The taboos and chains were gone, but so was the food.

The open societies had vanquished the closed, and lyrical prose had supplanted the dry. As Karl Popper taught me, the only society suitable for

fallible human beings was one capable of correcting its course after acknowledging its mistakes. A free press may fail to find those mistakes and
may fail to make itself useful or credible. But without free debate there can
be no experiment and no overcoming error.

Now the earth's political plates shifted faster than we could write. The
leaders of China, watching Gorbachev drown in his own reforms, recoiled
in fear, thinking they could modernize their economy while denying democracy. They will fail. Their children are already studying on the Inter-
net and breathing the free air of American campuses. Their barbed wire is
already cut, and their tanks will not protect them. As the Soviet Union
collapsed, so did the idiotic claim that Nelson Mandela was Moscow's
agent in South Africa. It became untenable to define white privilege as a
defense against communism, and so a remarkable man prevailed over the
armies of apartheid. In the Middle East, the disappearance of the Soviet
threat to Israel and of Soviet aid to the Palestinians forced reassessments
of their half century of conflict. The shift led directly to a handshake on
the White House lawn. And Fidel Castro welcomed the pope.

In America, predictably, a new and congenital insularity took hold.
The refugees who have always felt falsely safe aboard the ark America
once again hauled up the gangplank. No one cared much any longer who
ruled Japan, India, or Germany. Foreigners seemed important only if they
"stole" our jobs, crowded our cities, or devalued their currencies. And the
American extremists, who always need enemies, could make war only on
their own government.

———————

As the world turned, I turned our coverage in new directions, applied myself to *The Times*'s strategic plans, and encouraged like-minded colleagues
to prepare to succeed me. In all honesty, what stirred my heart as much as
the triumph of freedom and of our family has been the joy of waving that
baton across the pages of *The Times* and making so much glorious music.
But on my sixty-third birthday, I reminded Punch of his triple mandate: I
thought the paper was better than ever, his son's initiation well advanced,
and the newsroom as happy a place as it was ever likely to be. A gifted successor, Joe Lelyveld, deserved his own eight-year term, and I was ready to
step aside after I turned sixty-four, in mid-1994.

I yearned to sing again, to write something more than memos. I
yearned to paint again, to escape the bonds of tribe, and to reflect on my
craft and my journey. If I have learned from my times, I know something
of the future: It will rain again, on the world and on *The Times*. Those who

would truly stop the presses and seal the frontiers of nations and knowledge reappear in every generation, with tempting philosophies and contempt for humanity. By their press shall ye know them. They will cause
new floods.

But I have flown, like Noah's dove, with the spirit of the ark.

A Note About Quotes

Every memoir is a composite of records and recollections, including the recorded and recollected words spoken by others. Too few histories preserve the distinction. There is literary value in dialogue when it can be accurately reproduced or reasonably reconstructed, but for a journalist, a quotation mark must be sacrosanct. I have therefore used italics for words that I'm sure are close to those actually spoken; quotation marks have been placed around only those that I know to have been uttered precisely as they appear.

Acknowledgments

The story of a life has so many authors that no mere dedication or acknowledgment will ever do. This account of my passage is a miserable failure if it does not throb with gratitude to all who kept me afloat, above all my family, my teachers, and all my colleagues at *The New York Times*.

The packaging of this story had enormous help from Suzanne Grossman, my self-sacrificing assistant for more than two decades. It had essential encouragement and advice from my agent, Jane Gelfman, and my editor, Kate Medina, plus important editorial and design help from Random House's Ruth Fecych, Susan M. S. Brown, Meaghan Rady, Andy Carpenter, and Mercedes Everett.

My research was bolstered by the cheerful assistance of Linda Amster and her *Times* crew, notably Linda Lake and Lora Korbut, and by the proud *Times* librarians, Marilyn Annan and John Motyka. The files of my student journalism were dug up with the help of Paul Saronson, Philip Carrano, Lucy Wollin, and Constance Boykan of La Guardia (formerly Music & Art) High School, and Jean Ashton, Bernard Crystal, and Jane Siegel of the Rare Book Room of Columbia University's Butler Library.

The *Times* photographs were found with the help of Nancy Lee, Kathleen Wadlow, and Nancy Nielsen. The picture of Elsie Herrmann was happily preserved by Ann Sperry, and that of the two Arthur Sulzbergers was donated by Burk Uzzle. All the photos were lovingly shaped and reproduced by Karen Cunningham. The *Times* front pages came from the paper's archives and several, thanks to Tom Bodkin and Ed Gross, were reproduced from microfilm records.

The extensive use of *Times* materials throughout this book is the least of my debts to the Sulzberger family.

INDEX

ABOUT THE AUTHOR

MAX FRANKEL was born in 1930 in Gera, Germany. Raised in New York City, Frankel received his B.A. and M.A. from Columbia University. He has written for *The New York Times* for over forty years and received the Pulitzer Prize for international coverage in 1973. He served as executive editor of *The Times* from 1986 to 1994. This is his first book. He lives in New York City.

ABOUT THE TYPE

The text of this book was set in Janson, a misnamed typeface designed in about 1690 by Nicholas Kis, a Hungarian in Amsterdam. In 1919 the matrices became the property of the Stempel Foundry in Frankfurt. It is an old-style book face of excellent clarity and sharpness. Janson serifs are concave and splayed; the contrast between thick and thin strokes is marked.